ACCLAIM FOR THE
HOLLANDER TRANSLATION OF
THE INFERNO

"There has seldom been such a useful [version]. . . . The Hollanders . . .
act as latter-day Virgils, guiding us through the Italian text that is printed
on the facing page." —*The Economist*

"The virtues of prose raised to a quiet, sometimes stunning elegance. . . .
Reading Dante with Hollander could become addictive."
—Tom D'Evelyn, *The Providence Journal*

"A distinguished act of poetry and scholarship in one and the same breath,
the Hollander Dante, among the strong translations of the poet, deserves
to take its own honored place."
—Robert Fagles, translator of *The Iliad* and *The Odyssey*

"The present volume makes the poem accessible to the lay reader and ap-
pealing to the specialist: the translation is both faithful to the original and
highly readable; the introduction and notes are dense without being overly
scholarly; the bibliography consists predominantly of studies in English,
encouraging further investigation by English-language readers. . . . A
highly worthy new *Inferno* that is the mature fruit of years of scholarly,
pedagogical, and creative work." —*Choice*

"This new Hollander translation deserves to sweep the field. . . . Robert and Jean Hollander, both practicing published poets, have produced an English text of remarkable poetic sensitivity while never traducing the original Italian or pretending to supplant Dante's poem with one of their own. They have given us *The Inferno* in English, not a modern poetic medley on themes by Dante. And Robert Hollander has supplied precisely that kind of commentary the student or general reader needs—an economical and graceful edifice of explanatory notes resting firmly on a foundation, massive and deep, yet invisible and therefore not distracting to the reader's eye, of the erudition of a lifetime's study of the medieval Italian poets."   —John Fleming, Professor of English and Comparative Literature, Princeton University

JEAN HOLLANDER is a poet, teacher, and director of the Writers' Conference at the College of New Jersey.

ROBERT HOLLANDER, her husband, has been teaching Dante's *Divine Comedy* to Princeton students for forty years, and is the author of a dozen books and more than seventy articles on Dante, Boccaccio, and other Italian authors. He has received many awards, including the gold medal of the city of Florence, in recognition of his work on Dante.

They are at work on their translation of *Paradiso,* the conclusion of *The Divine Comedy.*

PURGATORIO

Dante Alighieri

PURGATORIO

A VERSE TRANSLATION BY JEAN HOLLANDER & ROBERT HOLLANDER

INTRODUCTION & NOTES BY ROBERT HOLLANDER

ANCHOR BOOKS
A Division of Random House, Inc.
New York

FIRST ANCHOR BOOKS EDITION, JANUARY 2004

The Library of Congress has cataloged the Doubleday edition as follows:
Dante Alighieri, 1265–1321.
[Purgatorio. English]
Purgatorio / Dante Alighieri; a verse translation by Jean Hollander and
Robert Hollander; introduction & notes by Robert Hollander.
p. cm.
Includes bibliographical references and index.
I. Hollander, Jean. II. Hollander, Robert. III. Title.
PQ4315.3 .H65 2003
851'.1—dc21   2002067100

Anchor ISBN: 0-385-49700-8

Author photographs © Pryde Brown
Book design by Pei Loi Koay
Map illustrated by Jeffrey L. Ward

www.anchorbooks.com

Printed in the United States of America
10   9   8   7   6   5   4   3

for J. V. F.

an ideal colleague,

a better friend

Since our goals in translating the second *cantica* of Dante's poem are not in substance different from those that animated our translation of the first, the reader is asked to consult the similar notice that precedes our translation of *Inferno* (Doubleday 2000; Anchor 2002). *Purgatorio* presents some challenges different from those encountered in *Inferno*, but we have again attempted to give as accurate a sense of the poetry and meaning of the Italian text as English allows. The language and style of this part of the poem is, in many respects, different from that to which we have become accustomed in the previous *cantica*. The "harsh and rasping" verse (*Inf.* XXXII.1) used to describe in particular the bottom reaches of hell is mainly lacking here, for the most part replaced by a more harmonious tone and diction. And the themes we encounter now are by and large quite different, as, entering the realm of the saved, we might expect. We need but think of the opening images of sunlight (unseen in *Inferno*), of the sense of divine grace operating before our eyes, of the fraternal love that replaces the hatred found in hell, of the light of the stars, of the singing so often heard and the smiling so often seen in this place, and, in general, of the theological virtue of hope (and its color, green), missing in even the best part of hell, Limbo (where, in Virgil's words, "without hope we live in longing" [*Inf.* IV.42]).

At the same time, things are not entirely different. The pain undergone by the penitents, it is true, is suffered to a joyous purpose, as Forese Donati makes plain: "I speak of pain but should say solace" (*Purg.* XXIII.72). Nonetheless, in form it is much as that suffered by the damned; all of these souls, too, have their *contrapasso* (*Inf.* XXVIII.142), the punishment that fits their crime, and it functions just as it did in hell, either by mirroring the sin it punishes (as in the choking smoke of wrath) or by being its opposite (as in upward-surging pride being crushed beneath a heavy burden). Also similar to those we found in *Inferno* are the narratives told by former sinners. The attitudes of these speakers and the resolutions of their lives are vastly different (we might compare Francesca [*Inf.* V] and Pia de' Tolomei [*Purg.* V], as many in fact do); however, the way in which their stories are presented is essentially the same, brief narratives, perhaps best considered Ovidian in origin, of the defining moment in a person's life. Perhaps no other feature of the *Comedy* is as reflective of the poetic essence of Dantean art as this one, as Robert Browning realized when he wrote his series of Dantesque monologues.

While surely we must acknowledge that *Inferno* and *Purgatorio* are very different poetic places, they nonetheless maintain some arrestingly similar elements. From the vantage point of *Paradiso* the second canticle looks much more like its predecessor than like its successor. But that is another story.

We are grateful to two friends born in Italy and born to Dante for their willingness to sample our translations and my comments with a knowing eye. Margherita Frankel, formerly a professor of Italian at New York University, was her usual careful and exacting self as she examined our materials. The same must be said of Simone Marchesi, who has studied with me as a graduate student at Princeton and now is about to begin teaching Dante in his own courses to fortunate students. We are pleased to be able here to express our gratitude to them both.

Gerald Howard, in addition to his more significant titles and duties at Random House, has been our editor for some years now. His support made publication of our work possible, and his continuing clearheaded and keen-eyed editorial supervision has helped keep the project on an even keel. And we are grateful as well to all at Random House and Anchor Books (including three former students of mine at Princeton) who have taken such pleasure in their association with this project.

March 2000 (Florence)–January 2002 (Tortola)

We have made some minor revisions in the translation, mainly stylistic in nature, for the first Anchor Books edition.

31 July 2003 (Hopewell)

1. Dante's works:

Conv.	*Convivio*
Dve	*De vulgari eloquentia*
Egl.	*Egloghe*
Epist.	*Epistole*
Inf.	*Inferno*
Mon.	*Monarchia*
Par.	*Paradiso*
Purg.	*Purgatorio*
Quest.	*Questio de aqua et terra*
Rime	*Rime*
Rime dub.	*Rime dubbie*
VN	*Vita nuova*

Detto	*Il Detto d'Amore* ("attributable to Dante")
Fiore	*Il Fiore* ("attributable to Dante")

2. Commentators on the *Commedia* (these texts are all either currently available or, as in the case of Bennassuti and Provenzal, should one day be available, in the database known as the Dartmouth Dante Project; dates, particularly of the early commentators, are often approximate):

Jacopo Alighieri (1322) (*Inferno* only)
Graziolo de' Bambaglioli (1324) (Latin) (*Inferno* only)
Jacopo della Lana (1324)

L'anonimo lombardo (1325[?]) (Latin) (*Purgatorio* only)
Guido da Pisa (1327) (Latin) (*Inferno* only)
L'Ottimo (1333)
L'anonimo selmiano (1337) (*Inferno* only)
Pietro di Dante (1340) (Latin) [also *Inferno* of 2nd & 3rd redactions]
Il codice cassinese (1350?) (Latin)
Chiose Ambrosiane (1355[?])
Guglielmo Maramauro (1369–73)
Chiose Cagliaritane (1370[?])
Giovanni Boccaccio (1373–75) (*Inferno* I–XVII only)
Benvenuto da Imola (1380) (Latin)
Francesco da Buti (1385)
"Falso Boccaccio" (1390[?])
L'anonimo fiorentino (1400)
Filippo Villani (1405) (*Inferno* I only)
Giovanni da Serravalle (1416) (Latin)
Guiniforto Barzizza (1440) (*Inferno* only)
Cristoforo Landino (1481) (up to *Inferno* XXI)
Alessandro Vellutello (1544) (up to *Purgatorio* X)
Pier Francesco Giambullari (1538–48)
Giovan Battista Gelli (1541–63)
Benedetto Varchi (1545) (*Paradiso* I & II only)
Trifon Gabriele (1525–41)
Bernardino Daniello (1547–68)
Torquato Tasso (1555–68)
Lodovico Castelvetro (1570)
Pompeo Venturi (1732)
Baldassare Lombardi (1791–92)
Luigi Portirelli (1804–5)
Paolo Costa (1819–21)
Gabriele Rossetti (1826–40) (*Inferno* & *Purgatorio* only)
Niccolò Tommaseo (1837)
Raffaello Andreoli (1856)
★Luigi Bennassuti (1864)
Henry W. Longfellow (1867) (English) (up to *Purgatorio* XXXIII)
Gregorio Di Siena (1867) (*Inferno* only)
Brunone Bianchi (1868)
G. A. Scartazzini (1874; but the 2nd ed. of 1900 is used)
Giuseppe Campi (1888)
Gioachino Berthier (1892)

Giacomo Poletto (1894)
Hermann Oelsner (1899) (English)
H. F. Tozer (1901) (English)
John Ruskin (1903) (English; not in fact a "commentary")
John S. Carroll (1904) (English)
Francesco Torraca (1905)
C. H. Grandgent (1909) (English)
Enrico Mestica (1921)
Casini/Barbi (1921)
Carlo Steiner (1921)
Isidoro Del Lungo (1926)
Scartazzini/Vandelli (1929)
Carlo Grabher (1934)
Ernesto Trucchi (1936)
★Dino Provenzal (1938)
Luigi Pietrobono (1946)
Attilio Momigliano (1946)
Manfredi Porena (1946)
Natalino Sapegno (1955)
Daniele Mattalia (1960)
Siro A. Chimenz (1962)
Giovanni Fallani (1965)
Giorgio Padoan (1967) (*Inferno* I–VIII only)
Giuseppe Giacalone (1968)
Charles S. Singleton (1973) (English)
Bosco/Reggio (1979)
Pasquini/Quaglio (1982)

★Not yet available

NB: The text of the *Purgatorio* is that established by Petrocchi, *Dante Alighieri: La Commedia secondo l'antica vulgata*, ed. Giorgio Petrocchi (Florence: Le Lettere, 1994 [1966–67]), vol. III. (This later edition has five minor changes to the text of this *cantica*, which is thus essentially the same as the earlier text.) All references to other works are keyed to the List of Works Cited found at the back of this volume (e.g., Aust.1933.1), with the exception of references to commentaries contained in the database known as the Dartmouth Dante Project, accessible online (telnet: ddp.dartmouth.edu; at the prompt type "connect dante"). Informational notes derived from Paget

Toynbee's *Concise Dante Dictionary of Proper Names and Notable Matters in the Works of Dante* (Oxford: Clarendon, 1914) are followed by the siglum **(T)**. References to the *Enciclopedia dantesca*, 6 vols. (Rome: Istituto della Enciclopedia Italiana, 1970–78) are indicated by the abbreviation *ED*. Commentaries by Robert Hollander are (at times) shorter versions of materials found in the Princeton Dante Project, a multimedia edition of the *Commedia* currently including most materials relevant to *Inferno* and *Purgatorio* (the last *cantica* is under development). Subscription (without charge to the user) is possible at www.princeton.edu/dante.

MAP OF DANTE'S PURGATORY

Earthly Paradise

Lust

Gluttony

Avarice (& Prodigality)

Sloth

Wrath

Envy

Pride

GATE OF PURGATORY

Late repentant:
loved the world too much
died violently
lethargic

Excommunicate

© 2002 Jeffrey L. Ward

(1) *History of Purgatory.*

It is important that a contemporary reader realize that the word "purgatory," as it is used in Dante's poem, while indicating a location in which suffering occurs, is used to denote the place in which every single soul is in progress toward salvation. Thus the current American slang use of the term to indicate an experience of harsh punishment—as though it were hell—is not a useful indicator of what the reader will find in the second part of Dante's *Comedy.* In that world, to come to purgatory is to arrive at the threshold of heaven, and to arrive there in a state of grace.

The idea of purgation has a far longer history as a concept than as a name for a place. Le Goff[1] finds the first use of the noun *Purgatorium* in a sermon of Petrus Comestor written between 1170 and 1180. Several biblical texts, however, combine to make two notions central: II Maccabees 12:39–45 suggests the efficacy of prayer for the dead, while Matthew (5:25–26, as well as 12:31–32) and Paul (I Corinthians 3:10–17) present at least a general sense of expiation postmortem.[2] In Paul's words (3:13), "Every man's work shall be made manifest: for the day shall declare it, because it shall be revealed by fire; and the fire shall try every man's work of what sort it is." Thus the purgatorial refining fire lay ready for later Christian thinkers as a way of conceptualizing the salvation of souls after the death of the body. This process bridges the time between death and the Last Judgment, a period that essentially remains a lacuna in the Bible itself. By Dante's time, theologians who attempted to deal with the lack of definition of the precise nature of "particular judgment," that is God's judgment of the individual soul upon the death of the body, realized that they needed to establish the nature of the divine decision that separated sinners from the saved immediately after death, since the Bible only posits the final judgment as described in the Book of Revelation. And once posthumous expiation and the prayers of the living became the crucial facts that clarify, for believers, both their own hopes and their responsibility with regard to their loved ones, it was almost inevitable that someone should invent a physical place in which this expiation of the souls of the dead might occur.

Adding to the store of images for the development of a place to be known as "purgatory" are a series of visions of the otherworld, studied by such scholars as Rajna,[3] Le Goff, and Morgan.[4] Le Goff demonstrates the lateness of the development of purgatory as a distinct place, beginning perhaps with Petrus Comestor and St. Bernard ca. 1170–80,[5] and underlines the major role of Dante in establishing the later sense of the place and of its function.[6] Cherchi[7] has shown that, among these writers, Gervase of Tillbury in particular presented a separate world of purgation that had a number of salient points in common with Dante's and which may have in fact suggested themselves to the poet, either because Dante knew his work (*Otia imperialia*, ca. 1210) or was acquainted with its tradition through other sources.

It is fair to say that by the thirteenth century Christian thinkers were ready to accept the idea that heaven and hell were not the only otherworldly kingdoms. Le Goff reminds us that, in a sermon in the early thirteenth century, no less a personage of the Church than Pope Innocent III referred to the realm of purgatory and that the Council of Lyons in 1274 called on Christians to believe in its existence. Such understandings surely lie behind Dante's: "Now I shall sing the second kingdom, / there where the soul of man is cleansed, / made worthy to ascend to heaven" (*Purg.* I.4–6). Dante's "second realm" thus accorded with the emerging general sense of exactly how the soul may increase its worthiness between death and the Last Judgment. (While Catholic doctrine allows that those who never actively sinned will bypass purgatory for direct access to paradise, Dante does not deal directly with this question; nonetheless, it seems likely that he shared this view.) We should recognize Dante's originality in setting the mount of purgatory at the antipodes of Jerusalem, the unique landmass in the southern hemisphere and the site of the birth of humankind. We should also be aware of his involvement in a search common to all Christians for an understanding of the nature of the soul's life between death and Judgment. Whether or not he may have been prompted, as D'Ovidio believed, by a passage in the *Aeneid* (VI.567–569), in which Rhadamanthus exacts confession of crimes from anyone who has delayed atonement until the final hours of life,[8] it seems clear that Dante is essentially responding to Christian formulations of the soul's pre-eternal afterlife. What is perhaps most surprising is that this lone poet's imagination of what this place must look like and how it functions simply became the standard source of information about purgation for many who thought of it after. Purgatory has many creators; its definitive shape, as most ordinary Christians eventually came to think of it, is essentially Dantean.

(2) Ante-purgatory.

Dante's second *cantica* (we will learn that name for each of the three parts of the work only at *Purg.* XXXIII.140, a few lines before the second canticle's conclusion) is divided into three large pieces: ante-purgatory (Cantos I–IX), purgatory proper (Cantos X–XXVII), and the earthly paradise (Cantos XXVIII–XXXIII). If the second of these has a tradition that predates Dante, the first is essentially his own creation.

In Dante's hands, the process of purgation presupposes the notion that some souls may have come farther along on the road to final penance than others, as we learn almost immediately from a comparison of the first two souls we meet who are involved in active purgation, Omberto Aldobrandesco and Oderisi d'Agobbio. It may seem surprising that Oderisi is less afflicted by Pride than Omberto,[9] even though he had died some forty years after him and thus had not been purging his pride as long as his companion. However, ante-purgatory itself is based upon a similar conception, one that may have been unique to Dante. While all the saved are, in some real sense, equally exalted (none of them wants more of heavenly bliss than he or she experiences, as we are told by Piccarda Donati),[10] their souls are in highly varied states of purification as they enter the afterworld. Indeed, some of them are not yet ready even to begin the process of repentance. And thus Dante has, as far as we can tell, invented this place of "prepurgation." His decision to do so reflects the notion that some saved sinners were less fully worthy than others and had to spend time on the lower slope of the mountain in order to make up for either of two conditions that impeded their freeing themselves from sin. The first of these groups gathers together the excommunicate, who must spend thirtyfold the amount of time that they were excommunicated in punishment for the insubordination that brought about their severance from the Church. Dante, however, gives back with the other hand what he has taken away with the first. We cannot imagine that many prelates would have acceded to the idea that anyone who had died under the ban of excommunication could possibly be saved. And that the first saved soul we meet after Cato of Utica (whose salvation remains a shock to readers even to this day) is that of the excommunicated, lecherous, murderous Manfred reminds us that Dante is not one readily to be swayed by ecclesiastical (or any other) authority. And Manfred is not here alone, but as the leader of a flock of other excommunicated souls, and the Christian image of a flock of sheep (*Purg.* III.79–87) that presents Manfred and his fellows itself stands as a reproof of the certainty of certain churchmen—including popes—in the justness of their judgments. Further, we learn from Manfred himself (at *Purg.* III.140–145) a crucial law of all of purgatory, that prayer from those still alive and in God's grace may reduce a soul's time in purgatory. The efficacy of prayer is thus another potential gift bestowed upon reformed sinners.

The second group in ante-purgatory includes all those who were saved despite the belatedness of their repentance. Their period of purgation is thirty times less onerous than that of the excommunicate, a single unit of time for each that they were behindhand on earth, moment for moment, year for year. These souls are themselves divided into three categories: those who were sluggish in their devotion to God; those who died unabsolved; and those who—and the largest group here involves negligent rulers—loved the world too much. Once again Dante is essentially relying on his own authority in the creation of this zone for his poem. And, as though the creation of ante-purgatory were not invention enough, Dante has added another area to purgatory, one even less potentially licensed by the Church, a sort of pre-ante-purgatory alluded to in the second canto. From Casella we learn (*Purg.* II.94–105) that there is a "staging area" somewhere near Ostia, the seaport of Rome, where saved souls gather before they are selected, with some having to wait their turn longer than others, for their journey through the Gates of Hercules across the seas to the huge mountain-island that stands, the highest point on earth, at the antipodes of Jerusalem.

(3) Purgatory.

The mountain's seven terraces reflect the tradition of the seven capital vices, also referred to as "mortal sins," or "deadly sins."[11] Pride, Envy, Wrath, Sloth, Avarice (and, in at least one case, Prodigality), Gluttony, Lust: these supply the seven terraces with their crowds. All terraces include the following features, mainly in the same order, as though part of a liturgical ritual for this churchlike place: (1) description of the physical aspect of the terrace, (2) exemplars of the virtue that counters the sin repented here, (3) description of the penitents, (4) recitation of their sins by particular penitents, (5) exemplars of the vice, (6) appearance to Dante of the angel representing the countering virtue. However, not only are there some subtle shifts and changes in the ordering of these elements, but there seems to be an individuated program of involvement for the protagonist. On four of the terraces he is untouched by the physical elements of penitence: he observes the envious, the slothful, the avaricious, and the gluttons without feeling their pain directly. However, among the prideful he himself bends down alongside them, thereby experiencing some of their condition; the smoke of Wrath stings his eyes, not only those of the penitents; and the flames of Lust burn him. Are we to understand that these sins are significantly his? Perhaps so. He is explicit about his pridefulness while claiming the merest touch of envious behavior (*Purg.* XIII.133–138), but those two other details—the blinding smoke and the afflicting flames—may associate him with Wrath and Lust, as what we know of his life and personality would lead us to believe.

Dante uses exemplary figures to represent both the virtue that directly opposes the vice repented and, ultimately, as *exempla* of the vice itself, the second a technique we are familiar with from *Inferno*. Thus the penitents are at first encouraged to love virtue and finally forced to confront the shame of their former vice. As Wenzel[12] and Delcorno[13] have established, Dante is heavily indebted to the writings of Peraldus on exemplary figures drawn from biblical texts.[14] This middle part of the canticle is the locus of the poem most dedicated to the use of exemplification, a technique of representation associated with ecclesiastical instruction and broadened by Dante to include classical literature and art.

The experience of purgation centers on a ritual performance of the final act of the sacrament of confession,[15] the giving of satisfaction on the part of the penitent sinner, the *satisfactio operis* (satisfaction by works) that alone may lead to absolution. It is of course true that each sinner who is saved has already, in one way or another, made amends to God for his former sinfulness. Salvation is certainly to be understood as impossible without that. Yet it would seem that Dante considered some amendment as having been tentative (thus accounting for such things as delays at Ostia and stays in ante-purgatory). In any case, the only souls who would seem to be exempt from atonement now are those who were utterly untouched by a given sin and thus do not need to purge themselves on that particular terrace. An individual's presence in penitence on any terrace indicates that person's need to proceed in an act of self-reproach, reflecting the contrition and confession that marked his or her freedom from sin on earth, as well as the words spoken to God's priest in promise of good works to come. And it seems to be only this last element that requires urgent attention here on the seven-storied mountain. Perhaps one way to think of this is that the offer of satisfaction, at least for some sinners, was more of a promise than an accomplishment, and that, for such as them, purgatory offers the opportunity for the fulfillment of that promise.

Unlike the denizens of *Inferno* and *Paradiso*, those in *Purgatorio* exist in real, present time. Inhabitants of the other two *cantiche* are in their eternal condition with one major exception: in both realms souls will receive their bodies to wear for eternity only at the Last Judgment. They are aware of time, but do not act in it (and those in hell are denied knowledge of the present—see *Inf.* X.97–108). All in ante-purgatory or purgatory are timebound[16] until such time as their penance is completed. This accounts for the leisurely sense—they are passing the time—we find in the characters in ante-purgatory, awaiting their turn for expiation, as well as for the intense and concentrated effort we observe in all those who are in active purgation higher up the mountain, pressing against the limits of time in their urgency.

At the core of this theological epic lies insistence on the free will's directing itself to the proper form of love. That will be the subject of the speeches of Marco the Lombard and of Virgil in the sixteenth and seventeenth cantos of this *cantica*. Our natural goodness, mirrored in our loving natures, is easily diverted from praiseworthy objects of affection. It is here in purgatory that the free will rediscovers its better affections.

(4)   *The Earthly Paradise.*
Once Dante's will "is free, upright, and sound" (*Purg.* XXVII.140), he is allowed to enter the sacred space "chosen for mankind as its nest" (*Purg.* XXVIII.78). The long process that accounts for the correction (initiated in the opening cantos of *Inferno*) and perfection of his will (announced by Virgil in the closing lines of the previous canto) is finally complete. The rest of the poem will have, at its dramatic center, the correction and perfection of his intellect,[17] overseen by Beatrice and finally by St. Bernard. How much his intellect is in need of correction is immediately made clear by his failure to understand the kind of affection offered by Matelda, who, as a modern Leah, represents the active life of virtue, but is misconstrued by the protagonist, who frames her offer of brotherly love in inappropriately carnal terms.

The climax of *Purgatorio* and, for many readers, of the entire poem occurs in the thirtieth canto when Beatrice, whose presence has been anticipated from the second canto of *Inferno* onward, finally appears. This scene seems to have been prepared as a kind of prothalamium, the preparation for a ceremony of marriage. But instead of preceding a wedding, it heralds a dressing down of the harshest kind. And now it is the living Dante's turn to do some urgent ritual purging of his sins, involving the rite of confession, contrition, and satisfaction. It is only then, having owned up to his sins against Beatrice (the nature of these remains less than clear to most readers, but they seem to have involved both sexual and intellectual transgressions), that he is allowed to proceed, under the guidance of the mysterious Matelda, toward his ritual absolution, which is accomplished in the final lines of the final canto of the poem called *Purgatory*. In this place where "the root of humankind was innocent" (*Purg.* XXVIII.142), Dante has regained his lost innocence and is only now prepared to ascend to the stars.

(5)   *Measurement of Time in* Purgatorio.
The opening of this three-part poem shows us its protagonist, lost in sin, coming back to his senses on a Wednesday night in late March or early April of the year 1300. He began his descent, led by Virgil, twenty-four hours later, on Friday evening. The journey to

the depths of *Inferno* takes exactly twenty-four hours, while the ascent back to the surface of the earth requires still another full day. The travelers thus arrive at the shore of purgatory at 6 PM on Sunday, Jerusalem time, or at 6 AM as time is reckoned at the antipodes. Telling the time in the heavenly regions of *Paradiso* is a less certain enterprise. The poet and his new guide, Beatrice, depart from the earthly paradise at noon of the following Wednesday and seem to spend, as we reckon time on earth, some thirty hours traversing the heavens, with the implicit return to this world occurring roughly one week after the scene in the dark wood with which this theological epic began. Time in purgatory, on the other hand, is frequently measured with elaborate precision.

In the fourteenth century the day was divided into readily remembered large periods, which may seem arbitrary to modern readers equipped with chronometers that are precise to the second. Dawn arrives at 6 AM; "tierce" is the third hour of the day, or 9 AM; the "sixth hour" is noon; "nones," the ninth hour, falls at 3 PM; the hour of Vespers arrives with the declining sun, between 3 PM and 6 PM (depending on the season); and evening arrives at 6 PM. Most of Dante's time indications are based on these convenient units.

The opening scene is played against the backdrop of the rising sun of Easter Sunday. In Canto III the early hours of morning brighten the landscape as the poets begin to climb. The meeting with Manfred is over by about 9 AM (*Purg.* III.15–16) and that with Belacqua at noon (IV.137–139). Virgil's conversation with Sordello concludes as the sun is moving downward, i.e., after 3 PM (VII.43). It is sunset in the Valley of the Princes (VIII.1–3) and 8:30 PM when Dante falls asleep. His dream occurs just before the dawn of Monday (IX.13) and he awakens just after 8 AM (IX.44). He and Virgil set out upon the first terrace a little after 9 AM (X.14–15) and reach the stairway to the second at noon (XII.81). They reach the third terrace at 3 PM (XV.1–6) and leave it just after nightfall (XVII.70–72). Their stay on the fourth terrace (Sloth) includes time for Virgil's lengthy discourse on love, which concludes at midnight (XVIII.76–78). Dante's second night's sleep and his second dream also occur on this terrace, the latter just before Tuesday's dawn (XIX.1–6). The dream is ended in the light of the sun, in which the two poets make their way toward the fifth terrace (XIX.38–39), where they stay, witnesses to Statius's completion of his purgation, until after ten o'clock (XXII.115–120). Since they reach the stairway to the seventh terrace at 2 PM (XXV.1–3), we realize that they have spent four hours among the penitents of Gluttony. Their stay on the seventh and final terrace (Lust) lasts approximately four hours as well, since the sun is setting (XXVII.61–68) as they leave it. They spend their final night in purgatory on the steps between the final terrace and the garden of Eden. It is on these steps that Dante has his third dream, again just before dawn, on Wednesday morning; he awakens with the dawn (XXVII.109). It is noon (XXXIII.103–105) as the description of the events observed in the garden of Eden comes to a close.

Robert Hollander
Tortola, 2 February 2002

1. Jacques Le Goff, *The Birth of Purgatory*, tr. A. Goldhammer (Chicago: University of Chicago Press, 1984 [1981]).

2. See citations and discussion in the introduction to *Purgatorio* by Nicola Fosca in the commentary to the *Commedia* that he is currently preparing.

3. Pio Rajna, *La materia e la forma della "Divina Commedia": I mondi oltraterreni nelle letterature classiche e nelle medievali*, ed. Claudia Di Fonzo (Florence: Le Lettere, 1998 [1874]).

4. Alison Morgan, *Dante and the Medieval Other World* (Cambridge: Cambridge University Press, 1990), pp. 144–65. Morgan's book also contains two useful appendices: a "Chronological table of principal representations of the other world," pp. 196–200, and "Written representations of the other world—summaries with background and bibliographical information," pp. 201–33.

5. Le Goff, pp. 163–65.

6. Ibid., pp. 334–55.

7. Paolo Cherchi, "Gervase of Tillbury and the Birth of Purgatory," *Medioevo romanzo* 14 (1989): 97–110.

8. Francesco D'Ovidio, *Nuovi studii danteschi: Il "Purgatorio" e il suo preludio* (Milan: Hoepli, 1906), pp. 404–12.

9. See *Purg.* XI.74–78 and note.

10. See *Par.* III.70–85.

11. See Morton W. Bloomfield, *The Seven Deadly Sins* (East Lansing: Michigan State College Press, 1952).

12. Siegfried Wenzel, "Dante's Rationale for the Seven Deadly Sins (*Purgatorio* XVII)," *Modern Language Review* 60 (1965): 529–33.

13. Carlo Delcorno, *Exemplum e letteratura: Tra Medioevo e Rinascimento* (Bologna: Il Mulino, 1989).

14. See note to *Purg.* XII.13–15.

15. See note to *Purg.* IX.94–102.

16. See Francis Fergusson, *Dante's Drama of the Mind* (Princeton: Princeton University Press, 1953), pp. 110–11.

17. See Robert Hollander, "The Invocations of the *Commedia*," *Yearbook of Italian Studies* 3 (1976): 235–40.

PURGATORIO I

Per correr miglior acque alza le vele
omai la navicella del mio ingegno,
3   che lascia dietro a sé mar sì crudele;

e canterò di quel secondo regno
dove l'umano spirito si purga
6   e di salire al ciel diventa degno.

Ma qui la morta poesì resurga,
o sante Muse, poi che vostro sono;
9   e qui Calïopè alquanto surga,

seguitando il mio canto con quel suono
di cui le Piche misere sentiro
12   lo colpo tal, che disperar perdono.

Dolce color d'orïental zaffiro,
che s'accoglieva nel sereno aspetto
15   del mezzo, puro infino al primo giro,

a li occhi miei ricominciò diletto,
tosto ch'io usci' fuor de l'aura morta
18   che m'avea contristati li occhi e 'l petto.

Lo bel pianeto che d'amar conforta
faceva tutto rider l'orïente,
21   velando i Pesci ch'erano in sua scorta.

I' mi volsi a man destra, e puosi mente
a l'altro polo, e vidi quattro stelle
24   non viste mai fuor ch'a la prima gente.

Goder pareva 'l ciel di lor fiammelle:
oh settentrïonal vedovo sito,
27   poi che privato se' di mirar quelle!

To run its course through smoother water
the small bark of my wit now hoists its sail,
leaving that cruel sea behind.

3

Now I shall sing the second kingdom,
there where the soul of man is cleansed,
made worthy to ascend to Heaven.

6

Here from the dead let poetry rise up,
O sacred Muses, since I am yours.
Here let Calliope arise

9

to accompany my song with those same chords
whose force so struck the miserable magpies
that, hearing them, they lost all hope of pardon.

12

Sweet color of oriental sapphire,
hovering in the calm and peaceful aspect
of intervening air, pure to the horizon,

15

pleased my eyes once more
as soon as I had left the morbid air
that had afflicted both my chest and eyes.

18

The fair planet that emboldens love,
smiling, lit up the east,
veiling the Fishes in her train.

21

I turned to the right and, fixing my attention
on the other pole, I saw four stars
not seen but by those first on earth.

24

The very sky seemed to rejoice
in their bright glittering. O widowed
region of the north, denied that sight!

27

Com' io da loro sguardo fui partito,
un poco me volgendo a l'altro polo,
30   là onde 'l Carro già era sparito,

vidi presso di me un veglio solo,
degno di tanta reverenza in vista,
33   che più non dee a padre alcun figliuolo.

Lunga la barba e di pel bianco mista
portava, a' suoi capelli simigliante,
36   de' quai cadeva al petto doppia lista.

Li raggi de le quattro luci sante
fregiavan sì la sua faccia di lume,
39   ch'i' 'l vedea come 'l sol fosse davante.

"Chi siete voi che contro al cieco fiume
fuggita avete la pregione etterna?"
42   diss' el, movendo quelle oneste piume.

"Chi v'ha guidati, o che vi fu lucerna,
uscendo fuor de la profonda notte
45   che sempre nera fa la valle inferna?

Son le leggi d'abisso così rotte?
o è mutato in ciel novo consiglio,
48   che, dannati, venite a le mie grotte?"

Lo duca mio allor mi diè di piglio,
e con parole e con mani e con cenni
51   reverenti mi fé le gambe e 'l ciglio.

Poscia rispuose lui: "Da me non venni:
donna scese del ciel, per li cui prieghi
54   de la mia compagnia costui sovvenni.

Ma da ch'è tuo voler che più si spieghi
di nostra condizion com' ell' è vera,
57   esser non puote il mio che a te si nieghi.

Once I had drawn my gaze from them,
barely turning toward the other pole
30   where the constellation of the Wain had set,

I saw beside me an old man, alone,
who by his looks was so deserving of respect
33   that no son owes his father more.

His beard was long and streaked with white,
as was his hair, which fell
36   in double strands down to his chest.

The rays of those four holy stars
adorned his face with so much light
39   he seemed to shine with brightness of the sun.

'What souls are you to have fled the eternal prison,
climbing against the dark and hidden stream?'
42   he asked, shaking those venerable locks.

'Who was your guide or who your lantern
to lead you forth from that deep night
45   which steeps the vale of hell in darkness?

'Are the laws of the abyss thus broken,
or has a new decree been made in Heaven,
48   that, damned, you stand before my cliffs?'

My leader then reached out to me
and by his words and signs and with his hands
51   made me show reverence with knee and brow,

then answered him: 'I came not on my own.
A lady descended from heaven and at her request
54   I lent this man companionship and aid.

'But since it is your will that I make plain
the true condition of our presence here,
57   it cannot be that I deny your wish.

Questi non vide mai l'ultima sera;
ma per la sua follia le fu sì presso,
60   che molto poco tempo a volger era.

Sì com' io dissi, fui mandato ad esso
per lui campare; e non lì era altra via
63   che questa per la quale i' mi son messo.

Mostrata ho lui tutta la gente ria;
e ora intendo mostrar quelli spirti
66   che purgan sé sotto la tua balìa.

Com' io l'ho tratto, saria lungo a dirti;
de l'alto scende virtù che m'aiuta
69   conducerlo a vederti e a udirti.

Or ti piaccia gradir la sua venuta:
libertà va cercando, ch'è sì cara,
72   come sa chi per lei vita rifiuta.

Tu 'l sai, ché non ti fu per lei amara
in Utica la morte, ove lasciasti
75   la vesta ch'al gran dì sarà sì chiara.

Non son li editti etterni per noi guasti,
ché questi vive e Minòs me non lega;
78   ma son del cerchio ove son li occhi casti

di Marzia tua, che 'n vista ancor ti priega,
o santo petto, che per tua la tegni:
81   per lo suo amore adunque a noi ti piega.

Lasciane andar per li tuoi sette regni;
grazie riporterò di te a lei,
84   se d'esser mentovato là giù degni."

"Marzïa piacque tanto a li occhi miei
mentre ch'i' fu' di là," diss' elli allora,
87   "che quante grazie volse da me, fei.

'This man has not yet seen his final sunset,
but through his folly was so close to it
60   his time was almost at an end.

'I was sent to him, as I have said,
for his deliverance. No other way
63   but this could he be saved.

'I have shown him all the guilty race
and now intend to let him see those spirits
66   who cleanse themselves within your charge.

'How I have led him would take long to tell.
Descending from on high a power aids me
69   to bring him here that he may see and hear you.

'May it please you to welcome his arrival,
since he's in search of liberty, which is so dear,
72   as he well knows who gives his life for it.

'You know this well, since death in Utica
did not seem bitter, there where you left
75   the garment that will shine on that great day.

'Not by us are the eternal edicts broken,
for this man lives and Minos does not bind me,
78   but I am of the circle where your Marcia

'implores with her chaste eyes, O holy breast,
that you still think of her as yours.
81   For love of her, then, I beseech you,

'allow us passage through your seven kingdoms.
I will report to her your kindness—
84   if you deign to be mentioned there below.'

'Marcia so pleased my eyes while I still lived,'
he said, 'that whatever favor
87   she sought of me, I granted.

Or che di là dal mal fiume dimora,
più muòver non mi può, per quella legge
90   che fatta fu quando me n'usci' fora.

Ma se donna del ciel ti move e regge,
come tu di', non c'è mestier lusinghe:
93   bastisi ben che per lei mi richegge.

Va dunque, e fa che tu costui ricinghe
d'un giunco schietto e che li lavi 'l viso,
96   sì ch'ogne sucidume quindi stinghe;

ché non si converria, l'occhio sorpriso
d'alcuna nebbia, andar dinanzi al primo
99   ministro, ch'è di quei di paradiso.

Questa isoletta intorno ad imo ad imo,
là giù colà dove la batte l'onda,
102   porta di giunchi sovra 'l molle limo:

null' altra pianta che facesse fronda
o indurasse, vi puote aver vita,
105   però ch'a le percosse non seconda.

Poscia non sia di qua vostra reddita;
lo sol vi mosterrà, che surge omai,
108   prendere il monte a più lieve salita."

Così sparì; e io sù mi levai
sanza parlare, e tutto mi ritrassi
111   al duca mio, e li occhi a lui drizzai.

El cominciò: "Figliuol, segui i miei passi:
volgianci in dietro, ché di qua dichina
114   questa pianura a' suoi termini bassi."

L'alba vinceva l'ora mattutina
che fuggia innanzi, sì che di lontano
117   conobbi il tremolar de la marina.

'Now that she dwells beyond the evil stream
she cannot move me any longer,
90   according to the law laid down at my deliverance.

'But if, as you say, a lady from Heaven
moves and directs you, there is no need of flattery.
93   It is enough you ask it in her name.

'Go then, make sure you gird him
with a straight reed and bathe his face,
96   to wipe all traces of defilement from it,

'for it would not be fitting to appear,
his eyes still dimmed by any mist,
99   before the minister, the first from paradise.

'This little island, at its lowest point,
there where the waves beat down on it,
102   grows reeds in soft and pliant mud.

'There no other plant can leaf,
or harden to endure,
105   without succumbing to the battering waves.

'After you are done, do not come back this way.
The sun, now rising, will disclose
108   an easier ascent to gain the peak.'

With that he vanished, and I stood up,
speechless. Coming closer to my leader,
111   I turned my eyes to him.

He began: 'My son, follow my steps.
Let us turn around, for this plain slopes
114   from here, down to its lowest edge.'

Dawn was overtaking the darkness of the hour,
which fled before it, and I saw and knew
117   the distant trembling of the sea.

Noi andavam per lo solingo piano
com' om che torna a la perduta strada,
120   che 'nfino ad essa li pare ire in vano.

Quando noi fummo là 've la rugiada
pugna col sole, per essere in parte
123   dove, ad orezza, poco si dirada,

ambo le mani in su l'erbetta sparte
soavemente 'l mio maestro pose:
126   ond' io, che fui accorto di sua arte,

porsi ver' lui le guance lagrimose;
ivi mi fece tutto discoverto
129   quel color che l'inferno mi nascose.

Venimmo poi in sul lito diserto,
che mai non vide navicar sue acque
132   omo, che di tornar sia poscia esperto.

Quivi mi cinse sì com' altrui piacque:
oh maraviglia! ché qual si scelse
l'umile pianta, cotal si rinacque
136   subitamente là onde l'avelse.

We went along the lonely plain,
like someone who has lost the way
120   and thinks he strays until he finds the road.

When we came to a place where the dew
can hold its own against the sun
123   because it is protected by a breeze,

my master gently spread
his hands upon the grass.
126   And I, who understood what he intended,

raised my tear-stained cheeks
and he restored the color
129   hell had obscured in me.

Now we came to the empty shore.
Upon those waters no man ever sailed
132   who then experienced his return.

There he girded me as it pleased Another.
What a wonder it was that the humble plant
he chose to pick sprang up at once
136   in the very place where he had plucked it.

1–3.   The opening metaphor of the new *cantica* relies on a topos famil-
iar from classical poetry and medieval reformulations (see Curt.1948.1,
pp. 128–30) that tie the *ingenium* (genius) of the poet, treating his mate-
rial, to the voyage of a ship over difficult waters. Dante's ship, for now,
is a small one (but cf. *Par.* II.1–3, where it is implicitly a much larger ves-
sel), raising its sails over better ("smoother") "water" than it traversed in
hell. While this metaphor will be important in *Paradiso* (II.1–18;
XXXIII.94–96), framing that *cantica* and representing the voyage as a
whole, it was only implicit in *Inferno* (as at *Inf.* I.22–24). Once again we
see Dante adding elements retroactively as the poem advances; we are
now asked to understand that it has been, in metaphor, a ship all along,
that hell is to be understood as a "sea" in retrospect.

4–6.   The second tercet encapsulates the entire *cantica*: purgatory is that
place in which the human spirit becomes fit for Heaven. There is no
longer a possibility, among the spirits whom we shall meet, of damna-
tion. Thus two-thirds of the *Commedia*, its final two *cantiche*, are dedi-
cated to the saved, first *in potentia*, then *in re*.

The words that reflect the presence of the poet derive generically
from classical poetry and perhaps specifically from the opening line of
the *Aeneid*, "Arma virumque *cano*" (Arms and the man I sing). Dante
presents himself as a singer of a kingdom, as other classical and medieval
poets identified themselves by the realms that they celebrated, the "mat-
ter of Troy," or the "matter of France," etc. But his "kingdom" is not of
this world, and no one has, at least in Dante's view, ever "sung" *this* king-
dom before.

7–12.   The third invocation of the poem now adds the attribute "holy"
to the Muses (who were unadorned "Muses" at *Inf.* II.7 and "those
ladies" at *Inf.* XXXII.10), implying that the art of this part of the *Comedy*
must keep a more religious sense to its poeticizing, since its subject from
here on is salvation. Most commentators identify Calliope as the ninth
and greatest (as representative of epic poetry) of the Muses. Dante surely
was aware of her being summoned both by Virgil (*Aen.* IX.525) and by
Ovid (*Metam.* V.338–340), the last as a part of the lengthy tale of the gods'
revenge on the nine daughters of Pierus, who, in their presumption,
imagined themselves better singers than the Muses themselves and chal-

lenged them to a vocal contest. Unwisely, they chose to sing of the re-
bellion of the giants (see *Inf.* XXXI.91–96); the Muses sang of the good-
ness of goddesses (Ceres and Proserpina). In Ovid's world of divine
assertion and vengeance, it is not difficult to imagine who won. The nine
girls were turned into raucous-sounding magpies. Identifying himself
with the pious Calliope, Dante, fully aware of his potential presumption
in singing the world of God's justice, makes a gesture of humility. That
precarious balance that a poet of divine revelation must manage is never
far from his (or our) concern. It will return as an even more evident and
central concern at *Purg.* XI.91–108. (For discussion of Dante's invocations
see note to *Inf.* II.7–9.)

Calliope is asked to rise up somewhat more than her eight sisters,
perhaps indicating her slight superiority to them or the relative higher
poetic level of *Purgatorio* to that of *Inferno* (yet not as high as that of the
cantica still to come).

The words *morta poesì* in verse 7 continue to cause occasional puz-
zlement. Do they mean "dead poetry" (i.e., poetry that had died with
the ancients and now is making a return under the pen of Dante)? Or
does it mean "poetry of the dead" (i.e., poetry concerned with the souls
of the damned)? The commentary tradition is enlightening. All the ear-
liest commentators supported the second interpretation. It was only
among "prehumanist" commentators and those who wrote in the
Renaissance (e.g., Pietro di Dante, Benvenuto da Imola, Vellutello) that
a "humanist" reading is found, one that selects the first alternative. From
the eighteenth century on nearly every commentator prefers the reading
found in our translation: Dante's poetry will rise from the subject of
damned souls to sing those of the saved. But for recent support of the
"humanist" reading see Balducci (Bald.1999.3), p. 13.

13.   The exordium and invocation combined, what we would call the
introduction to this *cantica*, occupy a mere twelve lines, where in *Paradiso*
they require thirty-six. The narrative begins with two noun phrases
(*dolce color* and *oriental zaffiro* [sweet color, oriental sapphire]) that we
would not expect to find in a description of anything seen in hell. This
part of God's kingdom, for all the pain of penance put forward in it, is a
brighter, happier place. Cioffi (Ciof.1985.1) argues for a biblical source of
Dante's gemstone (Exodus 24:10): the paved sapphire beneath the feet of
God when Moses and the seventy elders look upon Him.

For the sapphire in medieval gemology, see Levavasseur (Leva.1954.1),
pp. 57–59, indicating the stone's usual association with the Virgin.

14–18.   The word *mezzo* here has caused some problems. It would seem to mean the air between the lunar sphere and earth, that is, the "middle zone" between the first (lunar) celestial sphere and the surface of the earth. For Dante's own words to this effect see *Convivio* III.ix.12.

19–21.   The planet is Venus, whose astral influence "emboldens love." The rest of the tercet makes clear what sort of love: her brightness is veiling, as the dawn nears, the constellation Pisces (the fish was one of early Christianity's most frequent symbols for Christ, who asked his disciples to become "fishers of men" [Matthew 4:19]). Further, she is making the east seem to smile by her beauty, the east in which the sun is about to appear, a second reference to one of the constant images for Christ, the rising sun.

   This tercet has caused consternation in some readers ever since scholars understood that in the spring of 1300 Venus was not the morning star, in conjunction with Pisces, but the evening star, in conjunction with Taurus. For one way to resolve this difficulty see Hollander (Holl.2001.1), p. 196: "Emmanuel Poulle's article 'Profacio' (*ED* IV, p. 693) sketches out, with bibliographical indications, the central position of his study of the problem: Dante took his star charts from the *Almanach* of Prophacius Judaeus (ca. 1236–1304). The astronomical data found in the poem correspond only to the stars' positions during the dates 25 March–2 April 1301. If Poulle is right, Dante has privileged those dates in the calendar. As for 1301, it is inconceivable that the reader is supposed to believe that the date within the poem is other than 1300. However, if Dante was using Profacius's work, the star charts for 1300 fail to include data for the Sun and for Venus; Dante found March dates for them only in the charts for 1301. Since it took 700 years for someone to catch him out, we might surmise that, rather than calculate the missing data himself, he simply appropriated the charts for 1301 to his use." For the countering view that we are to understand that the *actual* date of the voyage is 1301 see Ceri (Ceri.2000.1), restating and refining his various previous insistences on this redating.

   Moore's discussion of the problem (Moor.1917.1), pp. 276–79, is based on the possibility that Dante misread the data in the *Almanach* and actually believed that Venus had been in Pisces in 1300. Moore's argument is somewhat weakened by his view that the action of the poem began on 8 April rather than 25 March (see note to *Inf.* I.1). Nonetheless, his conclusion, that the internal date of the vision is 1300, remains difficult to disprove (see Moor.1903.1, pp. 144–77).

22–24. Turning to face the south, even though he is at the antipodes, whence every direction is up, Dante looks at the heavens over the southern hemisphere and sees four stars not seen before except by Adam and Eve. Various other explanations of the *prima gente* (those first on earth) have been offered, the main one being that they were the inhabitants of the classical Golden Age. However, if one has to be in this spot to see these four stars, the only people ever to see them were, in consequence, the first two human souls, for once they fell from grace, they (mysteriously—and Dante never confronts the issue) ended up somewhere around Mesopotamia, and there began populating the earth with humankind. Singleton (Sing.1958.1), pp. 146–55, argues well for this view, basing his sense of the passage in what he considers Dante's understanding of the older Latin version of Genesis 3:24, in which Adam (as well as Eve) was sent "opposite Eden" right after he fell, i.e., into the antipodal hemisphere. And thus only Adam and Eve knew these stars.

That the four stars may represent the Southern Cross has long been considered a possibility. But how could Dante have known of them? Portirelli (in a lengthy, original, and fascinating passage in his commentary, ca. 1805, to vv. 22–30) speculates that Marco Polo, returned to Venice from his quarter century's sojourn in the Far East in 1295, was Dante's source. One can surely believe that Dante at least heard from others some of what the voyager reported. Nonetheless, neither Marco nor his book is ever mentioned by Dante. See Giuliano Bertuccioli, "Polo, Marco," *ED* IV (1973), p. 589.

Whatever the literal significance of these stars, their symbolic valence seems plain, and has so from the time of the earliest commentators: they represent the four moral (or cardinal) virtues: prudence, justice, fortitude, and temperance. What is important to understand (and for a fine exposition of the point in one of the most helpful essays on Dante's Cato ever written see Proto [Prot.1912.1]) is that these virtues were infused and not earned—which again points to Adam and Eve, the only humans born before Christ who had the virtues infused in their very making. In his commentary (1544), Vellutello both insists on Adam and Eve as the "first people" and nearly gives expression to the fact that, in them, these virtues were infused.

26. Our northern hemisphere is "widowed," deprived of the sight of these stars, because, as Chiavacci Leonardi suggests in her commentary (Chia.1994.1), it is like the "widowed" Jerusalem of Jeremiah (Ier. 1:1), separated permanently from its original condition of unalloyed goodness

(the condition, we may sometimes forget, that preceded that of original sin). Those who argue that our "widowhood" signifies that we know no goodness are defeated by the fact that some humans are indeed virtuous. What we have lost is more primitive and total than acquired virtue: absolute innocence.

29–30.   Dante looks north now, where the Big Dipper ("the Wain") is not seeable, given the fact that it is above the equator.

31.   The solitary figure of Cato is never named in the two cantos in which he appears (he was, however, referred to by name in *Inf.* XIV.15). Emerging details make his identity unmistakable. It would seem that Dante was fully aware of the puzzlement and outrage his salvation of Cato would cause; he thus apparently chose to leave the detective work to us, forcing us to acknowledge, from the details that he presents, that this is indeed the soul of Cato of Utica (95–46 B.C.), saved despite his suicide and his opposition to Julius Caesar, a sin in the last canto that damned Brutus and Cassius to the lowest zone of hell. (On this problem see Pasquazi [Pasq.1965.1], pp. 529–33.)

"Marcus Porcius Cato Uticensis, great-grandson of Cato the Censor, born B.C. 95; brought up as a devoted adherent of the Stoic school, he became conspicuous for his rigid morality. On the outbreak of the civil war in 49 he sided with Pompey; after the battle of Pharsalia he joined Metellus Scipio in Africa; when the latter was defeated at Thapsus, and all of Africa, with the exception of Utica, submitted to Caesar, he resolved to die rather than fall into Caesar's hands; he therefore put to an end his own life, after spending the greater part of the night in reading Plato's *Phaedo* on the immortality of the soul, B.C. 46" **(T)**.

It is vital to understand that no one other than Dante was of the opinion that Cato was saved. And that he is so to be construed escapes most early (and many later) commentators, who balk at this simple but offending notion and thus attempt to deal with Cato as an abstract quality rather than as a historical figure. Pietro di Dante's gloss (1340) to vv. 85–90 is one of the few places in which one may find a clear statement of the better view: Christ harrowed Cato from hell along with the faithful Hebrews; the Holy Spirit inspired Cato to believe in Christ to come and to seek absolution for his sins—or so Dante would like us to believe.

32–33.   Such strongly worded phrases of praise indicate the strength (and striking strangeness) of Dante's personal sense of identity with Cato. For some of his previous and later enthusiastic encomia of Cato the Younger see *Conv.* IV.xxviii.13–19 and *Mon.* II.v.15–17. And for the possibility that Dante saw in Virgil's line describing Cato, which appears in the description of the shield of Aeneas at *Aen.* VIII.670, his own name coupled with Cato's, see Hollander (Holl.1969.1), pp. 128–29: "his *dant*em iura *Cato*nem" ([italics added] and Cato giving them the laws).

34–36.   According to Lucan (*Phars.* II.372–376), Cato, sickened with sadness by the Caesar-inspired civil war in Rome, let his hair and beard grow untrimmed as a sign of grief. While he was only in his forties when he fought for the republican cause, Dante chooses to emphasize his age. However, and as Singleton says in his comment to verse 31, "it should be remembered that for Dante *la senettute* (old age) begins at forty-six (*Conv.* IV.xxiv.4)."

For the resemblances to Moses in Dante's portrait of Cato see Hollander (Holl.1969.1), pp. 124–26, and Carol Kaske (Kask.1971.1), pp. 2–3, 12–15.

37–39.   The general sense is clear: Cato's face is shining with light. Is this true because the four stars irradiate his face as though they were a sun shining upon him (the more usual interpretation), or is Dante saying that it was as though, in the brightness of Cato's face, the sun were shining before *him*? In our translation we have allowed the majority view, aware that the truncated grammatical logic of the line invites completion with "Cato" rather than "myself." However, we remain tempted by the minority view (restated by Giannantonio [Gian.1989.1], pp. 14–15), encouraged by, among other things, the fact that Dante had described the face of Lady Philosophy in the last ode of *Convivio* (vv. 59–62) as overcoming our understanding as the sun overcomes weak sight. Since the next canto will introduce the text of the second ode from *Convivio* for our consideration, it may be worth considering the appropriateness of that image to this scene.

40–45.   Cato's initial rigid and probing moral attitude may seem to indicate that he does not immediately understand the very grace that has brought him here. He reasons that Dante and Virgil, not arriving at his shores in the "normal" way (disembarking from the angel's ship that we shall see in the next canto), may have snuck into this holy land. He intuits that they have come up from the stream (the eventual course of Lethe?) that descends into hell (see *Inf.* XXXIV.129–132) and is eager to know how they could have done so without a very special grace indeed.

Nonetheless, in a manner totally unlike that encountered in the demons of Inferno, he at once allows for the possibility of grace. His second tercet immediately reveals what a different place we have now reached, one in which doubt and possibility exist even in the minds of its sternest keepers.

46–48.   His second set of questions maintains a similar balance: "Are you here because some newfangled ordinance of hell permits it, or has Heaven decreed a new law, permitting such unusual travel, that has been superimposed upon the New Law made by Christ?" That he refers to the cliffs of purgatory as his own shows that he is the keeper of the whole mountain, not just of its shore, a matter that used to cause debate.

49–51.   Cato's queries finally bring Virgil into the conversation. It is probably significant that the opening splendors of this Christian realm have been presented for Dante's sake alone. Only now does Virgil resume his role as guide.

The "signs" *(cenni)* with which he encourages his charge are probably facial gestures.

52–54.   Virgil's response echoes Dante's to Cavalcante de' Cavalcanti *(Inf.* X.61): "Da me stesso non vegno" (I come not on my own). There Dante reveals his debt to Virgil; here Virgil owns his subservience to Beatrice.

58–60.   Virgil's insistence on Dante's near-death condition at the outset of the poem may remind us of the possible connection between that condition and suicide (see note to *Inferno* XIII.24). The reflections of *Inferno* I and XIII in this canto, presided over by the "good" suicide, Cato, may produce an overtone of this concern.

Virgil's ascription of Dante's proximity to death to his *follia* may also remind the reader of Ulysses' *folle volo (Inf.* XXVI.125—the last text in which we have seen the word in its adjectival or nominal form). The younger Dante may have attempted to exercise options that he now regards as self-destructive. Cantos I, XIII, XXVI, and XXXIV of *Inferno* are perhaps those most present from that *cantica* in the verses of this opening canto of *Purgatorio*.

66.   That all the souls on the mountain are seen as being in Cato's charge makes it close to impossible to assign him a partial role, as do even some commentators who treat him as historical and not an allegory, one

in which he has authority only over the entrance at the shore or over that and the "vestibule" (ante-purgatory). He seems rather to be the guardian, appointed by God, of the entire mountain.

68. The "power" that leads Virgil from above was apparent to him when he first saw Beatrice in Limbo and she was "donna di virtù" (*Inf.* II.76).

71–74. Virgil's phrasing, which makes freedom *(libertà)* the key word connecting Dante and Cato, may also remind the reader of Christ, who gave His life for our freedom. For perhaps the first substantial understanding that there are significant figural relations between Christ and Cato see Raimondi (Raim.1962.1), pp. 78–83; for the compelling further notion that Dante would have seen confirmation of exactly such a reading in the text of Lucan itself, see Raimondi (Raim.1962.1, p. 80, and Raim.1967.2, p. 21) highlighting Cato's words (*Phars.* II.312): "Hic redimat sanguis populos" (and let my blood ransom the people). Barberi Squarotti eventually summarized this view as follows: "Cato, finally, comes to take on the function of a lay *figura* of Christ" (Barb.1984.1), p. 33. See also, in this vein, Wetherbee (Weth.1984.1), p. 135.

75. This line is so clear in its prediction of Cato's eventual salvation, when he will receive his glorified body in the general resurrection of the just that will follow the Last Judgment, that one has difficulty accepting Pasquazi's claim that the issue of Cato's salvation is left unresolved (Pasq.1965.1, p. 534). Pasquazi is closer to the mark than Andreoli, who, in his commentary (1856) to this verse, simply denies the possibility that Cato could be saved, arguing that Dante provides no grounds by which we might accept such a view. This is but another example of how the force of Dante's daring treatment of Cato has escaped his readers.

77. Virgil's self-serving reference to the fact that he was not an active sinner temporarily hides the further fact that he is damned.

78–84. Virgil's attempt at *captatio benevolentiae* (the winning of an audience's goodwill) probably sounds reasonable enough to most readers. Since he dwells in Limbo with Marcia, Cato's wife, he seeks to sway him with reference to her. Virgil has learned, we might reflect, how *captatio* functions in a Christian context from Beatrice, who practiced it upon him (*Inf.* II.58–60, II.73–74). If such rhetoric worked on him, he would seem to have surmised, perhaps it will now be effective with Cato. However, and as Di Benedetto (DiBe.1985.1), p. 175, has noted, "the mention of Marcia was something of a *gaffe*."

85–93.   Cato's rebuke of Virgil is gentle but firm: (1) Marcia pleased me well enough when I was mortal, but after I was harrowed from Limbo by Christ (the maker of the "New Law"), pity for the damned was no longer possible for me; (2) Beatrice's having interceded for you is all that is required—there is no need for flattery. Cato, unlike Orpheus, will not look back for his dead wife. He would seem rather to have Christ's words in mind: "For in the resurrection they neither marry, nor are given in marriage, but are as the angels of God in heaven" (Matthew 22:30), a passage Dante cites later in this *cantica* (*Purg.* XIX.137).

Cato's characterization of Virgil's words as *lusinghe* (flatteries) is harsh, but justified by Virgil's error. The name that would have worked (and still does) is Beatrice's, not Marcia's. Virgil has relied upon the power of the spiritually dead when he should have appealed to that of the saved.

94–99.   Turning from his admonition (which would have seemed gratu- itous had the author not wanted to call Virgil's sense of the situation into question), Cato now orders the Roman poet to gird Dante's loins with a symbol of humility. Pietro di Dante (commentary to vv. 134–136) refers to the sixth chapter of Matthew (he means Micah 6:14): "humiliatio tua in medio tui" (your casting down shall be in your midst), what Singleton's comment to verse 95 calls the *cingulum humilitatis* (cincture of humility). Dante's confirmation in humility must be joined with his purification (the cleansing of his face) so that he be pure in sight when he stands before the "admitting angel" at the gate of purgatory in Canto IX.

The *giunco schietto* (verse 95), the rush with which Virgil is ordered to bind his pupil, is, as Tommaseo (1837) was perhaps the first to suggest (in his commentary to vv. 94–96), meant to echo positively the horrible vegetation of the forest of the suicides (*Inf.* XIII.5), described as having branches that are *not* straight ("non rami schietti"), but contorted.

100–105.   Cato points Virgil (and Dante) toward a descent to the very shore of the island, its lowest point, truly a descent into humility, where the only vegetation is this most modest of plants, characterized by its plainness and its pliancy, and by its ability to grow in a landscape inhos- pitable to any other form of life.

107–108.   The guardian's reference to the nascent sunrise reminds us that this scene, until now, has been played in the hour just before dawn.

109.   Dante has been kneeling all through this scene (see verse 51) and only now arises.

115–117.   The beginning of this dawn, Easter Sunday 1300, resonates, as Tommaseo (1837) was perhaps the first to notice, with a similar phrasing from Virgil, "splendet tremulo sub lumine pontus" (the sea gleams beneath her flickering light—*Aen*. VII.9). The scene is the departure of Aeneas as he resumes his voyage toward Latium, but the source of that light is the moon, not the sun. In both works the passage marks a boundary of importance, the beginning of the "Iliadic" second half of the *Aeneid* and the preparation for Dante's journey upward toward God's kingdom.

118–120.   The comparison equates the protagonist and his guide alike with a person who finds the necessary (and hitherto obscured) path; yet we surely reflect that it applies far more forcefully to Dante, who is reported as having lost the true way at the poem's beginning ("ché la diritta via era smarrita"—*Inf.* I.3), and who now, and only now, is back on the path toward salvation.

121–123.   That is, once they had gotten closer to the sea, where the maritime breeze protects the dew from the heat of the sun more than it does higher up the slope.

124–129.   Virgil's cleansing of Dante's face removed the dark stain of the sins of hell from his visage and restored his white, or innocent (and faithful?), countenance. That we should think of the rite of baptism here may have been suggested by Benvenuto da Imola, whose gloss to vv. 121–125 refers to the *rugiada* (dew) as the "dew of divine grace, abundant when men humble their hearts before God and are cleansed of their habitual sinfulness."

   Pietro di Dante (1340) was the first (and remains one of the relative few) of the poem's commentators to insist on the redoing here of Aeneas's self-cleansing when he enters the Elysian fields (*Aen.* VI.635–636), a natural association for Dante to have had in mind. He too is entering a better precinct, having turned his attention away from "Tartarus," the place of the wicked.

130–132.   The reminiscence of Ulysses here has had a recent surge of appreciation, but notice of it is as ancient as the commentary of Benvenuto da Imola (followed, as he often was, by John of Serravalle). Citing St. Augustine's opinion (in *De civitate Dei,* Benvenuto [1380] says) that no one had ever lived at the antipodes who ever returned from there, Benvenuto goes on to suggest that this passage reflects the failed voyage of Ulysses. Some recent writers have also pointed out that the rhyme words in the passage *(diserto, esperto; acque, piacque, rinacque)* are also found in the Ulysses passage *(Inf.* XXVI.98f., XXVI.137f.).

133–136.   The triumphant wonder of the little miracle of the Christlike humble reed that renews itself concludes the canto with a proper Christian note. For Pasquazi (Pasq.1965.1), p. 537, the reed "expresses the beginning of an inner renewal, through which the poet, holding to the way of humility, opens himself to a new life." This canto is thus a canto of two "suicides," Cato and Jesus, each of whom voluntarily gave his life so that others might be free. For the way in which this scene counters the images of suicide found in *Inferno* XIII.31–32 see Hollander (Holl.1969.1), pp. 129–31. In the earlier scene, Dante, under Virgil's orders, breaks off a twig from the thornbush that is the damned soul of Pier della Vigna. Bits broken from some of the suicides do not grow back (see XIII.141–142), but strew the forest floor. Here the humble plant does indeed regrow. Wetherbee (Weth.1984.1), pp. 37–38, makes a similar observation. Pasquini (Pasq.1996.1), pp. 421–22, studies still other connections between Cato and Pier.

However, the major reference here is, as the early commentators were quick to realize, to the golden bough in the *Aeneid* (VI.143–144): "Primo avulso non deficit alter / aureus" (when the first is plucked, a second, golden too, does not fail to take its place). That scene offers a fitting parallel to this one, but with a major and governing difference: the classical object is artificial and precious, while the Christian one is natural and of little worth. Thus does the humility that inspires the Christian sublime help it outdo its classical forebear.

PURGATORIO II

Già era 'l sole a l'orizzonte giunto
lo cui meridïan cerchio coverchia
3   Ierusalèm col suo più alto punto;

e la notte, che opposita a lui cerchia,
uscia di Gange fuor con le Bilance,
6   che le caggion di man quando soverchia;

sì che le bianche e le vermiglie guance,
là dov' i' era, de la bella Aurora
9   per troppa etate divenivan rance.

Noi eravam lunghesso mare ancora,
come gente che pensa a suo cammino,
12   che va col cuore e col corpo dimora.

Ed ecco, qual, sorpreso dal mattino,
per li grossi vapor Marte rosseggia
15   giù nel ponente sovra 'l suol marino,

cotal m'apparve, s'io ancor lo veggia,
un lume per lo mar venir sì ratto,
18   che 'l muover suo nessun volar pareggia.

Dal qual com' io un poco ebbi ritratto
l'occhio per domandar lo duca mio,
21   rividil più lucente e maggior fatto.

Poi d'ogne lato ad esso m'appario
un non sapeva che bianco, e di sotto
24   a poco a poco un altro a lui uscìo.

Lo mio maestro ancor non facea motto,
mentre che i primi bianchi apparver ali;
27   allor che ben conobbe il galeotto,

The sun was nearly joined to that horizon
where the meridian circle at its zenith
stands straight above Jerusalem,

3

and night, circling on the other side,
was rising from the Ganges with the Scales
she drops when she is longer than the day,

6

so that, where I was,
the white and rosy cheeks of fair Aurora
were turning golden with time's ripening.

9

As yet we tarried by the seashore, like those
who think about the way and in their hearts go on—
while still their bodies linger.

12

And now, as in the haze of morning,
Mars, low on the western stretch of ocean,
sheds reddish light through those thick vapors,

15

there appeared to me—may I see it again!—
a light advancing swiftly on the sea:
no flight can match its rapid motion.

18

And in the moment I had turned away
to ask a question of my leader,
I saw it now enlarged and brighter.

21

Then on either side of it appeared
a whiteness—I knew not what—and just below,
little by little, another showed there too.

24

Still my master did not say a word
while the first whiteness took the shape of wings.
Then, once he saw the nature of the steersman,

27

gridò: "Fa, fa che le ginocchia cali.
Ecco l'angel di Dio: piega le mani;
30 omai vedrai di sì fatti officiali.

Vedi che sdegna li argomenti umani,
sì che remo non vuol, né altro velo
33 che l'ali sue, tra liti sì lontani.

Vedi come l'ha dritte verso 'l cielo,
trattando l'aere con l'etterne penne,
36 che non si mutan come mortal pelo."

Poi, come più e più verso noi venne
l'uccel divino, più chiaro appariva;
39 per che l'occhio da presso nol sostenne,

ma chinail giuso; e quei sen venne a riva
con un vasello snelletto e leggero,
42 tanto che l'acqua nulla ne 'nghiottiva.

Da poppa stava il celestial nocchiero,
tal che faria beato pur descripto;
45 e più di cento spirti entro sediero.

"In exitu Isräel de Aegypto"
cantavan tutti insieme ad una voce
48 con quanto di quel salmo è poscia scripto.

Poi fece il segno lor di santa croce;
ond' ei si gittar tutti in su la piaggia:
51 ed el sen gì, come venne, veloce.

La turba che rimase lì, selvaggia
parea del loco, rimirando intorno
54 come colui che nove cose assaggia.

Da tutte parti saettava il giorno
lo sol, ch'avea con le saette conte
57 di mezzo 'l ciel cacciato Capricorno,

he cried: 'Bend, bend your knees! Behold
the angel of the Lord and fold your hands in prayer.
30   From now on you shall see such ministers as these.

'Look how he scorns all human instruments
and wants no oar, nor other sail
33   beside his wings, between such distant shores.

'Look how those wings are raised into the sky,
fanning the air with his eternal pinions
36   which do not change like mortal plumage.'

Then, as the heavenly bird approached,
closer and closer, he appeared more radiant,
39   so that my eyes could not sustain his splendor,

and I looked down as he came shoreward
with a boat so swift and light
42   the water did not part to take it in.

At the stern stood the heavenly pilot—
his mere description would bring to bliss.
45   And more than a hundred souls were with him.

'In exitu Isräel de Aegypto'
they sang together with one voice,
48   and went on, singing the entire psalm.

Then he blessed them with the sign of Holy Cross.
They flung themselves upon the beach,
51   and he went off as swiftly as he came.

The crowd that stayed there had the look
of strangers to the place, gazing about
54   as though encountering new things.

Having driven Capricorn down from mid-heaven,
the sun, darting his rays in all directions,
57   brought on the day with his unfailing arrows

quando la nova gente alzò la fronte
ver' noi, dicendo a noi: "Se voi sapete,
60   mostratene la via di gire al monte."

E Virgilio rispuouse: "Voi credete
forse che siamo esperti d'esto loco;
63   ma noi siam peregrin come voi siete.

Dianzi venimmo, innanzi a voi un poco,
per altra via, che fu sì aspra e forte,
66   che lo salire omai ne parrà gioco."

L'anime, che si fuor di me accorte,
per lo spirare, ch'i' era ancor vivo,
69   maravigliando diventaro smorte.

E come a messagger che porta ulivo
tragge la gente per udir novelle,
72   e di calcar nessun si mostra schivo,

così al viso mio s'affisar quelle
anime fortunate tutte quante,
75   quasi oblïando d'ire a farsi belle.

Io vidi una di lor trarresi avante
per abbracciarmi, con sì grande affetto,
78   che mosse me a far lo somigliante.

Ohi ombre vane, fuor che ne l'aspetto!
tre volte dietro a lei le mani avvinsi,
81   e tante mi tornai con esse al petto.

Di maraviglia, credo, mi dipinsi;
per che l'ombra sorrise e si ritrasse,
84   e io, seguendo lei, oltre mi pinsi.

Soavemente disse ch'io posasse;
allor conobbi chi era, e pregai
87   che, per parlarmi, un poco s'arrestasse.

and the new people raised their faces
toward us, saying: 'If you know,
60   show us the road that leads up to the mountain.'

Then Virgil answered: 'Perhaps you think
we are familiar with this place,
63   but we are strangers like yourselves.

'We came but now, a little while before you,
by another road so rough and harsh
66   that now the climb to us will seem a pastime.'

The souls, who at my taking breath
could see that I was still alive,
69   turned pale with wonder,

and as people crowd to hear the news
around a messenger who bears an olive-branch,
72   and no one minds the crush,

so all these fortunate souls
kept their eyes fastened on my face,
75   as though forgetful of the road to beauty.

I saw one of them come forward
with such affection to embrace me
78   that I was moved to do the same.

Oh empty shades, except in seeming!
Three times I clasped my hands behind him
81   only to find them clasped to my own chest.

Surprise must have been painted on my face,
at which the shade smiled and drew back
84   and I, pursuing him, moved forward.

Gently he requested that I stop.
Then I knew him. And I asked him
87   to stay a while and speak with me.

Rispuosemi: "Così com' io t'amai
nel mortal corpo, così t'amo sciolta:
90 però m'arresto; ma tu perché vai?"

"Casella mio, per tornar altra volta
là dov' io son, fo io questo vïaggio,"
93 diss' io; "ma a te com' è tanta ora tolta?"

Ed elli a me: "Nessun m'è fatto oltraggio,
se quei che leva quando e cui li piace,
96 più volte m'ha negato esto passaggio;

ché di giusto voler lo suo si face:
veramente da tre mesi elli ha tolto
99 chi ha voluto intrar, con tutta pace.

Ond' io, ch'era ora a la marina vòlto
dove l'acqua di Tevero s'insala,
102 benignamente fu' da lui ricolto.

A quella foce ha elli or dritta l'ala,
però che sempre quivi si ricoglie
105 qual verso Acheronte non si cala."

E io: "Se nuova legge non ti toglie
memoria o uso a l'amoroso canto
108 che mi solea quetar tutte mie doglie,

di ciò ti piaccia consolare alquanto
l'anima mia, che, con la sua persona
111 venendo qui, è affannata tanto!"

"Amor che ne la mente mi ragiona"
cominciò elli allor sì dolcemente,
114 che la dolcezza ancor dentro mi suona.

Lo mio maestro e io e quella gente
ch'eran con lui parevan sì contenti,
117 come a nessun toccasse altro la mente.

'Even as I loved you in my mortal flesh,' he said,
'so do I love you freed from it—yes, I will stay.
90   And you, what takes you on this journey?'

'O Casella, I make this voyage to return
another time,' I said, 'here where I've come.
93   But why did it take you so much time to get here?'

To which he answered: 'No wrong is done me
if he, who takes up whom it pleases him and when,
96   has many times denied me passage,

'for righteous is the will that fashioned his.
It is three months now that he has taken,
99   acquiescent, all who would embark.

'And I, finally moving toward the shore
where Tiber's waters take on salt,
102   was kindly gathered in by him.

'To that estuary he now sets his wings,
for there the souls collect
105   that do not sink to Acheron.'

And I: 'If a new law does not take from you
memory or practice of the songs of love
108   that used to soothe my every sorrow,

'please let me hear one now to ease my soul,
for it is out of breath and spent,
111   joined to my body coming here.'

'Love that converses with me in my mind,'
he then began, so sweetly
114   that the sweetness sounds within me still.

My master and I and all those standing
near Casella seemed untroubled,
117   as if we had no other care. = divided will

Noi eravam tutti fissi e attenti
a le sue note; ed ecco il veglio onesto
120   gridando: "Che è ciò, spiriti lenti?

qual negligenza, quale stare è questo?
Correte al monte a spogliarvi lo scoglio
123   ch'esser non lascia a voi Dio manifesto."

Come quando, cogliendo biado o loglio,
li colombi adunati a la pastura,
126   queti, sanza mostrar l'usato orgoglio,

se cosa appare ond' elli abbian paura,
subitamente lasciano star l'esca,
129   perch' assaliti son da maggior cura;

così vid' io quella masnada fresca
lasciar lo canto, e fuggir ver' la costa,
com' om che va, né sa dove rïesca;
133   né la nostra partita fu men tosta.

We were spellbound, listening to his notes,
when that venerable old man appeared and cried:
120   'What is this, laggard spirits?

'What carelessness, what delay is this?
Hurry to the mountain and there shed the slough
123   that lets not God be known to you.'

As when doves, gathered at their feeding,
pecking here and there at wheat or tares,
126   without their usual display of pride—

should something suddenly make them afraid—
will all at once forget their food
129   because they are assailed by greater care,

thus I saw these new arrivals, their song cut short,
flee toward the mountain's slope
like those who take an unfamiliar road.
133   And we, with no less haste, departed.

1–9.   This elaborate way of telling time by the position of the sun and other stars in the heavens, inopportune in hell, where the sight of the sky is denied the travelers, will be a frequent feature of *Purgatorio*. The four main points of reference are, here (and on other occasions), Jerusalem, site of the Crucifixion and thus the most significant point on earth; the Ganges, 90 degrees to the east; the antipodes, 180 degrees to the south; and Cádiz, in Spain, 270 degrees around the circle of the meridian, a great-circle arc over Jerusalem. This makes a right angle in its intersection with the plane made by the equator, which extends into a similar great-circle arc known as the horizon. Each of the four equidistant points covered by the meridian is six hours from the other. Thus we are told that it was 6 PM in Jerusalem, midnight over India, and dawn here at the antipodes. The location of noon is left unexpressed, but we can understand that it is in fact over Cádiz, and may choose to understand that the omission forces us to supply this last indication and perhaps consider that this is the place associated with Ulysses' departure on his "mad flight" (*Inf.* XXVI.106–111), especially since the concluding verses of the last canto had so clearly reminded the reader of Ulysses' voyage (see note to *Purg.* I.130–132 and Holl.1990.1, pp. 32–33).

The phrase at vv. 4–6 is complicated, but eventually comprehensible. In the northern hemisphere, when the nights grow longer than the day after the autumn solstice, the sun appears in Libra, as a result no longer a nighttime constellation, and thus the Scales "fall from her [night's] hand." However, in the northern hemisphere it is now just after the spring solstice and the night is found in Libra, while the sun is in Aries.

10–12.   The mood of the travelers, compared by many, perhaps beginning with Benvenuto da Imola (1380), to pilgrims on their way to earn indulgence for their sins, is not particularly eager. Rather, they seem to hesitate. Vittorio Russo (Russ.1969.1), p. 243, cites Hebrews 11:13–16, with its insistence on the nature of life as a pilgrimage, as relevant to this tercet. That passage is contained in one of the most significant texts in the New Testament giving credence to the idea that those who were born before Christ were nonetheless responsible for and capable of believing in Christ to come (all of Hebrews 11 insists on the faith found in the great figures of the Old Testament). But our pilgrims seem more at home with

"Egypt" than they are eager for the New Jerusalem, as were the Hebrews themselves in the desert (see Exodus 14:11–12; 16:2–3; 17:3) because they lacked a full measure of zeal for their journey. For a discussion of the hesitance that suffuses this canto see Gorni (Gorn.1982.1). As Poletto (1894) was perhaps the first to note, the phrasing here reflects that of *Vita nuova* XII.6, where, in a simile, Dante is unsure about the path he should pursue.

13–18. This is, perhaps surprisingly, the first simile of *Purgatorio* (there was a brief comparison at *Purg.* I.119–120; another at verse 11, just above). While the first canto (vv. 19–21) involved a special relationship to Venus, this canto turns instead to Mars, treated here, as was Venus there, as morning star. In his *Convivio*, where Dante associates the first seven heavens with the liberal arts, he says (II.xiii.20–24) that Mars may be compared to Music. He concludes (24): "Moreover, Music attracts to itself the human spirits, which are, as it were, principally vapors of the heart, so that they almost completely cease their activity; this happens likewise to the entire soul when it hears music, and the virtue of all of them, as it were, runs to the spirit of sense, which receives the sound" (tr. Lansing). We shall see that these notions will come into play when Casella sings Dante's ode to the new pilgrims at the mountain's shore later in the canto. Bernardino Daniello was perhaps the first commentator (1568) to bring that passage in *Convivio* to bear on this text. But the valence of the passage as it is reflected here puts the alluring red light of Mars (and, later, listening to music, which is what Mars signifies in the earlier text) into a negative correspondence with the alacrity and whiteness of the swiftly approaching angel. Looking west toward Mars implies turning one's back on the sunrise to the east. Porena's commentary (1946) observes that Dante, as a Tuscan, was acquainted with this view of the sea, one found on the western—and not the eastern—shore of the Italian peninsula.

19–30. The gradual revelation of the approaching presence (more light, greater size, two elements of white that then resolve to three [two wings and the angel's "body"]) culminates in Virgil's recognition of the angelic nature of the steersman. For a brief account of the nature of and doctrinal problems inherent in Dante's angelology see Alison Cornish (Corn.2000.1).

The term *galeotto* (helmsman, steersman) has been used for Phlegyas, who carried Dante and Virgil across the Styx in his skiff (*Inf.* VIII.17—*ga-*

leoto). It had previously been used by Francesca (*Inf.* V.137), as a proper noun, to cast blame upon the character Gallehault in the Arthurian romance that led, according to her, to her undoing. The present *galeotto* is surely to be understood as a better-intentioned guide. Dante has been cleansed by Virgil to be in the purified condition fitting for his presence before exactly such a being, "il primo ministro . . . di paradiso" (*Purg.* I.98–99). Hell had its guardian demons; purgatory has guardian angels.

31–36.   Virgil's two balanced exclamations insist on the supernatural abilities of the angel. The first has the effect of reminding us of Ulysses. Where Ulysses made wings of oars (*Inf.* XXVI.135), this traveler over the same seas before the mount of purgatory requires neither oar nor sail. The word for "oar" was last heard in Ulysses' speech (as was the phrase "suol marino" [ocean floor] of verse 15 at *Inf.* XXVI.129). The word for poop deck, *poppa*, introduced to the poem to describe Ulysses' position as captain of his ship (XXVI.124, repeated at XXVI.140) now recurs to set this celestial steersman against his less worthy counterpart (verse 43). For this argument see Hollander (Holl.1990.1), pp. 34–35.

The second tercet, describing the heaven-directed wings of the angel, may remind us of Satan's (*Inf.* XXXIV.46–52) huge wings, if only by antithesis.

38.   Lombardi (1791) pointed out that the "uccel divino" (heavenly bird) stands in opposition to the demon Farfarello, a "malvagio uccello" (filthy bird) at *Inferno* XXII.96.

39.   This is the first time in the poem that Dante is "blinded by the light." Such scenes will recur for the rest of the final two *cantiche*.

42.   This detail almost necessarily reminds us of the contrary depiction of Charon's skiff in *Aeneid* VI.413–414, sinking into the water of the swamp beneath Aeneas's weight, as Daniello (1568) was perhaps the first to note explicitly. See also *Inferno* VIII.25–27, when Dante's weight makes Phlegyas's skiff sink in the muddy water of the Styx. And see the note to *Inferno* III.136.

44.   A much-debated text. The vast majority of codices and commentators prefer the variant not chosen by Petrocchi: "tal che parea beato per iscripto" (in such manner as to seem blessed by inscription). Petrocchi chooses the variant "tal che faria beato pur descripto" (in such a way as

to render blessed anyone who reads or hears him described). While we strongly side with the majority view, we have followed Petrocchi here as always. Were we to depart from him, our translation would run as follows: "whose look made him seem inscribed in blessedness." See this writer's earlier opinion (Holl.1990.1, p. 42): "My own view is that the verse should be read in the spirit of Landino's gloss, which holds that he seemed 'inscribed, that is, confirmed in bliss,' in the sense (also tentatively lent support by Portirelli) that he is written in the Book of Life" (see Apoc. 20:12 and discussion in Holl.1982.1).

45.   Dante's "more than a hundred" is a poet's allowable indefinite number, but one based on a very good number indeed, one hundred, number of God ($1+0+0 = 1$) and of the number of cantos in this poem.

46–48.   The arriving pilgrims, seated in the ship that carries them to purgation and eventual salvation, sing the Psalm of the Exodus, 114–115 in the modern Bible, 113 in the Vulgate. The text states clearly that they sing all of it in their shared exhilaration. For the informing pattern of the Exodus in this canto (and in the poem as a whole) see, among others, Singleton (Sing.1960.1), Tucker (Tuck.1960.1), Freccero (Frec.1986.1), pp. 14–15, 55–69, and Armour (Armo.1981.1).

For the program of Psalms and hymns utilized by Dante in the *Purgatorio* see Mastrobuono (Mast.1979.1), pp. 181–89, La Favia (LaFa.1984.1), and Ardissono (Ardi.1990.1).

49–51.   Like the heavenly messenger at the walls of Dis (*Inf.* IX.100–103), this angel, after blessing his flock, also moves away from those he has helped as quickly as possible, but on this occasion not from disgust at the place in which he finds himself, but to return to Ostia for more saved souls.

The souls fling themselves upon the shore *(si gittar)* just as the damned fling themselves *(gittansi)* upon Charon's boat (*Inf.* III.116), but with key elements in the scenes significantly reversed, though both groups are spurred by their desire for justice.

52–54.   The second scene of the canto begins with the mutual pleasure and confusion of the two groups that play the major roles in it, the crowd of pilgrims and the two travelers, both less (in Virgil's case) and more than saved souls, since Dante is destined to return and will then be a uniquely experienced penitent.

55–57.   As Bosco/Reggio (1979) point out in their commentary to these lines, all the images in them are derived from hunting. The sun (Apollo as archer), now risen above the horizon, shoots its rays (arrows) every-where, striking the constellation Capricorn, 90 degrees from Aries. Consequently, Capricorn moves several degrees down the sky from its highest point, where it was at dawn.

60.   For the resemblances of the mount of purgatory to Mt. Sinai see Carol Kaske (Kask.1971.1). For her the mountain is not only its former self, site of the divine gift of Ten Commandments to Moses, but a place of Christian pilgrimage under the New Law.

63.   Virgil's reply to the saved souls identifies himself and Dante as being "pilgrims," in the generic sense that they are travelers in a foreign land. In a more limited and Christian sense, only Dante and the new arrivals are truly on a pilgrimage. This is the first of nine uses of the noun or adjective *peregrino* that are distributed through the final two *cantiche*. For the view that the controlling idea of the *Commedia* is that of a pilgrimage see, among others, Demaray (Dema.1987.1), pp. 1–60; Basile (Basi.1990.1); Holloway (Holl.1992.3), esp. pp. 57–84; and Picone (Pico.1997.1).

65.   Virgil's recollection of the difficult journey up through hell is made to reflect the poet's own formulation in *Inferno* I.5 exactly: *aspra e forte* (dense and harsh), the adjectives there referring to the "dark wood" of the world in which Dante found himself at the outset.

66.   These are Virgil's last words in the canto. In fact he nearly disap-pears from the scene once Dante and Casella take over center stage. He will be mentioned as forming part of the group of those who are rapt by Casella's song (verse 115) and as departing in haste with Dante in the canto's final verse (133). In both cases he is behaving less like a guide than like a lost soul. In a sense, this is the protagonist's first solo flight in the *Commedia*, a moment in which he is potentially in command of the sit-uation. His success is hardly dazzling.

69.   Satan, with his three heads, had seemed a *maraviglia* to the protag-onist in *Inferno* XXXIV.37. In the last canto it was the miraculous "res-urrection" of the Christlike humble plant (verse 134) that had seemed a "wonder" to him. Now it is *he* who causes wonder in the onlookers, since he is present in the flesh.

70–74.   This second simile of the canto compares Dante's living visage to the olive branch carried by a messenger of peace. In other words, his very presence in this precinct is an additional assurance to the new souls that God's justice and promise of a kingdom of peace as the final haven for a Christian life was truly offered and truly kept. They have arrived, even if the way before them is uncertain and difficult, since they still have to perform their ritual cleansing of even the memory of sin. Commentators point to two possible Virgilian sources: *Aeneid* VIII.115–116 and XI.100–101. In the second, messengers from the camp of Turnus, holding up olive branches, seek permission of Aeneas to gather the bodies of the dead for burial; in the first it is Aeneas himself, standing upon the *puppis* (quarterdeck) of his ship, who holds forth the branch of peace to Pallas, son of Evander. Pallas is amazed (*obstipuit*—verse 121) by Aeneas's cordial gesture and accedes to it. The entire context there seems to fit the details of Dante's scene better, Dante as Aeneas "invading" the homeland of those with whom he will be allied.

76–78.   This as yet unidentified soul (we will learn his name, Casella, at verse 91) has recognized Dante and advances to embrace him; Dante, filled with a proper Christian affection, responds to his embracer's emotion without any personalization, returning love for love without earthly distinctions. It is a very good beginning for a pilgrim in purgatory.

79–81.   This much-admired scene is modeled on another, but which one? *Aeneid* II.792–794 and VI.700–702 contain three identical lines of verse describing a failed embrace. The first commentators opt for the latter, Aeneas's attempt to hold fast Anchises' paternal ghost. But John of Serravalle (1416) thinks, in a departure from that opinion, of Aeneas's identical effort to embrace the dead form of his wife, Creusa, in the second book. He was followed by Vellutello (1544). Modern commentators almost universally return to the more familiar scene in Book VI, and it has been rare in the last century of glossing to find anyone even contemplating the earlier scene involving Creusa. One would expect, perhaps, that commentators would at least discuss their options. But such is not the case. For reasons to prefer the less favored text, see Hollander (Holl.1990.1, p. 38), pointing out that (1) the poet will later and unmistakably refer to Aeneas's attempted embrace of Anchises (*Par.* XV.25–27) and arguing that it would be less than likely for him to do so here as well, since he had two such moments to choose from; (2) the context, in which Casella will shortly be singing a song of love to Dante, would argue for the greater appropriateness of Creusa than Anchises.

For the apostrophe of the "empty shades, except in seeming" see, as Tommaseo suggested in 1837, *Inferno* VI.36, the phrase "lor vanità che par persona" (their emptiness, which seems real bodies). The shades of the gluttons there and of all posthumous souls have this in common, but we must wait for Statius's long disquisition in Canto XXV to learn how the "aerial body" of the dead is produced.

83.   Casella's smile is the first one we have seen since Limbo, when Virgil smiled to see the poets of antiquity welcome Dante as they prepared to include him in their noble company (*Inf.* IV.99). Smiles, understandably absent from the visages of those in hell, will be more frequent in purgatory, some dozen of them, and still more so in paradise (two dozen).

85–87.   Only after Dante hears Casella's voice does he recognize him, so distant seems the world of earth. See the entirely similar moment with Forese Donati (*Purg.* XXIII.43–45) and one somewhat similar with his sister Piccarda (*Par.* III.58–63).

91.   Casella, finally named, was obviously, from the context of the scene, a musician. That is really all we know with any certainty about him. Nonetheless, it is clear that he is someone whom Dante actually knew. Whether he was from Florence or Pistoia (or even Siena—the commentators are puzzled and offer these possibilities, most of them plumping for Florence) we do not know. Whether he actually set one or more of Dante's poems to music, we do not know. For some sense of his possible identity and activity see Peirone, "Casella," *ED* I (1970), Bisogni (Biso.1971.1), and Elsheikh (Elsh.1971.1).

93.   Casella has evidently been dead some time (for at least slightly more than three months, as verse 98 will make plain) and Dante wonders why he has been so long between death and his first step toward salvation, arrival in purgatory. Beginning with Poletto (1894) and Moore (Moor.1896.1), p. 168, commentators have seen a connection here with Charon's unwillingness to take certain of the waiting shades across Acheron (they all are eager to be taken) and in fact picking and choosing among the waiting throng (*Aen.* VI.315–316). We might continue the thought: In Dante's poem Charon takes all bound for hell at once; only those bound for purgatory need to be winnowed by the transporting angel, with some having to stay longer in the world, near Ostia, thus

mirroring a sort of prepurgation that the poet has invented, offstage, as it were.

94–105.   Casella's startling narrative at times escapes the sort of attention it requires. This is what we learn: Before the Jubilee Year's plenary indulgence announced by Pope Boniface in February 1300 (retroactive to Christmas of 1299), all those who came to the region around Ostia, where the souls of the saved are gathered, had to await the pleasure of the angel to be taken aboard the ship that we have just seen Casella and the others disembark from. Before 25 December 1299, Casella was denied many times a seat in the ship. We are forced to understand that he was not gifted with a particularly energetic desire for God; i.e., he was a perfect "brother" to the Dante we meet at the beginning of this canto, a man like those "who think about the way and in their hearts go on—while still their bodies linger" (vv. 11–12). Purgatory thus has three places: the mountain of purgation itself, ante-purgatory, and "pre-ante-purgatory," located somewhere never described but at or near Ostia. And the laws of this place themselves underwent a change in late 1299, for after that date *anyone* who wanted to depart for the "holy land" would be accommodated by the angel. (Dante has apparently, on no authority but his own, decided that the plenary indulgence for sinners extended to the souls of the justified dead as well.)

    This requires that we understand that during the past three months Casella *did not want* to travel south toward heaven. Given his behavior once he arrives at the shore, however, this is not totally surprising. Finally, precisely three months after the merciful decree was made, he decided that he wanted to leave. The date: 25 March 1300, the Florentine New Year. Is it coincidence that this, the most likely date for the beginning of Dante's journey (see notes to *Inf.* I.1; I.11; *Purg.* I.19–21), is also that on which Casella probably set out? Whether or not it is, we have the delightful spectacle of these two miraculous voyagers, each starting somewhere in Italy, one gliding over the seas, the other moving under the earth, arriving at the antipodes within minutes of one another, reunited in friendship and peace. (Poletto's discussion [1894] of some of these problems is one of the few in which these complex matters are closely and suggestively examined.)

106–108.   The protagonist's language is laced with diametrically opposed terms: "new law" and "songs of love." Merely hearing them, one intuits that there is an oppositional relationship between them. Daniello's commentary (1568) asserts that there is indeed a "new law" in purgatory, where "one does not sing vain and lascivious things, but hymns and psalms in praise of God, and prays to Him." In this first confrontation, looking ahead to the song not yet sung, the 113th Psalm is that of the "New Law," and is juxtaposed against the love song that Dante wrote for a woman in the last century. It is this kind that, earthbound as he now again is, the protagonist longs for.

Petrocchi's text for verse 108 reads "doglie" (sorrows) and not "voglie" (longings). Hardly any Dantist currently admires this choice, and the vast majority urge a return to the 1921 reading, including the translators.

111.   Dante's soul, wearied by his bodily weight, remembers his condition at the beginning of *Inferno* (I.22): in simile, his mind, in stress, is like the breath of a man escaping from death by drowning, *affannata* (laboring). If he seems better off now than he was then, he is still in considerable difficulty.

112.   Casella's song is Dante's song, the second *canzone* found in *Convivio*. It was composed in celebration of Lady Philosophy. That sounds innocent or even positive. On the other hand, she is, early on in *Convivio*, specifically designated as having replaced Beatrice in Dante's affections. Within the confines of *Convivio* this is not problematic. In the *Commedia*, in which Beatrice is the moving force for so much, it is.

For discussions of the possibility that Casella actually set this *canzone* of Dante see Marti (Mart.1962.1), pp. 81–88, and Bisogni (Biso.1971.1).

113–114.   The sweetness of the song is memorable even now, says the poet. One can see why most readers of this scene take these words as confirming the poet's approval of a positive feeling. But see *Inferno* XXVI.19–24, where the poet "grieves again" as he "grieved then" for the lost Ulysses. Both Ulysses and his own Convivial ode are marked as temptations the strength of which are both still vividly felt by him, even though he now knows better than to accede to them.

118–121.   Cato's return was not in the program, as is clear from verse 106 in the previous canto. He evidently believed that this specially privileged Christian visitor to purgatory would know how to behave better than he does. But now he has not only backslid himself, but is involving the whole new contingent of the saved into behaving similarly. Cato sounds exactly like St. Paul, urging them all to "put off the old man and put on the new" (Ephesians 4:22; Colossians 3:9). For the closeness of Dante's thought here to Colossians 2 and 3 see Holl.1975.1, p. 357. See also Hollander (Holl.1990.1), pp. 40–41: "And Cato's identity here is not only Pauline, for the scene is clearly reminiscent of Moses's discovery of the falsely worshipping Hebrews before that golden calf (Exodus 32:18–19—see Kaske [Kask.1971.1]) which the text of Psalm 113 had already set before the minds of all who listened to what their own lips were singing only moments before. Echoing God's command and Moses's compliance ('neither let the flocks nor herds feed before that mount'—Exodus 34:3), Cato sends the music-lovers flying." For the Pauline references see also Rigo (Rigo.1994.1), pp. 93–94.

123.   Those who argue that Cato is being overzealous should pay closer attention to this strong charge he makes against the negligent spirits. Whatever the "slough" *(scoglio)* signifies, their adherence to it prevents their seeing God. In the world of the *Commedia* that can never be a slight problem.

124–132.   This third and final simile of the canto likens the new pilgrims to doves (for the three programmatic references to these birds in the *Commedia*, here and in *Inf.* V.82 and *Par.* XXV.19, see Shoaf [Shoa.1975.1]). See Hollander (Holl.1990.1), p. 41: "Their saved souls hunger on high, but their appetitive natures are not yet wrung dry of earthly longing. Thus they are careless in their ingestion (see Matthew 13:36–43 for the parable of the wheat and the tares alluded to in their failure to make a decision between 'biado o loglio'). If music be the food of love, there is also a heavenly music. We and the pilgrims know that this is true. They have sung it themselves in this very place."

133.   The final verse, in its understated brevity, conveys a feeling for the two travelers' guilty acceptance of Cato's command and their hasty departure in shame.

"The second canto of the *Purgatorio* dramatizes the need for interpretation by presenting two songs to its audience, the arriving pilgrims. It is clear that we comprise a still more crucial audience. Most of us have chosen to follow the lead of the one whom we take to be our leader, Dante himself. (His several intellectually or morally flawed responses as he moved through Inferno have not, apparently, been cogent enough sign of his frequent inadequacy as guide to our reactions.) He, lost in the beauty of his own old song, either fails to understand or else forgets the message of the new song which he has heard first, and which should have served as a rein on his enthusiasm. It is as old as Exodus and as new as the dawn which brings it, this Easter Sunday morning on the shore of the mountain" (Holl.1990.1, p. 41).

PURGATORIO III

III. *Manfred*

Avvegna che la subitana fuga
dispergesse color per la campagna,
3   rivolti al monte ove ragion ne fruga,

I' mi ristrinsi a la fida compagna:
e come sare' io sanza lui corso?
6   chi m'avria tratto su per la montagna?

El mi parea da sé stesso rimorso:
o dignitosa coscïenza e netta,
9   come t'è picciol fallo amaro morso!

Quando li piedi suoi lasciar la fretta,
che l'onestade ad ogn' atto dismaga,
12   la mente mia, che prima era ristretta,

lo 'ntento rallargò, sì come vaga,
e diedi 'l viso mio incontr' al poggio
15   che 'nverso 'l ciel più alto si dislaga.

Lo sol, che dietro fiammeggiava roggio,
rotto m'era dinanzi a la figura,
18   ch'avëa in me de' suoi raggi l'appoggio.

Io mi volsi dallato con paura
d'essere abbandonato, quand' io vidi
21   solo dinanzi a me la terra oscura;

e 'l mio conforto: "Perché pur diffidi?"
a dir mi cominciò tutto rivolto;
24   "non credi tu me teco e ch'io ti guidi?

Vespero è già colà dov' è sepolto
lo corpo dentro al quale io facea ombra;
27   Napoli l'ha, e da Brandizio è tolto.

Their sudden flight had scattered them
along the plain, toward the mountain
3   where Justice tries our souls,

and I drew closer to my true companion.
How would I have come this far without him?
6   Who would have led me up the mountain?

He seemed beside himself with self-reproach.
O pure and noble conscience,
9   how bitter is the sting of your least fault!

When he had slowed the hectic pace
that mars the dignity of any action,
12   my mind, at first withdrawn into itself,

now eagerly took in the wider landscape.
I fixed my gaze upon the highest hill
15   rising from the sea into the sky.

The sun, its rays like red flames at my back,
was cut off by my body
18   and threw the shadow of my shape before me.

Quickly I turned to look beside me,
afraid that I had been abandoned,
21   since the ground was dark in front of me alone.

And my comfort, turning, then began to speak:
'Why are you still distrustful?
24   Do you not believe I am with you and guide you?

'Evening has fallen there, where the body
that cast my shadow while I lived is buried.
27   Taken from Brindisi, Naples holds it now.

Ora, se innanzi a me nulla s'aombra,
non ti maravigliar più che d'i cieli
30   che l'uno a l'altro raggio non ingombra.

A sofferir tormenti, caldi e geli
simili corpi la Virtù dispone
33   che, come fa, non vuol ch'a noi si sveli.

Matto è chi spera che nostra ragione
possa trascorrer la infinita via
36   che tiene una sustanza in tre persone.

State contenti, umana gente, al *quia*;
ché, se potuto aveste veder tutto,
39   mestier non era parturir Maria;

e disïar vedeste sanza frutto
tai che sarebbe lor disio quetato,
42   ch'etternalmente è dato lor per lutto:

io dico d'Aristotile e di Plato
e di molt' altri"; e qui chinò la fronte,
45   e più non disse, e rimase turbato.

Noi divenimmo intanto a piè del monte;
quivi trovammo la roccia sì erta,
48   che 'ndarno vi sarien le gambe pronte.

Tra Lerice e Turbìa la più diserta,
la più rotta ruina è una scala,
51   verso di quella, agevole e aperta.

"Or chi sa da qual man la costa cala,"
disse 'l maestro mio fermando 'l passo,
54   "sì che possa salir chi va sanz' ala?"

E mentre ch'e' tenendo 'l viso basso
essaminava del cammin la mente,
57   e io mirava suso intorno al sasso,

'Do not wonder if I cast no shadow,
no more than that the heavenly spheres
30   do not cut off their rays from one another.

'The Power that fits bodies like ours
to suffer torments, heat, and cold
33   does not reveal the secret of its working.

'Foolish is he who hopes that with our reason
we can trace the infinite path
36   taken by one Substance in three Persons.

'Be content, then, all you mortals, with the *quia*,
for could you, on your own, have understood,
39   there was no need for Mary to give birth,

'and you have seen the fruitless hope of some,
whose very longing, unfulfilled,
42   now serves them with eternal grief—

'I speak of Aristotle and of Plato
and of many others.' And here he lowered his brow,
45   said nothing more, and seemed perturbed.

We now had come to the mountain's base.
There we found the cliff so steep
48   that nimble legs could not have climbed it.

The roughest, most deserted landslides
between Lèrici and Turbìa, compared with it,
51   seem like a wide and easy stairway.

'Who would know where the hill slopes gently,'
mused my master, coming to a halt,
54   'where someone without wings might climb?'

And while, his eyes cast down,
he was searching in his mind to find the way,
57   and I was looking up among the rocks,

da man sinistra m'apparì una gente
d'anime, che movieno i piè ver' noi,
60   e non pareva, sì venïan lente.

"Leva," diss' io, "maestro, li occhi tuoi:
ecco di qua chi ne darà consiglio,
63   se tu da te medesmo aver nol puoi."

Guardò allora, e con libero piglio
rispuose: "Andiamo in là, ch'ei vegnon piano;
66   e tu ferma la spene, dolce figlio."

Ancora era quel popol di lontano,
i' dico dopo i nostri mille passi,
69   quanto un buon gittator trarria con mano,

quando si strinser tutti ai duri massi
de l'alta ripa, e stetter fermi e stretti
72   com' a guardar, chi va dubbiando, stassi.

"O ben finiti, o già spiriti eletti,"
Virgilio incominciò, "per quella pace
75   ch'i' credo che per voi tutti s'aspetti,

ditene dove la montagna giace,
sì che possibil sia l'andare in suso;
78   ché perder tempo a chi più sa più spiace."

Come le pecorelle escon del chiuso
a una, a due, a tre, e l'altre stanno
81   timidette atterrando l'occhio e 'l muso;

e ciò che fa la prima, e l'altre fanno,
addossandosi a lei, s'ella s'arresta,
84   semplici e quete, e lo 'mperché non sanno;

sì vid' io muovere a venir la testa
di quella mandra fortunata allotta,
87   pudica in faccia e ne l'andare onesta.

there to the left I saw a company of souls
moving their steps in our direction,
60 not seeming to approach, they came so slow.

'Raise your eyes, master,' I said, 'look,
there are some who can offer us advice
63 if you can't puzzle out the way yourself.'

He looked up then and, reassured, replied:
'Let us go toward them, for they come slowly,
66 and you, dear son, hold to that hope.'

Even after we had walked a thousand steps
these souls were still quite far away—
69 about the distance a strong arm could throw—

when they all pressed against the solid wall
of the high bank, standing still and close together,
72 as men stop, taking stock, when they are puzzled.

'O you who have come to a happy end,
spirits already chosen,' Virgil began,
75 'by that peace which, I think, awaits you all,

'tell us where the mountain rises gently
so that we may begin the long ascent.
78 The more we know, the more we hate time's waste.'

As sheep come from the fold, first one,
then two, then three, and the rest stand timid,
81 bending eyes and muzzle to the ground,

and what the first one does the others copy,
pressing up behind it if it stops,
84 simple and quiet, not knowing why,

so, of that fortunate flock, I saw
the ones in front move shyly forward,
87 with solemn bearing and with modest looks.

Come color dinanzi vider rotta
la luce in terra dal mio destro canto,
90   sì che l'ombra era da me a la grotta,

restaro, e trasser sé in dietro alquanto,
e tutti li altri che venieno appresso,
93   non sappiendo 'l perché, fenno altrettanto.

"Sanza vostra domanda io vi confesso
che questo è corpo uman che voi vedete;
96   per che 'l lume del sole in terra è fesso.

Non vi maravigliate, ma credete
che non sanza virtù che da ciel vegna
99   cerchi di soverchiar questa parete."

Così 'l maestro; e quella gente degna
"Tornate," disse, "intrate innanzi dunque,"
102   coi dossi de la man faccendo insegna.

E un di loro incominciò: "Chiunque
tu se', così andando, volgi 'l viso:
105   pon mente se di là mi vedesti unque."

Io mi volsi ver' lui e guardail fiso:
biondo era e bello e di gentile aspetto,
108   ma l'un de' cigli un colpo avea diviso.

Quand' io mi fui umilmente disdetto
d'averlo visto mai, el disse: "Or vedi";
111   e mostrommi una piaga a sommo 'l petto.

Poi sorridendo disse: "Io son Manfredi,
nepote di Costanza imperadrice;
114   ond' io ti priego che, quando tu riedi,

vadi a mia bella figlia, genetrice
de l'onor di Cicilia e d'Aragona,
117   e dichi 'l vero a lei, s'altro si dice.

As soon as those in front could see the light
upon the ground was broken to my right, so that
90   my shadow stretched up to the cliff,

they stopped, drew back a little,
and all the rest that came behind,
93   not knowing why, did just the same.

'Without your asking I declare to you
this is a human body that you see,
96   which now divides the sun's light on the ground.

'Do not be amazed, but think
that not without a power sent from Heaven
99   does he attempt to scale this rocky wall.'

Thus the master. And those worthy souls replied:
'Turn, then, and go on before us,'
102   showing the way with the backs of their hands.

Then one of them began: 'Whoever you are,
as you continue walking, turn to look at me,
105   and think if ever you have seen me in the world.'

I turned and fixed my gaze on him.
He was blond, handsome, and of noble aspect,
108   but a blow had cleft one of his eyebrows.

When I had courteously disclaimed
ever to have seen him, 'Look here!' he said,
111   and showed me a wound high on his breast,

then, smiling: 'I am Manfred,
grandson of the Empress Constance.
114   Therefore I beg of you, when you return,

'make your way to my fair daughter,
mother of the pride of Sicily and Aragon,
117   and tell the truth if another tale is told.

Poscia ch'io ebbi rotta la persona
di due punte mortali, io mi rendei,
120   piangendo, a quei che volontier perdona.

Orribil furon li peccati miei;
ma la bontà infinita ha sì gran braccia,
123   che prende ciò che si rivolge a lei.

Se 'l pastor di Cosenza, che a la caccia
di me fu messo per Clemente allora,
126   avesse in Dio ben letta questa faccia,

l'ossa del corpo mio sarieno ancora
in co del ponte presso a Benevento,
129   sotto la guardia de la grave mora.

Or le bagna la pioggia e move il vento
di fuor dal regno, quasi lungo 'l Verde,
132   dov' e' le trasmutò a lume spento.

Per lor maladizion sì non si perde,
che non possa tornar, l'etterno amore,
135   mentre che la speranza ha fior del verde.

Vero è che quale in contumacia more
di Santa Chiesa, ancor ch'al fin si penta,
138   star li convien da questa ripa in fore,

per ognun tempo ch'elli è stato, trenta,
in sua presunzïon, se tal decreto
141   più corto per buon prieghi non diventa.

Vedi oggimai se tu mi puoi far lieto,
revelando a la mia buona Costanza
come m'hai visto, e anco esto divieto;
145   ché qui per quei di là molto s'avanza."

'After my body was riven
by two mortal blows, I turned
120   in tears to Him who freely pardons.

'Horrible were my sins,
but Infinite Goodness with wide-open arms
123   receives whoever turns to it.

'If the pastor of Cosenza, sent by Clement
on the hunt to take me down,
126   had read that page in God with greater care,

'my body's bones would still be sheltered
at the head of the bridge near Benevento
129   under the cairn of heavy stones.

'Now the rain washes and the wind stirs them,
beyond the Kingdom, near the Verde's banks, there
132   where he brought them with his torches quenched.

'By such a curse as theirs none is so lost
that the eternal Love cannot return
135   as long as hope maintains a thread of green.

'It is true that one who dies in contumacy
of Holy Church, even though repentant at the end,
138   must still endure outside this wall—

'for every year he spent in his presumption—
thirty, unless that sentence
141   is reduced by holy prayers.

'Now you know how you can make me happy:
reveal to my good Constance where you've seen me
and how long I am excluded—
145   for here much can be gained from those on earth.'

1–6.   The two "companions" are running, but not as quickly as the souls who precede them, while Virgil considers his previous inappropriate behavior and Dante his own (as we shall learn in vv. 7–9, 12–13). The poet, as though apologizing for what he is putting Virgil through in these scenes, reminds the reader of his enduring debt to the pagan poet, without whom this journey through the afterworld would have been impossible.

The word "ragione" in verse 3 does not mean "reason" but "justice," as is attested by Dante's earlier usage in *Convivio* (where it nine times refers to law, especially Justinian's codification of Roman statutes— see Vasoli's analytical index to *Convivio* [Vaso.1988.1], pp. 1011–12), and the entire commentary tradition (even if a small subset of commentators believes the word here means "conscience"). See also Marta Cristiani, "ragione," *ED* IV (1973), pp. 831–41, esp. 841. In this context it nearly certainly refers to divine justice.

7–9.   Virgil's remorse is self-caused. As Venturi (1732) remarked, Virgil rebukes himself even though he could not have been a target of Cato's anger, since he was not a soul on the way to purgation. And thus the little fault applies to him alone, not to Dante and the others (for all of whom it is considerably more serious).

10–11.   Virgil, here momentarily lacking *onestade* (dignity), is bracketed by the figures of Cato and the group containing Manfred; both of these are referred to as *onesto* (*Purg.* II.119; III.87).

12–13.   As Virgil is preoccupied with his minor failing, so Dante is troubled by his own guilty thoughts. Daniello (1568) points to Cato's rebuke (*Purg.* II.120–121) as the cause of his shame when he considers his hesitation in moving toward the necessary mountain.

15.   The verb *dislagarsi* (literally meaning "to unlake itself") is a Dantean coinage, a phenomenon that will grow as the poem progresses and flower in profusion in *Paradiso*.

16–18.   Dante's presence here in the body is a double-edged proposition, as it both emphasizes his extraordinary state of grace in being here in the flesh and his debilitated status, resulting from his fleshly view of things. For a study of this phenomenon and its development through the *cantica* see Berk (Berk.1979.1), who points out that, while we may feel that Dante in *Purgatorio* all too frequently presents himself as casting a shadow, he in fact does so only six times: here; later in this canto (vv. 88–90); then in *Purgatorio* V.4–6 and 25–27; XXVI.4–8; XXVII.64–69. Berk also makes the point that Dante's corporeal shadow finds a correspondence, later in the canto, in Manfred's wounds (vv. 108, 111), the signs of that soul's former mortality.

19–21.   Having noted his own shadow, the protagonist now is struck by the absence of Virgil's, and momentarily thinks he has been abandoned by his guide. While, as soon as the travelers reached the shore of the mount of purgatory and reentered the sunlight, the protagonist might have noted that none of the immortal denizens of this new place casts a shadow—not Cato, none of the pilgrims, not his guide—the poet reserves that recognition for this canto, so filled with reminiscence of the death of Virgil.

22–24.   Benvenuto da Imola's paraphrase of Virgil's rebuke begins with the words "modicae fidei": (*"you of little faith*, why have you so easily lost the faith and the hope that you ought and may have in me, who never left you behind in the city of the demons?"). Benvenuto is clearly thinking of the words of Christ in the Gospels (in the Latin Bible the phrase "modicae fidei" is found four times and only in Matthew [6:30; 8:26; 14:31; 16:8]). If Benvenuto has correctly heard that echo, its effect is noteworthy, for then the faithless Virgil is reproving his pupil, modeling his speech on the words of Christ, for *his* lack of faith, evident on occasion from the first canto of the *Inferno* until Virgil leaves the poem in *Purgatorio* XXX. Whether Virgil is citing Scripture or having Scripture placed in his mouth by his Christian author is a problem the reader has already encountered (see *Inf.* VIII.45 and note to VIII.40–45).

25–26.   Since it is shortly after dawn here in purgatory, it is shortly after sunset at the antipodes, Jerusalem. And since Italy, in Dante's geography, lies midway between Jerusalem and Gibraltar, it is sometime after 3 PM there, as evening *(vespero)* begins with the sun's last quarter, between 3 PM and 6 PM.

27.   Virgil died on 21 September 19 B.C. at Brindisi, a city in Apulia that still serves as a port for maritime travelers to and from Greece. Augustus was responsible for the transfer of his body from Brindisi to Naples, or actually, Pozzuoli, some ten miles distant, where it was interred in a grotto

in the vast tunnel, built by the ancient Romans, connecting Pozzuoli and the road to Naples. John of Serravalle (1416) records his having visited the site on 30 August 1413 and having held bones of Virgil in his hands. This passage begins what has been called "an antepurgatorial preoccupation with the body and its place of burial" (Heil.1972.1, p. 44).

Pietro di Dante was perhaps the first to cite Virgil's versified epitaph, as found in the *Vitae* of Virgil by Suetonius and Donatus:

Mantua me genuit, Calabri rapuere, tenet nunc
Parthenope: cecini pascua, rura, duces.

[Mantua gave me birth, Calabria took me off; now Naples holds me; I sang of pastures, fields, and kings.]

Virgil "sang" his *Eclogues, Georgics,* and *Aeneid.* For the possible reference to the three Virgilian subjects in the final hundred verses of the canto, see Hollander (Holl.1984.4), p. 114:

46–78:   The barren landscape of this scene *(rura)*
79–102:   the contumacious as sheep *(pascua)*
103–145: Manfred and empire *(duces)*

In this experimental formulation Dante would, in exactly one hundred lines, have deployed the three "spokes" of the stylistic *rota Vergilii* (the wheel of Virgil).

Carroll (1904) cites Plumptre for the opinion that this scene reflects the (unverified) tradition that St. Paul visited Virgil's grave at Naples and wept for the great poet, whom, had he but known him, he might have led to salvation.

28–30. Dante's heavens include the nine celestial spheres containing the Moon and, as they move higher, eventually no stellar bodies of any kind (the *primum mobile*). In *Paradiso* we will learn that, while they are material, they are also translucent. Something similar is also the case with respect to the shades here.

31–33. Virgil here touches on the nature of the "aerial bodies" of the dead in *Inferno* and *Purgatorio*. The Roman poet Statius will elaborate on the "physical" nature of shades in *Purgatorio* XXV.34–108.

34–36.   The "posthumous Christian" ruefully acknowledges, by pointing to reason as his means for attempting to know the essence of things, his failure to have had faith. The reference to reason does not indicate, as some commentators insist, that Virgil embodies or personifies Reason, especially since, in this context, Reason would then be commenting on the shortcomings of reason. Reason is a property (or, in Scholastic terms, an "accident") of the Roman poet, not his essence.

37.   The *quia* is a term deriving from Scholastic discourse. Benvenuto da Imola's paraphrase nicely conveys both that style and precisely what is meant here: "sufficiat vobis credere quia sic est, et non quaerere propter quid est" (let it suffice you to believe that something is so, without seeking to know why it is so), i.e., to accept things as they are, without attempting to understand their causes.

38–39.   Some commentators (e.g., Benvenuto) are of the opinion that these lines indicate that had humankind been able to know the final mysteries, Adam and Eve would not have fallen and Christ would not have been needed to save us. It seems far more likely that Dante's thought is more logically connected than such an analysis would indicate: had we known all, there would have been no need for Christ to come to bring us the final truth of things. The focus here is not moral so much as it is intellectual.

40–45.   Perhaps there is no passage in the poem that more clearly delineates the tragedy of Virgil, now studied by its protagonist himself. His own fourth *Eclogue*, which spoke of a virgin who would give birth to a son, but did not mean Mary and did not mean Jesus, is symptomatic of how near he came and thus how great was his failure, a result here addressed in an unspoken gesture—his lowering his head while holding back his tears. In the last canto, the newly arrived pilgrims looked up with hope ("la nova gente *alzò la fronte*" [the new people raised their faces]). The words describing Virgil's silence echo key words from that passage in a contrastive spirit (as noted by Holl.1990.1, p. 36): "e qui *chinò la fronte*, / e più non disse, e rimase turbato" (and here he lowered his brow, said nothing more, and seemed disturbed). As Benvenuto would have it, it is as though Virgil were saying: "And woe is me, I was among their number."

The words in rhyme position in these two tercets underline their message:

<table>
<tr><td></td><td>Maria</td><td>quetato</td></tr>
<tr><td>*quia*</td><td></td><td>Plato</td></tr>
<tr><td>via</td><td></td><td>turbato</td></tr>
</table>

One way leads up through faith to Christian truth, mediated by the mortal woman who gave birth to God in the flesh, the other down from this potential happiness, through rational attempts to know the rationally unknowable, to everlasting unhappiness. Mary and Plato are here the very emblems of the choices that we humans face.

46–48.   There is a sharp dividing line between the elegiac passage devoted to Virgil's consideration of his failure (vv. 22–45) and the scene that begins here, with the description of the sheer wall of the mountain and the first attempt at an ascent. For an appreciation of the nonetheless unitary nature of this canto as a whole, see Binni (Binn.1955.1), p. 9.

49–51.   Lerici and Turbia are settlements at either end of the Ligurian coast, to either side of Genoa, a region marked by rugged mountains sloping to the sea and, in Dante's roadless day, difficult of access.

52–57.   Virgil's question and attitude reveal a guide who has not taken *this* trip previously, as he had in *Inferno*. Further, while he falls back on the resource of his reason, the futility of which in certain situations has just been explored by the guide himself, his pupil, like the arriving penitents in the last canto (see note to vv. 40–45, above), does the intuitive and hopeful thing: he looks up.

58–60.   Having begun their attempt to ascend, Virgil and Dante begin moving leftward out of habit, we must assume. (They will only learn what direction they should be moving in at verse 101.) Our first glimpse of the souls of ante-purgatory marks them as unexcited and slow-moving, attributes that will gain in meaning when we learn more about them.

For helpful references to classical discussions of the morally charged nature of the directions of human movement (right, up, and ahead are all "good"; left, down, and behind are all "bad") see Stabile (Stab.1983.1), pp. 145–49.

61–63.   Underlining the difference between the guide's and the protagonist's ways of proceeding, Dante's remark, urging Virgil to look up, intrinsically reveals a reversal of roles, as was noted by Margherita Frankel (Fran.1989.1), pp. 120–21. It is not the master who is giving instructions but the pupil; throughout the little scene that follows, one can sense Virgil's effort to regain his attenuated authority.

72. The souls are puzzled by what they see, two figures moving in the wrong direction (to the left) on this holy mountain, as Benvenuto da Imola was perhaps first to suggest. Not only are they going in the wrong direction, they are also moving quickly, not at the reverential and thoughtful pace of penitence.

73–78. Virgil's *captatio benevolentiae* (the attempt to capture the goodwill of one's auditors) here, like the one he addressed to Cato in the first canto (*Purg.* I.70–84), reveals, as Frankel has been perhaps alone in arguing (Fran.1989.1, pp. 122–24), another example of his not understanding his own limitations. His epigrammatic concluding utterance, though taken *in bono* by commentator after commentator (and perhaps most pleasingly by Benvenuto, who goes on to claim that Dante himself was most prudent in using his time, so that he managed to get his *Commedia* finished before he died), shows him once again getting things a bit garbled. The self-assured turn of phrase, "The more we know, the more we hate time's waste," indicates that he is still without understanding of the positive aspects of *not* knowing, of *not* hurrying—two aspects of the saved souls whom he addresses that, as the following simile will make unmistakably clear, are praiseworthy in the Christian context of this scene.

79–87. The sole extended comparison of the canto centers attention on the need for faith untroubled by reason. These sheep, following and imitating their bellwether, are presented positively for their humility and faithfulness. See Lansing (Lans.1977.1), pp. 47–53, for a discussion of this simile, contrasting the humility exemplified here in Manfred (whom we shall soon come to understand is the "bellwether" in the simile), whose life was marked by the opposite vice, presumption, in his opposition to the Church. In one of his typical outbursts against his intellectual enemies in *Convivio*, Dante calls them stupid and compares them to sheep (I.xi.9–10), those sheep that follow their leader in jumping into a ravine a mile deep (is that phrasing, "mille passi," remembered in the same phrase at verse 68, above? Frankel [Fran.1989.1], p. 124, is of that opinion). Citation of this passage in *Convivio* was perhaps first brought into play by Daniello (1568), but it is only recently that readers have begun to understand that the ovine images in this simile work against the assertion found in the Convivial outburst. Its prideful, even presumptuous, tone is here countermanded by the poet's better understanding of the virtues of sheep, as the arrogance of prideful philosophizing gives way to Christian piety.

In his commentary to this passage, Singleton notes the appropriateness of the 77th Psalm (Psalm 77 [78]:52), recapitulating the Exodus with these words: "But [God] made his own people go forth like sheep, and guided them in the wilderness like a flock." It seems clear that such traditional Judeo-Christian images of the flock of the just govern this simile.

93.   If we had not sensed the importance of humble acts committed by those "not knowing why" in verse 84, the fact that the souls, now described directly, repeat what had been done within the simile reinforces the importance of the point.

94–96.   For Dante's shadow see note to vv. 16–18, above.

101–102.   The saved souls now express their concern: Dante and Virgil are heading in the wrong direction (see Fran.1989.1, pp. 121–22). They are thus aesthetically and morally disturbing as newcomers to purgatory.

The gesture that they make is puzzling to American readers, who give the sign for "Stop!" or "Go back!" by extending their palms outward. As Lombardi (1791) calmly points out, "The gesture referred to here by the poet is exactly the one with which we signal to others that they should turn and retrace their steps." Experience on Tuscan streets and paths even today will verify this.

103–105.   Manfred died (February 1266) some eight or nine months after Dante was born. His question is thus groundless, notwithstanding the exertions of commentators like Tommaseo (1837), Andreoli (1856), and Poletto (1894), who argue that Dante, as a deeply thoughtful man, looked old for his age. The utterly human perception that lies behind the poet's lending Manfred this question is that the great and famous are used to being recognized, and often assume that everybody has seen them, even if they themselves tend to have small recollection of the many whom they have encountered. On the other hand, his question may also be a hopeful one, i.e., if this living soul happens to recognize him, Manfred hopes that he will cause others to pray for him—see *Purgatorio* V.49–50, where other late-repentant souls make similar requests.

107–108.   The "realism" of the detail of this scarred eyebrow has drawn much admiration. Singleton's comment (1973) cites Augustine, *De civ. Dei* XXII.xix.3: "For, in the martyrs, such wounds will not be a deformity; they will have a dignity and loveliness all their own; and, though this radiance will be spiritual and not physical, it will, in some way, beam from their bodies." He goes on to suggest that Manfred, though excommunicated by the Church, nonetheless is treated here as a sort of martyr, "persecuted" by that very Church.

While a number of antecedents for Manfred's physical appearance have been proposed (e.g., David, Roland, Virgil's Marcellus), one seems most likely to have been on Dante's mind: the tragic figure of Deiphobus (*Aen.* VI.495–499), who attempts to *hide* his wounds from Aeneas, his mangled ears and his nose ("truncas inhonesto volnere naris" [his nostrils laid bare by a shameful wound—VI.498]). Deiphobus, desiring *not* to be recognized by his wounds, is, in this understanding, a foil to Manfred, eager to display the wound in his chest. Perhaps the first commentator to note this correspondence was Mattalia (1960); and see Hollander (Holl.1984.4), p. 119.

111.   Manfred's second wound (the poet will insist on the importance of the fact that he has *two* visible wounds in verse 119), perhaps reminiscent of the wound in Christ's side (John 19:34; 20:25), causes the reader to consider the possible significances of these two marks on his body. Perhaps we are to understand that the first wound, in his brow, traditionally and in Dante the locus of pride (see *Inf.* X.45 and XXXIV.35 and notes), is the sign of his pride brought low, his mark of Cain, as it were, now made good in his gesture of revealing his other wound, his mark of Christ, the seal of his humility. Torraca (1905) is nearly alone in seeing the resemblance, antithetic though it be, between the gestures of self-revelation in displaying wounds found in Manfred here and in Mohammed (*Inf.* XXVIII.29–31).

112.   Manfred's smile is part of a "program" of smiling found in the two final *cantiche* (see note to *Purg.* II.83). His way of naming himself seems to be part of a program limited to the ante-purgatory, the only part of the poem in which characters name themselves using this formula ("io son" followed by their own name). Manfred's smiling self-identification stands out from the evasive behavior in this regard exhibited by most of the sinners in hell. For the others who employ this formula see *Purgatorio* V.88 (Buonconte da Montefeltro), VI.34 (Sordello), VII.7 (Virgil). In the

less personal exchanges in *Paradiso* only St. Bonaventure uses a version of it: "Io son la vita di Bonaventura. . . ." There the great Franciscan identifies himself as a living heavenly soul.

Born ca. 1231, Manfred was the illegitimate son of the emperor Frederick II and Bianca Lancia, and thus the natural grandson of Emperor Henry VI and Constance of Sicily. He was also the father, by his wife Beatrice of Savoy, of Constance, who married King Peter III of Aragon (see vv. 115–116). When Frederick died in 1250, Manfred was appointed regent of Sicily in the absence of his brother, Conrad IV, involved elsewhere. When Conrad died, in 1254, leaving the realm to his three-year-old son, Conradin, Manfred again became regent. At the rumors of the child's death, in 1258 (he would in fact survive another ten years), Manfred was crowned king in Palermo. This did not sit well with the pope, and Alexander IV excommunicated him in 1258, as did Urban IV in 1261. Urban offered the vacated forfeited crown to Louis IX of France who, refusing it, opened the path to an invitation of Charles of Anjou, who accepted. Once Charles was crowned in Rome in January 1266, he set out to destroy Manfred, an aim that he accomplished the next month at the battle of Benevento. A lover of the "good life" at court, a fervent Ghibelline, a man charged (whether correctly or not) with a number of murders of his cofamiliars, supposedly undertaken to advance his political hopes, Manfred was not, at least not in Guelph eyes, a selection for salvation that could have been calculated to win sympathy to the work that contained such news. It is at least reasonable to believe that the first damned soul we see in hell is Celestine V (see note to *Inf.* III.58–60), a pope of saintly habits; here the first soul we find saved on the mountain is the excommunicated Manfred. Whatever else Dante enjoyed doing as he wrote this poem, he clearly delighted in shocking his readers—as though the salvation of Cato, with which the *cantica* begins, were not incredible enough for us.

On the problems raised for commentators by the salvation of the excommunicated Manfred see La Favia (LaFa.1973.1), who points out that a letter of Pope Innocent III dating from 1199 fully supports the notion that an excommunicate can eventually be saved, a position, as he demonstrates, that was not nearly as shocking to Dante's earliest readers as it would later become. La Favia produces the key portion of that Latin text (pp. 87–88).

113.   Manfred does not identify himself as his father's son (Frederick II is, after all, condemned to hell for heresy: *Inf.* X.119) but by reference to his paternal grandmother, Constance (1154–98). As Benvenuto uniquely

(among the early commentators) points out, Dante has borrowed this tactic from Polynices who, questioned about his lineage by the king of Argos, Adrastus, in Statius's *Thebaid*, prefers to omit the name of Oedipus in favor of that of his mother, Jocasta (I.676–681).

117.   The poet's self-awareness is unmistakable here. Hardly anyone in his time would have consented to the notion that Manfred had been saved. He places this reference to the imagined dubiety of those who might hear such news (i.e., by reading Dante's poem) in the mouth of his character and it is our turn to smile. Yet we can imagine how many Guelphs and churchmen would have fumed at this passage, adamant in their vehement and unflagging belief that Manfred had been damned.

121–123.   The sinners in hell, we must assume, failed exactly to do, even at the last moment of their lives, what Manfred did. While he is held back from purgation for the insubordination that resulted in his excommunication, he, too, is a late-repentant saved soul.

124–129.   The archbishop of Cosenza, in Calabria, enlisted by Pope Clement IV in his battles against Manfred's Ghibellines, was responsible, at the end, for disinterring his corpse, buried under the cairn of stones piled upon his body by Guelph troops after the battle of Benevento.
      There is some dispute as to the precise meaning of the word *faccia* here. Does it mean "face" or "page"? For the former, see Freccero (Frec.1986.1), p. 206. For "faccia" as page, see Frankel (Fran.1984.1), p. 107. The page in God's writing indicated here is perhaps found at Apocalypse 20:12, the reference to the Book of Life, in which are recorded the names of the saved, including, we must reflect, that of Manfred. However, three particulars lend support to those who argue for "page," *faccia* as an apocopation of *facciata*: (1) While most of the early commentators are vague in their readings of this verse, those who wrote in the Renaissance and after tend to find this interpretation more natural; (2) although modern commentators mainly prefer "face," they do so without the sort of convincing argument that might conclude the debate; (3) the archbishop of Cosenza, we might reflect, obviously had no direct experience of God's presence (at least not in Dante's mind), but he surely did have some kind of access to the Scripture, although he evidently—at least in Dante's eyes—understood it poorly.

130.   After Tommaseo (1837) many modern commentators suggest that there is a reference here to Virgil's Palinurus (*Aen.* VI.362): "Nunc me fluctus habet versantque in litore venti" (Now the waves have me and

the winds hurl me onto the beach). See notes to *Purgatorio* V.91–93 and VI.28–33.

131–135.   Adding insult to the injury of disinterment, the archbishop ordered Manfred's remains to be cast back into the world. They had first at least been allowed burial in unconsecrated ground with the ceremony prescribed for the excommunicate ("with torches quenched"). And so the corpse is put out of the Kingdom of Naples and Sicily onto a bank of the river Verde, today the Liri.

The name of the river, *Verde* (green), however, stands intrinsically opposed to such purpose, since it both traditionally represents the virtue of hope and happens to have been the color that Manfred himself favored. And thus the identical rhyme "Verde/verde" underlines the hopeful sign that Manfred's faith believed would come and his love longed for. The Church's human agents may not understand God's hidden disposition.

The final phrase here, "ha fior del verde," has caused much difficulty. Lombardi (1791) paraphrases the passage as follows: "so long as death does not entirely dry up hope, but leaves a single thread of it green."

139.   For a possible precursor for this period of delay see *Aeneid* VI.325–30, the one hundred years of wandering exacted of the souls of the unburied dead before they are permitted to cross Acheron, a connection perhaps first suggested by Daniello (1568). But this does not explain Dante's choice of the number thirty. It is not until the twentieth century that one finds a commentator wondering about the possible reasons for this choice: Grandgent (1909): "Why thirty? See E. G. Gardner in the *Modern Language Review*, IX, 63. In Deut. xxxiv, 8, we read: 'the children of Israel wept for Moses in the plains of Moab thirty days.' Hence the early Christian practice of saying prayers for the dead for thirty days after decease. Out of this grew the 'Trental of St. Gregory,' or thirty masses on thirty feast days through the year." Trucchi (1936) resuscitates a previously unnoted observation of Francesco da Buti, recalling the tale told by Gregory the Great in his *Dialogues*: the ghost of a monk named Justus who, buried excommunicate for having fathered children, was redeemed when thirty masses said by Gregory set things right. Another analogue, offered by a Princeton student, Gerald Dal Pan '82, in an examination paper in 1980, is worthy of discussion: the thirty years of Jesus's life before he was baptized and entered by the Holy Spirit, when He took on his mission in the world (Luke 3:25).

Torraca (1905) suggests that Manfred lived nine years under the ban of excommunication and thus had a sentence of 270 years in ante-purgatory when he died in 1266, thus leaving him 236 years to wait before commencing his purgation. However, since Dante's poem surely brought a storm of prayers to Heaven, he may have finished his penitential waiting much earlier than that.

143.   The third cantos of both *Purgatorio* and *Paradiso* are centrally involved with two women known as "Constance," here the grandmother and daughter of Manfred, there Piccarda Donati, whose name as a nun was Constance, and the other Constance, also a nun, who accompanies her when the two of them appear to Dante in the sphere of the Moon.

For a bibliography of discussions of this canto see Scorrano (Scor.2000.1), pp. 69–71.

PURGATORIO IV

Quando per dilettanze o ver per doglie,
che alcuna virtù nostra comprenda,
3   l'anima bene ad essa si raccoglie,

par ch'a nulla potenza più intenda;
e questo è contra quello error che crede
6   ch'un'anima sovr' altra in noi s'accenda.

E però, quando s'ode cosa o vede
che tegna forte a sé l'anima volta,
9   vassene 'l tempo e l'uom non se n'avvede;

ch'altra potenza è quella che l'ascolta,
e altra è quella c'ha l'anima intera:
12   questa è quasi legata e quella è sciolta.

Di ciò ebb' io esperïenza vera,
udendo quello spirto e ammirando;
15   ché ben cinquanta gradi salito era

lo sole, e io non m'era accorto, quando
venimmo ove quell' anime ad una
18   gridaro a noi: "Qui è vostro dimando."

Maggiore aperta molte volte impruna
con una forcatella di sue spine
21   l'uom de la villa quando l'uva imbruna,

che non era la calla onde salìne
lo duca mio, e io appresso, soli,
24   come da noi la schiera si partìne.

Vassi in Sanleo e discendesi in Noli,
montasi su in Bismantova e 'n Cacume
27   con esso i piè; ma qui convien ch'om voli;

When one of our faculties is given over
to pleasure or to pain,
our soul will focus on that one alone

and seem to pay no mind to any of its other powers—
revealing the error in the doctrine that maintains
among the souls within us one is more aflame.

And therefore when we see or hear a thing
that concentrates the soul,
time passes and we're not aware of it,

for the faculty that hears the passing time
is not the one that holds the soul intent:
the one that hears is bound, the other free.

This I truly understood,
listening to that spirit in amazement,
for the sun had already climbed fifty degrees

and I had failed to notice, when we came
to where these souls cried out as one:
'Here is the place you asked for.'

Often, at the time the grapes are darkening,
a peasant, with a pitchfork full of thorns,
will plug a larger opening

than the gap through which my leader
and I behind him climbed alone,
after the troop went on without us.

One may go up to San Leo or descend to Noli
or mount to the summits of Bismàntova or Cacùme
on foot, but here one had to fly—

3

6

9

12

15

18

21

24

27

dico con l'ale snelle e con le piume
del gran disio, di retro a quel condotto
30   che speranza mi dava e facea lume.

Noi salavam per entro 'l sasso rotto,
e d'ogne lato ne stringea lo stremo,
33   e piedi e man volea il suol di sotto.

Poi che noi fummo in su l'orlo suppremo
de l'alta ripa, a la scoperta piaggia,
36   "Maestro mio," diss' io, "che via faremo?"

Ed elli a me: "Nessun tuo passo caggia;
pur su al monte dietro a me acquista,
39   fin che n'appaia alcuna scorta saggia."

Lo sommo er' alto che vincea la vista,
e la costa superba più assai
42   che da mezzo quadrante a centro lista.

Io era lasso, quando cominciai:
"O dolce padre, volgiti, e rimira
45   com' io rimango sol, se non restai."

"Figliuol mio," disse, "infin quivi ti tira,"
additandomi un balzo poco in sùe
48   che da quel lato il poggio tutto gira.

Sì mi spronaron le parole sue,
ch'i' mi sforzai carpando appresso lui,
51   tanto che 'l cinghio sotto i piè mi fue.

A seder ci ponemmo ivi ambedui
vòlti a levante ond' eravam saliti,
54   che suole a riguardar giovare altrui.

Li occhi prima drizzai ai bassi liti;
poscia li alzai al sole, e ammirava
57   che da sinistra n'eravam feriti.

I mean with the swift wings and plumage
of great desire, following that guidance
30   which gave me hope and showed me light.

We climbed into a fissure in the rock.
The stony walls pressed close on either side.
33   We had to use our hands to keep our footing.

When we had reached the crag's high upper ledge,
out on the open hillside, 'Master,' I said,
36   'which path shall we take?'

And he to me: 'Do not fall back a single step.
Just keep climbing up behind me
39   until some guide who knows the way appears.'

The summit was so high that it was out of sight,
the slope far steeper than the line
42   drawn from midquadrant to the center.

Exhausted, I complained:
'Belovèd father, turn around and see
45   how I'll be left alone unless you pause.'

'My son,' he said, 'drag yourself up there,'
pointing to a ledge a little higher,
48   which from that place encircles all the hill.

His words so spurred me on
I forced myself to clamber up
51   until I stood upon the ledge.

There we settled down to rest, facing
the east, where we had begun our climb,
54   for often it pleases us to see how far we've come.

First I gazed upon the shore below,
then raised my eyes up to the sun and was amazed
57   to see its rays were striking from the left.

Ben s'avvide il poeta ch'ïo stava
stupido tutto al carro de la luce,
60 ove tra noi e Aquilone intrava.

Ond' elli a me: "Se Castore e Poluce
fossero in compagnia di quello specchio
63 che sù e giù del suo lume conduce,

tu vedresti il Zodïaco rubecchio
ancora a l'Orse più stretto rotare,
66 se non uscisse fuor del cammin vecchio.

Come ciò sia, se 'l vuoi poter pensare,
dentro raccolto, imagina Sïòn
69 con questo monte in su la terra stare

sì, ch'amendue hanno un solo orizzòn
e diversi emisperi; onde la strada
72 che mal non seppe carreggiar Fetòn,

vedrai come a costui convien che vada
da l'un, quando a colui da l'altro fianco,
75 se lo 'ntelletto tuo ben chiaro bada."

"Certo, maestro mio," diss' io, "unquanco
non vid' io chiaro sì com' io discerno
78 là dove mio ingegno parea manco,

che 'l mezzo cerchio del moto superno,
che si chiama Equatore in alcun' arte,
81 e che sempre riman tra 'l sole e 'l verno,

per la ragion che di', quinci si parte
verso settentrïon, quanto li Ebrei
84 vedevan lui verso la calda parte.

Ma se a te piace, volontier saprei
quanto avemo ad andar; ché 'l poggio sale
87 più che salir non posson li occhi miei."

The poet understood I was astounded
to see the road that chariot of light
60   was taking in its path between the north and us.

And so he said: 'If the mirror that moves its light
to either side of the equator
63   were in the company of Castor and of Pollux,

'the red part of the zodiac would show
still closer to the Bears
66   unless it were to leave its ancient track.

'If you would understand how this may be,
with your mind focused, picture Zion
69   and this mountain positioned so on earth

'they share the same horizon
but are in different hemispheres.
72   Then you shall see how, to his misfortune,

'the highway Phaeton failed to drive
must pass this mountain on the one side,
75   Zion on the other, if you consider it with care.'

'Indeed, my master,' I said,
'I did not understand what now is clear,
78   the point for which my wit was lacking:

'the mid-circle of that celestial motion,
which a certain science calls "Equator,"
81   and which always lies between the sun and winter,

'for the very reason you have given
is as far to the north from here
84   as the Hebrews saw it toward the torrid parts.

'But, please, tell me just how far
we have to go, for the hill rises
87   farther than my eyes can climb.'

Ed elli a me: "Questa montagna è tale,
che sempre al cominciar di sotto è grave;
90 e quant' om più va sù, e men fa male.

Però, quand' ella ti parrà soave
tanto, che sù andar ti fia leggero
93 com' a seconda giù andar per nave,

allor sarai al fin d'esto sentiero;
quivi di riposar l'affanno aspetta.
96 Più non rispondo, e questo so per vero."

E com' elli ebbe sua parola detta,
una voce di presso sonò: "Forse
99 che di sedere in pria avrai distretta!"

Al suon di lei ciascun di noi si torse,
e vedemmo a mancina un gran petrone,
102 del qual né io né ei prima s'accorse.

Là ci traemmo; e ivi eran persone
che si stavano a l'ombra dietro al sasso
105 come l'uom per negghienza a star si pone.

E un di lor, che mi sembiava lasso,
sedeva e abbracciava le ginocchia,
108 tenendo 'l viso giù tra esse basso.

"O dolce segnor mio," diss' io, "adocchia
colui che mostra sé più negligente
111 che se pigrizia fosse sua serocchia."

Allor si volse a noi e puose mente,
movendo 'l viso pur su per la coscia
114 e disse: "Or va tu sù, che se' valente!"

Conobbi allor chi era, e quella angoscia
che m'avacciava un poco ancor la lena,
117 non m'impedì l'andare a lui; e poscia

And he to me: 'This mountain is so fashioned
that the climb is harder at the outset

90   and, as one ascends, becomes less toilsome.

symbol for the will!

'When climbing uphill will seem pleasing—
as easy as the passage of a boat

93   that lets the current float it down the stream—

'at that point will this trail be done.
There look to rest your weariness.

96   This I know for truth. I say no more.'

As soon as he had said these words
a voice close by called out: 'Perhaps

99   you'll feel the need to sit before then.'

Hearing this, both of us turned around,
and saw to our left an enormous rock

102   that neither he nor I at first had noticed.

When we approached, we saw some people
resting in the shade behind the boulder

105   as men will settle down in indolence to rest,

and one of them, who seemed so very weary,
was sitting with his arms around his knees,

108   his head pressed down between them.

'O my dear lord,' I said, 'just look at him.
He shows himself more indolent

111   than if sloth had been his very sister.'

Then he turned and fixed his eyes on us,
barely lifting his face above his haunch,

114   and said: 'Go on up then, you who are so spry.'

At that I realized who he was,
and the exertion that still kept me short of breath

117   now did not keep me from his side.

ch'a lui fu' giunto, alzò la testa a pena,
dicendo: "Hai ben veduto come 'l sole
120   da l'omero sinistro il carro mena?"

Li atti suoi pigri e le corte parole
mosser le labbra mie un poco a riso;
123   poi cominciai: "Belacqua, a me non dole

di te omai; ma dimmi: perché assiso
quiritto se'? attendi tu iscorta,
126   o pur lo modo usato t'ha' ripriso?"

Ed elli: "O frate, andar in sù che porta?
ché non mi lascerebbe ire a' martìri
129   l'angel di Dio che siede in su la porta.

Prima convien che tanto il ciel m'aggiri
di fuor da essa, quanto fece in vita,
132   perch'io 'ndugiai al fine i buon sospiri,

se orazïone in prima non m'aita
che surga sù di cuor che in grazia viva;
135   l'altra che val, che 'n ciel non è udita?"

E già il poeta innanzi mi saliva,
e dicea: "Vienne omai; vedi ch'è tocco
meridïan dal sole, e a la riva
139   cuopre la notte già col piè Morrocco."

When I reached him he barely raised his head
to say: 'Have you marked how the sun
120   drives his car past your left shoulder?'

His lazy movements and curt speech
slowly shaped my lips into a smile, and I began:
123   'Belacqua, no longer need I grieve for you.

'But tell me, what keeps you sitting here?
Are you waiting for an escort,
126   or have you gone back to your old lazy ways?'

And he: 'Brother, what's the good of going up?
The angel of God who sits in the gateway
129   would not let me pass into the torments.

'I must wait outside as long as in my lifetime
the heavens wheeled around me
132   while I put off my sighs of penance to the end,

'unless I'm helped by prayers that rise
from a heart that lives in grace.
135   What good are those that go unheard in Heaven?'

And now, not waiting for me, the poet began
to climb the path, saying: 'Come along.
Look, now the sun is touching the meridian,
139   and on Morocco's shore night sets her foot.'

1–15.   This complex opening passage has its roots in classical and Scholastic discussions of the nature of the human soul. Commentators indicate passages known to Dante in Plato (*Timaeus*, putting forth a belief that there are three independent souls in man, a belief found also, in slightly different form, in the Manichees, and then repeated in Averroës), in Aristotle (*De anima*, arguing against Plato for a single soul, not a plurality of them), Albertus Magnus (*De spiritu et respiratione*), and Aquinas (*Summa theologica, Summa contra Gentiles*, and commentary on *De anima*) as these are reflected in Dante's *Vita nuova* (II.4–5—see DeRo.1980.1, pp. 31–32), *De vulgari eloquentia* (II.ii.6) and *Convivio* (III.ii.11–16). For some of these texts see Singleton's commentary (1973).

Following Aristotle and Aquinas, Dante believed that there was but a single soul in man, divided first into three faculties or powers (with this meaning, Dante uses, synonymously, the words *virtù* or *potenze*—he uses both of them in this passage): the vegetative (governing physical growth), the sensitive (governing the feelings), and the rational or intellective (governing thought). These are presented by Dante (*Conv.* III.ii.11) as "vivere, sentire e ragionare" (the force of life, of the senses, of the reason). Considering what happened within himself so that, absorbed by the words of Manfred for over three hours (50 degrees of the sun's ascent), he could so lose track of time, Dante uses the evidence of his senses to argue, as Aquinas had done before him, that the very fact that parts of the soul cease their function when one of them is fully enjoined proves that we have not a plurality of souls, for these would simply continue to function independently at all times. That is, had Dante's rational soul functioned unimpaired, he would have noted the passage of time even as he listened to Manfred.

The three faculties are all further divided into subsets, the sensitive soul into two, one of these including the five senses, and it is to this set (the senses of hearing and of sight) that Dante adverts here. See the commentary of Daniello (1568) to this passage and the discussion of *virtù* by Philippe Delhaye and Giorgio Stabile in *ED*, V (1976), pp. 1050–59, esp. pp. 1053–55.

Singleton suggests that the apparently forced diction, regarding an ability to *hear* the passage of time, in fact refers to the sound of bells, the primary means of telling time in the Middle Ages.

16–18.   This "flock of sheep" was made aware of Dante's desire to move upward in the last canto (verse 99). From behind the travelers they call out their courteous instruction, their "guidance" now at an end.

19–25. A pseudosimile only because its formal grammatical relations (e.g., "just as . . . so") are not expressed, these verses return to the countryside and the "humble style" that Dante has deployed in many of his similes in *Inferno* and that typified the sole simile found in the preceding canto (vv. 79–87). The farmer fixes his hedge, by filling holes in it with thorns, when the grapes come ripe so as to protect his vineyard from thieves. Steiner (1921) was perhaps the first commentator to note the reference to Matthew 7:14: "Because strait is the gate, and narrow is the way, which leads to life, and there are few that find it."

26–28. Here is another pseudosimile, even less grammatically ordered than the last, in which steep paths to towns or to mountain peaks in north and central Italy are compared to this path, which is even steeper.

37–39. Virgil, unacquainted with this place, gives sound provisional advice: it is best to keep moving up until some indication makes the way plain.

41–42. Beginning with Benvenuto da Imola there has been a small battle over the reference here. Is it to geometry, the line drawn from the apex of the triangle formed by bisecting the right angle of a quadrant of a circle? Or is it (as Benvenuto strongly believed) to the astronomical instrument, the quadrant, which is so called because it replicates precisely a quadrant of a circle? In either case the angle of ascent is even greater than 45 degrees.

50. It is no wonder, given the steepness of the slope, that Dante completes this part of the ascent by crawling on his hands and knees (*carpando*). For previous uses of the word *carpone* see *Inferno* XXV.141; XXIX.68.

52–54. This brief respite may, at least intrinsically, bring to mind the antithetic figure of Ulysses. Where he left the east behind him (*Inf.* XXVI.124) and always ventured forward, Dante now looks back to the east, whence the sun had risen. The eastern sky, locus of the sunrise, has a long tradition in Christianity of representing Jesus, the "light of the world" (John 8:12; 9:5).

55–57. Pietro di Dante (1340) was the first to cite, as a source for this detail, a passage in Lucan (*Phars.* III.247–248), where Arabs, coming south of the equator, marveled at the fact that the shadows of trees fell to their right, not to their left. Trucchi (1936) reminds the reader that, here in purgatory, *levante*, the place where the sun rises, is not east but west—from our perspective in the northern hemisphere.

Dante offers a more extended and entirely similar discussion of these matters in *Convivio* III.v.13–17.

58–60. *Aquilone* (line 60 in the Italian) is the north wind. The tercet repeats the protagonist's amazement upon seeing the morning sun to his left. The reader needs to understand that the poet imagines an "ideal" left and right in this and other particulars. That is, two people facing one another, in either hemisphere, would each claim that the sun is to the other hand. In the astronomical givens of the poem, above the Tropic of Cancer the sun is to the south of the imagined observer, to his or her right; "below" the Tropic of Capricorn (this is a northernizer's view, it should be noted) it is to the north, or left. Substituting "north" for "left" and "south" for "right," the reader may find this passage more readily understandable.

61–66. Virgil's explanation of the position of the sun in the morning sky may be paraphrased as follows: If the sun (the mirror), which moves from one side of the equator to the other, were in the constellation Gemini (Castor and Pollux, the celestial twins) and not Aries (where it is now—see *Inf.* I.37–40), Dante would see the sun's path (the red part of the zodiac) as close to the Bears (Ursa Major and Ursa Minor) and thus as far north as it ever gets (at the summer solstice, 21 June). It would do this, Virgil adds, in an apparently gratuitous detail (but see the next passage), unless it were to veer from its ordained path (which of course it will not in any normal expectation).

"Zodiac, a belt of the heavens eighteen degrees in breadth, extending nine degrees on either side of the Ecliptic, within which, according to the Ptolemaic system, the Moon, Mercury, Venus, the Sun, Mars, Jupiter, and Saturn perform their annual revolutions. It is divided into twelve equal parts of thirty degrees, called signs, which are named from the constellations lying within them" **(T)**.

67–75. Having made this much clear, Virgil goes on to offer Dante a "thought experiment" that in fact exactly replicates what was, in Dante's time, considered geographical actuality. For Dante, Jerusalem, upon the hill Zion, and the mount of purgatory are precisely antipodal and share a common horizon (the equator). From this "experiment" it quickly becomes clear that the path of the sun (the "highway" that Phaeton flew off when he lost control of the chariot of the sun—see note to *Inf.* XVII.106–108) must pass beneath (south) of Jerusalem and (in once more northcentric thinking), above (north) of the mount of purgatory. And thus we understand why Dante was surprised at the sun's leftness and why he should not have been.

The reference to Phaeton, now making clear the reason for the inclusion of reference to the possibility of the sun's *not* keeping its ordained path, is part of a "Phaeton program" in the poem (see Brow.1984.1). As Brownlee points out, Phaeton's presumptuous and failed heavenly voyage is set against Dante's ordained and successful voyage to the otherworld.

76–82.   The protagonist's rephrasing of what he has learned from Virgil is, one must admit, easier to grasp quickly than the master's presentation of it.

83–84.   The Hebrews used to see it from Jerusalem but do so no longer because of their diaspora.

85–87.   It is interesting that, in a canto in which the primary new character is the extremely lazy Belacqua, the protagonist is so strongly presented as wanting to rest—perhaps more so than in any other part of the poem (but see *Inf.* XXIV.43–45).

98–99.   The voice that breaks into what has by now become, for most readers, a rather labored and even fussily academic discussion will turn out to be that of Belacqua. Named only at verse 123, he was a "Florentine, contemporary of Dante, said by the old commentators to have been a musical instrument-maker; modern research has suggested his identification with one Duccio di Bonavia" **(T)**. According to Debenedetti (Debe.1906.1), Belacqua was dead before March 1302 but still alive in 1299. In other words, like Casella, he would seem to have been, in Dante's mind, a recent arrival.

His ironic and witty response to the conversation he has overheard immediately wins the reader's affection. (But, for a denial that this speech of Belacqua's is in fact ironic, see Petrocchi [Petr.1969.1], pp. 270–71.) For a moment we feel drawn out of the moralizing concerns and serious tones of the two poets. Manica (Mani.2000.1), p. 35, calls attention to the great importance of Dante's Belacqua to Samuel Beckett's fiction.

According to him, Belacqua becomes a contemporary myth of irony rather than a depiction of the loss of will; however, he may not sense how much of the Beckettian view of Belacqua is already present in Dante. Much of Beckett's work is a kind of rewriting of the Dantean universe from the point of view of Belacqua alone, a universe of waiting, boredom, question, and frustration, as in the early short story "Belacqua and the Lobster" and certainly including the rock-snuggled hoboes of *Waiting for Godot*. For at least a moment in this extraordinary exchange, Dante's Belacqua seems to control the situation. Of course he will have to be swept aside in the name of progress toward a Christian goal. But it is astounding (and heartwarming) to see how greatly Dante empathized with this character we like to imagine as being so antipathetic to him.

His first word, "perhaps," immediately reveals his character as being indecisive, at least where goals or noble purposes are concerned; what follows shows his wit, deftly puncturing the balloon of Dantean eagerness (for he is a man who longs to do some serious sitting—see verse 52, where he accomplishes that goal). As we shall see, Dante will fight back, and we will then have a scene that is reminiscent of the back-and-forth between Farinata and Dante in *Inferno* X.

105–111.   The word *negghienza* (indolence) begins a steady run of words expressing a desire not to do: *lasso* (weary—106), *sedeva* (was sitting—107), *negligente* (indolent—110), *pigrizia* (sloth—111). The words express the point of view of the protagonist, undoubtedly buoyed by his own recent enthusiasm for spiritual mountaineering, if perhaps conveniently forgetting his recent fatigue—of which Belacqua will enjoy reminding him. Dante has now returned Belacqua's delicate barb with a rather hefty blow.

The *tenzone*-like tone (see note to *Inf.* VIII.31–39) of jesting rivalry that marks the rest of this scene may have been previously set in real life. A tale has come down to us, first found in Benvenuto's commentary (1380), yet almost always cited by later commentators only from the Anonimo Fiorentino's more pleasing account (1400). According to him, Dante frequently reproached Belacqua for his sloth. One day Belacqua quoted Aristotle (the seventh chapter of the *Physics*, a passage also found in *Monarchia* I.iv.2): "The soul becomes wise when one is seated and quiet." To this Dante supposedly replied: "If sitting can make a man wise, no one is wiser than you."

115–117.   Rather than what we might expect, a counterthrust from Dante, we receive the information that he now, with brotherly affection, recognizes this saved soul and approaches him, despite the physical distress he still feels from that energetic climb of his.

121.   The poet's summarizing phrase puts his technique of presentation of Belacqua into relief: lazy movements and curt speech. In fact, Belacqua's three laconic speeches spread over only five lines (98–99, 114, 119–120), and not even the full extent of these. They make him out, as Dante almost certainly knew him, a familiar figure: a person of little physical energy and of incisive, biting wit.

122–123.   Dante's sympathy now governs the mood of the rest of the scene and puts an end to the aggressive sallies of the finally named Belacqua.

124–126.   Dante's last question is not without its barb; is Belacqua just being himself? Has nothing in him changed even in this state of grace?

127–135.   In what seems surprising length for so laconic a speaker (first three speeches, five lines; final speech, nine lines), Belacqua now reveals his other side, not that of a keen listener waiting for his "opponent" to fall into the net of his sharp wit, but of a lazy loser who can't quite get himself organized. It is, the more we reflect upon it, something of a miracle that God chose him to join the elect in Heaven (as the protagonist himself thought—see vv. 123–124).

127.   Belacqua's word of greeting, "frate," now used for the first time since we heard Ulysses—if with far different purpose (see note to *Inf.* XXVI.124–126)—address his men as his "brothers" (*Inf.* XXVI.112), establishes the bond of genuine community among the saved, and we shall hear it used to address one's fellow twelve more times in *Purgatorio* and five in *Paradiso*.

For an observation regarding the antithetic relationship between Belacqua and Ulysses see Frankel (Fran.1989.1), pp. 125–26.

Does it seem that Belacqua does not realize that Dante is still in the flesh, merely assuming that he and Virgil are headed up the mountain to purge themselves? It is possible to ask this question because, in this exchange, there is no reference to Dante's condition or to the identity or role of Virgil, subjects that have and will come up in other colloquies on the mountain.

130–131.   Where Manfred and his flock were eager to move on to their punishment and probably have far longer to wait, Belacqua exhibits a slothful hesitance even to consider shortening his time here. As the first of the late-repentant, he here establishes the rule that applies to all whom we meet in the remainder of ante-purgatory, that is, all between Cantos IV and VIII: there is a prescribed time of waiting for these former sinners, an equal amount to that which they spent unrepentant for their sins.

132.   Even his way of describing his last prayer, which in his view saved his soul, invokes a sense of laziness: it is composed, not of words, but of sighs, a lazy man's prayer if ever there was one.

133–135.   Acknowledging that other "law" of ante-purgatory, of which we have heard from Manfred in the last canto (vv. 138–141), Belacqua refers to the possibility that the sentences of the late-repentant, like those of the excommunicate, may be shortened by the prayers of the living. His way of phrasing the possibility makes us tend to agree with him that he will do the full term of his sentence, since it seems to him unlikely that any of *his* friends would seem to be possessed of "a heart that lives in grace." His speech trails off in dubiety; we reflect that his last negative words do not contain an appeal to Dante for help with the prayers of the living. It is no wonder that Beckett admired him so. He is the sole "Beckettian" character occupying a place in the purposeful and harmonious world of purgation and salvation.

136–139.   Virgil has had enough of this, perhaps revealing, in his stern tone, his own sense of the injustice of the salvation of the apparently undeserving Belacqua. His urgent summons to recommence the journey upward, abruptly terminating Dante's conversation with Belacqua before its formal conclusion (as Carroll [1904] observed), ends the canto with a note of timeliness that the episode has disrupted. Belacqua, saved, has all the time in the world; Virgil, damned, does not. Life, or grace, does not always seem fair.

It is now noon in purgatory and 6 PM in Morocco, across from Spain at Gibraltar. Since *Purgatorio* II.1–9, when it was dawn, the action on the mountain has consumed six hours (we learned that it was just after 9 AM at *Purg.* IV.15–16), just over two and a half of them spent in the difficult ascent and the meeting with Belacqua.

PURGATORIO V

Io era già da quell' ombre partito,
e seguitava l'orme del mio duca,
3   quando di retro a me, drizzando 'l dito,

una gridò: "Ve' che non par che luca
lo raggio da sinistra a quel di sotto,
6   e come vivo par che si conduca!"

Li occhi rivolsi al suon di questo motto,
e vidile guardar per maraviglia
9   pur me, pur me, e 'l lume ch'era rotto.

"Perché l'animo tuo tanto s'impiglia,"
disse 'l maestro, "che l'andare allenti?
12   che ti fa ciò che quivi si pispiglia?

Vien dietro a me, e lascia dir le genti:
sta come torre ferma, che non crolla
15   già mai la cima per soffiar di venti;

ché sempre l'omo in cui pensier rampolla
sovra pensier, da sé dilunga il segno,
18   perché la foga l'un de l'altro insolla."

Che potea io ridir, se non "Io vegno"?
Dissilo, alquanto del color consperso
21   che fa l'uom di perdon talvolta degno.

E 'ntanto per la costa di traverso
venivan genti innanzi a noi un poco,
24   cantando *"Miserere"* a verso a verso.

Quando s'accorser ch'i' non dava loco
per lo mio corpo al trapassar d'i raggi,
27   mutar lor canto in un "oh!" lungo e roco;

I had already parted from those shades,
following the footsteps of my guide,
when one behind me, pointing with his finger,

3

cried: 'Look how the sun's rays on the ground
are cut off to his left
and how he moves and seems like one alive.'

6

Hearing these words, I turned to look at them
and saw that they were staring in amazement
at me, at me and at the interrupted light.

9

'Is your mind so distracted,' asked the master,
'that you have slowed your pace?
Why do you care what they are whispering?

12

'Just follow me and let the people talk.
Be more like a sturdy tower
that does not tremble in the fiercest wind.

15

'For any man who lets one thought—
and then another—take him over
will soon lose track of his first goal.'

18

What could I answer but 'I come'?
I said it, blushing with such shame
as might make one worthy of his pardon.

21

And all this time in front of us
a group of shades advanced across the slope,
chanting *Miserere* line by line.

24

When they perceived my body stopped
the rays of the sun from shining through,
their voices faded to a hoarse and drawn-out 'Oh!'

27

e due di loro, in forma di messaggi,
corsero incontr' a noi e dimandarne:
30   "Di vostra condizion fatene saggi."

E 'l mio maestro: "Voi potete andarne
e ritrarre a color che vi mandaro
33   che 'l corpo di costui è vera carne.

Se per veder la sua ombra restaro,
com' io avviso, assai è lor risposto:
36   fàccianli onore, ed esser può lor caro."

Vapori accesi non vid' io sì tosto
di prima notte mai fender sereno,
39   né, sol calando, nuvole d'agosto,

che color non tornasser suso in meno;
e, giunti là, con li altri a noi dier volta,
42   come schiera che scorre sanza freno.

"Questa gente che preme a noi è molta,
e vegnonti a pregar," disse 'l poeta:
45   "però pur va, e in andando ascolta."

"O anima che vai per esser lieta
con quelle membra con le quai nascesti,"
48   venian gridando, "un poco il passo queta.

Guarda s'alcun di noi unqua vedesti,
sì che di lui di là novella porti:
51   deh, perché vai? deh, perché non t'arresti?

Noi fummo tutti già per forza morti,
e peccatori infino a l'ultima ora;
54   quivi lume del ciel ne fece accorti,

sì che, pentendo e perdonando, fora
di vita uscimmo a Dio pacificati,
57   che del disio di sé veder n'accora."

' and two of them, as messengers,
ran out to meet us and insisted:

30   'Tell us what you can of your condition.'

My master answered: 'When you go back
you may report to those who sent you:

33   this man's body is true flesh.

'If they stopped because they saw his shadow,
as I suppose, they have their answer.

36   It may profit them to do him honor.'

Never have I seen falling stars streak
across the placid sky nor, at nightfall,

39   lightning pulse within the clouds of August

as swiftly as these two ran upward
and, when they reached the others, they all,

42   like an unruly band, turned and charged toward us.

'These people crowding us are many
and they have come to seek your favor,' said the poet,

45   'but keep on walking, listening as you go.'

'O soul who go to blessedness
in the body you were born to,' they called

48   as they came up, 'here pause a while

'to see if one of us is known to you
that you may carry news of him into the world.

51   Ah, why do you go on? Why don't you stop?

'Sinners to the final hour,
we were all at the point of violent death

54   when a light from Heaven brought us understanding,

'so that, repenting and forgiving,
we parted from our lives at peace with God,

57   who with desire to see Him wrings our hearts.'

E io: "Perché ne' vostri visi guati,
non riconosco alcun; ma s'a voi piace
60   cosa ch'io possa, spiriti ben nati,

voi dite, e io farò per quella pace
che, dietro a' piedi di sì fatta guida,
63   di mondo in mondo cercar mi si face."

E uno incominciò: "Ciascun si fida
del beneficio tuo sanza giurarlo,
66   pur che 'l voler nonpossa non ricida.

Ond' io, che solo innanzi a li altri parlo,
ti priego, se mai vedi quel paese
69   che siede tra Romagna e quel di Carlo,

che tu mi sie di tuoi prieghi cortese
in Fano, sì che ben per me s'adori
72   pur ch'i' possa purgar le gravi offese.

Quindi fu' io; ma li profondi fóri
ond' uscì 'l sangue in sul quale io sedea,
75   fatti mi fuoro in grembo a li Antenori,

là dov' io più sicuro esser credea:
quel da Esti il fé far, che m'avea in ira
78   assai più là che dritto non volea.

Ma s'io fosse fuggito inver' la Mira,
quando fu' sovragiunto ad Orïaco,
81   ancor sarei di là dove si spira.

Corsi al palude, e le cannucce e 'l braco
m'impigliar sì ch'i' caddi; e lì vid' io
84   de le mie vene farsi in terra laco."

Poi disse un altro: "Deh, se quel disio
si compia che ti tragge a l'alto monte,
87   con buona pïetate aiuta il mio!

And I replied: 'However hard I gaze into your faces,
none do I recognize. But if in anything
60   I can please you, spirits born for bliss,

'by the very peace I seek
from world to world, following the steps
63   of such a guide, that I will do.'

And one of them began: 'Each of us trusts
in your good offices without your oath,
66   provided lack of power does not thwart your will.

'Therefore, speaking before the others do,
I beg you, should you ever see the region
69   between Romagna and King Charles's land,

'that you be kind enough to seek in Fano
heartfelt prayers for me
72   to help me purge my grievous sins.

'There I was born, but the deep wounds
that poured my blood out with my life
75   were given me among the sons of Antenor,

'where I most thought myself secure.
He of Este had it done, who was incensed
78   against me more than justice warranted.

'Had I but gone on to La Mira,
leaving Oriago, where I was found and taken,
81   I would still be back there where men breathe.

'I fled to the marsh. Entrapped in reeds
and mire I fell, and in that mud
84   I watched a pool of blood form from my veins.'

Then another spoke: 'Pray, so may the desire
be satisfied that draws you to this mountain,
87   do you with gracious pity help with mine.

Io fui di Montefeltro, io son Bonconte;
Giovanna o altri non ha di me cura;
90   per ch'io vo tra costor con bassa fronte."

E io a lui: "Qual forza o qual ventura
ti traviò sì fuor di Campaldino,
93   che non si seppe mai tua sepultura?"

"Oh!" rispuos' elli, "a piè del Casentino
traversa un'acqua c'ha nome l'Archiano,
96   che sovra l'Ermo nasce in Apennino.

Là 've 'l vocabol suo diventa vano,
arriva' io forato ne la gola,
99   fuggendo a piede e sanguinando il piano.

Quivi perdei la vista e la parola;
nel nome di Maria fini', e quivi
102   caddi, e rimase la mia carne sola.

Io dirò vero, e tu 'l ridì tra ' vivi:
l'angel di Dio mi prese, e quel d'inferno
105   gridava: 'O tu del ciel, perché mi privi?

Tu te ne porti di costui l'etterno
per una lagrimetta che 'l mi toglie;
108   ma io farò de l'altro altro governo!'

Ben sai come ne l'aere si raccoglie
quell' umido vapor che in acqua riede,
111   tosto che sale dove 'l freddo il coglie.

Giunse quel mal voler che pur mal chiede
con lo 'ntelletto, e mosse il fummo e 'l vento
114   per la virtù che sua natura diede.

Indi la valle, come 'l dì fu spento,
da Pratomagno al gran giogo coperse
117   di nebbia; e 'l ciel di sopra fece intento,

'I was of Montefeltro, I am Buonconte.
Not Giovanna nor another has a care for me,
90   so that I move among the rest with downcast brow.'

And I to him: 'What force or chance
took you so far from Campaldino
93   that your burial-place was never found?'

'Ah,' he replied, 'at Casentino's border
runs a stream called Archiano
96   that springs above the Hermitage among the Apennines.

'To where its name is lost I made my way,
wounded in the throat, fleeing on foot,
99   and dripping blood across the plain.

'There I lost sight and speech.
I ended on the name of Mary—there I fell,
102   and only my flesh remained.

'I will tell the truth—you tell it to the living.
God's angel took me, and he from hell cried out:
105   "O you from Heaven, why do you rob me?

' "You carry off with you this man's eternal part.
For a little tear he's taken from me,
108   but with the remains I'll deal in my own way."

'Surely you know how a column of moist air,
rising to colder heights, condenses
111   and once again is changed to water.

'That evil will, seeking only evil, he joined
with intellect, and with his natural powers
114   he roused the fog and wind.

'Then, when the day was spent, he shrouded
the valley from Pratomagno to the alps
117   in mist, and darkened the sky with clouds

sì che 'l pregno aere in acqua si converse;
la pioggia cadde, e a' fossati venne
120   di lei ciò che la terra non sofferse;

e come ai rivi grandi si convenne,
ver' lo fiume real tanto veloce
123   si ruinò, che nulla la ritenne.

Lo corpo mio gelato in su la foce
trovò l'Archian rubesto; e quel sospinse
126   ne l'Arno, e sciolse al mio petto la croce

ch'i' fe' di me quando 'l dolor mi vinse;
voltòmmi per le ripe e per lo fondo,
129   poi di sua preda mi coperse e cinse."

"Deh, quando tu sarai tornato al mondo
e riposato de la lunga via,"
132   seguitò 'l terzo spirito al secondo,

"ricorditi di me, che son la Pia;
Siena mi fé, disfecemi Maremma:
salsi colui che 'nnanellata pria
136   disposando m'avea con la sua gemma."

'so that the pregnant air was turned to water.
The rain fell and the overflow that earth
120   could not absorb rushed to the gullies

'and, gathering in surging torrents, poured
headlong down the seaward stream with so much rage
123   nothing could hold it back.

'At its mouth the swollen Archiano found
my frozen corpse and swept it down the Arno,
126   undoing at my chest the cross

'my arms had made when I was overcome by pain.
It spun me past its banks and to the bottom,
129   then covered and enclosed me with its spoils.'

'Pray, once you have gone back into the world
and are rested from the long road,'
132   the third spirit followed on the second,

'please remember me, who am La Pia.
Siena made me, in Maremma I was undone.
He knows how, the one who, to marry me,
136   first gave the ring that held his stone.'

1–3.   The canto begins with the protagonist's forward and upward propulsion but quickly reverses its sense of moral direction when Dante glances back, hearing the voice of one of the negligent behind him.

4–6.   Singleton (1973) argues that, because when Dante approached these late-repentant souls in the previous canto the sun was before him (IV.101), his shadow now fell behind him and, for this reason (or because, as Grabher [1934] noted, in the shade of the boulder he was out of the sun), was not observed by the onlookers until now when, moving away from them, he cast a shadow at an oblique angle. The sun was to Dante's left when he turned back toward the east (IV.52–57); now as he heads west it is to his right, casting his shadow to his left. (For the various moments in this *cantica* in which Dante's shadow is remarked upon, see note to *Purg.* III.16–18.)

7–8.   Dante does not stop, but he does slow his pace as he looks back, as Virgil's words will make clear (verse 11).

9.   How is the reader meant to take the poet's remembrance of his feelings at being recognized as a living soul? Was he guilty of the sin of pride? Some unknown early readers believed so, as we know because Benvenuto tacitly but strongly rebukes them. In his view Dante's excitement is not that of self-congratulation, but rather of joy in his having been chosen by God for this experience, exactly that feeling expressed by Paul when he said "thanks be to God I am what I am" (I Corinthians 15:10). Benvenuto's disciple, John of Serravalle (1416), however, does indeed see the taint of vainglory in Dante's memory of the intense gaze of the penitent souls.

10–18.   Discussing this passage, Frankel (Fran.1989.1), pp. 127–30, points out that Virgil's urgency in trying to get Dante to resume his forward movement is not found in Virgil himself when he encounters Sordello in *Purgatorio* VII and much enjoys his fellow Mantuan's interest and praise. And while, beginning perhaps with Tommaseo (1837), there have been other commentators who find Virgil's scolding excessive, the fact remains that the protagonist takes it most seriously (see vv. 19–21). Further, all that Virgil rebukes in Dante is his allowing his attention to wander, distracted by his admirers, from the prime purpose of the journey, i.e., he is acting to some degree like these negligent souls who were active Christians only near the end of their lives.

19–21.   Dante's blush of shame clearly justifies Virgil's indignation: the protagonist has been thinking of himself too much. And with this detail, indeed, the poem resumes its forward thrust, begun at vv. 1–2, but interrupted for seventeen lines.

23–24.   The new penitents enter singing the Psalm (50:1) that furnished the protagonist's own first word in the poem (*Inf.* I.65), *Miserere*, the first word of David's song of penance. Unlike the last group of late-repentant souls, lounging in the shade of their rock, these are moving in the same rightward direction that Virgil has urged Dante to follow.

25–27.   It is noteworthy that these penitents behave precisely as did the negligent, showing their astonishment and curiosity at Dante's embodied presence in the sacred precinct of the saved. It is also striking that this time Virgil will offer no rebuke to Dante for his interest in them, which will slow his forward movement. If one reflects that this encounter is part of the protagonist's "education" on the mountainside, the apparent contradiction begins to resolve itself. Dante's previous interest was in the negligent souls' reaction to him, not in what he could learn from them.

28–30.   Unlike other characters who enter the action of the poem unnamed but are later identified, these two messengers, seeking information about Dante's condition, will remain anonymous.

31–36.   For all the asperity of Virgil's response to the "messengers," it is clear that he is aware of and in favor of Dante's ability to help speed the progress toward purgation of these and other souls in ante-purgatory (verse 36).

37–40.   The similetic comparison may find its roots in Virgil's description of shooting stars in his *Georgics* (I.365–367), according to Tommaseo (1837) and, more recently, to Hermann Gmelin (Gmel.1955.1).

45.   Once again Virgil underlines the propriety of Dante's favorable response to requests for his intervention on behalf of the penitents as long as he continues his way up the mountain while he does so.

53.   As Chiavacci Leonardi (Chia.1994.1), pp. 143–44, points out, the phrase "sinners to the final hour" is probably meant to recall Matthew 20:1–16, the parable of the laborers in the vineyard, where even those who are summoned to work at the eleventh hour were paid the same as those who labored all the day: "So the last shall be first, and the first last: for many are called, but few are chosen" (20:16).

55.   It is noteworthy that salvation was possible for these sinners only after their own belated penitence *and* their forgiveness of those who had caused their deaths.

58–63.   Dante's acquiescence in being willing to bring news of their salvations pointedly includes those whom he does not know, encouraging them to make a request that might, to them, have seemed too bold. The words he uses for these souls, "spiriti ben nati" (spirits born for bliss) contrast sharply with the formulation for those who were described as "mal nati" in *Inferno* (V.7; XVIII.76; XXX.48).

64.   The speaker, never identified by name, either in his own speech of twenty-one lines (vv. 64–84) or by the narrator, is Jacopo del Cassero, born ca. 1260. "He was among the Guelf leaders who joined the Florentines in their expedition against Arezzo in 1288. He incurred the enmity of Azzo VIII of Este by his opposition to the designs of the latter upon Bologna, of which city Jacopo was Podestà in 1296. In revenge Azzo had him assassinated at Oriaco, between Venice and Padua, while he was on his way (in 1298) to assume the office of Podestà at Milan at the invitation of Maffeo Visconti. He appears to have gone by sea from Fano to Venice, and thence to have proceeded towards Milan by way of Padua; but while he was still among the lagoons, only about eight miles from Venice, he was waylaid and stabbed" **(T)**. Clearly Dante knew that he could count on Jacopo's renown and on his readers' fairly wide acquaintance with the details of his life and death.

69.   Jacopo refers to the Marches, the area between Romagna, to the north, and the kingdom of Naples, governed by Charles of Anjou in 1300, to the south.

71.   Should Dante ever find himself in Fano, in the March of Ancona, where Jacopo's relatives and friends survive, his news of Jacopo's salvation may, by causing them to pray for him, serve to shorten his time in ante-purgatory.

74.   Jacopo's blood, of which we shall hear more in his final lines, the seat
of the soul (see *Purg.* XXV.37–45), left his body through the wounds caused
by the murderous Paduans who waylaid him in 1298. Padua was founded
by Antenor, according to Virgil (*Aen.* I.242–249). Servius's comment on
these verses added the detail that Antenor, before he escaped from Troy,
had given the Greeks the Palladium, thus connecting him with betrayal of
one's country (and suggesting to Dante a name, Antenora, for the second
region of the ninth Circle of hell, *Inf.* XXXII.88).

77–78.   Azzo VIII d'Este became marquis of Este in 1293. Jacopo here
would seem to be suggesting that the Paduans who killed him were in
cahoots with Azzo, the ringleader of the plot. Dante's own former opin-
ion of Azzo was negative (see *Dve* I.xii.5, II.vi.4). Here Jacopo admits a
certain culpability in having aroused Azzo's wrath, reminding us that he
has had to forgive his slayer in order to have been saved. The commen-
tator Jacopo della Lana, in his gloss to vv. 70–72, gives some of the rea-
sons for Azzo's hatred of Jacopo. When Azzo wanted to make himself
ruler of Bologna, the Bolognesi called on Jacopo to be *podestà* of their
city. In opposing Azzo he, according to the fourteenth-century com-
mentator, was unceasing in his vilifications of his enemy, claiming, for in-
stance, that he had slept with his stepmother and was in fact the son of a
washerwoman.

      For the sin of wrath, in its hardened form, as a sin of will and not of in-
continence, see notes to *Inferno* VII.109–114 and XII.16–21 (last paragraph).
Because Azzo was alive in 1308, Dante could not place him in hell; it seems
likely that he would have considered setting him down among the murder-
ers in the company of his father, Obizzo, whom Azzo indeed, according to
many commentators, strangled in 1293. See *Inferno* XII.111–112.

79–80.   Jacopo, reconsidering his actions, realizes that he might have
made good his escape had he proceeded west in the direction of Milano
and headed for the town of La Mira, rather than stopping, off the main
road, between Venice and Padua at Oriago. Benvenuto believes that he
was on horseback (as seems reasonable) and thus could have made his es-
cape along the good road to La Mira, while the swampy overgrowth
made him easy prey for his attackers, stalking him on foot, when he
turned back to hide himself but was seen and attacked.

83–84.   Fallen (from his horse?) and apparently hacked to death by those
who pursued him on foot, Jacopo watches his blood (and thus his soul)
pass from his body.

88. Buonconte da Montefeltro (ca. 1250–89) was the son of the great Ghibelline leader, Guido da Montefeltro (*Inf.* XXVII.19–132; and see note to *Inf.* XXVII.4–6). "In June 1287 Buonconte helped the Ghibellines to expel the Guelfs from Arezzo, an event which was the beginning of the war between Florence and Arezzo; in 1288 he was in command of the Aretines when they defeated the Sienese at Pieve del Toppo; and in 1289 he was appointed captain of the Aretines and led them against the Guelfs of Florence, by whom they were totally defeated (June 11) at Campaldino, among the slain being Buonconte himself, whose body, however, was never discovered on the field of battle" **(T)**. It is important to remember that Dante himself was present at this battle as a cavalryman (see note to *Inf.* XII.75) in what was, for him and his fellow Florentine Guelphs, a great victory. Once again we sense his ability to identify with the loser (see note to *Inf.* XXI.95). There is not a trace of triumphalism in his exchange with the fallen leader of his enemies.

89–90. Unlike Jacopo del Cassero, who hopes that his relatives and friends will pray for him (verse 71), Buonconte realizes that his wife, Giovanna, and other family members have no concern for him. Unlike Jacopo and others of his band, he has been devoid of the hope that has urged the rest to petition Dante for his aid. Now he finds hope in this visitor from the world of the living. This poem, which summarizes its purpose as being to make the living pray better (*Par.* I.35–36), nowhere better indicates this purpose than in ante-purgatory in such scenes as these. It is undoubtedly the case that any number of people who read or heard the poem in the fourteenth century actually prayed for the souls of those whom Dante reports as needing such prayer.

91–93. Dante's desire for knowledge of what happened to Buonconte's body reflects the concern of others present at the battle of Campaldino. How could the body of so important a personage simply disappear? Several students of this passage have suggested that the poet here has in mind Virgil's portrait of Palinurus, so deeply troubled by his unburied state, and consider the protagonist's question a recasting of Aeneas's question to Palinurus: "Which of the gods, Palinurus, tore you from us and submerged you in the open sea?" (*Aen.* VI.341–342). While the linguistic fit is not a perfect one, both the circumstance and the fact that Dante seems to have the Palinurus passage in mind at *Purgatorio* III.130—and surely does so at VI.28–30—makes the reference at least plausible. Chiavacci Leonardi (Chia.1983.1), p. 88n., noted it, as now have Cioffi

(Ciof.1992.1) and Stefanini (Stef.1995.1). And for the view that Palinurus operates as a foil to Buonconte, see Picone (Pico.1999.2), pp. 78–80.

94–99.   The Casentino lies in the upper valley of the Arno. The torrent Archiano derives from sources above the valley near the monastery of Camaldoli, situated high in the mountains above the region. The battle of Campaldino took place on a plain below this higher valley and it is the place to which Dante imagines the wounded Buonconte to have made his way, just where the Archiano joins the Arno, several miles above the site of the battle.

104–108.   As commentators notice, the struggle of the good and wicked angel over the soul of Buonconte mirrors the similar scene that occurs at the death of his father, Guido da Montefeltro (*Inf.* XXVII.112–117), when St. Francis and a fallen Cherub struggle for the soul of Guido. Not even Francis can prevail against God's judgment—if we can accept Guido's narrative at face value.

A possible source for this scene is found in the Epistle of Jude (Iudae 9) in a passage that refers to the archangel Michael's struggle with the devil for the body of Moses. The relevance of this text to Dante's was perhaps first noted by Scartazzini in the 1870s. For discussion, see Pietropaolo (Piet.1984.1), who points out (p. 125) that, like Buonconte's, the whereabouts of Moses' actual burial place was not known (Deuteronomy 34:6).

Buonconte's tear (verse 107) reminds us of the similarly plangent Manfred (*Purg.* III.120).

109–111.   A number of recent commentators here note an echo of Virgil's first *Georgic* (I.322–324). For the view that this passage reflects the description of the storm that drives Aeneas's ships off course in the first book of the *Aeneid* see Carter (Cart.1944.1).

112–114.   Is Dante suggesting that evil forces have power only over the elements (and the dead bodies of humans—see verse 108)?

116.   The mountain ridge Pratomagno and the alpine protuberances referred to establish the confines of the Casentino at the southwest and northeast, respectively.

117.   Restoring a meaning offered in Benvenuto's commentary but perhaps never revisited and arguing against the scholarly exertions of others,

Pertile (Pert.1996.1), pp. 121–26, presents a strong case for the Tuscan form of the verb *intingere*'s past participle, *intinto* in its regular form, but also found as *intento* (darkened). We have accepted Pertile's reading in our translation.

122. Dante's term for "seaward stream" is *fiume real*, or "royal river," i.e., a river that ends in the sea.

126–127. The "cross" that Buonconte had made of his arms perhaps expresses both the gesture of a man in the throes of mortal pain and the sign of his hope for redemption.

128–129. Buonconte's body finally came to rest on the Arno's bed, along with the detritus that the rushing torrent had borne along with it until it, too, settled to rest, mingled with the body of the man.

130–136. The six verses devoted to Pia's speech have made her one of Dante's most remembered and admired portraits—even though we do not really know who she was, to whom she was married (nor how many times, but perhaps twice), or who killed her, or how. For the complicated, necessarily hypothetical, and eventually unknowable status of Pia's identity and story and the possible knowledge that Dante had of them, see Armour (Armo.1993.1), pp. 120–22. See also Giorgio Varanini, *ED* IV (1973), pp. 462–67.

133. Pia uses the "polite imperative," i.e., the impersonal subjunctive, to express her desire (i.e., "may it be remembered by you"): she hopes to be remembered by Dante once he is back on earth so that he can pray for her, as Vellutello (1544) suggests, or recall her to the minds of others for *their* prayers.

134. This line, celebrated for its brevity and power, has the lapidary quality of a headstone, perhaps because it represents one: the beginning of Virgil's epitaph, "Mantua me genuit, Calabri rapuere. . . ." (Mantua gave me birth, Calabria took me off), as Gmelin (Gmel.1955.1) was perhaps the first to suggest. See notes to *Purgatorio* III.27; VI.72. And see Hollander (Holl.1984.4), p. 119, n. 7.

Armour (Armo.1993.1), p. 116, suggests that, if she was defenestrated by her husband (or one of his agents), as many early commentators claim, then the hard earth of the Maremma actually did "undo" her, smashing her body when she hit it.

135–136.   These final verses of the canto have drawn numerous attempts at a clear understanding. However, without knowing the precise nature of the facts to which Dante has decided to allude, we cannot be certain. Among the more interesting suggestions for a source is Hermann Gmelin's (Gmel.1955.1): the verses reflect Dido's remark about her dead husband, Sichaeus, at *Aeneid* IV.28–29: "ille meos, *primus qui me sibi iunxit*, amores / abstulit; ille habeat secum servetque sepulchro" (He, who first joined me to him, has sealed up my love; may he have it with him and keep it in his grave). The italicized phrase seems close enough to Dante's "colui che 'nnanellata pria / disposando" to merit further thought, even if the contexts are not the same, a suffering wife and murderous husband replacing a loyal husband and a would-be loyal wife. Did Pia's husband himself give her a ring of betrothal before they married or, as Varanini suggests, did the man who eventually killed her, the representative of her husband (one Magliata di Pionpino), present the ring for him?

Endnote. The three "autobiographies" that make up the last and largest part of this canto are strikingly similar in their construction (for a somewhat different analysis of the structure of this "triptych" see Picone [Pico.1999.2], pp. 75–77), as the following table reveals. The central figure, Buonconte da Montefeltro, allows Dante the occasion to expand the model he had set for himself in the case of Jacopo del Cassero, and then Pia de' Tolomei offers an occasion to restrict that model, refining it to the very nub of possible composition in the form of a gesture that may remind contemporary readers of the minimalism found in the later works of Samuel Beckett. We should probably be aware that such artistic play is frequently found in medieval writers, who were accomplished practitioners in expansion *(amplificatio)* and contraction *(abbreviatio)* of passages in earlier texts.

JACOPO DEL CASSERO	BUONCONTE DA MONTEFELTRO	PIA DE' TOLOMEI
captatio (64–66)	*captatio* (85–87)	*captatio* (130–131)
homeland and hope for prayer there (67–72)	name, homeland: no hope for prayer there (88–90)	hope for prayer, name, homeland, and place of death (133–134)

place and cause of death (73–81)	place and cause of death (94–99)	cause of death (135–136)
moment of death (82–84)	moment of death (100–102)	moment of death (134)
	postlude (103–129)	

PURGATORIO VI

Continuation: seekers of prayer

1–12	simile: Dante as winner in a game of dice
13–24	six recently deceased souls seek his aid
25–27	Dante finally escapes their importuning

I. The efficacy of prayer

28–33	Dante accosts Virgil: doesn't the text of his poem assert that such prayers as these are vain?
34–42	Virgil denies this: (1) God's will is never forced, (2) pagan prayers were not addressed to the true God—
43–48	and Beatrice will make this plain

Interlude: timeliness

49–51	Dante's desire to continue the journey
52–57	Virgil on the limitations on their upward movement

*II. **Sordello***

58–60	Virgil indicates a soul, seated apart, who will show them the way
61–66	the modern poet's apostrophe of this "Lombard soul," who only silently took notice of their approach
67–69	Virgil asks for direction; the soul wants information
70–75	Virgil's mention of Mantua stirs Sordello to reveal his identity and the two townsmen embrace

"Digression": state of Italy

76–90	poet's apostrophe of "enslaved Italy":
	(a) Italy a ship adrift; a brothel (76–78)
	(b) embrace of Mantuans and civil war (79–87)
	(c) Justinian's empty saddle (88–90)

Quando si parte il gioco de la zara,
colui che perde si riman dolente,
3   repetendo le volte, e tristo impara;

con l'altro se ne va tutta la gente;
qual va dinanzi, e qual di dietro il prende,
6   e qual dallato li si reca a mente;

el non s'arresta, e questo e quello intende;
a cui porge la man, più non fa pressa;
9   e così da la calca si difende.

Tal era io in quella turba spessa,
volgendo a loro, e qua e là, la faccia,
12   e promettendo mi sciogliea da essa.

Quiv' era l'Aretin che da le braccia
fiere di Ghin di Tacco ebbe la morte,
15   e l'altro ch'annegò correndo in caccia.

Quivi pregava con le mani sporte
Federigo Novello, e quel da Pisa
18   che fé parer lo buon Marzucco forte.

Vidi conte Orso e l'anima divisa
dal corpo suo per astio e per inveggia,
21   com' e' dicea, non per colpa commisa;

Pier da la Broccia dico; e qui proveggia,
mentr' è di qua, la donna di Brabante,
24   sì che però non sia di peggior greggia.

Come libero fui da tutte quante
quell' ombre che pregar pur ch'altri prieghi,
27   sì che s'avacci lor divenir sante,

When the game of dice breaks up,
the loser, left dejected,
rehearses every throw and sadly learns,

while all the others crowd around the winner.
One goes in front, one grabs him from the back,
and, at his side, another calls himself to mind.

The winner does not stop, but listens first to one
and then another. Those to whom he gives his hand
then let him be, and so he gets away.

Such was I among that pressing throng,
turning my face this way and that,
and through my promises I freed myself of them.

The Aretine was there who met his death
at the fierce hands of Ghino di Tacco,
and the other who was drowned in the frenzied chase.

There Federico Novello was beseeching
with outstretched hands, and he of Pisa
who made the good Marzucco show his strength.

I saw Count Orso, and that soul severed
from its body both by spite and envy,
or so he said, and not for any crime—

Pierre de la Brosse. And let the Lady
of Brabant be mindful, while she remains on earth,
lest she be made to join a flock far worse.

As soon as I was free of all those shades,
whose only prayer it was that others pray
and speed them on to blessedness,

3

6

9

12

15

18

21

24

27

io cominciai: "El par che tu mi nieghi,
o luce mia, espresso in alcun testo
30   che decreto del cielo orazion pieghi;

e questa gente prega pur di questo:
sarebbe dunque loro speme vana,
33   o non m'è 'l detto tuo ben manifesto?"

Ed elli a me: "La mia scrittura è piana;
e la speranza di costor non falla,
36   se ben si guarda con la mente sana;

ché cima di giudicio non s'avvalla
perché foco d'amor compia in un punto
39   ciò che de' sodisfar chi qui s'astalla;

e là dov' io fermai cotesto punto,
non s'ammendava, per pregar, difetto,
42   perché 'l priego da Dio era disgiunto.

Veramente a così alto sospetto
non ti fermar, se quella nol ti dice
45   che lume fia tra 'l vero e lo 'ntelletto.

Non so se 'ntendi: io dico di Beatrice;
tu la vedrai di sopra, in su la vetta
48   di questo monte, ridere e felice."

E io: "Segnore, andiamo a maggior fretta,
ché già non m'affatico come dianzi,
51   e vedi omai che 'l poggio l'ombra getta."

"Noi anderem con questo giorno innanzi,"
rispuose, "quanto più potremo omai;
54   ma 'l fatto è d'altra forma che non stanzi.

Prima che sie là sù, tornar vedrai
colui che già si cuopre de la costa,
57   sì che ' suoi raggi tu romper non fai.

I began: 'O my light, it seems to me,
that in a certain passage you expressly contradict
30   that prayer can bend decrees of Heaven,

'and yet these people pray for that alone.
Will this their hope, then, be in vain,
33   or are your words not really clear to me?'

He answered: 'Plain is my writing
and their hopes not false
36   if with a sound mind you examine it,

'for not demeaned or lessened is high justice
if in one instant love's bright fire achieves
39   what they who sojourn here must satisfy.

'And there where I affirmed that point
defect was not made good by prayer
42   because that prayer did not ascend to God.

'But do not let these doubts beset you
with high questions before you hear from her
45   who shall be light between the truth and intellect—

'I don't know if you understand: I speak of Beatrice.
You shall see her above, upon the summit
48   of this mountain, smiling and in bliss.'

Then I: 'My lord, let us go on more quickly,
for now I am not wearied as I was,
51   and look, the hill already casts a shadow.'

'We will go on as long as this day lasts,'
he answered, 'as far as we still can,
54   but the truth is other than you think.

'Before you reach the top you'll see again
the one whose beams you do not break
57   because he is now hidden by the slope.

Ma vedi là un'anima che, posta
sola soletta, inverso noi riguarda:
60   quella ne 'nsegnerà la via più tosta."

Venimmo a lei: o anima lombarda,
come ti stavi altera e disdegnosa
63   e nel mover de li occhi onesta e tarda!

Ella non ci dicëa alcuna cosa,
ma lasciavane gir, solo sguardando
66   a guisa di leon quando si posa.

Pur Virgilio si trasse a lei, pregando
che ne mostrasse la miglior salita;
69   e quella non rispuose al suo dimando,

ma di nostro paese e de la vita
ci 'nchiese; e 'l dolce duca incominciava
72   "Mantüa . . . ," e l'ombra, tutta in sé romita,

surse ver' lui del loco ove pria stava,
dicendo: "O Mantoano, io son Sordello
75   de la tua terra!"; e l'un l'altro abbracciava.

Ahi serva Italia, di dolore ostello,
nave sanza nocchiere in gran tempesta,
78   non donna di province, ma bordello!

Quell' anima gentil fu così presta,
sol per lo dolce suon de la sua terra,
81   di fare al cittadin suo quivi festa;

e ora in te non stanno sanza guerra
li vivi tuoi, e l'un l'altro si rode
84   di quei ch'un muro e una fossa serra.

Cerca, misera, intorno da le prode
le tue marine, e poi ti guarda in seno,
87   s'alcuna parte in te di pace gode.

'But see that soul there seated all alone
who looks in our direction.
60   He will let us know the shortest way.'

We came up to him. O Lombard soul, how lofty
and disdainful was your bearing,
63   and in the calmness of your eyes, what dignity!

He did not speak to us
but let us approach, watching us
66   as would a couching lion.

Nevertheless, Virgil drew up closer,
asking him to point us to the best ascent.
69   To this request he gave no answer

but asked about our country and condition.
My gentle guide began: 'Mantua—'
72   and the shade, who had seemed so withdrawn,

leaped toward him from his place, saying:
'O Mantuan, I am Sordello of your city.'
75   And the two of them embraced.

Ah, Italy enslaved, abode of misery,
pilotless ship in a fierce tempest tossed,
78   no mistress over provinces but a harlot!

How eager was that noble soul,
only at the sweet name of his city,
81   to welcome there his fellow citizen!

Now your inhabitants are never free from war,
and those enclosed within a single wall and moat
84   are gnawing on each other.

Search, miserable one, around your shores,
then look into your heart,
87   if any part of you rejoice in peace.

Che val perché ti racconciasse il freno
Iustinïano, se la sella è vòta?
90   Sanz' esso fora la vergogna meno.

Ahi gente che dovresti esser devota,
e lasciar seder Cesare in la sella,
93   se bene intendi ciò che Dio ti nota,

guarda come esta fiera è fatta fella
per non esser corretta da li sproni,
96   poi che ponesti mano a la predella.

O Alberto tedesco ch'abbandoni
costei ch'è fatta indomita e selvaggia,
99   e dovresti inforcar li suoi arcioni,

giusto giudicio da le stelle caggia
sovra 'l tuo sangue, e sia novo e aperto,
102   tal che 'l tuo successor temenza n'aggia!

Ch'avete tu e 'l tuo padre sofferto,
per cupidigia di costà distretti,
105   che 'l giardin de lo 'mperio sia diserto.

Vieni a veder Montecchi e Cappelletti,
Monaldi e Filippeschi, uom sanza cura:
108   color già tristi, e questi con sospetti!

Vien, crudel, vieni, e vedi la pressura
d'i tuoi gentili, e cura lor magagne;
111   e vedrai Santafior com' è oscura!

Vieni a veder la tua Roma che piagne
vedova e sola, e dì e notte chiama:
114   "Cesare mio, perché non m'accompagne?"

Vieni a veder la gente quanto s'ama!
e se nulla di noi pietà ti move,
117   a vergognar ti vien de la tua fama.

If there is no one in your saddle, what good
was it Justinian repaired your harness?
90   Your shame would be less great had he not done so.

Ah, you who should be firm in your devotion
and let Caesar occupy the saddle,
93   if you but heeded what God writes for you,

see how vicious is the beast not goaded
and corrected by the spurs,
96   ever since you took the bridle in your hands.

O German Albert, who abandon her
now that she's untamed and wild,
99   you who should bestride her saddle-bow,

may the just sentence falling from the stars
upon your blood be strange enough and clear
102   that your successor may live in fear of it!

In that far land, both you and your father,
dragged along by greed, allowed
105   the garden of the empire to be laid waste.

Come and see the Montecchi and Cappelletti,
Monaldi and Filippeschi, those already wretched
108   and the ones in dread, you who have no care.

Come, cruel one, come and see the tribulation
your nobles suffer and consider their distress.
111   Then you shall see how dark is Santafiora.

Come and see your Rome and how she weeps,
widowed and bereft, and cries out day and night:
114   'My Caesar, why are you not with me?'

Come and see your people, how they love
one another, and, if no pity for us moves you,
117   come for shame of your repute.

E se licito m'è, o sommo Giove
che fosti in terra per noi crucifisso,
120   son li giusti occhi tuoi rivolti altrove?

O è preparazion che ne l'abisso
del tuo consiglio fai per alcun bene
123   in tutto de l'accorger nostro scisso?

Ché le città d'Italia tutte piene
son di tiranni, e un Marcel diventa
126   ogne villan che parteggiando viene.

Fiorenza mia, ben puoi esser contenta
di questa digression che non ti tocca,
129   mercé del popol tuo che si argomenta.

Molti han giustizia in cuore, e tardi scocca
per non venir sanza consiglio a l'arco;
132   ma il popol tuo l'ha in sommo de la bocca.

Molti rifiutan lo comune incarco;
ma il popol tuo solicito risponde
135   sanza chiamare, e grida: "I' mi sobbarco!"

Or ti fa lieta, ché tu hai ben onde:
tu ricca, tu con pace e tu con senno!
138   S'io dico 'l ver, l'effetto nol nasconde.

Atene e Lacedemona, che fenno
l'antiche leggi e furon sì civili,
141   fecero al viver bene un picciol cenno

verso di te, che fai tanto sottili
provedimenti, ch'a mezzo novembre
144   non giugne quel che tu d'ottobre fili.

Quante volte, del tempo che rimembre,
legge, moneta, officio e costume
147   hai tu mutato, e rinovate membre!

And if it is lawful to ask, O Jove on high,
You who were crucified on earth for us,
120   are Your righteous eyes turned elsewhere,

or, in Your abyss of contemplation
are You preparing some mysterious good,
123   beyond our comprehension?

For each Italian city overflows with tyrants
and every clown that plays the partisan
126   thinks he is the new Marcellus.

My Florence, you may well be pleased
with this digression, which does not touch you,
129   thanks to the exertions of your people.

Many others have justice in their hearts,
even if its arrow's late to fly from all their talking,
132   but yours have justice ready on their tongues.

Many others refuse the public burden. But yours
are eager with an answer without even being asked,
135   crying out: 'I'll take it on *my* shoulders.'

Count yourself happy then, for you have reason to,
since you are rich, at peace, and wise!
138   If I speak truth, the facts cannot deny it.

Athens and Sparta, which made the ancient laws
and had such civil order, gave only hints
141   of a life well lived compared to you,

who make such fine provisions
that the plans you've spun but in October
144   do not survive to mid-November.

How many times within your memory
have you changed laws, coinage, offices,
147   as well as customs, and renewed your members!

E se ben ti ricordi e vedi lume,
vedrai te somigliante a quella inferma
che non può trovar posa in su le piume,

151   ma con dar volta suo dolore scherma.

If you recall your past and think upon it clearly,
you will see that you are like a woman, ill in bed,
who on the softest down cannot find rest

151   but twisting, turning, seeks to ease her pain.

1–12. Frankel (Fran.1989.1), pp. 113–16, discussing this opening simile, deploys the argument that the figure of the loser within the simile equates with that of Virgil in the narrative. That so reasonable an interpretation took six and a half centuries to be developed is a mark of the continuing obstinately rosy view of Virgil and of his role in the poem among its interpreters. It was only in 1968 that any commentator tried to find a counterpart for the "loser"; Giacalone thinks he may correspond to Dante, because of the poet's many troubles at the hands of his enemies. Yet it is hard to see how Dante can be both winner (to whom he is explicitly compared) *and* loser. Singleton (1973 [at verse 2]) offers the following pronouncement: "This figure of the loser, though serving to make the whole scene more graphic, finds no correspondence in the second term of the simile." He is in part correct: both Dante and the crowd of petitioners do correspond to figures within the simile (winner and the crowd of spectators, respectively); that the reference to Virgil is suppressed, inviting the reader to supply it, makes it all the more telling. For support for Frankel's analysis see Hollander (Holl.1990.1), p. 31. Reviewing the commentators, we are able to witness centuries of avoidance behavior (e.g., Momigliano [1946]: the simile is produced "as a piece unto itself, with but slight regard for the context").

For information on the game of *zara* (from Arabic *zahr*, a die, through French *hazard* and Provençal *azar*) see Singleton's lengthy gloss in his commentary to the opening verse of the canto. Similar to the modern game of craps, *zara* involved betting on the numbers, from 3 to 18, resulting from the cast of three dice. The numbers 3, 4, 17, and 18 were, like 2 and 12 in the modern game, "craps," or *zara*, i.e., an undesirable result—unless the player called them out before he threw his dice. The game was apparently played by two players, as is reflected by Dante's reference to only a single winner and loser in this passage.

At verse 8 the reference is to the reward the winner traditionally bestowed upon the onlookers—a bit of his winnings (a practice found today in those at gaming tables who tip the croupier when they conclude their gambling happily).

13–24. These six males, all of whom died violently between 1278 and 1297, are presented as a sort of coda to the three developed figures who bring the preceding canto to its end (Jacopo, Buonconte, Pia), leaving us with the impression of the potentially more extensive narratives that might have accompanied their names, with still more resultant pathos. They also, as Chiavacci Leonardi (Chia.1994.1), p. 173, points out, remind us, in their violent deaths, of the unsettled political condition of Italy (even though the last of them, Pierre de la Brosse, is French), a subject that will dominate the final section of this canto.

13–14. The Aretine is Benincasa da Laterina, "(in the upper Val d'Arno), a judge of Arezzo; according to the old commentators, while acting as assessor for the Podestà of Siena, he sentenced to death a brother (or uncle) of Ghino di Tacco, a famous robber and highwayman of Siena; in revenge Ghino stabbed him while he was sitting in the papal audit office at Rome, whither he had got himself transferred from Siena, at the expiry of his term there, in order to be out of Ghino's reach" (T). Jacopo della Lana says (comm. to vv. 13–14) that Ghino cut off Benincasa's head in full view of the assembled papal court of Boniface VIII (ca. 1297) and somehow managed to make good his escape. Ghino di Tacco was of a Sienese noble family; exiled from his city, he became a famous highwayman. According to Boccaccio (*Decameron* X.ii), his nobility of character eventually resulted in his reconciliation with Pope Boniface before both of them died (in 1303). In Dante's reference to him here there is no such positive treatment; Benincasa, not Ghino, is presented as being saved.

15. This brief and unadorned reference is taken by nearly all the early commentators to refer to Guccio de' Tarlati di Pietramala, a Ghibelline of Arezzo, who was in an attacking party against the Bostoli, Aretine Guelphs in exile at the fortified castle of Rondine. Some assert that, when the forces of the Bostoli counterattacked, Guccio galloped, on a runaway horse, into the Arno, where he drowned. Others say that his death occurred while he was in pursuit of the enemy at that encounter. (The text would allow either interpretation.) Still others claim that his death occurred during the rout of Campaldino, shortly before the presence of the war party at Rondine, in 1289; but see the next note.

16–18. Federico Novello, son of Guido Novello of the Conti Guidi of Romena, in the Casentino (see note to *Inf.* XXX.58–61), died when he came to the aid of the Tarlati, besieging the Bostoli (see preceding note), ca. 1291. It would seem likely that Dante thought of both men as dying in the same effort.

The Pisan whom Dante observes is consistently identified as the son of Marzucco degli Scornigiani, a widely known and respected judge of Pisa until the time of Ugolino's joint rulership (with Archbishop Ruggieri—see note to *Inf.* XXXIII.1–3) in 1287. That Ugolino himself was involved in the political murder of Marzucco's son is attested by various early commentators. Whether the execution (by decapitation) was carried out under Ugolino's direct orders or not, it occurred in 1287 when Ugolino had returned to Pisa as its coruler, and necessarily would have, at the very least, suggested, in Dante's view, Ugolino's complicity.

Evidence for Marzucco's fortitude is ascribed to one of two anecdotes by the early commentators: either he astounded Ugolino by his calm demeanor when he, no longer a judge but a Franciscan novice, asked that the corpse of his son be taken up from the public square and buried (to which request the much impressed Ugolino assented) or he exemplified Christian forgiveness in his decision not to seek revenge for the judicial murder of his son. Both anecdotes may, however, be pertinent. In 1286, before these events, Marzucco had ended his long and distinguished career in Pisa as jurist (ca. 1249–86) to become a Franciscan and indeed eventually resided in the Franciscan house at Santa Croce in Florence from 1291 until his death in 1300 or 1301. It is possible that Dante knew him and heard of the events in Pisa and of Ugolino's involvement in them directly from "lo buon Marzucco" himself.

19–24.   The first of these two is Count Orso degli Alberti della Cerbaia, murdered by his cousin, Count Alberto da Mangona, ca. 1286. Their respective fathers, Napoleone and Alessandro degli Alberti da Mangona, have been seen locked in eternal hatred, in Caïna, as treacherous to kindred in *Inferno* XXXII.40–60. Like father, like cousin.

The only non-Italian in the group, and the first of them to die (in 1278), is the Frenchman, Pierre de la Brosse, "favorite and chamberlain of Philip III of France. On the sudden death in 1276 of the heir to the throne, Louis, Philip's son by his first wife, Isabella of Aragon, an accusation was brought against the Queen, Mary of Brabant, of having poisoned Louis in order to secure the succession of her own son, among her accusers being Pierre de la Brosse. Not long afterwards Pierre was suddenly arrested and imprisoned by order of the King. After being tried at Paris before an assembly of the nobles, he was hanged by the common hangman, June 30, 1278. The suddenness and ignominy of his execution appear to have caused great wonder and consternation, especially as the charge on which he was condemned was not made known. According to the popular account he had been accused by the Queen of an attempt upon her chastity. The truth seems to be that he was hanged upon a charge of treasonable correspondence with Alphonso X, King of Castile, with whom Philip was at war, the intercepted letters on which the charge was based having, it is alleged, been forged at the instance of the Queen" **(T)**. Dante seems to have believed the common version of the story, which would put Mary of Brabant (in our day a province of Belgium) not in purgatory, where her victim has his victory, but in hell (probably in the last of the Malebolge along with Potiphar's wife [*Inf.* XXX.97]) if she failed to repent her evildoing. Since she lived almost as long as Dante would (she died on 12 January 1321), one wonders if she became aware of this warning.

28–33. Dante's leading question puts Virgil on the spot. In *Aeneid* VI.376 the Sibyl answers Palinurus's request of Aeneas that he have his unburied corpse laid to rest by denying him such a hope: "desine fata deum flecti sperare precando" (cease hoping that decrees of the gods may be turned aside by prayer). Does this answer compel us to believe that the penitents are deluded in their hope for the efficacy of prayer? Dante's question is a necessarily tricky one for Virgil to have to deal with. See Hollander (Holl.1983.1), pp. 113–15.

34–42. Virgil's response seems casuistic, at least in part. In order not to deny Christians' belief in the efficacy of prayer, he first of all examines the notion that God's will has been bent by the desires of others if such prayer be acted upon. If God's will is won over in an instant by the loving prayer of others, that is as He wills, and there is only an apparent inconsistency. He has merely accepted in immediate payment the "sum" offered on behalf of the guilty party rather than insisting on an extended time of solitary penance. It is a bit difficult to reconcile this formulation, however, with the actual words in the *Aeneid*, which seem far less accommodating than this explanation of them. When Virgil goes on to explain that, in any case, Palinurus was not praying to the true God in the passage referred to in Book VI, our credulity is still more gravely tested. The statement of the Sibyl is totalizing, while Virgil now reconstructs it to have a meaning that it never could have had, i.e., *some* prayer is effective, some not. We witness another case in which the pagan author is forced to pay for his error in rather ungainly ways. Here Virgil confidently attacks inadequate Christian readings of the *Aeneid* as though *they* were the source of the poem's theological failure. "Plain is my writing" indeed!

43–48.   Virgil, having failed to develop a convincing case for his own expertise, now turns to Beatrice's authority in this matter.

61–63.   This figure will shortly (at verse 74) reveal himself to be Sordello, the thirteenth-century Italian poet, who wrote in Provençal. "Sordello was born (c. 1200) at Goito, village on the Mincio, about 10 miles NW of Mantua; shortly after 1220 he was resident at the court of Count Ricciardo di San Bonifazio of Verona, who had married (c. 1222) Cunizza, daughter of Ezzelino II da Romano (*Par.* IX.32). In or about 1226, Sordello, with the connivance of her brother, Ezzelino III (*Inf.* XII.109–110), abducted Cunizza, and took her to Ezzelino's court. Later he formed a liaison with her, and, to escape her brother's resentment, was forced to take refuge in Provence, where he made a lengthy stay at the court of Count Raymond Berenger IV (*Par.* IV.134). There he became acquainted with the Count's seneschal, Romieu de Villeneuve (*Par.* VI.128). While in Provence (c. 1240) Sordello wrote one of his most important poems, the lament for Blacatz, one of Count Raymond's Provençal barons, from which Dante is supposed to have taken the idea of assigning to Sordello the function of pointing out the various princes in Ante-purgatory (*Purg.* VII.49–136). After Count Raymond's death (1245) Sordello remained for some years at the court of his son-in-law, Charles of Anjou (*Purg.* VII.113). When the latter in the spring of 1265 set out on his expedition to Italy to take possession of the kingdom of Sicily, Sordello followed him. . . . Sordello was among those who shared in the distribution of Apulian fiefs made by Charles to his Provençal barons after his victories over the Hohenstaufen at Benevento and Tagliacozzo, to Sordello and his heirs being assigned several castles in the Abruzzi, under deeds dated March and June, 1269. No further record of Sordello has been preserved, and the date and place of his death are un-known. . . . Of Sordello's poems some forty have been preserved, besides the lament for Blacatz already mentioned, is a lengthy didactic poem, the *Ensenhamen,* or *Documentum Honoris*" (T).

Beginning perhaps with Torraca (1905), commentators have seen elements of Virgil's Elysian fields and the guide therein, the poet Musaeus (*Aen.* VI.666–678), in Dante's presentation of Sordello. See Hollander (Holl.1993.1), p. 302.

For Sordello's "scandalous love life" see Barański (Bara.1993.2), pp. 20–23 and notes (for bibliography).

64–65.   The intensity of the first four sets of encounters on the mountain has varied: the intense personalness of Manfred was countered by the quizzical distance of Belacqua, which in turn was balanced by the three intense self-narratives of Jacopo, Buonconte, and Pia. Sordello begins with a Belacqua-like reserve, only to be roused to a pitch of excitement by Virgil's revelation of his Mantuan homeland.

66. Sordello's pose may recall Genesis 49:9, where Judah, in Jacob's dying blessing, is described as a couching lion. Tommaseo was the first commentator to make this suggestion.

70. As Scartazzini (1900) pointed out, Sordello is unable to discern that Dante is here in the flesh because the sun is behind the mountain (see vv. 55–57) and he does not cast a shadow.

72. The word "Mantua" may have been intended, according to Benvenuto da Imola (followed by John of Serravalle), as the first word of Virgil's own Latin epitaph, "Mantua me genuit. . . ." See notes to *Purgatorio* III.27 and V.134.

73–75. The civic patriotism of Sordello is awakened when Virgil mentions their common homeland. Their resulting embrace has been, when coupled with Dante's failed attempt to embrace Casella (*Purg.* II.76–81), the source of considerable puzzlement when it is considered along with the decision not to embrace arrived at by Statius and Virgil. See note to *Purgatorio* XXI.130–136.

76–77. This passage begins what Benvenuto considers the third part of this canto, "a digression against Italy and the principal authors of her desolation." Dante himself at verse 128 refers to his "digression" here; but no one can possibly imagine that this "digression" is not central to his purpose. (On the subject of Dante's propensity to digress see Corsi [Cors.1987.1].) The poet will directly address Italy herself, the Church, the uncrowned Habsburg emperor Albert, God, and, finally, Florence.

As has long been noted, the sixth canto of each *cantica* is devoted to the treatment of political issues, those of Florence *(Inf.)*, of Italy *(Purg.)*, of the empire *(Par.)*—though these subjects are intertwined.

78. Bernardino Daniello (1568) was apparently the first to notice the now often-cited biblical source for Dante's phrase "donna di provincie" *(princeps provinciarum)* in the Lamentations of Jeremiah 1:1: "How does the city sit solitary, that was full of people! how is she become as a widow! she that was great among the nations, and *princess among the*

provinces, how is she become tributary!" Jeremiah's lament for Jerusalem had been a central reference point for the death of Beatrice, recorded in *Vita nuova* XXVIII.1.

83.   The evident recollection of the central image of Ugolino's punishment (*Inf.* XXXII.127–132) may owe its deployment here to the earlier concern with the Ugolino-related reference to the "good Marzucco" of Pisa. See note to vv. 16–18.

88–89.   The language here clearly derives from Dante's earlier expression of these sentiments, as Andreoli (1856) was perhaps the first to observe, in *Convivio* IV.ix.10: "Thus we might say of the Emperor, if we were to describe his office with an image, that he is the one who rides in the saddle of the human will. How this horse pricks across the plain without a rider is more than evident, especially in wretched Italy, which has been left with no means whatsoever to govern herself" (tr. Lansing).

"Justinian, surnamed the Great, Emperor of Constantinople, A.D. 527–565. During his reign the great general Belisarius overthrew the Vandal kingdom in Africa and the Gothic kingdom in Italy. Justinian, who is best known not by his conquests but by his legislation, appointed a commission of jurists to draw up a complete body of law, which resulted in the compilation of two great works; one, called *Digesta* or *Pandectae*, in fifty books, contained all that was valuable in the works of preceding jurists; the other, called *Justinianeus Codex*, consisted of a collection of the Imperial constitutions. To these two works was subsequently added an elementary treatise in four books, under the title *Institutiones*; and at a later period Justinian published various new constitutions, to which he gave the name of *Novellae Constitutiones*. These four works, under the general name of *Corpus Juris Civilis*, form the Roman law as received in Europe" **(T)**.

The empty chariot of the empire is reflected in the similarly empty chariot of the Church in the procession of the Church Militant, beset by all its external and internal enemies, in *Purgatorio* XXXII.

91–96.   The leaders of the Church are accused of having interfered in the civil governance of Italy, trying to guide its affairs by manipulating its "bridle" without having allowed the horse's rider to seat himself in the saddle. The passage may reflect Dante's unhappiness either with the intrigues of Pope Boniface VIII, maneuvering to bring about the accession of Albert in 1298, or with those of Pope Clement V, who managed to control the election of the next emperor, Henry VII, after the death of "German Albert" in 1308—or with both pontiffs' involvements in imperial politics. The language here reflects the biblical text that had greatest currency in the antipapal political arguments of the time, apparently claiming an indisputable right to govern for the monarch, Matthew 22:21: "Render unto Caesar the things that are Caesar's, and to God the things that are God's."

97–102. "German Albert, i.e. Albert I of Austria, son of Rudolf of Hapsburg, Emperor (but never crowned), 1298–1308; he was elected after having slain his predecessor, Adolf of Nassau, in a battle near Worms, his treason against Adolf having been condoned by Boniface VIII in consideration of the advantages of his alliance against the Pope's mortal enemy, Philip the Fair of France. Dante . . . foretells his violent death (which took place on May 1, 1308, when he was assassinated at Königstein, close to the castle of Hapsburg, by his nephew John)" **(T)**. It is also possible that Dante had in mind, as punishment of Albert's "blood," the death of his firstborn son, Rudolph, in 1307.

The image of Italy as uncontrolled animal, which has been operative since verse 89, now culminates in Sordello-like invective (see Perugi [Peru.1983.1]) against the Habsburg ruler.

Dante's *post-eventum* prophecy is clearly written after May 1308, but how much later? The really difficult problem facing anyone who wants to resolve this question involves the identity of Albert's "successor." Is the reference simply to *any* successor who will feel compelled by pressure to act in Italophile ways? Or does Dante have Henry VII of Luxembourg, elected in 1308, in mind? Various commentators (e.g., Tozer, Trucchi, Momigliano) argue for a date of composition between 1308 and July 1310, when Henry finally announced his intention of coming to Italy, the "garden of the empire." If such was the case, Henry had not yet begun his descent into Italy (autumn of 1310) and the rather cool tone of Dante's appeal for imperial action would make sense. For after the emperor's advent, Dante's words about him are, at least at first (Epistle V, composed in the last quarter of 1310) enormously warm and hopeful. We would then have three stages in Dante's responses to Henry: (1) initial dubiety (1308–10), (2) great excitement as the campaign to put Italy under the governance of a true Roman emperor begins (1310–11), (3) eventual wary enthusiasm (see the two political letters written in the spring of 1311 [Epistles VI and VII]), given the precariousness of Henry's military and political situation (1311–13). (For Dante's political epistles see Pertile

[Pert.1997.1]; for this view of Dante's changing enthusiasms about Henry's Italian mission see Hollander [Holl.2001.1], pp. 133–36.)

103.   Albert's father is Rudolph of Habsburg—see *Purgatorio* VII.94.

106–117.   The final four tercets of the poet's apostrophe of Albert all begin with mocking appeals to him to come to Italy (Albert was alive at the imagined date of the poem, 1300) to see "the garden of the empire laid waste."

106–108.   These first four names offer evidence of pandemic civil strife, exemplified by the Montecchi (Ghibellines) and the Guelph Cappelletti (Shakespeare's Montagues and Capulets), two political factions of the city of Cremona, still bearing the names of their founding families but no longer remaining family units (see Singleton's note to verse 106).

The Filippeschi, a Ghibelline family of Orvieto, were in continual combat with the Guelph Monaldeschi. The former, encouraged by Henry's presence in Italy, attempted to vanquish the Monaldeschi but failed and were themselves banished from Orvieto in 1312.

109–111.   "Santafiora, county in the Sienese Maremma, which from Cent. IX down to 1300 belonged to the powerful Ghibelline family of the Aldobrandeschi, who thence took their title of Counts of Santafiora. It was formerly an imperial fief, but at the time Dante wrote it was in the hands of the Guelfs of Siena" (T). We meet one of the counts of Santafiora, Omberto Aldobrandesco, in *Purgatorio* XI.55–72.

The language here reflects the Bible, as commentators since Daniello (1568) have noted, Jesus's words foretelling the destruction of Jerusalem (Luke 21:23), "For there shall be great distress *(pressura)* in the land."

112–114.   Dante's view of Rome's desire to have an emperor in the saddle is obviously at odds with the typical Guelph view.

115–117.   Albert's "people" are the Italians, bereft of their true leader; he would be shamed were he to hear what they say of him for abandoning them.

118–123.   The name "Jove" occurs variously in the poem, nine times in all, but here alone does it refer *only* to the Christian God (God is referred to as Jupiter in *Inf.* XXXI.45 in a similar usage). Although the poet realizes that his questioning of divine justice is out of bounds, he persists in it.

God's plan for Italy, in any case, arises from his divine counsel, which is beyond our knowing: see Psalm 35:7 [36:6]: "Iudicia tua abyssus multa" (Your judgments like the great deep), a citation first offered by Benvenuto da Imola.

124–126. Lacking an emperor, Italy is governed by local tyrants, while every yokel who joins a political party fancies himself the "new Marcellus." But which Marcellus? The debate continues. As Singleton points out, there were three contemporaneous Roman consuls named Marcellus and, among these, the most likely to be referred to here is Marcus Claudius Marcellus, consul in 51 B.C., and renowned for his hatred of Julius Caesar. It is possibly he to whom Lucan refers in *De bello civili* (I.313): "Marcellusque loquax et, nomina vana, Catones" (Marcellus, that man of words, and Cato, that empty name). This identification, which is supported by the majority of commentators (and given a magisterial first exposition by Benvenuto da Imola) and which apparently makes excellent sense in a context that certainly seems to inveigh against hostility to the emperor, is at least problematic: Lucan's words are part of Julius Caesar's infamous first speech to his troops, when he counsels their march on Rome (see note to *Inf.* XXVI.112–113), and they also ridicule Cato the Younger, surely Dante's greatest classical hero. In fact, the Lucanian Caesar unites Marcellus, Cato, and Pompey as three of his great enemies. Dante probably would have felt that anyone claimed as an enemy by Julius, about to destroy the Roman republic, was his friend. It would be strange for Dante to lend himself to Julius's view of these men, even if he defends the Caesarean inviolability of the eventual emperor and condemns Brutus and Cassius for murdering him. In any case, it is perhaps wise to consider other alternatives. An early tradition held that the text read "Metellus" (see *Purg.* IX.138) and not "Marcellus," but this possibility is no longer seriously considered. One other Marcus Claudius Marcellus, however, is worthy of consideration. He was consul in 222 B.C., successful in skirmishes against the great Hannibal, conqueror of Syracuse, welcomed back to Rome and referred to as "the Sword of Rome," the best known of all Romans of that name, and indeed mentioned in the *Aeneid* (VI.855) as one of Rome's greatest warriors, presented in the parade of heroes described by Anchises as preceding that latter-day Marcellus, the Emperor Augustus's adopted and very mortal son. Vellutello (1544) and Tommaseo (1837) both think of the earlier Marcus Claudius as the Marcellus most likely to be mentioned here. One potential advantage of this solution is that it broadens the base of Dante's political scorn: if the Marcellus is Lucan's, then only Guelph bumpkins, hating the emperor, are indicated; if Virgil's, then all enthusiastic amateurs, of whatever party, who think of themselves as great men.

127–129.   The fifth and final apostrophe is, naturally, of Florence herself, and is, naturally, dripping with sarcasm, reminiscent of the earlier apostrophe that opens *Inferno* XXVI, in which the city is asked to rejoice in her renown for having produced so many thieves who now disport themselves in hell. For the supposedly "digressive" nature of Dante's remarks, see note to vv. 73–75.

135.   The Florentine who shouts "I'll take it on *my* shoulders" is not expressing his respect for civic virtue so much as masking his intention to promote himself to "where the action is" under the guise of humble service.

139–147.   Dante's sardonic streak is rarely more evident than in this passage, in which the founding Western civic entities in Greece are seen by contemporary Florentines as pale and vapid precursors of their great city's version of political excellence. The Florentines are so good at governance, it seems, that they eschew any form of stability for rapid change, whether in their laws, coins, civic offices, political customs, and even citizenship, this last probably a reference to the sort of political act that banished the White Guelphs (including Dante) in 1302.

148–151.   The obvious sarcasm of the preceding seven tercets in "praise" of Florence now yields to a devastating image of the city as wealthy invalid wife, which is possibly derived from Augustine's *Confessions* (VI.16), as was perhaps first noted by Grandgent (1909). As Augustine nears conversion, at the very end of the sixth book, his soul still struggles to escape from God, to be free for "better" things; he describes its inner state as follows: "Whichever way it turned, on front or back or sides, it lay on a bed that was hard, for in you alone the soul can rest."

PURGATORIO VII

Poscia che l'accoglienze oneste e liete
furo iterate tre e quattro volte,

3   Sordel si trasse, e disse: "Voi, chi siete?"

"Anzi che a questo monte fosser volte
l'anime degne di salire a Dio,

6   fur l'ossa mie per Ottavian sepolte.

Io son Virgilio; e per null' altro rio
lo ciel perdei che per non aver fé."

9   Così rispuose allora il duca mio.

Qual è colui che cosa innanzi sé
sùbita vede ond' e' si maraviglia,

12   che crede e non, dicendo "Ella è . . . non è . . . ,"

tal parve quelli; e poi chinò le ciglia,
e umilmente ritornò ver' lui,

15   e abbracciòl là 've 'l minor s'appiglia.

"O gloria di Latin," disse, "per cui
mostrò ciò che potea la lingua nostra,

18   o pregio etterno del loco ond' io fui,

qual merito o qual grazia mi ti mostra?
S'io son d'udir le tue parole degno,

21   dimmi se vien d'inferno, e di qual chiostra."

"Per tutt' i cerchi del dolente regno,"
rispuose lui, "son io di qua venuto;

24   virtù del ciel mi mosse, e con lei vegno.

Non per far, ma per non fare ho perduto
a veder l'alto Sol che tu disiri

27   e che fu tardi per me conosciuto.

Once the courteous and joyful greetings
had been repeated a third time and a fourth,
3   Sordello drew back and asked: 'Who then are You?'

'Before souls worthy of ascent to God
could be directed to this mountain,
6   Octavian interred my bones.

'I am Virgil, and for no other failing
did I lose Heaven but my lack of faith.'
9   That was the answer that my leader gave.

Like one who of a sudden sees a thing before him
at which he wonders, who both believes and doesn't,
12   saying to himself: 'It is—but no, it cannot be,'

such seemed the other. He bowed his head,
humbly drew near again and, opening his arms,
15   bent down to clasp him deferentially.

'O glory of the Latins,' he exclaimed,
'through whom our language showed what it could do,
18   O eternal honor of the town where I was born,

'what merit or what grace brings you to me?
If I am worthy of your words, tell me
21   if you come from hell, and from what cloister.'

'Through all the circles of the woeful kingdom
I have made my way,' he answered. 'Power
24   from Heaven moved me and with that power I come.

'Not for what I did but what I did not do
I lost the vision of the lofty Sun you long for
27   and which I came to know too late.

Luogo è là giù non tristo di martìri,
ma di tenebre solo, ove i lamenti
30   non suonan come guai, ma son sospiri.

Quivi sto io coi pargoli innocenti
dai denti morsi de la morte avante
33   che fosser da l'umana colpa essenti;

quivi sto io con quei che le tre sante
virtù non si vestiro, e sanza vizio
36   conobber l'altre e seguir tutte quante.

Ma se tu sai e puoi, alcuno indizio
dà noi per che venir possiam più tosto
39   là dove purgatorio ha dritto inizio."

Rispuose: "Loco certo non c'è posto;
licito m'è andar suso e intorno;
42   per quanto ir posso, a guida mi t'accosto.

Ma vedi già come dichina il giorno,
e andar sù di notte non si puote;
45   però è buon pensar di bel soggiorno.

Anime sono a destra qua remote;
se mi consenti, io ti merrò ad esse,
48   e non sanza diletto ti fier note."

"Com'è ciò?" fu risposto. "Che volesse
salir di notte, fora elli impedito
51   d'altrui, o non sarria ché non potesse?"

E 'l buon Sordello in terra fregò 'l dito,
dicendo: "Vedi? sola questa riga
54   non varcheresti dopo 'l sol partito:

non però ch'altra cosa desse briga,
che la notturna tenebra, ad ir suso;
57   quella col nonpoder la voglia intriga.

'There is a place down there, not sad with torments
but only darkness, where lamentations sound,
30   not loud as wailing but soft as sighs.

'There I abide with the innocent little ones
seized in the fangs of death
33   before they could be cleansed of mortal guilt.

'There I abide with those who were not clothed
in the three holy virtues, yet, blameless,
36   knew the others and followed every one.

'But if you know the way and are permitted,
show us how to go, so that we may come sooner
39   where purgatory has its true beginning.'

He answered: 'We are set in no fixed place.
I may ascend and move about, and I will walk
42   with you and be your guide as far as I'm allowed.

'But see, already day is waning
and we may not ascend by night.
45   Now is the time to choose a resting place.

'There, to the right, are spirits set apart.
I will lead you to them, if you wish.
48   And not without pleasure shall you know them.'

'How is that?' was the reply. 'If a man should wish
to climb by night, would he be hindered,
51   or would he not ascend because he lacked the power?'

Good Sordello drew his finger through the dust
and said: 'See, you would not cross
54   even this line once the sun goes down,

'for nothing hinders the ascent
except the darkness of the night,
57   which binds the will with helplessness.

Ben si poria con lei tornare in giuso
e passeggiar la costa intorno errando,
60   mentre che l'orizzonte il dì tien chiuso."

Allora il mio segnor, quasi ammirando,
"Menane," disse, "dunque là 've dici
63   ch'aver si può diletto dimorando."

Poco allungati c'eravam di lici,
quand' io m'accorsi che 'l monte era scemo,
66   a guisa che i vallon li sceman quici.

"Colà," disse quell' ombra, "n'anderemo
dove la costa face di sé grembo;
69   e là il novo giorno attenderemo."

Tra erto e piano era un sentiero schembo,
che ne condusse in fianco de la lacca,
72   là dove più ch'a mezzo muore il lembo.

Oro e argento fine, cocco e biacca,
indaco, legno lucido e sereno,
75   fresco smeraldo in l'ora che si fiacca,

da l'erba e da li fior, dentr' a quel seno
posti, ciascun saria di color vinto,
78   come dal suo maggiore è vinto il meno.

Non avea pur natura ivi dipinto,
ma di soavità di mille odori
81   vi facea uno incognito e indistinto.

"Salve, Regina" in sul verde e 'n su' fiori
quindi seder cantando anime vidi,
84   che per la valle non parean di fuori.

"Prima che 'l poco sole omai s'annidi,"
cominciò 'l Mantoan che ci avea vòlti,
87   "tra color non vogliate ch'io vi guidi.

'After nightfall one might head back down
and wander lost around the hill
60   as long as the horizon hides the day.'

At that my lord, as in amazement, said:
'Lead us, then, to where you say
63   we may take pleasure in our rest.'

We had gone but a little way from there
when I observed the hill was hollowed out,
66   as valleys carve out hollows in our mountains.

'Let us go there,' said the shade,
'to where the slope sinks to a bowl,
69   and there await the coming of the day.'

A slanting path, connecting steep and flat,
brought us to the border of the glade
72   just where the rim around it falls away.

Gold and fine silver, carmine and leaded white,
indigo, lignite bright and clear,
75   an emerald after it has just been split,

placed in that dell would see their brightness fade
against the colors of the grass and flowers,
78   as less is overcome by more.

Nature had not only painted there in all her hues
but there the sweetness of a thousand scents
81   was blended in one fragrance strange and new.

Seated in the grass and flowers, I saw
souls not visible from beyond the sunken valley.
84   *'Salve Regina'* was the song they sang.

'Before the sun's rim sinks into its nest,'
began the Mantuan soul who'd brought us there,
87   'do not ask me to take you down among them.

Di questo balzo meglio li atti e ' volti
conoscerete voi di tutti quanti,
90   che ne la lama giù tra essi accolti.

Colui che più siede alto e fa sembianti
d'aver negletto ciò che far dovea,
93   e che non move bocca a li altrui canti,

Rodolfo imperador fu, che potea
sanar le piaghe c'hanno Italia morta,
96   sì che tardi per altri si ricrea.

L'altro che ne la vista lui conforta,
resse la terra dove l'acqua nasce
99   che Molta in Albia, e Albia in mar ne porta:

Ottacchero ebbe nome, e ne le fasce
fu meglio assai che Vincislao suo figlio
102   barbuto, cui lussuria e ozio pasce.

E quel nasetto che stretto a consiglio
par con colui c'ha sì benigno aspetto,
105   morì fuggendo e disfiorando il giglio:

guardate là come si batte il petto!
L'altro vedete c'ha fatto a la guancia
108   de la sua palma, sospirando, letto.

Padre e suocero son del mal di Francia:
sanno la vita sua viziata e lorda,
111   e quindi viene il duol che sì li lancia.

Quel che par sì membruto e che s'accorda,
cantando, con colui dal maschio naso,
114   d'ogne valor portò cinta la corda;

e se re dopo lui fosse rimaso
lo giovanetto che retro a lui siede,
117   ben andava il valor di vaso in vaso,

'From this bank you will more easily discern
their gestures and their features
90   than if you went among them down below.

'He who sits the highest—the one with the look
of a man who shirked his duty—not moving his lips
93   to match the singing of the rest,

'was Emperor Rudolph. He might have healed
the wounds that have brought Italy to death,
96   so that, for another to restore her, it is late.

'The next, who looks as if he gave him comfort,
ruled the land where the waters from the Moldau
99   flow into the Elbe, and from the Elbe to the sea.

'His name was Ottocar, and in his swaddling clothes
he was of greater worth than Wenceslaus,
102   his bearded son, who feasts on lust and idleness.

'And the one with the small nose, who seems in council
with the one who is so gracious in his looks,
105   died in flight, deflowering the lily.

'Look how he beats upon his breast!
And see the other, who rests his cheek
108   upon his palm and sighs:

'father and the father-in-law of the plague of France,
they know his foul and vicious life—
111   thus comes the grief that pierces them.

'He who looks so tall and sturdy and who sings
in time with him who bears a manly nose
114   was girt with the cord of every virtue.

'And if the youth who sits behind him
had come to power on his throne, then indeed
117   his virtue would have passed from vessel to vessel,

che non si puote dir de l'altre rede;
Iacomo e Federigo hanno i reami;
120   del retaggio miglior nessun possiede.

Rade volte risurge per li rami
l'umana probitate; e questo vole
123   quei che la dà, perché da lui si chiami.

Anche al nasuto vanno mie parole
non men ch'a l'altro, Pier, che con lui canta,
126   onde Puglia e Proenza già si dole.

Tant' è del seme suo minor la pianta,
quanto, più che Beatrice e Margherita,
129   Costanza di marito ancor si vanta.

Vedete il re de la semplice vita
seder là solo, Arrigo d'Inghilterra:
132   questi ha ne' rami suoi migliore uscita.

Quel che più basso tra costor s'atterra,
guardando in suso, è Guiglielmo marchese,
per cui e Alessandria e la sua guerra
136   fa pianger Monferrato e Canavese."

'which none can say of the other heirs.
James and Frederick hold their kingdoms,
120   but neither has the better heritage.

'Rarely does human worth rise through the branches.
And this He wills who gives it,
123   so that it shall be sought from Him.

'My words concern the large-nosed one no less
than Peter, who is singing with him,
126   so that Apulia and Provence are now in grief.

'As much is the plant poorer than its seed
that Constance may yet praise her husband
129   more than Beatrice and Margaret boast of theirs.

'See the king who led a simple life
sitting there alone, Henry of England.
132   His branches flower with better issue.

'Lowest among them, sitting on the ground
and looking up, is William the marquis,
because of whom Alessandria and its warfare
136   make Monferrato and Canavese weep.'

1–3.   The "digression" that fills almost exactly half of the last canto now yields to the continuance of the narrative that had related the embrace between the two Mantuan poets at *Purgatorio* VI.75. The formulation "a third time and a fourth" is, as has often been noted, Virgilian; since Scartazzini (1900) the reference is noted as being potentially triple: *Aeneid* I.94; IV.589; *Georgics* I.410. And Virgil, having been buffeted so unkindly in these early cantos of *Purgatorio*, is about to have his innings. Sordello asks about the provenance of both these travelers; once Virgil identifies himself, the contemporary Mantuan poet completely loses track of Dante. But the ancient Mantuan poet does so as well. In all his discussion with Sordello (VI.67–VIII.45) he never once refers to Dante as the reason for his own journey—as we have become accustomed to his doing (see *Purg.* I.52–69; III.94–99; V.31–33). It will only be in the next canto (VIII.62) that Sordello will understand that Dante is a living man.

4–6.   The reference to the redemption of sinners wrought by the Crucifixion seals Virgil's sense of his own doom, his bones buried (19 B.C.) during the rule of Augustus (63 B.C.–A.D. 14), whose reign coincided with the birth of Jesus.

7.   This is the sole occasion on which Virgil names himself in the *Commedia* (his name occurs thirty-one other times), thus answering in part Sordello's questions at *Purgatorio* VI.70, concerning the homeland and identity of these two travelers, one of which Virgil had already answered ("Mantua" at VI.72).

8.   To be without faith is to lack what is absolutely necessary in order to "win" salvation. The Anonimo Fiorentino cites St. Paul: "without faith it is impossible to be pleasing to God" (Hebrews 11:6), a passage explaining that Enoch was taken up alive into heaven because of his faith— as will be Dante soon, and as Virgil was not.

9–13.   The simile, another instance of what Tozer calls "similes drawn from mental experience" (see note to *Inf.* XXX.136–141), investigates the enormous pleasure of Sordello at meeting Virgil, a scene that will be reformulated for the meeting of Statius and Virgil in *Purgatorio* XXI.124–136.

Sordello's humility in lowering his brows ("e poi chinò le ciglia") is verbally reminiscent, if antithetically, of Farinata's pride (*Inf.* X.35: "s'ergea col petto e con la fronte" [was rising, lifting chest and brow]) and Satan's effrontery (*Inf.* XXXIV.35: "contra 'l suo fattore alzò le ciglia" [raised his brows against his Creator]). But it may also remind us of Virgil's own lowered brows when he is so filled with shame at his failure to believe in Christ to come (*Purg.* III.44: "e qui chinò la fronte").

15.   A small squall of disagreement disturbs the sea of commentary on this verse: does Sordello embrace Virgil just beneath his armpits? at the level of his thighs? at his knees? while lying prostrate at his feet? All four of these solutions continue to be put forward into the late twentieth century, while many commentators have been content to suggest that it is impossible to know exactly where this embrace is aimed. Vandelli (1929) supports the most popular hypothesis: Sordello bends his knees slightly so as to embrace Virgil under his arms, where the figure of lesser authority embraces his superior.

16–18.   Virgil, apostrophized by Sordello both as foremost among all Latin poets and as his greatest townsman, is here cast as the founder of all Romance poetry. The precise meaning of *lingua nostra* (our language) has been debated (see Mazzoni's summary of the debate [Mazz.1977.2], p. 164), and includes a wide range of possibilities: all human vernacular; Latin alone; all poetry, vernacular and Latin; and vernacular that is specifically developed from Latin. This last seems the most acceptable reading, making Latin the "mother tongue" of the Romance vernacular poets, as would also seem to be the case at *Purgatorio* XXI.94–99.

21.   Since Virgil has already (verse 8) confessed that he has "lost heaven," Sordello must assume that he is in hell. For a reading that sees the implicit rebuke to Virgil in Sordello's reference to his hellish situation see Picone (Pico.1998.1), pp. 65–66.

22–24.   Virgil's rejoinder rather surprisingly makes no reference to any reason for his being chosen for this journey; it is thus not surprising that Sordello believes his task is to guide Virgil, selected by God, to see these sacred precincts. Dante has become, temporarily, supernumerary.

25–27.   In *Purgatorio* XXI.18, Virgil will make clear to Statius that he must return to hell. Here it is also clear that he considers Limbo his final resting place, but he says as much in ways that invite speculation as to his possible salvation, since he claims now to know God and to have been aided by Him in coming this far. The absence of reference to Virgil's guidance of Dante allows Sordello to believe better of his townsman than the facts warrant.

28–36. The Roman poet puts the best possible face upon his presence in Limbo, attempting to establish a sort of "innocence by association," as it were, with the unbaptized infants and the other virtuous pagans.

40. At least since 1340 and Pietro di Dante's commentary it has been usual to cite *Aeneid* VI.673, "nulli certa domus" (no one has a preordained home), as a gloss on this verse. These are the words spoken by Musaeus to the Sibyl, who has asked where Anchises dwells, only to be told that he and the other virtuous souls live, free to roam, in the Elysian fields. Musaeus, like Sordello, offers to guide his charges up to see the assembled souls. This entire scene is closely modeled on that one.

44. Sordello seems to indicate that there is a law in ante-purgatory that prevents nocturnal movement upward. But see his further explantion, vv. 53–60.

46–48. Once again Sordello addresses only Virgil (and not Dante), and indeed, we can imagine, Virgil will enjoy seeing these Christian souls who are so reminiscent of his virtuous denizens of the Elysian fields.

49–51. Virgil, slow to understand the difference between external laws and inner will on this mountain, believes either that hellish demons would hinder a nocturnal climber or that such a climber would, with nightfall, lose his ability to ambulate upward.

52–60. Sordello's answer sets things straight: There are no external impediments and the inner will of the penitents makes them want to stay where they are, lest they wander to a lower station on the mountain, which would not be fitting. It seems that there would be no actual penalty for such behavior, but that no one would ever want to descend in any case. The "rule" of the mountain is more aesthetic than moral, since no harm can befall any of these saved souls. In this "club," no one would want to behave in so churlish a fashion.

64–66. Sordello will lead them among the souls gathered in the place that has come to be known as the Valley of the Princes, not among the early commentators, but at least by the time of Andreoli (1856) and his commentary to *Purgatorio* IX.54. It furnishes a certain foretaste of the garden of Eden, the pilgrim's eventual purgatorial destination.

73–78.   Much has been written about these verses. Beginning with Sapegno (1955), commentators have suggested a source in a *plazer* (a lyric poem describing the beauties of a place, person, or object) by Guido Cavalcanti, "Biltà di donna," verse 8: "Oro e argento, azzurro 'n orna-menti." (For Dante's earlier citation of this poem see note to *Inf.* XIV.30.) Dante is thus here understood to be joining the tradition of the *plazer* (cf. his own early poem, addressed to Cavalcanti, "Guido, i' vorrei") in de-scribing this particular *locus amoenus*, the idealized "pleasant place" since the Greek idyllic poems of Theocritus in classical antiquity. On a closely related theme see Giamatti (Giam.1966.1). For consideration of the deep resonance of "Biltà di donna" in this passage see Pico.1998.1, pp. 70–72. Picone notes the way in which Dante's description "outdoes" Guido's by merit of its supernatural Christian content.

For the emerald's association with hope (and its presence in the rest of the poem) see Levavasseur (Leva.1957.1), pp. 59–66. For the medieval lapidaries that Dante might have known see Cioffari (Ciof.1991.1).

79–81.   The supernatural nature of this place produces colors and odors that transcend, in their intensity and ability to give sensuous pleasure, their counterparts in the most exotic "normal" natural *loci*.

82–84.   The souls of the princes of the world invoke the merciful Queen of Heaven, underscoring their present humility. The text of this Marian evening hymn includes the fitting verses "to you we send up our sighs, mourning and weeping in this valley of tears." Poletto (1894) noted the echo here of another part of the scene presided over by Musaeus in *Aeneid* VI.656–658: the souls seated in the Elysian fields who sing songs of praise in that fragrant place.

For the association of the "Salve, Regina" with Compline see Heilbronn (Heil.1972.1), p. 50.

86.   The poet's diction reminds us of the fact that Virgil, *the* Mantuan, has temporarily been "demoted" in favor of Sordello.

87–90.   Here, too, the *Aeneid* (VI.754–755) makes its presence felt, as Vellutello (1544) noted: Anchises stations himself on a higher vantage point (with Aeneas and the Sibyl) so as to be able to discern the faces of those moving toward him in the pageant of Rome.

91–94. For the structural and moral force of Sordello's *planh*, or poem of lament, for the death of Blacatz reflected in Dante's composition of the rest of this canto see Picone (Pico.1998.1), pp. 73–77.

There are nine princes in the following "list," all of them ticketed for paradise, as there were nine who were saved at the last moment in Cantos V and VI. Both these groups of late-repentant sinners, the first of whom have in common death by violence, are seen as active (as opposed to the lethargic in Canto IV) in their attachment to the world. Rudolph of Austria, the only emperor (1273–91) in this group, father of the Albert so vilified in *Purgatorio* VI.97–102, is, however, censured most for his neglect of his Italian subjects. Rudolph "was born in 1218, and was the eldest son of Albert IV, Count of Hapsburg, and the founder of the imperial house of Austria. He first served under Ottocar, King of Bohemia, in his German wars, but in 1272, as he was encamped before the walls of Basle, he received the news that he had been elected Emperor, in preference to Ottocar and to Alphonso of Castile. Ottocar refused to acknowledge him as Emperor, but Rudolf, supported by powerful allies, made war upon him and compelled him to sue for peace. . . . A few years later Ottocar again rebelled, and was finally defeated and slain near Vienna, Aug. 1278. Rudolf allowed Ottocar's son, Wenceslaus, to succeed to the throne of Bohemia, but Austria, Styria, and Carniola he granted to his own sons, Albert and Rudolf" **(T)**.

Given the recorded behaviors of Rudolph (and of others in this group) it is surprising that Dante was willing to publish their salvations—or the fact that he even thought that they were saved.

95–96. Rudolph, had he served as he ought, might have spared Italy the divisions that occurred before 1291, culminating in the battle of Campaldino (1289), when Guelph supremacy solidified papal influence in Italian politics for a long time to come. The "wounds that have brought Italy to death" are most probably the ensuing disasters wrought by Boniface's (and then Clement's) political activities. Is Italy no longer capable of resuscitation? Will another leader's efforts be too late or might they come in the nick of time? The text is again problematic (see note to *Purg.* VI.100–102), first as to whether or not Henry VII is referred to, second as to the precise meaning of *tardi*, which can mean, in this context, either "at the last moment" or "too late to succeed." If, as many believe, this passage (1) was written in 1308–9 (along with *Purg.* VI.97–102), (2) refers to Henry VII, (3) uses *tardi* to mean "at the last moment," everything falls into place: Dante, not yet convinced that Henry will be the vigorous Italophile that he becomes in 1310, only dubiously puts forward the notion that Henry's election will have positive results. One proposing such an interpretation must admit that Dante, with only minor touches, could have revised both these passages in order to accommodate his post-1310 view of Henry. On the other hand, both at least allow the possibility of a more positive reading, and thus did not absolutely require such revision. And Dante's enthusiasm would only last for a short while, in any case. By September 1313, in the wake of the death of Henry, the disheartened reading, found in Benvenuto's commentary to these passages in *Purgatorio* VI and VII and in *Paradiso* XXX.133–138, would have become appropriate.

97–102.   The following five figures were all kings rather than emperors, beginning with Ottokar of Bohemia (1253–78), who was in fact killed by Rudolph in 1278. Just as Rudolph, for all his faults, is presented as saved, while his son Albert seems clearly not to be, so is Ottokar exalted while his son, Wenceslaus, is apparently headed for the second circle of hell (or lower).

Singleton points out that in the Elysian fields former enemies are also reunited in peace (*Aen.* VI.824–827).

103–111.   Philip III (the Bold) of France (1270–85) is seen in colloquy with Henry I of Navarre (1270–74), to whom he was related by marriage (his son, Philip IV [the Fair], "the plague of France," was married to Henry's daughter Juana). While Philip IV is also clearly referred to several other times in the poem, generally with bitter sarcasm (e.g., *Inf.* XIX.87; *Purg.* XX.91; *Purg.* XXXII.152–160 and XXXIII.45; *Par.* XIX.120), he is never named.

112–114.   Large-limbed *(membruto)* like Cassius (*Inf.* XXXIV.67), Pedro III, king of Aragon (1276–85), sings along with large-nosed Charles I of Anjou and Provence, king of Naples and Sicily (1266–85). Pedro had married Constance, daughter of Manfred (see *Purg.* III.115–116), in 1262, a relationship that gave him a claim to the crown of Sicily, which he assumed after the Sicilian Vespers (1282) and held until his death, despite the efforts of Charles, whom he had deposed and who died before Pedro, and thus without regaining his crown, in 1285. Once again we see enemies united in friendship.

115–117.   Dante refers, among Pedro's four sons, either to the firstborn, Alfonso III of Aragon, who reigned for six years (but not with happy result, according to the chroniclers) after his father's death (1285–91) and died at twenty-seven, or the last, Pedro, who did indeed die in his boyhood and was never put on. However, the text would seem clearly to indicate a son who did not succeed his father on the throne. Torraca (1905) makes a strong case for the unlikelihood of Dante's celebrating Alfonso, thus promoting the candidacy of Pedro (the "Marcellus" of Aragon, as it were). He has been followed by most commentators.

118–120.   Unlike their worthy brother (Pedro?), the other two sons of Pedro III, James and Frederick, do not possess their father's goodness, but only his territories. In fact, they went to war with one another over their claims to power in Sicily, with Frederick eventually winning out, leaving James to content himself with Aragon.

121–123.   Dante's sententious moralizing, issuing from the mouth of Sordello, has a precursor in his earlier words on the same subject in *Convivio* (IV.xx.5 and 7), as Poletto (1894) was perhaps first to point out. There Dante testified both that nobility does not descend into an entire family, but into individuals, and that it comes only and directly from God.

124–129.   Charles and Pedro, themselves noble of spirit, share the disgrace of degenerate offspring, the former's son, Charles II, king of Naples and count of Provence (1289–1309), singled out as being particularly vile. See Grandgent's (1909) explanation of these lines: "Charles II is as much inferior to Charles I as Charles I is to Peter [i.e., Pedro] III. Beatrice of Provence and Margaret of Burgundy were the successive wives of Charles I, Constance (daughter of Manfred) was the wife of Peter; and Charles I was not a devoted husband. 'The plant (the son) is inferior to the seed (the father) to the same extent that Constance boasts of her husband (Peter) more than Beatrice and Margaret boast of theirs (Charles).' " Dante, who has somewhat surprisingly treated Charles of Anjou with a certain dignity (see the harsh characterizations of him at *Purg.* XX.67–69 and *Par.* XIX.127), now takes some of that away, as Pedro and Charles are no longer treated with equal respect. Porena (1946) explains that Dante's gesture here is meant to show his objectivity; having saved Manfred (*Purg.* III), he now also saves Manfred's persecutor, Charles, despite his own political (and moral) disapproval.

130–132. Henry III of England (1216–72), disparaged by Sordello in his lament for Blacatz (as noted by Poletto [1894]), is here seen positively and, reversing the trend found in the last three "couples" of monarchs, his son (Edward I), known as "the English Justinian" for his compilation of English law, is seen as even more noble than he.

133–136. The final exemplar is, like Henry, seen alone, looking up in prayer (Bosco/Reggio). Marquis of Monferrato (1254–92), Guglielmo first welcomed Charles of Anjou when he descended into Italy, but then turned against him when he moved against Lombardy. Guglielmo's physical position is lowest in order to match his rank, as Rudolph, the only emperor in the group, was seated highest. His successful career as Ghibelline military leader in Lombardy and in Piedmont came to a dramatic halt when he was captured in Alessandria in 1290 and exhibited in a cage for a year and a half until he died. When his son, Giovanni, set out on a war of revenge, the result was disastrous for Monferrato and Canavese, the two regions that constituted the holdings of the marquisate.

PURGATORIO VIII

Era già l'ora che volge il disio
ai navicanti e 'ntenerisce il core
lo dì c'han detto ai dolci amici addio;

e che lo novo peregrin d'amore
punge, se ode squilla di lontano
che paia il giorno pianger che si more;

quand' io incominciai a render vano
l'udire e a mirare una de l'alme
surta, che l'ascoltar chiedea con mano.

Ella giunse e levò ambo le palme,
ficcando li occhi verso l'orïente,
come dicesse a Dio: "D'altro non calme."

"Te lucis ante" sì devotamente
le uscìo di bocca e con sì dolci note,
che fece me a me uscir di mente;

e l'altre poi dolcemente e devote
seguitar lei per tutto l'inno intero,
avendo li occhi a le superne rote.

Aguzza qui, lettor, ben li occhi al vero,
ché 'l velo è ora ben tanto sottile,
certo che 'l trapassar dentro è leggero.

Io vidi quello essercito gentile
tacito poscia reguardare in sùe,
quasi aspettando, palido e umìle;

e vidi uscir de l'alto e scender giùe
due angeli con due spade affocate,
tronche e private de le punte sue.

It was now the hour that melts a sailor's heart
and saddens him with longing on the day
3   he's said farewell to his beloved friends,

and when a traveler, starting out,
is pierced with love if far away he hears
6   a bell that seems to mourn the dying light,

and I began to listen less and fix my gaze,
intent upon a soul who suddenly stood up
9   and signaled for attention with his hand.

He lifted his clasped palms and fixed his eyes
upon the east as if he said to God:
12   'For nothing else do I have any care.'

'Te lucis ante' came forth from his lips
with such devotion and with notes so sweet
15   it drew me out from all thoughts of myself.

The others joined him then and sang
the whole hymn through with sweet devotion,
18   keeping their eyes upon the heavenly wheels.

Here, reader, set your gaze upon the truth,
for now the veil is drawn so thin
21   that piercing it is surely easy.

I watched that noble gathering
grow silent as they raised their eyes,
24   humble and pale with expectation.

And I saw issue from above and then descend
two angels holding flaming swords,
27   their pointed blade-tips broken off.

Verdi come fogliette pur mo nate
erano in veste, che da verdi penne
30   percosse traean dietro e ventilate.

L'un poco sovra noi a star si venne,
e l'altro scese in l'opposita sponda,
33   sì che la gente in mezzo si contenne.

Ben discernëa in lor la testa bionda;
ma ne la faccia l'occhio si smarria,
36   come virtù ch'a troppo si confonda.

"Ambo vegnon del grembo di Maria,"
disse Sordello, "a guardia de la valle,
39   per lo serpente che verrà vie via."

Ond' io, che non sapeva per qual calle,
mi volsi intorno, e stretto m'accostai,
42   tutto gelato, a le fidate spalle.

E Sordello anco: "Or avvalliamo omai
tra le grandi ombre, e parleremo ad esse;
45   grazïoso fia lor vedervi assai."

Solo tre passi credo ch'i' scendesse,
e fui di sotto, e vidi un che mirava
48   pur me, come conoscer mi volesse.

Temp' era già che l'aere s'annerava,
ma non sì che tra li occhi suoi e ' miei
51   non dichiarisse ciò che pria serrava.

Ver' me si fece, e io ver' lui mi fei:
giudice Nin gentil, quanto mi piacque
54   quando ti vidi non esser tra ' rei!

Nullo bel salutar tra noi si tacque;
poi dimandò: "Quant' è che tu venisti
57   a piè del monte per le lontane acque?"

Green as newly opened leaves, their garments,
stirred and fanned by their green wings,
30   swirled and billowed out behind them.

One came and took his stand there just above us
and one alighted on the other bank,
33   so that the company was set between them.

I could discern the angels' flaxen hair,
but looking at their faces dazzled me,
36   my power of sight undone by so much brightness.

'Both come from Mary's bosom,'
said Sordello, 'to guard the valley
39   from the serpent that will soon appear.'

Not knowing by what path,
I turned around, all chilled with fear,
42   and huddled closer to the trusted shoulders.

Sordello continued: 'Let us now go down
into the valley and speak with those great shades.
45   They will be pleased to have you join them.'

It seemed I had taken only three steps down
when I saw one who stared at me alone,
48   as if he tried to bring my name to mind.

It was now the hour when the air grows dark,
yet had not turned so dark it failed to show
51   his eyes and mine what had been hidden.

He moved toward me and I moved toward him.
Noble Judge Nino, what joy it was to me
54   when I saw you were not among the damned!

Between us no fair greeting was left unsaid.
Then he asked: 'How long is it since you came
57   over far waters to this mountain?'

"Oh!" diss' io lui, "per entro i luoghi tristi
venni stamane, e sono in prima vita,
60 ancor che l'altra, sì andando, acquisti."

E come fu la mia risposta udita,
Sordello ed elli in dietro si raccolse
63 come gente di sùbito smarrita.

L'uno a Virgilio e l'altro a un si volse
che sedea lì, gridando: "Sù, Currado!
66 vieni a veder che Dio per grazia volse."

Poi, vòlto a me: "Per quel singular grado
che tu dei a colui che sì nasconde
69 lo suo primo perché, che non lì è guado,

quando sarai di là da le larghe onde,
dì a Giovanna mia che per me chiami
72 là dove a li 'nnocenti si risponde.

Non credo che la sua madre più m'ami,
poscia che trasmutò le bianche bende,
75 le quai convien che, misera!, ancor brami.

Per lei assai di lieve si comprende
quanto in femmina foco d'amor dura,
78 se l'occhio o 'l tatto spesso non l'accende.

Non le farà sì bella sepultura
la vipera che Melanesi accampa,
81 com' avria fatto il gallo di Gallura."

Così dicea, segnato de la stampa,
nel suo aspetto, di quel dritto zelo
84 che misuratamente in core avvampa.

Li occhi miei ghiotti andavan pur al cielo,
pur là dove le stelle son più tarde,
87 sì come rota più presso a lo stelo.

'Oh,' I said to him, 'I came this morning
from the doleful regions. I am in my first life,
60   though by coming here I gain the other.'

And when they heard my answer
Sordello and he drew back,
63   like men suddenly bewildered.

One turned to Virgil, and the other called
to someone seated there: 'Rise, Currado,
66   come and see what God by His good grace has willed.'

Then, turning to me: 'By that special gratitude
you owe to Him who hides His primal purpose
69   so deep we cannot fathom it,

'when you are far from these wide waters,
ask my Giovanna to direct her prayers for me
72   to where the innocent are heard.

'I think her mother has not loved me
since she stopped wearing her white wimple,
75   which, in her coming misery, she may long for.

'There is an easy lesson in her conduct:
how short a time the fire of love endures in woman
78   if frequent sight and touch do not rekindle it.

'The viper that leads the Milanese afield
will hardly ornament her tomb as handsomely
81   as the cock of Gallura would have done.'

He spoke these words, his face stamped
with a look of righteous indignation
84   that burns with proper measure in the heart.

My hungry eyes were lifted toward the sky,
to that zone where the stars move slowest,
87   as does the spoke of a wheel close to the axle.

E 'l duca mio: "Figliuol, che là sù guarde?"
E io a lui: "A quelle tre facelle
90   di che 'l polo di qua tutto quanto arde."

Ond' elli a me: "Le quattro chiare stelle
che vedevi staman, son di là basse,
93   e queste son salite ov' eran quelle."

Com' ei parlava, e Sordello a sé il trasse
dicendo: "Vedi là 'l nostro avversaro";
96   e drizzò il dito perché 'n là guardasse.

Da quella parte onde non ha riparo
la picciola vallea, era una biscia,
99   forse qual diede ad Eva il cibo amaro.

Tra l'erba e ' fior venìa la mala striscia,
volgendo ad ora ad or la testa, e 'l dosso
102   leccando come bestia che si liscia.

Io non vidi, e però dicer non posso,
come mosser li astor celestïali;
105   ma vidi bene e l'uno e l'altro mosso.

Sentendo fender l'aere a le verdi ali,
fuggì 'l serpente, e li angeli dier volta,
108   suso a le poste rivolando iguali.

L'ombra che s'era al giudice raccolta
quando chiamò, per tutto quello assalto
111   punto non fu da me guardare sciolta.

"Se la lucerna che ti mena in alto
truovi nel tuo arbitrio tanta cera
114   quant' è mestiere infino al sommo smalto,"

cominciò ella, "se novella vera
di Val di Magra o di parte vicina
117   sai, dillo a me, che già grande là era.

And my leader: 'Son, what are you staring at?'
And I replied: 'At those three torches
90   with which this pole is all aflame.'

'The four bright stars you saw this morning,'
he said, 'are low upon the unseen sky
93   and these have risen where those others were.'

As he spoke, Sordello drew him closer,
saying: 'There is our adversary,'
96   and pointed his finger where to look.

In that place where the little valley
has no rampart, a snake appeared,
99   perhaps the one that gave to Eve the bitter fruit.

Through grass and flowers slid the evil streak,
turning its head from time to time to lick its back
102   like a beast that sleeks itself.

I did not see and therefore cannot tell
how the celestial falcons started up,
105   but I could plainly see them both in motion.

Hearing the green wings cleave the air,
the serpent fled. The angels wheeled around
108   and flew back up together to their posts.

The shade, who had drawn closer to the judge
when he called out, had not through that assault
111   at any time removed his gaze from me.

'So may the lantern leading you above
have ample wax in the candle of your will
114   to bring you to the enameled summit,'

he said, 'if you have true news of Valdimagra
or of the parts around, please tell me,
117   for there I once was great.

Fui chiamato Currado Malaspina;
non son l'antico, ma di lui discesi;
120   a' miei portai l'amor che qui raffina."

"Oh!" diss' io lui, "per li vostri paesi
già mai non fui; ma dove si dimora
123   per tutta Europa ch'ei non sien palesi?

La fama che la vostra casa onora,
grida i segnori e grida la contrada,
126   sì che ne sa chi non vi fu ancora;

e io vi giuro, s'io di sopra vada,
che vostra gente onrata non si sfregia
129   del pregio de la borsa e de la spada.

Uso e natura sì la privilegia,
che, perché il capo reo il mondo torca,
132   sola va dritta e 'l mal cammin dispregia."

Ed elli: "Or va; che 'l sol non si ricorca
sette volte nel letto che 'l Montone
135   con tutti e quattro i piè cuopre e inforca,

che cotesta cortese oppinïone
ti fia chiavata in mezzo de la testa
con maggior chiovi che d'altrui sermone,
139   se corso di giudicio non s'arresta."

'I was called Currado Malaspina,
not the old Currado but descended from him.
120   To my own I bore the love that here is purified.'

'Oh,' I said to him, 'never have I been there,
in your country. But where do men dwell,
123   anywhere in Europe, that it is not renowned?

'The fame that crowns your house with honor
proclaims alike its lords and lands—
126   even those who have not been there know them,

'and, as I hope to go above, I swear to you
your honored race does not disgrace
129   the glory of its purse and of its sword.

'No matter how a wicked chief may warp the world,
privileged both by nature and by custom,
132   your race alone goes straight and scorns the evil path.'

Then he said: 'Enough. Not seven times
shall the sun return to rest in the very bed
135   that the Ram covers and bestrides with all four feet

'before this courteous opinion
shall be nailed within your brain
by stronger nails than the words of others,
139   if the course of Judgment is not stayed.'

1–9. This pseudosimile (it has the effect but not the grammatical form of a simile) sets the protagonist apart from more usual mortal travelers. Using the two great metaphors for this journey and this poem, the voyage across a sea and the pilgrimage, the poet presents his earthbound counterparts as filled with all-too-human backward-looking sentiment. The protagonist pays attention to the event taking place before him, avoiding nostalgia, the sort of distraction we found him so attracted by in the second canto of *Purgatorio* when he encountered Casella and experienced associated memories of his former life.

Grabher's gloss (1934) to verse 5 runs as follows: "This is the bell for Compline, the last of the canonical hours of the day, when indeed the hymn *Te lucis ante terminum* ['Before the Ending of the Light'] is sung in order to invoke divine assistance against the temptations of the night." This hymn immediately follows the lesson in the service occurring after Vespers (the time between 3 PM and 6 PM), ideally accompanying the setting sun.

Tommaseo (1837) was perhaps the first to note the closeness to Dante's description of the pilgrims whom he observed in Florence, perhaps rapt in thoughts of the friends they had left behind at home (*Vita nuova* XL.2).

Byron's close translation of these much-admired verses in *Don Juan* III.108 is noted by Carroll (1904).

7–9. The opening passage is so beautiful and its readers so moved by it that most of them assume that the protagonist is being associated by the poet with the travelers it refers to. Yet it is clear that, unlike those travelers, he does not yield to the temptation of yearning for a past that is out of reach, even though this is *his* first evening in a distant, foreign place. Indeed, he may be drawing some of his attention from the hymn "Salve, Regina" in order to pay heed to the soul who calls for attention. Who this soul may be is a matter for which there are no grounds for discovery; we cannot even say whether it is male or female, although the entirely male cast of those identified in the Valley of the Princes makes the former possibility a more likely one. Commentators, including Scartazzini (1900), have been reminded of Acts 13:16: "Paul arose, motioning with his hand for silence" (Paul is addressing the Jews in the synagogue at Antioch; his main message is the Resurrection of Jesus).

10–12.   The praying figure is facing east, not because the sun is there (it is setting in the west), but because the east is traditionally associated with Christ as "rising sun." For the Virgilian provenance of his gesture see Tommaseo (1837): Dante's "levò ambo le palme" is indeed close to *Aeneid* X.844–845: "et ambas / ad caelum tendit palmas." However, Heilbronn (Heil.1972.1), pp. 56–57, points out that his action "imitates the words of Psalm 133:3: 'In noctibus extollite manus vestras in sancta, et benedicite dominum' [134:1–2: by night . . . lift up your hands in the sanctuary and bless the Lord]. At Compline, this psalm immediately precedes the hymn, *Te lucis*, as the gesture does in *Purg*. VIII."

13.   "Te lucis ante," an evening hymn, is sung in its entirety. As opposed to "Salve, Regina," which looks back upon the sadness of sin and exile, hoping for Marian intercession, "Te lucis ante" looks ahead and requests the Father's and the Son's protection from the dangers of the Satanic forces of the night. Thus, while surely there is nothing "wrong" with singing "Salve, Regina," in this context it is time to turn to the future, and this is what the protagonist does.

14–18.   Dante's reaction to this singing is reminiscent of his rapt response to the singing performed on his account by Casella in *Purgatorio* II (Poletto [1894] also notes this). The religious tone of this hymn and the "proper" behavior of this crowd gives us a very different perspective on this scene. There is no need of a Cato to come to reprimand these singers, whose eyes are fixed on heavenly things.

19–21.   This is the first of seven addresses to the reader in *Purgatorio* (see note to *Inf*. VIII.94–96). Most reminiscent, in its use of the language of allegory, of "veiled" truth, found in the second address in *Inferno* (IX.61–63), this passage also involves treating an action performed in the poem as though it were not "historical" but metaphoric (see note to *Inf*. IX.58–63).

25–30.   Most of the early commentators, following their natural inclination, allegorize the meaning of the two swords (often as God's justice and mercy), but Pietro di Dante (1340) turns to the Bible for their source, and presents a more interesting analysis. Yet it will only be with Lombardi (1791) that a later commentator turns to this most likely source. Genesis 3:24 records God's placing (two?) Cherubim at the east of the garden of Eden along with a flaming sword to keep sinful humans from the tree of life. Dante's redoing of the scene is careful and meaningful. The swords have no points because they do not need to do any harm, since the enemy has been defeated by Christ and need no longer be feared by those having faith in Christ; they are aflame with God's love for humanity, which has reversed the exclusionary rule of law in Genesis and reopened the garden with its tree of eternal life; the angels are green of wing and vestment because they give expression to the hope for salvation brought by Christ. Güntert (Gunt.2001.1), p. 109, notes the pivotal reversals of the scene in Genesis here.

37–39. Genesis 3:14–15 is another text visible behind the scenes of this drama (as Christopher McElroy, Princeton '72, suggested in a classroom many years ago), God's curse upon the serpent and the conjoined prophecy of the woman's seed who will bruise the serpent's head and have his heel bruised as a result, taken by Christian exegetes—and surely by Dante among them—to refer to the Crucifixion. Both these Cherubs come from the bosom of Mary, that "anti-Eve," to guard the valley, now safe from harm, as we shall see, against the serpent. This garden, foreshadowing the garden of Eden that lies above, has been reopened to humanity, as has been that higher place.

For the palindromatic opposition Ave/Eva see Pietro di Dante (1340) to *Paradiso* XXXII.4–6 (the locus of most commentators' discussion of this topos): "And the holy men say that, just as sickness was born from that most prideful one, that is, Eve, just so its cure springs from that most humble one, that is, Mary." And thus, Pietro continues, the "Ave" of the "Hail, Mary" counters the effect of Eve, whose name it spells backward.

40–42. On the basis of Sordello's description, the serpent sounds both real and threatening enough for Dante to be afraid, especially since he has not yet read the signs as well as he will eventually. There is only one other occasion in the poem in which Dante has been *gelato* (chilled): when he looks upon Satan (*Inf.* XXXIV.22). This serpent is indeed Satan in his "serpent suit" in the garden (Genesis 3:1 and passim).

43–45. Sordello's maneuver puts the appointment with the serpent on hold and occupies Dante's mind with other things. Now the Mantuan poet has Dante descend among the inhabitants of the valley—what he and Virgil specifically did not do in their first view of them (*Purg.* VII.88–90). The rest of the Edenic drama must wait until vv. 94–108.

46.   These three steps, unlike those at *Purgatorio* XXVIII.70, are taken by almost all commentators at face value. But even they, understood by most as indicating that it was but a short distance down into the valley (see *Purg.* VII.72), have made allegorists stir with interpretive excitement (e.g., Vellutello, Scartazzini). Poletto (1894) waxes hot against such attempts.

48.   Like the anonymous lethargic penitent at *Purgatorio* V.9, this penitent has eyes for Dante alone. On this occasion, however, it tells us more about him than it does about Dante. See note to vv. 109–111, below.

51.   From the distance, this soul and Dante could not recognize one another, but the darkness of nightfall is not yet so great as to prevent their doing so now.

52.   This "recognition scene" reestablishes Dante's role as "star" of the poem. Virgil has his Sordello, for whom Dante does not exist; Dante has his Nino, for whom Virgil does not exist.

53.   "Nino Visconti of Pisa, judge of the district of Gallura in Sardinia; he was grandson of Count Ugolino della Gherardesca, and in 1288 was chief of the Guelf party in Pisa; in that year he and the Guelfs were treacherously expelled from Pisa by Count Ugolino, whereupon he retired to Lucca, and in alliance with Genoa and the Lucchese and Florentine Guelfs made war upon Pisa, which he carried on at intervals for the next five years. In 1293, on the conclusion of peace between the Pisans and the Tuscan Guelfs, Nino betook himself to Genoa, and shortly after departed to his judgeship of Gallura. . . . Nino died in Sardinia in 1296" **(T)**. Nino fought at the battle of Campaldino and probably spent some time in Florence in the time between his exile from Pisa and his removal to Sardinia; it is possible that Dante came to know him then, as the conversation is clearly meant to be taken as one between old friends.

54.   Dante's surprise at Nino's salvation is not necessarily based on any specific knowledge of any particular sin; all are sinners and, if honest, are surprised to find themselves saved.

55–57.   The meeting between Dante and Nino contrasts with that between Virgil and Sordello, this one untinged by tragic notes. Nino assumes, almost correctly, that Dante is one of the saved; Sordello, guided by Virgil's admission that he has lost heaven, asks about Virgil's location in hell (*Purg.* VII.21).

Chiavacci Leonardi (Chia.1994.1), p. 241, cites Francesco D'Ovidio for the view that the phrase in verse 57, "over far waters," reflects, once again, a scene in the Elysian fields, when Anchises welcomes Aeneas (*Aen.* VI.692), who had journeyed "over wide seas" to experience that reunion.

58–60.   Dante finally is able to answer Sordello's question (*Purg.* VI.70) with regard to his own condition. These are the first words he has spoken since VI.51, a fact that underlines the way in which Sordello and Virgil have taken over the stage in these scenes. Now Dante is once again the "star" of the drama. See note to *Purgatorio* VII.1–3.

61–66.   Sordello and Nino are both surprised to learn that Dante is here in the flesh, is not yet dead, the one turning to his new companion, Virgil the Mantuan, the other, Nino, to his friend in God's grace, Currado, perhaps known to him from his recent travels in Tuscany. It is likely that Dante considered both Virgil and Sordello, champions of empire, sympathetic to the Ghibelline cause, while Nino was a Guelph and Currado, though a Ghibelline, was a cousin of Moroello Malaspina, with whom Dante had good relations and who was a Guelph. In the next world such divisive distinctions begin to break down.

Currado Malaspina was the grandson of Currado "l'antico" and son of Federigo of Villafranca. He died ca. 1294. His first cousin, Franceschino, was probably Dante's host in Lunigiana in 1306 (see vv. 133–139).

67–69.   Nino comments upon the unknown and unknowable purpose of God in bringing this living human soul into the immortal realm. He is content to accept the *quia*, the sheer fact of Dante's having been chosen to be here. See *Purgatorio* III.37.

71–72.   Nino hopes that Dante, returning to the world, will see his daughter, Giovanna, in Pisa and cause her, by recounting this meeting, to pray for his soul. Giovanna's innocence is the result at least of her age, since she was born in 1291 or so.

73–75.   Nino's unnamed wife was Beatrice d'Este. Sometime after his death in 1296 she stopped wearing widow's vestments, which featured white bands drawn around the head (her "wimple"), and eventually married, after a previous betrothal, a second husband, Galeazzo Visconti of Milan, in June 1300. The misery that awaits her is to share the exile of her new husband because of the expulsion of the powerful Visconti family from Milan in 1302.

77.   For early awareness of the citation of Virgil here, see the Anonimo Fiorentino (1400): *Aeneid* IV.569–570: "A woman is ever a fickle and a changeful thing."

79–81.   Nino's heraldic language suggests that the device of the Milanese Visconti's coat of arms, the viper, will not decorate her tomb as well as would have his family's device, the rooster, had she remained a widow and eventually died in Pisa.

Whether with a purpose or not, Dante plays off the situation that pertained in *Vita nuova* XXIV, when Guido Cavalcanti's Giovanna preceded Dante's Beatrice as John the Baptist preceded Christ. Here the innocent Giovanna is a foil to the unnamed but vicious Beatrice d'Este, her own mother. In the language of *King Lear* turned inside out, "bad wombs have borne good daughters."

82–84.   The poet underlines the fact, lest we fail to observe it, that Nino takes no pleasure in his former wife's coming tribulations, but merely notes God's justice in them.

85–93.   These three tercets distance the reader from the intense family drama narrated by Nino, as though to put that drama into a cosmic context. The protagonist gazes at the pole in the southern sky where, as on a wheel, that which is closest to the axle moves more slowly than points farther from it. The four stars, representing the four cardinal virtues (as almost all agree), seen by the travelers in *Purgatorio* I.23 near the pole, are now setting on the other side of the mount of purgatory and are thus shielded from view. They are replaced in their former position by these three. Nearly all, primarily because of their allegorical reading of the four, also insist that these represent the three theological virtues—faith, hope, and charity. However, some commentators, following Portirelli (1804), argue for a strictly literal and astronomical reference here, the three stars being among the brightest of two southern constellations, Dorado and Achernar in Eridanus; Canopus in Carina. (For Portirelli's notion that Dante knew about the southern heavens from Marco Polo, see note to *Purgatorio* I.22–24.) Beginning with Andreoli (1856), for half a century most commentators argue for a literal sense that indicates phenomena in the southern sky *and* an allegorical sense. But after Poletto (1894) most indicate only the allegorical meaning.

94–96.   Sordello interrupts Virgil's heavenly discourse to call his (and, once again, not Dante's) attention to the drama unfolding in the garden.

97–102.   We have seen this "snake" before, in *Inferno* XXXIV, imprisoned for his arrogant assault on God. Now we see him replaying his role in the Fall, licking himself in prideful self-absorption as he plans another assault, now that he has lost his first battle, upon humankind. Both Sordello's urgency in interrupting Virgil's notice of the heavens' beauties and the fact that no opposition has as yet deployed its forces have the effect of creating uncertainty (and fear) in the naïve onlooker and in the reader. This serpent seems dangerous indeed, as he was when he tempted Eve in Eden, but in fact is not, as we presently discover.

103–108.   Dante's attention to the snake kept the rapid defensive action of the angels from his view until they suddenly enter his field of vision, immediately thwarting the plans of the snake. We now see why their swords are blunted: they have no need of them because this serpent is powerless to offend. This drama is precisely that, a play, by which the onlookers, now safe in their potentially (but definitively) saved state, may be reminded of their sinful lives—their vulnerability to the serpent—and the grace that has rewarded their goodness with salvation. Mark Musa (Musa.1974.1) examines this scene as a representation of Christ's recurring second advent, as set forth by St. Bernard in his *First Sermon on the Advents*. Between His first (when He came to earth to save humankind) and final coming (at the end of time, to judge and rule the world), Christ is understood as coming into the heart of each successive believer. For Heilbronn (Heil.1972.1), who accepts Musa's view, the intervention of the angels represents "an allegorical enactment of the intermediate Advent—that is, the coming of Christ into the hearts of the faithful in this world" (p. 46).

109–111.   Heilbronn (Heil.1972.1), p. 55, argues that it is to Nino's companion's credit (we will shortly discover that this is Currado Malaspina) that he never takes his eyes from Dante, whose presence marks the really important event taking place here, against the backdrop of this now familiar play, in which nothing is really happening, for all its symbolic significance. The play reflects the past, Dante's physical presence in purgatory in the present, and the future—Dante's among Currado's family in Lunigiana and Currado's hopes for prayer from them, never expressed, but clear from all the similar requests we have already heard from others.

115–120.   The valley of the river Magra, flowing through Lunigiana, home of the Malaspina family. For Currado and his grandfather see note to vv. 61–66. Currado's disclaimer is probably meant to be taken as a sign of his modesty (his grandfather was the *real* Currado), as is his awareness that his love of the world must be purged above on the mountain.

121–129.   Dante's words in praise of the valor and generosity of the house of Malaspina in 1300 are in fact words of thanks for the hospitality of Franceschino Malaspina in Lunigiana in 1306 (and, according to Boccaccio, in his *Vita di Dante* [Bocc.1974.1], p. 483, of Moroello Malaspina as well [see Dante's letter to Moroello, his fourth Epistle, ca. 1307]).

130–132.   This verse has been variously interpreted. If we agree that *capo* is the subject (and not the object) of the sentence, as almost all do, then we may choose among the following solutions: the wicked chief who corrupts the world may be Satan, the pope (and then surely Boniface VIII), Rome (with its corrupt papacy and no emperor in her saddle), or bad governance in general. Whichever solution Dante may himself have had in mind, it is clear that any and all of these solutions "work," and are, in fact, interrelated. If Satan is the "prince of darkness" who leads most humans astray, his minions on earth (corrupt popes, pusillanimous emperors), or even corrupt leadership generally understood, all point to a common failing and a common cause: weak humans falling under the influence of those who govern poorly. From this failing only the Malaspina family is currently exempt.

133–139.   "Va" (or, literally, "Go") seems here to have the same sense that it sometimes has in Shakespeare, i.e., "Go to," meaning "Enough of such words." Currado, embarrassed by Dante's praise of his family, goes on to promise his interlocutor that he indeed will have cause to praise it more in 1306 (i.e., before the sun returns to the constellation Aries seven years from now).

PURGATORIO IX

La concubina di Titone antico
già s'imbiancava al balco d'orïente,
3   fuor de le braccia del suo dolce amico;

di gemme la sua fronte era lucente,
poste in figura del freddo animale
6   che con la coda percuote la gente;

e la notte, de' passi con che sale,
fatti avea due nel loco ov' eravamo,
9   e 'l terzo già chinava in giuso l'ale;

quand' io, che meco avea di quel d'Adamo,
vinto dal sonno, in su l'erba inchinai
12   là 've già tutti e cinque sedavamo.

Ne l'ora che comincia i tristi lai
la rondinella presso a la mattina,
15   forse a memoria de' suo' primi guai,

e che la mente nostra, peregrina
più da la carne e men da' pensier presa,
18   a le sue visïon quasi è divina,

in sogno mi parea veder sospesa
un'aguglia nel ciel con penne d'oro,
21   con l'ali aperte e a calare intesa;

ed esser mi parea là dove fuoro
abbandonati i suoi da Ganimede,
24   quando fu ratto al sommo consistoro.

Fra me pensava: "Forse questa fiede
pur qui per uso, e forse d'altro loco
27   disdegna di portarne suso in piede."

The concubine of old Tithonus,
fresh from her doting lover's arms,
3 was glowing white at the window of the east,

her forehead glittering with gems
set in the shape of that cold-blooded creature
6 that strikes men with its tail.

Where we were, night had made
two steps in her ascent and now the wings
9 of the third were already drooping,

when I, who had with me something of Adam,
lay down, overcome by sleep, there on the grass
12 where the five of us were seated.

At the hour near the verge of morning,
when the swallow begins her plaintive song,
15 remembering, perhaps, her woes of long ago,

and when our mind, more pilgrim
from the flesh and less caught up in thoughts,
18 is more prophetic in its visions,

in a dream I seemed to see an eagle,
with golden feathers, hovering in the sky,
21 his wings spread wide, ready to swoop.

And to me it seemed I was in the very place
where Ganymede abandoned his own kind
24 when he was caught up to the highest council.

And I pondered: —'Perhaps it is its habit
to strike only here, disdaining to pluck
27 from elsewhere any in its talons.'

Poi mi parea che, poi rotata un poco,
terribil come folgor discendesse,
30   e me rapisse suso infino al foco.

Ivi parea che ella e io ardesse;
e sì lo 'ncendio imaginato cosse,
33   che convenne che 'l sonno si rompesse.

Non altrimenti Achille si riscosse,
li occhi svegliati rivolgendo in giro
36   e non sappiendo là dove si fosse,

quando la madre da Chirón a Schiro
trafuggò lui dormendo in le sue braccia,
39   là onde poi li Greci il dipartiro;

che mi scoss' io, sì come da la faccia
mi fuggì 'l sonno, e diventa' ismorto,
42   come fa l'uom che, spaventato, agghiaccia.

Dallato m'era solo il mio conforto,
e 'l sole er' alto già più che due ore,
45   e 'l viso m'era a la marina torto.

"Non aver tema," disse il mio segnore;
"fatti sicur, ché noi semo a buon punto;
48   non stringer, ma rallarga ogne vigore.

Tu se' omai al purgatorio giunto:
vedi là il balzo che 'l chiude dintorno;
51   vedi l'entrata là 've par digiunto.

Dianzi, ne l'alba che procede al giorno,
quando l'anima tua dentro dormia,
54   sovra li fiori ond' è là giù addorno

venne una donna, e disse: 'I' son Lucia;
lasciatemi pigliar costui che dorme;
57   sì l'agevolerò per la sua via.'

Then it seemed to me that after wheeling awhile
it plunged down terrible as lightning,
30   and carried me straight to the sphere of fire.

There it seemed that it and I were both aflame,
and the imagined burning was so hot
33   my sleep was broken and gave way.

Not otherwise Achilles started up,
gazing with startled eyes around him,
36   not knowing where he was

that time his mother carried him,
sleeping in her arms, from Chiron to Scyros,
39   where later the Greeks would take him away—

than I awoke, the sleep gone from my eyes,
and then went deadly pale,
42   like a man frozen in his terror.

At my side there was no one but my comfort,
the sun more than two hours high.
45   My face was turned toward the sea.

'Do not be frightened,' said my lord,
'have confidence, for all is well with us.
48   Do not hold back, but rally all your strength.

'Now you have come to purgatory:
there you see the rock wall that encloses it
51   and, where that seems breached, the entrance.

'A short time ago, in the early light of dawn,
when your soul was asleep within you,
54   on the flowers that adorn the place below

'there came a lady who said: "I am Lucy.
Let me gather up this sleeping man
57   so I may speed him on his way."

Sordel rimase e l'altre genti forme;
ella ti tolse, e come 'l dì fu chiaro,
60   sen venne suso; e io per le sue orme.

Qui ti posò, ma pria mi dimostraro
li occhi suoi belli quella intrata aperta;
63   poi ella e 'l sonno ad una se n'andaro."

A guisa d'uom che 'n dubbio si raccerta
e che muta in conforto sua paura,
66   poi che la verità li è discoperta,

mi cambia' io; e come sanza cura
vide me 'l duca mio, su per lo balzo
69   si mosse, e io di rietro inver' l'altura.

Lettor, tu vedi ben com' io innalzo
la mia matera, e però con più arte
72   non ti maravigliar s'io la rincalzo.

Noi ci appressammo, ed eravamo in parte
che là dove pareami prima rotto,
75   pur come un fesso che muro diparte,

vidi una porta, e tre gradi di sotto
per gire ad essa, di color diversi,
78   e un portier ch'ancor non facea motto.

E come l'occhio più e più v'apersi,
vidil seder sovra 'l grado sovrano,
81   tal ne la faccia ch'io non lo soffersi;

e una spada nuda avëa in mano,
che reflettëa i raggi sì ver' noi,
84   ch'io dirizzava spesso il viso in vano.

"Dite costinci: che volete voi?"
cominciò elli a dire, "ov' è la scorta?
87   Guardate che 'l venir sù non vi nòi."

'Sordello stayed, as did the other noble souls,
and she took you and, as soon as it was day,
60   went up, and I then followed in her steps.

'Here she set you down, but first her lovely eyes
showed me that entrance, standing open.
63   Then she and sleep, as one, departed.'

Like a man who comes to see the truth
when he has been in doubt and now is reassured,
66   confidence replacing what in him was fear,

so was I changed. When my leader saw
that I was free of fear, he started up the path,
69   and I behind him, heading for the height.

Reader, you surely understand that I am raising
the level of my subject here. Do not wonder,
72   therefore, if I sustain it with more artifice.

We drew closer until we reached a place
where what at first had seemed a gap,
75   a breach that rends a wall,

I now saw was a gate, with three steps leading
up to it, each of a different color.
78   The keeper of that gate as yet said not a word.

And, when my eyes could make him out more clearly,
I saw that he was seated above the topmost step,
81   his face so bright I could not bear to look.

In his hand he held a naked sword,
which so reflected his bright rays
84   I often had to turn my eager eyes away.

'Say it from there, what do you want,'
he began, 'and where is your escort?
87   Beware lest your arrival cause you grief.'

"Donna del ciel, di queste cose accorta,"
rispuose 'l mio maestro a lui, "pur dianzi
90 ne disse: 'Andate là: quivi è la porta.' "

"Ed ella i passi vostri in bene avanzi,"
ricominciò il cortese portinaio:
93 "Venite dunque a' nostri gradi innanzi."

Là ne venimmo; e lo scaglion primaio
bianco marmo era sì pulito e terso,
96 ch'io mi specchiai in esso qual io paio.

Era il secondo tinto più che perso,
d'una petrina ruvida e arsiccia,
99 crepata per lo lungo e per traverso.

Lo terzo, che di sopra s'ammassiccia,
porfido mi parea, sì fiammeggiante
102 come sangue che fuor di vena spiccia.

Sovra questo tenëa ambo le piante
l'angel di Dio sedendo in su la soglia
105 che mi sembiava pietra di diamante.

Per li tre gradi sù di buona voglia
mi trasse il duca mio, dicendo: "Chiedi
108 umilemente che 'l serrame scioglia."

Divoto mi gittai a' santi piedi;
misericordia chiesi e ch'el m'aprisse,
111 ma tre volte nel petto pria mi diedi.

Sette P ne la fronte mi descrisse
col punton de la spada, e "Fa che lavi,
114 quando se' dentro, queste piaghe" disse.

Cenere, o terra che secca si cavi,
d'un color fora col suo vestimento;
117 e di sotto da quel trasse due chiavi.

'A lady from Heaven, who knows about such things,'
my master replied, 'said to us just now,
"Go that way, that way lies the gate." '

90

'And may she speed your steps to good,'
continued the courteous keeper of the gate.
'Come forward, then, to these our stairs.'

93

At that we moved ahead. The first step
was of clear white marble, so polished
that my image was reflected in true likeness.

96

The second was darker than the deepest purple,
of unhewn stone, looking as if it had been burned,
cracked through its length and breadth.

99

The third, resting its heavy mass above,
seemed to me porphyry, as flaming red
as blood that spurts out from a vein.

102

On this, seated on the threshold,
which seemed to be of adamant,
the angel of God rested both his feet.

105

Up the three steps my leader drew me
and I was glad for that. Then he said:
'Humbly petition him to slide the bolt.'

108

Devoutly I cast myself down at his holy feet.
I begged him for mercy and to let me enter,
but first, three times, I smote my breast.

111

With the point of his sword he traced seven P's
upon my forehead, then said: 'Once you are inside,
see that you wash away these wounds.'

114

Ashes or earth, when it is dug up dry,
would be the very color of his vestments.
Out from under them he drew two keys,

117

L'una era d'oro e l'altra era d'argento;
pria con la bianca e poscia con la gialla
120 fece a la porta sì, ch'i' fu' contento.

"Quandunque l'una d'este chiavi falla,
che non si volga dritta per la toppa,"
123 diss' elli a noi, "non s'apre questa calla.

Più cara è l'una; ma l'altra vuol troppa
d'arte e d'ingegno avanti che diserri,
126 perch' ella è quella che 'l nodo digroppa.

Da Pier le tegno; e dissemi ch'i' erri
anzi ad aprir ch'a tenerla serrata,
129 pur che la gente a' piedi mi s'atterri."

Poi pinse l'uscio a la porta sacrata,
dicendo: "Intrate; ma facciovi accorti
132 che di fuor torna chi 'n dietro si guata."

E quando fuor ne' cardini distorti
li spigoli di quella regge sacra,
135 che di metallo son sonanti e forti,

non rugghiò sì né si mostrò sì acra
Tarpëa, come tolto le fu il buono
138 Metello, per che poi rimase macra.

Io mi rivolsi attento al primo tuono,
e *"Te Deum laudamus"* mi parea
141 udire in voce mista al dolce suono.

Tale imagine a punto mi rendea
ciò ch'io udiva, qual prender si suole
quando a cantar con organi si stea;
145 ch'or sì or no s'intendon le parole.

one of gold, the other one of silver.
He touched the door, first with the white,
120   then the yellow, and thus my wish was satisfied.

'Any time one of these keys should fail
so that it does not turn inside the lock,'
123   he said to us, 'this portal does not open.

'One is more precious, but the other one requires
much skill and understanding before it will unlock,
126   for it is this one that unties the knot.

'From Peter do I hold them, and his instruction was
to err in opening rather than in keeping locked,
129   if but the soul fall prostrate at my feet.'

Then he pushed one door of the sacred portal open,
saying: 'Enter, but I warn you
132   he who looks back must then return outside.'

And when the linchpins of that sacred door,
which are of heavy and resounding metal,
135   were turning in their hinges,

the Tarpeian rock roared not so loud
nor proved so strident when good Metellus
138   was drawn away and it was then left bare.

I turned, intent on a new resonance,
and thought I heard 'Te Deum laudamus'
141   in voices mingled with sweet counterpoint,

giving me the same impression
one has when listening to singers
accompanied by an organ when the words
145   are sometimes clear and sometimes lost.

1–9.   Like *Inferno* IX, this ninth canto is both liminal, marking the boundary between two large areas, and filled with classical reference. And it is the first entire canto devoted to the transition from one poetic zone to another since *Inferno* XXXI. This sort of self-conscious poetic behavior puts us on notice, from the very outset, that we need to pay particular attention here.

Its reference to Aurora, surprisingly enough, has made this passage among the most hotly debated of the poem. In the "orthodox" version of the classical myth, Aurora, goddess of the dawn, arose from her couch, where she slept with her aged husband, Tithonus, to rise in the sky on her chariot, announcing the coming of day. A brief and incomplete summary of the debate yields the following (for a summary of the essential arguments over the passage and an attempt to restore Benvenuto da Imola's central and daring reading of it see Hollander [Holl.2001.2]): Moore (Moor.1903.1), pp. 74–85, essentially solved this problem almost a century ago, but in fact the early commentators (to whom Moore pays little attention) had already done so. Nearly all of them are quite sure that Dante has invented a second myth, one in which Tithonus is married to Aurora 1 (of the sun) but has a "relationship" with Aurora 2 (of the moon). The poetic facts are simple, according to Moore. The time is between 8:30 and 9 PM, the cold animal is the constellation Scorpio (and certainly not that belated other candidate, Pisces, arguments for which identification Moore competently dismantles), and thus the aurora we deal with is that of the moon.

For a review of these tormented verses and their tormentors (up to 1975) see Vazzana (Vazz.1981.1), pp. 180–85. And for one of the most interesting discussions of their meaning see Raimondi (Raim.1968.1), pp. 95–98. See also Cornish (Corn.2000.2), pp. 68–77.

7–9.   Much has been made of the phrase "where we were" by the "solar aurorans" in the hopes of counterposing the northern hemisphere (site of the solar Aurora at this hour in Italy) and the southern (where Dante and his companions are becoming sleepy). However, Dante is probably not contrasting the two hemispheres but the glow in the night sky of purgatory that spreads above them and the darkness of their surroundings as night advances. For a similar situation, consider *Purgatorio* II.8, the phrase "là dov' i' era" (there where I was) by which Dante refers to his situation in the southern hemisphere looking at the stars from there.

His figure of speech involves mixing metaphors, as the night is given feet, by which she measures her hours, and wings that do the same thing. The meaning is that the time is between 8:30 and 9 PM.

10–11.   Dante's Adamic sleepiness, that is, the heaviness brought on by his physical being, is adumbrated by a later passage (*Purg.* XI.43–44), in which Virgil comments upon the difficulties experienced by this living soul as he climbs the mountain in his flesh ("la carne d'Adamo"). But the theme is introduced in the first canto of *Inferno* (I.10–12) where Dante's "sleepiness" is associated with Adam's, according to Hollander (Holl.1969.1), p. 81n., suggesting a figural relationship between the fallen Adam, sent forth into his exile from the garden, and the sinful Dante.

13–15.   Dante's dream, occurring some nine hours after he fell asleep, takes place in the pre-dawn moments in which the swallow sings sadly *perhaps* (if we credit the mythographers, most certainly Ovid, *Metam.* VI.412–674) in memory of the rape of Philomel by her sister Procne's husband Tereus and her subsequent metamorphosis into a swallow (in Dante's version, where most others prefer the nightingale—see note to *Purg.* XVII.19–20, a passage that makes the swallow here necessarily Philomel). Tereus, like Tithonus, has had sexual concourse with each of two sisters—if we accept the notion that the opening passage of the poem posits a lunar aurora (see note to vv. 1–9, above).

16–18.   The greater truth, indeed the prophetic power, of dreams that came near morning was something of a commonplace in Dante's time. See note to *Inferno* XXVI.7. Beginning with Torraca (1905), twentieth-century commentators have reminded readers that in *Convivio* II.vii.13 Dante adduced our awareness of our own immortality from the fact that our dreams foretold the future for us.

19.   The formulaic expression (*mi parea + vedere*) is an earmark of Dante's description of seeing in dream; see also *Inferno* XXXIII.36; *Purgatorio* XV.85–87; XXVII.97–98. For the consistency in Dante's oneiric vocabulary, dating back to the *Vita nuova*, see Hollander (Holl.1974.1), pp. 3–4. For studies in English of the three purgatorial dreams see Hollander (Holl.1969.1), pp. 136–58; Cervigni (Cerv.1986.1), pp. 95–180; Barański (Bara.1989.1); see also Stefanini (Stef.1985.1).

20–21.   The reality corresponding to the eagle outside the dream is, naturally, St. Lucy (identified by Virgil in verse 55), who is bearing Dante higher up the mountain while he sleeps in her arms. But does this eagle have a symbolic valence? Some early commentators (the Ottimo the earliest) read the text strictly literally: the eagle is the bird of Jove (or, perhaps, Jove in the shape of an eagle). However, beginning with Pietro di Dante the eagle is allegorized as divine grace, and then, by various commentators up to and including Giacalone (1968), as one form of grace or another (e.g., prevenient, illuminating, etc.). In the twentieth century there was a vogue for a quite different allegorical reading, the eagle as symbol of empire. (To be sure, this is often, even usually, true in this highly political poem; in this context, however, it seems a forced reading.) It would seem most likely that a literal reading is the best procedure here, following the Ottimo (1333), and simply noting that this eagle is the one who flew off with Ganymede, as the context allows and encourages, i.e., Dante dreams that he was carried off by Jove.

22–24. John of Serravalle (1416), following Benvenuto, allegorizes the eagle as divine grace and then equates Dante and Ganymede, thus making Dante "one who lived with the gods." Casini/Barbi suggest that Dante had in mind Virgil's phrase in *Georgics* I.24–25, "deorum / concilia" (company of the gods) when he wrote "al sommo consistoro"; whether he did or not, his meaning seems clear. Within the dream there is a certain aura of violence and fear (implicit reference to the forcible rape of Ganymede by Jove as eagle—see *Aen.* V.252–257) masking the happier nature of the event: Dante being carried aloft gently by Lucy, and indeed, in a still happier understanding, on the way to the Empyrean, where he will, for a while, share the company of the immortal blessed.

25–27. The protagonist's thought within his dream is striking. Since, within the dream, Dante is "thinking like Ganymede," his thought refers to a place elevated from the normal, e.g., on this mountain near Troy. (Some commentators want to keep the usual imperial valence of the eagle by associating this Mt. Ida with Troy and thus empire; however, the point would rather seem to be that the place is elevated, not that it is Trojan.) And thus Dante would be thinking that only such extraordinary, i.e., "higher," mortals like Ganymede and Dante Alighieri are chosen by the gods for their delight. And this thought, perfectly in accord with what we will find out on the first terrace of purgatory proper, associates Dante with the sin of pride. Once again, however, the "reality" tells a different story: the true God is not interested in Dante's curly locks, but in his Christian soul; and He will pluck Dante up from the mount of purgatory for reasons better than those that motivated Jove.

The issue of Jove's homosexual desire for Ganymede is mainly avoided in the commentaries. It is, nonetheless, noteworthy that, of the many myths available to Dante that might express the love of the gods for a particular mortal, he has chosen this one. For the question of Dante's attitudes toward homosexuality see Hollander (Holl.1996.1). Durling (Durl.1996.1), pp. 559–60, on the basis of no known evidence, is of the opinion that Dante was of homosexual predisposition but had never acted on his desires. While that is probably more than can be shown to be true, the question of Dante's rather "unmedieval" view of homosexuality (see concluding note to *Inf.* XVI) has not been dealt with as openly as it ought to be.

28–30.   The eagle's descent may have still another Virgilian provenance: *Aeneid* XII.247–250, as Tommaseo (1837) was perhaps the first to suggest; he has been followed by a number of others. In that scene an eagle, described as "Jove's golden bird," offers an omen (arranged by Turnus's sister, the nymph Juturna) when it dives from the sky to snatch a swan out of the water and carries it off as its prey. (This much of the drama bodes ill for the Trojans, but they are heartened, unfortunately for them, in the final result, when the rest of the waterfowl attack the eagle and it drops the swan.) The language is pertinent: Jove's golden bird is attacking the "litoreas . . . avis turbamque sonantem / agminis aligeri" (the fowl along the shore, the clamorous crowd in their wingèd band). From among this *agmen aliger* the eagle picks one. For the pun available to Dante on his family name (Alighieri/*aliger*) see the note to *Inferno* XXVI.1–3. It seems possible that here Dante is conflating the two Virgilian passages in which a Jovian eagle seizes its prey and enjoying the coincidence that, in the last of them, that prey is associated with his own name, since he, too, while dreaming, is being lifted skyward in the talons of Jove.

The fire alluded to here is the ring of fire that was believed to surround the closer-to-earth sphere of air, just before one might reach the moon. That this is the "tanto . . . del cielo acceso" (so much of the sky set afire) of *Paradiso* I.79 was possibly first suggested by Lombardi (1791). Thereafter it became a commonplace in the commentaries.

31–33.   Once again the negative version of events put forth in the dream has a better meaning. It seemed that the eagle and Dante were consumed in the ring of fire high above the earth, while actually Dante and Lucia have risen to the gate of purgatory, as we shall shortly find out, and Dante is being awakened, not by the pain of death, but by the late-morning sun on his eyelids (verse 44). If there is a further significance to this detail, it would seem to refer to Dante's eventual arrival at the true "sphere of fire," the Empyrean.

34–42.   The poet describes the narrator's awakening in terms that recall Statius's text (*Ach.* I.247–250), describing the stratagem employed by Thetis, Achilles' mother, in order to keep him from being "drafted" into the Trojan War. Taking him from the care of his tutor, the centaur Chiron (see *Inf.* XII.71), Thetis carries him in her arms, sleeping, to the island of Scyros. Again Dante adverts to a mythic narrative that has a tragic result; Thetis's benevolent caution will not prevent the coming of Ulysses and Diomedes to Scyros and the eventual death of Achilles in the war. Dante's "comic" reality counters the Statian tragedy: Achilles is carried down from his mountain homeland to an island from which he will go off to his death; Dante is carried up a mountain situated on an island toward his eventual homeland and eternal life. Rarely in the *Commedia* is the contrast between classical and Christian views, between tragedy and comedy, more present than in these classicizing passages that open this canto. It is also true that the protagonist, as he experiences these new things, behaves very much as the "old" man that he still is, and assumes that terror is a valid response to these miraculous events that, the reader can see, speak only of God's love and protection for even such a sinner as Dante.

43–45.   Dante and Virgil have left their companions behind, down the mountain's slope, and are facing the east, the sun in their faces as the morning advances.

52–63.   As though to remind the reader that all the material relating to Dante's dream did have a counterpart in reality, Virgil's explanation "glosses" the dream as it explains the coming of Lucy, while Dante slept, at the solar aurora, nine hours after he had seen the lunar aurora. Sometime after dawn she began her ascent with Dante in her arms, leaving their companions in ante-purgatory.

55.   St. Lucy remains one of the more problematic presences in Dante's poem. Exactly who is she and why is she so important to him? Most commentators take her to be the early-fourth-century martyr from Syracuse, killed while Diocletian was emperor ca. A.D. 304. She is usu-

ally associated with the well-being of the eyes, and this may have had some resonance for Dante who, in *Convivio* III.ix.15, reports a severe bout of eye trouble in the same year that he was composing his ode "Amor che ne la mente mi ragiona." For whatever reason (and we shall probably never know it), Dante was obviously particularly devoted to the cult of this saint. She has a presence in three major scenes in the work, the "prologue in heaven" (*Inf.* II.97–108), the transport of Dante while he sleeps in this canto, and the prospect of the inhabitants of the "stadium-rose" (*Par.* XXXII.137).

Moore (Moor.1917.1), pp. 235–55, addresses the problem of an allegorical understanding of Lucy. Does she represent "illuminating grace"? "cooperating grace"? Gradually Moore undermines both these allegorical formulations and moves toward the notion of Lucy as Dante's "patron saint" (p. 241), offering in evidence the phrase "il tuo fedele" (*Inf.* II.98) that reappears variously (Dante as Beatrice's "fedele" in *Purg.* XXXI.134; Bernard as Mary's "faithful one" in *Par.* XXXI.102) to suggest that the expression "implies the relation of one person to another person *as such*, and not as a symbol or type" (p. 243).

64–67.   A final simile prepares us for the entrance to purgatory proper, comparing Dante to one who moves from dubiety to confidence, a movement that required that he reinterpret the dream and his associations in a positive light.

70–72.   At almost the precise midpoint of the canto Dante situates his second address to the reader of this *cantica* (see *Purg.* VIII.19–21 for the first). It has caused two major interpretive problems, twice dividing its readers into two basic groups. First, there are those who believe that it speaks of an increase of quality in the artistry employed by the poet, while others contend that it speaks rather of an increase of quantity. This dispute is most readily understood by referring to translations of the poem; those in the first group have Dante say that he will employ better art; those in the second, more of it.

A second question remains: does this heightening reflect just the scene that follows (as in the opinion of a minority) or all of the *Purgatorio* that is to come? For the latter opinion see Francesco da Buti (1385), who argues that, since the subject is now penitence, *that* is the higher matter that requires more art; in one form or another, this is the position taken by most commentators. In the opinion of this writer, the address to the reader refers to the description of the gate, its warder, and the three steps in the rite of confession, all of which need to be understood in the tradition of the allegory of the poets, as we shall see. It regards, in other words, matter both local and temporary. In a similar vein see Vazzana (Vazz.1981.1), pp. 177–80, arguing that what is at stake is the allegorical nature of what immediately follows.

80.   The angel is seated not *upon* (as some translate) the highest step but *above* it, as will become clear from verse 104, where we learn that he is seated on the threshold of the gate with his feet upon the third step.

81.   Beginning with Scartazzini/Vandelli, commentators resort to Matthew 28:3 for the stern brightness of the angelic countenance: "Erat autem aspectus ejus sicut fulgur" (His countenance was as the lightning).

82.   The warder's sword is "the sign of one who has authority to pronounce sentence," in the words of Singleton (1973), citing Benvenuto da Imola. Singleton goes on to add that it is also "reminiscent of the Cherubim with the flaming sword that were placed to guard Eden after Adam and Eve were driven forth."

85.   The warder's words of challenge, "Dite costinci" (Say it from there) repeat, as many note, the challenge of one of the centaurs to the approach of Virgil and Dante (*Inf.* XII.63) and, like that one, probably reflect Charon's similar words (fare age . . . iam istinc [tell me . . . right where you are]) to the invading Aeneas in *Aeneid* VI.389, as Daniello (1568) was perhaps the first to note.

86–93.   This scene represents an epitomizing replay of Virgil's and Dante's encounter with the guardian of all purgatory, Cato (*Purg.* I.40–93): challenge by the guarding presence, who wants to know if some higher authority permits this visit; Virgil's response indicating a female who had sent these "pilgrims" on their journey (this time with no attempt to flatter the warder); the warder's courteous acceptance of the aspirants' desire to enter a sacred precinct.

94–102.   The allegory of the three steps should be less difficult than it has proven to be. Considering this problem, Carroll (1904) cites Milton, describing the gate of heaven (*Paradise Lost*, III.516): "Each stair mysteriously was meant." But what exactly does each of Dante's steps "mean"? Catholic doctrine, as variously expressed, presents the path to absolution from sin as running, in the Sacrament of Penance, from **contrition** (the recognition and heartfelt rejection of a sin) to **confession** (of the sin, voiced to a priest), to **satisfaction** (in the promise to perform an act of penance as ordered by that priest, thus showing the genuineness of the confession). This is the psychologically correct order as well as the one given by "Scholastic and other Church writers uniformly" (Moore [Moor.1899.1], p. 47), i.e., one is contrite, confesses, and then performs acts that will lead to **absolution**, in the culmination of the sacrament. Dante's first commentators are, however, more or less evenly divided as to whether the three steps found here represent, in sequence, (1) contrition, (2) confession, (3) satisfaction (this group is saving Dante from himself, as it were, i.e., they record what he *should* have said) or (1) confession, (2) contrition, (3) satisfaction. However, it is fairly clear from the text that Dante has reinvented the order to suit his own purpose, beginning with confession and only then proceeding to contrition. That this is almost certainly true is confirmed by a later text. *Purgatorio* XXXI.31–90 offers a carefully orchestrated presentation of Dante's own penance before Beatrice, with the steps of that paralleling the steps found here, namely, confession, contrition, satisfaction, in that order. Moore also points out that Dante's presentation of the third stage, satisfaction, is unorthodox, since he represents it as the love that came from Christ's self-sacrifice. Thus, in Dante's scheme, the sinner first confesses his sin, then feels true contrition for it, and then moves beyond it in his imitation of and love for Christ. Why he should have wanted to repackage the elements of what was a standard body of doctrine and belief is not a subject that has received adequate attention. But we should not be surprised to find that this poet remakes any text or any doctrine to his own liking and for his own reasons. The one element that does run through Dante's version of this sacrament is that its priestly element is curtailed in favor of inward recognition and performance on the part of the sinner, i.e., confession in Dante seems more a private form of self-recognition than is generally the case, contrition contains mainly internal elements (if it must eventually be given voice), and satisfaction seems more attitudinal than performative. It also seems that Dante has moved elements of satisfaction into the second stage of the process, contrition.

94–96.   The first step, of white marble, serves as a mirror to the protagonist and thus seems associated with confession.

97–99.   The second, darker than the purple-black of the color perse and broken by a cruciform crack, represents the sinner's recognition of his "broken" state.

100–102.   The third, red with the color of spurting blood reminiscent of the sacrifice of Jesus Christ, is, like the first, of a stone of lofty character, porphyry (the second seems to be humble geological matter indeed), and suggests the sacrifice the sinner must make in imitation of the great sacrifice made by Christ.

103–105.   Only recently have commentators (Mattalia [1960], Fallani [1965], Bosco [1979]) turned, for the source of Dante's *diamante*, to Ezechiel's *adamantem*, when God gives his prophet a stony forehead to wear against his enemies (Ezechiel 3:9). And since the priestly angel, seated upon the adamant threshold, is iconographically related to St. Peter, a number of commentators think of Matthew 16:18, "You are Peter and upon this rock will I build my church."

109.   Either in December 1310 at Vercelli or in January 1311 at Milano, Dante was apparently presented to the new emperor, Henry VII (see Frugoni's notes in his edition of Dante's *Epistles*, p. 564). Dante himself reports that he embraced the emperor's feet (*Epist.* VII.9). It is at least conceivable that this verse remembers that experience, especially since, if it was written after the event, it was probably written soon after it. Once again we are unable to be certain, because of the uncertainties that attend dating the stages of the poem's composition.

111.   Dante's threefold beating of his chest has been glossed, since the time of the Ottimo (1333), as signifying "mea culpa, mea culpa, mea maxima culpa." Andrea Lancia (the probable author of that commentary) proceeds, followed in this, as well, by many later commentators, to say that these three in turn signify three kinds of sin: sins of thought, of the tongue, and in deed.

112.   The seven P's, generally understood as deriving from the first letter of *peccata* (sins), evidently stand for the seven mortal sins (or capital vices), but here, since the protagonist has learned to hate sin, they stand for what remains of the predisposition to these seven vices that is inherited by every mortal through Adam's (and Eve's) original sin. For the P's as deriving from the letter *tau* see Sarolli (Saro.1957.1), arguing for a source in Ezekiel 9:2–6, where God commands a scribe to write that letter—as a positive sign in that case—on the foreheads of all the inhabitants of Jerusalem who repent the abominations done in the city. In the following slaughter of the rest of the inhabitants, only Jeremiah and the

other just Jerusalemites are preserved. See also Apocalypse 7:3, for the true believers who bear the sign of God on their foreheads, and Apocalypse 13:16 and 20:4, where those who worship the Beast have *his* sign on their foreheads.

For some time now a debate among the commentators has involved the question of whether or not others on the mountain possess these P's (i.e., whether or not the P's on Dante's forehead are unique). Two differing reasons help us to be fairly certain that they are in fact unique to him, the first one positive: Dante is the sole visitor to purgatory who climbs there in the flesh; his uniqueness thus has this further sign. Second, and arguing from negative evidence, one may say that, since no other character is ever observed bearing these stigmata, one may reasonably conclude that none has them. See note to *Purgatorio* XXI.22–24.

114.   Sin as a "wound" is a biblical topos (see Isaiah 1:6 [first noted by Scartazzini in his comment to *Par.* VII.28]; Psalms 38:11 [39:10—as noted by Singleton commenting on this verse]).

115–116.   The color of the warder's garments is the gray of ashes and gives expression to his humility, despite his high office.

117–126.   Sensible allegorical expositions of the two keys are found variously, but of particular use is Poletto's gloss to vv. 115–117. The golden key denotes the authority to absolve granted by Christ directly; the silver, the judgment necessary in the priest to be sure the penitent is truly deserving of absolution. Poletto cites passages in St. Thomas to show Dante's closeness to them in this part of his description of the process of entering purgatory (*ST* III, Suppl., qq. 17–20). Once the priest has judged the penitent ready for absolution (using his silver key), he then uses the golden one to complete the opening of the door. The priest, of course, may err in wanting to allow an unfit soul to enter; in that case the golden key will not turn in the lock—but even so, God is disposed to err on the side of mercy and will overrule a prelate who is niggardly in pardoning.

The fact that a priest may err in his judgment makes it disturbing that this figure is presented as being literally an angel (who thus should be free of such weak discernment). It would seem more logical if we dealt here with an allegorical figure, Priestliness, the Petrine warder of the gate, a composite figure representing a class, not a particular historical being. And, indeed, the angel does not behave in any other way.

131–132.   See Christ's words to his disciples (Luke 9:62): "Nemo mittens manum suam ad aratrum, et respiciens retro, aptus est regno Dei" (No man, having put his hand to the plough, and looking back, is fit for the kingdom of God). This apt passage has been cited in this connection since the time of Pietro di Dante (1340). While Lot's wife (Genesis 19:17, 19:26) may also be remembered here, the passage from Luke's gospel is more closely related. The same may be said for the resonance of Orpheus's backward glance at Eurydice.

133–138.   This is the first part of one of the most difficult canto endings in the *Divine Comedy*. These lines remember a terrible moment of Roman history, while the second part (vv. 139–145) reflects the musical practice of Dante's day.

For hundreds of years Rome had kept a part of its treasure secure from any use, locked behind a portal that was never opened, until Caesar, in order to fund his pursuit of Pompey and Cato in 49 B.C., broke into the treasury and looted it, overcoming the resistance of a single brave republican, Metellus, loyal to Pompey. Dante's source here is the violently republican Lucan (*Phars.* III.108–168). It is worth reading the entire passage, which most commentators apparently do not do, for it drips with sarcasm about Julius Caesar, from its inception, in which Caesar, having marched on Rome and conquered by arms, has become everything and the senate has become a mouthpiece for this "private man," to its conclusion, in which the city is portrayed as being poorer than the one man who rules her as a result of his plundering the temple of Saturn, her treasury. There is nothing good here about Caesar, despite Dante's respect for him as the person he considered the first emperor of Rome (see Stull and Hollander [Stul.1991.1], pp. 33–43, for Dante's mainly negative, if mixed, views of Julius in the poem). And thus the sound that sounds so shrilly at Dante's entrance into purgatory is reminiscent of what, for Lucan and for Dante, is perhaps the nadir of Roman history, the accession of Caesar and the destruction of the republic. (For Dante's fervent belief in the republican virtues and form of government see Hollander and Rossi [Holl.1986.1].) Along with the passage in Lucan, undoubtedly Dante's main source here, Tommaseo (1837) brings into play *Aeneid* VI.573–574: "tum demum horrisono stridentes cardine sacrae / panduntur portae" (then at last, grating on their hinges, the impious gates swing open). Virgil is describing the gates of Tartarus, swinging open (the Sibyl and Aeneas do not enter, but she does tell him of the horrors of the punishments therein). Here, too, we can see how Dante has juxtaposed two similar objects, the gates of Tartarus, the pagans' hell, and those of purgatory, and make the reader aware of the crucial similarity that marks their utter difference.

What is the effect of such negative reminiscences as the protagonist begins to attain the Promised Land? One must conclude that we are dealing here with antithesis: as brutally shrill as was the sound of the squealing doors of the temple of Saturn, of the gates of Tartarus, exactly so terribly loud is the rare victory of a penitent being allowed to enter the kingdom of Heaven—or its vestibule. What was tragic in its consequence for Rome is marked by a sound exactly as loud and grating as this one that announces the victory of a new (and better) Caesar who enters not against the will of the warder, but in accord with it. Only the sounds are similar; all else is changed. And, as we have seen occur several times in the first half of this canto, tragic classical myth or history gives way to comic Christian narrative. In the words of Jesus (Luke 12:34), "There where your treasure is, there your heart is also." Caesar's treasure is far different from the treasure in Heaven sought and found by only relatively few Christians, their low numbers suggested by the infrequent screechings of this gate.

As for the positive resolution for the unpleasant sound of the opening gate, Heilbronn (Heil.1984.1) points out that medieval concepts of musical "sweetness" had more to do with harmony than with the sounds themselves. She (p. 4) gives the examples of the hurdy-gurdy and drum, both of which would hardly seem to be "sweet" to modern ears, but did to those of the time who recorded their responses. This point is a pivotal one for those who cannot bring themselves to see how the grating screech of a gate can be in harmony with another sound. Yet when we reflect, along with Heilbronn, that what the gate's sound announces is very sweet indeed, we may begin to understand Dante's strategy here.

134.   The noun *regge* represents a relatively rare term (one never used elsewhere by Dante) for the main portal of a church. Heilbronn (Heil.1984.1), p. 5, suggests that "like a cathedral door, the gate of Purgatory is the mystical image of the gate of heaven."

139–145.   This passage, too, has caused a great deal of difficulty. Heilbronn (Heil.1984.1), a Dante scholar with a musical background, has dealt with a number of the issues that have puzzled readers and offers a helpful review of the extensive discussion. Some of the essential matters in dispute involve the words *tuono, voce, suono*, and *organo*.

According to her, *tuono* (understood as "a note" and not as "thunder") should be seen as positive, since it is the sound that accompanies a soul's entrance into purgatory; *voce* and *suono* are, respectively, technical terms for the human voice and an inanimate, instrumental sound (pp. 6–7), while *organo* refers either to polyphonic singing or singing accompanied by an organ. Heilbronn is illuminating about the use of impressively large organs in churches in the tenth and eleventh centuries (pp. 8–10). Giacalone (1968) points out that Dante himself had described an organist as accompanying a song (*Dve* II.viii.5–6) and Bosco/Reggio, influenced by the paper given by Damilano in 1974, remind us that one of Dante's commentators, Cristoforo Landino (1481), grandnephew of the famous organist Francesco Landino, is of the opinion that the practice was to alternate passages of singing and organ-playing in church services and that this is referred to by Dante here.

Dante believes he hears the words of a hymn being sung (and we must imagine that, if there was actual singing to greet his coming [Dante only says that he *seemed* to hear voices], it was done by angels, since the penitents we eventually see in the next canto, the prideful, are bent under their weights and far from lyrical; however, this harmonious sound may issue from the gate itself). "Te Deum laudamus" has an interesting history in the commentaries. (For the text of the hymn in Latin and English see Singleton's gloss to verse 140.) Benvenuto claims that St. Ambrose wrote this hymn after he had served as St. Augustine's spiritual doctor and cured him of his terrible errors (in Milan shortly before Augustine's conversion); it is thus, Benvenuto continues, a most fitting accompaniment to Dante's—another great intellect's—turning to penance. Other early commentators also associate the hymn with Augustine's conversion, whether it was sung while he was being baptized or spoken by Ambrose in his sermon on that occasion or, indeed, according to Francesco da Buti, spontaneously spoken responsively by these two great men on that day. While in our time it is not believed to have been composed by Ambrose, in Dante's it was. That Dante should have chosen to present himself, entering purgatory, as a new (and better) Julius Caesar and as the new Augustine is both altogether extraordinary and completely Dantean. (For the opinion that Dante presents himself as being like Augustine in the sins he must conquer, lust and bad philosophizing, see Hollander [Holl.1969.1], p. 165n.)

PURGATORIO X
(*Pride*)

III. The penitent prideful

Poi fummo dentro al soglio de la porta
che 'l mal amor de l'anime disusa,
3   perché fa parer dritta la via torta,

sonando la senti' esser richiusa;
e s'io avesse li occhi vòlti ad essa,
6   qual fora stata al fallo degna scusa?

Noi salavam per una pietra fessa,
che si moveva e d'una e d'altra parte,
9   sì come l'onda che fugge e s'appressa.

"Qui si conviene usare un poco d'arte,"
cominciò 'l duca mio, "in accostarsi
12   or quinci, or quindi al lato che si parte."

E questo fece i nostri passi scarsi,
tanto che pria lo scemo de la luna
15   rigiunse al letto suo per ricorcarsi,

che noi fossimo fuor di quella cruna;
ma quando fummo liberi e aperti
18   sù dove il monte in dietro si rauna,

ïo stancato e amendue incerti
di nostra via, restammo in su un piano
21   solingo più che strade per diserti.

Da la sua sponda, ove confina il vano,
al piè de l'alta ripa che pur sale,
24   misurrebbe in tre volte un corpo umano;

e quanto l'occhio mio potea trar d'ale,
or dal sinistro e or dal destro fianco,
27   questa cornice mi parea cotale.

Once we had crossed the threshold of the gate
not used by souls whose twisted love
attempts to make the crooked way seem straight,

I knew that it had shut by its resounding.
And had I turned my eyes to look,
how could I have excused my fault?

We were climbing through a crevice in the rock,
which first bent one way, then another,
like a wave that ebbs and then comes rushing back,

when my leader said: 'Here we must use skill
in keeping close to one side or the other,
hewing to the side where the rock gives way.'

This so hindered our slow steps
the waning moon had gained its bed
and sunken to its rest

before we issued from that needle's eye.
But free above, out in the open
where the cliff draws back to leave a space—

I weary and both of us uncertain of our path—
we stopped at a flat and open spot
more solitary than a desert track.

From its edge, which borders on the void,
to the foot of the lofty bank in its sheer rise,
would measure thrice the body of a man.

And as far as my eye could wing its flight,
now toward the left, now to the other side,
the terrace stretched before me.

Là sù non eran mossi i piè nostri anco,
quand' io conobbi quella ripa intorno
30   che dritto di salita aveva manco,

esser di marmo candido e addorno
d'intagli sì, che non pur Policleto,
33   ma la natura lì avrebbe scorno.

L'angel che venne in terra col decreto
de la molt' anni lagrimata pace,
36   ch'aperse il ciel del suo lungo divieto,

dinanzi a noi pareva sì verace
quivi intagliato in un atto soave,
39   che non sembiava imagine che tace.

Giurato si saria ch'el dicesse *"Ave!"*;
perché iv' era imaginata quella
42   ch'ad aprir l'alto amor volse la chiave;

e avea in atto impressa esta favella
"Ecce ancilla Deï," propriamente
45   come figura in cera si suggella.

"Non tener pur ad un loco la mente,"
disse 'l dolce maestro, che m'avea
48   da quella parte onde 'l cuore ha la gente.

Per ch'i' mi mossi col viso, e vedea
di retro da Maria, da quella costa
51   onde m'era colui che mi movea,

un'altra storia ne la roccia imposta;
per ch'io varcai Virgilio, e fe'mi presso,
54   acciò che fosse a li occhi miei disposta.

Era intagliato lì nel marmo stesso
lo carro e ' buoi, traendo l'arca santa,
57   per che si teme officio non commesso.

Our feet had not yet stepped on it
when I perceived that the encircling bank,
30   steep and impossible to climb,

was of white marble carved with so much art
that Polycletus and Nature's very self
33   would there be put to shame.

The angel who came to earth with the decree of peace
that had been wept and yearned for all those years,
36   which opened Heaven ending God's long ban,

appeared before us so vividly engraved
in gracious attitude
39   it did not seem an image, carved and silent.

One would have sworn he said: *'Ave,'*
for she as well was pictured there
42   who turned the key to love on high.

And in her attitude imprinted were
the words: *'Ecce Ancilla Dei'*
45   as clearly as a figure stamped in wax.

'Do not fix your mind on one part only,'
said the kind master, who had me
48   on that side of him where we have our hearts.

At that I turned my face
and, looking beyond Mary, saw,
51   on the same side as he that prompted me,

another story set into the rock.
I went past Virgil and drew near
54   so that my eyes might better take it in.

There, carved into the marble, were the cart
and oxen drawing the sacred ark that makes men fear
57   to assume an office not entrusted to them.

Dinanzi parea gente; e tutta quanta,
partita in sette cori, a' due mie' sensi
60   faceva dir l'un "No," l'altro "Sì, canta."

Similemente al fummo de li 'ncensi
che v'era imaginato, li occhi e 'l naso
63   e al sì e al no discordi fensi.

Lì precedeva al benedetto vaso,
trescando alzato, l'umile salmista,
66   e più e men che re era in quel caso.

Di contra, effigïata ad una vista
d'un gran palazzo, Micòl ammirava
69   sì come donna dispettosa e trista.

I' mossi i piè del loco dov' io stava,
per avvisar da presso un'altra istoria,
72   che di dietro a Micòl mi biancheggiava.

Quiv' era storïata l'alta gloria
del roman principato, il cui valore
75   mosse Gregorio a la sua gran vittoria;

I' dico di Traiano imperadore;
e una vedovella li era al freno,
78   di lagrime atteggiate e di dolore.

Intorno a lui parea calcato e pieno
di cavalieri, e l'aguglie ne l'oro
81   sovr' essi in vista al vento si movieno.

La miserella intra tutti costoro
pareva dir: "Segnor, fammi vendetta
84   di mio figliuol ch'è morto, ond' io m'accoro";

ed elli a lei rispondere: "Or aspetta
tanto ch'i' torni"; e quella: "Segnor mio,"
87   come persona in cui dolor s'affretta,

The foreground, peopled by figures grouped
in seven choirs, made one sense argue 'No'
60   and the other: 'Yes, they sing.'

In just this way, the smoke of incense
sculpted there ~~put eyes and nose~~
63   in discord, caught between yes and no.

There the humble psalmist leaped in dance
before the blessèd vessel with his robe hitched up—
66   and was at once both more and less than king.

Opposite, a figure at the window
of a splendid palace, Michal looked on,
69   like a woman vexed and scornful.

I moved some steps from where I stood
to look more closely at another story
72   that I saw gleaming white beyond Michal.

Depicted there was the glorious act
of the Roman prince whose worth
75   urged Gregory on to his great victory—

I speak of the emperor Trajan,
with the poor widow at his bridle, weeping,
78   revealed in her state of grief—

the soil all trampled by the thronging knights.
Above, the eagles fixed in gold
81   seemed to flutter in the wind.

In their midst, one could almost hear the plea
of that unhappy creature: 'My lord, avenge
84   my murdered son for me. It is for him I grieve,'

and his answer: 'Wait till I return,'
and she: 'My lord,' like one whose grief is urgent,
87   'and if you don't return?' and his answer:

"se tu non torni?"; ed ei: "Chi fia dov' io,
la ti farà"; ed ella: "L'altrui bene
90 a te che fia, se 'l tuo metti in oblio?";

ond' elli: "Or ti conforta; ch'ei convene
ch'i' solva il mio dovere anzi ch'i' mova:
93 giustizia vuole e pietà mi ritene."

Colui che mai non vide cosa nova
produsse esto visibile parlare,
96 novello a noi perché qui non si trova.

Mentr' io mi dilettava di guardare
l'imagini di tante umilitadi,
99 e per lo fabbro loro a veder care,

"Ecco di qua, ma fanno i passi radi,"
mormorava il poeta, "molte genti:
102 questi ne 'nvïeranno a li alti gradi."

Li occhi miei, ch'a mirare eran contenti
per veder novitadi ond' e' son vaghi,
105 volgendosi ver' lui non furon lenti.

Non vo' però, lettor, che tu ti smaghi
di buon proponimento per udire
108 come Dio vuol che 'l debito si paghi.

Non attender la forma del martìre:
pensa la succession; pensa ch'al peggio
111 oltre la gran sentenza non può ire.

Io cominciai: "Maestro, quel ch'io veggio
muovere a noi, non mi sembian persone,
114 e non so che, sì nel veder vaneggio."

Ed elli a me: "La grave condizione
di lor tormento a terra li rannicchia,
117 sì che ' miei occhi pria n'ebber tencione.

'He who will take my place will do it,'
and she: 'What use to you is another's goodness
90   if you are unmindful of your own?'

And he then: 'Now take comfort, for I must discharge
my debt to you before I go to war.
93   Justice wills it and compassion bids me stay.'

He in whose sight nothing can be new
wrought this speech made visible,
96   new to us because it is not found on earth.

While I took pleasure in the sight
of images of such humility,
99   the lovelier to look at for their maker's sake,

'Here they come, though with slow steps,'
the poet murmured.
102   'They will direct us to the next ascent.'

My eyes, glad to gaze upon the marble,
quickly turned in his direction,
105   eager at the promise of new things.

Reader, I would not have you fall away
from good intentions when you hear
108   the way God wills the debt be paid.

Do not dwell upon the nature of the suffering.
Think what is to follow, think that at the worst
111   it cannot last beyond the final Judgment.

'Master,' I began, 'those that I see
moving toward us do not look like people—
114   whatever they may be, I cannot make them out.'

And he answered: 'The grave nature
of their torment contorts their bodies to a crouch,
117   so that at first my eyes were undecided.

Ma guarda fiso là, e disviticchia
col viso quel che vien sotto a quei sassi:
120   già scorger puoi come ciascun si picchia."

O superbi cristian, miseri lassi,
che, de la vista de la mente infermi,
123   fidanza avete ne' retrosi passi,

non v'accorgete voi che noi siam vermi
nati a formar l'angelica farfalla,
126   che vola a la giustizia sanza schermi?

Di che l'animo vostro in alto galla,
poi siete quasi antomata in difetto,
129   sì come vermo in cui formazion falla?

Come per sostentar solaio o tetto,
per mensola talvolta una figura
132   si vede giugner le ginocchia al petto,

la qual fa del non ver vera rancura
nascere 'n chi la vede; così fatti
135   vid' io color, quando puosi ben cura.

Vero è che più e meno eran contratti
secondo ch'avien più e meno a dosso;
e qual più pazïenza avea ne li atti,
139   piangendo parea dicer: "Più non posso."

'But look closer, disentangle
the figures bent beneath them from the stones.
120   Then you can see how each one beats his breast.'

O vainglorious Christians, miserable wretches!
Sick in the visions engendered in your minds,
123   you put your trust in backward steps.

Do you not see that we are born as worms,
though able to transform into angelic butterflies
126   that unimpeded soar to justice?

What makes your mind rear up so high?
You are, as it were, defective creatures,
129   like the unformed worm, shaped from the mud.

To hold up roof or ceiling, as a corbel does,
we sometimes see a crouching figure,
132   its knees pushed up against its chest,

and that unreal depiction may arouse
in him who sees it real distress,
135   such were these shapes when I could make them out.

They were indeed hunched over more or less,
depending on the burdens on their backs,
and even he that showed the greatest patience,
139   weeping, seemed to say: 'I can no more.'

1–6. The opening verses of the canto tell us that Dante is obeying the angel's warning (IX.132) not to look back (in this potentially resembling one of the disciples of Jesus even more than Lot's wife or Orpheus—see note to *Purg*. IX.131–132) and that the gate of purgatory makes such noise because it is so infrequently opened, since most human beings prefer to pretend that their crooked way is straight and spend eternity in hell as a result. This last image will be reinforced immediately by the undulating path through the rock that the travelers must follow, reminiscent of the sinful life they have left behind, and eventually, as Singleton points out, by the misconception that what is in fact crooked is straight in Dante's dream of the Siren (*Purg*. XIX.7–15).

Poletto's commentary (1894) to this passage reminds the reader of the total contrast between the solitary state of Dante and his guide, both when they approached the angelic warder and now, having proceeded farther up the mountain (see verse 21), and the vast crowds of damned sinners found both inside the gate of hell and before Minos in *Inferno* III.119–120 and V.12.

7–16. As opposed to the wide and easy entrance to hell (*Inf*. V.20), that to purgatory is narrow and difficult. For the reference to the "needle's eye" [verse 16]), see Christ's words to the disciples (Matthew 19:24): "And further I say to you, it is easier for a camel to pass through the eye of a needle, than for a rich man to enter the kingdom of heaven."

Virgil insists on the need for *arte*, or skill in navigating a tight spot, apparently so as not to allow Dante to be wounded by the sharp edges of the rock's outcroppings, and thus in not following the shortest path along this labyrinthine passageway, but the one that moves back and forth from the farther wall in order to avoid the protuberances on the nearer.

His reference to the waning moon (see *Inf*. XX.127, where we learn the moon was full on Thursday night) portrays the dark crescent in that body as leading it toward the horizon as it sets. It is now Monday morning; the moon was full 3.5 days ago and set in the western sky exactly at sunrise. With four days of retardation, fifty minutes per day, it is now setting approximately three hours and twenty minutes after sunrise. Since Dante awoke before the gate just after 8 AM (*Purg*. IX.44), it is perhaps slightly more than an hour later. In that time he has been admitted by the warder and made his way with Virgil through the "eye of the needle."

19. This verse distances Virgil from Dante by insisting on his freedom from the body's weight and yet equates the two travelers as being equally uninformed as to their impending choices. We have known that Virgil is not proficient in the ways of purgatory from the outset (*Purg.* II.61–63); now that we are in true purgatory the point is underlined.

22–23. See Toscano (Tosc.1989.1), pp. 207–8, on two debates among the commentators: Does this wall make a right or an obtuse angle with the smooth pavement? Do the penitents observe what is sculpted on the wall or not? Toscano strongly supports the notion that the wall is set at an obtuse angle so that the penitents are able to see what is depicted on it. If this were not the case, he continues, God's art would be wasted on them, unable to move their heads high enough to see the instructive decoration, which would, without their observation, be mere ornament. If the terraces are cut into the side of the mountain and if this verse, as many commentators believe, indicates that the inner bank of every terrace is part of the tapered shape of the mountain as a whole, then Toscano is correct. However, should we ever be forced to decide that, as Pietrobono (1946), Mattalia (1960), and Vazzana (Vazz.1970.1, pp. 65–67) believe, this terrace (and every other one?) has a perpendicular wall as its inner border, we would also probably deduce that, in God's realm, even stiff-necked penitents will somehow be able to see all of the sculpting that is put there for their instruction. (Dante's illustrators are not much help in this respect; if one examines the two illustrations of the purgatorial mount found in the *Dante Encyclopedia* [Lans.2000.1], pp. 725 and 729, one finds that one shows the first condition, the other, the second.) Since Dante never clarified this point and since the manuscript tradition of the line (verse 30) crucial to its interpretation itself has caused much uncertainty, we really cannot say what the meaning is. Bosco/Reggio (1979) contrive a compromise: the lower part of the wall is slanted, but the rest of it is perpendicular. This might solve certain problems, but cannot be supported by the text.

30. For some of the problems associated with this verse see note to vv. 22–23.

31–33. Art is clearly a major theme of this canto. We hear now of the aesthetic superiority of God's intaglios over the work of the sculptor Polycletus or the creative genius of nature herself. At verse 97 we learn, not of Dante's instruction, but of his delight in the intaglios. Near the canto's close we are told in a simile of the genuine distress that can be caused by our looking at a sculpted figure of a crunched human shape in a corbel (131–134). All these aesthetic moments have at their root the experience of art as moving its audience by its mimetic capacity. The morality of the art found on this terrace is not to be doubted, but in this canto (as opposed to the next) we at first find art treasured for purely aesthetic reasons (but see note to vv. 97–99).

The words that make their way through the three descriptions of intaglios in vv. 31–81 insist on the artistic nature of what the protagonist sees: forms of *intaglio*: 32, 38, 55; of *imagine*: 39, 41, 62; of *storia*: 52, 71, 73. This art of God, which some commentators have looked upon as uncannily predicting the eventual sculpture of Michelangelo, may be more advanced than that of mere mortals, and even of nature, but it somehow does not seem very far removed from that of Dante himself.

Polycletus, Athenian sculptor of the fifth century B.C., for Dante represented the height of classical Greek art. Torraca (1905) points out that previous thirteenth-century Italian writers cited him in a similar way. Sources of information about him were found in Cicero, Quintilian, and Pliny. And Aristotle, mentioning him in the *Nichomachean Ethics*, brought him to the attention of St. Thomas. And so, even if Italian vernacular writers of this period had never seen his work, they could refer to it as Dante does here.

34–45.   The first example of each virtue (here Humility), opposed to the capital vice purged on each of the seven terraces, is always Mary. These four tercets are spare and central in their presentation of the Annunciation: only Gabriel and Mary are seen, minus the "background" expected by any medieval reader, familiar with the iconography of this moment: dove, ray of light, garden, etc. As the Ottimo (1333) has it, the "long-standing ban" had been in effect since the time recorded in Genesis 3 (the Fall) and was only rescinded when Christ harrowed hell.

The sculpted forms are so vivid that they actually seem to speak. Thus does Dante recast the key spoken moments of Luke 1:26–38, Gabriel's charge and Mary's humble acceptance of it.

46–54.   Bosco/Reggio make explicit what is almost said by many of those commentators who deal with the phrase in verse 53, "varcai Virgilio" (I went past Virgil): it is a fine, realistic detail with no further significance. Yet this entire passage, in which Virgil gets Dante to stop enjoying so deeply the representation of Gabriel and Mary and to make himself available to more of God's art, has certain overtones that might cast a different light on the relationship between the two poets here. The Annunciation was nearly, we might reflect, the subject of Virgil's fourth *Eclogue*, the child to be born to a virgin that, had he only known which child and which virgin, might have saved him. It is this scene from which Virgil, in all innocence, pulls Dante away. And, while what follows merely describes Dante's moving past Virgil, who had been standing between him and the first intaglio, from left to right, so as better to inspect the next work, it also describes physically what has a moral status, that is, Dante surpasses Virgil as an artist because he is more available to the meaning of God's art. (In this vein see Barolini [Baro.1984.1], p. 278.)

55–69. As *Inferno* has readied us to observe, Dante will now couple his subordinate exemplary figures as scriptural and classical, more specifically Old Testament and Roman. This passage consolidates key elements of the narrative concerning David's bringing the Ark of the Covenant into Jerusalem: his dancing before it, his wife Michal's scorn, and her resultant barrenness (II Samuel 6:1–23).

56–57. Uzzah's presumption in attempting to assist Him who requires no help of any kind is related in II Samuel 6:6–7: he tried to steady the Ark when the movement of the oxen seemed about to topple it; for this God strikes him down immediately, killing him for his prideful insistence on a mission not enjoined. For Dante's complex and amusing acknowledgment, both here and, more specifically, in his eleventh *Epistle* that he is, in some ways, the "new Uzzah," see Barolini (Baro.1992.1), p. 132, and Hollander (Holl.1999.2).

60–63. The protagonist's ears assure him that the seven choirs in this panel are not singing, yet his eyes insist that they are. Just so his nose smells no perfume of incense, while his eyes can *see* that the smoke indeed has an aroma.

65. Perhaps no passage in a poem that refers to David more than to any other personage from the Old Testament (see Holl.1973.1) is more compelling in establishing the "figural relationship" between the two poets. Dante, too, is the "humble psalmist," David's modern counterpart. It seems just to say that no one has developed this observation as well as has Barolini (see especially Baro.1984.1, pp. 275–78). Tommaseo long ago (1837) dealt with this scene as a metaphor for great Dante's low vernacular poetry performed beneath the scornful gaze of pedantry: "But Dante is more than poet in certain respects, because he does not fear to

appear less than poet and dances with his robe hitched up; but princess Michal—I might call her 'pedantry'—sniffs from the window."

67–69.   Where David, down among the common people and dancing without kingly dignity, reflects the low comedic world, Michal, high above the crowd and separate from it, scornful, seems to represent the lofty, "tragic," or noble view. David here serves as a forerunner for Jesus, who will identify himself with humility, while Michal seems to be associated with all those who resist humility in the name of pride.

73–93.   The longest of these three scenes concerns Trajan, emperor of Rome in the years 98–117. Of those whom Dante depicts as being saved, to whom all or most Christians would deny, or at least question, that status (Cato [*Purg.* I.75], Statius [*Purg.* XXII.73], Trajan [*Par.* XX.44], and Ripheus [*Par.* XX.68]), only for Trajan does there exist a tradition that considered him saved. This result of St. Gregory's prayers is even allowed as possible by St. Thomas, in what seems an unusually latitudinarian gesture, recorded in the *Summa theologica* (as was perhaps first noted by Lombardi [1791]): *ST* III, Suppl., quaest. 71, art. 5, obj. 5 [for the text in English see Singleton's note to verse 75]). That what seems to modern ears an unbelievable story should have had the support of so rigorous a thinker as Thomas still astounds readers. Yet, if one looks closely, one sees that Thomas does hedge his bet: Trajan's salvation by Gregory's intervention is "probable" *(potest probabiliter aestimari)*; further, according to Thomas, "as others say" *(secundum quosdam)*, Trajan may have only had his punishment put back until Judgment Day. Dante betrays no such hesitation: the salvation of Trajan is Gregory's "great victory" (verse 75). Dante is in an enviable position, both possessing Thomas's support and being able to outdo him in enthusiasm.

For some of the many medieval texts that support the miraculous salvation of Trajan and for an array of possible sources for the dialogue between Trajan and the widow, including Trajan's column in Rome, see Vickers (Vick.1983.1), pp. 70–72, 75–79.

73.   For the term *storiata* see Singleton: "a depiction in art, even as stained-glass windows or initial letters in manuscripts or frescoed walls were said to be 'historiated' " with historical or legendary material.

75.   St. Gregory, known as Gregory the Great, was pope from 590 to 604. His lengthy commentary on the Book of Job (the *Moralia*), one of the most influential writings of the earlier Middle Ages, offers a different and happier

understanding of Job's story than is prevalent today, insisting that it has a truly "comic" resolution, rebinding Job to God and restoring his family. Dante mentions Gregory twice, here and in *Paradiso* XX.106–117, in connection with the salvation of Trajan, and he is referred to in the last sphere of the heavens as one of the saved (*Par.* XXVIII.133), despite the fact that he had made small errors in listing the orders of the angelic hierarchy (as had Dante himself in *Conv.* II.v.6) in the *Moralia*.

For information about which popes are saved and which are damned according to the *Commedia* see note to *Inferno* VII.46–48.

76. Having been told of Gregory's "great victory," we are now told in what it consisted: the pope has saved a (dead) pagan emperor. The way the text is handled reminds us of Dante's continuing hostility to the Church's insistence on the hierocrat position, in which the emperor is seen as totally dependent upon the Church for his authority. Gregory's intervention for a great Roman emperor has, in Dante's eyes, a different style and sets a better standard.

77–81. The rapid strokes that fill in the details of this intaglio show that Dante is fully capable of producing the scene in pictures. But in the following dozen verses, pushing the limits of the art he attributes to God, but which he has invented, he reports only the "visible speech" wrought by what he saw, that is, the words induced by the carving rather than the carving itself.

82–93. The exchange between the widow and Trajan, a sort of polite *tenzone*, involves six speeches. The widow seeks, Trajan denies; she seeks again and is again denied; she appeals to Trajan's moral character and he accedes, touched in those two treasured Roman inner qualities, respect for *iustitia* and *pietas*.

94–96. What is new to Dante is not so to God (but this does not reduce the novelty or the excitement of it for Dante [see verse 104] or for us).

For the program in the intaglios see Austin (Aust.1932.2); for ekphrasis in this canto see Heffernan (Heff.1993.1).

97–99. These images of humility reflect the pattern that we will find on each terrace: first *exempla* of the virtue that directly opposes the vice repented (here humility and pride), ultimately *exempla* of the vice itself (see *Purg.* XII.25–63). Thus the penitents are at first encouraged and finally warned lest they backslide.

100–102.   Dante's delectation has delayed the travelers long enough so that even this slow-moving band of penitents, coming along behind them, can become visible to Virgil (but not to the art-absorbed Dante), even though the path was totally bare when the two poets arrived on it (vv. 25–26). It is a curious fact of this art-filled canto that, of the two poets, Virgil has clearly the shorter attention span to give to art. He feels he has to urge Dante to take his eyes off Gabriel and Mary (verse 46) in order to examine David, and now interrupts Dante's delectation in the images of Trajan and the widow in order to get him to look at *real* souls. (He is obviously himself not nearly so absorbed by God's art.) It is a bit difficult to know what to make of these moments. Virgil resembles the less art-responsive member of a couple in a museum, waiting for his friend, totally absorbed, to finish looking so that their tour may continue. Further, the word used to describe Virgil's distracting locution is *mormorava* (murmured). Dante uses it seven other times in the poem, and it usually denotes some form of less-than-clear speech, uttered in this way because the speaker is in pain or distracted (in the only preceding occurrence, *Inf.* XXVI.86, it is the riven, speaking flame of Ulysses that murmurs). For Dante to put together the very word that for him most stands for eloquence, *poeta*, with "murmured" is striking. No one has, with the exception of Vickers, paid attention to the curious and disturbing notion that Virgil, of all people, should murmur. Here is her formulation, in partial response to that word: "The placing of Virgil face to face with divine assurance of the salvation of Trajan, a man of no more faith than he, cannot but emphasize the enigma of Virgil's situation" (Vick.1983.1, p. 72). She goes on to speculate that the salvation of Trajan by intervention of Gregory inevitably brings to mind another great medieval legend, that of St. Paul praying for the soul of Virgil at his tomb near Naples, a potential intervention on behalf of damned Virgil that, as far as everyone who has dealt with it is concerned, was obviously not successful.

103–105.   Vickers (Vick.1983.1), pp. 80–81, discusses Benvenuto's connecting the historiated walls of Carthage, with their account of the fall of Troy in *Aeneid* I.453–495, and this scene, and then goes on to suggest that "Aeneas is rapt in the esthetic experience and weeps; Dante the pilgrim is rapt and delights. The one reads defeat (emptiness); the other triumphs (fullness)."

106–111.   Dante's third address to us, his readers, is an appeal that we accept the necessity of treatment for our ills before we are eventually free of them. Since the "punishments" of the saved do not seem, at first blush, all that much more pleasant than the pains of the damned, the poet wishes to emphasize the great gulf that separates them: those in hell are eternal; these here are time-bound and will cease at least by the Day of Judgment.

112–120.   This passage has caused much discussion but is in fact not as difficult as it has been made to seem. The purpose of the entire passage is to get Dante to understand that what he is looking at is human and not merely a procession of mobile rocks. Virgil says he, too, had trouble making this fact out at first, but eventually could see that there were beings moving beneath the rocks. A single gesture makes this clear: they beat their breasts. And it is a gesture that accords with the penitential feelings of the penitent prideful, as Moore (Moor.1896.1), p. 49, clearly pointed out, citing Luke 18:13, where the publican beats his breast in humility.

121–129.   The poet's second apostrophe of the canto (see vv. 106–111 for the first) is not, strictly speaking, an address to the reader but rather a castigation of all those Christians (and thus, one would expect, *not* all his readers) who have turned away from God.

One of the most celebrated metaphors of the poem, the "angelic butterfly" that each of us has as a potential destiny, is what most of us will not become.

128.   While God wills that we, caterpillars that we are, become butterflies, Heaven-bound souls, we choose to be even less than those worms that are capable of that transformation, and have bent our wills to be such. As commentators have shown, *antomata* is Dante's version of Aristotle's creatures born, not of other creatures, but of the putrefaction of vegetable matter, as when the sun beats down on the mud—see *De generatione animalium* III.1, as cited by Benvenuto. See also Aristotle's *Historia animalium* V.19, as cited by Pasquini/Quaglio (1982), where Aristotle distinguishes, as Dante does here, between worms that can turn into butterflies and those, defective, which cannot. The meaning clearly seems to be that we are born worms, but turn ourselves into still lesser beings, formally imperfect worms, as though we had not been bred by creatures with rational souls. Benvenuto concludes by quoting Job (but actually the Psalms: 21:7 [22:6]): "Vermis sum ego et non homo" (I am a worm, not a man—Benvenuto may have conflated that passage with Job 25:6).

130–135.   In a canto so concerned with art, and highly mimetic art in particular, it seems only natural that the poet would have wanted to conclude with a simile, one of this artisan's specialties. We may be surprised to realize that this is the first one in this canto, that we have not seen one since well back in the last canto (*Purg.* IX.34–42). A corbel is a sculpted human figure, often crudely realistic, and thus part of the low-mimetic tradition, used to decorate the element that joins a weight-bearing column to the roof- or floor-beam that it supports.

The notion that an artifact can be so "realistic" that, although it is not real, but a fiction, as it were, it can cause an observer real distress, continues the mimetic concern so evident in this canto and also stands as a sort of emblem of the poem as a whole, with its insistence on its literal truth dizzyingly countered by its less evident but clear admission that it is in fact invented by a poet, if one who will only write fictions that seem (and claim) to be utterly true. For discussion of this passage in this light see Barolini (Baro.1992.1), pp. 125–26.

136–137.   We learn that, just as in hell there were sinners punished in differing degrees for the same sin, so in purging themselves penitents also reflect the degree of their former sinfulness.

138.   A small but continuing dispute in the commentaries debates whether *pazïenza* should be interpreted as "suffering" or "patience." Philologically there is probably no advantage to either solution. However, poetic logic points to a simple explanation (one shared by the vast majority of the commentators): what we face here is a relation of paradox rather than similarity. Even the most stoical of the sinners seemed to be expressing the thought (another case of "speech made visible") "I can no more." Of course the one who suffered most would be saying such a thing; that would not be worth mentioning. The point is that even the penitent least crushed by the weight of his former pride is suffering as much as one can possibly suffer.

Gerard Manley Hopkins offered, whether he wished to or not, a perfectly Dantean gloss to this verse. In his "terrible sonnet" named "Carrion Comfort" by Robert Bridges, Hopkins, more likely citing Shakespeare's *Antony and Cleopatra* (IV.xv.59) than Dante, has his speaking voice cry out, "Not, I'll not . . . cry *I can no more*. I can." While Antony says "I can no more" and dies, Hopkins's persona does not give in to despair and continues to strive toward God. Here, the penitents all seem to insist that they are at the end of their strength, yet all continue on the road toward making restitution to God by giving satisfaction for their sins and thus obtain their final absolution.

PURGATORIO XI
(Pride)

"O Padre nostro, che ne' cieli stai,
non circunscritto, ma per più amore
ch'ai primi effetti di là sù tu hai,

3

laudato sia 'l tuo nome e 'l tuo valore
da ogne creatura, com' è degno
di render grazie al tuo dolce vapore.

6

Vegna ver' noi la pace del tuo regno,
ché noi ad essa non potem da noi,
s'ella non vien, con tutto nostro ingegno.

9

Come del suo voler li angeli tuoi
fan sacrificio a te, cantando *osanna*,
così facciano li uomini de' suoi.

12

Dà oggi a noi la cotidiana manna,
sanza la qual per questo aspro diserto
a retro va chi più di gir s'affanna.

15

E come noi lo mal ch'avem sofferto
perdoniamo a ciascuno, e tu perdona
benigno, e non guardar lo nostro merto.

18

Nostra virtù che di legger s'adona,
non spermentar con l'antico avversaro,
ma libera da lui che sì la sprona.

21

Quest' ultima preghiera, segnor caro,
già non si fa per noi, ché non bisogna,
ma per color che dietro a noi restaro."

24

Così a sé e noi buona ramogna
quell' ombre orando, andavan sotto 'l pondo,
simile a quel che talvolta si sogna,

27

'Our Father, who are in Heaven,
circumscribed only by the greater love
You have for Your first works on high,

3

'praised be your name and power
by every creature, as is fitting
to render thanks for your sweet breath.

6

'May the peace of your kingdom come to us,
for we cannot attain it of ourselves
if it come not, for all our striving.

9

'As your angels make sacrifice to you
of their free wills, singing *hosanna*,
so let men make an offering of theirs.

12

'Give us this day the daily manna
without which he who labors to advance
goes backward through this bitter wilderness.

15

'And, as we forgive those who have wronged us,
do you forgive us in your loving kindness—
measure us not as we deserve.

18

'Do not put to proof our powers,
which yield so lightly to the ancient foe,
but deliver us from him who tempts them.

21

'This last petition, our dear Lord, is made
not for ourselves—for us there is no need—
but for the ones whom we have left behind.'

24

Thus praying for safe haven for themselves and us,
those shades trudged on beneath their burden,
the kind that sometimes weighs us down in dreams,

27

disparmente angosciate tutte a tondo
e lasse su per la prima cornice,
30   purgando la caligine del mondo.

Se di là sempre ben per noi si dice,
di qua che dire e far per lor si puote
33   da quei c'hanno al voler buona radice?

Ben si de' loro atar lavar le note
che portar quinci, sì che, mondi e lievi,
36   possano uscire a le stellate ruote.

"Deh, se giustizia e pietà vi disgrievi
tosto, sì che possiate muover l'ala,
39   che secondo il disio vostro vi lievi,

mostrate da qual mano inver' la scala
si va più corto; e se c'è più d'un varco,
42   quel ne 'nsegnate che men erto cala;

ché questi che vien meco, per lo 'ncarco
de la carne d'Adamo onde si veste,
45   al montar sù, contra sua voglia, è parco."

Le lor parole, che rendero a queste
che dette avea colui cu' io seguiva,
48   non fur da cui venisser manifeste;

ma fu detto: "A man destra per la riva
con noi venite, e troverete il passo
51   possibile a salir persona viva.

E s'io non fossi impedito dal sasso
che la cervice mia superba doma,
54   onde portar convienmi il viso basso,

cotesti, ch'ancor vive e non si noma,
guardere' io, per veder s'i' 'l conosco,
57   e per farlo pietoso a questa soma.

as they, unequally distressed,
plodded their weary round on that first ledge,
30   purging away the darkness of the world.

If good is always said of us up there,
what can be said and done for them on earth
33   by those whose wills have roots in good?

Surely we should help them wash away the stains
they carried with them, so that pure and light
36   they may approach the star-hung spheres.

'Please, so may justice and mercy soon
unburden you and give you wings
39   to lift you up as high as you desire,

'show us the shortest crossing to the stairs,
and if there is more than one passage,
42   let us know where the drop is not so steep,

'for he that comes here with me,
burdened with the weight of Adam's flesh,
45   though eager to ascend, is slow at climbing.'

It was not clear from whom now came
words spoken in response to those
48   voiced by the man I followed,

but we heard: 'Come with us on the bank,
keeping to the right, to find the stairs
51   a living man can climb.

'If I were not encumbered by the stone
that serves to bend my stiff-necked pride
54   so that I cannot lift my face,

'I would look at this man, still alive
but nameless, to see if he is known to me
57   and make him take pity for my heavy load.

Io fui latino e nato d'un gran Tosco:
Guiglielmo Aldobrandesco fu mio padre;
60   non so se 'l nome suo già mai fu vosco.

L'antico sangue e l'opere leggiadre
d'i miei maggior mi fer sì arrogante,
63   che, non pensando a la comune madre,

ogn' uomo ebbi in despetto tanto avante,
ch'io ne mori', come i Sanesi sanno,
66   e sallo in Campagnatico ogne fante.

Io sono Omberto; e non pur a me danno
superbia fa, ché tutti miei consorti
69   ha ella tratti seco nel malanno.

E qui convien ch'io questo peso porti
per lei, tanto che a Dio si sodisfaccia,
72   poi ch'io nol fe' tra ' vivi, qui tra ' morti."

Ascoltando chinai in giù la faccia;
e un di lor, non questi che parlava,
75   si torse sotto il peso che li 'mpaccia,

e videmi e conobbemi e chiamava,
tenendo li occhi con fatica fisi
78   a me che tutto chin con loro andava.

"Oh!" diss'io lui, "non se' tu Oderisi,
l'onor d'Agobbio e l'onor di quell' arte
81   ch'alluminar chiamata è in Parisi?"

"Frate," diss' elli, "più ridon le carte
che pennelleggia Franco Bolognese;
84   l'onore è tutto or suo, e mio in parte.

Ben non sare' io stato sì cortese
mentre ch'io vissi, per lo gran disio
87   de l'eccellenza ove mio core intese.

'I was Italian, a noble Tuscan's son.
Guglielmo Aldobrandesco was my father—
60   I do not know if you have ever heard his name.

'The ancient blood and gallant deeds
done by my forebears raised such arrogance in me
63   that, forgetful of our common mother,

'I held all men in such great scorn
it caused my death—how, all in Siena know,
66   and every child in Campagnatico.

'I am Omberto. Pride has undone
not only me but all my kinsmen,
69   whom it has dragged into calamity.

'And for this pride, here must I bear this burden—
here among the dead, since I did not
72   among the living—until God is satisfied.'

Listening, I bent down my face, and one of them,
not he who spoke, twisted himself
75   beneath the load that weighed him down,

saw me and knew me and called out,
with difficulty keeping his eyes fixed on me,
78   as I, all hunched, trudged on beside them.

'Oh,' I said to him, 'are you not Oderisi,
the honor of Gubbio and of that art
81   which they in Paris call illumination?'

'Brother,' he said, 'the pages smile brighter
from the brush of Franco of Bologna.
84   The honor is all his now—and only mine in part.

'Indeed, I hardly would have been so courteous
while I still lived—an overwhelming need
87   to excel at any cost held fast my heart.

Di tal superbia qui si paga il fio;
e ancor non sarei qui, se non fosse
90   che, possendo peccar, mi volsi a Dio.

Oh vana gloria de l'umane posse!
com' poco verde in su la cima dura,
93   se non è giunta da l'etati grosse!

Credette Cimabue ne la pittura
tener lo campo, e ora ha Giotto il grido,
96   sì che la fama di colui è scura.

Così ha tolto l'uno a l'altro Guido
la gloria de la lingua; e forse è nato
99   chi l'uno e l'altro caccerà del nido.

Non è il mondan romore altro ch'un fiato
di vento, ch'or vien quinci e or vien quindi,
102   e muta nome perché muta lato.

Che voce avrai tu più, se vecchia scindi
da te la carne, che se fossi morto
105   anzi che tu lasciassi il 'pappo' e 'l 'dindi,'

pria che passin mill' anni? ch'è più corto
spazio a l'etterno, ch'un muover di ciglia
108   al cerchio che più tardi in cielo è torto.

Colui che del cammin sì poco piglia
dinanzi a me, Toscana sonò tutta;
111   e ora a pena in Siena sen pispiglia,

ond' era sire quando fu distrutta
la rabbia fiorentina, che superba
114   fu a quel tempo sì com' ora è putta.

La vostra nominanza è color d'erba,
che viene e va, e quei la discolora
117   per cui ella esce de la terra acerba."

'For such pride here we pay our debt.
I would not be here yet, except, while living,
90   and with the means to sin, I turned to God.

'O vanity of human powers,
how briefly lasts the crowning green of glory,
93   unless an age of darkness follows!

'In painting Cimabue thought he held the field
but now it's Giotto has the cry,
96   so that the other's fame is dimmed.

'Thus has one Guido taken from the other
the glory of our tongue, and he, perhaps, is born
99   who will drive one and then the other from the nest.

'Worldly fame is nothing but a gust of wind,
first blowing from one quarter, then another,
102   changing name with every new direction.

'Will greater fame be yours if you put off
your flesh when it is old than had you died
105   with *pappo* and *dindi* still upon your lips

'after a thousand years have passed? To eternity,
that time is shorter than the blinking of an eye
108   is to one circling of the slowest-moving sphere.

'All Tuscany resounded with the name—
now barely whispered even in Siena—
111   of him who moves so slow in front of me.

'He was the ruler there when they put down
the insolence of Florence,
114   a city then as proud as now she is a whore.

'Your renown is but the hue of grass, which comes
and goes, and the same sun that makes it spring
117   green from the ground will wither it.'

E io a lui: "Tuo vero dir m'incora
bona umiltà, e gran tumor m'appiani;
120   ma chi è quei di cui tu parlavi ora?"

"Quelli è," rispuose, "Provenzan Salvani;
ed è qui perché fu presuntüoso
123   a recar Siena tutta a le sue mani.

Ito è così e va, sanza riposo,
poi che morì; cotal moneta rende
126   a sodisfar chi è di là troppo oso."

E io: "Se quello spirito ch'attende,
pria che si penta, l'orlo de la vita,
129   qua giù dimora e qua sù non ascende,

se buona orazïon lui non aita,
prima che passi tempo quanto visse,
132   come fu la venuta lui largita?"

"Quando vivea più glorïoso," disse,
"liberamente nel Campo di Siena,
135   ogne vergogna diposta, s'affisse;

e lì, per trar l'amico suo di pena,
ch'e' sostenea ne la prigion di Carlo,
138   si condusse a tremar per ogne vena.

Più non dirò, e scuro so che parlo;
ma poco tempo andrà, che ' tuoi vicini
faranno sì che tu potrai chiosarlo.
142   Quest' opera li tolse quei confini."

And I to him: 'Your true words pierce my heart
with fit humility and ease a heavy swelling there.
120   But who is he of whom you spoke just now?'

'That,' he replied, 'is Provenzan Salvani,
and he is here because in his presumption
123   he sought to have Siena in his grasp.

'Thus burdened he has gone, and goes on without rest,
ever since he died. Such coin he pays,
126   who is too bold on earth, in recompense.'

And I said: 'If the spirit that puts off
repentance to the very edge of life
129   must stay below, before he comes up here,

'as long as he has lived—
unless he's helped by holy prayers—
132   how was his coming here allowed?'

'While he was living in his greatest glory,' he said,
'he willingly sat in the marketplace
135   of Siena, putting aside all shame,

'and there, to redeem his friend
from the torment he endured in Charles's prison,
138   he made himself tremble in every vein.

'I say no more, and know my speech obscure.
It won't be long before they act, your townsmen,
in such a way that you'll know how to gloss it.
142   It was that deed which brought him past those confines.'

1–24. As Singleton points out in his gloss to this passage, this is the only complete prayer recited in the entire poem. And, as Bosco/Reggio point out, the three forms of expiation that are found on every terrace are prayer, suffering, and meditation (on examples of the vice's opposing virtue and on the vice itself). In this way the penitents attempt to accomplish their "satisfaction" (see note to vv. 70–72) before God for each particular offense into which they have fallen. (It will eventually become clear [e.g., *Purg.* XXIII.90] that not every sinner must purge every sin, although it is certainly possible that any given sinner would have sinned not only intrinsically but in fact in all seven categories.)

Dante's version of the Lord's Prayer (Matthew 6:9–13; Luke 11:2–4) is, as examination of the Vulgate reveals, an amalgam of the two passages, adapted so as to be particularly fit for the souls of those who are in essence saved but needful of purgation (as is made clear by vv. 22–24). It is clear that Dante is siding with those who have been involved in the vernacularization of the Bible, an activity fraught with danger in the late Middle Ages and early Renaissance. (The questions of the text of the Bible known to Dante and of his access to that text remain vital—and unanswered [see Angelo Penna, "Bibbia," *ED* 1 (1970), pp. 626–27].)

4–6. Giacalone (1968) was perhaps the first Italian commentator to point out that Dante's phrasing here ("laudato sia" [let your name be praised] . . . "da ogne creatura" [by every creature]) is not a translation from the Gospels but rather reflects the refrain of Francis of Assisi's *Laudes creaturarum.* For possible earlier citations by Dante of Francis's poem see note to *Inferno* I.26–27.

There is debate as to whether or not the Father is addressed as the Trinity or as Himself. Those who take the former position have apparent support in the word *vapore* (breath), which is often the sign of the Holy Spirit. Here, as some commentators, beginning with Lombardi (1791), believe, Dante is thinking along the lines found in Wisdom 7:25, where wisdom is described as "vapor . . . virtutis Dei" (aura of the power of God). Since the prayer is, indeed, the Paternoster, it is only natural that it be addressed to the Father, with whatever (inevitable) trinitarian overtones.

11. According to St. Augustine (*De doctrina* II.xi), *osanna* and other Hebrew words of exclamation are never translated in the Latin Bible.

(See Isidore of Seville on the untranslatability of interjections in the note to *Purg.* XXX.21.) This is the Hebrew word, used for a cry of joyful praise, most present in the *Commedia*, found a total of seven times.

13–15. We have heard (*Purg.* VII.58–60) that even souls in grace are capable of going downward and, while knowing that they will not as a result be "unsaved," nonetheless simply do not wish to move in a retrograde direction. Here the penitents of pride express a similar desire.

19–24. This last part of the adaptation is sung on behalf of earthly sinners, since those already on the mountain can no longer be overcome by Satan, as their earthly brethren all too easily are.

25. It is fair to say that no one is certain what the root of the word *ramogna* (translated here as "safe haven") is or what it really means (see Porena [Pore.1947.1] and the entry for the word in *ED* IV [1973], pp. 848–49). The early commentators mainly believed it meant a good journey, but on what authority one does not know. A plurality of modern commentators believe it means "good wishes," but it seems strange to argue that the souls are praying for good wishes, for that would come close to being a mere tautology. Our translation offers a variant of the earlier understanding.

27. The brief comparison equates the rocks carried by the penitents and our dreams of the incubus. The Codice cassinese (1350?) cites Virgil (*Aen.* XII.908–12) as an example of dreaming of suffocation under an enormous weight.

28. The souls are "unequally distressed" because they carry variously weighted burdens.

31–36. This is, as it were, an indirect address to the reader, hoping that all of us "whose wills have roots in good" will pray for these penitents as they indeed pray for us.

37–45. Virgil's single speech in this canto begins with a reprise of Trajan's climactic declaration of his willingness to help the widow, "*giustizia* vuole e *pietà* mi ritene" (justice wills it and compassion bids me stay), at *Purgatorio* X.93. It is as though Virgil, remembering the "visible speech" from the representation of Trajan's humility, had assumed these words worked wonders on Christian hearts, and now puts *giustizia* and *pietà* (found in the same verse only in these two scenes) to work on his and Dante's behalf.

46–48. The source of the words heard by the travelers is necessarily obscure, since the faces of all these souls are obscured by the rocks that they bear upon their backs. At the same time it is morally appropriate that a penitent in pride must speak without identification, since pride is an insistence on the self, while this anonymity erases it. However, to argue that all are speaking together, as some do, is to miss the patent fact that only one soul is speaking (v. 52).

53. Stiff-necked pride was a frequent complaint about the Hebrew people in the Old Testament, particularly in Exodus (32:9, 33:3, 33:5, 34:9) and Deuteronomy (9:6, 9:13, 10:16, 31:27).

58–69. The speaker is Omberto Aldobrandesco, second son of Guglielmo Aldobrandesco (dead by 1256), count of Santafiora (see *Purg.* VI.111) and head of this powerful Ghibelline family. Omberto was murdered by Sienese Guelphs outside his fortified castle in 1259. He lays the fault for his death and the need for his current penance on his family's pride in its name, which made the Aldobrandeschi consider themselves better than others merely by fact of being Aldobrandeschi.

The reference to every *fante* in Campagnatico, Omberto's feudal holding with its castle, where he died in battle, is variously interpreted. The word in Dante's Italian may mean (1) infantryman, (2) any man at all, especially one of the lower class, (3) a very young child. Most commentators support the third view (and we have followed them), but all three are potentially valid.

70–72. Omberto is the first penitent in purgatory proper who speaks to the travelers (we have only heard penitential prayer until now) and his last words clearly identify the purpose of purgation in the process of absolution (for Dante, necessarily preceded by confession, contrition, and satisfaction—see note to *Purg.* IX.94–102). What seems to be the case is that all those who have penance to perform on any particular terrace need precisely to give satisfaction (see the verb *sodisfaccia* in verse 71 [as Tozer (1901) duly noted]) before God for their transgressions on earth. This implies that others, those who do *not* need to do penance on a particular terrace, either were without that sin or else had given satisfaction while they were still alive. This is the view taken by Nicola Fosca in his unpublished commentary, portions of which he has kindly made available to this writer.

Porena (1946), in his commentary to *Purgatorio* IX.112–114, also says that the penitence observed on the mountain is the form that *satisfactio operis* takes in these eventually redeemed souls.

73. Dante's bending down his face is a natural action taken in order to see his interlocutor's face, yet it, too, reveals a moral significance (see note to vv. 46–48), as the protagonist's own words will later confirm (*Purg.* XIII.136–138), when he will admit that, once he returns to the mountain in the next life, his head will be lowered under the same load he now is able to observe upon the backs of others.

74–78. The next penitent is apparently less heavily weighted (and thus less burdened by pride) than Omberto, since he is able to move a little under his rock and thus twist his neck enough to get a glance at the features of Dante, now conveniently lowered by his desire to make out Omberto. As a result, Dante recognizes him.

Where the first penitent was still deeply involved in the feelings of the family pride that had afflicted him so greatly on earth, the next will represent all those who are prideful in their accomplishments (in this case, artistic ones); and we will see that he is more advanced in his penitence than Omberto.

79–81. Oderisi d'Agobbio is praised by Dante as the great Italian master of the art of illuminating manuscripts, an art particularly associated with the French and with Paris. "Oderisi, who was the son of Guido d'Agobbio (Gubbio [a hill town in the Apennines, not far from Perugia]), was in residence at Bologna in 1268, 1269, and 1271; he is said to have gone to Rome in 1295, and to have died there in 1299. Vasari, who possessed some of his drawings, states that he was a friend of Giotto, and that he and Franco of Bologna were employed by Boniface VIII to illuminate MSS. in the Papal library at Rome. It appears from the text that Dante and Oderisi were acquainted, or at least knew each other by sight" **(T)**.

82–87. Oderisi deflects Dante's compliment, thus showing that his pride is at least greatly abated (if not utterly vanquished—see verse 84). What is at stake here is artistic merit, not the cry of the vulgar, a subject that will be before us within ten lines. What Oderisi can now admit is that, as good as he was at illuminating, in his own opinion Franco of Bologna was superior to him in his craftmanship—a truth that he knew but never would have permitted himself to admit during his emulous life on earth. It is interesting that Benvenuto da Imola says that, from the examples he has seen, Franco really *was* a better illuminator. By being willing to *share* the honor with Franco (this is exactly the burden of *Purg.* XIV.86–87, the words of Guido del Duca: "O race of men, why do you set your hearts / on things that of necessity cannot be shared?"), Oderisi shows himself now different from the man bent on his own excelling to the cost of all others.

Little is known of Franco, who apparently lived until about 1310. His work was the subject of an exhibition in Bologna in 2000.

88–90.   If Oderisi was known by Dante to have died in 1299, he certainly had made his way up the mountain quickly, apparently spending very little time in ante-purgatory. Compare the case of Forese (*Purg.* XXIII.76–90), the most detailed information we are given in this *cántica* about passing over certain terraces on the way toward the summit. And see the note to vv. 127–132.

Oderisi, nonetheless, must have reformed his ways very early, since the late-repentant spend equal time in ante-purgatory as they did while they were unrepentant on earth. Or perhaps Dante thought or knew that he had died earlier than we think.

91–93.   Oderisi's outburst subtly changes the topic of his discourse from human talent and ability to its reception among other human beings. Where before he had spoken of Franco's honor, he now bewails the emptiness of these same talents as recipients of the praise conferred by fame.

The phrase "com' poco verde in su la cima dura" (literally: how briefly lasts the green upon the top) has never been adequately explained. What object does the poet have in mind for the noun *cima*? Hollander (Holl.1994.1) has argued—citing its next use in the poem, *Purgatorio* XV.13, where it refers to Dante's forehead, the space above his eyebrows—that it refers to exactly that part of our physiognomy here and that the green is the green of the laurel. The language of the passage, which addresses the question of the brief limits of fame unless a "dark age" allows fame to continue for longer than it usually does (by not producing other "winners" quickly), seems clearly to reflect exactly such a concern—one that was not far, as we know from *Paradiso* XXV.1–9, from this poet's mind.

94–96.   Giovanni Cimabue (ca. 1240–1308) was a highly praised Florentine painter. His pupil, Giotto di Bondone (ca. 1267–1337), is given credit by art historians for changing the nature of Italian painting, moving from the "flat" tradition to "roundness," representations that seemed more realistic than anything seen before him. (In this vein see Boccaccio's treatment of him in *Decameron* VI.v.5.)

The notion that Dante is in this passage putting Giotto's art ahead of Cimabue's is baseless, though widespread. Dante *may* himself have ad- mired Giotto's painting more than Cimabue's, but that is not the point here. All that Oderisi is saying is that, in accord with what he has just said about fame being brief unless a dark age assures the last "laureate" his continuing green reward, Cimabue had the public's cry but now Giotto has it. There is no evaluation of the relative worth of the work of these two masters stated or implied.

97–98.   Moving his attention from painting to poetry, Oderisi says the same thing about Guido Guinizzelli (ca. 1225–1276) and Guido Cavalcanti (ca. 1250–1300): one held the highest place in the public's es- teem until the other displaced him. A problem here arises from Dante's use of the noun *gloria*, which can mean "reputation, fame" in the vulgar sense, or "just renown for great deeds," or "heavenly glory" (as in the experience of paradise). The word occurs some twenty-two times in the poem and has this first meaning less frequently than it has either of the other two, e.g., in *Inferno* III.42, where it is explained that the neu- tral angels are not in hell lest they be placed lower than the rebel angels, who might then have "boasting rights" over them. But the word has just been used in its most negative form seven lines earlier: the "vana gloria" that prompts our desire for fame. In this reading, the more recent Guido (Cavalcanti) has taken the public's laurel from Guinizzelli.

99.   While there is still some dispute about the reference, most now agree that Dante is clearly pointing to himself as the one who will in turn replace Cavalcanti in the "nest" of the public's admiration.

Stierle (Stie.2001.1), p. 163, thinks Oderisi predicts Dante's "tri- umph" here and believes that Dante meant us to take from his words the understanding that he believes pride a necessary and positive aspect of his own *ingegno* and not entirely to be dispraised. To medieval readers this would surely have seemed an inappropriate reading. On the other hand, recent modern readers, with whose work Stierle seems not to be acquainted, have tried to make essentially the same case: Barolini

(Baro.1992.1), pp. 133–37, and Marks (Mark.1992.1). For a response see Hollander (Holl.1994.1).

100–108.   Oderisi's moralizing is pungent and clear: earthly fame is not worth even a moment's affection. It is difficult to justify any positive role for earthly fame in light of these forceful words.

105.   These are babytalk words for bread *(pappo = pane)* and money *(dindi = denaro)*.

109–114.   Without as yet naming him, Oderisi tells the cautionary tale of Provenzan Salvani, "Ghibelline of Siena, where he was at the head of affairs at the time of the great victory over the Florentine Guelfs at Montaperti, Sept. 4, 1260; it was he who at the Council of Empoli after the battle advocated the destruction of the city of Florence, which was averted by the firmness and patriotism of Farinata (*Inf.* X.91); he was Podestà of Montepulciano in 1261; he met his death in an engagement with the Florentines at Colle, in Valdelsa, June 11, 1269, when he was taken prisoner and beheaded" **(T)**. It is curious that, of these two great Ghibelline leaders, Dante has condemned Farinata (who saved the city) to hell and saved Provenzan (who wanted to destroy it).

115–117.   For the biblical passages that underlie this image of the fleetingness of grass as being similar to human ambitions in this life see the Old Testament (Isaiah 28:4, 38:27, 40:6; Psalms 89:6 [90:5–6]), as noted by Tommaseo (1837).

118–119.   This is Dante's first and not last (see *Purg.* XIII.133–138) admission of his pridefulness.

126.   Here again is the word *sodisfar*. See note to vv. 70–72. Provenzan is completing his *satisfactio operis* before Dante's eyes, so intent on it that he is not allowed a speaking part, but has Oderisi as his mouthpiece.

127–132.   If Provenzan died in 1269 and was (as is obvious) more than thirty-one years old when he died, the protagonist wants to know how, if the sentence in ante-purgatory is a year for each year spent in failure to repent and if Provenzan apparently, from Oderisi's narrative, died in his presumption, he can have come up here so quickly. We should remember that Dante was *not* surprised (see note to vv. 88–90) at Oderisi's

quick advent (perhaps less than a year separating his death and his ar-
rival), somehow understanding that Oderisi had purged his pride quite
early in his life and chosen to live for God. Why Dante might have
thought so is not known.

133–138.   Oderisi's third speech, devoted to Provenzan, shows Dante
that, in his lifetime, Provenzan had come to grips with his pride.

135.   The phrasing here has its roots in—is indeed a translation of—a
passage in Bonaventure's life of St. Francis, the *Legenda maior* (II.7),
"omni deposita verecundia," where Francis, setting aside all shame, be-
comes a mendicant. The attribution, which seems undeniable, has made
its way into the commentary tradition over the last one hundred years,
often unassigned. Bosco/Reggio and Marks (Mark.1992.1), p. 177 (n.
55), give credit to Passerini in 1898.

139–142.   And just as Provenzan humbled himself in public by his own
volition, Dante will have humility thrust upon him by his own people
when the Black Guelphs will exile him from Florence in 1302. For the
predictions of Dante's personal fortunes in the poem see note to *Inferno*
VI.64–66.

PURGATORIO XII
(Pride)

Di pari, come buoi che vanno a giogo,
m'andava io con quell' anima carca,
3   fin che 'l sofferse il dolce pedagogo.

Ma quando disse: "Lascia lui e varca;
ché qui è buono con l'ali e coi remi,
6   quantunque può, ciascun pinger sua barca";

dritto sì come andar vuolsi rife'mi
con la persona, avvegna che i pensieri
9   mi rimanessero e chinati e scemi.

Io m'era mosso, e seguia volontieri
del mio maestro i passi, e amendue
12   già mostravam com' eravam leggeri;

ed el mi disse: "Volgi li occhi in giùe:
buon ti sarà, per tranquillar la via,
15   veder lo letto de le piante tue."

Come, perché di lor memoria sia,
sovra i sepolti le tombe terragne
18   portan segnato quel ch'elli eran pria,

onde lì molte volte si ripiagne
per la puntura de la rimembranza,
21   che solo a' pii dà de le calcagne;

sì vid' io lì, ma di miglior sembianza
secondo l'artificio, figurato
24   quanto per via di fuor del monte avanza.

Vedea colui che fu nobil creato
più ch'altra creatura, giù dal cielo
27   folgoreggiando scender, da l'un lato.

As oxen go beneath their yoke
that overladen soul and I went side by side
as long as my dear escort granted.

But when he said: 'Leave him and hurry on,
for it is fitting here, with all your strength,
to speed your ship with wings and oars,'

I straightened up, erect,
as one should walk, but still my thoughts
remained bowed down and shrunken.

I set out, following gladly
in my master's steps, and our easy stride
made clear how light we felt.

And he to me: 'Cast down your eyes.
It will be good for you and calm you on your way
to look down at the bed beneath your feet.'

As gravestones set above the buried dead
bear witness to what once they were,
their carven images recalling them to mind,

making us grieve with frequent tears
when recollection pricks and spurs
the faithful heart with memories,

so were these figures sculpted there
along that road carved from the mountainside,
but in their artistry more true in their resemblance.

My eyes beheld the one, created nobler
than any other creature, fall like lightning
from the sky, over to one side.

Vedëa Brïareo fitto dal telo
celestïal giacer, da l'altra parte,
30   grave a la terra per lo mortal gelo.

Vedea Timbreo, vedea Pallade e Marte,
armati ancora, intorno al padre loro,
33   mirar le membra d'i Giganti sparte.

Vedea Nembròt a piè del gran lavoro
quasi smarrito, e riguardar le genti
36   che 'n Sennaàr con lui superbi fuoro.

O Nïobè, con che occhi dolenti
vedea io te segnata in su la strada,
39   tra sette e sette tuoi figliuoli spenti!

O Saùl, come in su la propria spada
quivi parevi morto in Gelboè,
42   che poi non sentì pioggia né rugiada!

O folle Aragne, sì vedea io te
già mezza ragna, trista in su li stracci
45   de l'opera che mal per te si fé.

O Roboàm, già non par che minacci
quivi 'l tuo segno; ma pien di spavento
48   nel porta un carro, sanza ch'altri il cacci.

Mostrava ancor lo duro pavimento
come Almeon a sua madre fé caro
51   parer lo sventurato addornamento.

Mostrava come i figli si gittaro
sovra Sennacherìb dentro dal tempio,
54   e come, morto lui, quivi il lasciaro.

Mostrava la ruina e 'l crudo scempio
che fé Tamiri, quando disse a Ciro:
57   "Sangue sitisti, e io di sangue t'empio."

My eyes beheld Briarèus, on the other,
transfixed by the celestial bolt,
30   now heavy on the earth in chill of death.

My eyes beheld Thymbraeus, Pallas, and Mars,
still armed, together with their father,
33   astounded by the giants' scattered limbs.

My eyes beheld Nimrod at the base of his great work,
as though bewildered, and the people,
36   who in Shinar shared his pride, all looking on.

Ah, Niobe, I saw you sculpted in the roadway,
your eyes welling up with grief,
39   amidst your dead, seven sons and seven daughters.

Ah, Saul, you too appeared there, dead
on your own sword in the mountains of Gilboa,
42   which never after knew the rain or dew.

Ah, mad Arachne, I saw you all but turned
to spider, wretched on the strands
45   you spun, which did you so much harm.

Ah, Rehoboam, now your image does not seem
to menace but to cower. A chariot bears it off—
48   and there is no one giving chase.

Now was shown, on that hard floor,
how Alcmaeon made that necklace, ill-omened,
51   seem not worth the price his mother paid.

Now was shown how his sons fell upon
Sennacherib inside the temple,
54   and how, slain, they left him there.

Now was shown the destruction and cruel slaughter
wrought by Tomyris when she said to Cyrus:
57   'You thirsted for blood. Now drink your fill.'

Mostrava come in rotta si fuggiro
li Assiri, poi che fu morto Oloferne,
60   e anche le reliquie del martiro.

Vedeva Troia in cenere e in caverne;
o Ilïón, come te basso e vile
63   mostrava il segno che lì si discerne!

Qual di pennel fu maestro o di stile
che ritraesse l'ombre e ' tratti ch'ivi
66   mirar farieno uno ingegno sottile?

Morti li morti e i vivi parean vivi:
non vide mei di me chi vide il vero,
69   quant' io calcai, fin che chinato givi.

Or superbite, e via col viso altero,
figliuoli d'Eva, e non chinate il volto
72   sì che veggiate il vostro mal sentero!

Più era già per noi del monte vòlto
e del cammin del sole assai più speso
75   che non stimava l'animo non sciolto,

quando colui che sempre innanzi atteso
andava, cominciò: "Drizza la testa;
78   non è più tempo di gir sì sospeso.

Vedi colà un angel che s'appresta
per venir verso noi; vedi che torna
81   dal servigio del dì l'ancella sesta.

Di reverenza il viso e li atti addorna,
sì che i diletti lo 'nvïarci in suso;
84   pensa che questo dì mai non raggiorna!"

Io era ben del suo ammonir uso
pur di non perder tempo, sì che 'n quella
87   materia non potea parlarmi chiuso.

Now was shown the Assyrians routed and in flight
after the slaying of Holofernes
60   and the leavings of that slaughter.

My eyes beheld Troy in ashes and in ruins.
Ah, Ilion, how reduced and shamed you were
63   now was shown within the carving.

What master of the brush and stylus
could have designed these forms and outlines
66   that would astound the most discerning talent?

Dead seemed the dead, living seemed the living.
He who beheld the real events on which I walked,
69   head bent, saw them no better than did I.

Wax proud then, go your way with head held high,
you sons of Eve, and no, do not bend down your face
72   and so reflect upon your evil path!

We had done more of the mountain's circle
and the sun had sped along its track
75   more than my mind, being bound, had reckoned,

when he, who always fixed his gaze before him
as he went, spoke out: 'Raise your head!
78   This is not the time for walking so absorbed.

'See the angel over there, preparing
to approach. See the sixth handmaid who returns
81   from her time of service to the day.

'Show reverence in your face and bearing
so that he may be pleased to send us upward.
84   Consider that this day will never dawn again.'

I was accustomed to his admonitions
not to waste my time, so that on this matter
87   his words were not obscure.

A noi venìa la creatura bella,
biancovestito e ne la faccia quale
90 par tremolando mattutina stella.

Le braccia aperse, e indi aperse l'ale;
disse: "Venite: qui son presso i gradi,
93 e agevolemente omai si sale.

A questo invito vegnon molto radi:
o gente umana, per volar sù nata,
96 perché a poco vento così cadi?"

Menocci ove la roccia era tagliata;
quivi mi batté l'ali per la fronte;
99 poi mi promise sicura l'andata.

Come a man destra, per salire al monte
dove siede la chiesa che soggioga
102 la ben guidata sopra Rubaconte,

si rompe del montar l'ardita foga
per le scalee che si fero ad etade
105 ch'era sicuro il quaderno e la doga;

così s'allenta la ripa che cade
quivi ben ratta da l'altro girone;
108 ma quinci e quindi l'alta pietra rade.

Noi volgendo ivi le nostre persone,
"Beati pauperes spiritu!" voci
111 cantaron sì, che nol diria sermone.

Ahi quanto son diverse quelle foci
da l'infernali! ché quivi per canti
114 s'entra, e là giù per lamenti feroci.

Già montavam su per li scaglion santi,
ed esser mi parea troppo più lieve
117 che per lo pian non mi parea davanti.

The fair creature, garbed in white,
came toward us. In his face there was what seemed
90   the shimmering of the morning star.

Opening his arms, he spread his wings
and said: 'Come, the steps are here at hand.
93   From here on up the climb is easy.

'They are very few who answer to this bidding.
O race of man, born to fly on high,
96   how can a puff of wind cause you to fall?'

He brought us where the rock was cleft,
there tapped my forehead with his wings,
99   then promised me that going on I would be safe.

Just as, to climb the hillside where the church is set
which, over Rubaconte, dominates
102   the justly governed city, there on the right

the sheer slope of the steep ascent is cut
by stairs that were constructed in a time
105   when registers and measures could be trusted,

even so the bank that sharply falls away
from the higher circle is made gentler, except
108   that here and there the towering rock scrapes close.

While we were moving off in that direction,
'Beati pauperes spiritu' a voice was singing
111   in tones that speech could not express.

Ah, how different these entrances from those of hell,
for here one's coming in is met with songs
114   but there with savage lamentation!

Now we were climbing on the hallowed stairs
and I felt so much lighter than before,
117   when the ground I trod was level,

Ond' io: "Maestro, dì, qual cosa greve
levata s'è da me, che nulla quasi
120   per me fatica, andando, si riceve?"

Rispuose: "Quando i P che son rimasi
ancor nel volto tuo presso che stinti,
123   saranno, com' è l'un, del tutto rasi,

fier li tuoi piè dal buon voler sì vinti,
che non pur non fatica sentiranno,
126   ma fia diletto loro esser sù pinti."

Allor fec' io come color che vanno
con cosa in capo non da lor saputa,
129   se non che ' cenni altrui sospecciar fanno;

per che la mano ad accertar s'aiuta,
e cerca e truova e quello officio adempie
132   che non si può fornir per la veduta;

e con le dita de la destra scempie
trovai pur sei le lettere che 'ncise
quel da le chiavi a me sovra le tempie:
136   a che guardando, il mio duca sorrise.

that I said: 'Master, tell me,
what weight has been lifted from me
120   that going on is hardly any effort?'

He answered: 'When the P's that still remain
upon your brow, though very faint, shall be,
123   as one already is, erased,

'your legs shall be so mastered by good will,
not only will they feel no effort going up,
126   but they will take delight in being urged to.'

Then I did as those who go along,
with something on their head, unknown to them,
129   unless its effect on others makes them wonder,

so that they reach up with their hand for answers.
Touching and searching they accomplish
132   the task that sight cannot achieve,

and, spreading the fingers of my right hand,
I found that, of the seven letters he of the keys
had traced upon my forehead, only six remained.
136   Observing this, my leader smiled.

1–3.　Dante and Oderisi are continuing their movement forward in humility, purging their pride in their differing ways until such time as Virgil will insist on Dante's pursuing other instruction. Strictly speaking, in ancient Greece a "pedagogue" was a slave whose task it was to guide children to school and supervise their conduct generally (but not to teach them); in ancient Rome the slave was frequently a Greek and had similar responsibilities, but also introduced the children to the beginning study of Greek. Dante's word, *pedagogo*, here in one of its first appearances in the Italian vernacular, according to the *Grande Dizionario* (Batt.1961.1), has a brief but important role (occurring twice) in a single biblical passage, Paul's Epistle to the Galatians 3:24–25 (Longfellow [1867] seems to have been the first to note the possible connection). In that passage Paul imagines us as having once been, under the Old Testament, guided by the *paedagogus* (the Law) but as now being taught by Christ, and thus as no longer requiring such guidance. This Dantean hapax (a word occurring only once in a given universe of words) may reflect that biblical near-hapax.

　　For the yoke that binds these two "oxen" see the commentary of Fallani (1965) and Scott's *lectura* (Scot.2001.1), p. 174: "For my yoke is easy and my burden light" (Matthew 11:29–30)—the words of Christ preaching to potential followers.

4–6.　Virgil's metaphor is probably developed, as Bosco/Reggio (1978) insist, on *Aeneid* III.520: "velorum pandimus alas" (we spread the wings of our sails), a passage cited by many commentators at *Inferno* XXVI.125, "de' remi facemmo ali" (we turned our oars to wings).

　　Petrocchi, in his reading of the line, overturns the previously favored opinion that Dante's text read *vele* (sails), but has the disadvantage of forcing the poet into a very mixed metaphor, "wings and oars." We would have followed the older reading, "sails and oars."

7–9.　The protagonist walks erect, as Ovid describes humans doing so as to be distinguished from brutes (*Metam.* I.84–86). Benvenuto cites Ovid's words and mentions the additional authority of Cicero, Sallust, and Juvenal on this matter in his comment to this passage.

　　The word *scemi*, which we have translated as "shrunken," has caused some discomfort. What exactly does it mean? Aurigemma (Auri.1970.1), pp. 109–10, claims that Oderisi's dour prophecy of Dante's future ills

(XI.140–141) leaves the protagonist feeling *monco* (incomplete) until such time as that disaster will finally confront him. He is following the nearly unanimous view found in the earliest commentators. However, since the time of Landino (1481) the more usual interpretation relates Dante's interior moral posture rather to his responses to Pride, whether in pity for the souls he now sees or in recognition of his own (former) pridefulness—the most usual version of that position today, expressed in the form that currently rules by Torraca (1905), who notes the "heavy swelling" (*Purg.* XI.119) of pride that Dante is getting under control. As a result, his thoughts are *scemi* in that they are lacking in pride. In other words, even if he has finally straightened up and begun walking as a confident human being, his thoughts remain bowed under the burden of the recognition of his pridefulness.

12.   Dante's new incredible lightness of being matches Virgil's usual state as soul unencumbered by body; getting his pride under control, the protagonist experiences the greatest and quickest spiritual growth we will observe in him during his ascent of the mountain.

13–15.   Now that Dante has experienced and embraced the positive exemplars of Humility, Virgil wants to confirm his new state by making him experience the negative exemplars of Pride in order to seal his "conversion" to humility. For exemplarity in the Middle Ages and in Dante see Delcorno (Delc.1989.1), esp. Chapter VI, "Dante e Peraldo," pp. 195–227. And for his discussion of the exemplars in this canto as deriving in part from William Peraldus's *Summa vitiorum*, see pp. 210–14; Delcorno shows that Dante's list of six biblical exemplars of Pride is related to Peraldus's first seven in his list of twelve biblical exemplars. Dante shares five of his six with Peraldus, substituting (for Adam) Nimrod (a choice, one might add, that underlines the poet's understandable concern with language—see note to *Inf.* XXXI.67). Then, in typical Dantean fashion, he adds six pagan exemplars to his shortened and revised version of Peraldus's list. For perhaps the first modern recognition of the importance of Peraldus's listing and description of the vices for Dante, see Wenzel (Wenz.1965.1), pointing out that Pietro di Dante's commentary to *Purgatorio* XVII (1340) relies strictly and extensively upon Peraldus's phrasing (wherever he found his version of Peraldus's text) for his description of the seven mortal sins.

16–24.   The figured pavement upon which the travelers walk is compared in simile to the gravestones set into church floors bearing the indications of the dead person's profession, family, or other identifying trait, as well as his or her likeness.

22–24. As was the case with God's art found in the intaglios upon the mountainside, here too divine art knows no human equal (cf. *Purg.* X.32–33).

25–63. Reading down the left-hand margin of the verses, we find a series of repeated letters beginning a series of tercets. They spell out a word. Lia Baldelli, "acrostico" (*ED* I [1970], p. 44), points out that perception of Dante's deployment of this technique escaped the attention of the early commentators; it was only in 1898 that Antonio Medin noticed the presence of the acrostic in these lines, the word VOM [or UOM, *uomo*, or "man"], while the presence of a similar acrostic, found at *Paradiso* XIX.115–141, yielding LVE [or LUE, "plague"], was only noted by Francesco Flamini in 1903. Most now accept the fact, despite a perhaps understandable modern distaste for such contrivance, that these two acrostics were deliberately constructed by the author (see, for more on Dante's acrostic proclivities, Scott [Scot.2001.1], p. 176 and n.). For a discussion of negative critical reactions to the acrostic on aesthetic grounds, as well as of its function in its context here, see Aurigemma (Auri.1970.1), pp. 113–19.

25–27. Naturally, the first exemplar of the sin of pride is Satan, its avatar (see note to *Inf.* XXXI.28–33 for his association with those other emblems of Pride, the giants who stormed Olympus). He is intrinsically opposed to the first exemplar of humility, the Virgin Mary, as is evident. When Dante drew near to the end of his poem (*Par.* XXXIII.2), he underlined this with a verse in description of Mary, "umile e alta più che creatura" (humble and exalted more than any creature), reflecting his description of (the unnamed) Lucifer here, who was more noble when he was created than any other creature. Trucchi (1936) observes Dante's borrowing from the Bible, his "folgoreggiando scender" (fall like lightning from the sky) echoing the similar phrase in Luke 10:18: "Satanam, sicut fulgur de coelo cadentem" ([I beheld] Satan as lightning fall from heaven).

28–30. We finally catch a glimpse of Briareus, so important an absence in the amusing business that occupies Dante and Virgil in *Inferno* XXXI.97–105 (and see the corresponding note), when Virgil denies Dante the sight of this giant, whom he has described, in his *Aeneid*, as having fifty heads and one hundred arms. Dante makes him, from what we can see, an "ordinary" giant, a pagan version of Lucifer for his presumption in challenging Jove. Briareus is mentioned in the three major martial epics that Dante knew and used, *Aeneid* X.565, *Thebaid* II.596, *Pharsalia* IV.596.

31–33.   Uniquely among the twelve sets of exemplars, the nonexemplary figures are the ones named (Apollo by his epithet Thymbraeus, Minerva by her second name [Pallas], and Mars), those who witnessed the defeat of the unnamed, exemplary giants (including Briareus), undone by the thunderbolts of Jove, their father. These exemplars are, in a wonderfully appropriate "punishment," present only as *disiecta membra*, the scattered remains of the outsized human creatures they once were.

34–36.   For Nimrod see the note to *Inferno* XXXI.70–81. He is accompanied by those who helped build the Tower of Babel on the plains of Shinar. See Genesis 10:8–10; 11:1–4.

37–39.   Niobe was the wife of Amphion, king of Thebes, and mother of seven sons and seven daughters. When she boasted that she was a better mother than Latona, who had but two offspring (even though these were Apollo and Diana), in the Ovidian world it is clear what will happen next: the two arrow-shooting siblings wipe out the children of Niobe who, turned to stone, nonetheless bewails their loss with eternal tears that flow perpetually as mountain streams (*Metam.* VI.148–312).

40–42.   Niobe's biblical counterpart is King Saul. Relieved of his kingship by Samuel for failing to keep God's commands, Saul fought against the Philistines at Gilboa. Mortally wounded and fearful of being captured by the enemy, he fell upon his sword (I Samuel 31:1–4). David's subsequent curse on the surrounding mountains, the witnesses of this scene (II Samuel 1:21), asks that neither rain nor dew reach this place in Samaria.

This exemplar of a prideful suicide throws into sharp relief the far different suicide of Cato the Younger, with reference to which *Purgatorio* opens.

43–45.   Arachne's presumption took the form of a challenge to Minerva in weaving. She (in this like Ovid himself? [*Metam.* VI.5–145]) produced a brilliant representation of the love affairs of the gods. Minerva, sensing herself unable to better this work of art, destroyed it, and Arachne determined to do away with herself. Minerva saved her life and turned the rope by which she was hanging herself into filament for this weaver turned spider.

46–48.   Rehoboam, a son of Solomon, was chosen to become king of Israel. His pride was manifest in the way he scornfully refused to lessen the tribute demanded of his people, at which ten of the twelve tribes of Israel rebelled. When his representative, Aduram, was slain by the rebellious Israelites, Rehoboam ran away with unseemly haste, even though he was not being pursued (see I Kings 12:1–18).

49–51.   In Statius's *Thebaid* (IV.187–213), Alcmaeon, son of Amphiaraus, the seer (who is, in a certain sense, a stand-in for Statius himself [see note to *Inf.* XX.31–39]), is left with the task of avenging his father's death. This came about after his wife, the mother of Alcmaeon, Eriphyle, betrayed his whereabouts to Polynices for the price of a necklace, with the result that Amphiaraus (see *Inf.* XX.31–36), who had foreseen the dreadful end of the civil war in Thebes and had hidden himself in order to escape his own death in it, ended up fighting and dying in the war. He pledged his son to avenge him, which indeed he did do by slaying his own mother. That the necklace, made by no less an artisan than Vulcan, had belonged to the goddess Harmonia marked Eriphyle's pride in thinking herself worthy of wearing it. As was the case for Lucifer, the first exemplary figure in this listing, Eriphyle is not named.

52–54.   "Sennacherib, King of Assyria, B.C. 705–681; after a reign of twenty-four years, in the course of which he twice 'went up against' Hezekiah, king of Judah, and besieged Jerusalem, he was assassinated, while at worship, by his two sons (I[V] Reg. 19:37)" **(T)**. The Vulgate (IV Regum 19:28) associates his anti-Jewish behavior with *superbia* (pride).

55–57.   In Paulus Orosius's *Historiae adversus paganos* (II.vii.6), Dante could have read of Cyrus the Elder, founder and king of the Persian Empire ca. 560 B.C. He died in battle against the Massagetae, in Scythia (529 B.C.), when he was ambushed by the queen of his enemies, Tomyris, who not only killed him, but had his decapitated head put into a vessel containing human blood and, according to Orosius, uttered words that closely resemble what Dante reports she said.

58–60.   The Assyrian general, Holofernes, was the victim of decapitation by the hand of Judith (see Iudith 13:1–13). "The leavings of that slaughter" are evidently the members of his decapitated body.

This last pair of classical/biblical parallels is painfully exact, with vainglorious military males opposed by skillful women who cut their heads off.

61–63. The final example serves as a sort of summary for the entire acrostic. For the medieval tradition that Troy was indeed prideful see Scott (Scot.2001.1), pp. 182–83. Dante's phrasing probably reflects *Aeneid* III.2–3, "superbum / Ilium," with the phrase to be read in a moralizing ("proud Troy") rather than an architectural ("lofty-towered Troy") manner. See note to *Inferno* I.75, discussing an earlier incidence of the same phenomenon.

64–69. Once again, concluding an ekphrastic presentation of some length (cf. *Purg.* X.94–99), the poet intervenes, now to praise the extraordinary mimetic quality of God's art, so precise in its representation that even an eyewitness of the original events saw them no more clearly than did Dante as he walked the terrace of Pride.

70–72. In *Purgatorio* X.121–129, in the wake of ekphrastic poetry, Dante addresses the prideful sinners among his readers; he now does a similar turn here, using the rhetorical trope of *antiphrasis*, i.e., expressing the opposite of what one says by means of a sarcastic tone of voice.

77. The phrase "Drizza la testa" was last heard, addressed to Dante by Virgil as it is here, in *Inferno* XX.31, when the guide wanted his pupil to take cognizance of Amphiaraus (see note to vv. 49–51).

78. Tommaseo (1837) was perhaps the first to cite the similar incitement, offered by the Sibyl to Aeneas, found at *Aeneid* VI.37 ("non hoc ista sibi tempus spectacula poscit" [this hour demands other sights than these]).

79–80. Singleton suggests that, since this is the only angel actually to move toward Dante, his gesture is meant to suggest humility. However, as Simone Marchesi has pointed out, responding to a draft of these notes, the Angel of Mercy even more certainly seems to approach Dante (*Purg.* XV.27–30).

81. The last signal of the time of day occurred at *Purgatorio* X.13–16, where we learned that it was sometime after 9 AM. Here, in metaphoric language that presents the hours of the morning as the handmaids of the

day, serving her highness one at a time and in succession, we learn that it is noon. Thus the time spent on this terrace is surprisingly short, a maximum of less than three hours and as little as two.

90.   That the angel comes as the morning star, Venus, otherwise known as Lucifer, sets him off in a polar relationship to Satan, the first exemplar of prideful behavior in the figured pavement.

94–96.   Who speaks these words, the Angel of Humility or the poet? The debate has been active for years. Aurigemma (Auri.1970.1), pp. 123–25, after reviewing various arguments, opts for the notion that it is Dante who speaks. The closeness of the sentiment expressed here to that found at X.121–129 (with its "angelic butterfly" at verse 125), which issues from the poet's mouth, would seem to support the idea that it is the poet who speaks here as well. Nonetheless, we have followed Petrocchi's punctuation, and it does not allow for the attribution of these lines to the poet. The main arguments for doing so are that for Dante to allude so clearly to his own special election is, even for him, a bit bold; further, the lack of indication of a second and new speaker and the abruptness that would result from such a shift both argue for Petrocchi's view; still further, only the angel could state as a fact that so few are chosen to rise this far. On the other hand, no other angel makes comments about humankind that are as harsh as these, since the seven angels of purgatory are celebrating the continuing ascent of this special visitor to the mountain. Perhaps the fullest, fairest, and most helpful gloss to the passage is Poletto's (1894) and he, after careful debate, comes down on the side of the attribution of these words to the angel.

98.   The angel's wing-clap has had a result that will only become known at vv. 121–126: one of the P's on Dante's brow has been removed. This is perhaps another reason to believe that Dante has not spoken the last words, which might seem more self-congratulatory than humble.

100–108.   The simile is redolent of the Florence left behind by the exiled poet. The site of the church of San Miniato al Monte, which is set above and across the Arno from the city, afforded then (as it does now) one of the surpassingly beautiful views of Florence. The Rubaconte Bridge (now known as the Ponte alle Grazie) was named for its builder in 1237, the podestà Rubaconte da Mandello da Milano, according to Giovanni Villani's *Cronica* (VI.26).

The phrase "the justly governed city" is obviously ironic. For Dante's only use of this word see the last (and incomplete) sentence in *De vulgari eloquentia* (II.xiv.2) where poets are seen as either writing in praise or in blame of their subjects, i.e. (among other categories), either *gratulanter* or *yronice*.

The poet remembers the "good old days" when "registers and measures could be trusted," i.e., before the civil authorities became corrupt, when they kept proper records and gave proper amounts of salt (without withholding some for their own profit). Documentation of these illicit activities may be found in ample detail in Singleton's commentary to vv. 104–105.

110.   The ritual occurring here, involving an adaptation of a Beatitude spoken by Jesus, will recur on the next six terraces as well. The Sermon on the Mount seems to include eight beatitudes (Matthew 5:3–10). For discussion of Dante's use of them, see Federigo Tollemache, "beatitudini evangeliche," *ED* I (1970). Tollemache points out that St. Thomas, whose discussion of the Beatitudes (*ST* I.ii.69.3 ad 5) seems to govern Dante's treatment of them, says there are seven, with "Blessed are the meek" (Matthew 5:5 [5:4 in the Vulgate]) omitted, while those that "hunger and thirst after righteousness" are remembered on separate terraces. Thomas considers "those who are persecuted for righteousness' sake" to refer to *all* of the first seven categories. Here the reference is to the first: "Blessed are the poor in spirit, for theirs is the kingdom of heaven." For a discussion of the program of the Beatitudes in *Purgatorio* see Chiavacci Leonardi (Chia.1984.2).

111.   The plural here is taken by the commentators as a singular, a stylistic liberty allowed for speech (perhaps because the words uttered are more than one). On all the terraces the fitting angel speaks his blessing unaccompanied. (For the program of angelic utterance in this *cantica* see note to *Purg.* XV.38–39.)

112–114.   This tercet is an evident return to the thematic opposition of *musica diaboli* and heavenly music (so present in purgatory once the gate is reached and entered in Canto IX). See note to *Inferno* XXI.136–139.

121–123.   It is a Christian commonplace, followed by Dante, that Pride is the root sin, notwithstanding the Pauline claim that "radix malorum est cupiditas" (avarice is the root of all evil—I Timothy 6:10). Clearly

Dante holds to the former notion, as we are here told that the removal of the P of Pride erases most of the indented marks made by each of the other six P's. For the question as to whether or not Dante uniquely has a P upon his forehead see notes to *Purgatorio* IX.112 and XXI.22–24.

127–136.   Anyone who has played the version of poker known as "hat-band" will immediately understand this concluding simile, the light-hearted tone of which culminates only logically in Virgil's smile. Having subdued his pride (and he knows how afflicted he is by this sin—see *Purg.* XIII.133–138), the protagonist feels lighter, better, as though his trip through purgation were half finished already. And thus this canto ends with a lighter and happier feeling than any that precedes it, offering a sort of foretaste of Edenic innocence.

PURGATORIO XIII
(Envy)

Noi eravamo al sommo de la scala,
dove secondamente si risega
3   lo monte che salendo altrui dismala.

Ivi così una cornice lega
dintorno il poggio, come la primaia;
6   se non che l'arco suo più tosto piega.

Ombra non lì è né segno che si paia:
parsi la ripa e parsi la via schietta
9   col livido color de la petraia.

"Se qui per dimandar gente s'aspetta,"
ragionava il poeta, "io temo forse
12   che troppo avrà d'indugio nostra eletta."

Poi fisamente al sole li occhi porse;
fece del destro lato a muover centro,
15   e la sinistra parte di sé torse.

"O dolce lume a cui fidanza i' entro
per lo novo cammin, tu ne conduci,"
18   dicea, "come condur si vuol quinc' entro.

Tu scaldi il mondo, tu sovr' esso luci;
s'altra ragione in contrario non ponta,
21   esser dien sempre li tuoi raggi duci."

Quanto di qua per un migliaio si conta,
tanto di là eravam noi già iti,
24   con poco tempo, per la voglia pronta;

e verso noi volar furon sentiti,
non però visti, spiriti parlando
27   a la mensa d'amor cortesi inviti.

We were at the summit of the stair
where the mountain that unsins us as we climb
is for the second time cut back.

There another terrace carves the hill,
just like the first, except its arc
is shorter and it makes a tighter curve.

There are no shades nor any carvings—
only the bank and the bare road
with the livid color of the stone.

'If we linger here to ask directions,'
the poet reasoned, 'before we choose our way,
I fear we may be long delayed.'

Then he fixed his eyes upon the sun
and made a pivot of the right side of his body
on which he swung his left side forward.

'O sweet light, in whose help I trust
as I set out upon this unknown road,' he said,
'give us whatever guidance here is needed.

'You shed your light upon the world and warm it.
Unless we find good reason to do other,
your rays must always be our guide.'

We had already gone as far
as here on earth would count a mile—
but quickly, for our will was eager—

when, flying toward us, spirits could be heard
but not be seen, sounding courteous invitation
to the table readied for the feast of love.

3

6

9

12

15

18

21

24

27

La prima voce che passò volando
"Vinum non habent" altamente disse,
30   e dietro a noi l'andò reïterando.

E prima che del tutto non si udisse
per allungarsi, un'altra "I' sono Oreste"
33   passò gridando, e anco non s'affisse.

"Oh!" diss' io, "padre, che voci son queste?"
E com' io domandai, ecco la terza
36   dicendo: "Amate da cui male aveste."

E 'l buon maestro: "Questo cinghio sferza
la colpa de la invidia, e però sono
39   tratte d'amor le corde de la ferza.

Lo fren vuol esser del contrario suono;
credo che l'udirai, per mio avviso,
42   prima che giunghi al passo del perdono.

Ma ficca li occhi per l'aere ben fiso,
e vedrai gente innanzi a noi sedersi,
45   e ciascun è lungo la grotta assiso."

Allora più che prima li occhi apersi;
guarda'mi innanzi, e vidi ombre con manti
48   al color de la pietra non diversi.

E poi che fummo un poco più avanti,
udia gridar: "Maria òra per noi":
51   gridar "Michele" e "Pietro" e "Tutti santi."

Non credo che per terra vada ancoi
omo sì duro, che non fosse punto
54   per compassion di quel ch'i' vidi poi;

ché, quando fui sì presso di lor giunto,
che li atti loro a me venivan certi,
57   per li occhi fui di grave dolor munto.

The first voice, flying by,
called loudly: *'Vinum non habent'*
30   and, having passed, called out the same again.

Before it was quite out of hearing
in the distance, there came another, crying:
33   'I am Orestes,' and it also did not stay.

'O father,' I said, 'what voices are these?'
And as I asked there came a third voice, saying:
36   'Love him who has done you wrong.'

And the good master said: 'This circle
scourges the sin of envy, and thus
39   the cords of the scourge are drawn from love.

'To rein in envy requires opposing notes.
Such other voices you will hear, I think,
42   before you reach the pass of pardon.

'Now fix your sight more steady through the air
and you will make out figures sitting there
45   in front of us along the rock.'

Then, opening my eyes still wider,
I looked ahead and now could see
48   shades wearing cloaks the color of the stone.

We had gone a little farther on,
when I heard voices crying: 'Mary, pray for us,'
51   then 'Michael,' 'Peter,' and 'All saints.'

I do not think there walks on earth today
a man so hard that he would not have been
54   transfixed by pity at what I saw next,

for when I had drawn close enough
so that their state grew clear to me
57   my eyes were overwhelmed by grief.

Di vil ciliccio mi parean coperti,
e l'un sofferia l'altro con la spalla,
60   e tutti da la ripa eran sofferti.

Così li ciechi a cui la roba falla,
stanno a' perdoni a chieder lor bisogna,
63   e l'uno il capo sopra l'altro avvalla,

perché 'n altrui pietà tosto si pogna,
non pur per lo sonar de le parole,
66   ma per la vista che non meno agogna.

E come a li orbi non approda il sole,
così a l'ombre quivi, ond' io parlo ora,
69   luce del ciel di sé largir non vole;

ché a tutti un fil di ferro i cigli fóra
e cusce sì, come a sparvier selvaggio
72   si fa però che queto non dimora.

A me pareva, andando, fare oltraggio,
veggendo altrui, non essendo veduto:
75   per ch'io mi volsi al mio consiglio saggio.

Ben sapev' ei che volea dir lo muto;
e però non attese mia dimanda,
78   ma disse: "Parla, e sie breve e arguto."

Virgilio mi venìa da quella banda
de la cornice onde cader si puote,
81   perché da nulla sponda s'inghirlanda;

da l'altra parte m'eran le divote
ombre, che per l'orribile costura
84   premevan sì, che bagnavan le gote.

Volsimi a loro e: "O gente sicura,"
incominciai, "di veder l'alto lume
87   che 'l disio vostro solo ha in sua cura,

They appeared covered with coarse haircloth.
Each propped up another with his shoulder,
60   and all of them were propped against the rock.

Just so the blind who lack for daily bread
at pardons take their place to beg for what they need,
63   one letting his head fall on another's shoulder

so that he may more quickly prompt to pity,
not only with the words that he is saying
66   but with his looks, which plead no less.

And as the sun is of no profit to the blind,
so Heaven's light denies its bounty
69   to the shades in the place of which I speak,

for iron wire pierces all their eyelids,
stitching them together, as is done
72   to the untrained falcon because it won't be calmed.

As I went on, it seemed to me that seeing others,
without my being seen, offended them,
75   so that I turned to my wise counsel.

Well he knew what my silence meant to say
and did not wait to hear me ask, but said:
78   'Speak, yet be brief and to the point.'

Virgil, moving along beside me on the terrace,
was at the edge, where one might fall
81   because no parapet encircled it.

At my other side were the shades in prayer
who, through those dreadful seams,
84   were wringing tears that bathed their cheeks.

I turned to them and I began:
'O people assured of seeing light on high—
87   sole object stirring your desire—

se tosto grazia resolva le schiume
di vostra coscïenza sì che chiaro
90   per essa scenda de la mente il fiume,

ditemi, ché mi fia grazioso e caro,
s'anima è qui tra voi che sia latina;
93   e forse lei sarà buon s'i' l'apparo."

"O frate mio, ciascuna è cittadina
d'una vera città; ma tu vuo' dire
96   che vivesse in Italia peregrina."

Questo mi parve per risposta udire
più innanzi alquanto che là dov' io stava,
99   ond' io mi feci ancor più là sentire.

Tra l'altre vidi un'ombra ch'aspettava
in vista; e se volesse alcun dir "Come?"
102   lo mento a guisa d'orbo in sù levava.

"Spirto," diss' io, "che per salir ti dome,
se tu se' quelli che mi rispondesti,
105   fammiti conto o per luogo o per nome."

"Io fui sanese," rispuose, "e con questi
altri rimendo qui la vita ria,
108   lagrimando a colui che sé ne presti.

Savia non fui, avvegna che Sapìa
fossi chiamata, e fui de li altrui danni
111   più lieta assai che di ventura mia.

E perché tu non creda ch'io t'inganni,
odi s'i' fui, com' io ti dico, folle,
114   già discendendo l'arco d'i miei anni.

Eran li cittadin miei presso a Colle
in campo giunti co' loro avversari,
117   e io pregava Iddio di quel ch'e' volle.

'so grace may soon dissolve the scum
that fouls your conscience, and the stream
90   of memory flow through it pure,

'tell me, for I shall hold it courteous and dear,
if any soul among you is Italian.
93   Perhaps for me to know might profit such a one.'

'O my brother, all of us are citizens
of the one true city. What you mean to say is,
96   "who, while still a pilgrim, lived in Italy." '

This it seemed to me I heard in answer
farther along from where I stood,
99   and I made myself heard by moving closer.

Among the rest I saw a shade that looked expectant,
and if any should ask 'how?', it was raising
102   its chin the way a blind man does.

'Spirit,' I said, 'who abase yourself to climb,
if you were the one who answered me,
105   make yourself known by your city or your name.'

'I was of Siena,' replied the shade,
'and with these others here I mend my sinful life,
108   weeping to Him that He may lend Himself to us.

'Sapìa was my name, though I was far from wise,
for I rejoiced much more at harm done others
111   than at my own good fortune.

'And, so that you know I do not lie,
hear me out when I tell how mad I was,
114   with the arc of my years already in decline.

'My townsmen were near Colle,
engaged in battle with their enemies, and I prayed
117   that God let happen what in fact He willed.

120
Rotti fuor quivi e vòlti ne li amari
passi di fuga; e veggendo la caccia,
letizia presi a tutte altre dispari,

123
tanto ch'io volsi in sù l'ardita faccia,
gridando a Dio: 'Omai più non ti temo!'
come fé 'l merlo per poca bonaccia.

126
Pace volli con Dio in su lo stremo
de la mia vita; e ancor non sarebbe
lo mio dover per penitenza scemo,

129
se ciò non fosse, ch'a memoria m'ebbe
Pier Pettinaio in sue sante orazioni,
a cui di me per caritate increbbe.

132
Ma tu chi se', che nostre condizioni
vai dimandando, e porti li occhi sciolti,
sì com' io credo, e spirando ragioni?"

135
"Li occhi," diss' io, "mi fieno ancor qui tolti,
ma picciol tempo, ché poca è l'offesa
fatta per esser con invidia vòlti.

138
Troppa è più la paura ond' è sospesa
l'anima mia del tormento di sotto,
che già lo 'ncarco di là giù mi pesa."

141
Ed ella a me: "Chi t'ha dunque condotto
qua sù tra noi, se giù ritornar credi?"
E io: "Costui ch'è meco e non fa motto.

144
E vivo sono; e però mi richiedi,
spirito eletto, se tu vuo' ch'i' mova
di là per te ancor li mortai piedi."

147
"Oh, questa è a udir sì cosa nuova,"
rispuose, "che gran segno è che Dio t'ami;
però col priego tuo talor mi giova.

'When they were routed and turned back
in bitter steps of flight, I watched the chase,
120   my heart filled with such boundless joy

'that recklessly I turned my face to God,
crying: "Now I do not fear you any more,"
123   as the blackbird said after a glint of sunshine.

'I sought my peace with God
at the very last, and penitence
126   would not have yet reduced the debt

'had it not been for Peter the comb-seller,
who in his charity was grieved for me
129   and remembered me in his devout petitions.

'But who are you who walk about inquiring
of our condition, with your eyes not sewn,
132   as I suspect, and speak with breath?'

'My eyes,' I said, 'will yet be taken
from me here, but for a short while only,
135   for small is their offense in looks of envy.

'Greater is the fear, which fills my soul with dread,   ⎫
of torments lower down, those heavy loads—   ⎬ *pride*
138   I can almost feel their weight upon me now.'   ⎭

And she: 'Who has led you here among us,
if you think that you'll return below?' And I:
141   'He that is with me here and does not speak.

'I am alive, and therefore ask of me,
you chosen spirit, if you would have me move
144   my mortal feet for your sake back on earth.'

'Oh,' she replied, 'how wonderful it is to hear
of this great token of God's love for you.
147   Since it is so, aid me sometime with a prayer.

E cheggioti, per quel che tu più brami,
se mai calchi la terra di Toscana,
150 che a' miei propinqui tu ben mi rinfami.

Tu li vedrai tra quella gente vana
che spera in Talamone, e perderagli
più di speranza ch'a trovar la Diana;
154 ma più vi perderanno li ammiragli."

'And I entreat you by what you most desire,
if ever you tread the soil of Tuscany,
150   to restore my name among my kinfolk.

'You will find them part of that vain people
who pinned their hopes on Talamone and will lose
more hope thereby than in their search for the Diana—
154   but it is their admirals who shall lose still more.'

1–3.   The whole mountain, by virtue of the way in which it is seven times sliced away, resembles a huge circular stairway cut in stone. The travelers' arrival at the second of these terraces coincides with a canto beginning. This is the only time that such a coincidence occurs in this *cantica*. It is as though Dante wanted to acknowledge the reader's expectation that the arrival at each terrace might coincide with the beginning of a canto, thus forcing that reader to speculate upon the aesthetic reasons for the poet's not being overly "neat."

The verb *dismalare* is almost certainly a Dantean coinage; we have tried to reflect its unusual character in our translation with an English coinage: "unsins."

7.   The verse "Ombra non lì è né segno che si paia" (There are no shades nor any carvings) has drawn some more complicated discussions than our translation would call for. As does Musumarra (Musu.1967.1), p. 442, we believe that the word *ombra* here means a "shade," and is to be distinguished from *segno*, which here means "designs," i.e., such as the intaglios that were found on the preceding terrace. In other words, the travelers see neither penitents nor carvings as they first examine this new space. Some others are of the opinion that both words refer to the shapes and designs on the wall of the terrace of Pride and not even the first of them to the penitents themselves. However, once the latter become manifest to Dante and Virgil, they are referred to as *ombre*; in fact this word is used as often in this canto as in any other of the poem. It appears here and then at vv. 47, 68, 83, 100; it is clear that all four of these later uses also refer to "shades."

8–9.   The barren "landscape" of the terrace of Envy contrasts with the highly wrought carvings that greet the travelers on that of Pride (*Purg.* X.28–33), as does the livid color of this place contrast with the gleaming whiteness found below. For all its vanity, Pride is a sin that has its vitality and brightness. Here all is the livid, or gray-blue (as in a bruise) color of stone. The sin of envy, as Dante has already acknowledged (*Inf.* I.111; and see accompanying note), was the cause of death's entering the world because of the envy Satan felt for God. This sin, much less present in the modern imagination than it was in the minds of medieval thinkers, was seen as particularly pernicious and widespread. Most of us tend to think of envy as a form of jealousy, motivated by the desire to possess a good that someone else holds. In Dante's time it represented, instead, the negative wish that this person lose his or her goods, his or her apparent advantage. It is thus not a form of avarice, but the expression of resentment against the perceived happiness of others. For a compelling modern example, see Prince Myshkin's words to the agonized and resentful Ippolit in Dostoevsky's *The Idiot*: "Forgive us our happiness." In the next canto, Guido del Duca will give it a similar expression (see *Purg.* XIV.82–84).

Fernando Salsano presents the salient features of this sin in Dante; see his entry "invidia," *ED* III (1971); for a discussion of the sin in English see Cassell, "Envy," in the *Dante Encyclopedia* (Lans.2000.1).

10–12.   Virgil again (as he did in *Purg.* III.52–56), seeing no one present who may give directions, assumes that the situation is worse than it actually is.

13–21.   Virgil's prayer to the sun (his only prayer in the poem) has drawn conflicting interpretations over the centuries. Is it, as most early commentators believed, a prayer to the Christian God (possibly for his grace), expressed in a metaphor (and surely the sun is a frequent metaphor for God in medieval culture and in this poem)? Is it directed to disembodied "speculative reason" as some other early commentators, followed by many moderns, believed? Or is it a prayer to the sun itself, unallegorized, for the light that will reveal the path that must be chosen? This is the position of a number of moderns, Porena (1946) perhaps the most convincing of these, citing *Purgatorio* I.107–108, where Cato tells the travelers that the sun's light will show them their way. Bosco/Reggio (1978), in a similar anti-allegorical vein, point out that the next lines (vv. 19–21) speak only of the physical properties of the sun's light, as was true in the verses spoken by Cato in the first canto of this *cantica*. It seems prudent to allow a literal meaning that makes sense to stand alone, without further interpretive scaffolding. Indeed, if, as Virgil says, the sun's light should serve as guide unless a better source be found, he cannot be speaking of any final authority, whether God or rational certainty, neither of which may be superseded by secondary causes.

25–27.   Virgil's prayer to the sun is not answered; instead, supernatural voices are heard flying overhead, bearing the identities of the positive exemplary figures of the virtue opposed to envy, charity. This "banquet" of affection recalls the controlling metaphor of Dante's unfinished treatise, *Convivio*.

28–30.   Mary's voice is—we are not surprised to discover, given our experience of the positive exemplars in *Purgatorio* X.40–45—the first whose words are represented by a flying voice. Dante never makes clear how these sounds are made or by whom, but we may be sure that their sources are not present on this terrace, as we know that Mary is in paradise (while one of the negative exemplars, Cain, in *Purg.* XIV.133, is probably in hell, since one of its final zones is named for him [see *Inf.* V.107 and XXXII.58]).

The biblical scene invoked is that of the marriage feast at Cana of Galilee when Mary tells Jesus there is no wine left for the guests ("Vinum non habent") and Jesus shortly thereafter turns water to wine (John 2:1–7).

31–33.   Orestes is known to Dante in two basic contexts, first as the avenger of his family honor as the killer of his adulterous mother, Clytemnestra; second, as the friend of Pylades. When, after these two friends have also killed the adulterous Aegisthus and Orestes is sought for capital punishment, Pylades cries out "Ego sum Orestes" (I am Orestes), while Orestes, not to be outdone, shouts "Immo enimvero ego sum, inquam, Orestes" (But I truly am, I say to you, Orestes—Cicero, *De finibus* V.xxii.63 [and see *De amicitia* VII.24]). According to the commentators, this second voice is either that of Orestes, of Pylades, or somehow relates to both of these. We believe the speaker is Pylades.

34–36.   The third exemplar is Jesus Christ, calling on his disciples to return love for hatred (see Matthew 5:44, where the words are a bit more expansive than they are here: "Diligite inimicos vestros, benefacite his qui oderunt vos [love your enemies, do good to those who hate you]). The first two voices are identical with their sources, the first, Latin word for Latin word; the second, a perfect Italian translation of the Latin original. The last, however, is a looser Italian version of the Vulgate's Latin.

37–42.   This is the first precise verbal formulation of the mode of purgatorial instruction by examples: first one is spurred to imitate the good, then dissuaded from following the bad, the goad and the bit that we have already encountered and will continue to come to know on each terrace. Having understood how these functions were experienced on the first terrace, Virgil now correctly surmises that, if the travelers have now heard the goad, they will hear the bit before they confront the angel with his blessing and leave this terrace.

43–48.   The coloration of the garments worn by the penitents in Envy is so close to that of the rocks themselves that it has taken Virgil a long while to make them out; he only now calls them to Dante's attention— and the protagonist has had no sense of their presence at all.

Envy, which is so clearly aware of difference, is cloaked in a uniform that makes distinction of difference nearly impossible. As Dante interacts with these penitents, it is clear that he has a hard time making out the features of any one of them.

49–51.   The voices we hear now emanate from the penitents on the terrace, not from unknown sources overhead. As Bosco/Reggio suggest, they cry out only the invocations of litanies because the rest of their texts would not be appropriate here, since these passages regard earthly ills and temptations, no longer of potential harm to these souls.

52–57.   Perhaps no passage indicates more clearly the disparity of attitude required of an onlooker in hell and purgatory. There the growth in the protagonist was measured, in part, by his ability not to respond pityingly; here compassion is an essential part of his ceremonial purgation. See the introduction to *Inferno*, pp. xxix–xxxiii.

58.   Haircloth, according to Francesco da Buti's gloss to this verse, both pricks the skin where it is knotted and leaves it chilled, because it has openings as does a net.

59–60.   The envious in life were not involved in supporting others; the contrary was their care. Now their communal attitude shows their penance—as does their mendicant pose, apparent in the following simile.

61–66.   Those who looked upon their fellows in unseeing ways (the sin *invidia* was etymologized in the Middle Ages as *in + videre*, i.e., more usually as "not seeing," but sometimes also understood as "seeing against," another being [see Bigongiari (Bigo.1964.1), pp. 90–91]) now hope for the opposite, to be looked upon with pity. Like Satan, the avatar of Envy, the envious soul is proud as well. And the proud cannot bear pity. These penitents show compassionate affection for one another as part of their purgation of Envy. The language of the simile reminds the reader of special occasions on which the Church offered indulgences to its flock on a given feast day or similar occasion; such "pardons" provided targets of opportunity to mendicants outside churches or other holy places. Dante's language also allows us to see the theatricality implicit in the act of begging; we are now, however, asked to believe in the wholehearted sincerity of these posthumous penitents.

67–72.   The aesthetic abnegation of this terrace is eased somewhat by these two back-to-back similes. Fastening our attention on the closed eyes of the envious, Dante compares them to the sewn-up eyes of sparrow hawks, captured in their maturity and temporarily blinded in this manner so that they remain docile in the presence of their handlers. The penitents' eyes are sewn, not with the thread used on hawks and falcons, but with iron wire.

73–78.   Dante, feeling sheepish about his position of privileged and unnoticed onlooker, is "read" by Virgil as he and Dante have been reading the feelings of the equally mute penitents. Virgil gives Dante permission to address them—and indeed withdraws from colloquy himself for the rest of this and nearly all the next canto (his next words will be heard only at *Purg.* XIV.143).

85–93.   The protagonist's labored and heavily rhetoricized *captatio* (including periphrastic references to the twin rivers of purgatory, Lethe and Eunoe) is perhaps meant to contrast with Sapia's far more immediate and direct response (vv. 94–96). He wants to find an Italian for his cast of characters and promises, in return, a prayer to speed the process of purgation. How ironically we are meant to take this speech is not clear, but Bosco/Reggio are derisive about Dante's "overblown rhetoric" here.

94–96.   The response by the shade who, we will soon discover, is Sapia, is a polite but incisive correction of the question she answers. (1) Dante had set the penitent souls apart from others, even from himself; Sapia joins them all in fellowship with a single word, *frate*. (2) Dante had spoken of earthly territories; Sapia makes all those beloved of God citizens of His city alone. (3) Dante had spoken of Italianness as a present condition; Sapia insists that geographical/political identities on earth were only fleeting and are now irrelevant.

102.   This physical gesture is familiar to anyone who has spoken with people who are blind, since they, guided by their ears, position their faces squarely in line with the source of the voice of their interlocutor.

105–108.   The protagonist's question receives its first answer, as nearly anonymous as it can be, with the exception of the identification of the speaker's homeland, and thus responding to only one part of the protagonist's request ("make yourself known by your city or your name"). Knowing only this much, our memories return to the last shade and, indeed, the last Sienese we encountered, Provenzan Salvani, his story recounted by Oderisi in *Purg.* XI.120–138. There we heard about his triumph in humility; here we will become aware, between the lines, of the horror of his death.

The word *rimendo* (verse 107), meaning "mending," "stitching back together," is Petrocchi's replacement for the former reading, *rimondo*, "cleansing," "purifying." There are those who continue to take issue with Petrocchi's emendation, e.g., Stephany (Step.1991.1), pp. 76–77.

109–111.   Punning on her name, she now identifies herself as Sapia if not *savia* (sapient) and speaks of her envious nature (see note to vv. 8–9).

For the history of the gradually more certain identification of Sapia, see Giorgio Varanini, "Sapia" (*ED* IV [1976], p. 26). Most now accept the work of nineteenth-century students of the problem, which demonstrated that she, born ca. 1210, was a noblewoman of Siena, an aunt of Provenzan Salvani (*Purg.* XI.121–142), and wife of one Ghinibaldo Saracini. After the battle of Colle Val d'Elsa in 1269 and before her death (sometime between 1275 and 1289) she gave much of her wealth to a hospital (S. Maria dei Pellegrini) that she and her husband (who had died before the great battle) had founded in 1265 in Siena.

112–123.   Sapia's narrative falls into two parts, this first containing the evidence of her former sinfulness, exemplified most savagely in her admission of her joy in witnessing the death of her own people, most probably Provenzan Salvani, her nephew.

As for Provenzan (a rough Sienese equivalent of the Florentine Farinata [*Inf.* X]), the man who led the Sienese Ghibellines in their triumph over the Guelphs of Florence at Montaperti in 1260 and the leading Ghibelline soldier of his city, he was captured in the battle of Colle Val d'Elsa, some ten miles northwest of Siena, and decapitated. According to Giovanni Villani (*Cronica* VII.31), his head, at the end of a pike, was then marched around the battlefield by his triumphant French and Florentine Guelph enemies. Since Sapia was also a Ghibelline it is difficult or impossible to know why she was so pleased by his death (most assume that Provenzan is among the "townsmen" whose death brought her so much pleasure). Since her sin was envy, it seems clear that Dante wants us to understand that she resented his and/or other townsmen's position and fame, that her involvement was personal, not political.

124–129.   Before her death, Sapia's change of heart brought her back to the love of God and her neighbor. As for Pier Pettinaio, whose second name is not a family name but an epithet denoting his profession, i.e., he sold combs to ladies (*pettine* means "comb"), it was his prayerful intervention after her death that reduced her time in ante-purgatory. Since she has been dead between twenty-five and eleven years, and since we would assume she would have spent at least a little time on the terrace of Pride, she has surely moved quickly up the mountain, sped by Pier's prayers. A "native of Campi in the Chianti district NE. of Siena, he was a hermit of the Franciscan Order, and dwelt in Siena, where he was renowned for his piety and miracles. Ubertino da Casale (*Par.* XII.124) in the prologue to his *Arbor Vitae Crucifixae Jesu* mentions that he had received spiritual instruction from him. Pier died on Dec. 5, 1289, and was buried at Siena, where he was long venerated as a saint, in a handsome tomb erected at the public expense" **(T)**.

130–132.   Sapia now, having satisfied Dante's question in both its points, asks after his identity. Having heard him breathe, she divines that he is present in the flesh (but has no sense of Virgil's presence as his guide, thus motivating the exchange that follows at vv. 139–142).

133–138.   Dante's admission of his culpability in Pride is a brilliant stroke, taking that stick out of his reader's hand and also, in some strange way, convincing us that this prideful poet has become, under the burden of this poem, humble—or something like that. It also serves to free him from the curse of every artist (as Oderisi knew): the emulous consideration of his or her competitors, from which he pronounces himself totally free.

143–144.   The protagonist fulfills the terms of the condition he had offered at verse 93: if an Italian will come forward, he will pray for that soul.

145–150.   Sapia's acceptance of Dante's offer of prayer, making him her second Pier Pettinaio, is accepted with a grace that is also morally telling: she may have envied Provenzan his prowess and his fame, but not Dante, who has won the greatest victory of anyone, coming to the afterworld in the flesh. She responds to his charity for her with charity.

151–154.   These four lines produce perhaps the most debated passage in this canto. Before approaching that controversy, it may be helpful to understand some of the rather recondite references in play here. In 1303, Siena purchased the seaport called Talamone, on the Mediterranean coast about fifteen miles away, in order to have better access to shipping routes; the problem was that the dredging necessary to keep the waters between Siena and the sea negotiable was an overwhelming problem. Consequently, the project had to be abandoned soon after the funds had been appropriated to support it. Similarly, another civic works project involved a search for an underground river (named Diana because the statue of the goddess had stood in the market square of the city); it too was a failure. The final *frecciata*, or gibe, of Sapia is to suggest that the biggest losers in the scheme to acquire a harbor on the sea will be the admirals. This word has been greatly debated: does Sapia refer to actual admirals? to investors in the scheme? to those who sold participation in the enterprise? It seems clear that Dante is making Sapia joke for him (Siena jokes being for Florentines what Harvard jokes are for Yalies). This writer's view is that the playfully nasty phrase is precisely similar to one still in use today: "the Swiss navy." The phrase requires that we recognize that the Swiss cannot have a navy because they do not have an ocean to put a navy on—exactly the same condition in which we find the Sienese. For a similar appreciation see Porena's lengthy discussion (1946) of these verses.

Sapia, as we have seen, is a moving figure, convincingly grappling with her former sin and seemingly in control of it. It seems clear that every verse she speaks in this canto is stamped by that change in her character, including her shrewd understanding of exactly what she was like within herself, precisely what she sounded like to others. It is a remarkable exercise in self-awareness. On the other hand, some argue that these final lines show that she is still very much in the grip of her old failing. Here, for example, is Singleton's analysis: "Thus, by this jibe at her fellow-townsmen, it is clear that Sapia can still be malicious and still has time to serve on this terrace, purging away such feelings." This is a fairly typical reaction. It should be observed that, if these last remarks present a soul still sinful, her sin is *not* Envy. She may be insensitive, perhaps, but not envious. First of all, she is speaking only of a few Sienese here, the would-be big shots in whose company Dante may find her decent relatives. Second, her remarks are not intended to affect these thieves and fools, but only (perhaps) to aid her relatives in fending off their wiles— if they are intended to have any practical worldly effect at all. Both Cassell (Cass.1984.1) and Stephany (Step.1991.1), pp. 83–86, support the view of Musumarra (Musu.1967.1), pp. 461–67, that Sapia's words are not to be read as evidence of her slipping back into the sin of Envy but rather as reflecting her desire to help her familiars and fellow citizens escape from the devastations that will befall them because of their misguided civic pride. In such readings, Sapia's last moment in the poem (and she has been given more of its space, forty-nine verses [106–154], than anyone encountered on the mountain except for Oderisi [XI.79–142—much of whose speech is devoted to the discussion of others] after the extended meeting with Sordello [*Purg.* VI–VIII]) is not offered up as a kind of recantation. Rather, this sharp-tongued, witty, and self-understanding woman ends her words with charity for all who have chosen the true way, along with acerbic wit for those who are governed by foolishness and pride. If that sounds like a description of the poet who created her, so be it.

PURGATORIO XIV
(Envy)

"Chi è costui che 'l nostro monte cerchia
prima che morte li abbia dato il volo,
3   e apre li occhi a sua voglia e coverchia?"

"Non so chi sia, ma so ch'e' non è solo;
domandal tu che più li t'avvicini,
6   e dolcemente, sì che parli, acco'lo."

Così due spirti, l'uno a l'altro chini,
ragionavan di me ivi a man dritta;
9   poi fer li visi, per dirmi, supini;

e disse l'uno: "O anima che fitta
nel corpo ancora inver' lo ciel ten vai,
12   per carità ne consola e ne ditta

onde vieni e chi se'; ché tu ne fai
tanto maravigliar de la tua grazia,
15   quanto vuol cosa che non fu più mai."

E io: "Per mezza Toscana si spazia
un fiumicel che nasce in Falterona,
18   e cento miglia di corso nol sazia.

Di sovr' esso rech' io questa persona:
dirvi ch'i' sia, saria parlare indarno,
21   ché 'l nome mio ancor molto non suona."

"Se ben lo 'ntendimento tuo accarno
con lo 'ntelletto," allora mi rispuose
24   quei che diceva pria, "tu parli d'Arno."

E l'altro disse lui: "Perché nascose
questi il vocabol di quella riviera,
27   pur com' om fa de l'orribili cose?"

'Who is this, circling our mountain
before he has been given wings by death,
who can open his eyes at will and shut them?'

'I don't know who he is but know he's not alone.
Question him, since you are closer,
and greet him courteously that he may answer.'

Thus two spirits, their faces almost touching,
conversed about me over to the right,
then turned their faces up to speak to me.

One said: 'O soul still rooted in the body,
making your way toward Heaven,
for the sake of charity relieve us, let us know

'where you come from and who you are,
for the grace bestowed on you has so amazed us
as something must that never was before.'

And I: 'Through the middle of Tuscany there flows
a winding stream that springs in Falterona—
one hundred miles still fail to curb its hungry course.

'From somewhere on its banks I bring this form.
To tell you who I am would be to speak in vain,
for my name as yet does not resound.'

'If my wit has truly grasped your meaning,'
he who had spoken first then answered,
'it is the Arno that you speak of.'

And the other asked him:
'Why did he conceal that river's name
just as one hides some dreadful thing?'

E l'ombra che di ciò domandata era,
si sdebitò così: "Non so; ma degno
30   ben è che 'l nome di tal valle pèra;

ché dal principio suo, ov' è sì pregno
l'alpestro monte ond' è tronco Peloro,
33   che 'n pochi luoghi passa oltra quel segno,

infin là 've si rende per ristoro
di quel che 'l ciel de la marina asciuga,
36   ond' hanno i fiumi ciò che va con loro,

vertù così per nimica si fuga
da tutti come biscia, o per sventura
39   del luogo, o per mal uso che li fruga:

ond' hanno sì mutata lor natura
li abitator de la misera valle,
42   che par che Circe li avesse in pastura.

Tra brutti porci, più degni di galle
che d'altro cibo fatto in uman uso,
45   dirizza prima il suo povero calle.

Botoli trova poi, venendo giuso,
ringhiosi più che non chiede lor possa,
48   e da lor disdegnosa torce il muso.

Vassi caggendo; e quant ella più 'ngrossa,
tanto più trova di can farsi lupi
51   la maladetta e sventurata fossa.

Discesa poi per più pelaghi cupi,
trova le volpi sì piene di froda,
54   che non temono ingegno che le occùpi.

Né lascerò di dir perch' altri m'oda;
e buon sarà costui, s'ancor s'ammenta
57   di ciò che vero spirto mi disnoda.

And the interrogated shade thus paid his debt:
'I do not know, but it is only fitting
that the name of such a valley perish,

30

'for from its source, where the wild mountain range,
from which Pelorus was broken off, rises to such height
that higher places are but few,

33

'down to where it surrenders to restore
what the sky draws from the sea,
so that the rivers are supplied in turn,

36

'all flee from virtue as if it were a snake,
an enemy to all, whether some curse
is on the place or evil habits goad them on,

39

'and those who live in that unhappy valley
are so altered in their nature it is as though
Circe were grazing them at pasture.

42

'Among filthy hogs, more fit to feed on acorns
than on any food that is prepared for men,
the water first directs its feeble course.

45

'Then, coming lower, it finds whelps that snarl
more than their powers warrant,
and so in scorn the river turns its snout from them.

48

'It goes on falling and the more it swells
the more does the accursed, ill-omened ditch
find that these dogs have been transformed to wolves.

51

'Having fallen through dark and deep-cut gorges,
it then finds foxes so very full of fraud
they have no fear that any trap can take them.

54

'Nor will I hold my peace because another hears me.
It will be wise of him to keep in mind
the truth the Spirit has revealed.

57

Io veggio tuo nepote che diventa
cacciator di quei lupi in su la riva
60   del fiero fiume, e tutti li sgomenta.

Vende la carne loro essendo viva;
poscia li ancide come antica belva;
63   molti di vita e sé di pregio priva.

Sanguinoso esce de la trista selva;
lasciala tal, che di qui a mille anni
66   ne lo stato primaio non si rinselva."

Com' a l'annunzio di dogliosi danni
si turba il viso di colui ch'ascolta,
69   da qual che parte il periglio l'assanni,

così vid' io l'altr' anima, che volta
stava a udir, turbarsi e farsi trista,
72   poi ch'ebbe la parola a sé raccolta.

Lo dir de l'una e de l'altra la vista
mi fer voglioso di saper lor nomi,
75   e dimanda ne fei con prieghi mista;

per che lo spirto che di pria parlòmi
ricominciò: "Tu vuo' ch'io mi deduca
78   nel fare a te ciò che tu far non vuo'mi.

Ma da che Dio in te vuol che traluca
tanto sua grazia, non ti sarò scarso;
81   però sappi ch'io fui Guido del Duca.

Fu il sangue mio d'invidia sì rïarso,
che se veduto avesse uom farsi lieto,
84   visto m'avresti di livore sparso.

Di mia semente cotal paglia mieto;
o gente umana, perché poni 'l core
87   là 'v' è mestier di consorte divieto?

'I see your grandson, who becomes a hunter
of the wolves that gather on the banks
60   of that wild stream and puts them all in terror.

'He sells their living flesh,
then slaughters them like old and useless cattle.
63   Many he robs of life and robs himself of honor.

'Covered in blood, he leaves that wretched wood
in such a state that not one thousand years
66   will make the trees grow green as once they were.'

As at the forecast of impending harm
the face of one who hears it shows distress,
69   no matter where the threat may bare its fangs,

the other soul, who had turned to listen,
became troubled and disheartened
72   once he had taken in the meaning of these words.

The speech of one and the expression of the other
made me want to know their names
75   and so I asked, entreating their response.

The spirit that had spoken first began again:
'You would have me do for you
78   what you do not consent to do for me.

'But since God wills His grace shine forth in you,
I will no longer hoard my answer:
81   Know, then, I was Guido del Duca.

'My blood was so consumed by envy
that, had I seen a man take joy in life,
84   you would have seen my skin turn livid.

'As I sowed, so now I reap such straw.
O race of men, why do you set your hearts
87   on things that of necessity cannot be shared?

Questi è Rinier; questi è 'l pregio e l'onore
de la casa da Calboli, ove nullo
90   fatto s'è reda poi del suo valore.

E non pur lo suo sangue è fatto brullo,
tra 'l Po e 'l monte e la marina e 'l Reno,
93   del ben richesto al vero e al trastullo;

ché dentro a questi termini è ripieno
di venenosi sterpi, sì che tardi
96   per coltivare omai verrebber meno.

Ov' è 'l buon Lizio e Arrigo Mainardi?
Pier Traversaro e Guido di Carpigna?
99   Oh Romagnuoli tornati in bastardi!

Quando in Bologna un Fabbro si ralligna?
quando in Faenza un Bernardin di Fosco,
102   verga gentil di picciola gramigna?

Non ti maravigliar s'io piango, Tosco,
quando rimembro, con Guido da Prata,
105   Ugolin d'Azzo che vivette nosco,

Federigo Tignoso e sua brigata,
la casa Traversara e li Anastagi
108   (e l'una gente e l'altra è diretata),

le donne e ' cavalier, li affanni e li agi
che ne 'nvogliava amore e cortesia
111   là dove i cuor son fatti sì malvagi.

O Bretinoro, ché non fuggi via,
poi che gita se n'è la tua famiglia
114   e molta gente per non esser ria?

Ben fa Bagnacaval, che non rifiglia;
e mal fa Castrocaro, e peggio Conio,
117   che di figliar tai conti più s'impiglia.

'This man is Rinier, this is the pride and honor
of the house of Càlboli, where no one since

90   has made himself an heir to his true worth.

'And not his blood alone—between Po and the mountains,
between Reno and the sea—is stripped of virtues

93   consonant with deeper thought and courtly pastime.

'For the land within these boundaries
is grown so dense with poisonous shoots

96   that even proper tillage now might come too late.

'Where is good Lizio, where Arrigo Mainardi,
Pier Traversaro and Guido di Carpigna?

99   O people of Romagna, how you've turned to bastards!

'When, in Bologna, does another Fabbro grow?
When, in Faenza, a Bernardin di Fosco,

102   noble branch sprung from a lowly weed?

'Do not marvel, Tuscan, if I weep
when, along with Guido da Prata, I recall

105   Ugolin d'Azzo, who lived among us,

'Federico Tignoso and his companions,
the house of Traversaro and of Anastagi—

108   both families now spent, without an heir—

'the ladies and the knights, the toils and sport
that love and courtesy inspired,

111   where now is found a waste of evil hearts.

'O Bertinoro, why do you not disappear,
since your best family, along with many others,

114   has fled you to escape corruption?

'Bagnacavallo does well to breed no more,
Castrocaro poorly and Conio worse,

117   obstinate in breeding such degenerate counts.

Ben faranno i Pagan, da che 'l demonio
lor sen girà; ma non però che puro
120 già mai rimagna d'essi testimonio.

O Ugolin de' Fantolin, sicuro
è 'l nome tuo, da che più non s'aspetta
123 chi far lo possa, tralignando, scuro.

Ma va via, Tosco, omai; ch'or mi diletta
troppo di pianger più che di parlare,
126 sì m'ha nostra ragion la mente stretta."

Noi sapavam che quell' anime care
ci sentivano andar; però, tacendo,
129 facëan noi del cammin confidare.

Poi fummo fatti soli procedendo,
folgore parve quando l'aere fende,
132 voce che giunse di contra dicendo:

"Anciderammi qualunque m'apprende";
e fuggì come tuon che si dilegua,
135 se sùbito la nuvola scoscende.

Come da lei l'udir nostro ebbe triegua,
ed ecco l'altra con sì gran fracasso,
138 che somigliò tonar che tosto segua:

"Io sono Aglauro che divenni sasso";
e allor, per ristrignermi al poeta,
141 in destro feci, e non innanzi, il passo.

Già era l'aura d'ogne parte queta;
ed el mi disse: "Quel fu 'l duro camo
144 che dovria l'uom tener dentro a sua meta.

Ma voi prendete l'esca, sì che l'amo
de l'antico avversaro a sé vi tira;
147 e però poco val freno o richiamo.

'The Pagani will do better when their "Devil"
shuffles off, yet not so well
120   that they will leave behind a stainless slate.

'O Ugolin de' Fantolin, your name is safe,
since no more sons are looked for
123   who might blacken it with their depravity.

'But now, Tuscan, be on your way,
for I would rather weep than speak,
126   so has our discourse wrung my mind.'

We knew those kindly spirits heard us moving off.
Their silence, for that reason,
129   confirmed that we were keeping to our path.

As we moved on by ourselves, a voice,
like lightning when it cleaves the air,
132   came down upon us, saying:

'Whoever finds me shall slay me,'
and fled, as thunder fades away,
135   after the sudden rending of its cloud.

As soon as our ears had some relief
a new voice followed with such clamor that it seemed
138   a thunderclap, delayed but for an instant:

'I am Aglauros who was turned to stone.'
At that, to draw closer to the poet,
141   I took a step to my right and not ahead.

Now that the air was quiet all around us,
he said to me: 'That was the bit and bridle
144   to keep a man within his bounds.

'But you mortals take the bait, so that the hook
of your old adversary draws you to him,
147   and then of little use is curb or lure.

Chiamavi 'l cielo e 'ntorno vi si gira,
mostrandovi le sue bellezze etterne,
e l'occhio vostro pur a terra mira;
151   onde vi batte chi tutto discerne."

'The heavens call to you and wheel about you,
revealing their eternal splendors,
but your eyes are fixed upon the earth.

151   For that, He, seeing all, does smite you.'

1–3. These words do not, as we might assume, issue from Sapia, but from a new speaker, the dominant presence in this canto. He is Guido del Duca, as we will discover at verse 81 (see note to that verse). His rather salty way of responding to the news (broadcast at *Purg.* XIII.142, when Guido overheard Dante speaking to Sapia) that Dante is here in the flesh, is a man "who can open his eyes at will and shut them," will turn out to be typical of his bluntness, which finds its foil in the indirect and extremely polite ways of his interlocutor, Rinieri da Calboli. Guido cannot see that Dante can see him (we recall that Dante was sensitive about his favored status in this respect at *Purg.* XIII.73–74) but surmises that, as a living soul, Dante has the ocular power that is taken from all those who are purging their envy on this terrace. This does not make him a source of envy for these souls, but of wonder (see vv. 13–14).

4–6. The second speaker, Rinieri da Calboli (see note to vv. 88–90), a sort of precursor of one of Marcel Proust's famously overpolite great-aunts, addresses Dante only through his companion, Guido. The characterization of the two respondents to Dante's presence is reminiscent, in its handling of such dramatically differing personalities, of the representation of character in the colloquy among Dante, Farinata, and Cavalcante in *Inferno* X.

7. We here learn that these are speakers we have not heard before. For a moment it is as though we were as "blind" as the penitents and dependent on what we hear said by the narrator to understand who is involved in this colloquy.

10–13. Sapia (*Purg.* XIII.130) had wanted to know Dante's identity; his response was to identify himself only as a person who had (at least until now) been prideful in his life. Now Guido (the speaker is not identified, but we safely assume, both from the rotation of speakers and from the forthright quality of his question, that it is he) asks to know both his homeland and his name; Dante will modestly offer only the first piece of information. He has learned, we surmise, something about Pride in his few hours on that terrace.

14–15. Guido's amazement at Dante's condition does two things quickly and neatly; it shows that he (and Rinieri) are not envious of his condi-

tion and it allows Dante not to have to insist pridefully on his unique-
ness, something that Guido has done for him. Once we find out who
these two are, we realize that these now fraternal souls were, on earth, a
Ghibelline (Guido) and a Guelph (Rinieri). These details may remind us
of the far less fraternal interaction between Farinata (a Ghibelline) and
Cavalcante (a Guelph) in *Inferno* X.

16–18. · The protagonist introduces its controlling image to the canto,
the river Arno. Its source is in the Apennines at Mt. Falterona and it then
makes its way, as we shall hear, through the Casentino, then the cities of
Arezzo, Florence, and Pisa, before it reaches the sea. Giovanna Ioli
(Ioli.1989.1), p. 210, points out that the verb *saziare* (slake) introduces the
theme of hunger to this description of the Arno. The river seems, in
order to satisfy its own appetites, not to extend far enough, despite all the
harm its approximately 150 miles (and not Dante's 100) produces.

19. The protagonist identifies himself as a Tuscan, not as a Florentine.
This is perhaps less the result of modesty than the poet's reflection on his
wandering condition in his exile, much of which was to be spent in
Tuscany, though not in Florence.

20–21. Dante's modesty here is gainsaid by his previous inclusion
among the great poets of all time in *Inferno* IV.100–102. There are those
who claim that in 1300 he had not indeed become particularly famous
and that this is the reason for his modesty here. It would rather seem to
be that he is keeping in mind the lessons in humility he has just learned
on the last terrace. Further, he clearly expects that fame will one day find
him. However, the only time his name is used in the *Commedia* it is spo-
ken, not for praise, but in denunciation of his disloyalty by Beatrice (*Purg.*
XXX.55).

22–24. The rhyme word *accarno*, a hapax, derives, as commentators
point out, from the word used to describe an animal that has caught an-
other and is biting into its flesh *(carne)*. Guido's third speech unravels the
fairly simple riddle that conceals the river's name.

25–27. Rinieri once again addresses Guido in order to pose a question
for Dante to answer. We can now see that this is the central trait of his
personality as explored in this canto. (He only speaks twice, a total of six
lines, and yet we feel we know him. We will see his sad expression in vv.
70–72 but he will not speak again.) Guido's peremptory, forward man-

ner in some ways matches, *in bono*, the Tuscan (western) side of the Apennines, presented as being ferocious; Rinieri's diffident attitude is perhaps meant to reflect his connection with the good folk (now long gone) from the eastern side of those mountains, in the Romagna.

28–30. Guido's opening verbal gesture of disdain sets the stage for his serial denunciation of the mountain hamlets and cities of the plain along the Arno. For the resonance of Job 18:17: "Memoria illius pereat de terra" (and may memory of him vanish from the earth) see Tommaseo (1837) on this tercet.

31–42. Guido first indicates the length of the entire river, from the mountain range (the Apennines) "from which Pelorus was broken off" to the sea on the other side of Pisa, where the river deposits its waters to replace that moisture drawn by the sun from the sea and subsequently dropped into the mountains where the Arno has its source. The natural cycle of renewal that typifies the river is not replicated by the inhabitants along it; these go from bad to worse as the river descends. (Compare the descent of the rivers that eventually make up the Po, falling from Lake Garda to the Adriatic Sea in *Inf.* XX.61–81.)

Pelorus, the promontory at the northeast end of Sicily, was believed to have been cut off by the sea (the Strait of Messina) from the southwest end of the Apennine range. Virgil testifies to this phenomenon at *Aeneid* III.410–419.

37–42. The word for "snake," *biscia*, deployed a third and final time (see also *Purg.* VIII.98 for its use to indicate the serpent in the garden) in the poem, recalls *Inferno* IX.77: the angelic messenger compared to a snake from which frogs flee.

The cause for the immoderate behavior of the valley's inhabitants, expressed as uncertain ("whether some curse / is on the place or evil habits goad them on"), is eventually explicitly identified as the result of the misapplied freedom of the will (i.e., the second cause alluded to here) by Marco Lombardo (*Purg.* XVI.67–83), as was pointed out, uniquely among the early commentators, by Benvenuto da Imola. All of the Arno-dwellers seem to have been turned to brutes by the sorceress Circe, most particularly those described in the next tercet.

43–45. This porcine part of the Casentino is associated with the Conti Guidi (see note to *Inf.* XXX.58–61) and in particular with the branch of the family that ruled in Porciano, a fortified town near Mt. Falterona along the shallow stream that will grow to become the Arno. Non-Tuscan readers may be surprised at commentators' certainty about the identities of all the unnamed towns or cities referred to in this part of the diatribe, but Dante counts on a reader familiar with the major points of habitation along the river.

46–48.   Next downstream is Arezzo, from which city the river turns sharply away in order to head northwest toward Florence as though it wanted to avoid the nasty "whelps" of Arezzo. Like the Texas rancher who is all hat and no cattle, these little dogs are all snarl or bark and no bite—or so the Ottimo (1333) thought.

49–51.   Florence seems to be associated, unsurprisingly, with avarice. (For the wolf as representing avarice see note to *Inf.* VII.8.)

52–54.   If Florence is associated with avarice, Pisa is presented as being full of fraud. Foxes are referred to in two other passages in the poem (*Inf.* XXVII.75: Guido da Montefeltro refers to his former "vulpine" strategies; *Purg.* XXXII.119: a fox, generally understood as heresy, invades the cart of the chariot of the Church).
    Pietro di Dante (1340) and Daniello (1568) both think of a passage in Boethius as Dante's source for the animals in Guido's outburst. See *De consolatione philosophiae* IV.iii (pr). 57–60: "You will say that the man who is driven by avarice to seize what belongs to others is like a wolf; the restless, angry man who spends his life in quarrels you will compare to a dog. The treacherous conspirator who steals by fraud may be likened to a fox; . . . the man who is sunk in foul lust is trapped in the pleasures of a filthy sow" (trans. Richard Green). (The accompanying poem in Boethius begins with Circe, who turned the companions of Ulysses into animals by means of her poisoned potions.)

55–57.   This passage offers the occasion for a dispute among the commentators: does *altri* refer to Rinieri or to Dante? (According to most early commentators, the former; to most later ones, the latter.) The major problem with the older hypothesis is that one has a hard time seeing what good it can do Rinieri to hear this news (and Guido's locution points to a potential benefit to his auditor), since he cannot intervene in worldly events, while Guido's unseen mortal interlocutor still has a life to live back on the earth—indeed in Tuscany—and may profit from this prophetic warning.

58–66.   Guido's prophecy concerns the grandson of Rinieri, Fulcieri da Calboli, "member of the illustrious Guelf family of that name at Forlì; he was Podestà of Florence in 1302/3, after the return of the Neri [the Black Guelphs] through the influence of Charles of Valois, and proved himself a bitter foe of the Bianchi" **(T)**. His enmity was shown not only to White Guelphs but to Ghibellines, as he had leaders of both these parties arrested and tortured and killed.

Fulcieri bargained with his employers (the Black Guelphs) over the fates of his prisoners, thus currying the favor of the Black leaders while shoring up his position as *podestà*; he eventually handed many of the captives over to be put to death by their enemies, selling them like cattle.

The metaphoric reference to Florence as a *trista selva* (wretched wood) in verse 64 may draw our attention back to the second verse of the poem, in which the protagonist discovers himself in a *selva oscura* (dark wood). The language of this tercet also identifies the better days of Florence as Edenic and suggests that the good old days are now gone for a very long time.

77–80.   Guido reminds Dante that he has not furnished his own name, but relents upon considering Dante's special relationship to the Divine plan that is manifest in his mere presence on the mountain in the flesh.

81.   "Guido del Duca, gentleman of Bertinoro, near Forlì, in Romagna, son of Giovanni del Duca of the Onesti family of Ravenna. The earliest mention of Guido occurs in a document dated May 4, 1199, in which he is described as holding the office of judge to the Podestà of Rimini. In 1202, and again in 1204, he is mentioned as playing an important part in the affairs of Romagna, both times in connexion with Pier Traversaro (*Purg.* XIV.98), whose adherent he appears to have been. In 1218, Pier Traversaro, with the help of his Ghibelline friends, and especially of the Mainardi of Bertinoro, made himself master of Ravenna, and expelled the Guelfs from the city. The latter, in revenge, seized Bertinoro, destroyed the houses belonging to the Mainardi, and drove out all Piero's adherents; among them was Guido del Duca, who at this time apparently, together with his family, betook himself to Ravenna, his father's native place, and resided there under the protection of Pier Traversaro. Some ten years later (in 1229) Guido's name appears as witness to a deed at Ravenna; he was alive in 1249. . . ." **(T)**.

82–84.   Guido's wry self-knowledge, similar to that of Sapia (*Purg.* XIII.110–111), practically defines the sin of envy as Dante understood it.

Pietro di Dante (1340) cites Horace (*Epistles* I.ii.57): "The envious man grows lean when his neighbor prospers." The citation is apt, even if Dante's knowledge of the *Epistles* is not assured. A more certain source is found in Aquinas, as is variously noted, first by Poletto (1894): *tristitia de alienis bonis* (sadness at another's possessions). But see Jacopo della Lana (1324), who attributes the phrase to John of Damascus (eighth century): "tristitia de bonis alienis."

For the gray-blue color of envy see the note to *Purgatorio* XIII.8–9.

85. The phrasing (sowing and reaping) is obviously biblical, as Lombardi (1791) was perhaps the first to note, citing St. Paul (Galatians 6:8): "Quae enim seminaverit homo, haec et metet" (For what a man sows, that shall he reap). Tommaseo (1837) cites another five biblical passages that also rely on this metaphor, but the passage in Paul is favored by the commentators once it enters the tradition. Here Guido, in purgation, harvests the straw of expiation for his sins on earth; his wheat awaits him in paradise.

86–87. Guido's denunciation, in the form of an apostrophe of the human race, places the blame for our envious lot in our not being able to seek goods that are shared. His phrase, "things that of necessity cannot be shared," will come back to be scrutinized in the next canto (XV.45), there offering Virgil occasion for a lengthy gloss (XV.46–75).

88–89. "Rinieri da Calboli, member of the illustrious Guelf family of that name at Forlì. . . . Rinieri, who played an important part in the affairs of Romagna, was born probably at the beginning of Cent. xiii; he was Podestà of Faenza in 1265 (the year of Dante's birth). In 1276 he made war upon Forlì, but was compelled to retire to his stronghold of Calboli, in the upper valley of the Montone, where he was besieged by Guido da Montefeltro (*Inf.* XXVII), at that time Captain of Forlì, who forced him to surrender, and destroyed the castle. In 1292, while for the second time Podestà of Faenza . . . , Rinieri captured Forlì, and expelled . . . many . . . powerful Ghibellines. Two years later, however (in 1294), Rinieri and his adherents were in turn expelled. In 1296 Rinieri and the Guelfs once more made themselves masters of Forlì, but the Ghibellines . . . quickly retook the city and killed many of the Guelfs, Rinieri among the number" **(T)**.

91–92. Guido now describes the boundaries of Romagna, a large area on the right-hand side of Italy, separated from Tuscany (subject of the first half of the canto's exploration of sins along the Arno) by the Apennines, lying south and west of Romagna. The rough boundaries include the river Reno, just to the west of Bologna, the river Po, flowing into the Adriatic north of Ravenna, the Adriatic at the eastern limit, and the hills of Montefeltro at the southern edge.

93–96.   Once virtuous, peopled by such as Rinieri, Romagna is now turned to an unweeded garden.

97–123.   Guido's second speech on a set topic, a version of the "ubi sunt?" (where are [the good folk of the past] today?) topos, as Sapegno (1955) insists, pointing to a general sense of source in the Bible and in medieval Latin hymns, includes references to ten additional worthy individuals, four families, and three towns, each of which is gone or has come upon hard times. The three categories are intermixed.

97.   **Lizio [di Valbona**, a castle near Bagno], a Guelph, fought alongside Rinieri in the losing battle at Forlì in 1276. Lizio is a character in one of the *novelle* (V.iv) of the *Decameron*. **Arrigo Mainardi**, a Ghibelline from Bertinoro, associated with Guido del Duca, was still living in 1228. Thus this first pair is divided equally between the two protagonists of the canto and their two political parties.

98.   **Pier Traversaro**, the most distinguished member of the powerful Ghibelline family of Ravenna and renowned for his patronage of poets, was an ally of Guido del Duca. At the end of his life in 1225 he was the unofficial ruler of Ravenna, where he had earlier been *podestà* for three separate terms, but his son Paolo, who succeeded him as the central political figure in the city, became a Guelph and, at his death in 1240, the Traversaro influence in Ravenna, which had been strong for nearly three hundred years, came to its end. **Guido di Carpigna**, a Guelph whose family was related to the counts of Montefeltro, was once *podestà* of Ravenna (in 1251).

99.   The relationship between the first four names and the present-day inhabitants of Romagna is oppositional, a notion that escaped some of the early commentators, who thought Dante was vilifying at least the next two names.

100.   **Fabbro [de' Lambertazzi]**, leader of the Bolognese Ghibellines, served as *podestà* of seven Italian cities (of three more than once) between 1230 and 1258.

101–102.   **Bernardin di Fosco**, sprung from ordinary folk (the Ottimo [1333] says he was a peasant), apparently exhibited such personal gentility that the nobles of Faenza eventually looked upon him as one of their own. While no commentator seems to know enough about him to present his political party, the fact that he seems to have been involved in the defense of Faenza against the emperor (Frederick II) in 1240 would ordinarily suggest that he was a Guelph; on the other hand he apparently was in the emperor's favor in 1248 and 1249 when he was made *podestà* of Pisa and then of Siena—positions that would suggest his alignment with the Ghibellines. However, Isidoro Del Lungo (1926), the only commentator to deal with the issue, simply states that he was a Guelph.

104.   Of **Guido da Prata** so little is known that one commentator, Luigi Pietrobono (1946), is of the opinion that, in light of the small amount of information that has come down to us, Dante had overestimated his worth. Prata is a village in the Romagna, between Forlì and Faenza; Guido seems to have been active in the political life of Ravenna.

105.   **Ugolino d'Azzo** was born in Tuscany, but at some point moved to Faenza (and thus, in Guido's words, "lived among us"). He was the son of Azzo degli Ubaldini and thus related to both the cardinal Ottaviano degli Ubaldini (*Inf.* X.120) and the archbishop Ruggieri degli Ubaldini (*Inf.* XXXIII.14). He was married to a daughter of Provenzan Salvani (*Purg.* XI.121) and died at a ripe old age in 1293.

106.   Of **Federigo Tignoso** practically nothing is known. Benvenuto says he was a rich nobleman of Rimini and that he had heard tell that Federigo had a great shock of yellow hair, so that his sobriquet, Tignoso, which is the adjective from the noun *tigna* (or "mange"), was a playful misnomer. Federigo's companions were, apparently, those who took part in his hospitable way of life. Those who attempt to date his life set it in the first half of the thirteenth century.

107–108.   Dante suddenly switches from munificent individuals to munificent families. Of the **Traversari** of Ravenna we have heard tell in the person of Piero (see note to verse 98); now we hear of another great Ghibelline family of that city, the **Anastagi**. When we consider that the last years of Dante's life were spent at Ravenna as a result of the hospitality of Guido Novello da Polenta it is striking that the Polentani, perhaps the greatest of all the families of Ravenna (along with the Traversari), are not mentioned here. Writing after 1317, Dante would surely have included them, since their Guelph allegiance would apparently have been no bar to being included in the cast assembled here, containing roughly as many Guelphs as Ghibellines.

Both these families have by 1300 nearly died out—a fate that is not the unmitigated disaster it might seem, as we shall soon see.

109–111.   These verses served Ariosto (1474–1533) as the model for the opening of his epic poem, *Orlando furioso*: "Le donne, i cavalier, l'arme, gli amori, / le cortesie, l'audaci imprese io canto" (Ladies and knights, weapons and love, courteous acts, bold-hearted deeds: all these I sing). The good old days have yielded to an iron age; it is perhaps better not to breed. That is the message that begins to be hammered home. For the themes of *cortesia* and *nobiltà* see Lo Cascio (LoCa.1967.1).

112–114.   **Bertinoro**, between Forlì and Cesena, was renowned for the generosity of its noble families, as the early commentators, beginning with the Anonymous Lombard (1322), told. The family referred to as having left may be the Mainardi (mentioned in verse 97) or some other; some commentators want to see the term as generic (i.e., *all* the good people of the town) but this is probably not warranted.

115.   **Bagnacavallo**, between Imola and Ravenna, a Ghibelline stronghold in Dante's time, is congratulated for not having male offspring by its counts (the Malvicini family), extinguished, in their male line, by 1300.

116–117.   **Castrocaro**, near Forlì, was a Ghibelline stronghold of the counts of Castrocaro until 1300, when it passed into the hands of the local Ordelaffi family and then, subsequently, into the possession of the Florentine Black Guelphs. **Conio**, a castle near Imola, was in the possession of Guelph counts. Both these strongholds are seen as breeding worse and worse stock.

118–120.   To conclude the brief list of families, Dante refers to the **Pagani**. They were Ghibelline lords of Faenza. Rather than praise their good early stock, Dante fixes on their "Devil," Maghinardo Pagano da Susinana, a truly impressive warrior and statesman. A Ghibelline, he also favored the Florentine Guelphs because of their decent treatment of him when he was a child and in their protection. On one side of the Apennines he fought on the side of Guelphs; on the other, of Ghibellines. What undoubtedly took any possibility of a dispassionate view of this extraordinary man from Dante was the fact that he entered the city in November 1301 at the side of Charles of Valois, the French conqueror of Florence (in collaboration with Corso Donati).

Maghinardo is the only name mentioned in this passage of a person alive at the imagined date of the vision (he died in 1302). Everyone else is of thirteenth-century provenance, and of the persons and events datable in this welter of historical material, nothing before 1200 or after 1293 is alluded to, thus reinforcing the notion that Dante is talking, through the mouth of Guido del Duca, of the "good old days" in Romagna. A similar and longer discourse in historical romanticism will be put forth by Cacciaguida in *Paradiso* XVI, an entire canto given over to the moral supremacy of a Florence that is now long gone.

121–123.   The last name to resound in Guido's list is that of **Ugolino de' Fantolini**. A Guelph from Cerfugnano, near Faenza, he was several times *podestà* of Faenza. Dead in 1278, he was survived by his two sons, both of whom died well before 1300, so that this Ugolino's name may be preserved from being sullied by any additional Fantolinian progeny.

125.   Guido's juxtaposition of tears and speech may remind the reader of Francesca's similar gesture—as well as Ugolino's. See *Inferno* V.126 and XXXIII.9, as is suggested by Mattalia (1960). And see note to *Inferno* XXXIII.9.

His final words of lament, after the extraordinary vivacity and range of his styles (noble, earthy, ironic, cynical, but always sharply honed), are the last word on Romagna, which was once so fair and now is foul, a transformation that leaves only grief in its wake.

133.   The voices overhead that greeted the travelers as they entered this terrace (*Purg.* XIII.25–27) return, again moving against the direction of their movement, but now presenting negative exemplars. Cain's words are translated from the Vulgate (Genesis 4:14): "Everyone who finds me shall slay me," spoken before God marked his forehead after the murder of his brother, Abel, so that he would not, indeed, be slain. For Cain's association with Envy, according to some fathers of the Church, see Cassell (Cass.1984.2), p. 17.

139.   See Ovid, *Metamorphoses* II.797–819, where Mercury turns Aglauros to stone because she wants him for herself and stations herself outside her sister Herse's door in order to prevent his entry to Herse's

bedchamber. Mercury then opens the door with a touch of his caduceus. That scene has already been (tacitly) present in *Inferno* IX.89–90, where the Mercury-like angel opens the gates of Dis to Virgil and Dante. See the note to that passage.

Cain and Aglauros share the condition of envy of a sibling, Cain of Abel, Aglauros of Herse. The second exemplar of Charity, Pylades, was in a brotherly relationship with Orestes, even though they were not related by blood (*Purg.* XIII.32).

140–141. It is noteworthy that the voices presenting the exemplars of Charity are courteous and inviting (*Purg.* XIII.25–27), while these, presenting exemplars of Envy, are like lightning and thunder and cause the protagonist to be fearful.

143–146. Virgil's language in this passage is biblical: Psalm 31:9 (32:9): "Be not as the horse, or as the mule, which have no understanding: whose mouth must be held in with bit [Vulgate: *camo*] and bridle [Vulgate: *freno*]. . . ." (a passage also cited by Dante in *Monarchia* III.xv.9, as was first noted by Tommaseo [1837]); Ecclesiastes 9:12: "as the fishes that are taken in an evil net [Vulgate: *hamo* (hook)], and as the birds that are caught in the snare; so are the sons of man snared. . . ." See *Purgatorio* XIII.40 for Dante's first use of *freno* on the terraces and see the note to XIII.37–42. The devil sets his snares or hooks to trap humankind. The next passage presents God's way of hunting us.

147–151. God's "lure" *(richiamo)*, a technical term from falconry, is part of this magnificent final image, which turns our human expectations upside down. God is seen as a falconer in the Empyrean spinning his lures, the stars that end each *cantica*, over his head, as it were, while we are falcons that are not drawn to this amazing bait, but look down to the earth for our temptations. Compare that other disobedient falcon, the monster Geryon, at *Inferno* XVII.127–132. The language of this passage is Boethian. See *De consolatione philosophiae* III.m8: "[Humans] dig the earth in search of the good, which soars above the star-filled heavens" (trans. R. Green).

PURGATORIO XV
(*Envy and Wrath*)

Quanto tra l'ultimar de l'ora terza
e 'l principio del dì par de la spera

3   che sempre a guisa di fanciullo scherza,

tanto pareva già inver' la sera
essere al sol del suo corso rimaso;

6   vespero là, e qui mezza notte era.

E i raggi ne ferien per mezzo 'l naso,
perché per noi girato era sì 'l monte,

9   che già dritti andavamo inver' l'occaso,

quand' io senti' a me gravar la fronte
a lo splendore assai più che di prima,

12   e stupor m'eran le cose non conte;

ond' io levai le mani inver' la cima
de le mie ciglia, e fecimi 'l solecchio,

15   che del soverchio visibile lima.

Come quando da l'acqua o da lo specchio
salta lo raggio a l'opposita parte,

18   salendo sù per lo modo parecchio

a quel che scende, e tanto si diparte
dal cader de la pietra in igual tratta,

21   sì come mostra esperïenza e arte;

così mi parve da luce rifratta
quivi dinanzi a me esser percosso;

24   per che a fuggir la mia vista fu ratta.

"Che è quel, dolce padre, a che non posso
schermar lo viso tanto che mi vaglia,"

27   diss' io, "e pare inver' noi esser mosso?"

As much as between the end of the third hour
and the first of day is seen of the sphere
that like a child is always darting here and there,

so much appeared now to remain
of the sun's course toward nightfall:
it was vespers there and midnight here on earth.

The rays were striking full upon our faces,
for we had circled so much of the mountain
that we were heading straight into the west,

when such great splendor overwhelmed my sight,
greater than any I had seen before,
that I was dazed by its unfamiliar brightness.

I raised one hand above my brow
and gave my eyes sufficient shade
to temper this excess of light.

As, when from water or a mirror, a reflected beam
leaps back the other way, rising
at the angle it took in its descent,

and from the plumb line of a stone
will deviate an equal distance,
as shown by science and experiment,

it seemed to me that I was struck
by such bright light reflected there before me
that my eyes were quick to turn away.

'What is that, gentle father,' I asked,
'from which I cannot even screen my eyes?
It seems to be moving toward us.'

3

6

9

12

15

18

21

24

27

"Non ti maravigliar s'ancor t'abbaglia
la famiglia del cielo," a me rispuose:
30   "messo è che viene ad invitar ch'om saglia.

Tosto sarà ch'a veder queste cose
non ti fia grave, ma fieti diletto
33   quanto natura a sentir ti dispuose."

Poi giunti fummo a l'angel benedetto,
con lieta voce disse: "Intrate quinci
36   ad un scaleo vie men che li altri eretto."

Noi montavam, già partiti di linci,
e *"Beati misericordes!"* fue
39   cantato retro, e "Godi tu che vinci!"

Lo mio maestro e io soli amendue
suso andavamo; e io pensai, andando,
42   prode acquistar ne le parole sue;

e dirizza'mi a lui sì dimandando:
"Che volse dir lo spirto di Romagna,
45   e 'divieto' e 'consorte' menzionando?"

Per ch'elli a me: "Di sua maggior magagna
conosce il danno; e però non s'ammiri
48   se ne riprende perché men si piagna.

Perché s'appuntano i vostri disiri
dove per compagnia parte si scema,
51   invidia move il mantaco a' sospiri.

Ma se l'amor de la spera suprema
torcesse in suso il disiderio vostro,
54   non vi sarebbe al petto quella tema;

ché, per quanti si dice più lì 'nostro,'
tanto possiede più di ben ciascuno,
57   e più di caritate arde in quel chiostro."

'Don't be surprised,' he answered me,
'if those who live in Heaven still can blind you:
this messenger invites us to ascend.

30

'Soon the sight of beings such as these
will not be burdensome, will give as much delight
as nature made you fit to feel.'

33

When we had reached the blessèd angel
he called out in a joyful voice: 'Now enter here
on a stairway far less steep than were the others.'

36

& tc. pride is the worst.

As we ascended, moving on from there,
we heard *'Beati misericordes'* sung behind us
and 'Rejoice, you who conquer.'

39

My master and I, alone again,
were climbing, and as we went along,
hoping to take some profit from his words,

42

I turned to him and asked:
'What did the spirit from Romagna mean
when he spoke of things that can't be shared?'

discourse on love.

45

He replied: 'Of his worst fault he knows the cost.
Thus it is no wonder he condemns it, in the hope
that fewer souls will have a reason to lament.

48

'Because your appetites are fixed on things
that, divided, lessen each one's share,
envy's bellows pushes breath into your sighs.

51

'But if love for the highest sphere
could turn your longings toward heavenly things,
then fear of sharing would pass from your hearts.

54

'For there above, when more souls speak of *ours*,
the more of goodness each one owns,
the more of love is burning in that cloister.'

57

"Io son d'esser contento più digiuno,"
diss' io, "che se mi fosse pria taciuto,
60 e più di dubbio ne la mente aduno.

Com' esser puote ch'un ben, distributo
in più posseditor, faccia più ricchi
63 di sé che se da pochi è posseduto?"

Ed elli a me: "Però che tu rificchi
la mente pur a le cose terrene,
66 di vera luce tenebre dispicchi.

Quello infinito e ineffabil bene
che là sù è, così corre ad amore
69 com' a lucido corpo raggio vene.

Tanto si dà quanto trova d'ardore;
sì che, quantunque carità si stende,
72 cresce sovr' essa l'etterno valore.

E quanta gente più là sù s'intende,
più v'è da bene amare, e più vi s'ama,
75 e come specchio l'uno a l'altro rende.

E se la mia ragion non ti disfama,
vedrai Beatrice, ed ella pienamente
78 ti torrà questa e ciascun' altra brama.

Procaccia pur che tosto sieno spente,
come son già le due, le cinque piaghe,
81 che si richiudon per esser dolente."

Com' io voleva dicer "Tu m'appaghe,"
vidimi giunto in su l'altro girone,
84 sì che tacer mi fer le luci vaghe.

Ivi mi parve in una visïone
estatica di sùbito esser tratto,
87 e vedere in un tempio più persone;

'I am more starved for answers,' I said,
'than if before I had kept silent,
60   since now my mind is filled with greater doubt.

'How can it be that a good, distributed,
can enrich a greater number of possessors
63   than if it were possessed by few?'

And he to me: 'Because you still
have your mind fixed on earthly things,
66   you harvest darkness from the light itself.

'That infinite and ineffable Good,
which dwells on high, speeds toward love
69   as a ray of sunlight to a shining body.

'It returns the love it finds in equal measure,
so that, if more of ardor is extended,
72   eternal Goodness will augment Its own.

'And the more souls there are who love on high,
the more there is to love, the more of loving,
75   for like a mirror each returns it to the other.

'And if my words do not requite your hunger,
you shall see Beatrice. She will deliver you
78   entirely from this and every other craving.

'Seek only that the five wounds healed
by being painful soon may be closed up,
81   as the other two already are.'

I was about to say: 'You give me satisfaction,'
when I saw that I had reached another terrace,
84   and my eager eyes made me keep silent.

There it seemed to me I was caught up
in an ecstatic, sudden vision
87   in which I saw a temple full of people

e una donna, in su l'entrar, con atto
dolce di madre dicer: "Figliuol mio,
90   perché hai tu così verso noi fatto?

Ecco, dolenti, lo tuo padre e io
ti cercavamo." E come qui si tacque,
93   ciò che pareva prima, dispario.

Indi m'apparve un'altra con quell' acque
giù per le gote che 'l dolor distilla
96   quando di gran dispetto in altrui nacque,

e dir: "Se tu se' sire de la villa
del cui nome ne' dèi fu tanta lite,
99   e onde ogne scïenza disfavilla,

vendica te di quelle braccia ardite
ch'abbracciar nostra figlia, o Pisistràto."
102   E 'l segnor mi parea, benigno e mite,

risponder lei con viso temperato:
"Che farem noi a chi mal ne disira,
105   se quei che ci ama è per noi condannato?"

Poi vidi genti accese in foco d'ira
con pietre un giovinetto ancider, forte
108   gridando a sé pur: "Martira, martira!"

E lui vedea chinarsi, per la morte
che l'aggravava già, inver' la terra,
111   ma de li occhi facea sempre al ciel porte,

orando a l'alto Sire, in tanta guerra,
che perdonasse a' suoi persecutori,
114   con quello aspetto che pietà diserra.

Quando l'anima mia tornò di fori
a le cose che son fuor di lei vere,
117   io riconobbi i miei non falsi errori.

and, at the door, about to enter, a woman,
with the sweet demeanor of a mother, who said:
90   'My son, why have you dealt with us like this?

'Behold, your father and I have searched
for you in sorrow.' Just as she now was silent,
93   so did that which brought her leave my sight.

Then there appeared to me another woman,
tears of grief still running down her cheeks
96   from anger at the one whom she disdained.

She said: 'If you are indeed lord of this city,
whose naming caused such strife among the gods
99   and from which so much knowledge lights the world,

'avenge yourself on those bold arms
that dared embrace our daughter, Pisistratus.'
102   And it seemed to me that lord gave gracious answer,

offered gently and with tranquil look:
'What shall we do to one who seeks our harm
105   if we condemn the one who loves us?'

Then I saw people, aflame with burning wrath,
stoning a youth to death,
108   and each one screaming to himself, 'Kill, kill.'

And I saw him sinking to the ground—
for death was heavy on him now—
111   but keeping his eyes open to Heaven,

as from his deepest agony he begged
the Lord on high to pardon his tormentors
114   with a look that must unlock compassion.

When my soul made its way back
to the things that are real outside it,
117   I came to know my errors were not false.

Lo duca mio, che mi potea vedere
far sì com' om che dal sonno si slega,
120   disse: "Che hai che non ti puoi tenere,

ma se' venuto più che mezza lega
velando li occhi e con le gambe avvolte,
123   a guisa di cui vino o sonno piega?"

"O dolce padre mio, se tu m'ascolte,
io ti dirò," diss' io, "ciò che m'apparve
126   quando le gambe mi furon sì tolte."

Ed ei: "Se tu avessi cento larve
sovra la faccia, non mi sarian chiuse
129   le tue cogitazion, quantunque parve.

Ciò che vedesti fu perché non scuse
d'aprir lo core a l'acque de la pace
132   che da l'etterno fonte son diffuse.

Non dimandai 'Che hai?' per quel che face
chi guarda pur con l'occhio che non vede,
135   quando disanimato il corpo giace;

ma dimandai per darti forza al piede:
così frugar conviensi i pigri, lenti
138   ad usar lor vigilia quando riede."

Noi andavam per lo vespero, attenti
oltre quanto potean li occhi allungarsi
141   contra i raggi serotini e lucenti.

Ed ecco a poco a poco un fummo farsi
verso di noi come la notte oscuro;
né da quello era loco da cansarsi.
145   Questo ne tolse li occhi e l'aere puro.

My leader, who could see that I was acting
like one who shakes himself from sleep, said:
120   'What's wrong with you that you can't walk straight

'but have come now more than half a league
with your eyes veiled and your legs entangled,
123   like a man overcome by wine or sleep?'

'O my dear father,' I said, 'if you'll but listen,
I will tell you exactly what I saw
126   when my legs were stolen from me.'

And he: 'If over your face you wore
a hundred masks, even your faintest thoughts
129   would not be hidden from my sight.

'These things were shown you so you would not refuse
to open your heart to the waters of peace
132   that pour from the eternal fountain.

'I did not ask "What's wrong?" for your resemblance
to a man who stares with but unseeing eyes
135   when his body lies insensate,

'but asked to put fresh vigor in your step.
So must the sluggard, slow to use his waking hours
138   even once these come, be spurred to act.'

We went along through the evening hour,
forcing our eyes to seek the farthest point ahead
141   against the bright late beams,

when, little by little, a smoke moved toward us,
black as night, and there was nowhere
we could escape from it. And first it took away
145   the pureness of the air and then our sight.

1–6.   This belabored opening has bothered any number of readers. Benvenuto, commenting on its six verses, remarks that all Dante means to say is that it is the hour of Vespers, and that he does so by means of circumlocution ("per unam circuitionem verborum"). However, Arnaldo Bonaventura (Bona.1902.1), pp. 9–10, chides Venturi (1732) for labeling the construction a "miserabile similitudine" (perfectly dreadful simile) and remarks that such lighthearted moments are also to be found in the Psalms of David and in the epics of Homer and of Virgil. Cachey (Cach.1993.1), pp. 212–14, following, as he says, Longfellow, and who speaks of Dante's poetry as being playful, has learned to enjoy the poetic playfulness of vv. 1–40, so long softly ridiculed and even characterized as a result of the poet's letting us see his worst (pedantic) side. Longfellow, bringing a fellow poet's perspective to the passage, had realized that Dante is not a stuffed owl and perceived that his fellow poet is having a little fun with himself and with us: "Dante states this simple fact with curious circumlocution, as if he would imitate the celestial sphere in this *scherzoso* movement. The beginning of the day is sunrise; consequently the end of the third hour, three hours after sunrise, is represented by an arc of the celestial sphere measuring forty-five degrees. The sun had still an equal space to pass over before his setting. This would make it afternoon in Purgatory, and midnight in Tuscany, where Dante was writing the poem." For a similar time-telling passage see *Purgatorio* III.25–26 and note. Here, however, Dante underlines his ludic propensity in his first rhyme: *terza-scherza*, as though to imply that this very *tercet* is itself *playful*.

It is to Cachey's credit that he builds his treatment of the entire canto on his sense of this initial burst of "childish" enthusiasm. Exuberance is the strand that ties together many elements of the canto, from its beginning to its end, juxtaposing youthful, innocent play against older "high seriousness." The morning sun is not currently shining on the mount of purgatory but is summoned in order to begin the canto, and is then followed by a series of benign presences: Dante (both as poet and as protagonist); the Angel of Mercy; Virgil's representation of the loving souls in paradise, including Beatrice; the twelve-year-old Jesus and his mildly chastising mother; the youth who kissed the daughter of Pisistratus and this nonjudgmental father; the youthful martyr Stephen; the "drunken" protagonist. The exuberant love of God and ecstatic awareness of His presence eventually fills the canto.

7–12.   The travelers, proceeding to their right as they climbed the mountain, have now moved some 90 degrees along the circle of which it is the center. The sun, at 3 PM, is thus to the northwest as it heads west ahead of them. Where it was behind them before (*Purg.* III.16–18), it now stands directly before them, brighter than it has been, to Dante's sight, at any point yet in the poem. This excess of light will carry forward into the brightness of the ecstatic light that is soon to flood the inner eye of the protagonist.

13–15.   Poletto (1894) calls attention to the passage in *Convivio* (III.ix.10) in which Dante says that Aristotle had confuted Plato's notion that our eyesight went out from us to take cognizance of external things, arguing (correctly, adds Dante) that things that we perceive through the eyes (*lo visibile*—the noun that Dante uses here) strike upon our senses, not the senses on them. See *Inferno* X.69.

16–24.   This simile introduces a "second sun" to Dante's dazzled glance, now the reflected radiance of the angel, as seems clear from the context and despite some early commentators who believe this is the direct beam of the light of God or of the sun itself. It seems to be neither, nor indeed the direct beam of brightness from the angel of this second terrace. As the elaborate simile and the sequential description of the light make plain enough, the light bounces down, and then up, under Dante's protective hand, so that the angle of incidence is the same as the angle of reflection (\ | /), notions established, for Dante, by such authorities as Euclid and Albertus Magnus. For Dante's knowledge of the phenomenon see *Convivio* II.iii.vi (where he refers to the science of perspective, or optics) and *Paradiso* I.49–50.

28–33.   Virgil's promise that eventually Dante's eyes, as his soul becomes more fit for the task, will be able to look upon angelic radiance without turning away is fulfilled at least in *Purgatorio* XXX.10 and XXX.18, where this word for "angel," *messo* (or *messaggiero*)—"messenger," is next (and for the last time) employed (it was introduced to the poem in *Inf.* IX.85).

36.   The "stairway" to the third terrace will be less steep than those to Pride and Envy. The slowly disappearing P's on Dante's brow, the increasing lightness of his being, the increasing ease of the ascent, all these elements underline the general improvement of the penitent's moral

condition, comparable to that of a patient who has survived a crisis and now grows rapidly stronger.

38–39.   A portion of the fifth Beatitude in Matthew (5:7), "Blessèd are the merciful, for they shall obtain mercy," is here accompanied by an Italian phrase. In one later moment (on the terrace of Gluttony, *Purg.* XXIV.151–154) Dante will set the angel's recasting of one of the Beatitudes in Italian. Here he offers biblical Latin conjoined with a subsequent Italian expression. Various issues have puzzled various commentators of this somewhat surprising conjunction. (1) What biblical text do these words paraphrase? (2) Who speaks, the angel or the penitents that Dante leaves behind? (3) Are the words directed to Dante or are they some sort of general expression? (4) Why does the speaker (whoever it is who speaks) resort to Italian?

(1) Most commentators after Daniello (1568) are drawn to the subsequent text in this chapter in Matthew's gospel (5:12), Jesus's conclusion of his sermon, in which he tells those who are true to Him to "*rejoice* (*gaudete*) and be exceeding glad, for great is your reward in heaven."

In order to answer the last three questions, it is probably necessary to consider the entire program of the angelic utterances to Dante during his penitential ascent of the mountain. These moments occur as follows: *Purgatorio* XII.110–111; XV.38–39; XVII.68–69; XIX.49–50; XXII.5–6; XXIV.151–154; XXVII.8–9. In all the last five of these the text clearly and specifically attributes the words to the angel. Only the first and second are, when we first read them, opaque. Nonetheless, it is at the very least probable that the angel speaks on these first two occasions as well. We should also take note of the facts that on the sixth terrace the angel paraphrases a Beatitude in Italian rather than reciting a phrase from it in Latin (*Purg.* XXIV.151–154) and that, on the seventh, his practice is exactly as we find it here: Latin for the citation of the Beatitude, Italian for his concluding advice to Dante (*Purg.* XXVII.8–9; 10–12). And there is one further common element in the second and seventh scenes: in all the others there is specific reference to the angel's wing or feathers erasing a "P" from Dante's forehead; in these two scenes there is no such description, thus leading us to speculate that the angel's Italian utterance is probably meant to coincide with the erasure. It seems likely that here the angel speaks, addressing Dante in Italian.

40–45.   The protagonist, now freed, as we perhaps are meant to understand, from the P of Envy, is rapidly improving. It is he, and not Virgil, who insists on using the traveling time for self-improvement; he would like, in a sort of postlude to the terrace of Envy, to understand the remark of Guido del Duca (*Purg.* XIV.86–87): "O race of men, why do you set your hearts on things that of necessity cannot be shared?" The moral consequence of such affection is to envy the possessor of what one longs for but cannot have; we remember that Satan, barely created (see *Par.* XXIX.55–57), immediately was prideful against his Maker (because of his envy of His power).

46–57. Virgil's gloss on Guido's words in the last canto distinguishes earthly desires for individual possessions from heavenly enjoyment of the common good. Commentators, beginning with Pietro di Dante (1340), cite the following passage from Augustine's *City of God* (XV.v): "nullo [enim modo] fit minor, accedente seu permanente consorte, possessio bonitatis, quam tanto latius quanto concordius individua sociorum possidet charitas" ([goodness] is in no way lessened when it is shared, whether fleetingly or permanently, but grows the more the love of it spreads in others—Latin quoted from the version found in Pietro's commentary).

58–63. If Dante's will to learn is good, his capacities still flag, held back by his earthly view of riches and of the very nature of possession, which he can only conceive as selfish. In *Convivio* (III.xv.10), Dante had understood very well what his fictive self here still does not comprehend: "li santi non hanno tra loro invidia" (the saints have no envious feelings about one another). Scartazzini (1900) was perhaps the first commentator to produce this citation in this context.

67–75. Virgil's final resolution of Dante's problem insists on the centrality of love as antidote to envy. Indeed, words for love (*amore, carità, amare, ama*) occur four times within seven lines. Barolini (Baro.1992.1), note 39, p. 330, also notes the insistence on *più* (more) in vv. 55–62 (an astounding eight occurrences in eight lines, the densest presence of a single word in any passage of the poem, one might add) and here (vv. 73–74), perhaps underlining the need for the incremental conceptual refinement necessary for the redefinition of human affection toward a better end.

69. Virgil's phrasing here relies on the notion that bodies of light themselves attract light.

70.   The word *ardore* is, for Wlassics (Wlas.1989.1), p. 166, the key word of this canto, uniting the notions of flame and of affection in its main significations.

77.   Beatrice's second naming in *Purgatorio* (see VI.46; XVIII.48). In her first nominal appearance (after *Inf.* II.70 and II.103, where she is first named by Virgil and then herself), she first seems to be associated with hope (VI.32; 35); in her third, with faith (XVIII.48). Is she here associated with charity? If she is, what is the consequence for the traditional identification of Beatrice as "Revelation" or "Theology" (and of Virgil as "Reason")? (Beatrice is named sixty-three times in all in the poem; Virgil, 31.) See note to *Purgatorio* XVIII.46–48.

79–81.   The clear reference here to the erasure of the second P earlier on calls attention to the problem that Dante has set for us, to determine exactly when this happened. See note to vv. 38–39.

82–84.   Dante's failure to respond to Virgil here perhaps prepares us for his more dramatic inability to communicate with his guide at the sudden appearance of Beatrice (*Purg.* XXX.43–51). It also has the effect of underlining the totally present and commanding nature of what he experiences in his *raptus:* there is nothing else that can hold his attention.

We now probably expect, on the basis of the experience we have had of the first two terraces, a description of the terrace upon which the travelers have just set foot (*Purg.* X.20–33, XIII.1–9). Its suppression here is obviously deliberate (we will find it, postponed as it is, only at the end of the canto at vv. 139–145 and then continuing into the next canto). In this way the poet underlines the heightened importance of the visionary experience granted to the protagonist on this terrace.

85–114.   The three visions that follow are set off from the narrative by a precise vocabulary of vision, one that Dante had established as early as in his *Vita nuova* (see Hollander [Holl.1974.1], pp. 3–7). This begins at once with the verse "Ivi mi parve in una visione . . ." (There it seemed to me . . . in a . . . vision . . .). The next line adds two crucial terms, the adjective *estatica* (ecstatic) and the verb *esser tratto* (to be drawn up). These technical terms, the first of which occurs only once in the poem's universe, establish the radical difference between this visionary experience and that obtained in conventional dreams, for here what is at stake is the sort of sight that was given to such as Paul and John in the New Testament (and, as we shall see in a few lines, to St. Stephen as well).

In Dante the verb *parere* can have two quite different meanings: "seem" (thus expressing a potentially limited or even nonexistent truthfulness) or "appeared" (to indicate something perceived that is actually present). The verbs *parere* and *apparire* are used throughout this passage (vv. 85, 93, 94, 102) to indicate presences that are experienced as being in fact present to the beholder in his ecstatic seeing; this is true as well of the verb *vedere* (vv. 87, 106, 109), used each time to indicate what has truly been made manifest to the beholder.

85–86. Pietro di Dante (1340) offers the following bit of medieval etymologizing for the word "ecstasy" *(extasis)*: "ab ex, quod est extra, et stasis, quod est status, quasi extra suum statum" (from *ex*, that is, outside, and *stasis*, that is, state: as though outside oneself). The word *visïone* modified by *estatica* denotes a very special kind of seeing, one that the poem will return to only with its final vision in the Empyrean. Thus the mode of presentation of the exemplars of meekness is, within the fiction, a preparation of the protagonist for his eventual opportunity to see God "face to face." Outside the fiction, it is a test of the reader's capacity to understand the nature of Dantean poetics, reliant upon claims that are, to say the very least, unusual for a poet to make for his poem, one that will finally offer us precisely *una visïone estatica*. Here the text offers us a foretaste of that final visionary moment.

87–93. The first exemplar is, as we have learned to expect, Mary. The narrative that clearly lies behind Dante's condensation of it is found in Luke's gospel (Luke 2:40–48). Mary, Joseph, and the twelve-year-old Jesus travel to Jerusalem at Passover and then the parents leave the city. In a remarkable moment, reflected in contemporary accounts of children left behind in cars or on school buses, they assume the boy is among their traveling companions and finally, discovering that he is not, return to Jerusalem to seek him out. Three days later they find him in the temple, explaining a thing or two to the rabbis.

Jesus as young genius is so palpably present that we need to remind ourselves that he is not the exemplary figure here; that is, indeed, his mother, who scolds him as gently as a scold may scold—as any former child will testify, remembering similar encounters with sterner mothers.

94–105. The second exemplar, once again a parent, is the sixth-century B.C. Athenian tyrant Pisistratus, known to Dante in this particular, according to many commentators (perhaps beginning with Pietro di Dante [1340]), from Valerius Maximus, author of that first-century compendium of classical history and lore, *Facta et dicta memorabilia*, who tells the tale almost precisely as Dante retells it here.

Like the first of these three examplary scenes, this one also begins with the portrait of a mother. Where the parents of Jesus are united in benevolence, those of the daughter of Pisistratus are divided; this mother, reminiscent of the haughty Michal (see *Purg.* X.65 and note), leaves the performance of a loving forgiveness to her husband.

97–99.   The wife of Pisistratus refers to the myth of the naming of Athens which Pietro di Dante (1340) says derives from Augustine's retelling of the myth, found earlier in Varro, in *De civitate Dei* XVIII.9. During the kingship of Cecrops, when Athena (Minerva) and Poseidon (Neptune) both wanted to name the city, the other gods chose Athena because her gift was the olive tree, seen as more useful to humans than Poseidon's gift of a spring. Pietro also refers to the version of the tale found in Ovid (*Metam.* VI.70–102).

106–114.   The artistry of Dante's treatment of the third and final exemplar, St. Stephen, the first martyr (Acts 7:54–59), is greatly admired. Among the three narratives exemplifying meekness, this is the only one in which that meekness is found in the youthful protagonist of the exemplary tale rather than in a parent. Arnaldo Bonaventura (Bona.1902.1), p. 29, sees that the progression of figures that benefit from the forgiveness which runs counter to wrath has a purposeful order: from a beloved son, to a relative stranger, to one's enemies. Anyone would forgive the twelve-year-old Jesus his "night out" in the temple; anyone, upon reflection, should perhaps forgive the youthful flamboyance of the amorous pursuer of a king's daughter; hardly anyone would choose to forgive his murderers.

107.   The youthfulness of Dante's portrayal of Stephen (as *giovinetto*) has caused controversy, beginning with Scartazzini's (1900) objection that here Dante had fallen into a small error, since the Book of Acts portrayed Stephen as a mature man (*homo, vir*: e.g., Acts 6:5, 6:13). In Scartazzini's view, in a lapse of memory Dante had conflated the descriptions of Stephen and St. Paul, present as the youthful *(adulescentis)* Saul as a witness to the martyrdom (Acts 7:57). To this argument Poletto (1894) objects, demonstrating that in Dante adolescence lasted until one is 25, while youth included the period between 25 and 45 (*Conv.* IV.xxiv.1–3), and also pointing out that Scipio and Pompey (*Par.* VI.52) are described

as "youths" *(giovanetti)*, 33 and 25 years old, respectively, at the time of those great victories to which Dante refers. Sarolli, "Stefano" *(ED* V [1976]), is also in this camp.

108.   In Acts the words of the maddened crowd supplied here by Dante are not given. Wlassics (Wlas.1989.1), p. 170, argues that Stephen's persecutors shout to themselves, not to one another, as almost all commentators (and translators) insist. Before him Casini/Barbi (1921) do allow for this possibility, but only Mattalia (1960) had previously chosen this option. This interpretation is supported by at least one pressing consideration: in the source text (Acts 7:56) the stoners of Stephen are specifically described as, having stopped up their ears, crying out with a loud voice and rushing upon their victim. They are shouting rather to screw up their courage than to exhort one another—they are shouting as do those who charge in battle, wrestling with their fear. Our translation preserves this understanding of the verse.

111.   What is seen by "the eyes that are open to Heaven" is described in the source text in Stephen's own words (it is notable that Dante suppresses the words spoken by the protomartyr and adds those spoken by his persecutors). Here is what he says he sees (Acts 7:56): "Behold, I see the heavens opened, and the Son of Man standing at the right hand of God." It is precisely these words, reporting his vision, that cause his murderers to stop up their ears and attack him in their offended rage. In this moment in the poem, we may reflect, Dante's eyes (referred to, just before the visions begin, as *luci vaghe* [eager eyes] at verse 84) are as open to Stephen's martyrdom as Stephen's are to *his* heavenly vision.

112–114.   The final action of these exemplary protagonists of mercy is obviously the most dramatic in the program: Stephen forgiving his murderers even as they murder him. His "look" would "unlock compassion" in anyone who beheld it—perhaps even his persecutors, but surely in any decent Christian soul witnessing his martyrdom, including, just now, the protagonist.

115–138.   On each terrace there is poetic space reserved for some sort of reaction on the part of the poet or protagonist (and, at times, his guide) to the experience of exemplarity. Of the thirteen other passages devoted to these transitional moments none is even nearly as lengthy as this one, twenty-four verses; in fact only once is such a passage as long as three tercets, while this one extends over eight. It is clear that the poet wanted to direct our attention to the importance of this exchange between guide and protagonist.

Virgil's reactions give rise to a number of questions. Does or does not Virgil see the visions vouchsafed Dante? Is his response (vv. 120–123) evidence that he does *not* understand the nature of Dante's experience (as Dante seems to believe at vv. 125–126)? If a reader believes that to be the case, how does that reader respond to Virgil's insistence that he indeed knows Dante's innermost thoughts (vv. 127–138)?

The structure of the fifteenth canto is formed by three moments of Virgilian interpretation of phenomena:

10–39:   Dante cannot behold the angel: Virgil explains the nature of the problem;

40–81:   Dante did not understand Guido del Duca's words in the last canto: Virgil gives the necessary commentary, acknowledging Beatrice's higher authority;

115–138:   Dante has a series of ecstatic visions: Virgil insists on explaining that he knows very well what they involved and says that he only calls attention to Dante's condition in order to spur him on.

In the first two scenes Virgil is clearly correct and thoroughly in control of the situation; in this last sequence he does not exactly issue triumphant.

115–117.   The literal sense is not difficult: Dante was not seeing that which was present before his fleshly eyes; from that point of view (the merely physical one) he is delusional, is seeing what does not exist, seeing erroneous phantasms instead of what his physical eyes would report. But such "errors" as these are the very heart of truth, or, in an extreme case of litotes (deliberate understatement), are, at the very least, "not false." See the discussion in Barolini (Baro.1992.1), pp. 151–53.

118–123.   Virgil's first response to Dante's "awakening" back in the world of lesser truth is a bit brutal in its colloquial insistence on a less than noble cause for his condition. For Dante's apparent drunkenness see Glending Olson (Olso.1999.1), pp. 25–26. Olson addresses the relationship between these and the seemingly "drunken" words of Boniface VIII, as described by Guido da Montefeltro in *Inferno* XXVII.99. The context of Acts 2:13 is clearly present here as well: witnessing the Apostles speaking in tongues after the descent of the Holy Spirit upon them, the cynical pronounce them to be "drunk with new wine." It is interesting to see that Virgil is associated, in his response to Dante, similarly filled with the Spirit, with those who denied the action of the Holy Spirit in the Apostles (see Seem [Seem.1991.1], p. 74). Here, Seem points out that Dante's "drunken" condition, shortly after he has heard Beatrice's name (XV.77), mirrors his being "come inebriato" (as though drunk) when he first saw Beatrice, as recorded in *Vita nuova* III.

124–126.   Dante's response to Virgil intrinsically explains his physical condition as the result of his being in a state which granted him the ability to see that which, apparently, Virgil did not and could not see. If Virgil did not know this before he asked his question, he does know this much now—not what Dante saw, but the nature of his seeing: ecstatic vision. Dante here shares the iconography of another closed-eyed visionary, John the Divine; see *Purgatorio* XXIX.143–144, where John, represented as the last book of the New Testament, Revelation, is seen, like Dante here, walking in a visionary state with his eyes closed, "dormendo."

127–129.   Virgil's claim for knowledge of even the least particular of Dante's mental awareness must be taken with skepticism (see discussion of Musa's arguments in the note to vv. 134–135).

130–132.   What does Virgil know? We have some information with which to answer this question. On the terrace of Pride, Virgil and Dante found the two sets of opposing exemplars displayed in marble carvings. Having seen the first set of these, once they had seen the second they could infer something about the structure of purgation and about its symbolic landscape. As a result, once Virgil hears the voices flying overhead, representing Charity, the virtue contrasted with Envy, he immediately understands that there will be a second set of sounds before the travelers leave the terrace (see note to *Purg.* XIII.37–42). His situation here is more difficult, for he has seen nothing to indicate this terrace's mode of exemplary instruction. According to him, he reads Dante's mind. Perhaps we should view his claim with a certain dubiety. Dante speaks, announcing that he is seeing things that are not visible; as soon as Virgil connects that information with the physical signs that his "drunken" charge is exhibiting, he understands: the *exempla* on this terrace are delivered through ecstatic vision, an experience reserved for only the elect. He knows that these visions must present positive figures of the opposing virtue, precisely "to open your heart to the waters of peace," as he tells Dante. No matter who may have been present in Dante's visions to represent meekness (and even Virgil may have by now divined that Mary will be the first of these), the meaning of the exemplars here will always be the same: to pour the water of peace upon the fires of wrath in the heart.

133–135. Bosco/Reggio (1979) are undoubtedly correct in suggesting that the debate in the commentaries over the literal sense of these verses is less than convincing and go on to plead that in these verses Dante uses "an imprecise expression." Salsano (Sals.1967.1), pp. 568–70, reflects upon the debate as it came into his time. Cachey (Cach.1993.1), pp. 222–23, offers a more up-to-date review of various interpretations. The only interpretation, however, that seems to offer a clear understanding of the difficult passage is one based on a comprehension of the tensions that exist here between the protagonist and his guide. Such a reading has been put forward by Lauren Seem (Seem.1991.1), who argues that what is at stake is Virgil's attempt to show that he has indeed known the nature of Dante's vision, that he did not think Dante was merely "drunk." And thus we can understand what he says as follows: "I did not ask what was wrong with you because you were having a vision—of course, I understood that—but only because it was now time to get you back on the track." As Musa has pointed out (see notes to *Inf.* XVI.115 and XXIII.25), there is no evidence in the poem, despite Virgil's claim in *Inferno* XXIII (repeated here), that he actually can read the protagonist's mind—a capacity reserved for Beatrice and the other saved souls who interview Dante in the heavens. Our reading of the entire passage eventually depends on whether we accept Virgil's protestations here or question them. For a step-by-step analysis of the difficult details that have so afflicted the commentators, see Seem (Seem.1991.1), pp. 75–80.

139–145. The description of this terrace, postponed from its expected space (see note to vv. 82–84), begins now, as we first perceive the black smoke of anger that will cover the travelers and the penitents for the entirety of the following canto, the darkest part of *Purgatorio*.

PURGATORIO XVI
(Wrath)

Buio d'inferno e di notte privata
d'ogne pianeto, sotto pover cielo,
3   quant' esser può di nuvol tenebrata,

non fece al viso mio sì grosso velo
come quel fummo ch'ivi ci coperse,
6   né a sentir di così aspro pelo,

che l'occhio stare aperto non sofferse;
onde la scorta mia saputa e fida
9   mi s'accostò e l'omero m'offerse.

Sì come cieco va dietro a sua guida
per non smarrirsi e per non dar di cozzo
12   in cosa che 'l molesti, o forse ancida,

m'andava io per l'aere amaro e sozzo,
ascoltando il mio duca che diceva
15   pur: "Guarda che da me tu non sia mozzo."

Io sentia voci, e ciascuna pareva
pregar per pace e per misericordia
18   l'Agnel di Dio che le peccata leva.

Pur *"Agnus Dei"* eran le loro essordia;
una parola in tutte era e un modo,
21   sì che parea tra esse ogne concordia.

"Quei sono spirti, maestro, ch'i' odo?"
diss' io. Ed elli a me: "Tu vero apprendi,
24   e d'iracundia van solvendo il nodo.

"Or tu chi se' che 'l nostro fummo fendi,
e di noi parli pur come se tue
27   partissi ancor lo tempo per calendi?"

Gloom of hell or of a night deprived
of all the stars, beneath a barren sky
which everywhere was overcast with clouds,

3

had never put so dark a veil across my eyes
or been so harsh and stinging to my sight
as was the smoke that covered us

6

so that I could not keep my eyelids open.
And then my wise and trusted escort
came up and offered me his shoulder.

9

Just as the blind man walks behind his guide
so that he does not stray or strike against
something that might hurt or even kill him,

12

thus did I move through that foul, bitter air
and listened to my leader, who kept urging:
'Make sure that you are not cut off from me.'

15

I heard voices and each one seemed to pray
for peace and mercy to the Lamb of God
who bears away our sins.

18

They all began with *Agnus Dei,*
and with one voice and intonation sang the words
so that they seemed to share complete accord.

21

I asked, 'Master, are these spirits that I hear?'
And he: 'You have it right. Here they undo
the knot that was their wrath.'

24

'But who are you that cleave our smoke?
You speak of us as though, even now,
you measured time in months and days,'

27

Così per una voce detto fue;
onde 'l maestro mio disse: "Rispondi,
30   e domanda se quinci si va sùe."

E io: "O creatura che ti mondi
per tornar bella a colui che ti fece,
33   maraviglia udirai, se mi secondi."

"Io ti seguiterò quanto mi lece,"
rispuose; "e se veder fummo non lascia
36   l'udir ci terrà giunti in quella vece."

Allora incominciai: "Con quella fascia
che la morte dissolve men vo suso,
39   e venni qui per l'infernale ambascia.

E se Dio m'ha in sua grazia rinchiuso,
tanto che vuol ch'i' veggia la sua corte
42   per modo tutto fuor del moderno uso,

non mi celar chi fosti anzi la morte,
ma dilmi, e dimmi s'i' vo bene al varco;
45   e tue parole fier le nostre scorte."

"Lombardo fui, e fu' chiamato Marco;
del mondo seppi, e quel valore amai
48   al quale ha or ciascun disteso l'arco.

Per montar sù dirittamente vai."
Così rispuose, e soggiunse: "I' ti prego
51   che per me prieghi quando sù sarai."

E io a lui: "Per fede mi ti lego
di far ciò che mi chiedi; ma io scoppio
54   dentro ad un dubbio, s'io non me ne spiego.

Prima era scempio, e ora è fatto doppio
ne la sentenza tua, che mi fa certo
57   qui, e altrove, quello ov' io l'accoppio.

I heard a voice say.
Then my master urged: 'Answer him,
30   and ask him if the way goes up from here.'

And I: 'O creature who purify yourself
to return in beauty to the One who made you,
33   you'll hear a wondrous story if you follow me.'

'I will follow as far as is permitted,'
he said, 'and if the smoke denies us sight,
36   hearing will keep us joined instead.'

And I began: 'With the very swaddling clothes
that death unwinds I make my way above,
39   and I have come through agony of hell.

'Since God has so received me in His grace
that He has willed that I shall see His court
42   in ways unknown to modern custom,

'do not conceal from me the life you led
before you died: tell it, and tell me if I'm headed
45   for the passage—your words shall be our escort.'

'I was a Lombard, known as Marco.
I knew the world and loved that valor
48   at which today all aim a slackened bow.

'You are on the path that leads you up.'
Thus he replied, then added: 'I pray you,
51   say a prayer for me once you are above.'

And I to him: 'I pledge to do your bidding.
But I will burst with my unspoken doubts
54   if I don't speak and free myself of them.

'A single doubt before, it is now paired
by what you said, which here confirms
57   what elsewhere I have heard, to which I couple it.

Lo mondo è ben così tutto diserto
d'ogne virtute, come tu mi sone,
60   e di malizia gravido e coverto;

ma priego che m'addite la cagione,
sì ch'i' la veggia e ch'i' la mostri altrui;
63   ché nel cielo uno, e un qua giù la pone."

Alto sospir, che duolo strinse in "uhi!"
mise fuor prima; e poi cominciò: "Frate,
66   lo mondo è cieco, e tu vien ben da lui.

Voi che vivete ogne cagion recate
pur suso al cielo, pur come se tutto
69   movesse seco di necessitate.

Se così fosse, in voi fora distrutto
libero arbitrio, e non fora giustizia
72   per ben letizia, e per male aver lutto.

Lo cielo i vostri movimenti inizia;
non dico tutti, ma, posto ch'i' 'l dica,
75   lume v'è dato a bene e a malizia,

e libero voler; che, se fatica
ne le prime battaglie col ciel dura,
78   poi vince tutto, se ben si notrica.

A maggior forza e a miglior natura
liberi soggiacete; e quella cria
81   la mente in voi, che 'l ciel non ha in sua cura.

Però, se 'l mondo presente disvia,
in voi è la cagione, in voi si cheggia;
84   e io te ne sarò or vera spia.

Esce di mano a lui che la vagheggia
prima che sia, a guisa di fanciulla
87   che piangendo a ridendo pargoleggia,

'The world is barren now
of every virtue, as you state,
60   and heavy with and overgrown by evil.

'Please point out to me the cause
that I may know it and make it known to others,
63   for both the heavens and the earth receive the blame.'

First he heaved a heavy sigh, which grief wrung
to a groan, and then began: 'Brother,
66   the world is blind and indeed you come from it. *discourse on free will*

'You who are still alive assign each cause
only to the heavens, as though they drew
69   all things along upon their necessary paths.

'If that were so, free choice would be denied you,
and there would be no justice when one feels
72   joy for doing good or misery for evil.

'Yes, the heavens give motion to your inclinations.
I don't say all of them, but, even if I did,
75   you still possess a light to winnow good from evil,

'and you have free will. Should it bear the strain
in its first struggles with the heavens,
78   then, rightly nurtured, it will conquer all. *habit-uation*

'To a greater power and a better nature you, free,
are subject, and these create the mind in you
81   that the heavens do not have in charge.

'Therefore, if the world around you goes astray,
in you is the cause and in you let it be sought.
84   In this I will now be your informant.

'From the hand of Him who looks on it with love
before it lives, comes forth, like a little girl
87   who weeps one moment and as quickly laughs,

l'anima semplicetta che sa nulla,
salvo che, mossa da lieto fattore,
90   volontier torna a ciò che la trastulla.

Di picciol bene in pria sente sapore;
quivi s'inganna, e dietro ad esso corre,
93   se guida o fren non torce suo amore.

Onde convenne legge per fren porre;
convenne rege aver, che discernesse
96   de la vera cittade almen la torre.

Le leggi son, ma chi pon mano ad esse?
Nullo, però che 'l pastor che procede,
99   rugumar può, ma non ha l'unghie fesse;

per che la gente, che sua guida vede
pur a quel ben fedire ond' ella è ghiotta,
102   di quel si pasce, e più oltre non chiede.

Ben puoi veder che la mala condotta
è la cagion che 'l mondo ha fatto reo,
105   e non natura che 'n voi sia corrotta.

Soleva Roma, che 'l buon mondo feo,
due soli aver, che l'una e l'altra strada
108   facean vedere, e del mondo e di Deo.

L'un l'altro ha spento; ed è giunta la spada
col pasturale, e l'un con l'altro insieme
111   per viva forza mal convien che vada;

però che, giunti, l'un l'altro non teme:
se non mi credi, pon mente a la spiga,
114   ch'ogn' erba si conosce per lo seme.

In sul paese ch'Adice e Po riga,
solea valore e cortesia trovarsi,
117   prima che Federigo avesse briga;

'the simple infant soul that has no knowledge
but, moved by a joyous maker,
90   gladly turns to what delights it.

'At first it tastes the savor of a trifling good.
It is beguiled by that and follows in pursuit
93   if guide or rein do not deflect its love.

'Therefore, there was need that laws be set
to act as curbs, need for a ruler to discern
96   at least the tower above the one true city.

'Yes, there are laws, but who takes them in hand?
No one, because the shepherd who precedes
99   may chew his cud, but does not have cleft hooves.

'The people, then, who see their leader lunge
only at the good for which they themselves are greedy,
102   graze on that and ask for nothing more.

'As you can plainly see, failed guidance
is the cause the world is steeped in vice,
105   and not your inner nature that has grown corrupt.

'Rome, which formed the world for good,
once had two suns that lit the one road
108   and the other, the world's and that to God.

'The one has snuffed the other out, the sword
is fastened to the crook, and these two,
111   forced to be together, must perforce go ill,

'since, joined, the one fears not the other.
If you don't believe me, think of a grain of wheat,
114   for by its seed each plant is known.

'In the land watered both by the Àdige and Po
valor and courtesy could once be found
117   before Frederick encountered opposition.

or può sicuramente indi passarsi
per qualunque lasciasse, per vergogna,
120   di ragionar coi buoni o d'appressarsi.

Ben v'èn tre vecchi ancora in cui rampogna
l'antica età la nova, e par lor tardo
123   che Dio a miglior vita li ripogna:

Currado da Palazzo e 'l buon Gherardo
e Guido da Castel, che mei si noma,
126   francescamente, il semplice Lombardo.

Dì oggimai che la Chiesa di Roma,
per confondere in sé due reggimenti,
129   cade nel fango, e sé brutta e la soma."

"O Marco mio," diss' io, "bene argomenti;
e or discerno perché dal retaggio
132   li figli di Levì furono essenti.

Ma qual Gherardo è quel che tu per saggio
di' ch'è rimaso de la gente spenta,
135   in rimprovèro del secol selvaggio?"

"O tuo parlar m'inganna, o el mi tenta,"
rispuose a me; "ché parlandomi tosco,
138   par che del buon Gherardo nulla senta.

Per altro sopranome io nol conosco,
s'io nol togliessi da sua figlia Gaia.
141   Dio sia con voi, ché più non vegno vosco.

Vedi l'albor che per lo fummo raia
già biancheggiare, e me convien partirmi
(l'angelo è ivi) prima ch'io li paia."
145   Così tornò, e più non volle udirmi.

'Now it may with impunity be crossed by anyone
who for shame would shun all discourse
120   with the virtuous or even coming near them.

'Three old men are left on earth,
longing for the better life when God will take them,
123   in whom the ancient times rebuke the new:

'Currado da Palazzo and the good Gherardo
and Guido da Castel, better called,
126   as say the French, the simple, honest Lombard.

'Spread the word, then, that the Church of Rome,
confounding in herself two governments, stumbles
129   in the mud, befouling herself and her burden.'

'O Marco mine,' I said, 'you reason well,
and now I understand just why the sons of Levi
132   were disbarred from their inheritance.

'But who is this Gherardo who, you say,
is left as an example of a race extinct,
135   thus rebuking this barbaric age?'

'Either your speech deceives me,' he replied,
'or it puts me to the test, for, speaking Tuscan,
138   how is it you know nothing of the good Gherardo?

'I know him by no other name unless
I were to take one from his daughter, Gaia.
141   May God be with you. I come with you no farther.

'You see the brightness shining through the smoke
already whitens, and I must take my leave
before the angel waiting there can see me.'
145   Then he turned back and would not hear me more.

1–7. This fiftieth canto of the *Divina Commedia* is literally its darkest; light finally glimmers only two lines from its conclusion (in verse 143) and its action is played completely in the smoke of Wrath. Technically, the numerical midpoint of the poem occurs between Cantos XVI and XVII, the latter of which also happens to be the middle canto of *Purgatorio*. Thus, as the poet prepares the entire poem and the *cantica* to reach their centers, it seems fitting that he first indicates the *Comedy*'s origin in hell: *Buio d'inferno* (Gloom of hell).

The sky is "barren" (literally "poor," or "impoverished") in that it is "deprived of its precious jewels," its stars (according to Benvenuto da Imola, mainly found in the eighth sphere but with one "planet" found in each of the first seven), are hidden behind layers of clouds.

The envious are made to repent by being denied their sight; the wrathful are being denied objects of sight because they were blinded by their anger for their enemies.

8–9. It seems that here Virgil has the power of sight, while the protagonist, like the penitents soon to be present, is effectively blind in the smoke. Is this a deliberate recasting of the situation in *Purgatorio* XV.115–138, where Dante can behold the ecstatic visions apparently denied to Virgil? Once again, Virgil's state would be marked off as different from that of saved souls.

The smoke that expresses the sin of Wrath on this terrace is referred to five times (XV.142; XVI.5, 25, 35, 142) and marks the last time in the poem that the noun *fummo* is used to describe a place. It clearly seems to be related to the smoke that marked the Circle of Anger in Inferno, where it is used three times, once (*Inf.* IX.75) with an adjective, *acerbo* (harsh), that seems to join it to the smoke we enter here. For the relationship between infernal anger and the purgation of Wrath see the note to *Purgatorio* XVII.19–39.

10–15. The simile presents an image of Dante walking behind Virgil with his hand upon the shoulder of his guide, otherwise present to him only as a voice. The image prepares us for what will happen once Marco Lombardo is his interlocutor: all he (and we) will be aware of is a voice, close to an ideal situation for a poet to contrive in order to gain undeflected attention on behalf of a presentation of moral philosophy.

19–21. We are presumably meant to understand that *all* the penitents pray on each of the previous terraces (see *Purg.* XI.1–24; *Purg.* XIII.49–51) and on this one as well. The pattern of communal liturgical prayer will be broken, for good reason, only by the slothful: *Purgatorio* XVIII.103–105.

Fallani (1965) discusses the prayer, instituted as part of the Mass by Pope Sergius I in the seventh century, comprised, once it became a part of the liturgy, of a single line that is then twice repeated: "Agnus Dei, qui tollis peccata mundi, miserere nobis" (Lamb of God who carry off the sins of the world, have mercy on us); in the third iteration the last phrase ("miserere nobis") gives place to the words "dona nobis pacem" (grant us peace), a particularly apt phrase for these penitents of Wrath, beseeching the serenity to which Virgil referred in *Purgatorio* XV.131, "the waters of peace."

25–27. The speaker can sense that the visitor is moving the smoke that he walks through and thus must be present in the flesh; for this reason, as he correctly assumes, the new arrival is still timebound. The souls on the mountain have their own temporality, but one in which all of time is but a necessary prolegomenon to eternity, when real life begins for them. Thus for them the months of the calendar are real but meaningless.

31–36. Dante's *captatio*, his attempt to gain his listener's goodwill (see note to *Inf.* II.58), celebrates the as yet unknown speaker's freedom from the flesh; his (rational) soul will soon be as it was when God breathed it into him (see *Purg.* XXV.70–75). The protagonist goes on to offer, in good rhetorical fashion, a reward for his auditor's collaboration. His insistence that this spirit follow him is predicated upon necessity: Dante's eyes are closed because his mortal flesh cannot bear the harshness of the smoke, with the result that he cannot see his interlocutor. The spirit, unlike Virgil, evidently cannot see in the darkness and therefore is only able to follow Dante's voice.

37–38. The image of the flesh as swaddling clothes, the protective cloth in which infants are wrapped, places emphasis on the soul as being the precious part of us, our bodies merely the wrapping that should keep it until it is ready for its better life.

41–42. This is the rather coy way that Dante refers to St. Paul's ascent to Heaven (II Corinthians 12:4) as being the last before his own. For

Dante, that somewhat strange word ("modern") is not a positive one. (The *Grande Dizionario* [Batt.1961.1] indicates this as the first recorded use of the word in Italian.) For Dante, in the battle between ancients and moderns, at least when it is waged on moral grounds, ancients are better. For the three subsequent uses of the word see *Purgatorio* XXVI.113, *Paradiso* XVI.33, *Paradiso* XXI.131.

46.   Marco the Lombard: to the many previous attempts to identify Marco (see Singleton's commentary) we must now add that of Giorgio Cracco (Crac.1984.1), who points out that a Venetian living in Lombardy wrote, ca. 1292, a (still unpublished) chronicle of the provinces of Venice. He names himself simply as "Marco" and his text contains a number of concerns and phrases that coincide with Dante's. That Dante allows him as limited identification as he does may indicate that he felt Marco's fame was great enough that his Christian name alone was sufficient to identify him.

47–48.   Marco's words make him seem a perfect courtier: worldly, but a lover of the good, and a user of soldier's language (that of bowmanship). Poletto (1894) also points out that his qualities would seem to mirror those of Ulysses—or at least those that Ulysses lends himself, his "fervor . . . to gain experience of the world and learn about man's vices, and his worth" (*Inf.* XXVI.97–99).

51.   Strangely enough, some commentators have taken the adverbial preposition *sù* ("above") to refer to the world at the antipodes (e.g., John of Serravalle [1416]) and one (Tommaseo [1837]), to the earthly paradise. However, it seems unmistakably clear that Marco, having learned of Dante's destination (verse 41), is the first spirit to ask him to pray for him once he is in Heaven. This request might seem to imply either that he is of a particularly holy disposition or that he believes that no one on earth whom Dante might meet loves anything that transcends the earthly (verse 48). But see Guido Guinizzelli's similar request (*Purg.* XXVI.127–130).

53–63.   Dante is bursting with a doubt, now made double by Marco's words: if the world is so thoroughly evil, wherein lies the cause? Dante wants to be informed so that he may pass the knowledge on to others, some of whom believe the cause is found on earth, while others think it is situated in the heavens. Is his doubt now "double" because he has heard from Guido del Duca (XIV.37–42) that all in the valley of the Arno flee virtue? That is Benvenuto's (1380) reasonable hypothesis, one that has many followers. Wanting to know the "cause" of evil (and his word, *malizia* [malice], is the word used in *Inf.* XI.22 to define the sins of the hardened will [see note to *Inf.* XI.22–27], those punished within the City of Dis), the protagonist triggers the heaviest use of this noun *(cagione)* in the poem; it occurs four times in forty-four lines, at vv. 61, 67, 83, and 104, thus underlining the centrality of this concern, to understand the root of human sinfulness, essential to the understanding of the concept of free will, as the next passage (Marco's rejoinder) and the next canto, when Virgil discourses on the nature of love, will both make plain.

64–66. Marco's earlier view of human depravity is obviously now deepened by the knowledge that most humans are not very bright, either, if even this specially selected mortal can ask such a stupid question.

67–129. Marco's speech, the only object of possible attention in the darkness, twenty-one *terzine* of moral philosophy, may be paraphrased as follows: If the heavens moved all things, there would be no free will; even if they did, you would still have the power to resist and conquer (67–78); to a greater power and better nature than the celestial heavens you, free, are subject, and that creates the mind [the rational soul] in you, which has nothing to do with those revolving spheres (79–83); let me expand: God lovingly created the (rational) soul in each of you; at its birth, since it was made by Him, even if it is a tabula rasa, it loves; and it loves anything at all if it is not guided or restrained; therefore, a leader and laws are necessary (84–96); laws exist, but who administers them? no one, because the pope is involved in temporal affairs and thus gives the wrong example that is much imitated (97–102); thus you can see that bad guidance and not corrupt human nature accounts for the wickedness of the world; Rome, which once made the world good, used then to have two suns which lit each path, secular and sacred (103–108); now, since the regal and pastoral functions have been conjoined, ill ensues—by their fruits shall you know them (109–114); in northern Italy, which once was the home of courtesy and valor before the Church opposed Frederick II, there are now but three good men, all of them old (115–126); thus you must make it known that the Church of Rome is befouled and befouling, arrogating unto itself both governments (127–129).

67–78. Marco's immediate and angry response (but his anger is meant to be taken as virtuous, as the righteous indignation of the just) lays the issue bare. "The fault is in the stars" was an earlier day's way of claiming "the dog [or computer] ate my homework" or "the devil made me do it." The celestial spheres, forming our tendencies, do incline us to various sensuous and sensual activities, but we are not forced to follow our appetites, since we have our will to direct our appetites. The concept of free will does not receive its full exposition until Beatrice's discourse upon it in *Paradiso* V.19–84, a moment marked by heavy seriousness because this concept lies at the very core of any Christian moral assertion. In Platonic (and Aristotelian) terms, our sensitive soul, which responds to such stimuli, is (or should be) governed by our rational soul.

79–81.   The great Christian paradox of our free submission to God's will stands before the reader here. Singleton (1973) suggests the relevance of Jesus' reference to himself as a yoke to be borne by his followers (Matthew 11:29) and Dante's own paradoxical formulation, "iugum libertatis" (the yoke of liberty) in his epistle (*Epist.* VI.5) to the Florentines who were in opposition to the emperor (Henry VII) in the autumn of 1310. God, the greater force and better nature, creates the third (rational) soul in us; it is *not* bound by celestial influences.

82–84.   Concluding the grand design of his argument, Marco triumphantly puts forward his *ergo*: any fault that we find when we examine human activity lies in us, not in our stars. And now he will expatiate on this paradigmatic equation.

85–90.   The image of the female child (its gender matching that of the word *anima* [soul]) heedless in her playfulness picks up the train of such images of youthful ebullience from the last canto, where the sun was disporting himself like a little boy (see note to *Purg.* XV.1–6). The rational soul, as yet unknowing, turns to anything that delights it without measuring the worth of that delight.

91–93.   This "ladder" of physically attractive objects, beginning with trifling goods, was earlier described by Dante in *Convivio* IV.xii.14–18, as was apparently first noted by Scartazzini (1900), when we begin, as children, longing for an apple, a little bird, pretty garments, then a horse, a mistress, riches, then greater riches, and finally enormous wealth. So does the corrupt human soul move from childhood to its "maturity"— unless such appetites are controlled.

94–96.   The "ruler" that Marco (not to mention Dante) seems to have in mind would not appear to be anything but secular. Some commentators recognize how radical an idea this is, while several of them (e.g., Benvenuto, Lombardi) simply assume that Dante must here be speaking of a religious leader. But the language is clear: the poet here is speaking of an emperor who, guiding our race as its leader (the *guida* [guide] of verse 93) and upholding the laws (the *fren* [rein] of that verse), will allow us to see at least the tower of the "true city." The question of whether this is meant to be understood as the City of God on earth or in Heaven, or indeed of an ideal secular city, draws some dispute. Whatever the solution of that part of the riddle, the forceful and (at least potentially) disturbing fact is that Dante, in search of moral leadership for mankind (rather than for individual humans), here looks to the state rather than to the Church.

97–99.   This tercet explains the vigorous and unusual Ghibelline turn in the preceding verses. The laws, left us by Justinian, exist but are not enforced. And this blame is laid upon the Church for keeping the emperor from power, since the pope may indeed ruminate, but does not distinguish between ecclesiastical and secular power. Tozer (1901) explains the reference as follows: "The terms here used refer to the tests by which beasts were determined to be clean under the Mosaic law, i.e., that they should chew the cud and divide the hoof (Leviticus 11:3). As applied to the Heads of the Church, the allegorical meaning of 'chewing the cud' seems to be the acquisition of wisdom by pondering on sources of knowledge; but in respect of 'dividing the hoof' the symbolism is twofold. . . . First, it signifies the practice of good morals, . . . and it is applied in this sense in vv. 100–105, where it is explained that it was the unprincipled conduct of the Roman Court which had demoralized the world. Secondly, the dividing of the hoof represents the separation of the temporal and spiritual powers, which principle the popes had ignored. This interpretation is found in vv. 127–129, where the Church of Rome is spoken of as a beast of burden, which falls in the mud in consequence of its not distinguishing between these two spheres of government, the reference obviously being to the support given to such animals in slippery ground by the divided hoof. The two allegorical applications are not wholly unconnected with one another, because it was greed of worldly gains which led to the appropriation of the temporal power by the Papacy."

100–102.   The reason that Dante here hopes only for temporal moral leadership is now completely clear: the current papacy leads mankind only in the example of unbridled appetite. Thus the Church, which is not to interfere with the City of Man on Earth (Augustine's negative phrase turned to a Dantean positive), cannot show the way to the City of God, either, and that task is turned over, in Dante's asseverations here, to the emperor. It is perhaps impossible to believe that he would have written such lines without having Henry VII in mind as the one who must accomplish these tasks of leadership. If Dante is writing between 1310 and 1313, it is more than likely that he did.

106–108.   The culminating image in Marco's discourse returns to the "good old days" when the early Church and the empire each performed their functions separately.

Dante is here, within the confines of a single tercet, entering polemically into one of the great political/theological debates of his time, the relative authority of emperor and pope. Against the hierocrats, who warmly supported papal claims to supremacy, Dante argues, on the basis of a revision in the hierocrats' central and polemical metaphor (pope as "sun," emperor as subordinate "moon"), that the two authorities are both supreme and have their authority independent of one another, both being established by the direct will of God. Singleton (1973) remembers, in this context, Dante's earlier and later precisions (*Conv.* IV.v.3–8; *Mon.* I.xvi.1–2) that when Christ was born under the rule of Augustus the world experienced a moment of perfection, what St. Paul calls *plenitudinem temporis* ("the fullness of time"—Galatians 4:4). Dante will later develop the metaphor of the "two suns" in a key chapter of *Monarchia* (III.iv). (For the date of *Monarchia* see the brief summary of the debate in Hollander [Holl.2001.1], pp. 150–51. Most currently interested in the problem believe that the work was composed ca. 1317, i.e., after the death of Henry VII, and after Dante had composed the early cantos of his *Paradiso*, since in *Monarchia* I.xii.6 he says "sicut in Paradiso Comoedie iam dixi" [as I have said in the *Paradiso* of my *Comedy*], referring to *Paradiso* V.19–24.)

On the entire subject of the authority of the emperor see the still essential work of Ernst Kantorowicz (Kant.1957.1).

109–114.   Dante laments the fact that now the Church's pastoral crook has taken into itself the imperial sword; his image, though of inanimate things, makes the resultant object seem a horrific animate hybrid, as does the reference to Matthew 7:16 or 7:20: "by their fruits you shall know them" (words spoken by Jesus to impugn false teachers).

115–120.   Dante's geographical reference is to the northeastern sector of Italy, not the territories associated with the presence of the emperor

Frederick, but Marco's home ground. For Dante, Frederick was the last emperor to take his role as emperor of all Europe seriously (see *Conv.* IV.iii.6, as Pietrobono [1946] suggests, where he is described as "the last emperor of the Romans"). It may seem strange that Dante should here support the kingship of Frederick II, seen among the heretics in hell (*Inf.* X.119). The issue, however, is not Frederick's personal worth, but his rights and privileges as emperor. These were grounds for contention between Frederick and the Church throughout his reign (1212–50).

121–126. Marco's three *vecchi*, all still alive in 1300, offer a Lombard counterpart to Cacciaguida's forty or so Florentine families from the "good old days" in that city that are listed in *Paradiso* XVI: Currado da Palazzo, from Brescia; Gherardo da Camino, from Padua; and Guido da Castello, from Reggio Emilia. All three of them had Guelph affiliations. Dante praises the last two in *Convivio* when he is discussing true nobility (*Conv.* IV.xiv.12; IV.xvi.6).

127–129. Marco's antipapal charge to Dante will be echoed and amplified in that given him by Beatrice in *Purgatorio* XXXII.103–105.

131–132. Dante shows his agreement with Marco's analysis of the church/state problem in contemporary Christendom in ancient Hebrew terms: the family of Levi, because they were, like the sons of Aaron, in a priestly function for Israel, were denied any right to inherit land because of their priestly privileges. See Numbers 18:20–32.

133–140. The protagonist's ignorance of Gherardo's virtues offers Marco (and the poet) a chance to replay the theme of the moment, that things are not what they used to be. The early commentators are uncertain whether or not the mention of Gaia is meant to be to her praise or blame. Jacopo della Lana (1324) and Benvenuto say she was well known as a loose woman. However, Benvenuto's self-proclaimed student, John of Serravalle (1416), who generally supports his *maestro*'s opinions, has only good to speak of her (and even claims that she wrote vernacular poetry). Most modern commentators argue that, since the argument at hand is that the old times bore at least some notable virtue while the present day is lacking in that respect, it would only make sense for Gaia's name to represent a descent from virtue. As several commentators suggest, until such time as some clearer evidence for Dante's opinion of Gaia is unearthed, it is impossible to be sure of the tone of the reference, wholehearted or ironic. The only two other uses of the word *gaio* (joyful)

in the poem are, however, totally positive: see *Paradiso* XV.60 and
XXVI.102.

141–145. Having walked through the smoke, they have now reached its
"edge," and so may soon regain the light of the sun. Thus we learn that
Marco and his colleagues, in repenting Wrath, all must measure their
pace so as not to walk either too slowly or too quickly in the smoke,
which is moving clockwise along the terrace. The smoke does not come
upon them, as it did Dante and Virgil; they inhabit it. Marco now re-
treats from the light, having walked too quickly in order to keep pace
with his new companions.

PURGATORIO XVII
(Wrath and Sloth)

Virgil's "Digression"

Ricorditi, lettor, se mai ne l'alpe
ti colse nebbia per la qual vedessi
3   non altrimenti che per pelle talpe,

come, quando i vapori umidi e spessi
a diradar cominciansi, la spera
6   del sol debilemente entra per essi;

e fia la tua imagine leggera
in giugnere a veder com' io rividi
9   lo sole in pria, che già nel corcar era.

Sì, pareggiando i miei co' passi fidi
del mio maestro, usci' fuor di tal nube
12   ai raggi morti già ne' bassi lidi.

O imaginativa che ne rube
talvolta sì di fuor, ch'om non s'accorge
15   perché dintorno suonin mille tube,

chi move te, se 'l senso non ti porge?
Moveti lume che nel ciel s'informa,
18   per sé o per voler che giù lo scorge.

De l'empiezza di lei che mutò forma
ne l'uccel ch'a cantar più si diletta,
21   ne l'imagine mia apparve l'orma;

e qui fu la mia mente sì ristretta
dentro da sé, che di fuor non venìa
24   cosa che fosse allor da lei ricetta.

Poi piovve dentro a l'alta fantasia
un crucifisso, dispettoso e fero
27   ne la sua vista, e cotal si moria;

Remember, reader, if ever in the mountains
you were trapped in fog and could not see
except as moles do, through their eyelids,

how, when the strands of mist, humid and dense,
began dispersing, the sun's disk
dimly glimmered through,

then you can readily imagine
how, on my seeing it again, the sun appeared,
now on the verge of setting.

Measuring my steps to the trusted steps
of my master, I came out of that haze
to beams already vanished from the shores below.

O imagination, which at times so robs us
of outward things we pay no heed,
though a thousand trumpets sound around us,

who sets you into motion if the senses offer
nothing? A light, formed in the heavens, moves you
either of itself or by a will that sends it down.

Of the impious deed of her whose shape was changed
into the bird that most delights to sing
a picture formed in my imagination.

At this my mind had so withdrawn into itself
there was no impulse from outside
that could impinge upon my senses.

Then there rained down into my lofty phantasy
one fastened to a cross, scornful
and fierce in looks, and in his death.

intorno ad esso era il grande Assüero,
Estèr sua sposa e 'l giusto Mardoceo,
30   che fu al dire e al far così intero.

E come questa imagine rompeo
sé per sé stessa, a guisa d'una bulla
33   cui manca l'acqua sotto qual si feo,

surse in mia visïone una fanciulla
piangendo forte, e dicea: "O regina,
36   perché per ira hai voluto esser nulla?

Ancisa t'hai per non perder Lavina;
or m'hai perduta! Io son essa che lutto,
39   madre, a la tua pria ch'a l'altrui ruina."

Come si frange il sonno ove di butto
nova luce percuote il viso chiuso,
42   che fratto guizza pria che muoia tutto;

così l'imaginar mio cadde giuso
tosto che lume il volto mi percosse,
45   maggior assai che quel ch'è in nostro uso.

I' mi volgea per veder ov' io fosse,
quando una voce disse "Qui si monta,"
48   che da ogne altro intento mi rimosse;

e fece la mia voglia tanto pronta
di riguardar chi era che parlava,
51   che mai non posa, se non si raffronta.

Ma come al sol che nostra vista grava
e per soverchio sua figura vela,
54   così la mia virtù quivi mancava.

"Questo è divino spirito, che ne la
via da ir sù ne drizza sanza prego,
57   e col suo lume sé medesmo cela.

With him were Ahasuerus, the great king,
Esther, his wife, and Mordecai the just,
30   so upright in his words and deeds.

And when this image broke up of itself,
just as a bubble does when it floats up
33   above the water from which it takes its form,

in my vision there arose a girl.
She was weeping bitterly, crying: 'O Queen,
36   why, in your anger, have you chosen not to be?

'Not to lose Lavinia have you killed yourself.
Now you have lost me and I am left to mourn
39   your death, mother, before the death of yet another.'

As sleep is broken when a sudden light
strikes on closed eyes and, broken,
42   flickers before it dies,

so my imaginings grew faint within me
as soon as a light, far brighter
45   than the light we know, struck my face.

I was turning to discover where I was
when a voice said: 'Here is your ascent,'
48   and drew me away from any other thought.

It raised in me the overwhelming wish—
a wish that cannot rest short of its goal—
51   to behold the one who spoke.

But as before the sun, which weighs upon our eyes,
veiling its form in an excess of light,
54   so, before him, my power of sight fell short.

'This divine spirit is directing us
toward the ascent without our even asking,
57   concealed in his own shining.

Sì fa con noi, come l'uom si fa sego;
ché quale aspetta prego e l'uopo vede,
60   malignamente già si mette al nego.

Or accordiamo a tanto invito il piede
procacciam di salir pria che s'abbui,
63   ché poi non si poria, se 'l dì non riede."

Così disse il mio duca, e io con lui
volgemmo i nostri passi ad una scala;
66   e tosto ch'io al primo grado fui,

senti'mi presso quasi un muover d'ala
e ventarmi nel viso e dir: "*Beati
69   pacifici*, che son sanz' ira mala!"

Già eran sovra noi tanto levati
li ultimi raggi che la notte segue,
72   che le stelle apparivan da più lati.

"O virtù mia, perché sì ti dilegue?"
fra me stesso dicea, ché mi sentiva
75   la possa de le gambe posta in triegue.

Noi eravam dove più non saliva
la scala sù, ed eravamo affissi,
78   pur come nave ch'a la piaggia arriva.

E io attesi un poco, s'io udissi
alcuna cosa nel novo girone;
81   poi mi volsi al maestro mio, e dissi:

"Dolce mio padre, dì, quale offensione
si purga qui nel giro dove semo?
84   Se i piè si stanno, non stea tuo sermone."

Ed elli a me: "L'amor del bene, scemo
del suo dover, quiritta si ristora;
87   qui si ribatte il mal tardato remo.

'He cares for us as we do for ourselves,
since one who sees another's need and awaits the asking
60   maliciously has set his mind upon refusal.

'We should accept so kind an invitation with our feet,
attempting the ascent before it darkens,
63   for then we cannot, until day returns.'

These were my leader's words, and we together
turned our footsteps toward a stairway.
66   As soon as I had reached the lowest step

I sensed beside me something like the motion
of a wing that fanned my face. I heard the words:
69   '*Beati pacifici*, those untouched by sinful wrath.'

Already the sun's last rays before the night
were slanting up so high above us
72   that stars were showing here and there.

'O my strength, why do you drain away?'
I said, but only to myself,
75   because I felt my legs had lost their power.

We had reached a point at which the stair
ceased rising higher and we stopped,
78   as does a ship that comes to shore.

For a little while I waited to discover
if my ears could make out sounds in this new circle.
81   Then I turned to my master and I said:

'Sweet father, tell me, what is the offense
made clean here in this circle that we've reached?
84   If our feet must rest, do not arrest your words.'

And he: 'A love of good that falls short
of its duty is here restored, here in this place.
87   Here the slackened oar is pulled with greater force.

Ma perché più aperto intendi ancora,
volgi la mente a me, e prenderai
90   alcun buon frutto di nostra dimora."

"Né creator né creatura mai,"
cominciò el, "figliuol, fu sanza amore,
93   o naturale o d'animo; e tu 'l sai.

Lo naturale è sempre sanza errore,
ma l'altro puote errar per malo obietto
96   o per troppo o per poco di vigore.

Mentre ch'elli è nel primo ben diretto,
e ne' secondi sé stesso misura,
99   esser non può cagion di mal diletto;

ma quando al mal si torce, o con più cura
o con men che non dee corre nel bene,
102   contra 'l fattore adovra sua fattura.

Quinci comprender puoi ch'esser convene
amor sementa in voi d'ogne virtute
105   e d'ogne operazion che merta pene.

Or, perché mai non può da la salute
amor del suo subietto volger viso,
108   da l'odio proprio son le cose tute;

e perché intender non si può diviso,
e per sé stante, alcuno esser dal primo,
111   da quello odiare ogne effetto è deciso.

Resta, se dividendo bene stimo,
che 'l mal che s'ama è del prossimo; ed esso
114   amor nasce in tre modi in vostro limo.

È chi, per esser suo vicin soppresso,
spera eccellenza, e sol per questo brama
117   ch'el sia di sua grandezza in basso messo;

'That you may understand more clearly,
pay close attention. Then you shall pluck
90   some good fruit from our stay.'

*discourse
on love II*

'Neither Creator nor His creature, my dear son,
was ever without love, whether natural
93   or of the mind,' he began, 'and this you know.

'The natural is always without error,
but the other may err in its chosen goal
96   or through excessive or deficient vigor.

'While it is directed to the primal good,
knowing moderation in its lesser goals,
99   it cannot be the cause of wrongful pleasure.

'But when it bends to evil, or pursues the good
with more or less concern than needed,
102   then the creature works against his Maker.

'From this you surely understand that love
must be the seed in you of every virtue
105   and of every deed that merits punishment.

'Now, since love cannot avert its face
from the welfare of its subject,
108   all creatures are secure against self-hatred,

'and since no being can conceive itself
as severed, self-existing, from its Author,
111   each creature is cut off from hating Him.

'It follows, if I'm right in these distinctions,
that the evil that is loved must be a neighbor's.
114   Three ways this love takes form within your clay.

'There is the one, hoping to excel by bringing down
his neighbor, who, for that cause alone, longs
117   that from his greatness his neighbor be brought low.

è chi podere, grazia, onore e fama
teme di perder perch' altri sormonti,
120 onde s'attrista sì che 'l contrario ama;

ed è chi per ingiuria par ch'aonti,
sì che si fa de la vendetta ghiotto,
123 e tal convien che 'l male altrui impronti.

Questo triforme amor qua giù di sotto
si piange: or vo' che tu de l'altro intende,
126 che corre al ben con ordine corrotto.

Ciascun confusamente un bene apprende
nel qual si queti l'animo, e disira;
129 per che di giugner lui ciascun contende.

Se lento amore a lui veder vi tira
o a lui acquistar, questa cornice,
132 dopo giusto penter, ve ne martira.

Altro ben è che non fa l'uom felice;
non è felicità, non è la buona
135 essenza, d'ogne ben frutto e radice.

L'amor ch'ad esso troppo s'abbandona,
di sovr' a noi si piange per tre cerchi;
ma come tripartito si ragiona,
139 tacciolo, acciò che tu per te ne cerchi."

'There is the one who fears the loss of power, favor,
honor, fame—should he be bettered by another.
120   This so aggrieves him that he wants to see him fall.

'And there is the one who thinks himself offended
and hungers after vengeance,
123   and he must then contrive another's harm.

'All these three forms of love cause weeping down below.
Now I would have you consider yet another,
126   which pursues the good in faulty measure.

'Everyone can vaguely apprehend some good
in which the mind may find its peace.
129   With desire, each one strives to reach it.

'If the love that draws you on is laggard
to know or have that peace, this terrace,   *Sloth.*
132   after just remorse, torments you for it.

'There is another good that fails to make men happy,
for it is not the essence or true source,
135   the root of happiness or its proper fruit.

'The excessive love which gives itself to that   *lust*
is mourned above us in three circles.   *gluttony*
Exactly how its parts are three I do not say,   *avarice*
139   so that you may consider for yourself.'

1–9.   This marks the first time that an address to the reader begins a canto, here just at the midpoint of the poem. (Two later cantos will, however, begin with such apostrophe: *Paradiso* II and XIII.) These opening lines are similetic in nature if not precisely so in form.

Dante is apparently countering certain contemporary views, which held that moles were completely sightless (see Brunetto Latini, *Tresor* I.197, cited by Scartazzini [1900]). Tozer (1901) cites Virgil, *Georgics* I.183: "oculis capti . . . talpae" (sightless moles). Benvenuto (1380), who says that he thought of this passage once, when he was caught in mountain mists between Florence and Bologna, understood that Dante meant that moles could see, if only weakly *(debiliter)*, through the skin that covers their eyes.

This entire section of the canto is dominated by words that often in Dante refer to a higher form of sight, in contrast with the darkness in which the scene begins. In the first forty-three verses we encounter words for seeing as follows: forms of *imagine (imagine, imaginativa, imaginar)* at vv. 7, 13, 21, 31, 43; of *vedere (vedessi, veder, vista, visïone)* at vv. 2, 8, 27, 34; the word *fantasia* at verse 25.

10–12.   The poet returns briefly to the narrative mode in order to set the scene for what is about to follow: it is just after sunset at the shore of the mountain, with the sun's rays still striking the higher reaches of its slopes.

13–18.   This passage gave birth, in the early commentators, to the repetition of a charming story. Dante, having found a book he had never seen before in Siena, read it just where he found it, in a street stall, so that he might fix it in his mind, and did so for more than three hours one afternoon. When someone later asked him whether he had been disturbed by the wedding festivities that had occurred during his reading, he expressed no awareness that any such things had occurred. This "incident" derives from Boccaccio's *Trattatello* and is also reported by Benvenuto (1380).

On these equivalent powers of the soul, the *phantasia* or *imaginatio*, see St. Thomas (*ST* I.lxxviii.4): "the phantasy or imagination is like a treasure house of images received by the senses" (cited by Mussetter, "Fantasy," in Lans.2000.1). Thus both "imagination" and "phantasy" have a far different meaning in the works of Dante than in anything written after the Romantic era, where the imagination, given its "esemplastic power" in the unforgettable phrase of Coleridge, rather than merely receiving them, *produces* images. For discussions of the imaginative faculty see Bundy (Bund.1927.1), Wolfson (Wolf.1935.1), and Baldelli (Bald.1985.1). See also Dumol, "Imagination," in Lans.2000.1.

As the Anonimo Fiorentino (1400) explains, what is experienced by the five senses is registered in the *senso comune* and then conserved, without its physical elements, in the imagination, which, in contrast to the *senso comune*, the recipient of sense impressions only so long as they are present, is able to preserve these impressions. To paraphrase Dante's ruminative question, he turns to the imaginative faculty within himself to ask, "How do you so remove our attention from outer reality that we do not even notice the most intrusive events? And what informs you if not a sense impression? A light that takes form in Heaven either naturally (i.e., through the natural influence of the stars) or through the will of God." It seems clear that the visions that follow, like those experienced by the protagonist two cantos earlier (see note to *Purg.* XV.85–86), are sent to him (and to the penitents on this terrace—but not to Virgil [see note to *Purg.* XV.130–132]) directly by God.

19–39. Is the division of the sin of violence in *Inferno* remembered here, with each of the three exemplary figures guilty of one of the sins of violence portrayed in *Inferno*: against others (Procne), against oneself (Amata), and against God (Haman)? For this possibility see notes to *Inferno* VII.109–114 and XII.16–21 (last paragraph), as well as Hollander (Holl.1969.1), pp. 310–11. Wrath is defined, later on in this canto (vv. 121–123), as involving the hardened will in a desire for revenge *(vendetta)*. It is clear that the sort of anger repented on this terrace is not the same sin that we encountered in *Inferno* VII–VIII, where we saw those who had been overcome by intemperate anger. Here we observe the results of wrathful behavior formed with deliberation.

It seems clear both that Dante has once again been favored by God-sent ecstatic visions and that Virgil now knows better than to attempt to inject himself into the proceedings: he is utterly silent throughout the scene, although we may imagine that Dante is once again manifesting "drunken" behavior to anyone who observes him (see *Purg.* XV.121–123).

19–21. For Dante's earlier advertence to Ovid's story of Philomel and Procne, see *Purgatorio* IX.13–15 and note. There Philomel is dealt with as a sympathetic figure; here Procne, her sister, is made exemplary of the sin of Wrath for murdering her own son, Itys, in order to take vengeance upon Tereus for raping her sister. It may seem odd to today's readers, but Dante thinks of Procne as the nightingale, Philomel as the swallow (see note to *Purg.* IX.13–15).

25.   There can be little doubt: the notion of these visions as having "rained down" into the image-receiving faculty of his soul cements the claim made for them. Here is part of Singleton's comment on this verse: "The phantasy, or *imaginativa*, is 'lofty' because of the experience of a vision coming from such a source. For this adjectival usage, cf. 'la morta poesì,' *Purg.* I.7; 'la scritta morta,' *Inf.* VIII.127; 'alto ingegno,' *Inf.* II.7; and again 'alta fantasia' in *Par.* XXXIII.142."

That the poet here uses the very phrase "alta fantasia," which will mark his final vision of the Trinity three lines from the end of the poem, underlines the importance of this "trial run" for his capacity as visionary protagonist (and eventually God-inspired poet).

26–30.   Once again one must know the story in order to understand the meaning of the vision, which is presented elliptically, a technique Dante employs in all three examples in these lines (19–39). In none of these is the exemplary figure named. This passage is perhaps the most striking in this respect, since the three "supporting players" are all named, while we must supply the name of Haman. Like Procne, Haman is enraged against another (Mordecai, for not bowing down to him, when he had been promoted to being Ahasuerus's prime minister: see Esther 3:5, where Haman is described as being "full of wrath" *[iratus est valde]*); like Procne, he tries to take revenge by killing others, deciding to put to death all the Jews in the kingdom of Ahasuerus. At Esther's urging Ahasuerus rescinds the decree Haman had wrung from him, thus saving God's people, the Jews in their Persian exile, and has Haman put to death on the gallows (*crux* in the Vulgate at Esther 5:14, thus accounting for Dante's *crucifisso* at verse 26).

31–33.   The "bubble" in Dante's vision breaks as a bubble does when it rises above the water that contained it, only to give place to another, the final vision of this terrace.

34–39.   Lavinia, anonymous at first but soon to name herself (verse 37), addresses her unnamed mother, Amata, the consort of Latinus, king of Latium, and reproaches her for her suicide. As Bosco/Reggio (1979) point out, Dante, in the spring of 1311, deals with this scene (*Aen.* XII.595–603) in his second epistle to Henry VII and refers correctly to the context of Amata's suicide (*Epist.* VII.24), i.e., she kills herself because she believes that her opposition to her daughter's marriage to Aeneas has resulted in a failed war and the death of Turnus (whom she wrongly assumes to have been killed when she sees the soldiers of Aeneas approaching the city without opposition). Following expressions of puzzlement with Dante's treatment of this Virgilian text by Porena (1946), Bosco and Reggio too are puzzled that Dante here develops the situation differently, and suggest that perhaps Dante wants here to make Amata a more sympathetic character. But perhaps he had simpler plans.

In *Aeneid* VII.286–405, Virgil presents the results of Juno's anger at Latinus's promise of Lavinia in marriage to Aeneas (and not to Turnus, the suitor preferred by Amata, described in verse 345 as a woman on fire, stirred by angers *[irae]*). Juno's wrath in turn stirs the Fury Alecto, who comes to earth and puts a venomous snake in Amata's breast. Poisoned by its venom, Amata goes mad with angry grief and, in the guise of a Bacchante, takes Lavinia to the countryside in the attempt to stop the marriage. All of this insubordination will, of course, eventually fail. It is not clear that Dante is reading the text of Virgil's twelfth book any differently now than he was when he wrote his second letter to Henry (whether that was written before or after this passage). At whom must Amata be angry, from the point of view of Lavinia? Aeneas, because he will now have Lavinia in marriage. In the epistle, Florence, rejecting her rightful ruler, Henry, is compared to suicidal Amata. There is no reason for such not to be Dante's understanding here. It is perhaps coincidental that the description of Amata's suicide is preceded in Virgil by a simile comparing the losing Latians to bees whose hive has been penetrated by the farmer's emetic smoke; nonetheless, our scene is also preceded by the smoke of anger. Amata, in this respect similar to the two previous exemplary figures, kills someone else in order to harm the person whom she truly hates, Aeneas. That someone else is herself. Hers is the secret of the terrorist, dying to let her enemy know the depths of her envious hatred.

The "death of yet another" with which the passage ends refers to Turnus in such a way as to indicate that Lavinia understood that her mother had incorrectly assumed that Turnus was already dead, just as she does in Virgil's poem.

40–45. The simile is not difficult or surprising. Just as a dreaming sleeper, awakened by a sunbeam, loses his hold on his dream in bits and pieces before it utterly disappears, so was Dante jarred from his visionary sleep by the sudden brightness of the Angel of Mercy. This angelic light outshines even that of the sun, explains Benvenuto (1380), "because an angel gives off light more splendid than any light found in the world."

This simile should be remembered in the reading of the final simile of awakening in the poem (*Par.* XXXIII.58–63). Dante's fascination with the state between dream and waking is a notable part of his program of investigating the mental state of humans (see note to *Inf.* XXX.136–141).

55–60. Perhaps a paraphrase of Virgil's remarks will be helpful: "This divine spirit does what we wish without our asking, hiding itself in its own radiance (and thus allowing us to see); and it deals with us as we deal with ourselves, for he who sees a need, and yet waits to be asked, unkindly predisposes himself toward denying the request." As Daniello (1568) noted, this is a restatement of a Senecan motto (*De beneficiis* II.i.3), concerning the grace of giving before one is asked, that Dante had already made his own in *Convivio* I.viii.16.

62–63. For the "rule" (apparently more consented to than insisted on) that governs nocturnal stasis on the mountain see Sordello's explanation (*Purg.* VII.53–60).

68–69. The Angel of Mercy draws upon the Beatitude found in Matthew 5:9, "Blessed are the peacemakers," yet does so in such a way as to indicate tacitly the distinction between "good" anger (righteous indignation) and the "bad" form of wrath *(ira mala)* that is fueled by desire for personal revenge.

70–72. The sun having set, its rays touch only the higher reaches of the mountain. It is after 6 PM and the first stars are visible.

73. The protagonist's inner apostrophe of his flagging power of locomotion shows his awareness of the special kind of nocturnal debility afflicting souls on this mountain. As we will see, his physical condition matches that of a man who is slothful.

79–80. Since, on the terrace of Wrath, Dante's learning experiences occurred in darkness, and since it is dark as he enters the fourth terrace, he assumes that he may be instructed in virtue by what he will hear.

82–87. Just as the poem is now entering its second half and this *cantica* is arriving at its midpoint, so the experience of the repentance of the seven capital vices has come to its central moment with Sloth. From Dante's question and Virgil's answer we also understand that there is a gulf separating the vices below, all of which begin in the love of what is wrongful, from the rest, all of which result from insufficient or improper desire to attain the good. The sin purged here is called *acedia* in Latin and *accidia* in Italian. (For a lengthy consideration see Wenzel's book [Wenz.1967.1.]; see also Andrea Ciotti's entry, which sometimes takes issue with Wenzel, "accidia e accidiosi" in *ED* I [1970]; for a wider view of *acedia* see Kuhn [Kuhn.1976.1], with special reference to Dante on pp. 56–59.) In the poem, the word will appear in the next canto, used retrospectively to indicate the sin repented here (*Purg.* XVIII.132); however, in adjectival form it was present earlier (*Inf.* VII.123—see note to *Inf.* VII.118–126). Scartazzini (1900) brings St. Thomas (*ST* I.lxiii.2) into play as the one who affords a clear understanding of this sin, a kind of spiritual torpor accompanied by (or even causing) physical weariness.

88–90. This second extended "diagram" is excused, as was the first (*Inferno* XI), by the need to linger awhile before continuing the journey. Compare verse 84 and *Inferno* XI.10–15.

91–139. The rest of the canto is given over, without interruption, to Virgil's discourse on the nature of love. It misses only by a little being the longest speech we have heard spoken in the poem since Ugolino's in *Inferno* XXXIII.4–75, beaten out by Sordello's recounting of the current denizens of the Valley of the Princes (*Purg.* VII.87–136) and of course by Marco the Lombard's discourse on the related failures of Church and empire (*Purg.* XVI.65–129).

91–92. The given of Virgil's whole speech is the universality of love. It proceeds from God in all His creation, and from all things that He has created. In the rational beings (angels and humans), it returns to Him; in the lower animals, to one another and to their habitat; in insentient bodies, to their habitat (e.g., water lilies on ponds) or place of origin (e.g., fire always wanting to reach the sky beneath the moon). See *Convivio* III.iii.2–5, cited by Singleton (1973).

93–96. Love is of two kinds, natural or "mental." Natural love always desires the utmost good, and for rational beings that is God. Thus all humans *naturally* desire the good. If that were the only love that motivated us, there would be no sin in the world. However, there *is* another kind of love, one reached by a mental effort, and thus found only in angels and humans. (Since angels have all made their will known, to love God eternally, only humans will be the subjects of Virgil's discourse.) Human beings, using their free wills, may fall into three kinds of sin: choosing the wrong object for their loves (sins repented on the first three terraces); loving the good deficiently (as do the slothful, whom we are about to encounter); loving the good excessively (the sins repented on the three highest terraces, Avarice, Gluttony, Lust). For discussion of the way in which Dante, unlike Andreas Capellanus and Guido Cavalcanti, is interested in affirming only spiritual love, see Pasquazi (Pasq.1970.1), pp. 227–31.

97–102.   The lines essentially repeat what has been established in vv. 91–96, as though Dante sensed the difficulty most readers would be likely to have with this conceptual poetry.

103–105.   The argument pauses for its first affirmation: whether we sin or use our (free) wills well, the results observed come from our ways of loving—and our merit or demerit accords with the nature of our loves.

106–111.   The first consequence of this doctrine is to remove two possible motivations from consideration: hatred of self or hatred of God, both of which are declared to be impossible. Singleton points out that sinners like Capaneus (*Inf.* XIV) and Vanni Fucci (*Inf.* XXV) indeed do demonstrate a hatred for God, a feeling possible only in hell, but not in this life on earth. The sins of suicide and blasphemy, however, surely seem to contradict this theoretical notion.

112–124.   Hatred of self or of God having been discarded as motivations for immoral human conduct, hatred of our neighbor remains, expressed in (1) prideful desire that his success be reversed so that we may be his superior, (2) in envious desire that his success be thwarted, (3) in wrathful desire to take revenge for the harm he has inflicted on us. We realize—although we are told it in case we might not—that these are the sins of Pride, Envy, and Wrath that we have just finished visiting.

118–119.   The actual midpoint of the poem lies between these two verses, numbers 7116 and 7117 of the poem's 14,233. For discussion of the debate surrounding the fact that the line lengths of the seven central cantos of the *Comedy* form an apparently deliberate pattern, see the Princeton Dante Project, commentary to *Purgatorio* XVII.133–139.

125–126.   These two verses refer to all of the other four sins as a group united in at least seeking the good (as was not the case for the first three), but imperfectly.

127–132.   Virgil now defines Sloth, the first of these two better kinds of sin, as "laggard love." Thus, by failing to respond to God's offered love more energetically, the slothful are more rebellious to Him than are the avaricious, gluttonous, and lustful, who are pursuing a secondary good rather than avoiding the primary one. In Dante's day, Sloth was a sin particularly identified with the clergy, with reference not so much to their physical laziness as to their spiritually laggard lives. See Kuhn (Kuhn.1976.1), pp. 39–64.

133–139.   This secondary good has been referred to earlier at verse 98 and will occupy Cantos XX through XXVII, broken into three categories: money, food, and sex.

PURGATORIO XVIII
(Sloth)

Posto avea fine al suo ragionamento
l'alto dottore, e attento guardava
3   ne la mia vista s'io parea contento;

e io, cui nova sete ancor frugava,
di fuor tacea, e dentro dicea: "Forse
6   lo troppo dimandar ch'io fo li grava."

Ma quel padre verace, che s'accorse
del timido voler che non s'apriva,
9   parlando, di parlare ardir mi porse.

Ond'io: "Maestro, il mio veder s'avviva
sì nel tuo lume, ch'io discerno chiaro
12   quanto la tua ragion parta o descriva.

Però ti prego, dolce padre caro,
che mi dimostri amore, a cui reduci
15   ogne buono operare e 'l suo contraro."

"Drizza," disse, "ver' me l'agute luci
de lo 'ntelletto, e fieti manifesto
18   l'error de' ciechi che si fanno duci.

L'animo, ch'è creato ad amar presto,
ad ogne cosa è mobile che piace,
21   tosto che dal piacere in atto è desto.

Vostra apprensiva da esser verace
tragge intenzione, e dentro a voi la spiega,
24   sì che l'animo ad essa volger face;

e se, rivolto, inver' di lei si piega,
quel piegare è amor, quell' è natura
27   che per piacer di novo in voi si lega.

My lofty teacher, having brought
his discourse to its end, now studied

·3 my face to see if I seemed satisfied,

while I, spurred on by yet another thirst,
kept silent, rehearsing in my mind the thought:

6 'Perhaps I trouble him with all these questions.'

But that true father, mindful
of the timid wish that I did not declare,

9 spoke and gave me courage to speak out.

Therefore I said: 'Master, your light so quickens
my mental sight that I discern in full

12 your argument's distinctions and its thesis.

'And thus I pray, dear, gentle father,
that you expound this love, from which you say

15 each good deed and its opposite derive.'

'Direct on me your intellect's keen eyes,'
he said, 'and the error of the blind

18 who set themselves as guides will be revealed.

'The mind, disposed to love at its creation,
is readily moved toward anything that pleases

21 as soon as by that pleasure it is roused to act.

'From real forms your perception draws
an image it unfolds within you

24 so that the mind considers it,

'and if the mind, so turned, inclines to it,
that inclination is a natural love,

27 which beauty binds in you at once.

Poi, come 'l foco movesi in altura
per la sua forma ch'è nata a salire
30   là dove più in sua matera dura,

così l'animo preso entra in disire,
ch'è moto spiritale, e mai non posa
33   fin che la cosa amata il fa gioire.

Or ti puote apparer quant' è nascosa
la veritate a la gente ch'avvera
36   ciascun amore in sé laudabil cosa;

però che forse appar la sua matera
sempre esser buona, ma non ciascun segno
39   è buono, ancor che buona sia la cera."

"Le tue parole e 'l mio seguace ingegno,"
rispuos' io lui, "m'hanno amor discoverto,
42   ma ciò m'ha fatto di dubbiar più pregno;

ché, s'amore è di fuori a noi offerto
e l'anima non va con altro piede,
45   se dritta o torta va, non è suo merto."

Ed elli a me: "Quanto ragion qui vede,
dir ti poss' io; da indi in là t'aspetta
48   pur a Beatrice, ch'è opra di fede.

Ogne forma sustanzïal, che setta
è da matera ed è con lei unita,
51   specifica vertute ha in sé colletta,

la qual sanza operar non è sentita,
né si dimostra mai che per effetto,
54   come per verdi fronde in pianta vita.

Però, là onde vegna lo 'ntelletto
de le prime notizie, omo non sape,
57   e de' primi appetibili l'affetto,

every love is not deserving of praise.

'Then, as fire, born to rise,
      moves upward in its essence,
30   to where its matter lives the longest,

'just so the mind, thus seized, achieves desire,
      a movement of the spirit never resting
33   as long as it enjoys the thing it loves.

'Now you see how hidden is the truth
      from those who hold that every love
36   is in itself deserving praise,

'perhaps because such love seems always good.
      But every seal is not a good one,
39   even if imprinted in good wax.'

'Your words and my responding wit,' I said,
      'have made love's nature clear to me,
42   but that has left me even more perplexed.

'For if love is offered from outside us
      and if the soul moves on no other foot,
45   it has no merit in going straight or crooked.'

And he to me: 'As far as reason may see in this,
      I can tell you. To go farther you must look
48   to Beatrice, for it depends on faith alone.

'Every substantial form that is at once distinct
      from matter and is, as well, united with it,
51   contains its own defining disposition.

'This is not perceived except in operation,
      nor ever demonstrated except by its effect, as,
54   in a plant, the force of life by its green leaves.

'In consequence, where we derive our knowledge
      of first principles and the inclination
57   to universal objects of desire, no one knows.

che sono in voi sì come studio in ape
di far lo mele; e questa prima voglia
60 merto di lode o di biasmo non cape.

Or perché a questa ogn' altra si raccoglia,
innata v'è la virtù che consiglia,
63 e de l'assenso de' tener la soglia.

Quest' è 'l principio là onde si piglia
ragion di meritare in voi, secondo
66 che buoni e rei amori accoglie e viglia.

Color che ragionando andaro al fondo,
s'accorser d'esta innata libertate;
69 però moralità lasciaro al mondo.

Onde, poniam che di necessitate
surga ogne amor che dentro a voi s'accende,
72 di ritenerlo è in voi la podestate.

La nobile virtù Beatrice intende
per lo libero arbitrio, e però guarda
75 che l'abbi a mente, s'a parlar ten prende."

La luna, quasi a mezza notte tarda,
facea le stelle a noi parer più rade,
78 fatta com' un secchion che tuttor arda;

e correa contra 'l ciel per quelle strade
che 'l sole infiamma allor che quel da Roma
81 tra ' Sardi e ' Corsi il vede quando cade.

E quell' ombra gentil per cui si noma
Pietola più che villa mantoana,
84 del mio carcar diposta avea la soma;

per ch'io, che la ragione aperta e piana
sovra le mie quistioni avea ricolta,
87 stava com' om che sonnolento vana.

'These are innate in you just like the zeal in bees
for making honey, and this primal inclination
60   admits no positing of praise or blame.

'That to this will all others may conform
there is innate in you the faculty that counsels
63   and ought to guard the threshold of assent.

'This is the principle in which is found
the measure of your merit, as it welcomes
66   and then winnows good from guilty loves.

'Those who in their reasoning reached the root
recognized this innate freedom
69   and thus bequeathed their ethics to the world.

'Let us posit as a given: every love
that's kindled in you arises of necessity.
72   Still, the power to restrain it lies with you.

'That noble power is called free will by Beatrice,
and so make sure that you remember this
75   if she should ever speak of it to you.'

Still brilliant after midnight, the moon
was blazing like a fiery bucket,
78   making the stars seem fewer than they were,

as in its course against the sky it followed
the tracks the sun inflames when seen from Rome,
81   setting between Sardegna and the Corsicans.

That noble shade through whom Pietola
is more renowned than any Mantuan town
84   had doffed the weight with which I'd burdened him,

so that I, having harvested his clear
and forthright answers to my questions,
87   remained like one who rambles in his drowsy mind.

Ma questa sonnolenza mi fu tolta
subitamente da gente che dopo
90   le nostre spalle a noi era già volta.

E quale Ismeno già vide e Asopo
lungo di sé di notte furia e calca,
93   pur che i Teban di Bacco avesser uopo,

cotal per quel giron suo passo falca,
per quel ch'io vidi di color, venendo,
96   cui buon volere e giusto amor cavalca.

Tosto fur sovr' a noi, perché correndo
si movea tutta quella turba magna;
99   e due dinanzi gridavan piangendo:

"Maria corse con fretta a la montagna;
e Cesare, per soggiogare Ilerda,
102   punse Marsilia e poi corse in Ispagna."

"Ratto, ratto, che 'l tempo non si perda
per poco amor," gridavan li altri appresso,
105   "che studio di ben far grazia rinverda."

"O gente in cui fervore aguto adesso
ricompie forse negligenza e indugio
108   da voi per tepidezza in ben far messo,

questi che vive, e certo i' non vi bugio,
vuole andar sù, pur che 'l sol ne riluca;
111   però ne dite ond' è presso il pertugio."

Parole furon queste del mio duca;
e un di quelli spirti disse: "Vieni
114   di retro a noi, e troverai la buca.

Noi siam di voglia a muoverci sì pieni,
che restar non potem; però perdona,
117   se villania nostra giustizia tieni.

ironic.

But suddenly this drowsiness was snatched away
by a crowd who were approaching,
having already rounded the terrace from behind us.

90

As once the rivers Ismenus and Asopus
saw a furious throng of revelers crowd their banks
on any night the Thebans felt the need for Bacchus,

93

such a throng cut their way, as does a sickle,
around that circle, and I could tell
that virtuous will and just love drove them on.

96

Soon they were upon us,
for the whole frenzied mob was running,
while two in front, weeping, cried out:

99

'Mary ran with haste into the mountains,'
and 'Caesar, to subdue Lèrida, thrust at Marseilles
and then raced on to Spain.'

102

'Quickly, quickly, lest time be lost for lack of love,'
the others cried behind them. 'Let our zeal
for doing good make grace grow green again.'

105

'O you who with keen fervor make amends,
perhaps for your past negligence and sloth
in being lukewarm to do good,

108

'this man, who is alive—indeed I do not lie—
is eager to ascend at day's first light.
Tell us, then, where is the nearest opening?'

111

These were my leader's words,
and one of those spirits answered:
'Follow us and you shall find the gap.

114

'We are so filled with our desire to keep on moving
we cannot rest. Pardon us, then,
if our just penance seems discourteous.

117

Io fui abate in San Zeno a Verona
sotto lo 'mperio del buon Barbarossa,
di cui dolente ancor Milan ragiona.

E tale ha già l'un piè dentro la fossa,
che tosto piangerà quel monastero,
e tristo fia d'avere avuta possa;

perché suo figlio, mal del corpo intero,
e de la mente peggio, e che mal nacque,
ha posto in loco di suo pastor vero."

Io non so se più disse o s'ei si tacque,
tant' era già di là da noi trascorso;
ma questo intesi, e ritener mi piacque.

E quei che m'era ad ogne uopo soccorso
disse: "Volgiti qua: vedine due
venir dando a l'accidïa di morso."

Di retro a tutti dicean: "Prima fue
morta la gente a cui il mar s'aperse,
che vedesse Iordan le rede sue.

E quella che l'affanno non sofferse
fino a la fine col figlio d'Anchise
sé stessa a vita sanza gloria offerse."

Poi quando fuor da noi tanto divise
quell' ombre, che veder più non potiersi,
novo pensiero dentro a me si mise,

del qual più altri nacquero e diversi;
e tanto d'uno in altro vaneggiai,
che li occhi per vaghezza ricopersi,
e 'l pensamento in sogno trasmutai.

120

123

126

129

132

135

138

141

145

'I was Abbot of San Zeno at Verona
under the rule of worthy Barbarossa,
120 of whom Milan still speaks with sorrow.

'And one there, with a foot already in the grave,
will soon bemoan that monastery
123 and regret his power over it,

'because he put his son, lame in body,
deformed in mind, and base of birth,
126 in the place of its true shepherd.'

I know not if he said more or was still,
he had already raced so far beyond us,
129 but this I heard and chose to keep in mind.

And he who was my help in every need
said: 'Turn around and see these two
132 who now come nipping at the heels of sloth.'

Coming behind the rest they chanted:
'The people for whom the Red Sea opened
135 were dead before the Jordan saw their heirs'

and 'Those who chose not to endure the toil
to its conclusion with Anchises' son
138 gave themselves to a life without renown.'

Then, when these shades were so far parted
from us we could no longer see them,
141 a new thought rose within me,

from which others, many and diverse, were born.
And I rambled so from one thought to another
that my eyes closed in drowsy wandering
145 and I transformed my musings into dream.

1.   This canto continues the flow of the last with no demarcation in the text itself of a terminus or of a new beginning. As Bosco points out in his introductory remarks to the two cantos, they form a unit developed on a chiastic pattern:

XVII.1–69   (NARRATIVE)

                       XVII.70–139   (INSTRUCTION)
                       XVIII.1–75   (INSTRUCTION)

XVIII.76–145   (NARRATIVE)

Further, these two cantos form a larger unit with *Purgatorio* XVI, which is similarly divided into two large blocks of material: 1–63 (narrative) and 64–145 (Marco's instruction). In this way the numerical center of the *Commedia*, cantos 49–51, is made more noticeable. (For the midpoint with respect to the number of lines in the poem see the note to *Purg.* XVII.118–119.)

Ricci (Ricc.1970.1), p. 252, suggests that Dante spreads Virgil's full canto's worth (145 verses) of speechifying over two cantos so as not to strain the reader's patience.

2–3.   Virgil's "Scholastic" credentials seem strong. See Tarozzi's appreciation (Taro.1901.1), p. 7: Virgil "here represents the idealized figure of the medieval docent." A close analysis of his discourse in the preceding canto, such as may be found, in English, in Singleton's commentary, reveals a line of argument that is closely based on Thomistic texts. In keeping with such discourse and for the first time since *Inferno* XVI.48, Virgil is saluted by his pupil as "professor" *(dottore)*. For the other terms used to describe Virgil's role as guide in the poem, see note to *Inferno* II.140.

In fact, Virgil has rarely been referred to or addressed by Dante with such fervent admiration as here and shortly later in this canto, when he will be "padre verace" (true father—7), "Maestro" (Master—10), and then "father" again (13). See note to vv. 17–18.

4.   In this and the next canto the protagonist's forward movement in understanding is underlined by the adjective *nuovo* (new): used here for his new "thirst," at verse 141 for his "new thought" in reaction to the departure of the penitents in Sloth, and at XIX.56, in his reference to the new dream he has just had on this terrace.

8.   Dante's "timid wish" should probably be considered related to intel-
lectual sloth (see *Purg.* XVII.130, *lento amore* [laggard love]). How could
Dante have considered himself "timid" in seeking the truth? Had he in-
volved himself in a less than urgent affection for the good, the charge
would seem appropriate. Since it is the author who makes the charge, it
might seem that he himself believed that he did not always display the
zeal necessary for loving well.

13–15.   Why, one might ask, after Virgil's long speech in the last canto,
should Dante want Virgil to "expound" love when he seems just now to
have finished (with suitable fanfare) doing precisely that? What the pro-
tagonist means is "expatiate upon," "explain more precisely," the argu-
ment just now presented. The word *dimostrare* is here, in fact, a verb
based on the Latin noun *demonstratio*, as used to refer to the development
of proofs by means of syllogistic demonstration. See *Paradiso* XXIV.96.

17–18.   Virgil's words reflect Matthew 15:14, where Jesus says that the
Pharisees are blind guides of the blind who follow them, adding that
guide and flock shall all end up falling into a ditch.

   In *Convivio* I.xi.4 Dante cites this passage, directing its barb against
"those wicked Italians who praise the vernacular of others while disparag-
ing their own" (*Conv.* I.xi.1) and who are therefore likewise headed
toward disaster. As Francesco Mazzoni argues ("Latini, Brunetto," *ED* III
[1971], p. 580b]), in this connection it is difficult not to think of Dante's
fellow Florentine Brunetto Latini, who wrote his encyclopedic *Tresor* in
French rather than in his native vernacular (see Pézard [Peza.1950.1] for
extensive development of this idea). Also to be considered are the words,
written shortly before or shortly after this passage (on the problems of dat-
ing *Dve* and *Conv.* see Hollander [Holl.2001.1], pp. 54–55), in *De vulgari
eloquentia* I.xiii.1, when Dante "exiles" Brunetto from the illustrious and
courtly vernacular that he is championing, relegating him to the ash heap
of the municipal vernacular, the "street talk" that is to be avoided by seri-
ous poets. In what seems to have been a change of heart, Brunetto, in the
fifteenth canto of *Inferno*, will be treated generously as Dante's vernacular
"teacher" (*Inf.* XV.85), just as Virgil was his first Latin guide. It seems clear
that these two are joined only by Guido Guinizzelli as explicitly paternal
figures of writerly authority for the Tuscan poet.

   Dante refers to, whether as protagonist or as poet, various "fathers"
in the course of the poem (this is to exclude "fathers" addressed by other
characters). The parenthetic reference is to the first appearance of each
"father."

(1)   Virgil (*Inf.* VIII.110)
(2)   Brunetto Latini (*Inf.* XV.83)
(3)   Cato of Utica (*Purg.* I.33)
(4)   Guido Guinizzelli (*Purg.* XXVI.97)
(5)   God (addressed as "good Apollo," *Par.* I.28)
(6)   St. Francis (*Par.* XI.85)
(7)   Cacciaguida (*Par.* XVI.16)
(8)   St. Benedict (*Par.* XXII.58)
(9)   the sun (*Par.* XXII.116)
(10)   St. Peter (*Par.* XXIV.62)
(11)   Adam (*Par.* XXVI.92)
(12)   St. Bernard (*Par.* XXXI.63)

19–21. Virgil, responding to Dante's request, carries his analysis of the loving human mind to the next level, the role of the rational soul in determining human choice and, therefore, action. This tercet establishes the subject of Virgil's difficult clarification (vv. 22–39): how mind (the rational soul, created directly by God and instilled in the embryo last [see *Purg.* XXV.67–75]) reacts appetitively to external things.

22–27. The *apprensiva* (power of perception), already implicitly referred to in Dante's apostrophe of the *imaginativa* (faculty of imagination) in *Purgatorio* XVII.13–15, is the faculty of perception that reacts to the capturing of an image (referred to here as an *intenzione*) of external reality in the *imaginazione* or *fantasia* (see note to XVII.13–18). The mind, as opposed to the "natural desire" of the senses (see *Purg.* XVII.93 for this distinction), which is always errorless, is responsible for its choices and may err. If its perception inclines toward what it contemplates, that is what we call love.

28–33. Desire, love in action, now continues by extending toward its goal and remaining in this state as long as it takes pleasure in its appetites. (For fire as an example of "natural desire," see note to *Purg.* XVII.91–92.) Thus here Dante is comparing intellectual desire to natural desire, but also insisting on the distance between them. Natural desire can never be culpable (e.g., fire always "desires" to rise—that is its natural inclination). There is perhaps no moment in the poem of greater danger to its essential philosophical position. Is human desire—for money, food, or sexual pleasure—not as "natural" as this? Does anyone *not* desire these things? Dante's attempt to persuade us, as he may well have realized, reflects that of another *dottore* and *maestro*, Jesus. He, as the Gospels amply testify, also spoke frequently, in his parables, in terms of human desires that all could understand, e.g., of money, agriculture, marriage. In all cases the listener is encouraged, even impelled, to understand that such pleasures, as great as they may be, will seem as nothing compared to the joys of Heaven.

Arriving at this point in the argument, a reader would have to be pardoned for believing that whatever good the spirit of love pursues is ipso facto good, just as the protagonist himself will shortly seem to believe (vv. 43–45). But what is the nature of the "moto spiritale" (movement of the spirit) of the "captive mind"? That question is reflected in the crucial and concluding portion of Virgil's discourse.

34–39. The main candidates for this unenviable denomination, the errant folk who believe that *all* love is good (a proposition, as we have seen, that we might have considered unassailable a moment ago), have been Epicureans. In the modern period this view is first offered by Scartazzini (1900) but then is held by many twentieth-century commentators. Grabher (1934) is of the opinion that this is the position of all love poets, including the younger Dante. His view, sometimes combined with that of Scartazzini, has grown increasingly attractive to recent commentators. Clearly, anyone who believes that love is in itself and always praiseworthy is among this group.

The "imprint" on the "wax" of our love becomes the crucial symbolic expression of the concept developed here. The "wax" clearly refers to the innate human potential to love, which is "stamped" by the image that the mind has extracted from reality; that "stamp" may either be worthy or unworthy, while the "wax" is always worthy.

40–45. It is, despite Virgil's last insistence on the (implicit) need for the proper exercise of the free will in choosing the objects of one's desire, understandable that Dante, up to this point, understands that the mind is completely responsive to internalized (by the *apprensiva*) external stimuli (the *intenzione*—see verse 23), and thus irreprehensible in whatever choice it makes.

46–48. This passage offers perhaps the only apparently material evidence in the poem that would tie both Virgil and Beatrice to an allegorical status, his role being that of Reason, hers, Faith. But see Hollander (Holl.1990.1), p. 42, n. 2: "It is from Virgil's lips that we first hear the name Beatrice . . . in *Purgatorio*: VI.46; XV.77; XVIII.48. In her first three nominal presences in this *cantica* . . . she is associated first with hope (VI.32), then with love (XV.68; XV.71; XV.74), then with faith." Thus associated with the three theological virtues, Beatrice can be seen as possessing all of them; she probably should not be seen as representing any one of them, or as having an "allegorical" status in this poem.

49–75.   The three cantos at the center of *Purgatorio* devote what may seem immoderate space to what Benedetto Croce disliked in Dante, his "non-poesia," his "structure," his mere *allotria* (the "extraneous matter" of philosophy or theology that Croce deprecated in Dante; opposing such views, Salsano [Sals.1967.1], p. 542, speaks of the *Comedy* as "un poema e non un libro di poesie"). Marco's long speech in XVI (65–129), Virgil's in XVII (91–139), and Virgil's concluding two in this canto (16–39; 49–75) should be looked upon, as should the related discursive portions of Cantos XXIV and XXV, as part of a continuing development of a complex statement about the nature and function of love, presented from different vantage points. In Canto XXIV, Dante's presentation of the Holy Spirit's creative role in helping to make the writings of a handful of poets acceptable to God prepares for the following treatment in Canto XXV of the way the Holy Spirit is breathed into all of us, thus explaining how eventually a very few of us may become acceptable to God as His saints in Paradise. In these three cantos Marco the Lombard explains the need for proper civil governance because our free will may elsewise lead us astray, while Virgil takes up a related topic, the need for us individually to use our free will correctly in choosing and responding to the objects of our attention and affection.

49–60.   The only "substantial form" to be both distinct from matter and joined to it is the human soul, which is formed by pure divine intellect (as are the angels) and by emotional and vegetative powers (as are the beasts). Its *specifica vertute* (defining disposition), as we learn at vv. 55–57, is composed of primal intellect and primal will, and is only perceptible in the action of the soul, not in itself. Now, leaving intellection out of consideration, Virgil continues: We have no recollection or current understanding of our original inclination (to love God), yet we do demonstrate its presence in us, as the eagerness of bees for making honey reveals their "defining disposition." This kind of (natural) will exists beyond and before moral assent.

61–66.   This innate will (see *Purg.* XXI.105, *la virtù che vuole* [the power that wills]) must accord with *la virtù che consiglia* (the faculty that counsels), the higher intellect that should govern all our choices; our ability to choose good and to discard evil affections is the ground for the measurement of our moral condition.

67–69.   Aristotle's *Ethics* is probably Dante's main source for his views on morality (a view supported by Benvenuto da Imola). However, to account for the plurality of the reference, Poletto (1894) sensibly refers to Dante's own earlier phrasing (found in the words of Virgil), "I speak of Aristotle and of Plato / and of many others" (*Purg.* III.43–44).

70–75.   Virgil's lengthy discourse concludes with his final insistence on the pivotal role of free will in individual moral responsibility and looks forward (as Benvenuto was perhaps the first to realize) to Beatrice's remarks on the subject in *Paradiso* V.19–24, asseverating that the freedom of the will is the greatest of God's gifts to humankind. Many of the early commentators find this a convenient place for them to reassert the "allegorical" valence of Beatrice, here interpreted as "Theology." In the past 150 years many commentators are content to leave the allegorical equation in abeyance, merely referring to Beatrice as herself.

76–81.   Returning to narrative, the poet returns to telling the time. The moon, as the slowest "planet" in Dante's astronomy, is fittingly the celestial body referred to on the terrace of Sloth. Its appearance is compared by Benvenuto to the semicircular fire in a lighthouse, glowing throughout the night.

The moon, Dante would seem to be saying, was roughly on the same path taken by the sun when it sets in the southwest (when seen from Rome) in late November, between Sardinia and Corsica.

82–84.   The protagonist's gratitude to Virgil is expressed with a salute to his birthplace, Pietola ("Andes" in Roman times). Some early commentators read the phrase "più che villa mantoana" to mean "more than the city Mantua," while the meaning is nearly certainly "more than any Mantuan town," i.e., any other town in the vicinity of the city, not Mantua itself, as Padoan (Pado.1967.1), p. 688n., agrees.

87–88.   Again a detail—Dante's somnolence—establishes a connection with Sloth.

89–90.   These penitents, as opposed to the wrathful, move in the same counterclockwise direction that is followed by Dante and Virgil. It would seem that, while the movement of Dante to the right is morally determined, that of the penitents is not, is rather the result of aesthetic considerations. Review of the various groups that are in motion suggests that such is the case. Below the gate, we see that the excommunicate are moving rightwards (*Purg.* III.59), while the late-repentant seem to be heading to the left (V.23). On the terraces, the prideful seem to be moving right (X.100), while the wrathful are headed left (XV.142). Here in Sloth the penitents come from behind Virgil and Dante but are moving in the same direction (XVIII.90). Farther up the mountain the penitent gluttons are also moving counterclockwise (XXIII.19–20), while the two distinct bands of the lustful proceed in two different directions (XXVI.29).

91–96. This is a fairly rare occurrence in *Purgatorio*, a simile based explicitly on classical materials (but see *Purg.* IX.34–42, for the similetic reference to Statius's Achilles). And there will not be another (now based on a passage in Lucan) until *Purgatorio* XXIV.64–69.

Ismenus and Asopus are names of rivers, the first flowing through the city of Thebes, the second near it. Beginning with Jacopo della Lana (1324), commentators have offered the opinion, from time to time, that Dante's source here is Statius (*Thebaid* IX). Ismenos is named at IX.404, his "brother" Asopos at IX.449. The passage includes two references to the orgiastic Bacchic rites (IX.434–436; 478–480) to which Dante here refers.

97–98. Running in a group to counteract the painful memory of their solitary slothful behaviors on earth, all these gathered penitents may put contemporary readers in mind of the massed crowds of runners in metropolitan marathons.

99–138. With the exception of the concluding interaction with the angel in the following canto, separated by Dante's sleep and dream from the action on the fourth terrace, all the usual "events" of any terrace are here condensed—in the compressed style appropriate to the description of the newly zealous—into these forty verses. All terraces include the following features in the same order: (1) description of the physical aspect of the terrace, (2) exemplars of the countering virtue, (3) description of the penitents, (4) recitation of their sins by particular penitents, (5) exemplars of the vice, (6) appearance to Dante of the angel representing the opposing virtue.

We might want to reflect on the extraordinary artisanship of the presentation of the exemplary material on the earlier terraces, things not matched by what we find in earlier medieval poems: the "speaking" (and odoriferous) intaglios of Pride, the voices streaking overhead in Envy, the ecstatic visions of Wrath. It is as though Dante had used up all the brilliant new techniques of presentation of which he could think and now, for the rest of the ascent, subsides to the perfectly acceptable artistic level of utterance, leaving us to marvel at what he had done before. On three of the last four terraces the names (sometimes accompanied by reference to significant deeds) of all exemplary figures are simply called out by the penitents, while on the terrace of Gluttony, in a variant, the two trees do the talking.

99–102.   Some of the earliest commentators believe that the reference is to the precipitous escape from Herod's decree and the flight of the holy family into Egypt (a misinterpretation that surfaced again in the Renaissance in the commentaries of Landino and Vellutello). However, beginning with Pietro di Dante (1340) the obvious citation of Luke 1:39 has been recognized as governing this example. Mary, having been told by Gabriel during the Annunciation of Elizabeth's miraculous pregnancy in her old age (which will result in the birth of John the Baptist), "abiit in montana cum festinatione . . . et salutavit Elisabeth" (went with good speed into the hill country . . . and offered her salutation to Elizabeth).

101–102.   The Roman example paired with Mary is none other than Julius Caesar. It is notable that in Lucan (*Phars.* III.453), Caesar's rushing off to do battle in Spain is not the result of military strategy but of his being bored *(inpatiens)* with the prolonged efforts to lay siege to Marseilles. Further, his eventual victory at Lerida is described by Lucan as being the result of fortunate changes in the weather (*Phars.* IV.48–49). Thus Dante's praise of him here is clearly at odds with Lucan's (always) withering scorn for the Great Man whom he so desperately despises. For the entire question of Dante's divided view of Julius Caesar, in one view the first, God-sent emperor of Rome, in another the destroyer of the Republic and of Roman virtue, see Stull and Hollander (Stul.1991.1), pp. 33–43. This is one of Julius's few positive moments in Dante's poem; and Dante needed to disregard Lucan's views in order to present him favorably. For Dante's previous and next far less favorable references to Julius, see the notes to *Purgatorio* IX.133–138 and XXVI.76–78.

103.   On every other terrace the penitents have a prayer that they speak in common when they are not interrupted by other forms of observance

or by conversation with Dante and Virgil (see *Purg.* XI.1–24; XIII.50–51; XVI.19; XIX.73; XXIII.11; XXV.121). The terrace of Sloth offers the only exception, as though the previous *acedia* of these penitents took from them the privilege of Christian prayer. The gloss of Carroll (1904) is interesting: "The idea seems . . . to be the danger of contemplation of good deeds, without an eager and immediate effort to imitate them. Mere 'study' of them may end in the 'little love' which produces sloth. It is only when 'study' is accompanied by action that it 'makes grace bud again.' " For Dante, a man devoted to the pursuit of the morally engaged active life, certain occasions for prayer perhaps appeared to offer a potential escape from one's civil and religious duty in the world. Men and women of such disposition are thus, here in their penitence, denied the comfort of prayer until such time as prayer will be totally zealous, not the occasion for a moment of repose from worldly responsibility or, for that matter, from proper monastic exertion. *Acedia* was frequently associated with improper monastic *otium*, a withdrawal from the world but from one's duty to God as well, surely a great temptation in the relative ease allowed by monastic life.

104–105. The phrase "per poco amor" (for lack of love) and the word "studio" (the Italian equivalent of the Latin word for "zeal") combine to underline the defining vice and virtue of this terrace.

107. Virgil's "perhaps" is a gentle act of *politesse* on his part: these penitents were guilty of precisely what he describes.

118–120. San Zeno, just outside the city of Verona (and, by common consent, one of the most beautiful churches in Italy), was also the site of a monastery. Its nameless abbot, who speaks here, is generally identified as "Gherardo II, who was abbot, in the time of the Emperor Frederick I, from 1163 till his death in 1187" **(T)**. Frederick Barbarossa, emperor from 1152 until his death in 1190 as Frederick I, was a grandfather of Frederick II (emperor 1215–50). Dante's overall opinion of him is difficult to measure, since he so rarely refers to him, but in the two passages that do invoke him, here and in *Epistle* VI.20, his destruction of Milan in 1162 for its anti-imperial activities is clearly applauded. On the question of Dante's views of Barbarossa see Nardi (Nard.1966.1).

For the less than likely possibility that the adjective "buon" (good) that precedes his name is here to be taken ironically, see Tommaseo (1837) on this passage. One may add that the thirty occasions in the

Commedia on which a reader finds the epithet combined with a name or title (e.g., "buon Marzucco," "buon maestro") do not reveal a single one in which an ironic reading seems warranted.

121–126. Dante, welcomed by the Scaligeri family to Verona in 1303–4, there enjoyed the first happy time of his exile. His memories of those rulers of the city give rise to a *post-eventum* prophecy. Alberto della Scala was lord of Verona until his death in 1301, by which time he had appointed his lame, illegitimate son, Giuseppe (1263–1313), to serve as abbot of the monastery (in 1292), for the rest of his days. Alberto was succeeded by his eldest legitimate son, Bartolommeo, nearly certainly Dante's first host in Verona. Upon Bartolommeo's death, in 1304, Alberto's second son, Alboino, became lord (many believe that Dante and Alboino did not get along, thus explaining Dante's departure from Verona around 1304), a position he held until his death in 1311, when he was succeeded by Cangrande della Scala, the third legitimate son and Dante's patron and host when the poet returned to Verona ca. 1314.

127–129. The nameless abbot is moving so quickly that Dante cannot tell whether he has finished speaking or has simply moved too far ahead to be heard while continuing to speak—a nice final touch to convey the zeal with which he pursued his penitence.

133–135. The first example of the sin of Sloth indicates the Hebrews who, having made the passage through the Red Sea, grew restive under Moses' guidance and died of plague before the completed exodus across Jordan into the Promised Land accomplished only by Joshua and Caleb. See Numbers 14:1–38 and Deuteronomy 1:26–40.

136–138. Similarly, some of Aeneas's companions, egged on by Iris, disguised as the wife of Doryclus, rebelled against the leadership of Aeneas and chose to remain in Sicily. The matrons set fire to the ships and Aeneas, having saved all but four of them from destruction, allows all who wish to stay behind to do so (*Aen.* V.604–761). Padoan (Pado.1967.1), p. 686, argues that Dante's treatment of *Aeneid* V here differs from that found in *Convivio* IV.xxvi.11, but the difference can be explained by the fact that in the earlier passage Dante focuses on the willingness of Aeneas to allow the discouraged to stay behind found in Virgil's text itself, while here he judges the malingerers from a different vantage point, the divinely sanctioned imperative to found new Troy in Latium.

141–142.   The protagonist's *novo pensiero* (new thought) has puzzled his commentators. Is it one triggered by what he has seen and heard? Or is he anticipating the matters he will rehearse in his dream in the next canto? Or is the poet merely describing, generically, the way in which the mind works as it flits from subject to subject on the way to sleep (a view that is much present in the commentaries)? In the next canto, a similar phrase will refer to a mental image already experienced (the *novella visïon* of XIX.56) in his previous dream. Thus here it is at least possible that the "new thought" is a response to what he has seen or heard. Could he have wondered whether he was himself more like the backsliding Hebrews and Trojans than he is like Joshua or Aeneas? This would seem possible, but not demonstrable. In any case, this unreported thought leads to still others, and these are clearly—because the text tells us so—the matter of his dream.

143.   The verb Dante uses to describe his floating state of consciousness, *vaneggiai* (rambled), picks up an earlier phrasing, when he compares himself to one who *sonnolento vana* (rambles in his drowsy mind—verse 87) after Virgil has finished his explanation of love and free will. There he is falling into a fatigue that mirrors the sin purged on this terrace. Here he finally gives in to that weight of somnolence.

145.   Dante's purgatorial dreams are described in cantos IX, XIX, and XXVII, but the second occurs here, in a single line, "e 'l pensamento in sogno trasmutai" (and I transformed my musings into dream). Since in *Vita nuova* he presents his age as having been nine, eighteen, and twenty-seven for his three main "encounters" with Beatrice, the poet perhaps wanted to retain those three nine-based and nine-spaced numbers for his three dreams that lead back to her now. For this calculation see Hollander (Holl.1969.1), p. 145.

PURGATORIO XIX
(*Sloth and Avarice*)

Ne l'ora che non può 'l calor dïurno
intepidar più 'l freddo de la luna,
3   vinto da terra, e talor da Saturno

—quando i geomanti lor Maggior Fortuna
veggiono in orïente, innanzi a l'alba,
6   surger per via che poco le sta bruna—,

mi venne in sogno una femmina balba,
ne li occhi guercia, e sovra i piè distorta,
9   con le man monche, e di colore scialba.

Io la mirava; e come 'l sol conforta
le fredde membra che la notte aggrava,
12   così lo sguardo mio le facea scorta

la lingua, e poscia tutta la drizzava
in poco d'ora, e lo smarrito volto,
15   com' amor vuol, così le colorava.

Poi ch'ell' avea 'l parlar così disciolto,
cominciava a cantar sì, che con pena
18   da lei avrei mio intento rivolto.

"Io son," cantava, "io son dolce serena,
che ' marinari in mezzo mar dismago;
21   tanto son di piacere a sentir piena!

Io volsi Ulisse del suo cammin vago
al canto mio; e qual meco s'ausa,
24   rado sen parte; sì tutto l'appago!"

Ancor non era sua bocca richiusa,
quand' una donna apparve santa e presta
27   lunghesso me per far colei confusa.

At that hour when the heat of day,
cooled by earth and at times by Saturn,
3   can no longer temper the cold of the moon,

when geomancers see their *Fortuna Major*
rise in the east before the dawn,
6   which does not long stay dark for it,

there came to me a woman, in a dream,
stammering, cross-eyed, splayfooted,
9   with crippled hands and sickly pale complexion.

I looked at her, and as the sun revives
cold limbs benumbed by night,
12   just so my gaze gave her a ready tongue

and then in very little time
straightened her crooked limbs
15   and tinged her sallow face as love desires.

And with her speech set free
she started singing in a way that would
18   have made it hard for me to turn aside.

'I am,' she sang, 'I am the sweet siren
who beguiles mariners on distant seas,
21   so great is their delight in hearing me.

'I drew Ulysses, eager for the journey,
with my song. And those who dwell with me
24   rarely depart, so much do I content them.'

Her lips had not yet closed
when at my side appeared a lady,
27   holy and alert, in order to confound her.

"O Virgilio, Virgilio, chi è questa?"
fieramente dicea; ed el venìa
con li occhi fitti pur in quella onesta.

30

L'altra prendea, e dinanzi l'apria
fendendo i drappi, e mostravami 'l ventre;
quel mi svegliò col puzzo che n'uscia.

33

Io mossi li occhi, e 'l buon maestro: "Almen tre
voci t'ho messe!" dicea, "Surgi e vieni;
troviam l'aperta per la qual tu entre."

36

Sù mi levai, e tutti eran già pieni
de l'alto dì i giron del sacro monte,
e andavam col sol novo a le reni.

39

Seguendo lui, portava la mia fronte
come colui che l'ha di pensier carca,
che fa di sé un mezzo arco di ponte;

42

quand' io udi' "Venite; qui si varca"
parlare in modo soave e benigno,
qual non si sente in questa mortal marca.

45

Con l'ali aperte, che parean di cigno,
volseci in sù colui che sì parlonne
tra due pareti del duro macigno.

48

Mosse le penne poi e ventilonne,
"Qui lugent" affermando esser beati,
ch'avran di consolar l'anime donne.

51

"Che hai che pur inver' la terra guati?"
la guida mia incominciò a dirmi,
poco amendue da l'angel sormontati.

54

E io: "Con tanta sospeccion fa irmi
novella visïon ch'a sé mi piega,
sì ch'io non posso dal pensar partirmi."

57

'O Virgil, Virgil, who is this?'
she asked, indignant. And he came forward

30   with his eyes fixed on that virtuous one.

The other he seized and, ripping her garments,
laid her front bare and exposed her belly.

33   The stench that came from there awoke me.

I was looking around, and the good master said:
'Three times at least I've called you. Arise and come.

36   Let us find the opening through which you enter.'

I stood up. All the circles of the holy mountain
were already filled with the advancing day

39   and we went on with the new sun at our backs.

With furrowed brow I followed him,
as though burdened with a thought that bent

42   my body like the half-arch of a bridge,

until I heard: 'Come, here is the passage,'
spoken in such gentle, gracious tones

45   as are not heard within these earthly confines.

With open wings that seemed a swan's
he that had spoken showed the way on up

48   between two walls of flinty stone

and, stirring his feathers, gently fanned us,
declaring those *qui lugent* to be blessed,

51   for their souls shall be comforted.

'What's wrong, that you keep staring at the ground?'
my guide began, once we were on our way,

54   leaving the angel just below.

'I am so distracted going on,' I said,
'because this strange new dream so weighs on me

57   I cannot keep it from my mind.'

"Vedesti," disse, "quell'antica strega
che sola sovr' a noi omai si piagne;
60   vedesti come l'uom da lei si slega.

Bastiti, e batti a terra le calcagne;
li occhi rivolgi al logoro che gira
63   lo rege etterno con le rote magne."

Quale 'l falcon, che prima a' piè si mira,
indi si volge al grido e si protende
66   per lo disio del pasto che là il tira,

tal mi fec' io; e tal, quanto si fende
la roccia per dar via a chi va suso,
69   n'andai infin dove 'l cerchiar si prende.

Com' io nel quinto giro fui dischiuso,
vidi gente per esso che piangea,
72   giacendo a terra tutta volta in giuso.

"*Adhaesit pavimento anima mea*"
sentia dir lor con sì alti sospiri,
75   che la parola a pena s'intendea.

"O eletti di Dio, li cui soffriri
e giustizia e speranza fa men duri,
78   drizzate noi verso li alti saliri."

"Se voi venite dal giacer sicuri,
e volete trovar la via più tosto,
81   le vostre destre sien sempre di fori."

Così pregò 'l poeta, e sì risposto
poco dinanzi a noi ne fu; per ch'io
84   nel parlare avvisai l'altro nascosto,

e volsi li occhi a li occhi al segnor mio:
ond' elli m'assentì con lieto cenno
87   ciò che chiedea la vista del disio.

'You saw,' he said, 'that ancient witch
who alone is purged with tears above us here.
60 And you saw how man is freed from her.

'Let that be enough. Press your heels
into the ground. Raise your eyes to the lure
63 the Eternal King whirls with His majestic spheres.'

Like the falcon that at first looks at its feet,
and only then turns to the call and stretches up
66 in its desire for the food that draws it,

such I became and, so impelled, I went
as far as the cleft rock allowed for the ascent
69 to where the circling starts again.

When I came out onto the ledge
of the fifth round, I saw people on it
72 lying face down on the ground and weeping.

'Adhaesit pavimento anima mea'
I heard them say with such deep sighs
75 the words could hardly be distinguished.

'O chosen ones of God, whose sufferings
both hope and justice make less hard,
78 direct us to the steps that lead us up.'

'If you are here exempt from lying prostrate
and wish to find the quickest way,
81 keep to the right along the outer rim.'

Thus the poet asked and thus came the response
from a little way ahead, and I could tell who spoke
84 although his face was hidden.

I turned my eyes to the eyes of my lord.
With a pleased sign he consented
87 to what my pleading look had asked.

Poi ch'io potei di me fare a mio senno,
trassimi sovra quella creatura
90   le cui parole pria notar mi fenno,

dicendo: "Spirto in cui pianger matura
quel sanza 'l quale a Dio tornar non pòssi,
93   sosta un poco per me tua maggior cura.

Chi fosti e perché vòlti avete i dossi
al sù, mi dì, e se vuo' ch'io t'impetri
96   cosa di là ond' io vivendo mossi."

Ed elli a me: "Perché i nostri diretri
rivolga il cielo a sé, saprai; ma prima
99   *scias quod ego fui successor Petri.*

Intra Sïestri e Chiaveri s'adima
una fiumana bella, e del suo nome
102   lo titol del mio sangue fa sua cima.

Un mese e poco più prova' io come
pesa il gran manto a chi dal fango il guarda,
105   che piuma sembran tutte l'altre some.

La mia conversïone, omè!, fu tarda;
ma, come fatto fui roman pastore,
108   così scopersi la vita bugiarda.

Vidi che lì non s'acquetava il core,
né più salir potiesi in quella vita;
111   per che di questa in me s'accese amore.

Fino a quel punto misera e partita
da Dio anima fui, del tutto avara;
114   or, come vedi, qui ne son punita.

Quel ch'avarizia fa, qui si dichiara
in purgazion de l'anime converse;
117   e nulla pena il monte ha più amara.

When I was free to do what I desired
I drew away and stood above that soul
90   whose words had first made me aware of him,

saying: 'Spirit in whom weeping ripens
that without which there is no return to God,
93   for my sake just a while neglect your greater care.

'Tell me who you were and why you lie face down
and whether there is something I might do
96   for you back there, where I set out alive.'

And he to me: 'Why Heaven turns our backs
against Itself, that you shall know, but first
99   *scias quod ego fui successor Petri.*

'Between Sestri and Chiàvari there runs down
a lovely stream and with its name
102   the title of my line has marked its shield.

'In a month and little more I learned how heavy
the mantle weighs on one who keeps it from the mud,
105   making any other burden seem a feather.

'My conversion, alas, came late—
but when I became the shepherd of Rome,
108   I discovered a life full of lies.

'I saw that there the heart was not at peace,
nor was preferment possible in that life,
111   and for this higher state my love was kindled.

'Until that moment I was a wretched soul,
cut off from God, and filled with avarice.
114   Now, as you see, I am punished for that here.

'The work of avarice is here proclaimed
in the purging of the down-turned souls,
117   and the mountain gives no punishment more bitter.

Sì come l'occhio nostro non s'aderse
in alto, fisso a le cose terrene,
120   così giustizia qui a terra il merse.

Come avarizia spense a ciascun bene
lo nostro amore, onde operar perdési,
123   così giustizia qui stretti ne tene,

ne' piedi e ne le man legati e presi;
e quanto fia piacer del giusto Sire,
126   tanto staremo immobili e distesi."

Io m'era inginocchiato e volea dire;
ma com' io cominciai ed el s'accorse,
129   solo ascoltando, del mio reverire,

"Qual cagion," disse, "in giù così ti torse?"
E io a lui: "Per vostra dignitate
132   mia coscïenza dritto mi rimorse."

"Drizza le gambe, lèvati sù, frate!"
rispuose; "non errar: conservo sono
135   teco e con li altri ad una podestate.

Se mai quel santo evangelico suono
che dice 'Neque nubent' intendesti,
138   ben puoi veder perch' io così ragiono.

Vattene omai: non vo' che più t'arresti;
ché la tua stanza mio pianger disagia,
141   col qual maturo ciò che tu dicesti.

Nepote ho io di là c'ha nome Alagia,
buona da sé, pur che la nostra casa
non faccia lei per essempro malvagia;
145   e questa sola di là m'è rimasa."

'Just as we failed to lift our eyes on high
because they were fixed on earthly things,
120   so justice here has turned them to the earth.

'As avarice quenched our love of worthy things,
wasting our chance to do good works,
123   so justice here has bound us fast.

'Securely bound are our hands and feet.
As long as it shall please the righteous Lord
126   so long shall we, unmoving, lie here prone.'

I had kneeled and was about to speak,
but as soon as I began and he perceived,
129   only by listening, that I in reverence had knelt,

'Why,' he asked, 'did you kneel down that way?'
And I: 'Because the dignity of Your high office
132   stung my conscience as I stood erect.'

'Straighten your legs, stand up, brother,'
he replied, 'make no mistake. I am a fellow-servant
135   with you, and with the others, of a single Power.

'If ever you did understand the holy passage
in the gospel where it tells us *"Neque nubent,"*
138   you may well perceive just why I say this.

'Now go your way. I would not keep you longer,
for your being here prevents the tears
141   with which I ripen that of which you spoke.

'On earth I have a niece who is called Alàgia—
she is still virtuous if indeed our house
has not by its example made her wicked,
145   and she alone is left to me back there.'

1–3.   Dante apparently believed that the rays of the moon, in his time considered a "cold planet" (e.g., by Jacopo della Lana [1324]), enhanced the natural nocturnal cooling of the earth, its temperature further decreased whenever another "cold" planet, Saturn, was visible above the horizon. The hour is just before dawn on Tuesday, the beginning of Dante's third day at the antipodes. For an earlier Dantean reference to the coldness of Saturn see *Convivio* II.xiii.25.

4–6.   The early commentators who deal with the problems encountered here are in fairly close accord. Beginning with Benvenuto da Imola they indicate the following: geomancers are diviners who create charts based on random points on the earth's surface and drawn in the sand (and later copied onto paper or in sand on a tabletop) that can be linked in such a way, by joining various of these points with lines, to create a number of figures (Daniello [1568], following Landino, names sixteen of these). The facts behind the passage seem to be pretty much as Grandgent (1909) said: " 'Geomancers' foretold the future by means of figures constructed on points that were distributed by chance. Their specialty was the selection of favorable spots for burial. They were the first in Europe to use the compass. One of their figures, called *fortuna major*, or 'greater fortune,' resembled a combination of the last stars of Aquarius and the first of Pisces. As these constellations immediately precede Aries, in which the sun is from March 21 to April 21, the figure in question can be seen in the east shortly before sunrise at that season." The name geomancer reflects the fact that such an adept draws his figures in the sand (or earth— Greek *ge*) and that he is a diviner (Greek *mantis*). The configuration known as *Fortuna maior* is illustrated by Benvenuto and others as shown here:

★ ★

★ ★

★ ★

Whatever the precise nature of the practices of geomancers, it seems clear that Dante has not taken six lines to indicate that the time was shortly before dawn without purpose. Surely the unpleasant and unsavory connotations of coldness and of divination (we remember the treatment of diviners in *Inferno* XX) color our reception of the dream that shortly follows. We should also remember that this dream occurs on the terrace of Sloth, thus suggesting that it may reflect Dante's own former tardiness in seeking the good. Insofar as that affliction also encouraged his involvement in cupidity, the dream may also look back to some sort of misdirected love.

7–9.   This second purgatorial dream is at least as difficult to interpret as the first (see note to *Purg.* IX.19). For a brief and cogent review of classical, scriptural, patristic, and scholastic views of the nature of dreams see Armour (Armo.1990.1), pp. 13–16.

Small seas of ink have been poured out in the quest for the source and meaning of this unpleasant woman. The far from convincing results previously obtained probably should warn anyone against advancing an opinion. On the other hand, it seems to some that the problem is easier to understand than are the attempts to solve it. The poem itself, in the words of Virgil, tells us precisely who the stammering woman is: she represents the conjoined sins of excessive love, avarice, gluttony, lust— the sins of the flesh or, in the language of Dante's first *cantica*, the sins of incontinence. (See Virgil's words at vv. 58–59: "You saw . . . that ancient witch / who alone is purged with tears above us here.") Dante's dream, nonetheless, must surely also have specific meaning for him. If the woman is the object of his affection, she must have particular reference to lust, since the poem nowhere offers any indication that Dante considered himself ever to have been avaricious (or prodigal, for that matter) or gluttonous. The "good that fails to make men happy" (*Purg.* XVII.133), in Dante's case, must then nearly certainly be understood as involving wrongful sexual desire.

Consideration of the *femmina balba* (stammering woman) has caused readers to seek out some fairly recondite sources. For a general analysis of this passage see Cervigni (Cerv.1986.1), pp. 123–35.

What has rarely been noted in modern commentaries (but see Mattalia [1960] and, citing him, Giacalone [1968]) is the fact that *balbus* is the contrary of *planus*, the word that describes Beatrice's speech in *Inferno* II.56 (see the note to *Inf.* II.56–57). Cf. the entry *balbus* in Lewis and Short's *Latin Dictionary*, where this view is confirmed.

10–15.   The woman, we learn from the preceding tercet, stammers, is crooked in her glance as well as in her extremities, and sickly in her complexion. That is her natural condition. Dante, in the logic of the dream, redresses each of these sets of flaws, making her speech fluent, straightening her limbs, and making her facial complexion the color that love desires to find in a woman (commentators debate whether this is red or white, but only since the time of Tommaseo [the early commentators do not treat the question]); Tommaseo (1837) opts for the darker hue (purple, red); Bianchi, citing *Vita nuova* XXXVI.1, where the "color of love" is the pallor Dante finds in the *donna gentile*, the woman who replaces dead Beatrice in his affections, chooses the lighter: white. While the commentators remain divided, opting for a shade of red, a whiteness, or a combination of the two (all of which may be found in the lengthy tradition of the "colors of love," at least from Ovid onward), the context of *Vita nuova*, which sponsors pallor as the "color of love," supports only the second possibility.

16–18.   That Dante's glance has transformed her may further suggest that the song she sings is, in some sense, of his composition also, as was the tempting song sung by Casella (*Purg.* II.112), the second *canzone* included in Dante's *Convivio*, addressed to the *donna gentile* (and not to Beatrice).

For the view that the *femmina balba* reflects not only the potentially various flesh-and-blood ladies of Dante's sexual transgressions but also the *donna gentile* of *Convivio*, see Hollander (Holl.1969.1), pp. 136–44, 162–63. It seems more likely that Dante here means to refer to the first and carnal lady for whom he betrayed Beatrice, the lady of the last section of *Vita nuova*, the lady who, he later claimed, was only an allegory for the unchallengeably virtuous Lady Philosophy. Thus the main thrust of his self-correction is aimed at the straying recorded in the earlier work; but, naturally enough, it would also hold in contempt that later allegorized lady as well, also presented as an "enemy" of Beatrice in the first three treatises of *Convivio*. Both move the lover from affection for his true beloved in service of one far less worthy.

20–21.   The phrasing that expresses the Siren's power over men may put us in mind of the condition of Dante in the opening verses of the poem, when he, *nel mezzo del cammin*, was off his course and resembled a sailor who had nearly drowned. Does he now see himself as having been seduced by a "siren"? Insofar as the she-wolf represents the sins of Incontinence, and thus, for Dante, lust (see note to *Inf.* I.32–54), the essential reason for his having lost the true way would now seem to be predominantly related to his sexual affections.

22–24. A tormented tercet: what does *vago* mean? to whom or what does it refer? who is the *serena* who claims so to have held Ulysses' attention? As Barbi (Barb.1934.1), p. 228, maintained, in this poem the adjective *vago* always (it is used thirteen other times) means *bramoso* (desirous of) and is, as here, used with the genitive (cf. *Purg.* XXVIII.1). Thus, while the commentators are divided roughly evenly, with more early ones opting for *vago* as modifying *cammin* (and meaning "wandering, indirect"), and more modern ones, beginning with Torraca (1905), believing that it modifies Ulysses (and means "eager"), one is more likely to be convinced, as was Mezzadroli (Mezz.1990.1), p. 29, that the context and Dante's general practice allow us to resolve the first two questions as did Barbi (this woman drew Ulysses from the journey he was so eager to pursue). But what of this "Siren" who so beguiled Ulysses? Commentators have at times forgotten that Dante did not know Homer's account (*Odyssey* XII.39–200) of Ulysses' escape from the Sirens' seductive wiles. We should probably understand, following Moore (Moor.1896.1) that, from Cicero's *De finibus* V.xviii.48–49, Dante decided that Ulysses had indeed been tempted by the Sirens. In any case, that is how he has the Siren portray Ulysses, and he offers no textual support for any other view. For that matter, in Beatrice's later opinion, Dante himself is seen in exactly the same light, as yielding to the temptation of the Sirens when he withdrew his attention from her in order to fall under the spell of another lady or ladies (*Purg.* XXXI.43–48).

26–27. Attempting to identify this lady, Fedele Romani (Roma.1902.1), pp. 15–18, one hundred years ago opted for Beatrice, but has had few followers.

Among more recent proponents of Beatrice's candidacy see Poletto (1894), who clearly prefers her as best fitting what happens in the poem, while ultimately not being quite certain, and Giacalone (1968), who offers the fullest and best defense of Beatrice as being the lady in question.

28–30. If this is Beatrice, then it is hardly surprising that she would recognize Virgil, in the dreamer's estimation, since he knows from what he was told in *Inferno* II.53 that Beatrice came to Virgil in Limbo. And as for the identity of the lady here, characterized as being "onesta" (virtuous), it is probably worth remembering that Beatrice is later compared to a "donna onesta" (chaste lady) in *Paradiso* XXVII.31.

31–33. What is the subject of the verb *prendea* (seized)? Some have argued that it is the holy lady. A sense of grammatical structure indicates, instead, that it is Virgil, subject of the previous verb (*venìa* [came forward]) that is in parallel with it. Further, if the lady indeed represents Beatrice, it would be highly unlikely that she would do the dirty work herself. Just as she, in *Inferno* II, called on Virgil to make Dante aware of the foulness of the sins punished in hell, so now she stands to one side while Virgil reveals the noxious nature of her rival, the *femmina balba*.

The stench that arises from the naked belly of the *femmina* has, according to Hollander (Holl.1983.3), pp. 84–86, a familiar source, not one that must be sought in out-of-the-way medieval treatises, but in Virgil's description of the Harpies in *Aeneid* III.216–218: "virginei volucrum vultus, foedissima ventris / proluvies, uncaeque manus, et pallida semper / ora fame" (maidenly of countenance, yet winged; most foul the discharge of their bellies; their hands taloned; their faces always pale with hunger). The particular similarity of the stinking bellies of Dante's Siren and Virgil's Harpies is surely striking. A further similarity lies in the purpose both creatures have in the works that contain them, which is to draw the hero away from his task, whether from proceeding to Italy or from pursuing Beatrice to a destination in Christ. In this sense both are counselors of despair. In Dante's case, it is his duty to confess that he himself had created, out of what should have been repulsive, what he came to worship; out of a Harpy he had formed a Siren. Unlike Ulysses' Siren, Dante's *femme fatale* is not even beautiful to begin with. It is no wonder that she will be brought back into play in his worst moment of guilt in the entire poem when he is censured by Beatrice in *Purgatorio* XXXI.43–48, warning him not to be lured by the "Sirens" ever again.

34–35.   In Dante's "Surgi e vieni" (Arise and come), Mattalia (1960) seems to have been the first commentator (and few have subsequently joined him) to hear what is clearly a biblical echo, even if his hearing is a little dull. He cites Matthew 9:5–6, where Jesus urges the paralyzed man to walk; perhaps more applicable is Matthew 26:36–46, where Jesus three times leaves his disciples in Gethsemane in order to pray in a place apart and three times comes back to find them sleeping, finally arousing them with "Surgite, eamus" (Rise, let us be going), for His betrayal (by Judas) is at hand. The rhythm of those three disheartening visits to those who should have been awake is preserved in Dante's "Three times at least I've called you," as was suggested in 1969 by two undergraduate students at Princeton, John Adams and Christopher McElroy. Lost in his dream, Dante is like the disciples who sleep while their Lord suffers alone.

37–42. Dante has slept late, unsurprisingly, given his late-night activities on the terrace of Sloth (*Purg.* XVIII.76–78), and now finds the sun, at his back, risen above the horizon.

43–45. The Angel of Zeal's words ("Come, here is the passage") may not be like any heard here on earth, but they do resemble those spoken by Beatrice when she was described by Virgil as being "soave e piana" (gentle and clear) in her speech (*Inf.* II.56), as Poletto (1894) suggested.

49–51. The nine verses devoted to the presence of the angel here represent the briefest scene yet devoted to the interplay between angel and mortal (but see note to *Purg.* XXII.1–6). The Beatitude referred to, Matthew 5:4 (5:5 in the Vulgate), "Blessed are they that mourn, for they shall be comforted," has caused some to wonder what specific relevance these words have to those formerly guilty of Sloth. Federigo Tollemache, "beatitudini evangeliche," *ED* I (1970), p. 540b, explains that, given Thomas Aquinas's definition (*ST* II.ii.35.2) of *accidia* as *tristitia de spirituali bono* (dejection over one's spiritual health), the phrase "qui lugent" (those who mourn) is relevant. For the program of the Beatitudes in this *cantica* see the note to *Purgatorio* XII.110.

52–60. The exchange clearly reflects that between Virgil and Dante in *Purgatorio* XV.120–126. Once again Virgil begins by asking Dante "che hai?" (what's wrong?), not at first understanding his charge's removal from present reality. Once again Dante insists on his other-mindedness. In the first instance Virgil quickly understood that Dante was having a visionary experience; now he becomes aware that Dante has been having a dream of what his guide's words had prepared him for, coming to grips with the "good that fails to make men happy" (*Purg.* XVII.133).

Virgil's formulation causes a problem for those who would argue that the holy lady is Beatrice, since it generalizes the nature of the lady who opposes the *femmina balba* and makes Dante's dream applicable to all sinners, no others of whom, we may assume, are lovers of Beatrice. For this reason Parenti's understanding (Pare.1996.1), pp. 62–63 (resuscitating Torraca's opinion [1905]), that the holy lady equates with Charity, seems the most adequate solution, good love that operates against the forces of "the good that fails to make men happy" (*Purg.* XVII.133). Charity may well be the general meaning of the lady in the dream; for Dante, however, that theological virtue is the core of the meaning of Beatrice.

63–69. Virgil's metaphoric expression and the poet's following simile return to falconry (see note to *Inf.* XVII.127–136), now in as central an image of the basic movement of the entire poem as may be found. Mortals look down, consumed by their own concerns, while God, the falconer, wheels his lure (the celestial heavens) around his "head," thus drawing us back to Him. Dante had been looking at the earth (verse 52) and Virgil urges him to push off against it in order to move on (verse 61); in the simile the falcon, too, looks down, perhaps to see if he is still bound to the falconer's wrist now that his hood has been removed (or merely in his habitual attitude, his head inclined downward, resting on his breast). Both bird and Dante, urged on, look up and travel upward, in Dante's case by climbing through the passageway in the rock so that he may resume his circling of the mountain on his approach to God.

The image of the star-filled heavens as God's lures for us, his falcons, is central to the progress of the poem that concludes each of its *cantiche* with the word *stelle* (stars).

70–72. Dante's arrival on the fifth terrace, that of Avarice and Prodigality, is immediately greeted by the sight of those who are purging themselves there, prostrate on the earth. This terrace is unique in that it is a stage for three increasingly lengthy conversations, first with a pope (Adrian V) in this canto, with a kingly figure (Hugh Capet) in the next, and finally with a poet (Statius) in XXI and XXII, a sample of callings that reflects Dante's most pressing concerns: Church, empire, and letters.

73–75. The penitents' cries, muffled because they lie facedown on the floor of the terrace and are uttering them through painful sighs, are "my soul cleaves to the earth" (Psalm 118 [119]:25). The Ottimo (1333) connects this confessional outpouring with Virgil's earlier remark to Dante ("Press your heels / into the ground" [verse 61]), thus suggesting that the avaricious repent their longing for the things of the earth, exactly what Virgil is urging Dante to do.

76–77. The terms in which Virgil puts his request may remind us that his own condition in Limbo lacks precisely what these penitents enjoy: hope in the justice of God for eventual salvation. Virgil and the other inhabitants of Limbo long for that justice, but without any possible hope of achieving it (*Inf.* IV.42).

79.   As Singleton (1973) observes, this is the first time we learn that some penitents do not have to spend penitential time on every terrace, since the nameless speaker (we will learn that he was a pope at verse 99) assumes, from Virgil's request for help, that both of these newcomers are saved souls exempt from the sin of avarice (or of prodigality) who are ascending to a destination higher up the mountain without having to stay here.

84.   Dante cannot make out the identity of the speaker, but is able to individuate the source of the words he has just heard; he seeks Virgil's permission to question him.

92.   Dante's circumlocution, "that without which there is no return to God," refers to the satisfaction each penitent must offer to God, showing that he or she is finally pure of the traces of the defiling sin purged on each terrace.

94–96.   Dante's three questions will be the basis for this penitent's speech, which will fill most of the rest of the canto, vv. 97–126 and 142–145. He wants to know the identity of his interlocutor, the nature of the sin reflected in his prone posture, and, as is customary, what service he (as living soul) can perform back on earth for him.

99.   The speaker, in good papal Latin ("Know that I was a successor of Peter"), informs Dante that he was once a pope, not boastfully, but humbly and ashamedly, as though to say "I, of all people, who should have known better." Benvenuto (1380) makes a similar point; it is as though he said he was a successor of Peter "sed non pauper ut Petrus" (but not a poor man, as was Peter).

100–105.   Geographical indications (two towns on the Ligurian coast and the stream taken by members of the Fieschi family for their title: they are "counts of Lavagna") leave no doubt as to the identity of the pope who speaks: "Adrian V (Ottobuono de' Fieschi of Genoa), elected Pope at Rome, in succession to Innocent V, July 11, 1276; died at Viterbo on Aug. 16 following, before he had been crowned" **(T)**; thus Dante's "a month and little more" to indicate Adrian's term of office. Longfellow (1867) reports the following papal remark: "When his kindred came to congratulate him on his election, he said, 'Would that ye came to a Cardinal in good health, and not to a dying Pope.' "

104.   See *Purgatorio* XVI.127–129 for Dante's earlier view of the papacy's descent into the "mud" of wrongful activity.

Bosco (1979) draws attention to the parallels between the previous nineteenth canto and this one, both deeply involved with the papacy in both similar and opposed spirits. At least here we understand what the papacy might be if the pope were an Adrian V. It is perhaps by design that the first saved pope whom we meet in the poem (there will be more [see note to *Inf.* VII.38–39]) should be distinguished by having died shortly after his election and thus without having served "officially" at all.

106–114.   Adrian's remarks have caused a certain puzzlement, since historical records give no sense of his involvement in avaricious behavior (nor, consequently, of his turning from that sin only once he was elected pope); as Scartazzini (1900) observed, such notice derives only from this passage in Dante's poem and from his perhaps too gullible commentators. Bosco (Bosc.1942.1), pp. 136–43, followed by Sapegno (1955), argues that Dante thought that what he had read in John of Salisbury's *Policraticus* (VIII.xxiii.814) or, more likely, since Petrarch later also made the same mistake, in some (unknown) later source that created this error, about the twelfth-century pope Adrian IV, concerned instead his thirteenth-century namesake.

106.   Conversion here signifies any turning to God. Even confirmed Christians are likely to experience a continuing need for "conversion." See Singleton (Sing.1958.1), pp. 39–56.

115–126.   Adrian here answers Dante's second question, why these souls are in the posture Dante sees them in, by explaining their *contrapasso*: since they sought the things of earth energetically, they now are face-down on that earth and restrained, immobile, upon it.

127–132.   Dante's reverent kneeling before Adrian is apparent from his voice, which sounds louder because his face is now closer to the recumbent pope's body. The interruption in Adrian's answers allows this little exchange that offers a lesson in fellowship that trumps Dante's gesture of respect.

131.   Adrian earns one of Dante's relatively few uses of the honorific "voi" (see note to *Inf.* X.49–51). In the first *cantica* only Farinata,

Cavalcante, and Brunetto have this honor bestowed upon them. Adrian, the fourth of seven to share the honor, will be joined only by Guinizzelli (*Purg.* XXVI.112) and Beatrice (first at *Purg.* XXXI.36) in this *cantica*, and then by Cacciaguida (first at *Par.* XVI.10) in the next.

133.   Adrian's response is so urgent that he only gets to his fraternal salute, nearly always found, elsewhere in the poem, at the beginning of direct address and never at its end, last. His "frate," rhyming with "dignitate," is the answer to the hierarchy underlined by that second term and by Dante's kneeling. In God's kingdom there is no specialness, only brotherhood of the equally special.

134–135.   From the time of Benvenuto (1380) it has been understood that this scene clearly replays a similar scene in the Bible: Apocalypse 19:9–10, where the angel addresses John, commanding him to write of the blessedness of those who share the marriage supper of the Lamb. When John falls before the feet of the angel to worship him, the angel says: "You must not do that; I am your fellow-servant *(conservus)*." Dante's hapax, *conservo*, surely cements the relationship between the two texts.

136–138.   The next biblical reference is to Matthew 22:23–30, "neque nubent" (nor do they marry), a passage in which Christ deals with the sardonic and hairsplitting Sadducees, who do not believe in resurrection and who wish, cynically, to know which of six brothers, who had in turn married an eldest brother's widow, would be her resurrected husband. Jesus answers them by saying that after the Resurrection there will be no marrying in Heaven, where all will share, one might add, in the marriage supper of the Lamb as equals, where all are married to all and to none. Adrian's insistence on the lack of hierarchical distinction is his version of Jesus' saying.

141.   "That of which you spoke" refers to Dante's previous understanding (verse 92) of Adrian's desire to complete his penance and thus achieve purification.

142–145.   Answering the third element in Dante's question, regarding what Dante might do for him, Adrian can supply only the name of a niece, Alagia, who might pray for him, thus suggesting that his avaricious former life had much in the way of familial bad company among all the rest of his relatives.

Alagia was married to Moroello Malaspina, with whom Dante was on friendly terms, and thus his good words about her probably reflect a positive impression gained from personal knowledge and may also serve to express gratitude for the Malaspina family's hospitality in Lunigiana in the early years of Dante's exile.

PURGATORIO XX
(Avarice)

Contra miglior voler voler mal pugna;
onde contra 'l piacer mio, per piacerli,
3   trassi de l'acqua non sazia la spugna.

Mossimi; e 'l duca mio si mosse per li
luoghi spediti pur lungo la roccia,
6   come si va per muro stretto a' merli;

ché la gente che fonde a goccia a goccia
per li occhi il mal che tutto 'l mondo occupa,
9   da l'altra parte in fuor troppo s'approccia.

Maladetta sie tu, antica lupa,
che più che tutte l'altre bestie hai preda
12   per la tua fame sanza fine cupa!

O ciel, nel cui girar par che si creda
le condizion di qua giù trasmutarsi,
15   quando verrà per cui questa disceda?

Noi andavam con passi lenti e scarsi,
e io attento a l'ombre, ch'i' sentia
18   pietosamente piangere e lagnarsi;

e per ventura udi' "Dolce Maria!"
dinanzi a noi chiamar così nel pianto
21   come fa donna che in parturir sia;

e seguitar: "Povera fosti tanto,
quanto veder si può per quello ospizio
24   dove sponesti il tuo portato santo."

Seguentemente intesi: "O buon Fabrizio,
con povertà volesti anzi virtute
27   che gran ricchezza posseder con vizio."

The will strives ill against a worthier will.
Therefore, against my wish but granting his,
I drew the sponge, not full yet, from the water.

I moved on and my leader picked his way,
keeping to the clear path near the rock
as one must walk on ramparts, tight against the wall,

for the people from whose eyes dissolves,
drop by drop, the evil filling all the world
were crowded near the outer edge's rim.

May you be cursed, you age-old wolf,
who take more prey than any other beast
to feed your bottomless appetite!

O heavens, whose wheels transmute
the state of those on earth, as some believe,
when will he come from whom the wolf shall flee?

We made our way with scant, slow steps,
my attention fixed upon those weeping shades
as I listened to their piteous lamentations,

when by chance I heard one up ahead call out
'Sweet Mary!' through his tears,
even as a woman does in labor,

and I heard the voice go on:
'How poor you were is witnessed by the inn
where you set down your holy burden.'

After that I heard: 'O good Fabricius,
you chose poverty with virtue
rather than possess great wealth in wickedness.'

Queste parole m'eran sì piaciute,
ch'io mi trassi oltre per aver contezza
30   di quello spirto onde parean venute.

Esso parlava ancor de la larghezza
che fece Niccolò a le pulcelle,
33   per condurre ad onor lor giovinezza.

"O anima che tanto ben favelle,
dimmi chi fosti," dissi, "e perché sola
36   tu queste degne lode rinovelle.

Non fia sanza mercé la tua parola,
s'io ritorno a compiér lo cammin corto
39   di quella vita ch'al termine vola."

Ed elli: "Io ti dirò, non per conforto
ch'io attenda di là, ma perché tanta
42   grazia in te luce prima che sie morto.

Io fui radice de la mala pianta
che la terra cristiana tutta aduggia,
45   sì che buon frutto rado se ne schianta.

Ma se Doagio, Lilla, Guanto e Bruggia
potesser, tosto ne saria vendetta;
48   e io la cheggio a lui che tutto giuggia.

Chiamato fui di là Ugo Ciappetta;
di me son nati i Filippi e i Luigi
51   per cui novellamente è Francia retta.

Figliuol fu' io d'un beccaio di Parigi:
quando li regi antichi venner meno
54   tutti, fuor ch'un renduto in panni bigi,

trova'mi stretto ne le mani il freno
del governo del regno, e tanta possa
57   di nuovo acquisto, e sì d'amici pieno,

These words gave me such pleasure
that I pressed forward to encounter
30   the spirit who I thought had spoken

and he went on to tell the generous gifts
that Nicholas conferred upon the maidens
33   to guide their youthful innocence to honor.

'O soul that speak of so much goodness,
tell me who you were,' I said, 'and why you alone
36   rehearse these deeds so fit for praise.

'Your words shall not go unrewarded
if I return to finish my brief journey
39   in that life which rushes to its ending.'

And he: 'I will tell you, not for any comfort
I await from there, but for the grace that shines
42   in you, reflected evén short of death.

'I was the root of the evil tree
that casts its shadow over all the Christian lands
45   so that good fruit is rarely gathered there.

'If Douai, Lille, Ghent, and Bruges
but had the power, there would soon be vengeance—
48   and this I beg of Him who judges all.

'On earth I was known as Hugh Capet.
Of me were born the Philips and the Louis
51   who lately have been rulers over France.

'I was the son of a butcher of Paris.
When the ancient line of kings had all died out,
54   except for one, a gray-robed monk,

'I found the reins to govern all the kingdom
firm in my hands, and soon had in possession
57   such power and so very many friends

ch'a la corona vedova promossa
la testa di mio figlio fu, dal quale
60   cominciar di costor le sacrate ossa.

Mentre che la gran dota provenzale
al sangue mio non tolse la vergogna,
63   poco valea, ma pur non facea male.

Lì cominciò con forza e con menzogna
la sua rapina; e poscia, per ammenda,
66   Pontì e Normandia prese e Guascogna.

Carlo venne in Italia e, per ammenda,
vittima fé di Curradino; e poi
69   ripinse al ciel Tommaso, per ammenda.

Tempo vegg' io, non molto dopo ancoi,
che tragge un altro Carlo fuor di Francia,
72   per far conoscer meglio e sé e ' suoi.

Sanz' arme n'esce e solo con la lancia
con la qual giostrò Giuda, e quella ponta
75   sì, ch'a Fiorenza fa scoppiar la pancia.

Quindi non terra, ma peccato e onta
guadagnerà, per sé tanto più grave,
78   quanto più lieve simil danno conta.

L'altro, che già uscì preso di nave,
veggio vender sua figlia e patteggiarne
81   come fanno i corsar de l'altre schiave.

O avarizia, che puoi tu più farne,
poscia c'ha' il mio sangue a te sì tratto,
84   che non si cura de la propria carne?

Perché men paia il mal futuro e 'l fatto,
veggio in Alagna intrar lo fiordaliso,
87   e nel vicario suo Cristo esser catto.

'that to the widowed crown
my son's head was put forward.
60   His issue is entombed as consecrated bones.

'As long as the great dowry of Provence
had not yet stripped my house of feeling shame,
63   it counted little, but at least it did no harm.

'Then, with fraud and pillage, the rape began
and afterwards, to make amends,
66   my heirs took Ponthieu, Normandy, and Gascony.

'Charles came into Italy and, to make amends,
made Conradin a victim and then,
69   to make amends, drove Thomas back to Heaven.

'I see a time, not very long from now,
that brings another Charles away from France
72   to make himself and then his kin more known.

'He comes alone, armed only with the lance
that Judas used for jousting. And with one thrust
75   he bursts the swollen paunch of Florence.

'From this he shall acquire, not land,
but sin and shame, so much the heavier for him
78   the lighter he considers such disgrace.

'Still another Charles: once led, a prisoner,
from his own ship, I see him sell his daughter
81   after haggling, as pirates do for female slaves.

'O avarice, what greater harm can you do,
since my blood is so attached to you
84   it has no care for its own flesh?

'That past and future evil may seem less,
I see the fleur-de-lis proceed into Anagni
87   and, in His vicar, make a prisoner of Christ.

Veggiolo un'altra volta esser deriso;
veggio rinovellar l'aceto e 'l fiele,
90   e tra vivi ladroni esser anciso.

Veggio il novo Pilato sì crudele,
che ciò nol sazia, ma sanza decreto
93   portar nel Tempio le cupide vele.

O Segnor mio, quando sarò io lieto
a veder la vendetta che, nascosa,
96   fa dolce l'ira tua nel tuo secreto?

Ciò ch'io dicea di quell' unica sposa
de lo Spirito Santo e che ti fece
99   verso me volger per alcuna chiosa,

tanto è risposto a tutte nostre prece
quanto 'l dì dura; ma com' el s'annotta,
102   contrario suon prendemo in quella vece.

Noi repetiam Pigmalïon allotta,
cui traditore e ladro e paricida
105   fece la voglia sua de l'oro ghiotta;

e la miseria de l'avaro Mida,
che seguì a la sua dimanda gorda,
108   per la qual sempre convien che si rida.

Del folle Acàn ciascun poi si ricorda,
come furò le spoglie, sì che l'ira
111   di Iosüè qui par ch'ancor lo morda.

Indi accusiam col marito Saffira;
lodiamo i calci ch'ebbe Elïodoro;
114   e in infamia tutto 'l monte gira

Polinestòr ch'ancise Polidoro;
ultimamente ci si grida: 'Crasso,
117   dilci, che 'l sai: di che sapore è l'oro?'

'I see Him mocked a second time.
I see renewed the vinegar and gall—
90   between two living thieves I see Him slain.

'I see that this new Pilate is so brutal
this does not sate him, and, unsanctioned,
93   I see him spread his greedy sails against the Temple.

'O my Lord, when shall I be gladdened
at the sight of vengeance that, as yet concealed,
96   hidden in your mind, makes sweet your wrath?

'The words that I called out before,
of the Holy Spirit's one and only bride,
99   which made you turn to me for explanation,

'are the response, as long as it is day,
in all our prayers, but when night falls
102   we then intone an opposite refrain.

'Then we recall Pygmalion,
whose all-devouring lust for gold
105   made him a traitor, thief, and parricide,

'and the misery of avaricious Midas
that came on him for his intemperate demand
108   and must always be a cause for laughter.

'Each then remembers reckless Achan
and how he stole the spoils, so that the wrath
111   of Joshua seems here to strike at him again.

'Then we accuse Sapphira with her husband.
We celebrate the hoof-blows that Heliodorus bore.
114   In disgrace the name of Polymnestor,

'for slaying Polydorus, circles all the mountain.
Last, the cry is: "Tell us, Crassus,
117   since you know, what is the taste of gold?"

Talor parla l'uno alto e l'altro basso,
secondo l'affezion ch'ad ir ci sprona
120   ora a maggiore e ora a minor passo:

però al ben che 'l dì ci si ragiona,
dianzi non era io sol; ma qui da presso
123   non alzava la voce altra persona."

Noi eravam partiti già da esso,
e brigavam di soverchiar la strada
126   tanto quanto al poder n'era permesso,

quand' io senti', come cosa che cada,
tremar lo monte; onde mi prese un gelo
129   qual prender suol colui ch'a morte vada.

Certo non si scoteo sì forte Delo,
pria che Latona in lei facesse 'l nido
132   a parturir li due occhi del cielo.

Poi cominciò da tutte parti un grido
tal, che 'l maestro inverso me si feo,
135   dicendo: "Non dubbiar, mentr' io ti guido."

"Gloria in excelsis" tutti "Deo"
dicean, per quel ch'io da' vicin compresi,
138   onde intender lo grido si poteo.

No' istavamo immobili e sospesi
come i pastor che prima udir quel canto,
141   fin che 'l tremar cessò ed el compiési.

Poi ripigliammo nostro cammin santo,
guardando l'ombre che giacean per terra,
144   tornate già in su l'usato pianto.

Nulla ignoranza mai con tanta guerra
mi fé desideroso di sapere,
147   se la memoria mia in ciò non erra,

'Sometimes one speaks loud, another low,
according to the zeal that spurs our speech,
120   at times with greater, at times with lesser force.

'Therefore, in giving voice to goodness,
as here we do by day, I was not alone just now,
123   even though no other raised his voice nearby.'

We had already left him there behind us
and strove to pick our way
126   as nimbly as the narrow path allowed,

when I felt the mountain tremble
as though it might collapse, and a chill,
129   like the chill of death, subdued me.

Surely Delos was not so shaken
before Latona built her nest
132   and there gave birth to the twofold eyes of heaven.

Then there rose up a great cry all around us
so that my master drew up closer to me,
135   saying: 'Have no fear while I'm your guide.'

'Gloria in excelsis Deo' all were shouting
from what I understood from those nearby,
138   where their outcry could be better heard.

We stood stock still and in suspense,
like the shepherds who first heard that song,
141   until the trembling ceased and the song ended.

Then we continued on our holy path,
our eyes cast down to see the shades along the ground,
144   who had returned to their accustomed weeping.

Never did ignorance attack me with such fury
against so great a need to know—
147   if in this my memory does not err—

quanta pareami allor, pensando, avere;
né per la fretta dimandare er' oso,
né per me lì potea cosa vedere:
così m'andava timido e pensoso.

151

as then I felt deep in my thoughts.
But, since we had to hurry, I dared not ask,
nor could I of myself find answers there.
151   I went on, afraid to ask and full of thought.

1–3. The metaphoric sponge (his knowledge of this pope's experience) will not be as thoroughly saturated as the protagonist would have liked because he wishes no longer to distract Adrian, acceding instead to his clear desire to return to his penance.

4–9. Virgil and Dante move along close to the wall of the mountain, away from the shades of the penitents, so thickly strewn upon this terrace but mainly near the outer edge. That avarice has affected an enormous number of souls was also clear from *Inferno* VII.25. And while Pride is often accounted the "root sin," another tradition gives Avarice that role. See Trucchi (1936) and Giacalone (1968), the latter citing the passage in I Timothy 6:10 ("Radix omnium malorum est cupiditas" [avarice is the root of all evil]) that helped form that tradition.

10–12. Virgil addresses Plutus, standing over the avaricious in the fourth Circle of hell, as "maladetto lupo" (accursèd wolf—*Inf.* VII.8); the she-wolf *(lupa)* who blocks Dante's upward path in *Inferno* I.49–54 is widely understood to represent the sin of Avarice. Here there can be no doubt: the poet apostrophizes that sin as being the most widespread among mortals.

13–14. The poet's second apostrophe seeks aid from above in the hope of defeating the scourge of avarice. Mattalia (1960) sees these astral influences as executors of the will of God. Woody (Wood.1977.1), p. 122, puts a finer point upon this view, arguing that Dante is here referring to the conjunction of the planets Saturn and Jupiter every twenty years. One such had occurred in Dante's birth year, 1265, in the constellation of Gemini (and thus in the period of Dante's birth); the next was scheduled for 1325, also in Gemini.

15. Even from the very beginning of the exegetical tradition, commentators, e.g., the Anonymous Lombard (1322) and Jacopo della Lana (1324), believe that this opaque question refers to the *veltro* (hound) in Virgil's prophecy at *Inferno* I.101, thus from this vantage point lending that passage a decidedly imperial caste. It is striking to find so much unanimity here, and so little there. However, if there the political figure was (as some believe) Cangrande della Scala, here it would seem to be an ac-

tual emperor, Henry VII, not merely a supporter of the Ghibelline position. Dante would have felt that Henry's advent was still in the offing, as it was until the autumn of 1310, when the emperor announced his decision to come to Italy; or else, if the passage was written in the spring of 1311, the poet, as in the view of Trucchi (1936), was urging Henry to do what he had up to now failed to do, despite his presence in Italy: capture the city of Florence. In his seventh Epistle, Dante's initial enthusiasm for the imperial enterprise has been reduced to overexcited and dubious hope. See notes to *Purgatorio* VI.97–102 and VII.95–96.

These two apostrophes in the mouth of the poet (vv. 10–12 and 13–15) are suggestively coupled; the first deprecates avarice while the second calls for divine intervention in the form of an imperial presence. We have just met a pope, who conquered the avarice that threatened to ruin him, but who, despite his best intentions, left the papacy vulnerable to the depredations of the *lupa* of avarice; we are about to meet a just king (in Dante's mind not in fact a king, but the father of a line of kings), whose France, in his wake, will do everything it can to collaborate with the corrupt papacy in its struggle against the forces of imperial righteousness.

19–24. The exemplars on this terrace are presented in an artistic medium that is parsimonious when compared to those we have been treated to on the first three terraces (see note to *Purg.* XVIII.99–138): here, a (temporarily) anonymous voice crying out the name and a single action of those who were noteworthy for their generosity of spirit. As usual, the first is Mary, here remembered for giving birth to the Son of God in a stable (Luke 2:7).

25–30. "Caius Fabricius, famous Roman hero, Consul B.C. 282, 278, Censor 275. During the invasion of Italy by Pyrrhus, King of Epirus, he was sent to the latter to negotiate an exchange of prisoners. Pyrrhus used every effort to gain him over, but Fabricius refused all his offers. On a later occasion he sent back to Pyrrhus the traitor who had offered to poison him, after which he succeeded in arranging terms for the evacuation of Italy by the former. He and his contemporary Curius Dentatus are lauded by Roman writers for their frugality, and probity in refusing the bribes of the enemy" **(T)**. The protagonist's special pleasure in hearing of him reflects some of the poet's nearly constant enthusiasm for models of Roman republican virtue. (For the extraordinary importance of Roman republicanism to Dante see Davis [Davi.1984.1], pp. 224–89; and see Hollander and Rossi [Holl.1986.1], p. 75, for Fabricius's presence in four of the five collections of republican heroes offered by Dante in *Convivio*, *Commedia*, and *Monarchia*.)

31–33.   Nicholas, whose gift-giving eventually made him the patron of Christmas, was a bishop in Asia Minor in the reign of Constantine in the fourth century. His renown for generosity is based upon his kindness in offering dowries of gold for the three daughters of an impoverished noble friend, who had been planning to sell them into prostitution in order to maintain them and himself. In the first two examples, poverty was itself seen as a sort of nobility, preferred both by Mary and by Fabricius to worldly wealth. Here things are a bit different, as Nicholas allows his friend to escape from poverty by arranging for his daughters' dowries.

34–39.   Dante's two questions ("Who were you? Why do you alone cry out?") are accompanied by a promise to repay the favor of replies by procuring prayers for this penitent on earth. These three elements will structure the rest of the canto, given over almost entirely to the words of this as yet unnamed speaker.

The protagonist's last phrase, concerning the brevity of human life, is memorably echoed near the conclusion of this *cantica* (*Purg.* XXXIII.54: " 'l viver ch'è un correre a la morte" [the life that is a race to death]).

40–42.   Hugh Capet (we can infer that this is he from the next tercet, while he will offer a clear statement of his identity at verse 49) answers with the style of a man practiced in the ways of the political world. As a gentleman, he will respond to Dante only out of the goodness of his heart because he can see that Dante lives in grace; at the same time, like the pope who spoke before him (*Purg.* XIX.142–145), this father of a line of kings realizes there are few or none below who honor his memory. As he converses with Dante, we can observe that half of him lives in this new world of grace while half of him remembers the world he left behind.

43–45.   As the ancestor of a line of kings of France, Hugh had a crucial role in ruling the land that now casts its desiccating shadow over the "garden of the empire" (*Purg.* VI.105). We can imagine that to Dante, exiled as a result of French intervention in the affairs of Florence in collaboration with Boniface VIII in 1302, these words have a particularly bitter ring.

46–48.   For the series of events in Flanders that culminated in the uprising of the Flemish cities in 1302, see Singleton's commentary. While the French did manage to hold on to some of the territory of Flanders, their military defeat at Courtrai in July 1302 must have seemed to Dante in some respects a punishment for what was done to Florence in the same year. Hugh's words ring out as a prophetic hope to see his descendants justly punished, but have a particular resonance for an Italian auditor. See Santelli (Sant.2001.1), pp. 21–23, for the political atmosphere of the Italy in which Dante was composing this very political canto.

49.   The speaker at last fully identifies himself as Hugh Capet, who was in fact king of France (987–96), even if Dante did not know him as such. "The statements put by Dante into the mouth of Hugh Capet as to the origin of the Capetian dynasty are in several respects at variance with the historical facts, and can only be explained on the supposition that Dante has confused Hugh Capet with his father, Hugh the Great, . . . The facts are as follows: Hugh the Great died in 956; Louis V, the last of the Carlovingians, died in 987, in which year Hugh Capet became king; on his death in 996, he was succeeded by his son Robert, who had previously been crowned in 988 [to assure a Capetian continuity upon Hugh's eventual death]. Dante makes Hugh Capet say: firstly, that he was the son of a butcher of Paris (verse 52), whereas common tradition assigned this origin not to Hugh Capet, but to his father, Hugh the Great; second, that when the Carlovingians came to an end he was so powerful that he was able to make his son king (vv. 53–60), whereas on the failure of the Carlovingian line Hugh Capet himself became king (987); and third, that with his son the Capetian line began (vv. 59–60), whereas in fact it began with himself" **(T)**. Hugh's control of the power over kingship is the alpha of which the rule of Philip the Fair, the French king as Dante was writing, is the omega.

50–51.   Bosco/Reggio (1979) offer a list of the ten kings who followed Hugh to the throne between 996 and 1314. Four of these indeed bore the name "Philip" and four, "Louis," but it is the last in each of these groups who may be of greatest interest. Louis IX (1226–70) is one of the major figures of the Middle Ages, a great crusader, king, and saint. Of him Dante is—perhaps not surprisingly, given his hatred of France—resolutely silent; of Philip IV (the Fair—1285–1314), he is loquacity itself, vituperating him several times in this canto, but also in a number of other passages (*Inf.* XIX.85–87; *Purg.* VII.109–110; XXXII.155–156; *Par.* XIX.118–120).

52.   For Dante's repetition of this common error concerning Hugh's paternity see Toynbee's remarks in the note to verse 49.

53–54.   Again Dante is misled, perhaps confusing events in the eighth century surrounding the last days of the Merovingian line, when Pippin the Short *did* put away his last possible political rival in a monastery. What Hugh had done was to have the last of the Carolingians, the Duke of Lorraine, imprisoned in 991. He remained in prison until his death a year later. See Bosco/Reggio's comment on verse 54.

55–60.   Hugh's account of himself as kingmaker is, once again, not in accord with history (see Toynbee, above in the note to verse 49): it was immediately after he himself was made king that he had his son, Robert, anointed as his successor. Thus his account of himself as father of the first of the line is an unwitting act of modesty, since he himself was the first in it.

61–66.   Hugh offers a brief and allusive recapitulation of four centuries of French expansionism, beginning with the continuing efforts to annex Provence, which avoided this fate until 1246, when a marriage between the brother of Louis IX, Charles of Anjou, was arranged with Beatrice, daughter of Raymond Berenger IV of Provence. And then, to make amends for this perfidy (*per ammenda* will be repeated, with increasing sarcasm, to create a triple identical rhyme, twice in the following tercet), France consolidated its territories by annexing three other territories that had been independent.

67–81.   And now the really dreadful deeds begin: a descent into the Italian peninsula where a series of members of the French royal house named Charles are given employment by being sent into Italy: Charles of Anjou, who is blamed for killing Conradin (the last hope of Italian Ghibellinism) at Tagliacozzo in 1268 (see *Inf.* XXVIII.17–18) and for poisoning Thomas Aquinas in 1274 (a rumor that appears to have been made out of whole cloth as part of Italian anti-French propaganda, but which Dante seems only too willing to propagate). Then Charles de

Valois will take (we are once again in the realm of *post-factum* prophecy) Florence in 1301 on behalf of an alliance among the French, the papacy of Boniface, and the Black Guelphs of Corso Donati; it is not difficult to imagine Dante's outrage at the intervention of this second Charles. Finally, the third of these wretched Frenchmen, Charles II, son of Charles of Anjou and king of Naples, is brought onstage to suffer Dante's taunts, delivered by this French version of Dante's ancestor Cacciaguida (see *Par.* XV–XVII), a benevolent ancestor of (in this case) an undeserving descendant. This Charles is portrayed as—after having lost a calamitous naval battle during the Sicilian Vespers in 1284 and, as a result, being held prisoner on his own ship—selling his daughter (there having been no intervention from St. Nicholas on his behalf, we may assume) into matrimony with Azzo VIII of Este in 1305.

82–84. Hugh's first apostrophe of Avarice parallels Dante's at vv. 10–12.

85–90. And now the worst of all the French arrives for his excoriation, King Philip IV (see note to *Purg.* VII.103–111 and to vv. 50–51, above). This king, who had been excommunicated by Boniface as a result of their dispute over the French king's desire to tax the clergy, had his revenge. In September 1303, the king's representative, William of Nogaret, accompanied by an Italian ally, Sciarra Colonna, a member of the family that Boniface, aided by the advice of Guido da Montefeltro, had harmed (see *Inf.* XXVII.102), arrived in Anagni with a force of soldiers and, after physically assaulting the elderly pope, imprisoned him in his own palace, which they sacked. Boniface was eventually freed in a popular uprising against these intruders and made his way to Rome. But the insult to his person, both physical and spiritual, was apparently so great that he died on 12 October 1303. For a description in English of the outrage done to Boniface see Carroll's commentary (1904).

Dante was no admirer of Boniface. The French attack upon the person of the pope, however, was an attack upon the holy office itself, and thus upon the Mystical Body of Christ, the Church. And thus Boniface is compared to Christ betrayed by Pontius Pilate and crucified, while the agents of Philip become the two thieves present at that event, but now represented as part of the torture administered to their victim.

For the possible dependence of Dante's verses here on a poetic prayer to the Virgin composed by Boniface see Moore (Moor.1889.1), pp. 396–97; for the text of this poem see Artinian (Arti.1967.1).

91–93.   The "new Pilate" now directs his rage against the Templars. (For a more balanced view than Dante's of Philip's motives see Scott [Scot.1996.1), pp. 174–77.) "The Knights Templars were one of the three great military orders founded in Cent. xii for the defence of the Latin Kingdom of Jerusalem. After having existed as a powerful and wealthy order for nearly two centuries they were in 1307 accused by Philip the Fair of heresy, sacrilege, and other hideous offences, in consequence of which he ordered their arrest, and by means of diabolical tortures wrung from them confessions (for the most part undoubtedly false) of their alleged enormities. Five years later, at Philip's instigation, they were condemned by Clement V, and the order was suppressed by decree of the Council of Vienne (May, 1312); in the following year the Grand Master, Du Molay, was burned alive at Paris in the presence of the king. The French king's motive in aiming at the destruction of the Templars was, it can hardly be doubted, a desire to get possession of the immense wealth of the order, as is implied by Dante, and stated in so many words by Villani (viii.92)" **(T)**. When did Dante write this passage? Clearly sometime after 1307; and, perhaps nearly as clearly, before 1312. It is notable that none of the details of the denouement of this ugly scheme reached Dante's page: *sanza decreto* (unsanctioned) the king sets out without the papal support necessary to justify such an action (it would come from that other detested Frenchman, Pope Clement V, only in 1312).

94–96.   Hugh's second apostrophe parallels Dante's (vv. 13–15) in hoping for divine vengeance to descend from above and smite the guilty, in this case most particularly Philip the Fair.

There are questions as to whether the poet meant the reader to think of the "vengeance" as reflecting his defeats in Flanders in 1302 (see Singleton [1973]), or Philip's death while hunting, when his horse was overturned by a charging boar, in 1314 (the opinion of John of Serravalle [1416]), or neither of these events. As Trucchi (1936) points out, Dante clearly refers with joy to Philip's death in November 1314 at *Paradiso* XIX.118–120. The notion that God's vengeance for the events at Anagni in 1303 occurred in Flanders in 1302 hardly seems acceptable. Further, as Bosco/Reggio (1979) argue, since Dante does refer to Philip's death in the next *cantica*, it only makes sense to believe that he did not yet know of it when he wrote this passage, for it would have been much too tempting a piece of information not to include. In any case, the result is as Dante probably would have wanted anyway; here he predicts only that such outrageous behavior will receive God's eventual vengeance—it is but a matter of time. This seems the best understanding. The gleeful passage in *Paradiso* banks the promissory note that Dante writes us here.

At verse 35, Dante had inquired as to the speaker's identity; it has taken Hugh sixty-two lines to answer him by including the history of France's decline as a narrative of a family's woe, from his virtue to Philip's savagery, in just over three hundred years. Needless to say, for Dante, Hugh's tale is still more important as the record of what went wrong for Italy, drawing her from her Roman-imperial destiny toward her near death (see *Purg.* VII.94–96), because of France's malfeasance.

97–102. To answer Dante's second question, caused by his sense that only one penitent seemed to be crying out the names of the generous, Hugh is equally contorted and long-winded, only clearing up Dante's miscomprehension at vv. 118–123. When he uttered the name of Mary (verse 19) he did what he and his companions do during the day, i.e., name the exemplars of generous lives; at night they turn from names that serve as "goads" to those that serve as "bridles," those of the avaricious.

For Mary as "bride of the Holy Spirit," Singleton (1973) cites Matthew 1:20: "For that which is begotten of her is of the Holy Spirit."

103–117. This is Dante's most "crowded" group of exemplary figures in *Purgatorio*, eight of them presented in fifteen lines. Once again he divides his cast into biblical and pagan personages, here not in parallel pairings (as in *Purg.* XII.25–60) but chiastically:

PYGMALION (VIRGIL)
MIDAS (OVID)
         ACHAN (OT)
                  ANANIAS (NT)
                  SAFFIRA (NT)
         HELIODORUS (OT)
POLYMNESTOR (VIRGIL, OVID)
CRASSUS (CICERO?)

103–105. Virgil's tale of Pygmalion's avarice (*Aen.* I.340–364) is narrated by Venus to Aeneas. Pygmalion was king of Tyre and brother of Dido, married to wealthy Sychaeus. Pygmalion secretly murdered Sychaeus, whose shade then appeared to reveal everything in a dream to Dido, who consequently made off, with Sychaeus's hidden stores of wealth, to her new life in Carthage, thus depriving Pygmalion of the gold he sought.

106–108. Two back-to-back Ovidian narratives involving Midas (*Metam.* XI.100–193) may here be condensed into a tercet. In the first Bacchus allows Midas his famous "touch," turning all to gold with disastrous results once he realizes he can no longer eat nor drink, and has to ask to have his gift withdrawn; in the second, Apollo metamorphoses Midas's ears into the enormous ears of an ass because Midas, alone among the listeners, insisted on his opinion that Pan's piping was more beautiful than Apollo's playing of his lyre. Dante refers to this scene in his second *Eclogue* (*Egl.* II.50–53). It is not clear whether Midas is laughable only for his foolish avarice or for his ass's ears as well.

109–111. Achan's theft of the treasure of the Israelites and its result (his being stoned to death by command of Joshua) is the subject of the entire seventh chapter of Joshua (7:1–26).

112. Ananias and his wife, Sapphira, having sold some of their land to make a donation in support of the young Church, kept back part of the price for themselves. Peter, reading their hearts, tells first Ananias and then his wife that he realizes they have lied; as a result, each drops dead before him from shame (Acts 5:1–11).

113. Heliodorus was sent by his king, Seleucus IV of Syria, whom he served as treasurer, to take possession of the treasure in the temple in Jerusalem. Entering the sacred precinct for such purpose, he is assaulted by a terrifying figure on horseback and by two young men who beat him (II Maccabees 3:7–40).

114–115. Polymnestor murdered Polydorus for the gold of Troy that the young son of Priam was sent with, while supposedly under the protection of the Thracian king (see *Inf.* XIII.31–39 and note; *Inf.* XXX.18–19). Dante's sources include Virgil (*Aen.* III.22–48) and Ovid (*Metam.* XIII.429–438).

116–117. Marcus Licinius Crassus, known as "Dives" (the rich man), the name reflecting his reputation for avarice. He had a successful political career, becoming triumvir with Caesar and Pompey in 60 B.C. (all three were reconfirmed in 56). In 55 he became proconsul in Syria. Trapped in an ambush by the warring Parthians, he was killed, and his severed head and one hand were sent back to the Parthian king, Orodes, who then had his mouth filled with molten gold. There is unresolved discussion of Dante's likely source for this tale, with candidates being Paulus Orosius, *Historiae adversus paganos*; Lucius Annaeus Florus, *Epitome de Tito Livio*; Cicero, *De officiis*. The Latin phrasing most cited is "aurum sitisti, aurum bibe" (you thirsted for gold, now drink it) used to refer to the Parthian king's treatment of Crassus's head. For the importance of Florus as source for much of Dante's Roman history, see Antonio Martina, "Floro," *ED* II (1970), pp. 948–52. For Dante's earlier readings in *De officiis* see Marchesi (Marc.2001.1).

118–123.   Hugh finally explains the reasons for his seeming to have spoken alone when Dante first observed him. What can we deduce from the fact that he, of all the penitents, is the most moved to call upon the positive examples of generosity? Perhaps we are meant to understand that he, burdened by his thoughts of the terrible avarice of his French descendants, is the one most moved at this particular moment.

124–126.   In contrast to his unenthusiastic departure from Pope Adrian, Dante's leaving of Hugh Capet is quick and purposive. Perhaps the difference in the two interviews is that this one has come to a sense of completion, while Dante still longed to know more of Adrian's life at the end of his discourse.

127–129.   The sudden shift in focus to Dante's fearful condition in response to this earthquake opens an entirely new chapter in the narrative, a unique one. As Philip B. Miller observed in conversation many years ago, Statius's completion of penance is the only genuine event that occurs involving a damned or a saved soul in the entire *Commedia*. (Discussion of Statius awaits the next canto.) All else in the poem that passes for narrative action pertains to demons or angels interacting with Dante, Virgil, or the souls whom they help to punish or serve, to Dante's own difficulties or successes in moving on, or else represents some form of ritual performance by the souls in the afterworld for the benefit of onlooking Dante. Dante, still a stranger on this magic mountain, responds by feeling like a man in fear of death. We shortly learn that he is witness to a moment of completion, of resurrection. It takes a while for this to become clear.

130–132.   Benvenuto (1380) understands the simile as having the following meaning: "Just as that most renowned island, Delos, once sent forth the two most famous luminaries into the sky [Apollo and Diana, the sun and the moon], so now this most renowned mount of Purgatory was sending into the heavens two very famous poets, one ancient, i.e., Statius, and one modern, i.e., Dante. I speak not of Virgil, for he did not go to heaven." The commentary tradition is, nonetheless, a seedbed of confusion for interpreters of these verses. The following things are among those variously said: (1) Delos was made stable by Jove so that Latona, pursued by jealous Juno, could give birth in peace; (2) before Latona gave birth, Delos suffered no such quaking; (3) the island became stable only when Latona arrived to give birth on it; (4) Apollo later made the wandering island stable out of *pietas* (the version sponsored by *Aeneid* III.73–77). Either the third or this last, partly because of its Virgilian authority, seems the best to follow. The mountain's wild quaking reminds the poet of the agitated condition of the floating island, which welcomed Latona for her parturition, before it was made fast, either by her arrival or, later, by Apollo.

For passages in the Old Testament anticipating Dante's supernatural earthquake see Boyde (Boyd.1981.1), pp. 93–95.

133–135.   Once again a tercet is devoted to Dante's apparent fear and now to Virgil's miscomprehension of what is happening, since he, too, thinks that fearful thoughts now are understandable, if not welcome.

136–141.   The passage in Luke 2:13–14 presenting angelic praise of God at the birth of Jesus ("Glory to God in the highest, and on earth peace among men of good will") is cited first by Pietro di Dante (1340). By comparing himself and Virgil to the shepherds that first heard the angelic *Gloria* (Luke 3:15), Dante has underlined the connection between Jesus and Statius, which will be evident in the next canto as well. The birth of Jesus stands as a sign for the rebirth of this soul, who has finished his purgation and is prepared to ascend to the Father. All on the mountain apparently cease their own penitential activity to celebrate the event in this song, and do so until the quaking stops; we are led to imagine that this is true each time a soul arrives at this joyful moment of freedom from even the memory of sin, a condition that is formally completed with the passage through the waters of Lethe in the earthly paradise.

142–144.   At the cessation of the celebrative singing all return to their usual practice, including the two travelers.

145–151.   Dante for the first time underlines his unusual (even for him) curiosity to know the meaning of the things he has just felt and heard. Tommaseo (1837) noted the echo here of Wisdom 14:22, "in magno viventes inscientiae bello" (they live in a great war of ignorance).

The need to press on leaves Dante suspended—and the reader, as well.

PURGATORIO XXI
([*Avarice &*] *Prodigality*)

IV. The speakers (3)

La sete natural che mai non sazia
se non con l'acqua onde la femminetta
samaritana domandò la grazia,

mi travagliava, e pungeami la fretta
per la 'mpacciata via dietro al mio duca,
e condoleami a la giusta vendetta.

Ed ecco, sì come ne scrive Luca
che Cristo apparve a' due ch'erano in via,
già surto fuor de la sepulcral buca,

ci apparve un'ombra, e dietro a noi venìa,
dal piè guardando la turba che giace;
né ci addemmo di lei, sì parlò pria,

dicendo: "O frati miei, Dio vi dea pace."
Noi ci volgemmo sùbiti, e Virgilio
rendéli 'l cenno ch'a ciò si conface.

Poi cominciò: "Nel beato concilio
ti ponga in pace la verace corte
che me rilega ne l'etterno essilio."

"Come!" diss' elli, e parte andavam forte:
"se voi siete ombre che Dio sù non degni,
chi v'ha per la sua scala tanto scorte?"

E 'l dottor mio: "Se tu riguardi a' segni
che questi porta e che l'angel profila,
ben vedrai che coi buon convien ch'e' regni.

Ma perché lei che dì e notte fila
non li avea tratta ancora la conocchia
che Cloto impone a ciascuno e compila,

3

6

9

12

15

18

21

24

27

The natural thirst that never can be quenched
except with that water the woman of Samaria
3   begged to be given as a special grace

tormented me. And in haste I followed my leader
over bodies strewn along the way,
6   still grieved at their just punishment.

And lo, as Luke sets down for us that Christ,
just risen from the cave that was His sepulcher,
9   revealed himself to two He walked with on the road,

there appeared a shade, coming up behind us
while we, intent upon the crowd prone at our feet,
12   were not aware of him until he spoke

and said: 'O my brothers, may God grant you peace.'
We turned at once and Virgil answered him
15   with the gesture that befits this greeting

and then began: 'May the unerring court
that confines me in eternal exile
18   bring you in peace to the assembly of the blessed.'

'What?' the other asked—even as we hurried on—
'if you are shades whom God does not deem worthy,
21   who has led you up so far along His stairs?'

And my teacher said: 'If you behold the signs
that this man bears, traced by the angel,
24   you will know that he must reign among the good.

'Since she that spins both day and night
had not used up the flax that for each mortal
27   Clotho loads and winds upon the distaff,

l'anima sua, ch'è tua e mia serocchia,
venendo sù, non potea venir sola,
30   però ch'al nostro modo non adocchia.

Ond' io fui tratto fuor de l'ampia gola
d'inferno per mostrarli, e mosterrolli
33   oltre, quanto 'l potrà menar mia scola.

Ma dimmi, se tu sai, perché tai crolli
diè dianzi 'l monte, e perché tutto ad una
36   parve gridare infino a' suoi piè molli."

Sì mi diè, dimandando, per la cruna
del mio disio, che pur con la speranza
39   si fece la mia sete men digiuna.

Quei cominciò: "Cosa non è che sanza
ordine senta la religïone
42   de la montagna, o che sia fuor d'usanza.

Libero è qui da ogne alterazione:
di quel che 'l ciel da sé in sé riceve
45   esser ci puote, e non d'altro, cagione.

Per che non pioggia, non grando, non neve,
non rugiada, non brina più sù cade
48   che la scaletta di tre gradi breve;

nuvole spesse non paion né rade,
né coruscar, né figlia di Taumante,
51   che di là cangia sovente contrade;

secco vapor non surge più avante
ch'al sommo d'i tre gradi ch'io parlai,
54   dov' ha 'l vicario di Pietro le piante.

Trema forse più giù poco o assai;
ma per vento che 'n terra si nasconda,
57   non so come, qua sù non tremò mai.

'his soul, which is your sister—mine as well,
could not attempt the climb unaided
30   because it cannot see things quite as we do.

'I, for this reason, was drawn from hell's wide jaws
to be his guide, and I shall guide him
33   as far as my own teaching will allow.

'But tell us, if you can, why did the mountain shake
so hard just now and why did it emit
36   such clamor, down to its wave-washed base?'

With this question he threaded the needle of my wish
with such precision that, with but hope
39   for an answer, he made my thirst less parching.

The other offered this response:
'The mountain's holy law does not allow
42   anything disordered or that violates its rule.

'Here nothing ever changes.
Only by that which Heaven gathers from Itself,
45   and from nothing else, can any change be caused,

'so that not rain nor hail nor snow
nor dew nor hoarfrost falls above
48   the gentle rise of those three steps below.

'Clouds, dense or broken, do not appear,
nor lightning-flash, nor Thaumas' daughter,
51   who appears in many places in the sky down there,

'nor does dry vapor rise above the highest
of those three steps of which I spoke,
54   where Peter's vicar sets his feet.

'Lower down, perhaps, it trembles more or less,
but from the wind concealed in earth
57   it has not, I know not why, ever trembled here above.

Tremaci quando alcuna anima monda
sentesi, sì che surga o che si mova
60   per salir sù; e tal grido seconda.

De la mondizia sol voler fa prova,
che, tutto libero a mutar convento,
63   l'alma sorprende, e di voler le giova.

Prima vuol ben, ma non lascia il talento
che divina giustizia, contra voglia,
66   come fu al peccar, pone al tormento.

E io, che son giaciuto a questa doglia
cinquecent' anni e più, pur mo sentii
69   libera volontà di miglior soglia:

però sentisti il tremoto e li pii
spiriti per lo monte render lode
72   a quel Segnor, che tosto sù li 'nvii."

Così ne disse; e però ch'el si gode
tanto del ber quant' è grande la sete,
75   non saprei dir quant' el mi fece prode.

E 'l savio duca: "Omai veggio la rete
che qui vi 'mpiglia e come si scalappia,
78   perché ci trema e di che congaudete.

Ora chi fosti, piacciati ch'io sappia,
e perché tanti secoli giaciuto
81   qui se', ne le parole tue mi cappia."

"Nel tempo che 'l buon Tito, con l'aiuto
del sommo rege, vendicò le fóra
84   ond' uscì 'l sangue per Giuda venduto,

col nome che più dura e più onora
era io di là," rispuose quello spirto,
87   "famoso assai, ma non con fede ancora.

'Here it trembles when a soul feels it is pure,
ready to rise, to set out on its ascent,
60   and next there follows that great cry.

'Of its purity the will alone gives proof,
and the soul, wholly free to change its convent,
63   is taken by surprise and allows the will its way.

'It wills the same before, but holy Justice sets
the soul's desire against its will,
66   and, as once it longed to sin, it now seeks penance.

'And I, who have been prostrate in this pain
five hundred years and more, just now felt
69   my freed will seek a better threshold.

'That is why you felt the earth shake
and heard the pious spirits of this mountain
72   praise the Lord—may He soon raise them!'

Thus he spoke to us, and since it is true
the greater the thirst the more the drinking pleases,
75   I cannot begin to tell the benefit to me.

And my wise leader: 'Now I see the net
that here ensnares you and how you are released,
78   why the earth trembled and why you rejoiced.

'May it please you to tell me who you were
and to let me understand from your own words
81   why you have lain here for so many centuries.'

'In the time when worthy Titus,
aided by the King most high, avenged the wounds
84   from which had poured the blood that Judas sold,

'on earth I bore the name that most endures
and honors most,' replied that spirit.
87   'Fame I had found, but not yet faith.

Tanto fu dolce mio vocale spirto,
che, tolosano, a sé mi trasse Roma,
90   dove mertai le tempie ornar di mirto.

Stazio la gente ancor di là mi noma:
cantai di Tebe, e poi del grande Achille;
93   ma caddi in via con la seconda soma.

Al mio ardor fuor seme le faville,
che mi scaldar, de la divina fiamma
96   onde sono allumati più di mille;

de l'Eneïda dico, la qual mamma
fummi, e fummi nutrice, poetando:
99   sanz' essa non fermai peso di dramma.

E per esser vivuto di là quando
visse Virgilio, assentirei un sole
102   più che non deggio al mio uscir di bando."

Volser Virgilio a me queste parole
con viso che, tacendo, disse "Taci";
105   ma non può tutto la virtù che vuole;

ché riso e pianto son tanto seguaci
a la passion di che ciascun si spicca,
108   che men seguon voler ne' più veraci.

Io pur sorrisi come l'uom ch'ammicca;
per che l'ombra si tacque, e riguardommi
111   ne li occhi ove 'l sembiante più si ficca;

e "Se tanto labore in bene assommi,"
disse, "perché la tua faccia testeso
114   un lampeggiar di riso dimostrommi?"

Or son io d'una parte e d'altra preso:
l'una mi fa tacer, l'altra scongiura
117   ch'io dica; ond' io sospiro, e sono inteso

'So sweet was my poetic recitation,
Rome drew me from Toulouse and deemed me worthy
90   to have my brows adorned with myrtle.

'Statius is my name. On earth men often say it.
I sang of Thebes and then of great Achilles,
93   but fell along the way with the second burden.

'The sparks that kindled the fire in me
came from the holy flame
96   from which more than a thousand have been lit—

'I mean the *Aeneid*. When I wrote my poems
it was my *mamma* and my nurse.
99   Without it, I would not have weighed a dram.

'To have lived on earth when Virgil lived
I would have stayed one year's sun longer than I owed
102   before I came forth from my exile.'

These words made Virgil turn to me
with a look that, silent, said: 'Keep silent.'
105   But the power that wills cannot do all it wills,

for laughter and tears so closely follow feelings
from which they spring, they least can be controlled
108   in those who are most truthful.

I only smiled, like one who gives a hint,
at which the shade was silent, probing my eyes,
111   where the soul's expression is most clearly fixed.

'So your great labor may end in good,'
he said, 'why did your face just now
114   give off the sudden glimmer of a smile?'

Now I am caught between one side and the other:
one bids me hold my tongue,
117   the other urges me to speak,

dal mio maestro, e "Non aver paura,"
mi dice, "di parlar; ma parla e digli
120   quel ch'e' dimanda con cotanta cura."

Ond' io: "Forse che tu ti maravigli,
antico spirto, del rider ch'io fei;
123   ma più d'ammirazion vo' che ti pigli.

Questi che guida in alto li occhi miei,
è quel Virgilio dal qual tu togliesti
126   forte a cantar de li uomini e d'i dèi.

Se cagion altra al mio rider credesti,
lasciala per non vera, ed esser credi
129   quelle parole che di lui dicesti."

Già s'inchinava ad abbracciar li piedi
al mio dottor, ma el li disse: "Frate,
132   non far, ché tu se' ombra e ombra vedi."

Ed ei surgendo: "Or puoi la quantitate
comprender de l'amor ch'a te mi scalda,
quand' io dismento nostra vanitate,
136   trattando l'ombre come cosa salda."

so that I sigh and my master understands.
'Don't be afraid to speak,' he says to me,
120   'yes, speak—tell him what he is so keen to know.'

And I begin: 'Perhaps you wonder,
ancient spirit, at my smiling,
123   but I would have a greater wonder seize you.

'This one who guides my eyes on high
is the very Virgil from whom you took the power
126   to sing of men and of the gods.

'If you believed another reason caused my smile,
dismiss that as untrue and understand
129   it was those words you spoke of him.'

Already he was stooping to embrace my teacher's feet,
but Virgil said: 'Brother, do not do so,
132   for you are a shade and you behold a shade.'

And the other, rising: 'Now you can understand
the measure of the love for you that warms me,
when I forget our emptiness
136   and treat our shades as bodied things.'

1. From at least the time of Tommaseo (1837), commentators dealing with this opening verse have cited the opening (and other passages) of Dante's *Convivio* (I.i.1): "As the Philosopher [Aristotle] says in the beginning of the First Philosophy [*Metaphysics* I.i], all of humankind naturally desires to know." Bosco/Reggio (1979), however, make an important distinction. Since here the protagonist is presented with a miracle, the moment in which a soul is finally prepared to rise to God, the following reference (vv. 2–3) to the waters of eternal life in the episode in John's gospel "confirms the notion that the natural desire for knowledge cannot be satisfied except by Revelation, thus going beyond the affirmations found in *Convivio* (I.i.1; I.i.9; III.xv.4) normally cited by the commentators, which are limited to philosophical knowledge."

2–3. The obvious reference to the passage in John's gospel (John 4:5–15) has not escaped many readers. The Samaritan woman who finds Jesus, unprepared for the task of drawing water, at her well, ends up being eager to taste the "water" that he offers as replacement for that which seems so necessary at noon of a warm day in the desert, for it "fiet in eo fons aquae *salientis* in vitam aeternam" ([italics added] shall become in him a fountain of water springing up into life everlasting). In the Vulgate the present participle *salientis* may refer to the water or indeed to the drinker, rising up into eternal life. It is worth keeping this potential grammatical ambiguity in mind, for that second reading applies precisely to the condition of Statius, who has just now come to that moment in his posthumous existence: he is ready to take on the life of a soul in paradise; he himself is ready to *salire* (rise up). In most interpretations, the water that the Samaritan woman asks for is that of eternal life, which comes alone from the grace of God.

As some commentators have pointed out, John's word for the Samaritan is *mulier* (woman), while Dante has used a diminutive *(femminetta)*. Giacalone (1968) thinks of the form more as a "commiserative" than as a "diminutive," i.e., we are to think of this woman's absolute ordinariness as an encouragement to our own need for exactly such satisfaction of our "thirst."

4–6. Dante has rarely portrayed his protagonist as being beset by so many distractions. He desperately wants to understand the meaning both

of the earthquake and of the song accompanying it; he and Virgil are try-
ing to move ahead as quickly as possible, picking their way among the
clutter of the penitents; he continues to feel a sense of grief at their pun-
ishment, despite its obvious rightness.

7–9. Announced with its solemn biblical stylistic flourish (*Ed ecco* [And
lo]), the reminiscence of Luke 24:13–16 (a passage that begins "Et ecce")
reminds the reader of two of Christ's disciples (Dante's first commenta-
tors at times incorrectly identify them as James and John; it is clear that
one of the two is named Cleopas [24:18], while the other is perhaps his
wife [24:29], in which case she may well have been known as Mary
[John 19:25]), walking on the road to Emmaus when Christ joined them
and walked with them, unrecognized.

10–14. Statius's unmistakable resemblance to Christ risen, his figural re-
lation to Jesus, makes him, technically, not a "figure" of Christ but a
"fulfillment" of Him, which is theologically awkward. Hollander
(Holl.1969.1), pp. 67–70, argues for the technical reference of the word
ombra (shade) here, grounded in the language of the Christian interpre-
tation of Scripture, discovered, indeed, in this very chapter of Luke's
gospel (24:27), when Jesus teaches his disciples the figural method of un-
derstanding the Old Testament. (See the section on allegory in the in-
troduction to *Inferno*. And see Heilbronn [Heil.1977.1], p. 58, for a
completely similar view.)

Statius's first words join him to the tradition of fraternal purgatorial
greeting on the part of the penitents we have so far heard addressing
Dante: Belacqua (*Purg.* IV.127); Oderisi (*Purg.* XI.82); Sapia (*Purg.*
XIII.94); Marco (*Purg.* XVI.65); Adrian (*Purg.* XIX.133). See notes to
Purg. IV.127 and *Purg.* XIX.133.

For the source of Statius's greeting, see the words of Christ to his
apostles, the second scene of his resurrected life on earth in Luke's gospel
(Luke 24:36): "Pax vobis: ego sum, nolite timere" (Peace unto you: I am,
have no fear). In the next verse of Luke the apostles indeed do show fear;
and we may remember how fearful Dante was when the earth shook be-
neath him at the end of the last canto (vv. 128–129; 135).

14–15. The nature of the *cenno* (sign) made in response by Virgil has
long puzzled the commentators. We can say one thing with something
like certainty: Virgil's gesture is not a spoken one, since he makes some
sort of gesture and *then* begins to speak (verse 16). Many early and some

later commentators have liked the idea that in response Virgil said "et cum spiritu tuo" (and with your spirit as well), a liturgical reply. Yet it surely seems impossible that Dante would have first presented Virgil as speaking and then immediately afterwards as *beginning to speak*. And so it is clearly preferable to understand that Virgil made some sort of physical gesture. (For clear examples of facial gestures as *cenni* in this very canto, see verse 104, Virgil's look that calls for silence, and verse 109, Dante's smile that is a hint.)

16–18. Virgil's wish for Statius is touching, in part because it has been accomplished, since Statius is already substantially one of the blessed, only awaiting a change in his accidental state, which will be accomplished in less than a day. While the poem does not show him there, its givens make it plain that, had Dante chosen to do so, Statius could have been observed seated in the rose in *Paradiso* XXXII; he is there by the time Dante ascends into the heavens at the beginning of the next *cantica*, or so we may assume.

Virgil's insistence on his own eternal home is a moving reminder of his tragic situation in this comic poem. Statius's salvation comes closer than anyone else's in showing how near Virgil himself came to eternal blessedness, as the next canto will make clear. And, once we learn (*Purg.* XXII.67–73) that it was Virgil who was responsible, by means of his fourth *Eclogue*, for the conversion of Statius, we consider these lines with a still more troubled heart.

19–21. For Statius's miscomprehension of Dante's condition, see the note to the next tercet. The physical reason for it is that, because the travelers are out of the sun's rays on the far side of the mountain, Dante's body casts no revealing shadow, and Statius takes Virgil's confession of his own plight to apply to both of these "shades."

22–24. Virgil's remarks suggest to Statius that the (remaining three) P's on Dante's forehead indicate a special status, namely that he is bound for Glory—just as is Statius. But did Statius have these marks incised on *his* forehead? Had he, they would now all be erased but for this last, which would probably disappear, along with Dante's, before the beginning of the next canto (see *Purg.* XXII.3, where we learn the angel has wiped Dante's fifth P from his brow). He would have spent, we will be able to compute from information gleaned from verse 68 and from *Purgatorio* XXII.92–93, as many as 300 years in ante-purgatory and/or on some or all of the first three terraces, since it is 1,204 years since his death in the year 96 and he has had to remain over 400 years on the fourth terrace and over 500 on this one. Thus, had he borne signs on his forehead, these would originally have been as many as five and as few as two. However, there is no reason to believe that he, or any other penitent not here in the flesh, has had his brow incised with P's. (See the note to *Purg.* IX.112.) For other reasons to believe that only Dante is incised, see Hollander (Holl.2002.1); for an opposing view see Fosca (Fosc.2002.2).

25–30. The circumlocution describes Lachesis, the second of the three Fates of classical mythology. "At the birth of every mortal, Clotho, the spinning fate, was supposed to wind upon the distaff of Lachesis, the alotting fate, a certain amount of yarn; the duration of the life of the individual being the length of time occupied in spinning the thread, which, when complete, was severed by Atropos, the inevitable fate" **(T)**. For Atropos, see *Inferno* XXXIII.126. This is Virgil's long-winded way of saying that Dante was still in the body when he was summoned to guide him through the afterworld. For Dante's likely dependence upon Statius for the names of the three Fates see Ettore Paratore, "Stazio," *ED* V (1976), pp. 422b–423a.

33. What exactly Virgil means by his *scola* (teaching of Dante) has been a matter of some debate, featuring predictable allegorizations, e.g., Virgil as reason, Statius as moral philosophy, Beatrice as theology. None of these has the merit of being immediately (or eventually?) convincing. The last time we have heard the word was at *Inferno* IV.94, where the poet referred to the group of poets *(la bella scola)* headed by Homer, and perhaps, "reading Dante by Dante," we should keep this simplest explanation in clear view. Virgil, informed by all that a pagan poet can know, will guide Dante as best he can. Once we reach the question of the nature of the human soul, in Canto XXV, he will give way to Statius, who, as a Christian, understands things about the nature of the human soul's relationship to divinity of which Virgil is simply ignorant. There is no reason to believe, one might add, that Beatrice could not have instructed Dante about this question, or that Statius could not have told him anything that Beatrice will reveal in *Paradiso*. All saved Christians, in this poem, are capable of knowing all things in God. The rewards of Heaven are not only affective, but intellectual.

We should also be aware of Beatrice's use of the same word, *scola*, in *Purgatorio* XXXIII.85 to denigrate Dante's own nearly disastrous adventures in what she seems to consider his overbold philosophizing.

34–39. At last Virgil asks Statius the two questions that have so vexed Dante; for a third time the importance of the salvation of Statius is underlined. See notes to *Purgatorio* XX.145–151 and to vv. 4–6 of this canto.

40–60. Statius first establishes the meteorology of the mountain. There is no "weather" encountered above the upper limit of ante-purgatory, but below that limit there is. Up here the only celestial force having any effect is the direct influence of the heavens.

Thaumas's daughter is Iris, for classical poets the personification of the rainbow, appearing variously above the earth and not in one fixed place.

The wind hidden inside the earth (verse 56, first referred to as "dry vapor" in verse 52) refers to what Dante, in keeping with one medieval view (see *Inf.* III.130–136), believed to be the cause of earthquakes. Statius's point is that there are no natural earthquakes on the upper reaches of the mountain, but that there are "supernatural" ones. This one, accompanying the completion of Statius's penance and marking his liberation from sin, may remind us of the earthquake that greeted Dante's "supernatural" descent into the underworld at the conclusion of *Inferno* III, itself perhaps also meant to remind the reader of the earthquake at the Crucifixion (referred to at some length by Virgil in *Inf.* XII.31–45). These three earthquakes, all caused by Christ-centered spiritual events, would clearly seem to be related.

61–66. The self-judging quality of the penitents is here made plain. We saw the same phenomenon among the damned in the confessions that they offered to Minos (see note to *Inf.* V.8).

Words for "will" and "willing" occur five times in nine lines (61–69), the densest block of *volere* and *volontà* found in the poem. In *Paradiso* III the examples of Piccarda and Costanza will afford the opportunity to study the divergence between the absolute will, always striving toward the good, and the conditional (i.e., "conditioned") will, which, when guided by desires for lesser goods, chooses unwisely. Here Dante plays the changes on that basic understanding of the will's role. In purgatory the conditional will does not elect the lesser good, but instead desires to repent its former movement in that direction. This is a "rule" of purgatory that has no precedent in Christian lore, since Dante's purgatory is so much his own invention; nonetheless, it makes intuitive sense. It is thus that the poet suggests that his reader understand why a penitent, while naturally desiring to cease the act of penance, simultaneously feels a still stronger and countering desire to complete it, as is made clear here.

For a soul to "change its convent," in this context, means for it to move from purgatory to paradise.

67–72. His use of the first person here is the first instance of an autobiographical bent on the speaker's part, but his self-identification still awaits. He only now formally concludes his response to Dante's insistent and paired questions, first alluded to in the last canto (XX.145–151); in a gesture typical of purgatorial brotherhood, his next thought is for his fellow penitents (cf. Virgil's similar wish at vv. 16–18). (For Statius's various sins and the time spent purging them on the mountain, see notes to vv. 22–24 and to *Purg.* XXII.92–93.)

73–75. After telling us three times how eagerly he wanted to know more about these strange signs on the mountain (see note to vv. 34–39), the poet now once again underlines their importance. The singular importance of the salvation of Statius is insisted on in such a way as to let us understand that what matters is not only the importance of the finishing of purgation for any soul, but Statius's astounding role in Dante's poem, which will gradually become more clear as the two cantos devoted to him continue to unfold their mysteries.

78. Tommaseo (1837) rightly suggests that *congaudere* (rejoice) is a biblical word; further precision was offered by Campi (1888), citing I Corinthians 12:26: "sive gloriatur unum membrum, congaudent omnia membra" (if a single member glories, then all members rejoice along with it). St. Paul is developing the analogy between parts of the human body and the individual members of the Mystical Body of Christ, the Church.

81. Virgil's specific question at last elicits a sort of *vita poetae* from his interlocutor. See note to *Inferno* I.67–87 for the similar *vita Virgilii* found there.

82–93. Publius Papinius Statius (45–96) was born in Naples and not in Toulouse, birthplace of a different Statius, a rhetorician; Dante's error was a common one (perhaps deriving from the glosses by Lactantius [ca. 300] to the poems of Statius) and he helped propagate it, since he is probably responsible for the mistaken birthplace found both in

Boccaccio and in Chaucer. Statius's *Thebaid*, an epic in twelve books, composed in the years between between 80 and 92, was the source of a good deal of Dante's sense of what for us is the "Oedipus story," in Statius seen as the civil war between the forces loyal to one or the other of Oedipus's royal sons.

Dante's reference to Statius's laureation is problematic. Since it seems clear, despite an occasional argument to the contrary, that Dante did not know Statius's collection of his "fugitive" poems, the *Silvae* (see the note to verse 90), he could not have read (in *Silvae* III.v.28–31) that, while the emperor (Domitian) had crowned Statius with gold at an "arts festival" at Alba, he had not done so at Rome, i.e., Statius did not get the laurel for his epic. And thus it remains possible but seems unlikely that he ever received the laurel; however, his dedication of the *Thebaid* to Domitian, coupled with the opening lines of the *Achilleid* (I.9–11), where he asks Apollo for laureation and intimates that he had been previously coronated, might have made Dante think he had been. This second epic, which he did not finish, getting only as far as into the second book, was the source of most of what Dante, Homerless, knew about Achilles.

82–84. Born around A.D. 45, Statius was thus about twenty-five when Titus, son of the emperor Vespasian, destroyed in A.D. 70 the Second Temple in Jerusalem as part of his attack upon the Jews, an event to which Dante will advert in *Paradiso* VI.92 (for Dante's sense of the "just retribution" involved in this event, see the note to that passage). Titus succeeded Vespasian as emperor (79–81).

85–87. The "name" to which the speaker refers is that of poet. The surprising, even shocking, culmination of his statement of his debt to Virgil in the next canto (verse 73: "through you I was a poet, through you a Christian") is adumbrated here, where Statius owns himself (at the age at which Dante suffered the loss of Beatrice, twenty-five) to have achieved fame as a poet but not yet faith in Christ.

88. Dante had already referred to Statius as "lo dolce poeta" (the sweet poet) at *Convivio* IV.xxv.6, as Tommaseo (1837) pointed out. Pietro di Dante (1340) was the first to suggest that the source for the phrase lay in Juvenal's *Satires* (VII.82–87). For strong support of this notion, see Ronconi (Ronc.1965.1), pp. 568–69; see also Tandoi (Tand.1969.1). Ettore Paratore, "Giovenale," *ED* III (1971), pp. 197–202, offers proba-

bly the most balanced and useful introduction to the problem of Dante's knowledge of Juvenal.

90.   There has been much confusion over the meaning of Statius's reference to being crowned with myrtle leaves. The myrtle tree was sacred to Venus (see, e.g., *Aen.* V.72). And, indeed, Statius himself, in his *Silvae* (IV.vii.10–11), asks to be crowned as a lyric poet (and not as a writer of epic) with myrtle leaves. However, as nearly all admit, or even insist, Dante could not have been acquainted with the *Silvae*. Then what does Dante mean us to understand by Statius's insistence that he was crowned with myrtle? As Daniello (1568) notes, Virgil speaks of both laurel and myrtle (*Egl.* II.54): "You, too, o laurels *(lauri)*, I will pluck, and you, neighboring myrtle *(myrte)*"; Daniello believes that Statius is associated with myrtle because he was a poet of love. Disagreeing with him, Tommaseo (1837) thinks that the phrase, for Dante, meant that the myrtle wreath was secondary to the laurel, an opinion followed by Porena (1946) and developed by Mattalia (1960), who argues that, while Dante himself makes Statius one of the *poete regolati* (i.e., the classical Latin poets worthy of emulation [*Dve* II.vi.7]), it is Statius who speaks now, and he wants to show his awareness of his dependence upon Virgil, of his role as secondary poet following in the wake of a master. See verses two lines from the ending of the *Thebaid* (XII.816–817), which explicitly make a highly similar claim: "do not attempt to rival the divine *Aeneid*, but follow at a distance, always worshiping its footsteps." Moore (Moor.1896.1), p. 243, was perhaps the first to suggest that this passage was being cited here in vv. 94–97. For its possible earlier relevance, see the note to *Inferno* XXIII.145–148.

93.   Statius's "second burden" was his unfinished *Achilleid*.

94–96.   For the relationship of Statius's text to these lines, see the concluding remarks in the note to verse 90. The image of the *Aeneid* as being the divine torch that has set aflame many another poem, including this one, similarly "divine," if surely in different ways, will be explored as this scene unfolds.

97–99.   The appearance of the word *mamma* here is stunning, for we find it, a spectacular instantiation of the low vernacular (see the last item in the note to *Inf.* XXXII.1–9, the passage in which it has had its only previous appearance), used in the same verse with the word that may have represented for Dante the height of classical eloquence, *Eneïda*, the title of the greatest classical poem, here in its only use in the *Comedy*.

The passage applies to Statius, but increasingly students of this passage have been convinced that Statius's fictive biography serves as a sort of stand-in for Dante's genuine one, that is, in Statius's words here about his dependence on Virgil we are also reading Dante's confession of his own debt to the Roman poet. For this view see, among others, Paratore (Para.1968.1), pp. 72–73; Padoan (Pado.1970.1), p. 354; Hollander (Holl.1980.2), pp. 123–24, 205n.; Stephany (Step.1983.1), p. 151; Picone (Pico.1993.2), p. 330. In the next canto the extent of that debt will assume staggering proportions.

A dram is the equivalent of one-eighth of an ounce.

100–102.   While some have understood that Statius's gesture offers a single day of lingering (first, the Anonimus Lombardus [1322]) and others a solar cycle of twenty-eight years (first, Jacopo della Lana [1324]), most, after the Ottimo (1333), believe that he means one more year.

103–114.   The first of these two adjacent and charming passages to return to earlier moments in the canto adverts to the discussion of the absolute and conditional wills in vv. 61–69. Here we see that Dante's absolute will is conquered by his emotions. In the second, Dante's smile is probably to be understood as exactly such a sign as Virgil gave to arriving Statius at vv. 14–15.

One does not want to read in too moralizing a light this extraordinary little scene. There is no serious consequence if Dante gives away Virgil's little secret, or if Statius becomes overenthusiastic once it is known. The three poets share a moment of common freedom from the constraints of their missions. It is typical of this great and securely serious theological poet that he can indulge himself and his readers in moments of such moving happiness. This is perhaps as close to experiencing Christian fellowship as Virgil ever comes.

125–126.   The protagonist's understanding of Statius's debt to Virgil is obviously not yet fully developed. In his formulation it was from the greater poet that Statius learned "to sing of men and of the gods," an adequate description of the work of a pagan writer of epic. We will learn in the next canto that, behind the façade of pagan trappings, Statius was in fact a secret Christian. See note to *Purgatorio* XXII.67–73.

130–136. With regard to the supposed "failed embrace" between Statius and Virgil, Hollander has argued (Holl.1975.1), p.359, that Dante's failed attempt to embrace Casella (*Purg.* II.76–81), pointing to a physical impossibility, is countered in the successful exchange of embraces between Sordello and Virgil, both shades (*Purg.* VII.2, 15). In both of those scenes there is a desire to embrace that is either frustrated or accomplished. Here Statius desires to embrace Virgil but, once advised against doing so by the author of the *Aeneid*, wills not to. Since we know from Sordello's and Virgil's shared embraces that in fact shades are capable of embracing, we may not properly say, as most who deal with the scene do, that Virgil and Statius, "being shades, cannot embrace," or that they "are not capable of embracing" (Cecchetti [Cecc.1990.2], p. 107). They are perfectly capable of embracing; Virgil convinces Statius that it is not a fitting gesture in this higher realm. For another view of the supposedly problematic program of embraces see Iliescu (Ilie.1971.1). And see the note to *Purgatorio* XIX.134–135 for the probable biblical source of a similar scene: Pope Adrian's refusal to accept Dante's obeisance. In the end Statius won't embrace Virgil because up here souls do not behave "that way," just as Virgil did not want to have his identity revealed for a similar reason.

PURGATORIO XXII
([*Avarice*] & *Prodigality; Gluttony*)

Già era l'angel dietro a noi rimaso,
l'angel che n'avea vòlti al sesto giro,
avendomi dal viso un colpo raso;

3

e quei c'hanno a giustizia lor disiro
detto n'avea beati, le sue voci
con *'sitiunt,'* sanz'altro, ciò forniro.

6

E io più lieve che per l'altre foci
m'andava, sì che sanz'alcun labore
seguiva in sù li spiriti veloci;

9

quando Virgilio incominciò: "Amore,
acceso di virtù, sempre altro accese,
pur che la fiamma sua paresse fore;

12

onde da l'ora che tra noi discese
nel limbo de lo 'nferno Giovenale,
che la tua affezion mi fé palese,

15

mia benvoglienza inverso te fu quale
più strinse mai di non vista persona,
sì ch'or mi parran corte queste scale.

18

Ma dimmi, e come amico mi perdona
se troppo sicurtà m'allarga il freno,
e come amico omai meco ragiona:

21

come poté trovar dentro al tuo seno
loco avarizia, tra cotanto senno
di quanto per tua cura fosti pieno?"

24

Queste parole Stazio mover fenno
un poco a riso pria; poscia rispuose:
"Ogne tuo dir d'amor m'è caro cenno.

27

The angel who had shown the way
to the sixth circling now was left behind,
3   having erased another swordstroke from my brow

as he declared that those who long for righteousness
are blessed, ending on *sitiunt*
6   without the other words he might have said.

And now I could move on, lighter
than at the other entrances, so that I followed
9   the swifter spirits up with ease,

when Virgil began: 'A love that is kindled by virtue
has always ignited another, as long as its flame
12   was shining where it could be seen.

'From the hour, therefore, when Juvenal descended
into the limbo of hell, among us,
15   and made your affection known to me,

'my good will toward you was as great
as anyone has ever felt for someone never seen,
18   so that to me these stairs will now seem short.

'But tell me—and as a friend forgive me
if with too much assurance I relax the reins,
21   and as a friend speak with me now—

'how could avarice find room
amidst such wisdom in your breast,
24   the wisdom that you nourished with such care.'

These words made Statius smile a little
before he answered: 'Every word of yours
27   is to me a welcome token of your love.

Veramente più volte appaion cose
che danno a dubitar falsa matera
per le vere ragion che son nascose.

30

La tua dimanda tuo creder m'avvera
esser ch'i' fossi avaro in l'altra vita,
forse per quella cerchia dov' io era.

33

Or sappi ch'avarizia fu partita
troppo da me, e questa dismisura
migliaia di lunari hanno punita.

36

E se non fosse ch'io drizzai mia cura,
quand'io intesi là dove tu chiame,
crucciato quasi a l'umana natura:

39

'Per che non reggi tu, o sacra fame
de l'oro, l'appetito de' mortali?',
voltando sentirei le giostre grame.

42

Allor m'accorsi che troppo aprir l'ali
potean le mani a spendere, e pente'mi
così di quel come de li altri mali.

45

Quanti risurgeran coi crini scemi
per ignoranza, che di questa pecca
toglie 'l penter vivendo e ne li stremi!

48

E sappie che la colpa che rimbecca
per dritta opposizione alcun peccato,
con esso insieme qui suo verde secca;

51

però, s'io son tra quella gente stato
che piange l'avarizia, per purgarmi,
per lo contrario suo m'è incontrato."

54

"Or quando tu cantasti le crude armi
de la doppia trestizia di Giocasta,"
disse 'l cantor de' buccolici carmi,

57

'But, in truth, things often are misleading
when their true causes remain hidden,
30   thus leading us to false conclusions.

'Your question shows me you believe,
perhaps because of the terrace I was on,
33   that I was avaricious in the other life.

'Know then that avarice was much too far
removed from me and that this lack of measure
36   lunar months in thousands now have punished.

'And had I not reformed my inclination
when I came to understand the lines in which,
39   as if enraged at human nature, you cried out:

' "To what end, O cursèd hunger for gold,
do you not govern the appetite of mortals?"
42   I would know the rolling weights and dismal jousts.

'Then I learned that we can spread
our wings too wide with spending hands,
45   and I repented that and other sins.

'How many more will have to rise again, hair shorn
through ignorance, which takes away repentance
48   of this sin in life and in the hour of death!

'Note this also: the fault that runs
directly counter to a sin
51   is here grouped with it and is withered of its green.

'Therefore, if I, to purge my sins, have been
among those shades who weep for avarice,
54   this has befallen me for the opposing fault.'

'But, when you sang the savage warfare
between the twofold sorrows of Jocasta,'
57   said the singer of the *Eclogues*,

"per quello che Clïò teco lì tasta,
non par che ti facesse ancor fedele
60   la fede, sanza qual ben far non basta.

Se così è, qual sole o quai candele
ti stenebraron sì, che tu drizzasti
63   poscia di retro al pescator le vele?"

Ed elli a lui: "Tu prima m'invïasti
verso Parnaso a ber ne le sue grotte,
66   e prima appresso Dio m'alluminasti.

Facesti come quei che va di notte,
che porta il lume dietro e sé non giova,
69   ma dopo sé fa le persone dotte,

quando dicesti: 'Secol si rinova;
torna giustizia e primo tempo umano,
72   e progenïe scende da ciel nova.'

Per te poeta fui, per te cristiano:
ma perché veggi mei ciò ch'io disegno,
75   a colorare stenderò la mano.

Già era 'l mondo tutto quanto pregno
de la vera credenza, seminata
78   per li messaggi de l'etterno regno;

e la parola tua sopra toccata
si consonava a' nuovi predicanti;
81   ond' io a visitarli presi usata.

Vennermi poi parendo tanto santi,
che, quando Domizian li perseguette,
84   sanza mio lagrimar non fur lor pianti;

e mentre che di là per me si stette,
io li sovvenni, e i lor dritti costumi
87   fer dispregiare a me tutte altre sette.

'it does not seem, from what you wrote with Clio's help,
that you had found as yet the faith,
60   that faith without which good works fail.

'If that is so, what sun, what candles
dispelled your darkness so that afterwards
63   you hoisted sail, following the fisherman?'

And the other answered him: 'It was you who first
set me toward Parnassus to drink in its grottoes,
66   and you who first lit my way toward God.

'You were as one who goes by night, carrying
the light behind him—it is no help to him,
69   but instructs all those who follow—

'when you said: "The centuries turn new again.
Justice returns with the first age of man,
72   and new progeny descends from heaven."

'Through you I was a poet, through you a Christian.
But, that you may see better what I outline,
75   I will set my hand to fill the colors in.

'Already all the world was pregnant
with the true faith, inseminated
78   by the messengers of the eternal kingdom,

'and the words of yours I have just recited
did so accord with the new preachers
81   that I began to visit them.

'More and more they seemed to me so holy
that when Domitian started with his persecutions
84   their weeping did not lack my tears.

'While I remained on earth,
I gave them comfort. Their upright ways
87   made me despise all other sects.

E pria ch'io conducessi i Greci a' fiumi
di Tebe poetando, ebb' io battesmo;
90   ma per paura chiuso cristian fu'mi,

lungamente mostrando paganesmo;
e questa tepidezza il quarto cerchio
93   cerchiar mi fé più che 'l quarto centesmo.

Tu dunque, che levato hai il coperchio
che m'ascondeva quanto bene io dico,
96   mentre che del salire avem soverchio,

dimmi dov' è Terrenzio nostro antico,
Cecilio e Plauto e Varro, se lo sai:
99   dimmi se son dannati, e in qual vico."

"Costoro e Persio e io e altri assai,"
rispuose il duca mio, "siam con quel Greco
102   che le Muse lattar più ch'altri mai,

nel primo cinghio del carcere cieco;
spesse fïate ragioniam del monte
105   che sempre ha le nutrice nostre seco.

Euripide v'è nosco e Antifonte,
Simonide, Agatone e altri piùe
108   Greci che già di lauro ornar la fronte.

Quivi si veggion de le genti tue
Antigone, Deïfile e Argia,
111   e Ismene sì trista come fue.

Védeisi quella che mostrò Langia;
èvvi la figlia di Tiresia, e Teti,
114   e con le suore sue Deïdamia."

Tacevansi ambedue già li poeti,
di novo attenti a riguardar dintorno,
117   liberi da saliri e da pareti;

'I was baptized before, in my verses,
I had led the Greeks to the rivers of Thebes,
90   but, from fear, I stayed a secret Christian,

'long pretending I was still a pagan.
More than four centuries, because I was lukewarm,
93   I circled the fourth terrace.

'You, then, who have raised the veil
that hid from me the great good I describe,
96   tell me, while there is time in this ascent,

'where is our ancient Terence, where Cecilius,
Plautus, Varius, if you know.
99   Tell me if they are damned and in what place.'

'Those, Persius, and I, and many more,'
replied my leader, 'are with that Greek
102   the Muses suckled more than any other,

'in the first circle of the dark prison.
We often talk about that mountain
105   where those who nursed us ever dwell.

'Euripides is with us there and Antiphon,
Simonides and Agathon and many other Greeks
108   whose brows were once adorned with laurel.

'Among those from your works who may be seen
are Antigone, Deïphyle, Argia,
111   and Ismene, still sad as once she was.

'She that revealed Langìa also may be seen,
as well as the daughter of Tiresias,
114   and Thetis, and Deïdamìa with her sisters.'

Both the poets now were silent,
again intent on looking all around them,
117   freed from the constraint of stairs and walls.

e già le quattro ancelle eran del giorno
rimase a dietro, e la quinta era al temo,
120   drizzando pur in sù l'ardente corno,

quando il mio duca: "Io credo ch'a lo stremo
le destre spalle volger ne convegna,
123   girando il monte come far solemo."

Così l'usanza fu lì nostra insegna,
e prendemmo la via con men sospetto
126   per l'assentir di quell' anima degna.

Elli givan dinanzi, e io soletto
di retro, e ascoltava i lor sermoni,
129   ch'a poetar mi davano intelletto.

Ma tosto ruppe le dolci ragioni
un alber che trovammo in mezza strada,
132   con pomi a odorar soavi e buoni;

e come abete in alto si digrada
di ramo in ramo, così quello in giuso,
135   cred' io, perché persona sù non vada.

Dal lato onde 'l cammin nostro era chiuso,
cadea de l'alta roccia un liquor chiaro
138   e si spandeva per le foglie suso.

Li due poeti a l'alber s'appressaro;
e una voce per entro le fronde
141   gridò: "Di questo cibo avrete caro."

Poi disse: "Più pensava Maria onde
fosser le nozze orrevoli e intere,
144   ch'a la sua bocca, ch'or per voi risponde.

E le Romane antiche, per lor bere,
contente furon d'acqua; e Daniello
147   dispregiò cibo e acquistò savere.

Already four handmaids of the day were left behind
and the fifth was at the chariot-shaft,
120   guiding its gleaming tip still higher,

when my leader said: 'It might be better if we turned
our right side's shoulders to the outer edge,
123   circling the mountain as we are accustomed.'

Thus habit was our teacher there,
and we took our way with less uncertainty
126   because that other worthy soul encouraged us.

They went along in front and I, alone,
came on behind, listening to their discourse,
129   which gave me understanding of the art of verse.

But soon their pleasant talk was interrupted
by a tree found in the middle of the path,
132   with fruits that smelled both savory and good,

and as a fir tree narrows as it branches upward,
this one tapered down from branch to branch,
135   so that, I think, no one could climb it.

On that side, where our way was blocked,
from the high rock fell pellucid water,
138   which was dispersed among the upper leaves.

As the two poets neared the tree
a voice from among the boughs called out:
141   'This is a food that you shall lack.'

And then it said: 'Mary gave more thought
that the marriage-feast be decorous and complete
144   than for the mouth with which she pleads for you.

'The Roman matrons of antiquity
were glad to have but water as their drink,
147   and Daniel scorned banquets and acquired wisdom.

Lo secol primo, quant' oro fu bello,
fé savorose con fame le ghiande,
e nettare con sete ogne ruscello.

150

Mele e locuste furon le vivande
che nodriro il Batista nel diserto;
per ch'elli è glorïoso e tanto grande
quanto per lo Vangelio v'è aperto."

154

'The first age was as beautiful as gold.
Its acorns were made savory by hunger
150   and thirst made nectar flow in every brook.

'Honey and locusts were the food
that nourished John the Baptist in the desert,
for which he is glorious and as great
154   as in the Gospel is revealed to you.'

1–6.   The scene with the angel, which we expect, having experienced such a scene at the end of the description of each terrace, is here done retrospectively and as briefly as possible. The giving of directions to the next terrace and the removal of Dante's (fifth) P are referred to simply as having occurred. The remembered angelic recital of a Beatitude (here the fourth, Matthew 5:6, "Blessèd are they who hunger and thirst after righteousness [justice, *iustitiam*, in the Vulgate], for they shall be filled") is given in truncated form. Responding to this economy, Benvenuto (1380) refers to Dante's "novum modum scribendi" (new way of writing). What exactly was omitted from the Beatitude has been a subject of discussion, but it clearly seems to be "hunger and" (saved to be deployed, words more appropriate to Gluttony, at *Purg.* XXIV.154) and perhaps the ending as well ("for they shall be filled"), possibly omitted in both utterances.

It is as though the poet were clearing every inch of available space for the second scene with Statius, and indeed the arrival at the Terrace of Gluttony will be postponed for over a hundred lines (until verse 115), the longest such intermezzo we find among the seven terraces.

From verse 3 it seems inferentially clear that Statius does not have what would have been his final P removed. Dante describes his own letter being removed from his brow by the angel ("avendo*mi* dal viso un colpo raso" [having erased another swordstroke from my brow]). Had he wanted to include Statius as having the same experience, he would only have to have written "avendo*ci*" (from *our* brows). Thus, like all "regular" penitents, it seems most likely that Statius did not have his brow adorned by the writing of the warder at the gate of purgatory. See the note to *Purgatorio* XXI.22–24.

7–9.   We are reminded of Dante's increasing similarity to the unburdened souls of the disembodied. Traversing two more terraces will make him as light as they.

10–18.   Dante's charming fiction has it that Juvenal (for the reason behind the choice of him as praiser of Statius see the note to *Purg.* XXI.88), arriving in Limbo ca. A.D. 140, told Virgil of Statius's great affection, which then caused a similar affection in Virgil for the unknown Statius. Benvenuto (1380) offers a sweet-tempered gloss to this passage: "Often we love a virtuous man, even if we have never met him—and in just this way do I love dead Dante."

19–24. Virgil wraps his delicate yet intrusive question in pledges of friendship, and then asks Statius how such as he could have been stained by the sin of avarice. The phrase "tra cotanto senno" (amidst such wisdom) recalls the identical words found at *Inferno* IV.102, and thus reminds us of the five classical poets encountered there by Dante. It may also remind us that Limbo is precisely where anybody else would have assumed Statius would spend eternity.

25–26. As Benvenuto says, "Statius now smiles at Virgil's mistake just as Dante had smiled, earlier [*Purg.* XXI.109], at Statius's mistake." Statius is also obviously allowed to be pleased to have been guilty of prodigality rather than avarice, no matter how seriously Dante took the latter sin.

28–35. A paraphrase may help make clear the general sense of these lines: "As my situation among the avaricious made you take me for one of them—and a better understanding shows the opposite sin to pertain, just so did your text seem to be condemning avarice—until my personal understanding revealed that it condemned my own prodigality." On the problem of the belatedness of prodigality's appearance as a subject on this terrace, of which it is supposedly the cotitular occupant, see Barnes (Barn.1993.1), pp. 288–90.

36. Statius has already said (*Purg.* XXI.68) that he had to spend five hundred years and more on this terrace, thus more than six thousand months.

38. The verb used by Statius to indicate his comprehension of Virgil's text will turn out to be pivotal, in that he does not say "when I read" but "when I understood," i.e., allowing us to comprehend his latent meaning: "when I construed your text so that it matched my need."

40–41. The meaning of these lines, clearly a translation of a text of Virgil (*Aen.* III.56–57), is the subject of much debate involving questions about the exact nature of what Dante wrote ("Per che" or "perché"?) and what he took Virgil to mean (or decided to make Virgil say). Here, as always, we have followed Petrocchi's text in our translation, even though in this case we are in particularly strenuous disagreement with him. Here are the texts, Virgil's first:

> **Quid** non mortalia pectora *cogis*,
> auri <u>sacra</u> fames?

(to what do you not drive human hearts, impious hunger for gold?)

As for Dante's text, it may be either of the following:

> **Per che** non *reggi* tu, o <u>sacra</u> fame
> de l'oro, l'appetito de' mortali?

(**to what end,** O <u>cursèd</u> hunger for gold, do you not *govern* [drive] the appetite of mortals?)

or

> **Perché** non *reggi* tu, o <u>sacra</u> fame
> de l'oro, l'appetito de' mortali?

(**why** do you not *govern* mortal appetites, O <u>holy</u> [i.e., temperate] hunger for gold?)

It is true that the Latin adjective *sacer* can mean either "holy, sacred" or "unholy, impious." However, the meaning of Aeneas's outcry, recounting the horrific deed committed by Polymnestor against Polydorus (see note to *Inf.* XIII.31–39) is clear to all; he means "impious." But what of Dante's text? The "traditional" reading has him maintaining the negative valence of Virgil's *sacer* (which would then be the only occurrence among twelve in which *sacro* does not mean "holy" in his poem). Perhaps no early reader, among those who understood Statius as deliberately misreading Virgil, was as "modern" and "revisionist" as Francesco da Buti (1385), who simply argued that Dante was deliberately giving Virgil's text another meaning than it held because it suited his purpose to do so. Bianchi (1868) is the first to appreciate the absurdity of the notion that Dante had used the verb *reggere* (to govern) in a pejorative sense. The debate continues into our own day, mainly propelled by the notion that Dante could not possibly have misunderstood Virgil's words and therefore did not grossly misrepresent them. This, however, is to overlook the fact that it is the character Statius who is understanding them as they took on significance for him, guilty of prodigality, not of avarice. And just as he will later reveal his "misinterpretation" of Virgil's fourth *Eclogue* at vv. 70–72, a "misreading" that saved his soul, so now he shows how his moral rehabilitation was begun when he "misread" a passage in the *Aeneid*. The debate is finally in such condition that this view, present in some of the earliest commentators but energetically attacked over the centuries, now may seem only sensible. See, among others, Ronconi (Ronc.1958.1), pp. 85–86; Groppi (Grop.1962.1), pp. 163–68; Paratore (Para.1968.1), pp. 73–75; Hollander (Holl.1980.1), pp. 212–13, and (Holl.1983.1), pp. 86–89, completely in accord with Shoaf's earlier and nearly identical reading (Shoa.1978.1). They are joined by Barolini (Baro.1984.1), p. 260, and, at length, by Martinez (Mart.1989.2). A similar, if less developed argument, is found in Mazzotta (Mazz.1979.1), p. 222. And, for wholehearted acceptance of Shoaf's argument, see Picone (Pico.1993.2), pp. 325–26. Neglected, by all but Barolini and Shoaf, is Austin (Aust.1933.1). Mainly forgotten as well is the then daring support of Francesco da Buti by Alfredo Galletti (Gall.1909.1), pp. 17–18. Among Italian students of the problem who accept this basic view of its resolution see Chiamenti (Chia.1995.1), pp. 131–37, who offers most of the essential bibliography for the problem but is, however, surprisingly unaware of the support for his position available in his American precursors' analyses of what he considers "the most beautiful example of free translation in Dante" (p. 134). For the general question of Dante's Statius see Brugnoli (Brug.1969.1) and Rossi (Ross.1993.1); for more recent bibliography see Glenn (Glen.1999.1), p. 114, and Marchesi (Marc.2002.1), an extended discussion of the possible Augustinian sources of the "aggressive" reading of Virgilian text attributed to Statius by Dante.

46. Statius's description of the prodigal as having shorn hair repeats that element in the description of those damned for prodigality in *Inferno* VII.57.

47. The fact that, according to Statius, the prodigal do not understand that their behavior is sinful underlines the importance of Virgil's words about the "holy" hunger for gold in bringing about his own salvation. Their ignorance of their own sinfulness may help explain why there is so little reference to their form of sin on this terrace. See discussion in the note to vv. 52–54.

49–51.   The reference of the adverb "qui" (here) in this tercet is a matter of debate. One should be aware that the notion that it refers to all of purgatory (rather than to this terrace alone) is of recent vintage and is intelligently opposed by Bosco/Reggio (1979). Further, if one examines all eighteen uses of the adverb by penitents who have speaking roles on the mountain, it is plain that only twice does it not refer to the particular terrace on which the speaker is found. In short, there is every reason to believe that the reference is only to this particular terrace, the only one on which a particular sin and its opposite are purged.

52–54.   We can begin to understand that Dante has constructed this terrace in a way that is much different from that in which he structured the Circle of Avarice and Prodigality in *Inferno*. There the two sins are treated, at least approximately, as equals, each of them sharing literally half the realm. Here it would seem (one cannot be certain) that there is no set place for the penitent prodigal nor any exemplary figures that refer directly to their sin. In fact, this is the terrace of Avarice on which prodigals seem to be gathered, too. Since the only one we know of—and he refers to no others in his condition—is Statius, we have no way of knowing or guessing how many others there are like him, or even whether there are any others at all, although, from vv. 49–51, there seem to be.

55–63.   Virgil is referred to as the author of the *Eclogues*, the fourth of which will shortly come into prominent play in Statius's narrative of his conversion (vv. 70–73). His question reveals that Dante treats him as having read—and with some care—Statius's *Thebaid*, a work written roughly one hundred and ten years after his death. (We have observed a similar bit of business in *Inf.* XXXI.115–124, where Virgil borrows from the texts of Lucan as he attempts to flatter Antaeus [see Hollander (Holl.2000.2)].) Do we imagine, as more than one discussant has, that Virgil had read Lucan (or Statius) in Limbo? Or do we realize that Dante is a poet and takes liberties when he wishes to?

55–56.   The sons of Jocasta (by her son Oedipus) are Eteocles and Polynices. Their fraternal rivalry results in the civil war in Thebes that is the main subject of Statius's only completed epic.

58.   Statius twice invokes Clio, as the muse of history, in the *Thebaid* (I.41; X.630). Virgil's question suggests that the text of the epic, while

historically valid, does not seem to him to yield any hint of Statius's Christian faith. But see the note to vv. 64–73.

Lombardi (1791) was perhaps the first commentator to suggest the (debated but viable) idea that *tastare* here means "pluck the strings of the lyre" in accompaniment of the poet's song.

61–63. Virgil would like to know what sun (God?) or what candles (human sources of enlightenment?) enlightened Statius, removing him from the darkness of paganism in Domitian's Rome so that he could "set sail," following the Church's instruction. St. Peter, the rock on which Jesus built that church, is portrayed as a "fisher of souls" in Mark 1:17.

The Castalian spring, source of poetic inspiration in classical myth, had its own source among the caves of Mt. Parnassus.

64–73. Statius's response surprises Virgil and continues to surprise nearly everyone. It was Virgil whose example made him want to be a poet and Virgil who brought him to love the true God. The culminating verse of his answer begins by restating the first part of the equation, to which no one can object, and then the second ("per te cristiano"). There is no external authority, competent or otherwise, who would have brought Dante to believe such a thing.

However, if Dante believed, or had decided to believe, that Statius was a Christian, when did he think he first converted? Virgil's own remark about his not finding any evidence in the text of the *Thebaid* that supports a Statian conversion to Christianity is perhaps a clue to what we should do in examining that text. That is, the "dating" of such a conversion might have seemed ascertainable from Statius's texts themselves. Mariotti (Mari.1975.1) discussed Poliziano's view that a passage in the *Thebaid* (IV.514–518, naming the mysterious "high lord of the triple world" [Demogorgon?]) seemed to authorize understanding of a Christian intent on the part of its author. Mariotti's argument did not convince Hollander (Holl.1980.2), pp. 206–7, who argued instead that a passage early on in the work (*Thebaid* II.358–362) revealed, unmistakably, a reference to the key prophetic text in Virgil's fourth *Eclogue*. (He might have argued that there is an even more precise reference at V.461, the phrase "iam nova progenies" [and now a new race] that matches exactly Virgil's key phrase in the *Eclogue* [IV.7].) Thus, if for Dante the phrase in Virgil that converted Statius is that one, it only makes sense that, finding it in the text of Statius's epic, he could argue that, by the time he was writing its second book, Statius was already a closet Christian. For a discussion see also Chiamenti (Chia.1995.1), pp. 205–8.

On the continuing complexity of the problem of Statius's supposed Christianity see, among many others, Brugnoli (Brug.1988.1), Scrivano (Scri.1992.1), and Heil (Heil.2001.1), pp. 52–101. For the narrower discussion of the dependence of Dante's view on putative existing medieval sources for such a belief, see Padoan (Pado.1959.1), Ronconi's rejoinder (Ronc.1965.1), and Padoan's continuing insistence (Pado.1970.1). It seems clear that Ronconi's view, that the conversion of Statius is entirely Dante's invention, is the only likely solution to an intriguing problem.

65. In classical myth the Castalian spring, flowing in the grottoes of Parnassus, is the source of poetic inspiration in those who drank from it.

70–72. Dante's translation of the crucial lines of the fourth *Eclogue* (5–7) deforms them just enough to show how a Christian might have found a better meaning in them than did Virgil himself:

> magnus ab integro saeclorum nascitur ordo.
> iam redit et Virgo, redeunt Saturnia regna;
> iam nova progenies caelo demittetur alto.

> (The great line of the centuries begins anew;
> now the Virgin returns, the reign of Saturn returns;
> now new progeny descends from heaven on high.)

From *Monarchia* I.xi.1 we know that Dante believed that Virgil's *Virgo* was not a woman named Mary but Astraea, or Justice. Still, primal justice was the condition of humankind in the prelapsarian Eden, that "first age of man" *(primo tempo umano)*, which is open to a wider interpretation than Virgil's "Saturnia regna." Statius's version of Virgil had to rearrange very little (and that seems to be Dante's hard-edged intention) to make the prophecy a Christian one. Dante's identical rhymes *(ri-nova, ciel nova)* add a repeated word that has a deeply Christian ring to it, "new," thus pointing to the concept that *almost* emerges from Virgil's text. He came very close, but he failed.

74–75. The phrasing is self-conscious in the extreme. Dante, having invented a Christian Statius, now hints that it is a fabrication of his own by putting the language of portraiture (and not of history) into the mouth of his creation. See Hollander (Holl.1980.2), p. 206.

76–81. Soon Virgil's words seemed so to confirm the message of the preachers who followed Christ's apostles that Statius began to frequent these Christians.

82–87. Statius's epic is dedicated (fulsomely) to the emperor. Thus Dante, believing that Domitian persecuted Christians and that Statius was a Christian, had to resolve that problem by imagining a conversion that only bloomed *after* he had begun writing the *Thebaid*. "Domitian (Titus Flavius Domitianus Augustus), Roman Emperor, younger son of Vespasian and successor of his brother, Titus; he was born at Rome A.D. 51, became Emperor in 81, and was murdered in 96. Among the many crimes traditionally imputed to him was a relentless persecution of the Christians, which is mentioned by Orosius (*Hist.* VII.x.1), who was doubtless Dante's authority" **(T)**. Orosius, however, puts this persecution late in Domitian's reign, while Dante would seem to have believed that it occurred earlier, i.e., at the very least before Statius had reached the seventh book of his epic. While later historians question either the severity or the very existence of Domitian's persecution of Christians (and Jews [see the Ottimo (1333)]), Dante's early commentators, who may reflect traditions known also to him, insist that Domitian was only the second emperor (after Nero) to persecute Christians. The Anonimo Fiorentino (1400) states that Domitian's persecutions began in the fourth year of his reign (81–96) and that in 89, when they reached their height, they had made martyrs of such notable Christians as St. Clement. If Dante was aware of the traditional timetable for the composition of the *Thebaid*, 80–92, his life of Statius, supplied in these verses, would match well with those particulars.

88–89. Baptism, we remember from the last time we heard the word in the poem (*Inf.* IV.35), was precisely what Virgil and his fellow pagans in Limbo lacked. Statius indicates that by the time he was writing the seventh book of his epic, when the exiled Theban forces, returning, prepared their assault on the city, he had been baptized.

90. Dante's secret-Christian topos has its roots in John's gospel (John 19:38–39) in the figures of Joseph of Arimathea (Singleton [1973]) and Nicodemus (Benvenuto [1380]), both of whom come only secretly to Christ's tomb.

92–93. Statius's four hundred years and more on the terrace of Sloth are the fitting result of his tardiness in making an open declaration of the faith to which he had, *mirabile dictu*, been led by Virgil's *Eclogue*. For slothful behavior as being slowness to love correctly see *Purgatorio* XVII.130 and XVIII.8, and see Carroll's remarks, quoted in the note to *Purgatorio* XVIII.103.

94–95. Statius's remark inevitably reminds Virgil that, even though he is surely the greater poet, he has lost the most important contest in life. Modesto (Mode.1995.1), p.11, compares his role to that of Brunetto in *Inferno* XV.123–124, who seems to be a winner but who has, in fact, lost everything.

96. This "throwaway line," insisting on the plethora of time available for Statian discourse, again reminds the reader of the unusual nature of the entire Statius episode, displacing "normal" events and procedures in order to give maximum importance to this remarkable invention on Dante's part.

97–108. Virgil now adds nine classical poets to the named population of Limbo (five poets and thirty-five others). Added to the "school" of Homer ("that Greek / the Muses suckled more than any other") are five Latins: Terence, Caecilius Statius (of whom no texts survive), and Plautus (all wrote in the second century B.C.); Dante's knowledge of their works was mainly nonexistent, with the barely possible exception of Terence (see notes to *Inf.* IV.88–90 and XVIII.133–135); Varro is either Publius Terentius Varro or Lucius Varius Rufus, both Roman poets of the first century B.C. Dante's source for these names is debated, with Horace (*Ars poetica* 54–55) the leading candidate. On the three Latin comic poets see Barański (Bara.1993.1), who also suggests (p. 233) that Varro is associated with tragedy and Persius with satire, thus rounding out the three major Latin styles.

   The names of the four Greeks whom Virgil goes on to mention, derived from the writings of Aristotle, St. Thomas, and perhaps still others, were nearly all that Dante knew of them, three tragedians of the fifth century B.C., Euripides, Antiphon, and Agathon, and one lyric poet, Simonides.

   Their conversation, Virgil reports, is of Mt. Parnassus, home of the Muses, the mountain that Statius (verse 65) says Virgil first led him toward in making him desire to be a poet. They and Virgil learn too late about this better Christian mountain.

109–114. Virgil adds eight more souls to Limbo, now not those of poets, but of virtuous women. All of them are to be found in Statius's two epics (the last two in the *Achilleid*) and all are also to be understood, as they were by Giovanni Boccaccio, as exemplifying filial piety (see Hollander [Holl.1983.1], pp. 208–12). "She that revealed Langia" is Hypsipyle (see *Inf.* XVIII.92 and *Purg.* XXVI.95). "La figlia di Tiresia" is, almost all now agree, Manto, thus causing a terrible problem for Dante's interpreters, the sole "bilocation" in his poem (for her first appearance see *Inf.* XX.52–102). Did he, like Homer, "nod"? Are we faced with an error of transcription? Or did he intentionally refer here to Statius's Manto, while Virgil's identical character is put in hell? For the second view, see the work of Kay and Hollander referred to in the note to *Inferno* XX.52–56.

118–120.   The personified hours of the day (see note to *Purg.* XII.81) are now between ten o'clock and eleven, with the fifth hour, presented as a chariot's yoke, aimed upward in the sky toward the sun.

121–123.   Virgil's remark reveals how much he (and we) are taken by the story of Statius, so much so that the continued penitential circling seems almost an afterthought. Statius has consented to keep the penitential Dante and his revered guide company. He is free, they are bound.

127–129.   The two poets (*poeti*, vv. 115, 139) are speaking of making poetry (*poetar*) while Dante listens; it is a scene reminiscent of that in *Inferno* IV.103–105, on which occasion Dante does more than only listen to the discussion.

130–135.   Many early commentators believed that this tree is upside down, with its roots in the air and its tip in or on the ground. It seems better to understand that its "branches" bend downward (rather than reaching upward, as do those of earthly trees) and are longer the higher they are found on the trunk, so as to prevent anyone from climbing. However that matter may be resolved (and the text would seem to support this second view, as Scartazzini [1900] argues), it seems clear that this tree is portrayed as being a shoot from the Tree of Life (Genesis 2:9). While a good deal of debate surrounds this point, strong arguments for this identification are found in Scartazzini (1900).

136–138.   This tree is nourished from above, through its leaves, not from below, through its root system. Since it is an evergreen, and indeed a mystical representation of a supernatural tree, it does not require nourishment at all. The water that moistens its branches may thus be symbolic of the water of Life that came to fulfill the function of the Tree of Life in Jesus, who restored to humankind the immortality lost in Eden.

140–141. Like the tree, the voice from within it is mysterious as well; it would rather seem to be the "voice" of the tree itself than anything else. What the voice says at first may seem to be a version of God's prohibition of the fruit of the Tree of the Knowledge of Good and Evil to Adam (Genesis 2:17, a passage Mattalia [1960] believes is repeated at *Purg.* XXIV.115—but see the note to that passage). However, it seems far more likely that this voice speaks of the result of Original Sin, humankind's loss of eternal life, symbolized here in the unavailability of the fruit (described in verse 132) of this tree, the Tree of Life.

142–154. The rest of the canto is dedicated to the exemplars of Temperance, the virtue opposed to Gluttony, thirteen verses spoken by, as far as we can tell, the tree itself.

142–144. Mary is presented as wanting to be sure others are fed properly at the marriage feast in Cana of Galilee (the same biblical scene [John 2:1–7] that furnished, in *Purg.* XIII.29, her charitable answer to Envy); she was not herself interested in eating, and her mouth is rather presented as being preserved for her later task, as intercessor, of intervening for sinners with her prayers.

145–147. Roman matrons of the old days, probably in Dante's mind those associated with republican Rome, before the excesses that characterized the reign of the Caesars, are paired with Daniel who, in Daniel 1:8, is presented as being uninterested in the food of the king's table or in wine. This is the first time that Dante uses a group as exemplary, a choice that he will make again in the next pairing.

148–154. The inhabitants of the golden age of Saturn are described by Ovid (*Metam.* 1.103–106), in which men, before tillage, happily consumed berries and acorns. Once again a classical group is paired with a Hebrew individual, John the Baptist, similarly temperate. Shoaf (Shoa.1978.1), p. 197, refers to "the hunger of Temperance" in another context, but the phrase is apt here.

It is possible that Daniello (1568) was the first to cite, in support of John's "greatness," the apt passage in Matthew 11:11 (some others will later also cite the nearly identical one in Luke 7:28): "Among those who are born of women there is not a greater prophet than John the Baptist." It is striking that no commentator gathered in the DDP who cites this passage ever goes on to cite its concluding sentence, which fits the context here so very well, where Virgil has served as prophet of Christ for Statius but not for himself (for Virgil's role in the poem as reflecting that of John the Baptist, see the note to *Inf.* I.122): "But he that is least in the kingdom of God is greater than he."

PURGATORIO XXIII
(Gluttony)

Mentre che li occhi per la fronda verde
ficcava ïo sì come far suole
3   chi dietro a li uccellin sua vita perde,

lo più che padre mi dicea: "Figliuole,
vienne oramai, ché 'l tempo che n'è imposto
6   più utilmente compartir si vuole."

Io volsi 'l viso, e 'l passo non men tosto,
appresso i savi, che parlavan sìe,
9   che l'andar mi facean di nullo costo.

Ed ecco piangere e cantar s'udìe
"Labïa mëa, Domine" per modo
12   tal, che diletto e doglia parturìe.

"O dolce padre, che è quel ch'i' odo?"
comincia' io; ed elli: "Ombre che vanno
15   forse di lor dover solvendo il nodo."

Sì come i peregrin pensosi fanno,
giugnendo per cammin gente non nota,
18   che si volgono ad essa e non restanno,

così di retro a noi, più tosto mota,
venendo e trapassando ci ammirava
21   d'anime turba tacita e devota.

Ne li occhi era ciascuna oscura e cava,
palida ne la faccia, e tanto scema
24   che da l'ossa la pelle s'informava.

Non credo che così a buccia strema
Erisittone fosse fatto secco,
27   per digiunar, quando più n'ebbe tema.

While I was peering through green boughs,
even as do men who waste their lives
3   in hunting after birds,

my more than father said to me: 'My son,
come along, for the time we are allowed
6   should be apportioned to a better use.'

I turned my face, and my steps as quickly,
to follow the two sages, whose discourse
9   made my going on seem easy,

when with weeping we heard voices sing
'*Labïa mëa, Domine*' in tones
12   that brought at once delight and grief.

'O sweet father, what is that I hear?' I asked,
and he: 'Shades, perhaps, who go their way
15   loosening the knot of what they owe.'

Just as pilgrims, absorbed in thought,
overtaking strangers on the road,
18   turn toward them without coming to a halt,

so, coming up behind us at a quicker pace than ours
and passing on, a group of souls,
21   silent and devout, gazed at us with wonder.

Their eyes were dark and sunken,
their faces pale, their flesh so wasted
24   that the skin took all its shape from bones.

I do not believe that Erysichthon had become
so consumed, to the very skin, by hunger
27   when he was most in terror of it.

Io dicea fra me stesso pensando: "Ecco
la gente che perdé Ierusalemme,
30   quando Maria nel figlio diè di becco!"

Parean l'occhiaie anella sanza gemme:
chi nel viso de li uomini legge "omo"
33   ben avria quivi conosciuta l'emme.

Chi crederebbe che l'odor d'un pomo
sì governasse, generando brama,
36   e quel d'un'acqua, non sappiendo como?

Già era in ammirar che sì li affama,
per la cagione ancor non manifesta
39   di lor magrezza e di lor trista squama,

ed ecco del profondo de la testa
volse a me li occhi un'ombra e guardò fiso;
42   poi gridò forte: "Qual grazia m'è questa?"

Mai non l'avrei riconosciuto al viso;
ma ne la voce sua mi fu palese
45   ciò che l'aspetto in sé avea conquiso.

Questa favilla tutta mi raccese
mia conoscenza a la cangiata labbia,
48   e ravvisai la faccia di Forese.

"Deh, non contendere a l'asciutta scabbia
che mi scolora," pregava, "la pelle,
51   né a difetto di carne ch'io abbia;

ma dimmi il ver di te, dì chi son quelle
due anime che là ti fanno scorta;
54   non rimaner che tu non mi favelle!"

"La faccia tua, ch'io lagrimai già morta,
mi dà di pianger mo non minor doglia,"
57   rispuos' io lui, "veggendola sì torta.

I said to myself in thought:
'Behold the people who lost Jerusalem
30   when Mary set her beak into her son!'

The sockets of their eyes resembled rings
without their gems. He who reads 'omo'
33   in men's faces would easily make out the 'm.'

Who, if he did not know the reason, would believe
the scent of fruit and smell of water
36   could cause such craving, reducing shades to this?

I was wondering what makes them so famished,
since what had made them gaunt, with wretched
39   scaling skin, was still unknown to me,

when out of the deep-set sockets in his head
a shade fixed me with his eyes and cried aloud:
42   'What grace is granted to me now!'

I never would have known him by his features,
but the sound of his voice made plain to me
45   what from his looks had been erased.

That spark relit the memory
of his changed features
48   and I knew Forese's face.

'Ah,' he begged, 'pay no attention
to the withered scab discoloring my skin
51   nor to this lack of flesh on me,

no mourning his state like in hell.

'but give me news about yourself
and tell me of those two souls over there,
54   escorting you. Do not hold back your answer.'

'Your face, over which I wept when you were dead,
now gives me no less cause for tears,
57   seeing it so disfigured,' I responded.

Però mi dì, per Dio, che sì vi sfoglia;
non mi far dir mentr' io mi maraviglio,
ché mal può dir chi è pien d'altra voglia."

Ed elli a me: "De l'etterno consiglio
cade vertù ne l'acqua e ne la pianta
rimasa dietro, ond' io sì m'assottiglio.

Tutta esta gente che piangendo canta
per seguitar la gola oltra misura,
in fame e 'n sete qui si rifà santa.

Di bere e di mangiar n'accende cura
l'odor ch'esce del pomo e de lo sprazzo
che si distende su per sua verdura.

E non pur una volta, questo spazzo
girando, si rinfresca nostra pena:
io dico pena, e dovria dir sollazzo,

ché quella voglia a li alberi ci mena
che menò Cristo lieto a dire 'Elì,'
quando ne liberò con la sua vena."

E io a lui: "Forese, da quel dì
nel qual mutasti mondo a miglior vita,
cinqu' anni non son vòlti infino a qui.

Se prima fu la possa in te finita
di peccar più, che sovvenisse l'ora
del buon dolor ch'a Dio ne rimarita,

come se' tu qua sù venuto ancora?
Io ti credea trovar là giù di sotto,
dove tempo per tempo si ristora."

Ond' elli a me: "Sì tosto m'ha condotto
a ber lo dolce assenzo d'i martìri
la Nella mia con suo pianger dirotto.

'In God's name, tell me what so withers you away.
Don't make me speak while I am so astounded,
60   for a man intent on other things speaks ill.'

And he to me: 'From the eternal counsel
a power falls onto the tree and on the water
63   there behind us. By it am I made so thin.

'All these people who weep while they are singing
followed their appetites beyond all measure,
66   and here regain, in thirst and hunger, holiness.

'The fragrance coming from the fruit
and from the water sprinkled on green boughs
69   kindles our craving to eat and drink,

'and not once only, circling in this space,
is our pain renewed.
72   I speak of pain but should say solace,

'for the same desire leads us to the trees
that led Christ to utter *Elì* with such bliss
75   when with the blood from His own veins He made us free.'

And I to him: 'Forese, from that day
when you exchanged the world for better life,
78   five years have not wheeled by until this moment.

'If your power to keep on sinning ended
just before the hour of blessèd sorrow
81   that marries us once more to God,

'how did you come so far so fast?
I thought that I might find you down below,
84   where time must be repaid with equal time.'

And he answered me: 'It is my Nella
whose flooding tears so quickly brought me
87   to drink sweet wormwood in the torments.

Con suoi prieghi devoti e con sospiri
tratto m'ha de la costa ove s'aspetta,
90   e liberato m'ha de li altri giri.

Tanto è a Dio più cara e più diletta
la vedovella mia, che molto amai,
93   quanto in bene operare è più soletta;

ché la Barbagia di Sardigna assai
ne le femmine sue più è pudica
96   che la Barbagia dov' io la lasciai.

O dolce frate, che vuo' tu ch'io dica?
Tempo futuro m'è già nel cospetto,
99   cui non sarà quest' ora molto antica,

nel qual sarà in pergamo interdetto
a le sfacciate donne fiorentine
102   l'andar mostrando con le poppe il petto.

Quai barbare fuor mai, quai saracine,
cui bisognasse, par farle ir coperte,
105   o spiritali o altre discipline?

Ma se le svergognate fosser certe
di quel che 'l ciel veloce loro ammanna,
108   già per urlare avrian le bocche aperte;

ché, se l'antiveder qui non m'inganna,
prima fien triste che le guance impeli
111   colui che mo si consola con nanna.

Deh, frate, or fa che più non mi ti celi!
vedi che non pur io, ma questa gente
114   tutta rimira là dove 'l sol veli."

Per ch'io a lui: "Se tu riduci a mente
qual fosti meco, e qual io teco fui,
117   ancor fia grave il memorar presente.

'With her devoted prayers and with her sighs,
she plucked me from the slope where one must wait
90   and freed me from the other circles.

'So much more precious and beloved of God
is my dear widow, whom I greatly loved,
93   the more she is alone in her good works.

'For the Barbagia of Sardegna
shelters many more modest women
96   than does that Barbagia where I left her.

'O sweet brother, what would you have me say?
In my vision even now I see a time,
99   before this hour shall be very old,

'when from the pulpit it shall be forbidden
for the brazen ladies of Florence
102   to flaunt their nipples with their breasts.

'What barbarous women, what Saracens,
have ever needed spiritual instruction
105   or other rules, to walk about in proper dress?

'But if these shameless creatures knew
what the swift heavens are preparing, even now
108   their mouths would be spread open in a howl.

'For if our foresight here does not deceive me
they shall be sorrowing before hair grows
111   on cheeks of babes still soothed by lullabies.

'Pray, brother, conceal your tale no longer.
Look, not only I but all these people
114   gaze in wonder where you veil the sun.'

At that I said to him: 'If you recall
what you were with me and I was with you,
117   that memory now would still be painful.

Di quella vita mi volse costui
che mi va innanzi, l'altr' ier, quando tonda
120   vi si mostrò la suora di colui,"

e 'l sol mostrai; "costui per la profonda
notte menato m'ha d'i veri morti
123   con questa vera carne che 'l seconda.

Indi m'han tratto sù li suoi conforti,
salendo e rigirando la montagna
126   che drizza voi che 'l mondo fece torti.

Tanto dice di farmi sua compagna
che io sarò là dove fia Beatrice;
129   quivi convien che sanza lui rimagna.

Virgilio è questi che così mi dice,"
e addita'lo; "e quest' altro è quell' ombra
per cuï scosse dianzi ogne pendice
133   lo vostro regno, che da sé lo sgombra."

'He who precedes me made me give over
that life but several days ago, when the sister
120   of him'—and I pointed to the sun—

'appeared round to you. He it is who led me
through the deep night of the forever dead
123   in this my solid flesh that follows him.

'With his support I have left all that behind,
climbing and circling the terraces of the mountain
126   that straightens those made crooked by the world.

'He promises to keep me company
until I shall encounter Beatrice.
129   Then I must be left without him.

'It is Virgil who tells me this'—I pointed to him—
'and the other is the shade for whom just now
your kingdom quaked in all its slopes,
133   shaking him from itself to set him free.'

3.   For *perdere la vita* as meaning simply "to spend one's life," and as not necessarily implying any negative moralizing judgment, see Jenni (Jenn.1972.1), p. 1n. The context here (Virgil's gentle chiding), however, would seem to support the more usual interpretation, one that sees the phrase as negative ("waste one's life").

4.   The phrase that would make Virgil "more than father" to Dante, according to the early commentators, praises his instruction of Dante in virtue, here redirecting his attention to the immediate task (and back from mere curiosity, in Carroll's view [1904]). It may also reflect the Roman poet's extraordinary ability to bring a pagan—and perhaps even this backsliding Christian—to Christ, as Statius's narrative has established (and see *Purg.* XXX.51, Dante's ultimate gesture of farewell to his "father": "Virgil, to whom I gave myself for my salvation").

5–6.   Virgil has broken off his conversation with Statius in order to address Dante (with an Italian version of the Latin vocative case: "figliuole," verse 4). As Singleton (1973) points out, all three of the similar warnings on the part of the protagonist's guide that the journey must be completed within a definite period occur in the "next-to-last circle of each of the three realms" (see also Inf. XXIX. 10–12; *Par.* XXII. 124 [the eighth of the nine heavenly spheres]).

8–9.   Dante does not find that having to resume his difficult task is unpleasant for a single reason: because the subject under discussion is poetry (see *Purg.* XXII. 127–129).

10–12.   "O Lord, open my lips, and my mouth shall proclaim your praise." The song of the penitents in Gluttony derives from the defining moment of David's repentance, not for gluttonous behavior, but for lust (Psalm 50:17). For the admixture of delight and grief typical of expressions of penitence on this terrace, see Trone (Tron. 1995. 1).

Beginning with Jacopo della Lana (1324), commentators have noted that this verse of the Psalm corrects the former sins of those who were gluttons because of its insistence on this better use of mouths—in songs of praise—than on the pleasures of the table. See the clear formulation of this idea in the presentation of Mary as exemplar of Temperance in the previous canto (*Purg.* XXII. 142–144).

13–15.   Dante's question and Virgil's tentative answer are necessitated by the fact that, as the following simile will make plain, the penitents here are currently *behind* the travelers. On the previous terrace they had become accustomed to looking upon stationary souls, prostrate on the ground before them. Here, as on the terraces of Pride, Wrath, and Sloth (and Lust, still ahead of them), the penitents are in motion. (Only in Envy and Avarice are they not.)

22–24.   The brief description of the gaunt visages of these penitents establishes the precise nature of the *contrapasso* here: starvation.

25–30.   The first reference is to Ovid's narrative concerning Erysichthon, who, having cut down trees in a sacred grove, was driven by its offended deity, Ceres, into boundless appetite that only ended when he engorged his own flesh (*Metam.* VIII. 738–878). The second, as was noted by several of the early commentators, is to an incident recorded in the sixth book of Josephus's *De bello judaico (Concerning the Jewish War)* in which a young woman named Mary, during the general starvation brought about by Titus's siege of Jerusalem in A.D. 70, killed, cooked, and ate her infant son. It is noteworthy that the poet explicitly adds exemplars to those "found" on the seven terraces.

32–33.   In the faces of the penitents, hollow-eyed, pale, skeletal, an observer might read only the "m," formed by the combination of cheekbones, eyebrows, and nose, but not the "o"s of the eyes, shrunken from view. Longfellow (1867), Scartazzini (1900), and others present a passage from one Berthold, a Franciscan of Regensburg (Germany), which describes the "letters" found in human faces, first the "omo" (latin *homo*) that is man's name and then the "dei" (Latin genitive of *deus*, "of God"); our faces announce that each of us is a "man of God." For the text of his remarks in English see the commentary of Longfellow or of Singleton to this passage.

34–36.   For the fruit of the tree and the water flowing over its leaves that cause such appetite, see *Purgatorio* XXII.137–138; and see the later reference in this canto (vv. 62–63). That this desire is good but not yet realizable would seem again to point to the notion that this tree is descended from the Tree of Life. See note to *Purgatorio* XXII.130–135.

39.   The "scaling skin" of these penitents, a sign of their advanced "starvation," will again be insisted on at vv. 49 and 58.

42–48.   The penitent's quick and gentle recognition of Dante, whose visage is in its normal human condition, plays off the gradual recognition on the part of the protagonist of his interlocutor. This is his old friend, Forese Donati. He was the brother of two other personages referred to in his remarks: Piccarda (encountered by Dante in the heaven of the Moon in *Par.* III), praised generously (*Purg.* XXIV.13–15), and Corso, denounced savagely (*Purg.* XXIV.82–87). The interplay between these fellow Florentines develops as one of the most tender scenes in the entire poem.

It is perhaps worth noting that the words that Forese and the others have been singing (verse 11) happen to come from the very fiftieth Psalm that opens with what serves as the protagonist's first spoken word in the *Comedy, Miserere* (*Inf.* I.65). The stories of Forese and of Dante are certainly meant to show God's great mercy.

61–71.   Forese begins by glossing for us the meaning of the tree and water encountered on the previous terrace. Both of these are informed by divine power with the promise of eternal life—object of the true hunger of these penitents. As the expiation of their former gluttony leads to this better hunger, they have their pangs renewed at another tree as well. Many commentators have believed that the text here invites us to believe that there is a multitude of trees stationed along the rest of the terrace, an idea that probably must be discarded because we will in fact find only one more (in the next canto). Since the two that we do discover in the text are so dramatically emblematic of the two trees of Genesis, and since no other tree along this terrace is alluded to, it is almost certainly wise to reject that theory, as D'Ovidio (Dovi.1926.1), p. 206, insisted.

72–75.   The text used by most of the early commentators apparently offered a form of *albore*, "tree" in the singular. Petrocchi's note, however, shows a preponderance of plural forms and all modern editors agree. We have seen the offshoot of the Tree of Life (and if the early commentators should happen to be correct in believing that the reference here is to a single tree, it would be to that one [see note to *Purg.* XXII.130–135]). In the next canto (vv. 113–117) we shall come upon a second, clearly descended from the Tree of the Knowledge of Good and Evil. The most direct explanation of vv. 73–74, "the same desire leads us to the trees / that led Christ to utter *Elì* with such bliss," is that the first sin of Adam and Eve, eating of the fruit of that tree, deprived them of the fruit of the

other, eternal life. Thus Christ's sacrifice is doubly restorative, redeem-
ing the sin and restoring the reward.

See Matthew 27:46 for "Eli, Eli, lamma sabacthani?" (My God, My
God, why have you forsaken me?), Christ's last words on the cross, ut-
tered in Aramaic. (See also Mark 15:34, with the variant "Eloi.") Many
of the early commentators discuss the passage in light of Jesus' request
that the "cup" (of crucifixion) pass from him, but then accepting it joy-
fully in favor of the resultant redemption of humankind. The human in
Him momentarily despairs, but then the God in Him rejoices.

For the notion that the penitents, like Jesus on the cross, simultane-
ously wish and do not wish to suffer in order to achieve redemption, see
Trone (Tron.1995.1).

76–84.   The entire context of this intimate recollection invites us to be-
lieve that Forese (to leave to one side the question of Dante's own be-
havior), in his life on earth, had behaved in ways that suggested to his
friend that his salvation was not exactly to be expected. Dante's question
is amusing. Since Forese, dead for less than four years (he died in July
1296), had lived most of his life a sinner (and thus was late in his repen-
tance), why did Dante not find him down on the lower slopes of the
mountain in ante-purgatory? (This is possibly a sort of compromise, a far
more polite question than "Why did I not find you in hell?")

85–93.   The prayerful tears of Forese's wife, Nella, demonstrate emphat-
ically that the efficacy of prayer is not limited to the benefit of the souls
found in ante-purgatory, but extends to those involved in active purga-
tion as well.

In a famous exchange of sonnets in a *tenzone*, a sort of poetic con-
test in the form of a series of exchanged insults, Dante and Forese heaped
calumnies upon one another for sexual and other inadequacies. While
there is continuing dispute concerning the authenticity of these poems
(see note to vv. 115–117), in which, among other things, poor Nella is
presented as being cold at night because of the lack of sexual interest on
the part of her impotent husband, this exchange between the two men
would seem to be based on some personal reminiscence of a similar na-
ture.

Nella continues Dante's "legends of good women" here in purga-
tory, tales of women who lived thoroughly virtuous lives. Such as these
begin with Pia de' Tolomei (*Purg.* V.130–136), continue with Gaia (if one
reads her character positively) in *Purgatorio* XVI.140, and Alagia in

Purgatorio XIX.142–145, include in the briefest of mentions virtuous pagan women (*Purg.* XXII.109–114, adding eight more to the earlier eight found in Limbo), possibly include the enigmatic reference to "Gentucca" in the next canto (*Purg.* XXIV.37), and conclude with Piccarda, Costanza, and St. Clare in the third canto of *Paradiso*. None of the other three prominent women who are seen in these realms of salvation, Sapia (*Purg.* XIII) and then both Cunizza and Rahab (*Par.* IX), quite fill the bill, since at least portions of their lives on earth were spectacularly sinful. As for Lucy (*Purg.* IX), Matelda (*Purg.* XXVIII), Beatrice, the Hebrew matriarchs seen seated in the heavenly Rose (*Par.* XXXII), and the Virgin Mary, they are all creatures of a still higher order of saintly virtue. For discussions of the women of the *Commedia* see Ferrante (Ferr.1975.1), Jacoff (Jaco.1988.1), and Kirkham (Kirk.1989.2).

94–96. Forese compares the sexually provocative women of Florence with the women of a wild region of Sardinia, renowned (according to some of the early commentators) for their crude behavior and indecent dress.

98–111. For the sumptuary laws (laws governing attire) reflected in Forese's prediction and which were contained in the *Constitutions of Florence* drawn up by the new bishop of the city, Antonio d'Orso Biliotti, in 1310, see Cassell (Cass.1978.1), p. 79. Cassell argues that the exiled Dante, writing only a few years later, nevertheless had ample time to have gotten word of these.

115–119. What activities do Dante's words indicate? The first commentators believed that he refers to, in the phrase of Benvenuto, their mutual pursuit of *delectabilia non honesta* (improper pleasures). No commentator before the Anonimo Fiorentino had apparently read or heard of their *tenzone* (one of the main reasons that those who deny its authenticity do so). And it was only in the late nineteenth century that some offered the opinion that this passage referred to the *tenzone*. Nearly all of the more recent discussants are firmly of the opinion, agreeing with the first commentators, that Dante is referring to the actual relationship he had with Forese and the sort of *delectabilia non honesta* that they shared in their companionship. It is not clear exactly what activities the poet has in mind, but it is clear that his own are seen as afflicting him when Virgil rescued him from sin and led him into the afterworld. This is the first time we have any indication that Dante's sins on earth might be characterized as having involved moral turpitude.

There has been a continuing effort to deny the authenticity of the *tenzone*. This began with Domenico Guerri's debate with Michele Barbi in the early 1930s, which Guerri's student, Antonio Lanza, reopened in the early 1970s. His opposition to authenticity is currently supported by *his* student, Mauro Cursietti (Curs.1995.1). (Their position is supported by Stefanini [Stef.1996.1].) For a recent overview of the current debate, with necessary bibliography and polemical insistence on inauthenticity, see Lanza (Lanz.1997.1); see also Cursietti (Curs.1997.1 and Curs.2000.1). But see Fabian Alfie's (Alfi.1998.1) arguments for retention of the *tenzone* in the Dantean canon on the basis of the evidence of the manuscripts. The debate is probably far from over.

120–121.   See *Inferno* XX.127–129 for the moon being full in the opening scene of *Inferno*. While there is discussion as to whether the particle *vi* (which may mean "there" or "you") here refers to the dark wood of *Inferno* I or to the penitents on this mountain, our translation follows Daniello (1568) in accepting the first possibility. We are reminded that the action of the poem began on a Friday and that it is now Tuesday afternoon, the fifth day of the journey.

126.   The phrasing here is reminiscent of that describing both Dante's errant soul (*Purg.* XVIII.43) and its love for the "stammering woman" (*Purg.* XIX.8 and 13), language depending on the notion of making what is straight crooked, or the obverse.

128–133.   Forese is the only penitent to whom Dante names Beatrice, thus perhaps indicating that he was aware, in the period of their shared improper behavior, that Dante was not being loyal to her. Similarly, Forese is, once again uniquely among all penitents (Statius has just gone beyond that state when Dante names Virgil for him [*Purg.* XXI.125]), allowed to hear the name of Virgil from Dante's lips. That Dante does not here refer to Statius by name might seem to indicate (at least hypothetically) that, while the two men spoke of Virgil in their earthly conversations, they had not discussed Statius.

PURGATORIO XXIV
(Gluttony)

V. Exemplars of Gluttony

VI. The Angel of Temperance

Né 'l dir l'andar, né l'andar lui più lento
facea, ma ragionando andavam forte,
3   sì come nave pinta da buon vento;

e l'ombre, che parean cose rimorte,
per le fosse de li occhi ammirazione
6   traean di me, di mio vivere accorte.

E io, continüando al mio sermone,
dissi: "Ella sen va sù forse più tarda
9   che non farebbe, per altrui cagione.

Ma dimmi, se tu sai, dov' è Piccarda;
dimmi s'io veggio da notar persona
12   tra questa gente che sì mi riguarda."

"La mia sorella, che tra bella e buona
non so qual fosse più, trïunfa lieta
15   ne l'alto Olimpo già di sua corona."

Sì disse prima; e poi: "Qui non si vieta
di nominar ciascun, da ch'è sì munta
18   nostra sembianza via per la dïeta.

"Questi," e mostrò col dito, "è Bonagiunta,
Bonagiunta da Lucca; e quella faccia
21   di là da lui più che l'altre trapunta

ebbe la Santa Chiesa in le sue braccia:
dal Torso fu, e purga per digiuno
24   l'anguille di Bolsena e la vernaccia."

Molti altri mi nomò ad uno ad uno;
e del nomar parean tutti contenti,
27   sì ch'io però non vidi un atto bruno.

Walking did not slow our talk, nor did the talking
slow our motion, as conversing we moved swiftly,
3   like ships driven by a favoring wind.

And the shades, that seemed things dead twice over,
stared at me, amazed, from the sockets of their eyes,
6   once they saw I was alive.

And I, continuing, remarked:
'Perhaps he climbs more slowly than he'd like
9   because someone else is with him.

'But tell me, if you know, where Piccarda is.
And tell me if I am seeing anyone of note
12   among these people who are staring at me so.'

'I cannot say whether my sister was more virtuous
than she was beautiful. On high Olympus
15   she already triumphs, rejoicing in her crown.'

This he said first and then:
'Here it's not forbidden to call us by our names,
18   since our features are sucked dry by fasting.

'He there'—and he pointed with his finger—'is
Bonagiunta, Bonagiunta of Lucca, and that one
21   just beyond him, the face more cracked and scaly

'than the rest, held Holy Church within his arms.
He was from Tours and now by fasting purges
24   eels from the Bolsena served *alla vernaccia.*'

He named many another, one by one,
and each seemed happy to be named—
27   I did not see a scowl on any face.

Vidi per fame a vòto usar li denti
Ubaldin da la Pila e Bonifazio
30   che pasturò col rocco molte genti.

Vidi messer Marchese, ch'ebbe spazio
già di bere a Forlì con men secchezza,
33   e sì fu tal, che non si sentì sazio.

Ma come fa chi guarda e poi s'apprezza
più d'un che d'altro, fei a quel da Lucca,
36   che più parea di me aver contezza.

El mormorava; e non so che "Gentucca"
sentiv' io là, ov' el sentia la piaga
39   de la giustizia che sì li pilucca.

"O anima," diss' io, "che par sì vaga
di parlar meco, fa sì ch'io t'intenda,
42   e te e me col tuo parlare appaga."

"Femmina è nata, e non porta ancor benda,"
cominciò el, "che ti farà piacere
45   la mia città, come ch'om la riprenda.

Tu te n'andrai con questo antivedere:
se nel mio mormorar prendesti errore,
48   dichiareranti ancor le cose vere.

Ma dì s'i' veggio qui colui che fore
trasse le nove rime, cominciando
51   *'Donne ch'avete intelletto d'amore.'* "

E io a lui: "I' mi son un che, quando
Amor mi spira, noto, e a quel modo
54   ch'e' ditta dentro vo significando."

"O frate, issa vegg' io," diss' elli, "il nodo
che 'l Notaro e Guittone e me ritenne
57   di qua dal dolce still novo ch'i' odo!

I saw, gnashing his teeth on nothing in his hunger,
Ubaldino dalla Pila, and Bonifazio,
30   who with his crozier led and fed a multitude.

I saw Messer Marchese, who once took his leisure,
drinking in Forlì with less cause for thirst
33   and yet could not be satisfied.

But as a man might look around and take more note
of one than of another, so I did with him from Lucca,
36   who clearly seemed to know me.

He was muttering and all I could make out
was a word like 'Gentucca' coming from his mouth,
39   where he felt most the justice that so wastes them.

'O soul,' I said, 'who seem so keen to speak with me,
speak in a manner I can understand
42   and with your speech thus satisfy us both.'

'A woman is born and wears not yet the wimple,'
he said. 'She shall make my city please you,
45   however men revile it.

'Take your way with this prophecy in mind
and, if you have mistook my muttering,
48   events themselves will make it plain to you.

'But tell me if I see before me
the one who brought forth those new rhymes
51   begun with *Ladies that have intelligence of love.*'

And I to him: 'I am one who, when Love
inspires me, take note and, as he dictates
54   deep within me, so I set it forth.'

'O my brother,' he said, 'now I understand the knot
that kept the Notary, Guittone, and me
57   on this side of the sweet new style I hear.

Io veggio ben come le vostre penne
di retro al dittator sen vanno strette,
60   che de le nostre certo non avvenne;

e qual più a gradire oltre si mette,
non vede più da l'uno a l'altro stilo";
63   e, quasi contentato, si tacette.

Come li augei che vernan lungo 'l Nilo,
alcuna volta in aere fanno schiera,
66   poi volan più a fretta e vanno in filo,

così tutta la gente che lì era,
volgendo 'l viso, raffrettò suo passo,
69   e per magrezza e per voler leggera.

E come l'uom che di trottare è lasso,
lascia andar li compagni, e sì passeggia
72   fin che si sfoghi l'affollar del casso,

sì lasciò trapassar la santa greggia
Forese, e dietro meco sen veniva,
75   dicendo: "Quando fia ch'io ti riveggia?"

"Non so," rispuos'io lui, "quant' io mi viva;
ma già non fïa il tornar mio tantosto,
78   ch'io non sia col voler prima a la riva;

però che 'l loco u' fui a viver posto,
di giorno in giorno più di ben si spolpa,
81   e a trista ruina par disposto."

"Or va," diss' el; "che quei che più n'ha colpa,
vegg' ïo a coda d'una bestia tratto
84   inver' la valle ove mai non si scolpa.

La bestia ad ogne passo va più ratto,
crescendo sempre, fin ch'ella il percuote,
87   e lascia il corpo vilmente disfatto.

'I clearly understand that your pens follow
faithfully whatever Love may dictate,
60   which, to be sure, was not the case with ours.

'And he who takes the next step sees in this
what separates the one style from the other.'
63   Then, as though with satisfaction, he was silent.

As birds that spend the wintertime along the Nile
sometimes gather in a flock high in the air,
66   then, flying faster, form a line,

so all the people gathered there
turned from us, hurrying away,
69   light as they were through leanness and desire.

And, as one exhausted by his run
lets his companions race ahead while he but walks
72   until the heaving of his chest is eased,

so Forese let the holy flock pass by
and came along with me behind them. He asked:
75   'How long until I see you here again?'

'I do not know,' I said, 'how long I'll live.
But my return could not occur so soon
78   that I will not in thought return before,

'since the place where I was put to live
day by day despoils itself of every good
81   and seems disposed to certain ruin.'

'How true,' he said, 'and I see him who bears
the greatest blame dragged behind a beast
84   toward the valley where there is no absolution.

'The beast goes faster with each step,
and faster, until it hurls him to the ground
87   and leaves his body horribly disfigured.

Non hanno molto a volger quelle ruote,"
e drizzò li occhi al ciel, "che ti fia chiaro
90   ciò che 'l mio dir più dichiarar non puote.

Tu ti rimani omai; ché 'l tempo è caro
in questo regno, sì ch'io perdo troppo
93   venendo teco sì a paro a paro."

Qual esce alcuna volta di gualoppo
lo cavalier di schiera che cavalchi,
96   e va per farsi onor del primo intoppo,

tal si partì da noi con maggior valchi;
e io rimasi in via con esso i due
99   che fuor del mondo sì gran marescalchi.

E quando innanzi a noi intrato fue,
che li occhi miei si fero a lui seguaci,
102   come la mente a le parole sue,

parvermi i rami gravidi e vivaci
d'un altro pomo, e non molto lontani
105   per esser pur allora vòlto in laci.

Vidi gente sott' esso alzar le mani
e gridar non so che verso le fronde,
108   quasi bramosi fantolini e vani

che pregano, e 'l pregato non risponde,
ma, per fare esser ben la voglia acuta,
111   tien alto lor disio e nol nasconde.

Poi si partì sì come ricreduta;
e noi venimmo al grande arbore adesso,
114   che tanti prieghi e lagrime rifiuta.

"Trapassate oltre sanza farvi presso:
legno è più sù che fu morso da Eva,
117   e questa pianta si levò da esso."

'Those wheels do not have long to turn'—
and he looked skyward—'until that which my speech
90   has left obscure shall be made plain to you.

'Now I must leave you here, for time
is precious in this realm so that I lose too much
93   by moving at your pace, slow step by step.'

As sometimes a horseman dashes at a gallop
from a troop of riders to attain
96   the honor of the first encounter,

he went away from us with longer strides,
and I continued on with those two souls
99   who were such noble leaders of the world.

After he had raced so far ahead
that my eyes could not make out his shape
102   any more than my mind made out his words,

suddenly a second tree, its branches green
and weighted down with fruit,
105   caught my eye as we came nearer.

I saw a crowd beneath it raising up their hands
and calling—I don't know what—up at the foliage,
108   like headlong, foolish children

who beg, but he from whom they beg does not reply
and, to make their longing even stronger,
111   holds the thing they want aloft and does not hide it.

Then they went away as if enlightened,
and it was our turn to approach the lofty tree
114   that turns away so many prayers and tears.

'Pass on, do not come any closer.
This is the offshoot of that tree above
117   from which Eve plucked and ate the fruit.'

Sì tra le frasche non so chi diceva;
per che Virgilio e Stazio e io, ristretti,
120   oltre andavam dal lato che si leva.

"Ricordivi," dicea, "d'i maladetti
nei nuvoli formati, che, satolli,
123   Tesëo combatter co' doppi petti;

e de li Ebrei ch'al ber si mostrar molli,
per che no i volle Gedeon compagni,
126   quando inver' Madïan discese i colli."

Sì accostati a l'un d'i due vivagni
passammo, udendo colpe de la gola
129   seguite già da miseri guadagni.

Poi, rallargati per la strada sola,
ben mille passi e più ci portar oltre,
132   contemplando ciascun sanza parola.

"Che andate pensando sì voi sol tre?"
sùbita vóce disse; ond' io mi scossi
135   come fan bestie spaventate e poltre.

Drizzai la testa per veder chi fossi;
e già mai non si videro in fornace
138   vetri o metalli sì lucenti e rossi,

com'io vidi un che dicea: "S'a voi piace
montare in sù, qui si convien dar volta;
141   quinci si va chi vuole andar per pace."

L'aspetto suo m'avea la vista tolta;
per ch'io mi volsi dietro a' miei dottori,
144   com' om che va secondo ch'elli ascolta.

E quale, annunziatrice de li albori,
l'aura di maggio movesi e olezza,
147   tutta impregnata da l'erba e da' fiori;

I do not know whose voice spoke out among the leaves,
but Virgil and Statius and I drew closer,
120   moving on beside the rising cliff.

'Remember,' the voice went on, 'those accursèd creatures,
formed in the clouds, their chests both beast and man,
123   who, drunk with wine, made war on Theseus,

'and those Hebrews whose thirst revealed them slack,
so that Gideon would not take them with him
126   when he charged from the hills against Midian.'

Thus, staying close to one edge of the path,
we passed on, hearing sins of gluttony
129   that long ago received their wretched wages.

Then, more separate along the road now empty,
we moved ahead at least a thousand paces,
132   each of us silent, deep in thought.

'What are you thinking as you walk along,
you three there by yourselves?' a sudden voice inquired,
135   at which I started, as do timid, drowsy beasts.

I raised my head to make out who it was,
and never was glass or metal in a furnace
138   ever seen so glowing and so red

as the one I saw who said: 'If you wish
to mount above, here is where you turn.
141   This is the road for those who would find peace.'

His shining face had blinded me,
so that I turned and walked behind my teachers
144   like someone led by only what he hears.

And as, announcing dawn, the breeze of May
stirs and exudes a fragrance
147   filled with the scent of grass and flowers,

tal mi senti' un vento dar per mezza
la fronte, e ben senti' mover la piuma,
150   che fé sentir d'ambrosïa l'orezza.

E senti' dir: "Beati cui alluma
tanto di grazia, che l'amor del gusto
nel petto lor troppo disir non fuma,
154   esurïendo sempre quanto è giusto!"

just such a wind I felt stroking my brow
and I could feel the moving of his feathers,

150   my senses steeped in odor of ambrosia.

I heard the words: 'Blessed are they
whom grace so much enlightens that appetite
fills not their breasts with gross desires,

154   but leaves them hungering for what is just.'

1–3.   The conversation between Forese and Dante continues. We have not heard Virgil's voice since the fifteenth verse of the last canto. We will not hear it again until the next canto (XXV.17). This is his longest silence since he entered the poem in its first canto (see note to *Inf.* XXX.37–41). He would seem to have been moved aside in response to Dante's interest in the encounter with Forese and concern with exploring the nature of his own most particular poetic practice, the subject at the core of this canto.

4.   For the phrase "things dead twice over" see the Epistle of Jude. The context is worth noting. Jude is declaiming against those who have infiltrated the ranks of the true believers, those "ungodly men" (*homines . . . impii*—Iudae 4) who are compared to, in succession, the unbelieving Israelites, the fallen angels, the sinners of Sodom and Gomorrah, as well as those great sinners Cain, Balaam (Numbers 22–25 and 31:16), and Korah (Numbers 16). The presence of these ungodly ones is then portrayed (Iudae 12) as a blemish upon the feasts of Christians gathered in charity. Interlopers, they are described as "feeding themselves without fear: clouds they are without water, carried about by the winds; trees whose fruit withers, without fruit, twice dead *(bis mortuae)*, plucked out by the roots." Several commentators refer to this passage, but only Poletto (1894) does so with some attention to the context, also graciously giving credit to the commentary of Antonio Cesari (Cesa.1824.1) for the earliest citation. The *contrapasso* here is thus more related to gluttony than at first may seem apparent, calling attention to an arid feasting that has no regard for the condition of the soul. These penitents thus purge themselves as though in memory of Jude's gluttonous "ungodly men."

8–9.   Once again (see note to *Purg.* XXI.103–114) we see that Statius is portrayed as putting off his Christian zeal in order to give himself to affectionate admiration of Virgil.

10.   Dante asks after Forese's sister, Piccarda, whom we shall meet as the first presence of *Paradiso* (see note to *Par.* III.46–49). The Donati family, like others in the poem, is variously dispersed in the afterworld. Later in this canto (verse 84) we will hear of Forese's brother, Corso, who is des-

tined for hell. In ante-purgatory we met a member of another similarly dispersed family, Buonconte da Montefeltro (*Purg.* V.88), son of the damned Guido (*Inf.* XXVII.67).

13–15.   Forese's touching words of praise for his sister, already joyous in the presence of God in the Empyrean (the Christian version of Mt. Olympus, home of the gods in classical mythology), brought the following misogynist comment from Benvenuto (1380): "And that is great praise, for it is a rare thing to find in the same woman harmony between comely form and chaste behavior."

Piccarda, who was dragged from her life as a nun into matrimony against her will, eventually puts us in mind of Pia de' Tolomei (*Purg.* V.133–136), who also was forced into a marriage she did not welcome. And both of them may send our thoughts back to Francesca da Rimini, similarly mistreated (*Inf.* V.100–107). The first three women present in each of the three *cantiche* have this experience in common.

16–18.   "Here" surely refers to this terrace (see note to *Purg.* XXII.49–51). Since there is no prohibition against naming names on any other terrace, commentators worry about Forese's motive in speaking this way. Most currently agree that he is using exaggerated understatement (the trope *litotes*) to make his point: i.e., on this terrace one *must* use names to identify the penitents because they are unrecognizable (as was Forese to Dante at *Purg.* XXIII.43–48) as a result of their emaciation.

19–20.   Bonagiunta Orbicciani degli Overardi da Lucca (1220?–1297?), notary and writer of lyric poems, composed mainly in imitation of the Provençal poets. He was involved in polemic against the poetry of Guido Guinizzelli and was attacked by Dante in his treatise on vernacular eloquence (*Dve* I.xiii.1) for writing in a dialectical rather than the lofty ("curial") vernacular. Some three dozen of his poems survive and a group of these has been re-edited and re-presented by Gianfranco Contini (Cont.1960.1), vol. I, pp. 257–82.

21–24.   Simon de Brie, who "married" Holy Church as Pope Martin IV (1281–85), was French. He was not born in Tours, but had served as treasurer of the cathedral of St. Martin in Tours. He briefly served as chancellor of France before becoming a cardinal in 1261. And his French connection was further apparent when Charles of Anjou was instrumental in securing the papacy for him. His gluttonous affection for eels from

Lake Bolsena caused him, according to Jacopo della Lana (1324), to have them, still alive, drowned in white wine from Liguria (the town of Vernazza) and then roasted. The commentator also reports that, as pope, coming from meetings dealing with Church business, he would cry out, "O Lord God, how many ills must we bear for Your holy Church! Let us have a drink!" and head for table to console himself.

Not only did this gluttonous pope support French political designs in Italy, he was the man who promoted Benedetto Caetani to the rank of cardinal, thus greatly facilitating his eventual elevation as Pope Boniface VIII (a promotion that Dante could not have regarded with equanimity, given his personal sufferings at the hands of this pope [see note to *Inf.* XIX.52–53]). In the light of such things, why did Dante decide that Martin was among the saved? Trucchi (1936) suggests that, as the successor to the nepotistic and venal Nicholas III (see *Inf.* XIX. 69–72), Martin put an end, for a time, to the practice of simony in the papacy. It is for that reason, in his opinion, that Dante overlooked his other flagrant sins to save him.

26–27.   The act of naming being particularly necessary on this terrace (see note to vv. 16–18), it brings pleasure (Dante again employs *litotes*: it does not cause scowls) to those who are named and thus may hope for relieving prayer from the world, once Dante returns to it. It hardly needs to be pointed out that many of the sinners in hell were less pleased at being recognized.

29.   "Ubaldino degli Ubaldini of La Pila (castle in the Mugello, or upper valley of the Sieve, tributary of the Arno, north of Florence), member of the powerful Ghibelline family of that name. Ubaldino, who was one of those who voted for the destruction of Florence (*Inf.* X.92), and was a member of the Consiglio Generale, after the battle of Montaperti (Sept. 4, 1260), was brother of the famous Cardinal Ottaviano degli Ubaldini (*Inf.* X.120), uncle of Ugolino d'Azzo (*Purg.* XIV.105), and father of the Archbishop Ruggieri of Pisa (*Inf.* XXXIII.14); he died in 1291" **(T)**.

29–30.   Bonifazio has been "identified by modern commentators with Bonifazio dei Fieschi of Genoa, Archbishop of Ravenna, 1274–1295. . . . The ancient pastoral staff of the Archbishops of Ravenna, which is still preserved, bears at the top an ornament shaped like a chess 'rook' [rather than the conventional curved crosier], hence the term *rocco* used by

Dante. Bonifazio . . . is known to have been immensely wealthy, but there is no record of his having been addicted to gluttony" **(T)**.

While some debate whether or not the reference to the archbishop's pastoral care is meant to be taken ironically, it seems difficult, in light of the descriptions of the other penitent gluttons, to take it any other way. The flock he is envisioned as leading would seem to be less the faithful of Ravenna than his guests to dinner.

31–33. "Marchese (or Marchesino) degli Orgogliosi of Forlì . . . was Podestà of Faenza in 1296" **(T)**. Embellishing an incident he probably first heard from his teacher, Benvenuto da Imola, John of Serravalle (1416) recounts it this way: "One day [Marchese] asked of his servant, 'What do the people say of me? What is my reputation among them?' And the servant answered, 'O my lord, they say that you are noble and wise,' etc. And so he spoke again to his servant, saying, 'Now tell me the truth, what do they really say?' In reply the servant said, 'Since you wish it, I will tell you the truth; people say you are a great drinker of wine.' At which [Marchese] responded, 'These people speak truthfully; but they really ought to add that I am always thirsty—and that is a fact, for I thirst continually.' " Bonagiunta was also a lover of the grape, according to Benvenuto (1380), who characterized him as "a deft contriver of rhymes and a ready imbiber of wines."

34–36. Dante's attention was drawn to Bonagiunta da Lucca because, he says, Bonagiunta seemed to know him. We may reflect that Dante the poet's interest in Bonagiunta centered on his desire to stage, clued by the utterance of this lesser poet, his own *ars poetica*, as we shall shortly understand. Including Dante, the interaction among those speaking or being noticed in this canto involves two poets, two religious figures, and two politicians. And then there are the two classical poets who are not even mentioned once in this very "modern" canto (it is notable that Pope Martin, dead only fifteen years, is the senior ghost among the five gluttons in this group).

37–39. For Dante's use of the verb *mormorare* (murmur), see the note to *Purgatorio* X.100–102. This passage has long been problematic. Does Bonagiunta refer to his fellow Lucchesi in an unfavorable way, calling them *gentucca* or *gentuccia* (a deprecating way of referring to his people, or *gente*)? Or is he mentioning a kindly woman of that name who will be welcoming to Dante when, in his exile, he will come to Lucca? In this case he would be referring to the *femmina* referred to in vv. 43–45. Beginning with Francesco da Buti (1385), who states that Gentucca was the name of a woman from Rossimpelo, most commentators believe that the reference is to someone who was benevolent to Dante in Lucca during a stay there. We have, however, no confirming evidence for this sojourn in Lucca (see Michele Messina, "Lucca," *ED* III [1971]), which, if it took place, probably did so in 1308–9, and certainly no hard facts establishing her identity. Nonetheless, this remains the best hypothesis. Still others have attempted to make a case for Gentucca as a woman with whom Dante had some sort of sexual liaison, an interpretation that seems venturesome at best. On the entire question see Giorgio Varanini, "Gentucca," *ED* III (1971).

40–42.   Dante encourages Bonagiunta, for whom speech is made difficult by the pain he feels in his mouth, the orifice by which he offended in gluttony, to speak more plainly.

43–48.   If this woman is, as some contemporary students of the question suggest, Gentucca di Ciucchino Morla, she was the wife of Buonaccorso Fondora. In that case she wore the black wimple, worn by wives, not the white, reserved for widows. Nino Visconti's widow, Giovanna, according to him, made the mistake of remarrying badly, putting off the white wimple (*Purg.* VIII.74). However, we cannot be sure whether Bonagiunta is referring to an as yet unmarried woman, or to a married one whose husband, soon to die, is still alive. In any case, this woman will make Lucca seem pleasant to Dante, no matter how others may blame it (as Dante himself had done in *Inf.* XXI.40–42).

49–51.   Having recognized Dante earlier (vv. 35–36), Bonagiunta now presses him about the nature of his poetry. Is he the poet who drew forth from within himself the new poems that began with the *canzone* "Ladies that have intelligence of love"? This is the first long poem of the three that help give structure to the *Vita nuova*, announcing the beginning of its second stage, in which Dante chooses to give over the style of "complaint," borrowed from Cavalcanti, in order to turn to the style of praise, with its debt to Guinizzelli. Dante composed this poem around 1289. From this remark, we learn at least one important thing. Whatever the determining features of Dante's new poetry, it was different—at least according to him, using Bonagiunta as his mouthpiece—from *all* poetry written before it, including Dante's own. This precision evades many who discuss the problem, who continue to allow poems by Dante and other poets written before *Donne ch'avete* to share its status. It seems clear that Dante's absolute and precise purpose is to rewrite the history of Italian lyric, including that of his own poems, so that it fits his current program.

52–54. There is perhaps no more debated tercet in this poem than this one, and perhaps none that has more far-reaching implications for our general understanding of Dante's stance as a poet. Does he refer to Amore as the god of Love? or as the name of the true God in His Third Person, the Holy Spirit? Dantists are deeply (and fiercely) divided by this issue. The bibliography of work devoted to it is immense. Readers who know Italian will want to refer to three papers composed for the Third International Dante Seminar (Florence, 2000) by members of the panel concerning the currently vexed question of Dante's attitude toward Cavalcanti and its relationship to his view of his own poetic as this is given voice here (see Anto.2001.1, Durl.2001.1, and Leon.2001.1). For the views of this writer, which are at some variance especially from those of the first and third of these, see Holl.1992.2 and Holl.1999.1. In the most recent of these two studies, the case is made for our understanding that Dante indeed presents himself as writing under the inspiration of the Holy Spirit, a view that causes understandable distress, but which is fundamental, in one line of thought, to a better comprehension of his purposes.

55–63. Bonagiunta's response may be paraphrased as follows: "Now I understand the nature of the knot that held back the Notary [Giacomo da Lentini], Guittone [d'Arezzo], and me from the sweet new style that at this very moment I am hearing! Now I clearly understand how your pens [plural] followed strictly after the words of the 'dictator,' something that ours did not; and in that lies the entire difference between your [Dante's] 'new style' and ours." He falls silent, as though, it seems, satisfied with his utterance.

What exactly does Dante mean by the phrase "sweet new style"? This is surely one of the key questions presented in the poem, and not one of the easiest. Further, who else wrote in that "style"? And what is the significance of the fact that Bonagiunta says that he hears it *now* (in listening to Dante here in purgatory? in current Tuscan poems composed on earth? [but how would he *hear* these?])? What follows is a series of hypotheses that sketch out this writer's views of the major aspects of a difficult question.

(1) The passage, probably written ca. 1311–12, marks the first time

that the beguiling phrase "dolce stil novo" had ever been used in the vernacular that we call "Italian." That it was meant to refer to or to identify an actual "school" of poets that existed before the date of its inscription in Dante's text may not be assumed (see Bigi [Bigi.1955.1] and Favati [Fava.1975.1]), although it frequently is.

(2) On the other hand, the author's (or Bonagiunta's) plural "vostre" should be seen as including not only himself, but also Cino da Pistoia (the one fellow poet who, Dante believed, had understood the theological significance of his Beatrice), if perhaps no one else (see Hollander [Holl.1992.2] and Brugnolo [Brug.1993.2]).

(3) The significance of the poetic stance struck in the phrase should be understood in theological terms. Dante is not presenting himself as a usual love poet, but as one who serves as God's scribe in recording the result of God's love for him through the agency of Beatrice. Dante and others had previously written in a "sweet" style; but only he, now, in his *Comedy*, writes in this "sweet new style" that creates a theologized poetry that is like almost no one else's (see Mazzotta [Mazz.1979.1], pp. 197–210; Barański [Bara.2001.2], pp. 392–94).

(4) The word "style" here has a broader connotation than it usually does in discourse about poetry, indicating not only a way of writing, but a subject for writing, as was apparent when his new style of praise in *Vita nuova* was presented as requiring new "matter" (see Holl.1999.1, pp. 271–72; Aversano [Aver.2001.1], p. 131: the poem is "sweet artistically because it is new poetically"). The "new style" not only sounds different, it *is* different (but see the differing view of Leonardi [Leon.2001.1], p. 334). The very phrasing of the element that sets, in Bonagiunta's understanding (vv. 58–59), this "style" apart from all others—copying out exactly what was spoken by the "dictator"—points not at all to style, but rather to content.

(5) We should probably also understand that the phrase "dolce stil novo" refers to some of Dante's earlier poetry (only the *canzone* "Donne ch'avete intelletto d'amore" for certain), some of Cino's poems (at least and perhaps only the *canzone* upon the death of Beatrice, "Avegna ched el m'aggia più per tempo"), and to Dante's *Comedy*, thus presenting the author's claims for a theological grounding of his poem's inspiration as being joined to certain of his earlier poems that he felt either had, or could be construed as having, the same character. This is the crux of a continuing disagreement with those who argue that the *Comedy* is a poem that goes *beyond* the *stil novo* (e.g., Pertile [Pert.1993. 1]), rather than being a continuation of it. In short, while Dante and others (Guido

Cavalcanti perhaps the most capable among them) had previously written in a "sweet" style, Dante alone developed, on the model of Guinizzelli's lyrics, poems of praise of a theologized lady, Beatrice.

56.   In a single line Bonagiunta crosses off the list of illustrious precursors two of the great poetic figures that preceded Dante, Giacomo da Lentini (died ca. 1250) and Guittone d'Arezzo (ca. 1230–94). Giacomo was the first major Italian practitioner of lyric, and is looked upon as the inventor of the sonnet and as the founder of the so-called Sicilian School, the first group of writers of lyric in Italian, taking their models from the writers of lyric in Provençal. Dante is later still harder on Guittone (see *Purg.* XXVI. 124–126 and note), who, as Dante came to poetry in the 1280s, was perhaps the preeminent Tuscan poet.

64–74.   The two similes, piled one upon the other, return to a technique not observed in some time: a comparison based on an antique source coupled with a completely "vernacular" and "ordinary" one. See *Inferno* XXIV. 1–15, where ancient and contemporary elements are combined in a single simile, and *Inferno* XXVI. 25–39, where local Tuscan agriculture and Elijah's ascent to heaven are the contrasting elements in two neighboring similes.

The first of this pair derives, fairly obviously to today's reader, instructed by the notes in the text, from Lucan (*Phars.* V.711–716), a description of cranes fleeing winter's cold to winter on the Nile. Nonetheless, for all the certainty in recent commentators that this is a reminiscence of Lucan, it was only with Torraca (1905) that it seems first to have been observed. Lucan's passage is revisited even more plainly at *Paradiso* XVIII.73–78.

75.   Forese's remark is perhaps the high point in the fraternal affection found in purgatory, as he looks forward to Dante's death as the necessary precondition for their next meeting in the afterlife.

76–81.   Notable is Dante's calm assurance that he will be saved. This may seem prideful, but is rather the natural result, or so he would have us believe, of his having been chosen for such an experience of the afterworld. God, he would ask us to imagine, would not have selected as His scribe one destined to die in sin.

82–90.   Corso Donati, brother of Forese, was, in Dante's eyes, the Black Guelph who bore "the greatest blame" for Florence's problems (and for his own) because of his alliance with Pope Boniface VIII, the "beast" who will drag him to hell—as Dante will see before much time passes. In fact, through the magic of post-event prophecy (Corso was killed on 6 October 1308), Forese is able to promise the protagonist this happy vengeance.

Corso had supervised the murderous taking of the city by the Black Guelphs after Charles of Valois had led his French troops into Florence in November 1301. In a political reversal that is not totally unlike Dante's own, he was condemned to death by the priors for trying to take power into his own hands in a supposed arrangement involving the Tuscan Ghibelline leader Uguccione della Faggiuola, to whose daughter he was married.

While the "beast" in Forese's account is clearly metaphorical, Corso apparently did die while trying to escape, either in a fall from his horse or by being lanced by one of his captors once he had fallen—or even as he was hanging from a stirrup, dragged along the ground.

94–99.   The military simile fits the tone of the death scene of Corso that has just been narrated by his brother. Here, by way of returning to the rigors of his penance, Forese is allowed to assume the role of the cavalryman who goes out to make the first contact of battle. Virgil and Statius, described by a word perhaps never seen before in Italian, "marshals," are left behind, but are calmly directing the battle, as it were. As for Dante, that retired cavalryman (see note to *Inf.* XXI.95), it is not clear what role he plays, but he is a subordinate to these two marshals, those great poets who led other humans into knowledge and virtue through their works.

100–102.   Forese has rounded the terrace and is now beyond the reach of Dante's sight, just as his prophecy, obscure now in 1300 before the event of Corso's death, has escaped Dante's understanding.

103–105.   Moving along the terrace with his eyes fixed on Forese, Dante does not at first see the tree that his own movement forward has brought him to. The second tree of this terrace has caused less puzzlement than the first one (*Purg.* XXII.131–135); the succeeding verses (116–117) answer most questions that one might have (see note to vv. 115–117): this tree is an offshoot of the Tree of the Knowledge of Good and Evil.

Jenni (Jenn.1972.1), pp. 12–13, argues that the sight of the water from above causing the leaves to shine makes the penitent gluttons even hungrier. As was the case with the first tree, this one is also apparently watered from above (see *Purg.* XXII. 137–138).

106–111.   This simile possibly reflects a passage from *Convivio* (*Conv.* IV.xii.16) in which Dante speaks of the natural love of human souls for God, their maker, which is easily drawn off course: "Thus we see little children setting their desire first of all on a fruit, and then, growing older, desiring to possess a little bird, and then still later desiring to possess fine clothes, then a horse, and then a woman, and then modest wealth, then greater riches, and then still more" (tr. Lansing). The central elements of this image (a man catching the hungry attention of a child by holding up a fruit) are deployed again in *Purgatorio* XXVII. 45.

112–114.   The penitents (as will be the poets) are urged to turn aside, apparently by the same voice from within the tree that will warn off the poets (and since the names of exemplary figures are recited by this voice, we probably correctly assume it speaks to all, triggered by its sense that someone is approaching, that is, not only in response to these special visitors). They are "enlightened" (in the sense that their first opinion, that the fruit of this tree is desirable, is changed) when they realize that this tree is a branch from that beneath which humankind first fell into sin, and thus willingly move away.

115–117.   Once again an unseen and unidentified divinely authorized voice speaks from within the foliage of a tree (see *Purg.* XXII.140–154). This is an offshoot of the tree of which Eve (and then Adam, who had also been warned not to [see note to *Purg.* XXII.140–141]) ate the fruit.

   Porena (1946) is one of those who unaccountably believe that there must be still other trees upon this terrace. If, indeed, Dante is referring to the two most significant trees in the original garden, the Tree of Life and the Tree of the Knowledge of Good and Evil (Genesis 2:8), it would seem unlikely that he would have wanted us to imagine there might be others scattered along the terrace. Porena denies that the first speaking tree (*Purg.* XXII.141) is an offshoot of the Tree of Life, but believes that it, too, is derived from the Tree of Knowledge, an opinion that may seem difficult to justify.

   Bosco/Reggio raise a question in their commentary: Why was the first tree (*Purg.* XXII.139) approachable, while this one is not? Would it not seem reasonable that the fruit of the Tree of Life should be precisely what purgation is preparing penitents to receive? At the same time, it would also seem reasonable that they should prepare for their reward by ceremonially avoiding the site of humanity's original sin.

121–126.   The voice reminds the travelers (and the penitents, we assume) first of the "Centaurs, mythical race, half horses and half men, said to have been offspring of Ixion, King of the Lapithae, and a cloud in the shape of Hera [Juno]" (**T**). The Centaurs fought against the Lapiths and Theseus at the wedding feast for Pirithoüs (the friend of Theseus and their half brother) and his bride Hippodamia. The Centaurs attempt to rape the bride and bridesmaids but are prevented by Theseus and others. The final three hundred lines of the scene, which served as Dante's source, in Ovid (*Metam.* XII.210–535) represent a kind of tumultuous and comic redoing of the battle scenes in the *Iliad* (and in the *Aeneid*), with plenty of body parts and blood.

For the double nature of the Centaurs (beast and man at once), see *Inferno* XII.84.

The Hebrews selected by Gideon to make war upon the Midianites were those who lifted water to their mouths in their cupped hands, as opposed to those who cast themselves down to a stream to drink directly with their mouths (see Judges 7:2–8). The ones remembered here are not the 300 whom he chose to fight, but the 9,700 who were sent back to their tents. These were "slack" in that they gave in totally to their desire to drink, while the 300 displayed a more controlled demeanor, more fitting to those who would require composure even in the heat of battle.

133–134.   This voice, we shortly come to understand, comes from the Angel of Temperance.

137–138.   Singleton (1973) points out that the description of this angel is indebted to John's Revelation (Apocalypse 1:9–20). The passage, prologue to John's vision, tells how the apostle was ordered to write it by Jesus, a scene described in terms that at times closely resemble these.

145–150.   The last of the similes in a canto rich with them compares the waft of air from the angel's wing felt by Dante on his brow to the sweet-smelling breeze of May. Tommaseo (1837) suggested a source in Virgil's fourth *Georgic* (IV.415): "Haec ait et liquidam ambrosiae diffundit odorem" (She spoke, giving off the flowing fragrance of ambrosia).

Cyrene is encouraging her despondent son, Aristaeus, to learn his fate from Proteus.

151–154. Dante now "finishes" the Beatitude (Matthew 5:6) begun in *Purgatorio* XXII. 4–6, "Beati qui esuriunt et sitiunt iustitiam, quoniam ipsi saturabuntur" (Blessed are those who hunger and thirst after righteousness, for they shall be satisfied). In the first context, applying to those who "thirst" for riches, only *sitiunt* was heard, while here we have the echo only of the word for hunger, *esuriunt*.

PURGATORIO XXV
(Lust)

now informs the soul of the
new being in the female; (4)
but how this soul becomes a
human being is not yet clear;
67–78 once the fetal brain is formed,
God, delighted with Nature's
work, breathes into it the
[rational] soul, which blends
with the already existent soul
and makes a single entity, as
wine is made by the sun;
79–108 at the moment of death the
soul leaves the body but carries
with it the potential for both
states, the bodily one "mute,"
the rational one more acute
than in life, and falls to
Acheron (if damned) or Tiber
(if saved), where it takes on its
"airy body," which, inseparable
as flame from fire, follows it
wherever it goes; insofar as this
new being "remembers" its
former shape, it takes on all its
former organs of sense and
becomes a "shade"

Ora era onde 'l salir non volea storpio;
ché 'l sole avëa il cerchio di merigge
3   lasciato al Tauro e la notte a lo Scorpio:

per che, come fa l'uom che non s'affigge
ma vassi a la via sua, che che li appaia,
6   se di bisogno stimolo il trafigge,

così intrammo noi per la callaia,
uno innanzi altro prendendo la scala
9   che per artezza i salitor dispaia.

E quale il cicognin che leva l'ala
per voglia di volare, e non s'attenta
12   d'abbandonar lo nido, e giù la cala;

tal era io con voglia accesa e spenta
di dimandar, venendo infino a l'atto
15   che fa colui ch'a dicer s'argomenta.

Non lasciò, per l'andar che fosse ratto,
lo dolce padre mio, ma disse: "Scocca
18   l'arco del dir, che 'nfino al ferro hai tratto."

Allor sicuramente apri' la bocca
e cominciai: "Come si può far magro
21   là dove l'uopo di nodrir non tocca?"

"Se t'ammentassi come Meleagro
si consumò al consumar d'un stizzo,
24   non fora," disse, "a te questo sì agro;

e se pensassi come, al vostro guizzo,
guizza dentro a lo specchio vostra image,
27   ciò che par duro ti parrebbe vizzo.

It was the hour when the ascent did not permit delay,
for the sun had left the meridian to the Bull,
and night had left it to the Scorpion.

Therefore, like one who does not stop
but, urged on by the spur of need,
plods along his way no matter what,

we thrust into the gap, one before the other,
single file, up stairs so narrow
they separate those who climb them.

And as a baby stork may raise a wing,
longing to fly, but does not dare
to leave its nest and lowers it again,

such was I, my desire to question kindled
and then put out, moving my mouth
like a man who prepares himself to speak.

Despite our rapid pace, my gentle father said:
'Relax the bent bow of your speech,
now stretched to the arrow's iron point.'

At that, with confidence I opened my mouth to ask:
'How can it be that one grows thin
here where there is no need for nourishment?'

'If you recall how Meleager was consumed
in the time it took to burn a log-end,' he said,
'this will not be difficult for you to understand.

'And if you consider how at your slightest motion
your image moves within the glass,
a concept that seems hard would then seem easy.

Ma perché dentro a tuo voler t'adage,
ecco qui Stazio; e io lui chiamo e prego
che sia or sanator de le tue piage."

30

"Se la veduta etterna li dislego,"
rispuose Stazio, "là dove tu sie,
discolpi me non potert' io far nego."

33

Poi cominciò: "Se le parole mie,
figlio, la mente tua guarda e riceve,
lume ti fiero al come che tu die.

36

Sangue perfetto, che poi non si beve
da l'assetate vene, e si rimane
quasi alimento che di mensa leve,

39

prende nel core a tutte membra umane
virtute informativa, come quello
ch'a farsi quelle per le vene vane.

42

Ancor digesto, scende ov' è più bello
tacer che dire; e quindi poscia geme
sovr' altrui sangue in natural vasello.

45

Ivi s'accoglie l'uno e l'altro insieme,
l'un disposto a patire, e l'altro a fare
per lo perfetto loco onde si preme;

48

e, giunto lui, comincia ad operare
coagulando prima, e poi avviva
ciò che per sua matera fé constare.

51

Anima fatta la virtute attiva
qual d'una pianta, in tanto differente,
che questa è in via e quella è già a riva,

54

tanto ovra poi, che già si move e sente,
come spungo marino; e indi imprende
ad organar le posse ond' è semente.

57

'But, to soothe you and to grant your wish,
here is Statius. I call on him, I beg him,
30   to be the healer of your wounds.'

'If I unfold the eternal plan before him
in your presence,' answered Statius,
33   'let my excuse be that I can't refuse you.'

Then he began: 'Son, if your mind treasures
and takes in my words,
36   they will explain how what you ask may be.

'The perfect blood, which is never drunk
by the thirsty veins and remains untouched,
39   like the food one removes from the table,

'gathers in the heart and carries
formative power to all members, like the blood
42   that, flowing through, becomes a part of them.

'Again digested, it descends where silence
is more fit than speech and from there later
45   drops into the natural vessel on another's blood.

'There the one is mingled with the other,
one fitted to be passive and the other active,
48   owing to the perfect place from which it springs,

'and this one, so conjoined, begins to function,
first coagulating, then quickening that which,
51   as its future matter, it has already thickened.

'The active force, having now become a soul—
like a plant's but differing in this: it is still
54   on the way, while the plant has come to shore—

'next functions, moving now and feeling,
like a sea-sponge, and from that goes on, producing
57   organs for the faculties of which it is the seed.

Aristotle's theory

Or si spiega, figliuolo, or si distende
la virtù ch'è dal cor del generante,
60   dove natura a tutte membra intende.

Ma come d'animal divegna fante,
non vedi tu ancor: quest' è tal punto,
63   che più savio di te fé già errante,

sì che per sua dottrina fé disgiunto
da l'anima il possibile intelletto,
66   perché da lui non vide organo assunto.

Apri a la verità che viene il petto;
e sappi che, sì tosto come al feto
69   l'articular del cerebro è perfetto,

lo motor primo a lui si volge lieto
sovra tant' arte di natura, e spira
72   spirito novo, di vertù repleto,

che ciò che trova attivo quivi, tira
in sua sustanzia, e fassi un'alma sola,
75   che vive e sente e sé in sé rigira.

E perché meno ammiri la parola,
guarda il calor del sol che si fa vino,
78   giunto a l'omor che de la vite cola.

Quando Làchesis non ha più del lino,
solvesi da la carne, e in virtute
81   ne porta seco e l'umano e 'l divino:

l'altre potenze tutte quante mute;
memoria, intelligenza e volontade
84   in atto molto più che prima agute.

Sanza restarsi, per sé stessa cade
mirabilmente a l'una de le rive;
87   quivi conosce prima le sue strade.

'Now unfurls, now spreads the force, my son,
that comes straight from the heart of the begetter,
60   there where nature makes provision for all members.

'But how from animal it turns to human
you do not see as yet. This is the point
63   at which a wiser man than you has stumbled → Aristotle

'in that his teaching rendered separate
the possible intellect from the soul,
66   because he could not find the organ it could live in.

'Open your heart to the truth that follows
and know that, once the brain's articulation
69   in the embryo arrives at its perfection,

'the First Mover turns to it, rejoicing
in such handiwork of nature, and breathes
72   into it a spirit, new and full of power,

'which then draws into its substance
all it there finds active and becomes a single soul
75   that lives, and feels, and reflects upon itself.

'And, that you may be less bewildered by my words,
consider the sun's heat, which, blended with the sap
78   pressed from the vine, turns into wine.

'When Lachesis runs short of thread, the soul
unfastens from the flesh, carrying with it
81   potential faculties, both human and divine.

'The lower faculties now inert,
memory, intellect, and the will remain
84   in action, and are far keener than before.

'Without pausing, the soul falls, miraculously,
of itself, to one or to the other shore.
87   There first it comes to know its road.

Tosto che loco lì la circunscrive,
la virtù formativa raggia intorno
90   così e quanto ne le membra vive.

E come l'aere, quand' è ben pïorno,
per l'altrui raggio che 'n sé si reflette,
93   di diversi color diventa addorno;

così l'aere vicin quivi si mette
e in quella forma ch'è in lui suggella
96   virtüalmente l'alma che ristette;

e simigliante poi a la fiammella
che segue il foco là 'vunque si muta,
99   segue lo spirto sua forma novella.

Però che quindi ha poscia sua paruta,
è chiamata ombra; e quindi organa poi
102   ciascun sentire infino a la veduta.

Quindi parliamo e quindi ridiam noi;
quindi facciam le lagrime e ' sospiri
105   che per lo monte aver sentiti puoi.

Secondo che ci affliggono i disiri
e li altri affetti, l'ombra si figura;
108   e quest' è la cagion di che tu miri."

E già venuto a l'ultima tortura
s'era per noi, e vòlto a la man destra,
111   ed eravamo attenti ad altra cura.

Quivi la ripa fiamma in fuor balestra,
e la cornice spira fiato in suso
114   che la reflette e via da lei sequestra;

ond' ir ne convenia dal lato schiuso
ad uno ad uno; e io temëa 'l foco
117   quinci, e quindi temeva cader giuso.

'As soon as space surrounds it there,
the formative force radiates upon it,
90   giving shape and measure as though to living members.

'And as the air, when it is full of rain,
is adorned with rainbow hues not of its making
93   but reflecting the brightness of another,

'so here the neighboring air is shaped
into that form the soul, which stays with it,
96   imprints upon it by its powers.

'And, like the flame that imitates its fire,
wherever that may shift and flicker,
99   its new form imitates the spirit.

'A shade we call it, since the insubstantial soul
is visible this way, which from the same air forms
102   organs for each sense, even that of sight.

'Through this we speak and through this smile.
Thus we shed tears and make the sighs
105   you may have heard here on the mountain.

'And, as we feel affections or desires,
the shade will change its form, and this
108   is the cause of that at which you marvel.'

But now we had come to the final circling
and, turning to the right,
111   we were attentive to another care.

There the bank discharges surging flames
and where the terrace ends, a blast of wind shoots up
114   which makes the flames recoil and clear the edge,

so that we had to pass along the open side,
one by one, and here I feared the fire
117   but also was afraid I'd fall below.

Lo duca mio dicea: "Per questo loco
si vuol tenere a li occhi stretto il freno,
però ch'errar potrebbesi per poco."

120

"*Summae Deus clementïae*" nel seno
al grande ardore allora udi' cantando,
che di volger mi fé caler non meno;

123

e vidi spirti per la fiamma andando;
per ch'io guardava a loro e a' miei passi,
compartendo la vista a quando a quando.

126

Appresso il fine ch'a quell' inno fassi,
gridavano alto: "*Virum non cognosco*";
indi ricominciavan l'inno bassi.

129

Finitolo, anco gridavano: "Al bosco
si tenne Diana, ed Elice caccionne
che di Venere avea sentito il tòsco."

132

Indi al cantar tornavano; indi donne
gridavano e mariti che fuor casti
come virtute e matrimonio imponne.

135

E questo modo credo che lor basti
per tutto il tempo che 'l foco li abbruscia:
con tal cura conviene e con tai pasti
che la piaga da sezzo si ricuscia.

139

My leader said: 'Along this path
a tight rein must be kept upon the eyes,
120   for here it would be easy to misstep.'

'Summae Deus clementiae' I then heard sung
in the heart of that great burning,
123   which made me no less eager to turn back,

and I saw spirits walking in the flames,
so that I watched them and my footsteps,
126   dividing my attention, now there, now here.

After the hymn was sung through to its end
they cried aloud: *'Virum non cognosco,'*
129   then, in softer tones, began the hymn again.

When it was finished, next they cried:
'Diana kept to the woods and drove Callisto out
132   for having felt the poisoned sting of Venus.'

Then they again began to sing,
calling on wives and husbands who were chaste,
135   even as virtue and matrimony urge.

And this way they go on, I think,
for as long as the fire burns them.
With such treatment and with just such diet
139   must the last of all the wounds be healed.

1–3.   The constellations Taurus and Scorpio are 180 degrees apart. The sun at the antipodes has now moved roughly two hours, from shining down from in front of the constellation Capricorn, then Sagittarius, and now Taurus, or from noon to two o'clock (as, half the world away, in Jerusalem it is two in the morning). Since the travelers had entered this terrace at roughly ten in the morning (*Purg.* XXII.115–120), it results that they have spent roughly four hours among the penitents of Gluttony and will spend approximately the same amount of time from now until they leave the penitents of Lust (see *Purg.* XXVII.65–66), the first two hours traversing the distance between the two terraces (see *Purg.* XXVI.4–6).

4–9.   The simile stresses the renewed urgency of the climb, with the three poets, led by Virgil, mounting in single file. Statius is, as will eventually be made plain, in the middle position (see *Purg.* XXVII.48), from which he will shortly respond at length to Dante's question about the aerial body.

17–18.   Virgil's metaphor has Dante drawing the bowstring of his question so hard and far that the iron tip of his arrow is touching the shaft of his bow. These are the first words spoken by Virgil since *Purgatorio* XXIII.15 (see the note to *Purg.* XXIV.1–3).

20–21.   Dante's question, which has been in the back of his mind since *Purgatorio* XXIII.37–39, addresses the apparent incongruity of the fact that the souls of the penitents of Gluttony seem to grow thin from not ingesting food. Such a phenomenon, he has wrongly assumed, should be associated only with the experience of starvation in a mortal body.

22–24.   The reference is to Ovid's near-epic narrative of the hunt for the Calydonian boar with its unhappy outcome for Meleager (*Metam.* VIII.260–546). He, son of the king of Calydon and of Althaea, killed this rampaging animal and gave its skin to Atalanta, with whom he was in love. Althaea's two brothers, Plexippus and Toxeus, take the remains of the beast back from her. Enraged at the insult to his honor, Meleager kills them. Seeing the corpses of her brothers brought into the temple where she was giving thanks for her son's victory, and learning who had killed them, Althaea is moved to take vengeance, even upon her own son. When he was born, the three Fates had determined that he would live only so long as a firebrand remained unconsumed in a fire into which it had been cast. Hearing this, Althaea snatched the burning log-end from the fire and doused it in water. Now she took up again this piece of wood, which she had preserved, and cast it into a fire, thus causing the death of her own son. Virgil's point is that if Dante had understood this principle, that there is a vital relationship between what seem unrelated phenomena (e.g., the burning of a log-end and the death of a man), he would have already understood the relationship between body and soul here in purgatory.

25–27.   As a second instance of this principle, Virgil offers the example of a person's movements being reflected in a mirror; once again, to an ignorant observer, the two phenomena might seem to have independent and unrelated causes if the observer did not understand the principle of reflection (e.g., two Marx brothers in sleeping garments facing each other in an open doorway and moving in harmony).

28–30.   It is as though Virgil himself understands that his explanations, relying on physical laws, do not explain the deeper principles involved in the fact that these souls respond with physical symptoms to a moral sensation. Dealing with this passage, Pietro di Dante (1340) allegorizes Virgil as "rational philosophy" and Statius, "a Christian poet," as "moral philosophy." It might seem more to the point to realize that Statius, as a saved Christian, simply knows by revelation some mysterious things that are not known by others, e.g., all ordinary mortals and all souls who are not saved.

31–33.   Statius excuses himself for revealing an essential Christian mystery in the presence of a pagan because of his love for this particular pagan. John of Serravalle (1415) speaks of Virgil's belief (learned from Plato's *Timaeus*, according to Benvenuto's commentary on *Inf.* I. 10–12) that the souls of humans come from the stars and return to them. While we cannot be certain that Dante shared the first part of this view (and see *Par.* IV.22–24 for his denial of the second), the "eternal plan" is at significant variance from Plato, as Statius's lecture will make plain.

34–108.   For a summary of the main points of Statius's lecture on embryology, see the Outline of this canto, above. For extremely useful notes on Dante's sources in these verses (37–88), Aristotle, Avicenna, Averroës, Albertus Magnus, Aquinas, along with reference to Bruno Nardi's important contribution to our awareness of Dante's schooling in such matters, see Singleton's commentary to them. This "lecture" is put to the task of justifying Dante's presentation of spiritual beings as still possessing, for the purposes of purgation, their bodily senses even though they have no bodies. Souls in Heaven, we will discover, have no such "aerial bodies," but are present as pure spirit.

37–42. The "perfect blood" is the end result of a series of four "digestions" within the body: in the stomach, the liver, the heart, the members. Sperm is what remains after the "fourth digestion" of the blood, which informs the various members of the body (e.g., heart, brain).

48. "The perfect place from which it springs" is the heart, from which it flows to become sperm.

52–54. The vegetative soul is the first one formed. Unlike the vegetative soul of things that have no higher nature, ours is only the beginning—our soul has not yet "come to shore," its "voyage" has only begun. The vegetative soul enables the growth of the physical body. This capacity we share with animate matter (things that grow, e.g., plants, as opposed to inanimate matter, e.g., rocks) and the animals.

56–57. Now, at first resembling the lowest form of animate life, the seasponge, the animal soul begins to take life. This second soul is known as the "sensitive soul," and is the seat of human emotion, a capacity we share with the animals.

61. What Dante has not yet heard (and thus cannot understand) is how this "animal" embryo can and does become a human being, i.e., how it receives its rational soul. The word "fante," here translated "human," strictly speaking means "one who speaks." Thus an "infant" *(in-fans)* is a human who cannot yet speak. Here Dante, through Statius, is speaking precisely, but not technically. He means to indicate that the rational soul, once it is joined to the embryo, only then makes this new creature potentially fully human. And this third capacity of the soul we share with no other mortal beings (angels are nothing but rational soul, having no bodily form). For these three faculties as found in each single human soul, see the note to *Purgatorio* IV.1–15.

62–66. The question of the "possible intellect" was of considerable interest in Dante's day and was variously addressed, even among "orthodox" Christian thinkers (Albertus Magnus and his pupil Thomas Aquinas had major disagreements about it), partly because its most visible champion was Averroës (see *Inf.* IV.144), the twelfth-century Islamic philosopher who had decided that the possible intellect, which is the potential capacity to perceive universal ideas, existed apart from any particular human agent. An eventual result of such a view was to question or deny the immortality of the individual human soul. Dante's solution was to make the possible intellect coterminous with the rational soul, breathed into the embryo directly by God. It is not surprising that Dante, whose ways are often extremely freewheeling, simply appropriated the term to his own purpose and, in these few lines, makes the possible intellect "orthodox." See Cesare Vasoli, "intelletto possibile," *ED* III (1971).

67–75. These three tercets mark the climax of the argument and nearly shimmer with affection as they describe God's love for his human creatures, consummated in the breathing in of the rational soul, which immediately fuses with the vegetative and sensitive souls to form a single and immortal entity, capable of intellection and of will.

76–78. God's love for us creates a new entity, an immortal soul, out of the raw material of nature just as the sun creates a new entity, wine, out of the moisture drawn up from the earth by the grapevine (Jacopo della Lana [1324]). The emphasis is on the new entity's relation to its formative cause: a human being is the residue of God's spirit interacting with flesh; wine is a distillation of sunlight and matter.

79–84. At the moment of death (for the role of Lachesis and her two sister Fates, see note to *Purg.* XXI.25–30) the lower faculties of the soul are once again in potential (rather than active) state. The higher faculties of the rational soul, on the other hand, are immediately said to be *in atto* (in action, i.e., fully existing), and more vigorously so than when they were inhibited by the lower souls.

There are three constitutive parts of the intellectual (or rational) soul according to St. Augustine, *De Trinitate* X.18, cited by Daniello (1568): "The memory, the intellect, and the will are the components of a single mind." These seem to be the sources of Dante's formulation here.

85–99. The "afterlife" of a shade is compared to its taking the form of a rainbow when the soul "imprints" itself upon the surrounding air to make itself reassemble the memory of its former body out of thin air. It is as inseparable from the higher soul as a flame is from its fire.

100–108.   The conclusion of Statius's demonstration of the nature of a shade's aerial body relies, as readers since Pietro di Dante (1340) have realized, on Virgil's description of the condition of the souls in his afterworld, *Aeneid* VI.730–751. Among the details found there are the smiles and tears of which Dante speaks here (see *Aen.* VI.733 and vv. 103–104).

109.   The word *tortura* (translated as "circling") here perhaps has two meanings: "turning" and "torture," thus describing both the spatial and the punitive aspects of the terrace: one makes a tighter circle there as one burns. An interpreter is free to choose either alternative; a translator is forced to decide on one.

112–117.   Some readers have difficulty visualizing what Dante here describes. Flames shoot out from the wall of the cliff, at first horizontally, but then driven back and up by a wind moving sharply upward from below at the edge of the terrace, thus making the flames move up and past the face of the wall and freeing a narrow path that is flame-free at the outer edge of the terrace.

121.   The hymn sung by the penitents of Lust has caused some confusion in the modern age because the hymn *"Summae Deus clementiae"* ("God of supreme clemency") does not seem appropriate to the recriminations of the lustful, while the hymn *"Summae Parens clementiae"* does. However, the early commentators knew this hymn by the same first line as we today know the former. Its text, in a form that is probably close to or identical with that known by Dante, is found in the commentary of Jacopo della Lana (1324). The third stanza hopes for God's annealing fire to combat the passion of lust.

128.   "I know no man." These are part of Mary's words in answer to the angel's announcement (Luke 1:34) that she will bear a child: "How shall this be, since I know no man?" This is Mary's seventh appearance on the mountain as the primary exemplar of a virtue opposing the relevant vice. Edward Moore (Moor.1899.1), pp. 63 and 194, suggests that Dante may have derived his idea of having Mary represent the "antidote" to each of the seven sins from St. Bonaventure *(Speculum Beatae Mariae Virginis).*

130–132.   The second exemplar of Chastity is Diana, her story drawn from Ovid (*Metam.* II.401–530), the tale of the wood nymph Helice

(Callisto), who paid for Jupiter's seduction and impregnation of her when, at the request of outraged Juno, Diana banished her from her woodlands. She was turned into a bear by Juno, and then, by the now more kind Jupiter, into the constellation Ursa Major.

133–135. See Pertile (Pert.2001.1), p. 62, for discomfort with Dante's unique use of anonymous exemplars here. Porena (1946) was perhaps the first commentator to give voice to a similar disquiet (Bosco/Reggio [1979] do also), suggesting that we expect a third example drawn from the Judeo-Christian tradition but receive instead exemplars that he rightly characterizes as being "indeterminate" and "impersonal." John S. Carroll (1904), while not dealing with this anomaly directly, may have found a reason for Dante's decision in a desire to champion the importance of marriage and the acceptability, indeed the desirability, of sexual concourse between husbands and wives. In this formulation Dante resorts to anonymity for his married couples in order to justify sexual pleasure for all who are married, in covert polemic against such overly zealous clerics as those who called for even marital abstinence.

138–139. The word *piaga* (wound) is used here, as it was used at *Purgatorio* XXIV.38 for Bonagiunta and his companions, to refer to the "wound" of sin. Does it also refer to the letter P incised on them? Those who believe that all the penitents on the mountain bear this sign would naturally believe so (see notes to *Purg.* IX.112, XXI.22–24, and XXII.1–6). On the other hand, if only Dante bears this letter on his forehead, the reference would be to the inner wound of sin, as would seem more natural, and as Portirelli (1804) believed, arguing that the *cura* (treatment) represented the external application of fire and *pasti* (diet), the internal process of reflection upon the exemplars of the chaste life.

PURGATORIO XXVI
(*Lust*)

Mentre che sì per l'orlo, uno innanzi altro,
ce n'andavamo, e spesso il buon maestro
3   diceami: "Guarda: giovi ch'io ti scaltro";

feriami il sole in su l'omero destro,
che già, raggiando, tutto l'occidente
6   mutava in bianco aspetto di cilestro;

e io facea con l'ombra più rovente
parer la fiamma; e pur a tanto indizio
9   vidi molt' ombre, andando, poner mente.

Questa fu la cagion che diede inizio
loro a parlar di me; e cominciarsi
12   a dir: "Colui non par corpo fittizio";

poi verso me, quanto potëan farsi,
certi si fero, sempre con riguardo
15   di non uscir dove non fosser arsi.

"O tu che vai, non per esser più tardo,
ma forse reverente, a li altri dopo,
18   rispondi a me che 'n sete e 'n foco ardo.

Né solo a me la tua risposta è uopo;
ché tutti questi n'hanno maggior sete
21   che d'acqua fredda Indo o Etïopo.

Dinne com' è che fai di te parete
al sol, pur come tu non fossi ancora
24   di morte intrato dentro da la rete."

Sì mi parlava un d'essi; e io mi fora
già manifesto, s'io non fossi atteso
27   ad altra novità ch'apparve allora;

One before the other, we walked along the edge,
and often the good master said to me:
3   'Careful now, pay attention to my warning.'

The sun was beating down on my right shoulder,
for now its beams were changing
6   the aspect of the west from blue to white,

and as my shadow made the flames appear more glowing
I saw that many of the shades, as they went past,
9   took note of that faint sign.

It was this that made them speak of me,
and they began by telling one another:
12   'This man's body does not seem made of air.'

Then some of them came up as near me
as they could, always careful not to venture
15   beyond the burning of the flames.

'O you who go along behind the others,
not from sloth but, it may be, with reverence,
18   answer me, since I burn with thirst and fire.

'It is not I alone who crave your answer.
All these others thirst for it more than the Indian
21   or Ethiopian who craves cold water.

'Tell us, how is it that your body makes
a wall against the sun, as if you were
24   not yet entangled in the net of death?'

asked one of them. I would have then
made myself known had I not been intent
27   on another strange new sight that now appeared,

ché per lo mezzo del cammino acceso
venne gente col viso incontro a questa,
30   la qual mi fece a rimirar sospeso.

Lì veggio d'ogne parte farsi presta
ciascun' ombra e basciarsi una con una
33   sanza restar, contente a brieve festa;

così per entro loro schiera bruna
s'ammusa l'una con l'altra formica,
36   forse a spïar lor via e lor fortuna.

Tosto che parton l'accoglienza amica,
prima che 'l primo passo lì trascorra,
39   sopragridar ciascuna s'affatica:

la nova gente: "Soddoma e Gomorra";
e l'altra: "Ne la vacca entra Pasife,
42   perché 'l torello a sua lussuria corra."

Poi, come grue ch'a le montagne Rife
volasser parte, e parte inver' l'arene,
45   queste del gel, quelle del sole schife,

l'una gente sen va, l'altra sen vene;
e tornan, lagrimando, a' primi canti
48   e al gridar che più lor si convene;

e raccostansi a me, come davanti,
essi medesmi che m'avean pregato,
51   attenti ad ascoltar ne' lor sembianti.

Io, che due volte avea visto lor grato,
incominciai: "O anime sicure
54   d'aver, quando che sia, di pace stato,

non son rimase acerbe né mature
le membra mie di là, ma son qui meco
57   col sangue suo e con le sue giunture.

for in the middle of the flaming road
came people moving in the opposite direction
30   who had me staring, all absorbed.

There I can see that every shade of either group
makes haste to kiss another, without stopping,
33   and is content with such brief salutation,

just as, within their dark-hued files,
one ant will put its face up to the other's,
36   perhaps to inquire of its path and fortune.

When they have ceased their friendly greeting,
before they take a new step to continue,
39   each makes an effort to outshout the rest.

The new ones cry: 'Sodom and Gomorrah!'
and the others: 'Pasiphaë crawls into the cow
42   so that the bull may hasten to her lust.'

Then, as though cranes were flying, some toward
cool Riphean mountains and some toward desert sands,
45   these shunning frost and those the sun,

the one crowd goes, the other nears,
and all return, weeping, to their former song
48   and to the cry that most befits them.

Then the same shades who had entreated me
drew closer, as they had before,
51   and seemed all eagerness to hear me out.

Having twice been made aware of their desire,
I began: 'O souls secure of gaining,
54   whenever it may be, the state of peace,

'my limbs have not been left on earth,
whether green or dried, but are here with me
57   intact, in all their blood and joints.

Quinci sù vo per non esser più cieco;
donna è di sopra che m'acquista grazia,
60   per che 'l mortal per vostro mondo reco.

Ma se la vostra maggior voglia sazia
tosto divegna, sì che 'l ciel v'alberghi
63   ch'è pien d'amore e più ampio si spazia,

ditemi, acciò ch'ancor carte ne verghi,
chi siete voi, e chi è quella turba
66   che se ne va di retro a' vostri terghi."

Non altrimenti stupido si turba
lo montanaro, e rimirando ammuta,
69   quando rozzo e salvatico s'inurba,

che ciascun' ombra fece in sua paruta;
ma poi che furon di stupore scarche,
72   lo qual ne li alti cuor tosto s'attuta,

"Beato te, che de le nostre marche,"
ricominciò colei che pria m'inchiese,
75   "per morir meglio, esperïenza imbarche!

La gente che non vien con noi, offese
di ciò per che già Cesar, trïunfando,
78   'Regina' contra sé chiamar s'intese:

però si parton 'Soddoma' gridando,
rimproverando a sé com' hai udito,
81   e aiutan l'arsura vergognando.

Nostro peccato fu ermafrodito;
ma perché non servammo umana legge,
84   seguendo come bestie l'appetito,

in obbrobrio di noi, per noi si legge,
quando partinci, il nome di colei
87   che s'imbestiò ne le 'mbestiate schegge.

'I climb from here no longer to be blind.
A lady is above through whom I gained the grace
60   to bring my mortal parts into your world.

'But, so may your greatest longing
soon be satisfied and the heaven take you in
63   that is so full of love and holds the widest space,

'tell me, that I may trace it on my pages,
who you are and who is in that throng
66   which is even now receding at your backs?'

Not less astounded is the mountaineer,
struck dumb and staring all around him
69   when rough and rustic he comes into a town,

than each shade seemed from its expression.
But once they had recovered from amazement,
72   which is quickly overcome in noble hearts,

he who had questioned me began again:
'Blessed are you, who, to die a better death,
75   here take on board the knowledge that you gain.

'Those, who come not with us, all offended
the same way Caesar did, for which, in triumph,
78   he once heard "queen" called out against him.

'Thus they move on crying "Sodom,"
as you heard, in self-reproach.
81   And with their shame they fan the flames.

'Hermaphroditic was our sin.
Because we did not follow human law,
84   but ran behind our appetites like beasts,

'when, in our disgrace, we move off from the others
we shout her name who made herself a beast
87   inside the beast-shaped rough-hewn wood.

Or sai nostri atti e di che fummo rei:
se forse a nome vuo' saper chi semo,
90   tempo non è di dire, e non saprei.

Farotti ben di me volere scemo:
son Guido Guinizzelli, e già mi purgo
93   per ben dolermi prima ch'a lo stremo."

Quali ne la tristizia di Ligurgo
si fer due figli a riveder la madre,
96   tal mi fec' io, ma non a tanto insurgo,

quand' io odo nomar sé stesso il padre
mio e de li altri miei miglior che mai
99   rime d'amor usar dolci e leggiadre;

e sanza udire e dir pensoso andai
lunga f ïata rimirando lui,
102   né, per lo foco, in là più m'appressai.

Poi che di riguardar pasciuto fui,
tutto m'offersi pronto al suo servigio
105   con l'affermar che fa credere altrui.

Ed elli a me: "Tu lasci tal vestigio,
per quel ch'i' odo, in me, e tanto chiaro,
108   che Letè nol può tòrre né far bigio.

Ma se le tue parole or ver giuraro,
dimmi che è cagion per che dimostri
111   nel dire e nel guardar d'avermi caro."

E io a lui: "Li dolci detti vostri,
che, quanto durerà l'uso moderno,
114   faranno cari ancora i loro incostri."

"O frate," disse, "questi ch'io ti cerno
col dito," e additò un spirto innanzi,
117   "fu miglior fabbro del parlar materno.

'Now you know our deeds and know our guilt.
If, perhaps, you would like to know our names,
there is no time to tell and I would not know how.

'About myself, indeed, I'll satisfy your wish.
I am Guido Guinizzelli, come so far in my purgation
because I felt true sorrow well before the end.'

As the two sons became on seeing their mother
caught in Lycurgus' outraged grief,
so I became, if with less abandon,

when he gave his name and I knew he had been
father to me and to others, my betters,
who always used love's sweet and graceful rhymes.

For a long time, deep in thought, I went on
without listening or speaking as I gazed at him,
but did not, for the fire, move closer.

Once my eyes were satisfied,
I owned myself ready to do him service
with such assurance as compels belief.

He answered: 'All that I hear you tell
leaves so deep and clear a trace in me
that Lethe cannot wash it out or make it dim,

'but if your words just now have sworn the truth,
tell me what has caused you to disclose
by speech and look that you still hold me dear.'

And I to him: 'Your sweet verses,
which as long as modern custom lasts,
will make their very ink seem precious.'

'O brother,' he said, 'that one whom I point out—
and he pointed to a spirit just ahead—
'was a better craftsman of the mother tongue.

90

93

96

99

102

105

108

111

114

117

Versi d'amore e prose di romanzi
soverchiò tutti; e lascia dir li stolti
120   che quel di Lemosì credon ch'avanzi.

A voce più ch'al ver drizzan li volti,
e così ferman sua oppinïone
123   prima ch'arte o ragion per lor s'ascolti.

Così fer molti antichi di Guittone,
di grido in grido pur lui dando pregio,
126   fin che l'ha vinto il ver con più persone.

Or se tu hai sì ampio privilegio,
che licito ti sia l'andare al chiostro
129   nel quale è Cristo abate del collegio,

falli per me un dir d'un paternostro,
quanto bisogna a noi di questo mondo,
132   dove poter peccar non è più nostro."

Poi, forse per dar luogo altrui secondo
che presso avea, disparve per lo foco,
135   come per l'acqua il pesce andando al fondo.

Io mi fei al mostrato innanzi un poco,
e dissi ch'al suo nome il mio disire
138   apparecchiava grazïoso loco.

El cominciò liberamente a dire:
"Tan m'abellis vostre cortes deman,
141   *qu'ieu no me puesc ni voill a vos cobrire.*

Ieu sui Arnaut, que plor e vau cantan;
consiros vei la passada folor,
144   *e vei jausen lo joi qu'esper, denan.*

Ara vos prec, per aquella valor
que vos guida al som de l'escalina,
sovenha vos a temps de ma dolor!"
148   Poi s'ascose nel foco che li affina.

'In verses of love and tales of romance
he surpassed them all, and let the fools go on
120   who think that fellow from Limoges was better.

'They favor hearsay over truth
and thus arrive at their opinions
123   without the use of skill or reason.

'The same was true of many long ago about Guittone,
voice after voice shouting praise of him alone,
126   until for most the truth at last prevailed.

'Now, if you possess such ample privilege
that you are licensed for the cloister
129   where Christ is abbot of the brothers,

'say a Paternoster there for me,
as much of it as we have need in this our world,
132   where we no longer have the power to sin.'

Then, perhaps to make room for another
who was near him, he vanished through the fire
135   as fish glide to the bottom through the water.

I edged forward a little toward the other
who had been pointed out and said that my desire
138   prepared a place of welcome for his name,

to which he readily made answer:
'Your courteous question pleases me so much
141   I neither can nor would conceal myself from you.

'I am Arnaut, weeping and singing as I make my way.
I see with grief past follies and I see,
144   rejoicing, the joy I hope is coming.

'Now I pray you, by that power
which guides you to the summit of the stairs,
to remember, when the time is fit, my pain.'
148   Then he vanished in the fire that refines them.

3. Virgil's brief admonition will be his only utterance in this canto, which, like the twenty-fourth, is heavily involved in questions regarding vernacular poetry, thus necessarily marginalizing Virgil's presence.

4–6. Dante, according to the calculations of Trucchi (1936), having begun his climb of the mountain at due east at the antipodes, has now reached a point some 25 degrees short of due west. As for the time, it has apparently taken a bit more than two hours to climb between the two terraces (see note to *Purg.* XXV.1–3).

7–9. A shadow cast upon flames does indeed make them glow a darker color. (See Abrams [Abra.1985.1] for a consideration of this image as emblematic of the themes of this canto.) Once again Dante's presence in the body serves as a provocation to a group of penitents.

12. At *Inferno* VI.36 the poet speaks of the shades of the gluttons as "lor vanità che par persona" (their emptiness, which seems real bodies). Here the penitents remark at Dante's condition; his body does not seem to be, like theirs, "fictitious," airy (about which state we have just heard Statius's lengthy disquisition).

15. Their impulse, reversing Dante's, is *not* to leave the searing flames. Again we sense the eagerness of penitents to undergo their purgation. See the remark of Forese Donati, "I speak of pain but should say solace" (*Purg.* XXIII.72).

16–20. The speaker is Guido Guinizzelli (see note to verse 92), the previous Italian poet to whom, we will learn, Dante now feels the greatest allegiance. While Guido may or may not be correct in thinking Dante is following the two other souls out of reverence rather than from lack of zeal (or fear of the flames that he must enter), what he cannot know (and never discovers) is that these are the great shades of Virgil and Statius. We, however, do know and realize that this scene is the last in a series that began in the cantos devoted to Statius (XX–XXII), a program devoted to an exploration of the nature of Dante's poetics in relation to those of other poets: Statius, Bonagiunta (who throws in Giacomo da Lentini and Guittone d'Arezzo for good measure), and, in this canto, Guinizzelli (adding Giraud de Borneil and poor Guittone again) and

Arnaut Daniel. No other part of the poem is as extensively or as richly concerned with the purposes of poetry.

There is some debate among the commentators about the metaphoric or literal nature of the thirst to which Guido refers: "answer me, since I burn with thirst and fire" (verse 18). While hunger and thirst were the natural penalties undergone by the penitent gluttons, there is no such *contrapasso* here. Further, Guido's description of his cosufferers' "thirst" (vv. 20–21) is surely metaphoric, thus suggesting that this first mention of thirst is also. For this view, among others, see Pertile (Pert.1993.3), p. 381. On the other hand, the fire of which he speaks is literal enough, as Dante will find out in the next canto (*Purg.* XXVII.49–51), and his aerial body surely allows him to feel such sensations.

31–36.   This remarkable simile, a rare medieval manifestation of a moment of fraternal affection between heterosexuals and homosexuals, is striking. The passage probably reflects Paul's admonition in Romans 16:16: "Greet one another with a holy kiss," as was suggested by Scartazzini (1900). For the ants, see Virgil's memorable simile in *Aeneid* IV.402–407. Aeneas's men, preparing their ships for departure from Carthage, are described as follows: "Just so do ants, when winter's on their mind, pillage great stores of grain and fill their houses to the beams. Over the fields moves a black column, carrying their spoil through the grass along their narrow path; some heave the huge seeds upon their shoulders, some shape up the columns, rebuking their delay. All the path fairly shines with labor."

40.   Those who have argued that the sin punished in *Inferno* XV and XVI is not homosexuality (see the endnote to *Inf.* XVI) are hard pressed to account for the obvious reference of the word "Sodom" repeated here, found first in *Inferno* XI.50 to refer to the sinners on the barren sands of homosexuality. The early commentators have no doubt whatsoever about all this. See, for example, John of Serravalle (1416): "And from this city, Sodom, the sin against nature took its name, just as simony did from Simon [Magus]." Each group cries out the appropriate exemplar(s) of its sin, the first the homosexuals, calling out the names of these two "cities of the plain" (see Genesis 19:1–28), the *locus classicus* for homosexual lust, where the men of Sodom ask Lot to give them for their sexual pleasure the two angels who have come to Lot and whom they take for men (Genesis 19:4–11).

What has long been problematic is the fact that, in *Inferno*, we find the heterosexual lustful punished in the realm of Incontinence, while those guilty of homoerotic behavior are in that of Violence (against nature, in their case). That these two groups are now purging themselves on the same terrace may be the result of the changed ground rules for the sins of the two *cantiche* more than of any supposed change of heart on Dante's part, that is, Dante no longer has the option of fitting these two different bands onto an Aristotelian/Ciceronian grid, but must associate them with one of the seven capital vices, which leaves him little choice. Nonetheless, no matter what his intentions, the effect is to make the reader feel that the poet has now softened his views. The notion of Pertile (Pert.1993.3), p. 388, that the impulse to love is the same in hetero- and homosexuals and that, since in purgatory only the impulse (or predisposition) toward sin is purged, there is no longer any need to distinguish between them, is interesting but difficult to accept. In *Inferno* homosexuality is treated as a sin of hardened will, and one would be hard pressed to show that this does not make the "impulse" that drives it different from that behind the sins of Incontinence.

41–42. The heterosexuals call out the name of Pasiphaë (see *Inf.* XII.12–13 and note), the wife of Minos, king of Crete, who had Daedalus build for her a wooden frame covered with a cowhide so that she could be mounted by a bull. The child of this union was the Minotaur. Pasiphaë here is clearly meant to represent the animalistic nature of unrestrained lust, not some sort of sodomy.

43–48. The hypothetical nature of this simile is underlined by Dante's use of the subjunctive mood for its main verb *(volasser)*. Cranes do not and would not migrate simultaneously in two different directions, north to the Riphean mountains and also south to the sands of the (Libyan?) desert. Dante has developed the passage on the model, perhaps, of some of Lucan's similes concerning cranes (see note to *Purg.* XXIV.64–74), but the resemblance does not seem more than casual, if the closest would seem to be that found at *Pharsalia* VII.832–834.

The "former song" of the penitents is the hymn *"Summae Deus clementiae"* punctuated by the words of Mary at the Annunciation and those regarding Diana's chaste anger at Callisto (*Purg.* XXV.121–132). Each subgroup also then sends up "the cry that most befits" it, that is, either "Sodom and Gomorrah" or "Pasiphaë."

55–66. Dante at last responds to the request of the penitents, if only to some degree, since he does not fully identify himself, in keeping with his avoidance of doing so on other terraces. He defines himself in terms of his intermediate age (neither youthful and unripe nor ancient and ripe), tells them what they suspected (he is here in the flesh, not in the aerial body), and that Beatrice (not named, and decidedly not the sort of woman penitents here "do time" for) draws him heavenward. Thus he admits to his miraculous presence among them, but gives no information that might genuinely satisfy their curiosity. In return for relatively little he asks to know the identity of those with whom he speaks and the condition of the group that has moved away from them.

His evasive behavior here allows him to avoid naming himself uselessly to those who do not know him (see his similar avoidance with Sapia [*Purg.* XIII.133–138], Guido del Duca [*Purg.* XIV.20–21], and Marco the Lombard [*Purg.* XVI.37–42]). Those who recognize Dante in purgatory are as follows: Casella (*Purg.* II.76–78); Belacqua (recognized by Dante at *Purg.* IV.109–123; it would seem that he knows Dante but does not, in his laconic, sardonic way, reveal that he does); Nino Visconti (*Purg.* VIII.46–57); Oderisi (*Purg.* XI.76); Forese (*Purg.* XXIII.40–42); and Bonagiunta (*Purg.* XXIV.35–36).

64–65. See Benvenuto's (1380) paraphrase: "as though to say, so that I may write of you souls and give your true reputation, in case there should remain in the world infamous word of your lust." Dante's way of promising to record the penitents' presence on the road to salvation (we must remember that his charitable offer is made without knowing the identity of any of the souls whom he here addresses) so that it may draw prayers from the living and thus hasten their passage to bliss will be enlarged in Guido's final request of Dante (vv. 130–132), where he hopes for prayers of intercession on his behalf in Heaven itself.

The language here reflects the mode of preparing a manuscript for inscription, the penciling in of guidelines that can be erased once ink is set to vellum or paper. Dante imagines, from the vantage point of his progress through the second kingdom of the afterworld, the preparation, by his own hand, of the manuscript of the *Comedy* once he is back in the world. Here the preparation of the page equates with its completion, the inscription of Guido Guinizzelli in the Book of Life. See *Inferno* XXIX.54–57 and note; see also the less generous, but similar, offer made to Bocca degli Abati at *Inferno* XXXII.93. Bocca is also recorded, but in the Book of the Dead.

75. Guido uses a nautical metaphor to praise Dante's on-loading of this precious cargo of knowledge, paraphrased by Benvenuto (1380) as fol-

lows: Dante is one who "gathers and assembles in the bark of his wit" the mountain's source of knowledge that will allow him a better chance for salvation.

76.   Guido now addresses Dante's question (vv. 65–66), brought on by the sight of the second group of penitents that had caught his attention (vv. 25–27).

77–78.   As part of his rather cruel treatment of Julius Caesar, who has already been put forward as a *positive* exemplary figure of zeal (see *Purg.* XVIII.101–102 and note), Dante now makes him an "informal exemplar" (this practice is observable elsewhere only once on the mountain: see note to *Purg.* XXIII.25–30) of homosexual lust (that is, he is not a part of the "official" program of those who are presented to all penitents, but is mentioned only to Dante by Guido). This makes him perhaps the only exemplary figure in *Purgatorio* to have both positive and negative valences. Again we can see how complex, troubling, and unremitting Dante's response to Julius was.

Benvenuto (1380) dutifully and ashamedly reports Caesar's one known homosexual experience but surrounds it, in his perplexity and discomfort, with a list of Julius's (at times outrageous) sexual encounters with women. In a similar mode, John of Serravalle (1416) insists that Julius was a mere fourteen years old at the time of this misadventure. Dante's source for poor Julius's escapade in Bithynia may eventually be found in Suetonius's *Life of the Caesars* (chapter 49), as Daniello reports (1568), citing the lines that were supposedly cried out against him when he returned from Gaul in triumph: "See how Caesar triumphs, having conquered Gaul; Nicomedes triumphs not, but he made Caesar fall." What had happened? Apparently, when Julius was young and serving in Bithynia, the king, who admired him, got him drunk and had sexual relations with him. Other tales make Caesar a more willing accomplice to the king's desire, e.g., Suetonius, attributing the story to Cicero, cites the report that he was dressed in purple as the queen of the realm at a wild party that ended in his "deflowering," etc. Later Dante commentators (e.g., Oelsner [1899]) suggest that Dante's source was a much condensed version of the events in Bithynia found in Uguccione of Pisa's entry for "triumph" in his *Magnae derivationes*, which adverts to Bithynia and to Caesar's being called both "king" and "queen" during one of his triumphs.

82.   The word "hermaphrodite" here doubtless means (and only means) "heterosexual" (from Ovid's tale of Salmacis and the son of Hermes

[Mercury] and Aphrodite [Venus], Hermaphroditus [*Metam.* IV.285–388], in which their two genders are eventually included in a single double-sexed human being). If "hermaphrodite" here means other than that, the only souls saved from the sin of Lust would have been homosexual and bisexual, that is, there would be no heterosexual penitents on the mountain. The commentary tradition yields some hilarious missteps on this subject. Francesco da Buti (1385), selecting "hermaphrodite" (in the sense of bisexual) as the second category of the penitent lustful on the mountain, tells the tale of a person he had seen, while he was a youth, who dressed as a man but who sat at the distaff and spun wool, using the name "Mistress Piera." It is only with Gabriele (1525) and Daniello (1568) that commentators get the problem cleared up: these are the penitent heterosexual lovers. There was still so much confusion three centuries later that even Scartazzini (1900) felt that he had to do a full review of the question. It should be said that it was provocative for Dante to have used the myth as he chose to. Ovid's original tale is quite startling in its sexual role reversals: Salmacis behaving like a traditional slavering male while Hermaphroditus behaves like a traditional inviting female (even performing an unintended striptease before the excited Salmacis, peeping from her hiding place in the woods). The tale seems fully intended to serve as the foundation myth of hermaphroditism. That was not enough, however, to protect it from Dante's by now unsurprisingly elastic and eclectic reading of classical material. His meaning for the word is clear: "heterosexual"; to arrive at that unriddling, he probably foresaw, would cause his readers some exertion.

83–87.   These lines themselves possess the capacity to settle a problem that some readers prefer to keep open. How can the name of Pasiphaë, who was involved not in heterosexual lust between humans, but in sodomy (sexual contact between human and beast), be used here to indicate the former? He and his companions, Guido makes plain, did *not* commit "unnatural" sexual acts, but broke the laws that govern human sexual concourse, specifically those of marriage, and did so with an untamed energy that is more fit for beasts than humans, and is thus symbolized by a woman who conspired to be entered by a bull.

90.   The large number of those who repine their former lust seems to be commensurate with those who are condemned forever to relive it; see *Inferno* V.67–69, where Virgil points out to Dante a vast number of identifiable sinners—and this after we have already seen huge flocks of essentially anonymous lovers (*Inf.* V.40–42). And these sinners here, like

those among whom we find Francesca and Paolo, are also compared to cranes (vv. 43–45; *Inf.* V.46–49).

92.   The speaker finally reveals himself as Guido Guinizzelli. "The most illustrious of the Italian poets prior to Dante, he belonged to the family of the Principi of Bologna, in which city he was born ca. 1230. In 1270 he was Podestà of Castelfranco; in 1274, when the Ghibelline Lambertazzi were expelled from Bologna, Guido with the rest of the Principi, who belonged to the same party, was forced to leave his native city; he is said to have died in exile at Verona in 1276" **(T)**. His most famous poem is the *canzone* "Al cor gentil rempaira sempre amore" ("Love always finds shelter in the noble heart"). It sets out the doctrine, embraced by Dante in the fourth treatise of *Convivio*, that true nobility is not determined by birth but by inner virtue.

93.   Since Guido had died ca. 1276, he has made his way from Ostia in very good time indeed, passing through ante-purgatory and the first six terraces in less than a quarter century. Such speedy passage through purgation is a feature common to all the major figures whom Dante meets on the mountain, one forced on him by his predilection for the recently dead (Statius being the only ancient of note upon the slopes of the mountain allowed a speaking part, while Hugh Capet is the oldest "modern"). However, we have no idea how long any of the souls whom we see will be at their penance (if Statius is a model, a good long time, since he spent more than twelve hundred years purging himself [see note to *Purg.* XXI.22–24]). We simply have no idea how long Guido must stay in the fire for his lust. Time is not over for any of these sympathetic figures, and the mysteries of penance and redemption leave such concerns unresolved. For all we know, Manfred or Belacqua may finish purgation before Guido does.

94–96.   In a striking example of *abbreviatio*, Dante boils down a lengthy scene in Statius's *Thebaid* (V.499–730) to two lines. The story to which he refers runs roughly as follows. Hypsipyle was daughter of the king of Lemnos, whom she saved from death when the women of the island determined to kill all the males on it. She was subsequently seduced and abandoned by Jason (*Inf.* XVIII.88–95), by whom she had twin sons, Thoas and Euneus. When the Lemnian women discover that their king is still alive, Hypsipyle flees, and after a misadventure with pirates ends up in the service of the king of Nemea, Lycurgus. While caring for

Archemorus, the king's son, she was approached by the seven exiled warriors marching against Thebes in civil war. Since they were thirsty, she agreed to show them to water (the fountain of Langia—see *Purg.* XXII.112), but left the baby behind long enough for him to be killed by a snake. Lycurgus would have killed her but for the chance arrival of her twin sons. Once they have quelled the attempt on their mother's life, they embrace her eagerly, more eagerly than Dante will move to embrace Guido, because he fears the flames.

97–99. Benvenuto (1380) remembers the reference to Guido's having been "driven from the nest" at *Purgatorio* XI.97–99, and that he had been cast forth precisely by Dante. But who are these other poets who wrote (the verb is in the past tense) better poems than Dante? While most commentators simply avoid this problem, those who deal with it tend to favor Guido Cavalcanti and Cino da Pistoia. For the later reappearance of the adjective "sweet," see verse 112 and note.

107. Guido, like Bonagiunta, refers to hearing Dante's voice with the relative clause "ch'i' odo" (that I hear). See *Purgatorio* XXIV.57. Both clauses draw attention to the importance that each of these predecessor poets places on listening to the living voice of this extraordinary visitor to their realm.

109–111. Beginning in these lines, words for truth and for speaking or for writing poetry wend their way through twenty-two lines: *ver* in vv. 109, 121, 126; *dir* or its derivative *detto* (poem) in vv. 111, 112, 119, 130. The conjunction reminds the reader of the importance of the issue of the possibility of poetic truth, given the traditional view that poets are liars. It may be helpful to know that in Dante's day a poet in the vernacular was known as a *dicitore per rima*, a "speaker in rhyme."

112. For the rarity of Dante's use of the honorific *voi*, here given to Guido, see the note at *Purgatorio* XIX.131.

If Guido's poems are *dolci* (sweet), in what way are they different from those of Dante that are written in the "sweet new style" (*Purg.* XXIV.57)? This is a question that has had a variety of answers. Some make Guido the first practitioner of the "sweet new style" (which is impossible, in Dante's view, given his precisions at *Purg.* XXIV.49–51 that make his own *canzone* "Donne ch'avete," written at least ten years after Guido's death, the first of the "new" poems that constitute the *dolce stil*

novo). The better understanding is that Guido Guinizzelli, Guido
Cavalcanti, others among the Tuscans, and surely Dante himself, all
wrote in the "sweet style" (the most effective demonstration of this is
found in Leonardi [Leon.2001.1]). But what both Guidos, the early
Dante, and just about everybody else failed to do was to find the "new
style" that Dante developed from his understanding of Guinizzelli's sweet
style of praise, a mode that he took one step further when he developed
his own theologized poetics of Beatrice.

In that he was the first, and had perhaps no more than one com-
panion (Cino da Pistoia, who also wrote "theologically" of Beatrice after
her death). This is what the evidence of the texts seems to suggest. In
short, Dante honors Guinizzelli for being what he was, as far as the
younger poet was concerned, the "father" of the *dolce stil novo*, but not
one of its practitioners. Thus we may understand that a number of poets
wrote in the "sweet style," but hardly any of them achieved the *new*
"sweet style" that is the hallmark of Dante's praise of Beatrice. In all as-
pects of this debate, it is essential to remember that we are trying (or
should, at any rate, be trying) to negotiate an answer from what Dante
said happened, not from what actually happened (or what we imagine
actually happened).

113–114.   Dante's affectionate remark bestows less than it may seem to
do, for all his unquestionable admiration of Guido. In *Purgatorio*
XI.97–108 we are told both that this Guido had been eclipsed by Guido
Cavalcanti in the public's esteem and that fame for artistic excellence
does not last very long, in any case. In short, "modern custom" is not
enduring. As long as such poems (i.e., those in the Italian vernacular) are
written, Guido's will be read; he will have an honored place amongst the
vernacular poets. Dante, partly because of his own endeavors on Guido's
behalf, got it right. His praise, however, is not of the order of his praise
of Virgil; according to Beatrice *his* fame will last as long as the world lasts
(*Inf.* II.59–60), a life that even Dante probably thought would be longer
than that enjoyed by the Italian vernacular (see *Par.* XXVI.133–138). For
Dante's relationship to Guido see discussions in Marti (Mart.1966.1),
Folena (Fole.1977.1), Moleta (Mole.1980.1), and Barolini (Baro.1984.1),
esp. pp. 125–36.

115–116.   Guido now, in a moment of evidently heartfelt humility, insists
on Arnaut Daniel's superiority in the vernacular, but in the vernacular of
Provence, an area in the southeast of what is now France; it only came
under the official rule of the French kings in 1245.

"Arnaut Daniel, famous Provençal poet (fl. 1180–1200); but little is known of his life beyond that he belonged to a noble family of Ribeyrac in Périgord, that he spent much of his time at the court of Richard Coeur-de-Lion, and that he visited Paris, where he attended the coronation of Philip Augustus, as well as Spain, and perhaps Italy. His works, such as they have been preserved, consist of eighteen lyrical poems, one satirical, the rest amatory" **(T)**.

Arnaut's poems are brilliantly difficult, written in the so-called *trobar clus* (a modern translation could be "hermetic verse"), typified by its harsh tones and challenging phrasing; in other words, he avoids the *trobar leu* (a more open style, easier and more mellifluous). On Dante's knowledge and use of Arnaut's poems see Perugi (Peru.1978.1). For a brief overview in English of Dante's relations with Provençal poets and poetry see Bergin (Berg.1965.1). And for a substantial study of Dante's response to previous modern poets, Provençal and Italian, see Barolini (Baro.1984.1), pp. 85–187.

117–118.   What does it mean to say that Arnaut was "a better craftsman of the mother tongue"? Not, it would appear, that he wrote poems that were better in substance than those of others, but better in style, better made. It is possible that Guinizzelli's language reflects the claim that lay latent (but clear enough) in some poems of Cavalcanti, who liked to use the image of the file *(limo)*, an instrument used to refine one's handiwork, to suggest the careful nature of his own poeticizing. Dante here would seem to be, through the testimony of Guinizzelli, taking some of that distinction away from the other Guido and, in a sense, replacing him with Arnaut, a craftsman not only better than he, but better than Cavalcanti, too.

The "mother tongue" here not only refers to Arnaut's *langue d'oc*, his native Provençal, but to *any* Latin-derived vernacular (see Sordello's similar remark, addressed to Virgil, at *Purg.* VII.16–17, which also makes Provençal the child of Latin: "O glory of the Latins . . . through whom our language showed what it could do").

119–120.   "Giraut de Borneil, one of the most famous troubadours of his century, born at Essidueil, near Limoges, ca. 1175, died ca. 1220" **(T)**. Dante refers to him a number of times in *De vulgari eloquentia* and once in *Convivio*, never slightingly—quite the opposite is true. Hence Dante's about-face here is dramatic. In *De vulgari* (II.ii.9) he had made Giraud his own Provençal counterpart: Dante presented himself as the leading poetic celebrant of virtue in Italian, while Giraut was presented in exactly the same role for his language group.

124–126. "Guittone del Viva, more commonly known as Fra Guittone d'Arezzo, one of the earliest Italian poets, was born ca. 1240 at Santa Firmina, about two miles from Arezzo. But little is known of the details of his life, a great part of which was spent in Florence, where Dante may have known him. About the year 1266 Guittone, who was married and had a family, entered the Order of the Frati Gaudenti [Jovial Friars, see *Inf.* XXIII.103]. In 1293 he helped to found the monastery of Sta. Maria degli Angeli at Florence, in which city he appears to have died in the following year" **(T)**. Dante, surely unfairly, is getting even, less perhaps with Guittone than with his admirers, who were many (and continue to exist today). It was not enough for him to have Bonagiunta (*Purg.* XXIV.56) include him, along with himself, among those who failed to come up to Dante's measure. Now Dante uses the great Guinizzelli (who had indeed come to dislike Guittone's poetry in reality) to skewer Guittone a second time, and much more harshly. As early as *De vulgari eloquentia* (e.g., I.xiii.1; II.vi.8), Dante had been deprecating Guittone. One may sense a certain "anxiety of influence" at work here, especially since Guittone did so many of the things that Dante himself took on as his own tasks: love lyrics, moral *canzoni*, and eventually religious poems.

   On Dante's rejection of Guittone see Contini (Cont.1976.1), pp. 60–61, the contributions of Gorni, Antonelli, and Mazzoni in the volume devoted to studies of Guittone edited by Picone (Pico.1995.1), and Barolini (Baro.1997.1).

127–132. Guido's request speaks now of a better kind of poetry, the Lord's Prayer, that this other poet can offer in his name in Heaven. He concludes by suggesting an "edit" in the text, namely of that part which speaks of leading not into temptation and delivering from evil (Matthew 6:13; Luke 11:4). Similarly, in *Purgatorio* XI.19–24 the penitents *do* sing this part of the text, but only on behalf of their earthly brethren, since it no longer pertains to them.

133–135. Guido's departure reminds the reader that those who speak with Dante need to come to the edge of the flame, without leaving it, in order to be visible (see vv. 13–15). His disappearance back into the flames like a fish from the surface of a pond recombines images of fire and water, as did his opening sally to Dante, in which he speaks of his thirst, while he burns in flame, to know of a living man's reason for being here.

140–147. That Arnaut's speech forms a little Provençal poem eight lines in length may reflect, according to Nathaniel Smith (Smit.1980.1), pp.

101–2, the fact that this was generally a favored stanza length for Provençal poets and indeed of six of the eleven Provençal poems cited by Dante in *De vulgari eloquentia*. Smith also demonstrates that Dante's *pastiche* of Provençal lyric is wider than an imitation of Arnaut, and reflects numerous other poems and poets in the *lingua d'oc*. He also comments on the deliberate "dumbing down" of Dante's version of Arnaut's language (recognized by its difficult and elliptical style) in which almost every word of this invented poem has an obvious Italian (or Latin) cognate (pp. 106–7).

Arnaut, like Guido, is now more interested in salvation than in dazzling the world with verse. These are penitential moments, not ones that encourage thoughts of emulous poetic striving. Giacalone (1968) says it this way: "The poet of the *trobar clus*, who was ever at the ready to make his poems 'concealing,' now at the end conceals himself, but in the penitential fire." There seems no question but that Dante was staggered by Arnaut's virtuosity; and surely we were staggered, in turn, by Dante's perhaps most virtuosic versification, heavily indebted to Arnaut, found in the last cantos of *Inferno*. But now there is no dwelling on the excellence of poetic technique, but rather on prayer and hopes for the joys of Heaven. Guido's last words (vv. 92–93), which seem to imply that, unlike Dante, he came to God *not* in his poetry but even in spite of it, and Arnaut's Provençal stanza, which also speaks to life rather than to art, are matched by Dante's own "sweet new style" here, singing of salvation, the subject it took this poet some time to find again after his first attempt in the concluding chapter of his *Vita nuova*. In this sense Guido's words about prayer as poem and Arnaut's poem, which is a request for prayer, posthumously join these two poets to Dante's new style, a poetry in tune with God.

PURGATORIO XXVII
(Lust)

Sì come quando i primi raggi vibra
là dove il suo fattor lo sangue sparse,
3   cadendo Ibero sotto l'alta Libra,

e l'onde in Gange da nona rïarse,
sì stava il sole; onde 'l giorno sen giva,
6   come l'angel di Dio lieto ci apparse.

Fuor de la fiamma stava in su la riva,
e cantava *"Beati mundo corde!"*
9   in voce assai più che la nostra viva.

Poscia "Più non si va, se pria non morde,
anime sante, il foco: intrate in esso,
12   e al cantar di là non siate sorde,"

ci disse come noi li fummo presso;
per ch'io divenni tal, quando lo 'ntesi,
15   qual è colui che ne la fossa è messo.

In su le man commesse mi protesi,
guardando il foco e imaginando forte
18   umani corpi già veduti accesi.

Volsersi verso me le buone scorte;
e Virgilio mi disse: "Figliuol mio,
21   qui può esser tormento, ma non morte.

Ricorditi, ricorditi! E se io
sovresso Gerïon ti guidai salvo,
24   che farò ora presso più a Dio?

Credi per certo che se dentro a l'alvo
di questa fiamma stessi ben mille anni,
27   non ti potrebbe far d'un capel calvo.

As when it strikes with its first rays
there where its Maker shed His blood,
while the Ebro lies beneath the lofty Scales

3

and noon burns down on the waters of the Ganges,
so stood the sun. And thus day was departing
when the blissful angel of the Lord appeared.

6

He stood beyond the flames there on the terrace
and sang *'Beati mundo corde!'*
with a voice more radiant than ours.

9

'There is no going on, you blessèd souls,
without the fire's stinging bite. Enter,
and do not stop your ears against the distant song,'

12

he said to us once we were near,
so that, hearing him, I felt
like a man who has been put into his grave.

15

I bent forward over my outstretched hands
and stared into the fire, my mind fixed on the image
of human bodies I once saw being burned.

18

Then my kindly escorts turned to me
and Virgil said: 'My son,
here you may find torment, but not death.

21

'Keep it in mind, keep it in mind—
if even on Geryon I conveyed you safely,
what shall I do now we are nearer God?

24

'You must believe that if you were confined
in the very belly of this flame a thousand years
it would not singe a single hair upon your head.

27

E se tu forse credi ch'io t'inganni,
fatti ver' lei, e fatti far credenza
30   con le tue mani al lembo d'i tuoi panni.

Pon giù omai, pon giù ogne temenza;
volgiti in qua e vieni: entra sicuro!"
33   E io pur fermo e contra coscïenza.

Quando mi vide star pur fermo e duro,
turbato un poco disse: "Or vedi, figlio:
36   tra Bëatrice e te è questo muro."

Come al nome di Tisbe aperse il ciglio
Piramo in su la morte, e riguardolla,
39   allor che 'l gelso diventò vermiglio;

così, la mia durezza fatta solla,
mi volsi al savio duca, udendo il nome
42   che ne la mente sempre mi rampolla.

Ond' ei crollò la fronte e disse: "Come!
volenci star di qua?"; indi sorrise
45   come al fanciul si fa ch'è vinto al pome.

Poi dentro al foco innanzi mi si mise,
pregando Stazio che venisse retro,
48   che pria per lunga strada ci divise.

Sì com' fui dentro, in un bogliente vetro
gittato mi sarei per rinfrescarmi,
51   tant' era ivi lo 'ncendio sanza metro.

Lo dolce padre mio, per confortarmi,
pur di Beatrice ragionando andava,
54   dicendo: "Li occhi suoi già veder parmi."

Guidavaci una voce che cantava
di là; e noi, attenti pur a lei,
57   venimmo fuor là ove si montava.

'And if you think, perhaps, that I deceive you,
go close to it and test it, holding out
30   the hem of your garment in your hands.

'From now on put away, put away all fear,
head in this direction, come, and boldly enter.'
33   But, against my will, I stood stock still.

When he saw me stay, unmoved and obstinate,
he said, somewhat disturbed: 'Now look, my son,
36   this wall stands between Beatrice and you.'

As at the name of Thisbe, though on the point of death,
Pyramus raised his lids and gazed at her,
39   that time the mulberry turned red,

just so, my stubbornness made pliant, I turned
to my wise leader when I heard the name
42   that ever blossoms in my mind,

at which he shook his head and said: 'Well,
are we going to stay on this side?' then smiled
45   as one smiles at a child won over with a fruit.

Then, ahead of me, he was immersed in the fire,
asking Statius, who for a long way now
48   had walked between us, to come through last.

As soon as I was in I would have thrown myself
straight into molten glass to cool myself,
51   so beyond measure was the burning there,

and my sweet father, to comfort me,
kept speaking of Beatrice as he went,
54   saying: 'Even now I can almost see her eyes.'

Guiding us was a voice that sang beyond the flame.
We gave it our rapt attention,
57   and came forth from the fire where the ascent began.

"Venite, benedicti Patris mei,"
sonò dentro a un lume che lì era,
60 tal che mi vinse e guardar nol potei.

"Lo sol sen va," soggiunse, "e vien la sera;
non v'arrestate, ma studiate il passo,
63 mentre che l'occidente non si annera."

Dritta salia la via per entro 'l sasso
verso tal parte ch'io toglieva i raggi
66 dinanzi a me del sol ch'era già basso.

E di pochi scaglion levammo i saggi,
che 'l sol corcar, per l'ombra che si spense,
69 sentimmo dietro e io e li miei saggi.

E pria che 'n tutte le sue parti immense
fosse orizzonte fatto d'uno aspetto,
72 e notte avesse tutte sue dispense,

ciascun di noi d'un grado fece letto;
ché la natura del monte ci affranse
75 la possa del salir più e 'l diletto.

Quali si stanno ruminando manse
le capre, state rapide e proterve
78 sovra le cime avante che sien pranse,

tacite a l'ombra, mentre che 'l sol ferve,
guardate dal pastor, che 'n su la verga
81 poggiato s'è e lor di posa serve;

e quale il mandrïan che fori alberga,
lungo il peculio suo queto pernotta,
84 guardando perché fiera non lo sperga;

tali eravamo tutti e tre allotta,
io come capra, ed ei come pastori,
87 fasciati quinci e quindi d'alta grotta.

'*Venite, benedicti Patris mei*' resounded
from a dazzling light that blinded me
60   so that I could not bear to look.

'The sun departs and evening comes,'
it continued, 'do not stop, but hurry on
63   before the west grows dark.'

The way went straight up through the rock
so that my body blocked the last rays of the sun,
66   now low in the sky, from my path.

We had tried only a few of the steps when we,
I and my sages, understood, as my shadow faded,
69   that the sun had set behind us.

And before the horizon, in all its vast expanse,
had taken on a single hue
72   and night had claimed all parts of her domain,

each of us made, of a step, a bed,
for the nature of the mountain took from us
75   the power and the urge for climbing higher.

As goats that have been quick and reckless
on the heights before they grazed
78   now peacefully chew their cud,

silent in the shade while the sun is burning,
guarded by the shepherd, leaning on his staff,
81   who lets them take their rest,

and as the herdsman who lives out in the open
passes the night beside his quiet flock,
84   watching lest a wild beast scatter them,

such were the three of us,
I like a goat and they like shepherds,
87   shut in on all sides by walls of rock.

Poco parer potea lì del di fori;
ma, per quel poco, vedea io le stelle
90   di lor solere e più chiare e maggiori.

Sì ruminando e sì mirando in quelle,
mi prese il sonno; il sonno che sovente,
93   anzi che 'l fatto sia, sa le novelle.

Ne l'ora, credo, che de l'orïente
prima raggiò nel monte Citerea,
96   che di foco d'amor par sempre ardente,

giovane e bella in sogno mi parea
donna vedere andar per una landa
99   cogliendo fiori; e cantando dicea:

"Sappia qualunque il mio nome dimanda
ch'i' mi son Lia, e vo movendo intorno
102   le belle mani a farmi una ghirlanda.

Per piacermi a lo specchio, qui m'addorno;
ma mia suora Rachel mai non si smaga
105   dal suo miraglio, e siede tutto giorno.

Ell' è d'i suoi belli occhi veder vaga
com' io de l'addornarmi con le mani;
108   lei lo vedere, e me l'ovrare appaga."

E già per li splendori antelucani,
che tanto a' pellegrin surgon più grati,
111   quanto, tornando, albergan men lontani,

le tenebre fuggian da tutti lati,
e 'l sonno mio con esse; ond' io leva'mi,
114   veggendo i gran maestri già levati.

"Quel dolce pome che per tanti rami
cercando va la cura de' mortali,
117   oggi porrà in pace le tue fami."

Only a small space could be seen beyond them,
but in that space I saw the stars
90   bigger and brighter than usually they are.

Amidst such sights and thoughts
I was seized by sleep, which often knows
93   what is to be before it happens.

In the hour, I think, when Cytherea,
who always seems aflame with fire of love,
96   first shone on the mountain from the east,

in a dream I seemed to see a lady,
young and lovely, passing through a meadow
99   as she gathered flowers, singing:

'Let anyone who asks my name know I am Leah,
and here I move about, using my fair hands
102   to weave myself a garland.

'To be pleased at my reflection I adorn myself,
but my sister Rachel never leaves her mirror,
105   sitting before it all day long.

'She is as eager to gaze into her own fair eyes
as I to adorn myself with my own hands.
108   She in seeing, I in doing, find our satisfaction.'

And now, along with the predawn splendors
that, rising, become more welcome to the traveler,
111   as, returning, he lodges a little nearer home,

the shadows all around were being put to flight
and my sleep with them. And I rose up,
114   seeing the great masters already risen.

'That sweet fruit which mortals, with great effort,
seek on so many different boughs
117   shall today give peace to all your cravings.'

Virgilio inverso me queste cotali
parole usò; e mai non furo strenne
120   che fosser di piacere a queste iguali.

Tanto voler sopra voler mi venne
de l'esser sù, ch'ad ogne passo poi
123   al volo mi sentia crescer le penne.

Come la scala tutta sotto noi
fu corsa e fummo in su 'l grado superno,
126   in me ficcò Virgilio li occhi suoi,

e disse: "Il temporal foco e l'etterno
veduto hai, figlio; e se' venuto in parte
129   dov' io per me più oltre non discerno.

Tratto t'ho qui con ingegno e con arte;
lo tuo piacere omai prendi per duce;
132   fuor se' de l'erte vie, fuor se' de l'arte.

Vedi lo sol che 'n fronte ti riluce;
vedi l'erbette, i fiori e li arbuscelli
135   che qui la terra sol da sé produce.

Mentre che vegnan lieti li occhi belli
che, lagrimando, a te venir mi fenno,
138   seder ti puoi e puoi andar tra elli.

Non aspettar mio dir più né mio cenno;
libero, dritto e sano è tuo arbitrio,
e fallo fora non fare a suo senno:
142   per ch'io te sovra te corono e mitrio."

Such were Virgil's words to me,
and never was there promise of a gift
120   that might bring equal pleasure.

Desire upon desire so seized me to ascend
that with every step
123   I felt that I was growing wings for flight.

When the stairs had all run past beneath us
and we were on the topmost step,
126   Virgil fixed his eyes on me

and said: 'The temporal fire and the eternal
you have seen, my son, and now come to a place
129   in which, unaided, I can see no farther.

'I have brought you here with intellect and skill.
From now on take your pleasure as your guide.
132   You are free of the steep way, free of the narrow.

'Look at the sun shining before you,
look at the fresh grasses, flowers, and trees
135   which here the earth produces of itself.

'You may sit down or move among these
until the fair eyes come, rejoicing,
138   which weeping bid me come to you.

'No longer wait for word or sign from me.
Your will is free, upright, and sound.
Not to act as it chooses is unworthy:
142   over yourself I crown and miter you.'

1–5.   Dante's simile here, perfect in form, masks its formal vacuity: "as is the sun in a certain position, so was it then" (e.g., "as a commentator scratches his head in complaint, so did he complain"). Dante enjoys using this sort of comparison. See the note to *Inferno* XXX.136–141, in which reference is made to the study of this phenomenon (sometimes referred to as "false simile" or as "pseudo-simile") by Eric Mallin (Mall.1984.1).

Using his usual four coordinates, each 90 degrees apart from the next (Jerusalem, Spain, India, the antipodes), Dante, like clocks on the wall in an air terminal, tells us the global condition of the time. It is 6 PM now on the mountain. At the start of the *cantica* a similar passage described dawn (*Purg.* II.1–9), with the sun's position, with regard to all these coordinates, 180 degrees distant from where it is now.

3.   The river Ebro in Spain is now beneath the constellation Libra, i.e., it is midnight in Spain.

6–8.   The Angel of Chastity, standing outside the flames along the far edge of the terrace, intones part of the sixth Beatitude (Matthew 5:8), "Blessèd are the clean of heart [for they shall see God]."

10–12.   This angel has a unique function, since he, like the warder at the gate below, supervises a border beyond which purgation is not performed; however, unlike the warder, he functions within the territory of his terrace and his task is not replicated by an angel on any other terrace. He supervises what seems to be a form of final expiation and acceptance that mirrors Christ's baptism by fire (Matthew 3:11), as promised by John the Baptist: the Lord whom he serves will baptize "with the Holy Ghost and with fire." Absent as far as one can tell from the commentary tradition, this citation was suggested by an undergraduate at Princeton (Joseph Taylor '70) many years ago. The angel seems to be addressing "blessèd souls" whether *in re* (Statius) or *in potentia* (Dante); Virgil, of course, is excluded from blessedness.

Trucchi (1936) observes that this angel seems to be working in collaboration with a second one (the voice that sings from beyond the fire to draw the finally fully penitent souls to their new lives in grace), so that we find on this terrace, uniquely, two angels. See note to vv. 55–57.

13–15. Most recent commentators believe that Dante here refers to a corpse being laid in a grave (e.g., "I became so terrified that I looked like a dead man": Benvenuto's reading). Others, beginning with Lombardi (1791), argue that this *fossa* (pit, grave [it can mean either; in its last appearance at *Purg.* XVIII.121 it meant "grave"]) refers to the deeper and narrower pit that is used to bury a criminal alive and to which Dante has earlier referred (*Inf.* XIX.46–47). However, this form of punishment, *propagginazione*, involves suffocating a criminal by covering him with earth after he has been placed upside down in a pit, a posture that does not seem germane to this passage. Perhaps for this reason most (but not all) recent discussants read the line as we do.

16. Exactly what Dante's physical posture here is has been variously understood. Bosco/Reggio (1979) review a number of these discussions and make the sensible suggestion that Dante is holding his hands toward the fire, feeling its heat on them and attempting to keep the rest of his body as far as possible from the flame behind those extended hands, while he bends his head toward it, peering into it. Those who argue that Dante has joined his hands do not deal with the fact that the other three times in the *Comedy* when he uses a form of this past participle of *commettere* (to commit) it never means "join together," as most take it to mean here. See *Inferno* VII.62 and XIX.47, as well as *Purgatorio* X.57. In other words, he has "committed" his hands to the fire, i.e., stretched them out toward it.

17–18. The currently most favored reading of these lines is already found in Tozer (1901): "Burning was a mode of punishment at Florence at this period, and Dante himself had been condemned to be burnt alive at the time of his banishment." In short, Dante, having seen human beings burned alive in the public square, and having been promised exactly such treatment should he ever attempt to return to Florence from his exile, is understandably frozen by fear. For him, a man in the flesh, the danger of the fire seems, naturally enough, far greater than it must have to those who were there in spirit only. They, to be sure, suffer mental anguish as they purge their sin of lust in the flames; Dante understandably imagines that the fire will work quite differently upon him.

19. Although it is Virgil who speaks, the narrator again reminds us of Statius's continuing presence, even though he has not spoken since Canto XXV.108, when he finished his lecture on the aerial body. He will, in

fact, not speak again, though his actions and presence will be recorded until a few lines from the end of the *cantica* (*Purg.* XXXIII.135).

21–23. Virgil is at pains to remind Dante that here in purgatory the dangers are not those encountered in Inferno. He will not perish in these flames, while he might have been destroyed by Geryon's envenomed tail or by falling from his back (*Inf.* XVII.83–84; 95–96; 121). And so, Virgil asks, if Dante could trust him then, how much more can he trust him now?

25–27. See Luke 21:18: "Yet not a hair on your head shall perish." Jesus is speaking of the terrible time of tribulation that awaits his followers, which they shall nonetheless survive. Scartazzini (1900) also cites Paul's words to his followers, terrified in a storm at sea (Acts 27:34): "For not a hair shall fall from the head of any of you."

28–30. Virgil, having failed to convince Dante even a little, now resorts to scientific experiment, asking him to test a hem of his clothing in this spiritual fire. As Torraca (1905) pointed out, *far credenza* (perform a test), was a phrase (found in the second book of Boccaccio's *Filocolo*) used for the practice of having a prince's (or other important person's) food sampled by animals or by servants, expressly charged with this task, to be sure it had not been poisoned.

33. In a wonderfully wrought sequence, Virgil has given, rapid-fire, a series of convincing proposals and arguments, along with a concluding volley of encouragement (vv. 20–32). The poet's description of the protagonist, in a single line, Dante's version of "the soul indeed is willing but the flesh is weak" (Matthew 26:41), shows that he is now as reluctant as he has ever been: "against my will, I stood stock still."

37–42. In Ovid's story (*Metam.* IV.55–166), the myth that accounts for why the fruit of the mulberry tree is red, Pyramus and Thisbe are neighbors in the Babylon of Queen Semiramis (see *Inf.* V.58). They are in love. Since their parents forbid them to marry, they speak to one another lovingly through a little gap in the common wall of their houses. They conspire to meet one night at the tomb of Ninus, the dead king, former husband of Semiramis. Thisbe arrives first but, as luck would have it, a lioness, fresh from the kill and covered in the blood of the cattle she had slain, seeking a fountain to slake her thirst, frightened Thisbe away. The beast, returning from her drink and finding the cloak that fleeing Thisbe had dropped on the ground, soils that garment with her bloody maw. Pyramus, arriving late for his assignation, finds the bloodied cloth and assumes the worst. Blaming himself for Thisbe's putative death, he kills himself with his sword. His spurting blood colors the white fruit of the mulberry red. Returning, Thisbe finds the body of her beloved. In anguish she calls out his name and her own, and he opens his eyes and recognizes her just before he dies. In turn, she uses the sword of Pyramus to take her life.

The simile that Dante contrives from this material gives the name of Beatrice the same role as that of Thisbe. Virgil speaks her name just as Thisbe had spoken her own. In Dante's case it revives the will to continue toward salvation in a lover who has felt he was at the verge of death, while in the case of Pyramus there is no larger sense of redemption, only a moment of tragic recognition. Why does Dante construct this similetic moment out of such antithetic material? His love for Beatrice leads to life, Pyramus's love for Thisbe, to death. When we hear Dante's name on the lips of Beatrice (*Purg.* XXX.55), we are in a better position to see the complex relations between these two acts of naming and two kinds of love.

On the relations between the mulberry and the Tree of the Knowledge of Good and Evil from which Eve and then Adam ate, as well as the cross on which Christ died and hung like bloodied fruit, see Moevs (Moev.2000.1), pp. 218–19.

45.   For a passage from *Convivio* (*Conv.* IV.xii.16), relevant here also as an indication of Virgil's pleasure in regaining his role as Dante's teacher and guide, see the note to *Purg.* XXIV.106–111.

47–48.   We had previously known that Dante was following the two other poets (*see Purg.* XXVI.16–18) and now we learn that Statius has been nearest him, with Virgil in the lead. As Bosco/Reggio point out (1979), Virgil's tactic here is reminiscent of his staying behind Dante to protect him from Geryon's sting (*Inf.* XVII.83–84). Here, however, one might add, Virgil is not worried about protecting Dante, but by the possibility that he would try to flee back through the flames. And thus Statius is deployed as a rearguard, not against any enemy, but against the questionable will of the protagonist. Further, Virgil, by making Dante come closer, arranges things so that it is easier to control him.

54.   Virgil will probably not see those eyes, since he will be dismissed from the poem just as Beatrice appears (see *Purg.* XXX.49), even though

he had been subjected to the heat of the fire when he guided Dante through it.

55–57.   The scene we expect, as the protagonist completes his ritual purging on a terrace, is the removal of one (in this case the seventh and last) P from his forehead. Apparently the poet decided to avoid representing this climactic moment, allowing it either to be intrinsic, or else perhaps allowing us to believe that the fire itself cleansed the protagonist of his predisposition toward lust. But this is the moment (not before the entrance to the fire, as some believe) at which the ritual act should be performed, just before the upward movement to the next area of the mountain, as it has been on the other terraces (see an associated discussion of the angels' recitations of the Beatitudes in the note to *Purg.* XV.38–39).

Trucchi (1936) counts the angels who serve God's ends in *Purgatorio* and comes up with ten (the "perfect number," as he remarks): the Christian Mercury who brings the living dead to the mountain (*Purg.* II.43), the angelic warder at the gate (*Purg.* IX.104), the seven who are associated with the virtues opposed to the vices repented at the end of the experience of each terrace, and now this one.

This final angel of purgatory (in paradise we see Gabriel circling the Virgin [*Par.* XXIII.103] and then the angelic hierarchy in *Paradiso* XXVIII) acts as a sort of positive Siren, drawing souls away from lust and setting them free.

58.   As, among the early commentators, only he who speaks from the pages of the Codice Cassinese pointed out, the passage reflects the words that Christ will speak to the just at the Day of Judgment: "Then shall the King say unto them on his right hand, 'Come, blessèd of my Father, take possession of the kingdom prepared for you from the [time of the] foundation of the world' " (Matthew 25:34). In the twentieth century, notice began again to be paid to this absolutely relevant text. As Singleton reports (1973), Wilkins (Wilk. 1927.1), p. 5, pointed out that a mosaic in the Florentine Baptistery showed a gate guarded by an angel who welcomes a newly arrived soul, while a second angel leads a group of the saved and carries a banner that is inscribed "Come, blessèd of my Father, possess what has been prepared." Dante's second and singing angel would certainly seem to be modeled on that second angel and his words. And that there are two angels on this terrace may reflect his memory of the mosaic.

61–63. The angel's words, as many now note, are a sort of paraphrase of John 12:35: "Walk while you have the light, that darkness may not overtake you." Poletto (1894) seems to have been the first commentator to notice the correlation. That it should have waited so long to be observed is comprehensible, since it is not a literal citation so much as a recasting of John's thought. This second angel, exactly like the first on this terrace, first speaks in Latin and then in the vernacular. See, again, the note to *Purgatorio* XV.38–39.

64–66. Bosco/Reggio (1979) point out that, since this stair runs from due west to due east and since at the outset of the ascent (*Purg.* III.16–18) Dante had his back to the east, he has now gone exactly halfway around the mountain's circumference, or 180 degrees. Naturally the actual circumference keeps decreasing as the mountain goes higher, like that of a snail's shell.

67. Dante's phrase *levare i saggi* (tried) suggests a literal sense of taking a sample of rock, as in geological studies.

76–87. Dante's playfulness is for some reason particularly evident in his similes, which often and deliberately have "something wrong" in them, incomplete grammatical relations, mixtures of styles, and other apparent "defects." Here, on the other hand, we have a perfectly developed and complex "classical" simile: "Just as . . . and just as . . . so." Anyone examining the passage closely is likely to perceive that there are things "wrong" here as well. Let us consider the components of the simile:

	Dante (singular)	*Virgil and Statius (plural)*
76–81	goats (plural)	shepherd (singular)
82–84	flock (plural)	herdsman (singular)
85–87	goat (singular)	shepherds (plural)

Several things are worth remarking. This simile is mainly unadulterated vernacular pastoral with a few Latinate words (and perhaps a phrase from Virgil at line 77 from *Georgics* IV.10, according to Daniello [1568] and many of those who followed him). But why does Dante not get his singulars and plurals straight in the first two elements, only to correct them in the third? Why does he include the second element at all, since he excludes it from his summarizing and concluding third element? And why, as Torraca (1905) wondered, is the shepherd standing up (if leaning on his stick) while Virgil and Statius are lying down? Is that why, Torraca continued to wonder, Dante included the second element, in which the herdsman is at least closer to lying down? The purpose of these questions is to focus attention on how much Dante expects of his reader. These little touches, reminding us of his artistic freedom, make us aware of that.

77.   The phrase *rapide e proterve* in verse 77 (which we have translated as "quick and reckless"), according to some commentators, beginning with Benvenuto (1380), means "rapaces et temerariae" (rapacious and bold). Others have objected to the first of these terms, more fitting to describe the appetite of a wolf, as being inapplicable to goats. On the other hand, if we understood the word to mean "voracious," there would be no such problem. We, however, believe that Dante is referring to the way a free-roaming goat moves, rather than to the way it eats, but have no quarrel with those who follow Benvenuto.

89–90.   The stars look bigger and brighter because Dante is higher up and closer to them than he has ever been in his life. There may be a moral atmosphere at work here as well, in that he has lost the obscuring mantle of sin that is our normal lot (see *Purg.* XXX.3), and that also would make them seem brighter. For exactly such a twofold understanding see John of Serravalle (1416).

94–99.   It is now before dawn on Wednesday morning, the last day on the mountain, from which Dante will depart at noon.

"Cytherea" is a proper noun formed from the epithet used of the "maritime" Venus, the lustful goddess born of the spume of the sea near the island Cythera. Dante here presents her as the morning star, as she was seen at the opening of the *cantica*. However, and as has been pointed out in recent years with increasing insistence, in 1300, Venus was the evening star at this period of the year, and the morning star only in 1301. See the discussion in Vescovini [Vesc.2002.1], pp. 292, 300n., who resists the temptation to "redate" the poem to 1301, believing that Dante is merely taking advantage of poetic license. And see the note to *Purgatorio* I.19–21.

For the formulaic nature of Dante's preparation of his three dream narratives in *Purgatorio* see Hollander (Holl.1969.1), p. 149. All the dreams are preceded by "an astronomical reference to the hour of the morning at which the dream occurs" and then by the distinct vocabulary of dream vision, as in the second of these tercets: "in sogno mi parea / donna vedere" (in a dream I seemed to see a lady).

100–108. The dream of Leah and Rachel is the most transparent of the three dreams in *Purgatorio* (see *Purg.* IX.13–33 and XIX.1–33). Leah and Rachel, the daughters of Laban in Genesis, were understood by Christian interpreters to represent, respectively, the active life and the contemplative life (and thus Rachel's staring into the mirror is not to be taken as narcissistic self-admiration but contemplation in a positive sense). It is clear that Dante is making use of that tradition here. However, he is also making use of biblical typology in his treatment of Leah, who is related to Eve in her as yet unfallen condition in that she is doing what Adam and Eve were told to do, "ut *operaretur* et custodiret illum" (to dress [the garden] and keep it—Genesis 2:15). Dante's verb in the last line of Leah's speech, which concludes the dream, remembers the biblical verb in his *ovrare*, the working in this garden that points back to the tasks of that one before the Fall (see Holl.1969.1, p. 153). For the balanced relationships between the pair Leah and Rachel and a second pair, Matelda and Beatrice, the two central female presences in the earthly paradise, see Pacchioni (Pacc.2001.1).

It is probably also fair to say that the text intrinsically presents Dante as a new Jacob: "As Jacob toiled for seven years in order to gain the hand of Rachel, only to be given that of Leah (Genesis 29:10f.), so Dante has toiled up seven terraces of purgation with the promise of Beatrice, only to find Matelda" (Holl.1969.1, pp. 151–52). Pascoli (Pasc.1902.1), p. 462, had much earlier suggested that Dante, "the new Aeneas," was also the "new Jacob."

110–111. Awakening, the protagonist (and Statius, but Virgil only problematically so) is associated with travelers who are getting nearer home. It is quite clear that "home" now is at the very least the garden of Eden, and perhaps the true paradise that lies above. There are no thoughts of Florence here. In these lines the true pilgrimage becomes a journey from God, into the world, and back to God. It is interesting to compare the beautiful and sad opening of the eighth canto of this *cantica*, with its traveler whose thoughts are on friends left behind in the world. This pilgrim/traveler has apparently learned a good deal on the mountain.

112. For the resonance of a phrase found in the Song of Songs in this verse, "le tenebre fuggian da tutti lati" [the shadows all around were

being put to flight]: "Donec aspiret dies et *inclinentur umbrae*" [Until the day break and *the shadows flee away*] (Canticle 2:17 and 4:6), see Eleanor Cook (Cook.1999.1), p. 5.

122–123. This is as close as the poet comes to telling us that the protagonist's last P has been removed. He feels as light as his "feathers."

125. Since the garden of Eden seems to be just slightly below the level to which the travelers have now climbed (see *Purg.* XXVIII.4), this topmost step of the stair is the highest point on earth attained by Dante, and by Virgil as well, but he has no further rising to do.

127. Beginning with Scartazzini (1900), commentators have cited St. Thomas to the effect that the pains of the damned are eternal while the fire of purgatory is temporary.

131. If Dante's will is as good as Virgil will shortly say it is, he can take pleasure as his guide because he will only want that which reason will want. Nothing sinful would any longer tempt him.

135. The self-sufficient nature of the vegetation of the garden will be insisted on at *Purgatorio* XXVIII.109–120.

139–141. It is perhaps useful to consider an attempt to see how the poem may be divided into four large units, as follows:

	Dante's development	*locus*	*guide*
I.	correction of the will	*Inf.* I–XXXIV	Virgil
II.	perfection of the will	*Purg.* I–XXIX	Virgil
III.	correction of the intellect	*Purg.* XXX–*Par.* XXX	Beatrice
IV.	perfection of the intellect	*Par.* XXX–end	Bernard

See Hollander (Holl.1976.2). And for the possible contribution of St. Bernard to this schema, see note to *Paradiso* XXXIII.127–132.

It is at this moment that Virgil gives over the instructional task that has been his since *Inferno* I, presiding over the correction and perfection of Dante's will.

142.   The precise meaning and reference of this concluding verse has been the subject of much discussion. The metaliterary sense that he has of the canto as a whole leads Picone (Pico.1987.2), pp. 400–401, to allegorize the crown and miter that Virgil awards Dante as (1) the triumphant laurel of the modern poet and (2) the Christian truth that he can add to Virgil's store of pagan wisdom and poetic technique. As Fasani (Fasa.2001.1), p. 432, points out, although the modern discussion has tended to treat the terms as synonyms, as long ago as in the commentaries of the Ottimo (1333) and of Francesco da Buti (1385) they were understood as separate entities. To the Ottimo they signified "rector and shepherd"; to Francesco, laurel crown ("*corono*; di laurea, come poeta") and bishop's miter ("come vescovo e guidatore dell'anima tua a l'eterna salute" [as bishop and guide over your own soul, bound for eternal salvation]), two very different sorts of adornment for Dante's head. Fasani opts for the crown as a sign of Dante's active life, his temporal (and decidedly imperial) political mission, and sees the miter as an image of his contemplative life, the poet's spiritual mission.

Virgil can make Dante neither an emperor nor a bishop (and surely not a pope). He is metaphorically crowning Dante for now having, in his will, the ability to rule himself morally, as the world, were it only better governed, would be ruled by two powers, emperor and pope. Dante is now said by Virgil to be in complete command of the powers of his will, a microcosmic image of the world made just (improbable as Dante would have thought such a happy state) under its two prime authorities.

PURGATORIO XXVIII
(Garden of Eden)

sun might not harm his creature, this part of the
mountain was raised above the realm of weather.
Here the air you feel follows the circling of the
primo mobile; when it strikes a plant, the plant puts
its potency back into the breeze, which then
scatters it to the appropriate parts of the earth,
where a diversity of flora is found; thus on earth
no one should be surprised that plants spring up
without being sown; and where you are now,
every seed is found, including those the fruit of
which is unknown to earthlings

118–133 "As for the water, it's not natural either,
evaporating and condensing, but flows constantly
from a source by God's will in two currents, one
having the capacity to take away the memory of
sin (Lethe), while the other (Eunoe) has the
power to bring back the memory of every good
deed; and it must be tasted in that order in order
to have such effect

134–144 "And, even if to know that much would
completely answer your question, I will tell you
still more by way of a corollary: this is the place
the ancient poets had in mind when they sang of
a golden age, perhaps dreaming of it in Parnassus;
here the first people were innocent, and here
spring is eternal, and every fruit; this is the nectar
of which the poets told"

145–148 Dante turns to his right to the poets, who are
smiling, and then turns back to Matelda

Vago già di cercar dentro e dintorno
la divina foresta spessa e viva,
3   ch'a li occhi temperava il novo giorno,

sanza più aspettar, lasciai la riva,
prendendo la campagna lento lento
6   su per lo suol che d'ogne parte auliva.

Un'aura dolce, sanza mutamento
avere in sé, mi feria per la fronte
9   non di più colpo che soave vento;

per cui le fronde, tremolando, pronte
tutte quante piegavano a la parte
12   u' la prim' ombra gitta il santo monte;

non però dal loro esser dritto sparte
tanto, che li augelletti per le cime
15   lasciasser d'operare ogne lor arte;

ma con piena letizia l'ore prime,
cantando, ricevieno intra le foglie,
18   che tenevan bordone a le sue rime,

tal qual di ramo in ramo si raccoglie
per la pineta in su 'l lito di Chiassi,
21   quand' Ëolo scilocco fuor discioglie.

Già m'avean trasportato i lenti passi
dentro a la selva antica tanto, ch'io
24   non potea rivedere ond' io mi 'ntrassi;

ed ecco più andar mi tolse un rio,
che 'nver' sinistra con sue picciole onde
27   piegava l'erba che 'n sua ripa uscìo.

Eager to explore the sacred forest's boundaries
and its depth, now that its thick and verdant foliage
3   had softened the new day's glare before my eyes,

I left the bank without delay
and wandered slowly through the countryside
6   that filled the air around with fragrance.

A steady gentle breeze,
no stronger than the softest wind,
9   caressed and fanned my brow.

It made the trembling boughs
bend eagerly toward the shade
12   the holy mountain casts at dawn,

yet they were not so much bent down
that small birds in the highest branches
15   were not still practicing their every craft,

meeting the morning breeze
with songs of joy among the leaves,
18   which rustled such accompaniment to their rhymes

as builds from branch to branch
throughout the pine wood at the shore of Classe
21   when Aeolus unleashes his Sirocco.

Already my slow steps had carried me
so deep into the ancient forest
24   I could not see where I had entered,

when I was stopped from going farther by a stream.
Its lapping waves were bending to the left
27   the grasses that sprang up along the bank.

Tutte l'acque che son di qua più monde,
parrieno avere in sé mistura alcuna
verso di quella, che nulla nasconde,

30

avvegna che si mova bruna bruna
sotto l'ombra perpetüa, che mai
raggiar non lascia sole ivi né luna.

33

Coi piè ristetti e con li occhi passai
di là dal fiumicello, per mirare
la gran varïazion d'i freschi mai;

36

e là m'apparve, sì com' elli appare
subitamente cosa che disvia
per maraviglia tutto altro pensare,

39

una donna soletta che si gia
e cantando e scegliendo fior da fiore
ond' era pinta tutta la sua via.

42

"Deh, bella donna, che a' raggi d'amore
ti scaldi, s'i' vo' credere a' sembianti
che soglion esser testimon del core,

45

vegnati in voglia di trarreti avanti,"
diss' io a lei, "verso questa rivera,
tanto ch'io possa intender che tu canti.

48

Tu mi fai rimembrar dove e qual era
Proserpina nel tempo che perdette
la madre lei, ed ella primavera."

51

Come si volge, con le piante strette
a terra e intra sé, donna che balli,
e piede innanzi piede a pena mette,

54

volsesi in su i vermigli e in su i gialli
fioretti verso me, non altrimenti
che vergine che li occhi onesti avvalli;

57

All the streams that run the purest here on earth
would seem defiled beside that stream,
30 which reveals all that it contains

even though it flows in darkness,
dark beneath perpetual shade
33 that never lets the sun or moon shine through.

Though my feet stopped, my eyes passed on
beyond the rivulet to contemplate
36 the great variety of blooming boughs,

and there appeared to me, as suddenly appears
a thing so marvelous
39 it drives away all other thoughts,

a lady, who went here and there alone, singing
and picking flowers from among the blossoms
42 that were painted all along her way.

'Pray, fair lady, warming yourself in rays of love—
if I am to believe the features
45 that as a rule bear witness to the heart,'

I said to her, 'may it please you
to come closer to this stream,
48 near enough that I may hear what you are singing.

'You make me remember where and what
Proserpina was, there when her mother
51 lost her and she lost the spring.'

As a lady turns in the dance
keeping her feet together on the ground,
54 and hardly puts one foot before the other,

on the red and yellow flowers
she turned in my direction,
57 lowering her modest eyes, as does a virgin,

e fece i prieghi miei esser contenti,
sì appressando sé, che 'l dolce suono
60 veniva a me co' suoi intendimenti.

Tosto che fu là dove l'erbe sono
bagnate già da l'onde del bel fiume,
63 di levar li occhi suoi mi fece dono.

Non credo che splendesse tanto lume
sotto le ciglia a Venere, trafitta
66 dal figlio fuor di tutto suo costume.

Ella ridea da l'altra riva dritta,
trattando più color con le sue mani,
69 che l'alta terra sanza seme gitta.

Tre passi ci facea il fiume lontani;
ma Elesponto, là 've passò Serse,
72 ancora freno a tutti orgogli umani,

più odio da Leandro non sofferse
per mareggiare intra Sesto e Abido,
75 che quel da me perch' allor non s'aperse.

"Voi siete nuovi, e forse perch' io rido,"
cominciò ella, "in questo luogo eletto
78 a l'umana natura per suo nido,

maravigliando tienvi alcun sospetto;
ma luce rende il salmo *Delectasti*,
81 che puote disnebbiar vostro intelletto.

E tu che se' dinanzi e mi pregasti,
dì s'altro vuoli udir; ch'i' venni presta
84 ad ogne tua question tanto che basti."

"L'acqua," diss' io, "e 'l suon de la foresta
impugnan dentro a me novella fede
87 di cosa ch'io udi' contraria a questa."

and, attending to my plea, came closer
so that the sound of her sweet song
60   reached me together with its meaning.

As soon as she was where the grass is merely
moistened by the waters of the lovely stream,
63   she granted me the gift of raising up her eyes.

I do not think such radiant light blazed out
beneath the lids of Venus when her son by chance,
66   against his custom, pierced her with his arrow.

Straightening up, she smiled from the other shore,
arranging in her hands the many colors
69   that grow, unplanted, on that high terrain.

The river kept us just three steps apart,
yet the Hellespont where Xerxes crossed—
72   a bridle still on human pride—

was not more hated by Leander for its tossing waves
between Sestos and Abydos than I did hate
75   that rivulet for not parting then.

'You are new here,' she began, 'and,
perhaps because I'm smiling in this place
78   chosen for mankind as its nest,

'you are perplexed and filled with wonder,
but the psalm *Delectasti* offers light
81   that may disperse the clouds within your minds.

'And you who stand in front and who entreated me,
say if you'd hear more, for I have come
84   ready to answer every question you might have.'

'The water and the sound of wind among the trees
contradict what I was told and had accepted,'
87   I said, 'about the nature of this place.'

Ond' ella: "Io dicerò come procede
per sua cagion ciò ch'ammirar ti face,
90   e purgherò la nebbia che ti fiede.

Lo sommo ben, che solo esso a sé piace,
fé l'uom buono e a bene, e questo loco
93   diede per arr' a lui d'etterna pace.

Per sua difalta qui dimorò poco;
per sua difalta in pianto e in affanno
96   cambiò onesto riso e dolce gioco.

Perché 'l turbar che sotto da sé fanno
l'essalazion de l'acqua e de la terra,
99   che quanto posson dietro al calor vanno,

a l'uomo non facesse alcuna guerra,
questo monte salìo verso 'l ciel tanto,
102   e libero n'è d'indi ove si serra.

Or perché in circuito tutto quanto
l'aere si volge con la prima volta,
105   se non li è rotto il cerchio d'alcun canto,

in questa altezza ch'è tutta disciolta
ne l'aere vivo, tal moto percuote,
108   e fa sonar la selva perch' è folta;

e la percossa pianta tanto puote,
che de la sua virtute l'aura impregna
111   e quella poi, girando, intorno scuote;

e l'altra terra, secondo ch'è degna
per sé e per suo ciel, concepe e figlia
114   di diverse virtù diverse legna.

Non parrebbe di là poi maraviglia,
udito questo, quando alcuna pianta
117   sanza seme palese vi s'appiglia.

And she: 'I will explain that what you marvel at
has its own special cause
90   and thus disperse the fog assailing you.

'Supreme Goodness, pleased in Itself alone,
made man good and to do good only. This place
93   He gave to him as token of eternal peace.

'Through his own fault his sojourn here was brief.
Through his own fault he changed lighthearted frolic
96   and unblemished joy for toil and tears.

> very ironic — so that
> fulfills our
> natures
> after all!?

'So that the turbulence below,
created by the vapors rising both from land and sea
99   toward the sun's heat as far as they can rise,

'should do no harm to man,
this mountain rose just high enough toward heaven
102   to tower free of it above the bolted gate.

'Now, since all the air revolves in a circle
with the first circling, unless
105   its revolution is at some point blocked,

'that movement strikes upon this summit,
standing free in the living air, and makes
108   the forest, because it is so dense, resound.

'The wind-lashed plants have such fecundity
that with their power they pollinate the air,
111   which after, in its circling, scatters seed abroad.

'Your earth below, according to its qualities
and climate, conceives and then brings forth
114   from various properties its various plants.

'If this were understood, it would not seem
so marvelous on earth each time a plant
117   takes root without its seedling being known.

E saper dei che la campagna santa
dove tu se', d'ogne semenza è piena,
120 e frutto ha in sé che di là non si schianta.

L'acqua che vedi non surge di vena
che ristori vapor che gel converta,
123 come fiume ch'acquista e perde lena;

ma esce di fontana salda e certa,
che tanto dal voler di Dio riprende,
126 quant' ella versa da due parti aperta.

Da questa parte con virtù discende
che toglie altrui memoria del peccato;
129 da l'altra d'ogne ben fatto la rende.

Quinci Letè; così da l'altro lato
Eünoè si chiama, e non adopra
132 se quinci e quindi pria non è gustato:

a tutti altri sapori esto è di sopra.
E avvegna ch'assai possa esser sazia
135 la sete tua perch' io più non ti scuopra,

darotti un corollario ancor per grazia;
né credo che 'l mio dir ti sia men caro,
138 se oltre promession teco si spazia.

Quelli ch'anticamente poetaro
l'età de l'oro e suo stato felice,
141 forse in Parnaso esto loco sognaro.

Qui fu innocente l'umana radice;
qui primavera sempre e ogne frutto;
144 nettare è questo di che ciascun dice."

Io mi rivolsi 'n dietro allora tutto
a' miei poeti, e vidi che con riso
udito avëan l'ultimo costrutto;
148 poi a la bella donna torna' il viso.

'And you should know the holy ground
on which you stand is filled with every kind of seed
120 and gives forth fruit that is not plucked on earth.

'The water you see here does not spring from a vein
that is restored by vapor when condensed by cold,
123 like a river that gains and loses flow,

'but issues from a sure, unchanging source,
which by God's will regains as much
126 as it pours forth to either side.

'On this side it descends and has the power
to take from men the memory of sin.
129 On the other it restores that of good deeds.

'Here it is called Lethe and on the other side
Eünoè, but its water has no effect
132 until they both are tasted.

'The second surpasses every sweetness.
And even though your thirst might have been slaked
135 were I to reveal no more to you,

'I will offer a corollary as a further gift,
nor do I think my words will be less welcome
138 if they extend beyond the promise that I made.

'Those who in ancient times called up in verse
the age of gold and sang its happy state
141 dreamed on Parnassus of perhaps this very place.

'Here the root of humankind was innocent,
here it is always spring, with every fruit in season.
144 This is the nectar of which the ancients tell.'

I turned around then to my poets
and saw that they had listened
to her final utterance with a smile.
148 Then I turned back to the fair lady.

1.   We enter the third and final part of the *cantica*. These divisions, *antipurgatorium* (the first naming of "ante-purgatory" in the commentaries), *purgatorium*, and *postpurgatorium*, are found in Benvenuto da Imola (1380).

Dante's first word, *vago* (eager) ties him to Ulysses, eager for adventure (for the word *vago* see note to *Purg.* XIX.22–24). Virgil had told him, in his final instruction (*Purg.* XXVII.138), that in the garden he will be free either to sit (thus imitating Rachel, the contemplative life) or to move about (thus imitating Leah, the active life). We should not be surprised that Dante makes the latter choice. Since, as we shall see, his contemplative faculties are at this point faulty at best, his choice will be reflected in his intellectual difficulties with understanding the nature of the love represented by the beautiful woman he will shortly meet (and who is eventually identified as Matelda).

Matelda will only be named at *Purgatorio* XXXIII.119. It may be helpful to the reader to deal with her identity and her role in the poem before then. However, the reader should not forget that Dante has presented this woman as nameless, perhaps, among other reasons, to make us pay attention to what she means rather than concentrating on who she is. For the question of her identity, see the note to vv. 40–42.

2.   This forest is sacred, in the words of Andrèoli (1856), "because it was planted by the very hands of God." Many discussants of the opening of this canto realize that the poet is drawing a line across the page between the last canto and this one. Dante has finished the first half of the journey and now he finds himself in a very different sort of forest from the dark wood in which he came to his senses at the opening of *Inferno*. That wood was "aspra e forte" (dense and harsh [*Inf.* I.5]) while this forest is "spessa e viva" (thick and verdant).

It is instructive and amusing to consider the opening remarks of Benvenuto da Imola (1380) as he addresses this canto: "Before I come to its literal meaning, I would like you first to note that this entire chapter is figurative and allegorical, for otherwise it would in large measure be fatuous and untrue." Benvenuto is essentially denying the claim made by the poet that this is the actual garden of Eden. He goes on to assert that the garden signifies "the happy state of man in the perfection of his virtue, as much as is possible in this miserable life of ours." Benvenuto's commentary, which remains one of the most intelligent and helpful ever written, has a blind eye for many of Dante's theological strategies.

5. In this forest Dante the sightseer can move *lento lento* (very slowly), enjoying his surroundings. Here he will not be subject to the fear that afflicted him in the *selva oscura*.

7–9. The gentle breeze, as we shall learn (vv. 85–87), surprises Dante, who had expected to find no meteorological disturbance of any kind in the garden. It strikes upon his brow, perhaps reminding us that that was where the seven P's were inscribed on him by the warder of the purgatorial gate (*Purg.* IX.112). He is, as was Adam when he found himself in this place 6,499 years ago (see *Par.* XXVI.119–123), innocent. Unlike Adam, Dante will not fall in it.

10–12. From the westward movement of the boughs of the trees we learn that the wind in the garden blows from the east, a propitious source, since it is associated with the rising sun and thus with Christ, often represented as the sun climbing the sky, resurrected from the darkness of death.

13–18. The morning breeze does not disturb the birds plying their crafts (singing and nesting, according to John of Serravalle [1416], but surely flying as well). Lest the reader believe these birds are actually birds, Benvenuto (1380) reveals what they "really" represent: "wise and virtuous men, who rise to the heights of virtue and joyfully sing their praise of God." An allegorical temper can steal the joy from any poem.

   The harmony of birdsong and forest murmur, treble and bass, respectively, reveal the favorable conjunction of art (the birdsong) and nature (the wind in the trees) in Eden.

19–21. The sound of the forest is compared to that made by the trees in the great pine forest near Ravenna when it is stirred by the strong wind from Africa, released, at least in myth, from Aeolus's bag of the winds.

   The image of wind making melody on a natural instrument, the Aeolian harp, became a staple of Romantic literature.

22–24. Insisting again on the slowness, and thus the calm, of his progress (see verse 5), Dante implicitly contrasts his entrance into the world of sin in the first canto of the poem with his arrival in the garden. Here, just as there, he takes stock by looking back through a wood toward his point of entrance: "How I came there I cannot really tell, / I was so full of sleep / when I forsook the one true way" (*Inf.* I.10–12), but the differences between the two places overwhelm their similarities.

25–27.   This stream is Lethe, the river of oblivion in classical literature, in which Christians in Dante's Eden leave the memory of their sins behind them for eternity, as Matelda will explain (vv. 127–128).

32–33.   Beginning with Tommaseo (1837), commentators have suggested a source in Ovid (*Metam.* V.388–391) for the shaded garden here, the Sicilian scene of Proserpina's rape (see vv. 49–51), where the forests above the pools in the hills of Enna keep them protected from Apollo's rays.

40–42.   The fascination of the character introduced anonymously here (we will not find out her name until *Purgatorio* XXXIII.119) has proven so great that in Dante studies there is practically a separate industry devoted to problems associated with her identity and her significance. The position taken in what follows is based on the following given: Matelda (that is the name that we eventually hear, and it is spelled with an "e" [and not an "i"] in all the manuscripts consulted by Petrocchi) is not "allegorical" but historical. Almost all the early commentators believe that she is Matilda of Tuscany (1046–1115). Their cases pleaded from ca. 1860 on, the two principal other historical claimants to the role are thirteenth-century German nuns, Mechthild of Magdeburg and Mechthild of Hackeborn, but they have both been mainly abandoned in recent and current discussions. Starting in the nineteenth century there was a reaction against all such historical figures and, led by Scartazzini, once he came over to this view, an attempt to establish her identity as one of the other women in Dante's *Vita nuova*, a position given support in our own era by so eminent a student of the *Commedia* as Contini (Cont.1976.1), pp. 173–74. A calmer and more sensible survey than Scartazzini's is found in Moore (Moor.1903.1), pp. 210–16; he ends up cautiously maintaining the claim of Matilda of Tuscany. As opposed to the nuns, who are contemplatives, Matelda's service to the Church is clearly related to the active life, based precisely on the Church's own favorite mode of the laity's involvement: financial support. None of the young women in the *Vita nuova* are easily understood in any such role.

Matilda of Tuscany, by mere virtue of having so much support in the early commentaries (the first real opposition to her occurs only in Venturi [1732]), is probably the most intelligent choice. For an attempt to restore her identity see Villa (Vill.1987.1). However, she is nonetheless problematic for at least three reasons. (1) She was fiercely supportive of the political claims of the Church against the emperor; (2) she is presented here as a beautiful young woman, which little accords with her descriptions in the chronicles, which make her seem little less than a virago, a female soldier, and surely less "romantic" than would accord with such a portrait as Dante's; (3) since the function she performs in the garden seems to be universal (but there is debate about this, with some believing that she is only here for Dante's visit [see note to *Purg.* XXXIII.128–135]), the fact that she could not have begun her task until 1115 is a bar to her candidacy. This, however, is true for *all* candidates, as it was not, for instance, for that other *genius loci,* Cato (presiding over purgatory as Matelda presides over Eden), who died before Christ harrowed hell, before there were any souls in purgatory, and who thus was able to take up his function only when there were those who required it.

Someone (it may have been Charles Singleton) once made the remark that if we did not know Matelda's name we would know much more readily who she is. In her role in the garden of Eden she is, there can hardly be a doubt, a representation of unfallen Eve.

As the "new" (or "original old" or "perpetually new") Eve, she makes sense. She represents the active life that Leah led us to expect in her (as Rachel associates Beatrice with the contemplative life) and she can have been here from the beginning of purgation. And it is also true that, in Genesis, unfallen Eve is never named; she is only named *after* the fall, when Adam calls his wife "Eve" (Genesis 3:20). Matelda, too, is named belatedly.

43–51. Here the reader should probably be aware of a distinction between what the poet knows of Matelda's significance and what the character makes of her. A strategic awareness of the evident difference in perspective between narrator and character as a general aspect of the poem is, surprisingly enough, a fairly recent development. See Spitzer (Spit.1946.1), pp. 414–22; Singleton (Sing.1949.1), p. 25; Contini (Cont.1976.1 [1958]), pp. 33–62; Montano (Mont.1962.1), pp. 367–76.

43–48. Dante sees that Matelda is "in love" and wants to understand what she is singing. The response of Venturi (1732) indicates that the current debate was already in progress nearly three hundred years ago. He takes Matelda to be singing "of divine love and not, as some ignorant fools understand, of the bestial kind." However, many commentators, aroused by the sensual tone of the protagonist's responses, disagree.

The first major use of Guido Cavalcanti's poem, "In un boschetto trova' pasturella" (In a little wood I came upon a shepherd girl), to amplify the meaning of this scene was made by Charles Singleton (Sing.1958.1), pp. 214–16, even if he was not the first to call attention to its importance here (see Scartazzini [1900]). This *ballata* is in a genre worked previously by dozens of French and Provençal poets, a genre in which poets who more usually wrote songs about unattainable ladies had their "revenge," as it were. The *pastourelle* or *pastorella* (the genre is named for the willing and socially unimportant shepherdess it celebrates) generally, as in Cavalcanti's lyric, has a highborn protagonist ride into a clearing in a wood where he finds a lovely and willing young woman who gives him sexual pleasure at his merest request (indeed, in Cavalcanti's poem, it is she who proposes the amorous encounter to him). Any study of this *ballata* makes it immediately clear that Dante had it on his mind as he composed this canto.

Once we see Guido's poem behind Dante's we can also discern an authorial strategy behind its presence. Matelda does not come as a shepherdess, but as the unfallen Eve, virginal, upright, completely uninterested in sex. It is the protagonist, his head full of Cavalcantian sexuality, who imagines she is in love with him, just like a pretty *pastorella*. It will take him some time to discover the wrongness of his view of her, and some of his readers still have not made that discovery.

49–51. The protagonist first associates Matelda with Ovid's Proserpina (*Metam.* v.391–401), seen, grasped, and carried off by Pluto. Dante, who has begun this scene believing that Matelda is in love with him, now lets his erotic misinterpretation show; he thinks he is in the role of Pluto to her Proserpina because he thinks she is a *pastorella*.

52–58. Playing off Dante's carnal appreciation of her meaning, Matelda comes closer so that he can hear the words of her song, thus acceding to his request. She is portrayed, in simile, as being as chaste as virginity itself.

59–60. Dante's wish, expressed at verse 48, to make out the words of Matelda's song is here granted. Few texts in the poem have been as poorly treated by the commentators as this one. The protagonist's wish made *us* want to know what Matelda was singing; and here we learn that Dante now can make out her words. However, the poet does not tell us what she sang. It is at least possible that he expected us to puzzle out the identity of her song. No one has. Perhaps it is the Psalm to which she refers at verse 80, perhaps it is another song altogether. Our teachers, with only one exception, are silent, merely saying the obvious, that Dante understood what she was singing, and, with only the exceptions of Isidoro Del Lungo (1926) and Charles Singleton (1973), not even bothering to point out that the poet refuses to share this information with us. About all that can safely be said is that she probably sings a song that is kindred in spirit to the Psalm to which she later refers (see note to vv. 80–81).

64–66. Matelda's gaze, the poet remembers, was like the amorous gaze of Venus, wounded by mistake by the arrow of her son, Cupid, and consequently madly in love with Adonis, in a second Ovidian reminiscence (*Metam.* X.525–532).

67–69. Matelda, resuming her role as a latter-day Leah (and Eve as well), picks the self-seeding plants the nature of which she will disclose to Dante at vv. 109–120.

70–75. The first reference is to the Persian king Xerxes, who found a way to cross the wide Hellespont in 480 B.C. by having his vast army build a bridge out of ships lashed together; defeated by the Greeks whom he was attacking, he had to sail home in ignominy in a small boat.

The sight of this lady moved the protagonist, the poet informs us, to lustful thoughts like those of Leander, unable to cross the rough seas of the Dardanelles from Abydos to make love to his girlfriend Hero at Sestos, the third Ovidian reference, this time to the *Heroides* (XVIII). Leander finally drowned in his attempt to swim to Hero.

These three classical allusions to destructive sexual passions, aligning Matelda, in the protagonist's eyes, with Proserpina, Venus, and Hero, and himself with Pluto, Adonis, and Leander, function, as Hollander suggested (Holl.1969.1), pp. 154–58, much as did the associations with the dream in *Purgatorio* IX, in which three classical references, involving rape or other destructive behavior, were balanced and corrected by the Christian benevolence of St. Lucy. Here the protagonist's sexualized vision of Matelda yields to a better understanding once she reveals the nature of her love: Christian charity. Once she does so, the protagonist, whose will came through his self-produced temptation well enough (he does not attempt to cross the narrow stream to be with her), finally has his understanding corrected and no longer thinks of Matelda in sexual terms for the rest of his six cantos in the garden.

70. Some readers have found the three paces that must not yet be crossed allegories of the three "steps" of confession, contrition, and satisfaction that await Dante later when he must deal with Beatrice's accusation in Cantos XXX and XXXI. Others think they are only indicative of a short distance and have no deeper meaning.

76–80. Matelda, who has appeared at verse 40, finally speaks. Addressing all three poets (we have surely forgotten about the presence of Statius and of Virgil—as has Dante), she says things that at least Statius and Dante are able to understand. They are "new" (in the sense that they have never been here before but also in that they are "new men," remade, sinless) and perhaps expect to hear a lament for the Fall, for the loss of this place by the human race because of original sin. Her message, however, is not the tragic message of the Fall but the comic one of recovery, of paradise regained.

76. With regard to the word *rido*: Matelda is probably not laughing, as some hold, but smiling; see König (Koni.2001.1), p. 441, citing *Convivio* III.viii.1 for a smile as the shining forth of delight in the soul.

80–81. Psalm 91 (92), "A Psalm or Song for the sabbath day," begins as follows: "It is a good thing to give thanks unto the Lord, and to sing praises unto your name, O most High." The verse that Matelda refers to, 91:5 in the Vulgate, runs as follows in the English Bible: "For you, Lord, have made me glad *(delectasti me)* through your work: I will triumph in the work of your hands" (92:4). Matelda is expressing her Leah-like devotion to the active life, her delight in "dressing and keeping the garden" as Eve was enjoined to do (but did not, eating the forbidden fruit instead). She is once again joined in our understanding to the unfallen Eve, her constant typological referent in Dante's garden of Eden. If we ever had any doubt about the nature of the love she feels, we do so no longer. She is "in love" with God, not with Dante except as she loves him in God, as we shall see all the saved loving one another (and Dante) in *Paradiso*.

In his *Monarchia* (*Mon.* III.xv.7), Dante says that the earthly paradise signifies the *beatitudo huius vitae* (the blessedness of the earthly life).

82–84. Having cleansed Dante's mind of its impurities, Matelda now assumes, as a sort of handmaid of Beatrice, the role of teacher, leaving her sexuality a forgotten thought in Dante's formerly clouded mind.

85–87.   Dante's double question refers to the explanation of Statius (*Purg.* XXI.43–72) that the earthquake marking his liberation from the memory of sin was not, as Dante had imagined, a natural meteorological event, but a supernatural one. Just so the running water of the stream and the constant breeze, Matelda will explain, are not natural phenomena but supernatural ones, heavenly artifices to harmonize the physical attributes of this place with its spiritual essence.

90.   Once again Matelda refers to Dante's mental processes as "beclouded" or "befogged"; first he did not understand the nature of her love (verse 81) and now he does not understand the nature of the garden.

91–102.   Matelda essentially repeats what Statius had said below (see note to vv. 85–87): God limits the natural meteorology of the mountain to the ante-purgatory. The first humans, Adam and Eve, were placed in this spot free of any such disturbance; but they themselves, in their disobedience, disturbed the laws of eternal nature in the garden (vv. 94–96).

103–120.   The "weather" here is thus not the sign of some kind of disturbance, but was, from the Beginning, the sign of the harmonious essence of the created universe. The breeze in the garden, limited to this upper reach of the mountain, was (and is) caused by the movement of the highest sphere in the heavens, the *primum mobile*, the first moving (which, we will learn eventually, in *Paradiso*, moves toward God in desire and by so doing creates the movement of all the heavens below it). That breeze scatters the seeds of most (but not all) of the plants of Eden down onto the earth below. And this is why, she explains, that mortals at times cannot find the source of a plant new to their experience; it has been carried by the wind from Eden and then somehow across the seas of the southern hemisphere and deposited in the landmass half a world away. And this is why Dante will also see some plants here that have no counterpart on earth.

121–126.   Having explained the source and result of the constant breeze in the garden, Matelda turns to the equally constant water, which also does not suffer the changes of water in our world, condensing and then being released from the clouds (consider the transformations of the Arno's waters in *Purg.* XIV.34–36). What the rivers here "lose" as they run out of Eden is not restored from the clouds, but from an eternal fountain in the garden, put into operation by God Himself.

127–132.   Having answered both of Dante's questions (vv. 85–87) Matelda now turns her attention to the twofold river in this garden. The Bible says there are four rivers in Eden: the Phison (Ganges), Gehon (Nile), Tigris, and Euphrates (Genesis 2:10–14). Dante says there are two, Lethe and Eunoe. The first of these is looked forward to by Virgil (*Inf.* XIV.136–138) in response to Dante's wrongful assumption that it is a river in hell. The second, Eunoe, appears to be no less than a Dantean invention. Thus Dante has first of all reduced the number of the garden's rivers from four to two.

Lethe is the classical river of oblivion, present in the poets best known to Dante: Virgil (*Aen.* VI.713–715, where drinking from it deprives the soul of its entire remembered experience and thus prepares it for another life), Ovid (*Metam.* XI.602–604), Statius (*Theb.* I.296–298), Lucan (*Phars.* V.221–222). As for the word Eunoe, a Dantean Greek-derived coinage, Tommaseo (1837, in his comment to *Purg.* XXXIII.127–129) was perhaps the first commentator to consider Dante as having cited himself (*Convivio* II.iii.11), when he says that the Empyrean heaven was formed by the divine mind alone, or Protonoe (*protos* = first; *nous* = mind). Here Dante reformulates that Greek term, itself derived by Uguccione da Pisa from Martianus Capella (see Vasoli [Vaso.1988.1], p. 138n.), into *eu* (good) and *nous* (mind—or here perhaps "memory").

133.   There is some disagreement among the commentators as to whether the rivers' water taken as a whole (i.e., that of both Lethe and Eunoe) is sweeter than any other taste, or whether Eunoe's water is even sweeter than Lethe's, as our translation indicates that we believe.

136.   Chiamenti (Chia.1999.2), pp. 214–15, citing Lewis and Short's *Latin Dictionary*, argues for the classical Latin meaning for the word "corollary" here, a present or gratuity (e.g., a gift of money offered in exchange for a garland of flowers), as filtered through Old French poems describing ladies in gardens. While we have left the term intact in our translation, we agree with Chiamenti's inclination to read it in the floral tradition of Romance poems, since the whole passage is so redolent of such scenes.

139–141.   When they were inspired on their holy mountain, Parnassus (that is, when they were most inspired by their muses), the classical poets sang of the age of gold (e.g., Ovid in the beginning of the *Metamorphoses*,

Virgil in his fourth *Eclogue*). In doing so, they perhaps had some intimation of this place, scene of the true "golden age," where mankind was created in innocence and joy.

142–144.   Ovid's description of the classical "Eden" (*Metam.* I.89–112) is remembered closely in this tercet. One of its particulars is arresting. Where Dante makes his springtime eternal, in Ovid (*Metam.* I.107) it became ephemeral and now leaves us every year: "ver *erat* aeternum" (the spring *was* everlasting). The drama of the Fall and Resurrection is reflected in this tercet. In this garden humankind was created innocent and fell; nonetheless, the garden awaits our redemption in its eternal unfallen condition, filled with the nectar and ambrosia of the classical Golden Age in its Edenic form: fruit and water (see *Purg.* XXII.148–150).

Singleton (Sing.1958.1), pp. 192–99, points out that the virgin Astraea, or Justice, is a significant presence in both Ovid's and Virgil's presentations of the Golden Age, the last goddess to leave the earth in Ovid's myth, only to return in Virgil's prophecy. And just so, for Singleton, does Matelda serve in the role of Astraea here in Dante's garden, representing original justice (as well as our memory of the unfallen Eve).

146–147.   The protagonist's series of smiles (beginning at *Purg.* XXI.109), caused by his pleasure in the prospect of the joy that Statius will experience once he discovers that he is in the company of Virgil, is now matched by the two smiling countenances of those two poets as they understand, through Matelda's "corollary," that they have finally found the true Golden Age.

PURGATORIO XXIX
(Garden of Eden)

82–87	1) 24 elders crowned with lilies
88–96	2) four living creatures, each with six wings full of eyes
97–105	address to the reader: since Dante must conserve poetic space he will not describe the four creatures
106–114	3) among these four is a griffin drawing a two-wheeled triumphal car; his wings rise up through the middle of the bands without harming them; his bird-parts are gold while his lion-parts are red and white
115–120	the poet exclaims that neither Scipio nor Augustus had so splendid a car, no, not even the sun
121–129	4) at the right wheel of the chariot are three ladies, red, green, and white
130–132	5) at the left wheel four ladies in purple, led by the one of them who has three eyes
133–141	6) next come two men, one a doctor, caring for mankind, the other showing hostility in his sword
142	7) four men of humble aspect
143–144	8) an old man, sleeping, his face alert
145–150	these last three "groups" dressed like the first one except, where those were crowned with lilies, these are crowned with roses and other red flowers
151–154	as the car reaches Dante, a thunderclap seems to be the cause of everything coming to a complete halt

Cantando come donna innamorata,
continüò col fin di sue parole:
"Beati quorum tecta sunt peccata!"

3

E come ninfe che si givan sole
per le salvatiche ombre, disïando
qual di veder, qual di fuggir lo sole,

6

allor si mosse contra 'l fiume, andando
su per la riva; e io pari di lei,
picciol passo con picciol seguitando.

9

Non eran cento tra ' suoi passi e ' miei,
quando le ripe igualmente dier volta,
per modo ch'a levante mi rendei.

12

Né ancor fu così nostra via molta,
quando la donna tutta a me si torse,
dicendo: "Frate mio, guarda e ascolta."

15

Ed ecco un lustro sùbito trascorse
da tutte parti per la gran foresta,
tal che di balenar mi mise in forse.

18

Ma perché 'l balenar, come vien, resta,
e quel, durando, più e più splendeva,
nel mio pensier dicea: "Che cosa è questa?"

21

E una melodia dolce correva
per l'aere luminoso; onde buon zelo
mi fé riprender l'ardimento d'Eva,

24

che là dove ubidia la terra e 'l cielo,
femmina, sola e pur testé formata,
non sofferse di star sotto alcun velo;

27

After she had finished speaking
like a lady touched by love she sang:
3   *'Beati quorum tecta sunt peccata!'*

And like the nymphs that wandered all alone
through shaded forests, one seeking to find,
6   another to escape, the sun,

she moved against the current's flow,
walking along the bank, while I on my side
9   tried to match her shorter steps with mine.

We had not taken a hundred steps between us
when the two banks curved as one around a bend
12   so that once more I was headed toward the east.

And we had not gone far in that direction
when the lady turned and faced me,
15   saying: 'My brother, look and listen.'

Suddenly a shining brightness
flared through all the forest
18   so that I thought it must be lightning.

But since lightning is gone even as it flashes
and that light, shining on, became more lustrous,
21   I asked myself: 'Now what is this?'

Through the luminous air there came a melody
so sweet that I was mastered by a worthy zeal
24   to reprimand the impudence of Eve:

there when earth and heaven were still obedient,
how she, a woman, alone and just then given shape,
27   could not resist, not stay beneath the veil.

sotto 'l qual se divota fosse stata,
avrei quelle ineffabili delizie
30   sentite prima e più lunga fïata.

Mentr' io m'andava tra tante primizie
de l'etterno piacer tutto sospeso,
33   e disïoso ancora a più letizie,

dinanzi a noi, tal quale un foco acceso,
ci si fé l'aere sotto i verdi rami;
36   e 'l dolce suon per canti era già inteso.

O sacrosante Vergini, se fami,
freddi o vigilie mai per voi soffersi,
39   cagion mi sprona ch'io mercé vi chiami.

Or convien che Elicona per me versi,
e Uranìe m'aiuti col suo coro
42   forti cose a pensar mettere in versi.

Poco più oltre, sette alberi d'oro
falsava nel parere il lungo tratto
45   del mezzo ch'era ancor tra noi e loro;

ma quand' i' fui sì presso di lor fatto,
che l'obietto comun, che 'l senso inganna,
48   non perdea per distanza alcun suo atto,

la virtù ch'a ragion discorso ammanna,
sì com' elli eran candelabri apprese,
51   e ne le voci del cantare *"Osanna."*

Di sopra fiammeggiava il bello arnese
più chiaro assai che luna per sereno
54   di mezza notte nel suo mezzo mese.

Io mi rivolsi d'ammirazion pieno
al buon Virgilio, ed esso mi rispuose
57   con vista carca di stupor non meno.

Had she remained submissive there beneath it,
I should have tasted these ineffable delights
30   much sooner and a longer time.

While I walked on among so many first fruits,
this foretaste of eternal bliss, enchanted
33   though desiring joys still greater,

beneath the green boughs the air before us
seemed to become a blazing fire
36   and that sweet sound could now be heard as song.

O sacred Virgins, if fasting, cold, or sleepless nights
I've ever suffered for your sake,
39   necessity drives me to call for my reward.

Now let the springs of Helicon pour forth
and let Urania help me with her choir
42   to put in verse things hard for thought.

A short way on, seven golden trees
seemed to appear, an illusion caused
45   by the space that separated them from us.

But when I had come close enough,
distance no longer could deceive the senses
48   nor distort the common object's proper shape,

and the faculty that readies reason for its matter
knew them as candelabra, which indeed they were,
51   and in the voices of the chant I heard 'Hosanna.'

From above flared the glorious array,
far brighter than the moon, bright
54   at mid-month in a midnight sky.

Full of wonder, I turned to my good Virgil
and he answered with a look
57   no less charged with amazement.

Indi rendei l'aspetto a l'alte cose
che si movieno incontr' a noi sì tardi,
60   che foran vinte da novelle spose.

La donna mi sgridò: "Perché pur ardi
sì ne l'affetto de le vive luci,
63   e ciò che vien di retro a lor non guardi?"

Genti vid' io allor, come a lor duci,
venire appresso, vestite di bianco;
66   e tal candor di qua già mai non fuci.

L'acqua imprendëa dal sinistro fianco,
e rendea me la mia sinistra costa,
69   s'io riguardava in lei, come specchio anco.

Quand' io da la mia riva ebbi tal posta,
che solo il fiume mi facea distante,
72   per veder meglio ai passi diedi sosta,

e vidi le fiammelle andar davante,
lasciando dietro a sé l'aere dipinto,
75   e di tratti pennelli avean sembiante;

sì che lì sopra rimanea distinto
di sette liste, tutte in quei colori
78   onde fa l'arco il Sole e Delia il cinto.

Questi ostendali in dietro eran maggiori
che la mia vista; e, quanto a mio avviso,
81   diece passi distavan quei di fori.

Sotto così bel ciel com' io diviso,
ventiquattro seniori, a due a due,
84   coronati venien di fiordaliso.

Tutti cantavan: "*Benedicta* tue
ne le figlie d'Adamo, e benedette
87   sieno in etterno le bellezze tue!"

Then I raised my face again to the high mysteries.
They moved so slowly toward us
60   even newly wedded brides would have outpaced them.

The lady scolded: 'Why is your desire so set
on the display of living lights
63   that you have failed to note what comes behind them?'

Then I saw people, clad in white, who followed,
as though led by the lights, their garments
66   of a whiteness never seen on earth.

The water to my left was all aglow
and like a shimmering glass gave back
69   an image of my left side if I turned to look.

When I was at a point on my edge of the bank,
where only the river flowed between us,
72   I paused to have a better view

and saw the flames advance,
leaving behind them painted air
75   as though they had been brushes in a painter's hand,

so that above us blazed in streaks
the seven bands in all the hues the sun
78   takes for his bow and Delia for her girdle.

These banners stretched beyond my sight.
As near as I could judge,
81   the outermost were set ten paces from each other.

Beneath so fair a sky as I describe
twenty-four elders, two by two,
84   came crowned with lilies.

All were singing: 'Blessèd are you
among the daughters of Adam
87   and blessèd is your loveliness forever!'

Poscia che i fiori e l'altre fresche erbette
a rimpetto di me da l'altra sponda
90   libere fuor da quelle genti elette,

sì come luce luce in ciel seconda,
vennero appresso lor quattro animali,
93   coronati ciascun di verde fronda.

Ognuno era pennuto di sei ali;
le penne piene d'occhi; e li occhi d'Argo,
96   se fosser vivi, sarebber cotali.

A descriver lor forme più non spargo
rime, lettor; ch'altra spesa mi strigne,
99   tanto ch'a questa non posso esser largo;

ma leggi Ezechïel, che li dipigne
come li vide da la fredda parte
102   venir con vento e con nube e con igne;

e quali i troverai ne le sue carte,
tali eran quivi, salvo ch'a le penne
105   Giovanni è meco e da lui si diparte.

Lo spazio dentro a lor quattro contenne
un carro, in su due rote, trïunfale,
108   ch'al collo d'un grifon tirato venne.

Esso tendeva in sù l'una e l'altra ale
tra la mezzana e le tre e tre liste,
111   sì ch'a nulla, fendendo, facea male.

Tanto salivan che non eran viste;
le membra d'oro avea quant' era uccello,
114   e bianche l'altre, di vermiglio miste.

Non che Roma di carro così bello
rallegrasse Affricano, o vero Augusto,
117   ma quel del Sol saria pover con ello;

When the flowers and the verdant grasses
across the river on the other bank
90   were left barren of those chosen people,

as, in the heavens, light comes after light,
four living creatures followed them,
93   each crowned with green-leaved wreaths,

and every one had six wings as his plumage,
wings so full of eyes that the eyes of Argus,
96   were they to come alive, would be just like them.

To describe their forms, reader, I do not spend
more rhymes, for other outlay so constrains me
99   I cannot deal more lavishly in this.

Go read Ezechiel who depicts them as he saw them,
descending from the frigid zone
102   in wind and cloud and fire.

And just as you shall find them on his pages,
such were they there—but for the wings,
105   where John accords with me and not with him.

These four marked off a space that held
a two-wheeled chariot of triumph,
108   drawn along behind a griffin's neck.

The griffin lifted both its wings between
the middle band of light and the two sets of three
111   so that it did not cut through any band,

wings raised so high that they were lost to sight.
Its parts were golden where it was a bird,
114   and all the rest of it was white, with some vermilion.

Never did Rome give joy to Africanus,
nor indeed Augustus, with such a splendid car.
117   Compared to it, the sun's would seem but poor—

quel del Sol che, svïando, fu combusto
per l'orazion de la Terra devota,
120 quando fu Giove arcanamente giusto.

Tre donne in giro da la destra rota
venian danzando; l'una tanto rossa
123 ch'a pena fora dentro al foco nota;

l'altr' era come se le carni e l'ossa
fossero state di smeraldo fatte;
126 la terza parea neve testé mossa;

e or parëan da la bianca tratte,
or da la rossa; e dal canto di questa
129 l'altre toglien l'andare e tarde e ratte.

Da la sinistra quattro facean festa,
in porpore vestite, dietro al modo
132 d'una di lor ch'avea tre occhi in testa.

Appresso tutto il pertrattato nodo
vidi due vecchi in abito dispari,
135 ma pari in atto e onesto e sodo.

L'un si mostrava alcun de' famigliari
di quel sommo Ipocràte che natura
138 a li animali fé ch'ell' ha più cari;

mostrava l'altro la contraria cura
con una spada lucida e aguta,
141 tal che di qua dal rio mi fé paura.

Poi vidi quattro in umile paruta;
e di retro da tutti un vecchio solo
144 venir, dormendo, con la faccia arguta.

E questi sette col primaio stuolo
erano abitüati, ma di gigli
147 dintorno al capo non facëan brolo,

the chariot of the sun, which, gone astray,
at the pious prayer of Earth
120   was quite consumed in Jove's mysterious justice.

Then came three ladies dancing in a round
near the right wheel, one so flaming red
123   she hardly would be noticed in a fire.

Another seemed as though her flesh and bones
were made of emerald, while the third
126   seemed white as is new-fallen snow.

Sometimes it seemed the white, and now the red,
led in the dance. And from the red one's song
129   the others took their movements, quick or slow.

Four other ladies, dressed in purple,
were dancing at the left, keeping to the cadence
132   the three-eyed one among them set.

Behind the group I have described
I made out two old men, unlike in their attire
135   but alike in bearing, honorable and grave.

One showed himself conjoined with those
who follow great Hippocrates,
138   whom nature shaped for creatures she loves most,

while the other showed a different disposition,
his sword so bright and sharp
141   that even from across the stream it made me fear.

Then I saw four, humble in their aspect,
and, after them, an old man came alone and walked
144   as though he slept, despite his keen expression.

All seven of these were dressed just like the group
that first appeared, except they did not have
147   garlands of lilies around their heads—

anzi di rose e d'altri fior vermigli;
giurato avria poco lontano aspetto
150   che tutti ardesser di sopra da' cigli.

E quando il carro a me fu a rimpetto,
un tuon s'udì, e quelle genti degne
parvero aver l'andar più interdetto,
154   fermandosi ivi con le prime insegne.

theirs were of roses and other crimson flowers.
From just a little farther off one would have sworn
150   that they were all on fire above the eyebrows.

And when the chariot stood across the stream from me
a thunder-clap was heard and all that worthy throng
seemed forbidden to go farther and they stopped
154   behind the banners that had come before them.

1–3.   Echoing Guido Cavalcanti (see the note to *Purg.* XXVIII.43–48), the poet begins this canto by returning to the situation that we found early in the last one: Dante thinking that a beautiful young woman was in love with him. Now the poet himself seems to confirm this. We, nonetheless, probably realize that the song Matelda sings is once again utterly different from the sexually charged *pastorella* and is indeed once again a Psalm (31:1 [32:1]): "Blessed are they whose transgressions are forgiven, whose sins are covered." As Singleton (1973) points out, St. Paul (Romans 4:3–8) interprets this Psalm as indicating God's reward for just humans. However, this is not, in short, to "fuse" the "theme of profane love" with that of "charity, love of a higher order" (Singleton [1973]), but simultaneously to include and supersede it. Matelda is a very different sort of "shepherd girl" from the one we found in Cavalcanti; that seems to be Dante's main point. She does indeed love the protagonist, but she is not in love with him, as he at first believed. The word that describes her affective state, *innamorata* (touched by love), here appears for the first time in the poem. It seems to collocate itself in the Cavalcantian world of sexual love. However, as a graduate student at Princeton, Sheila Colwell, pointed out in the spring of 1984, the verb *innamorare*, in an inflected form or as a past participle, will be used eight more times in *Paradiso*, always to indicate, as we may realize either now or retrospectively, heavenly affection.

4–6.   Why are these two groups of nymphs made part of the simile, when Dante and Matelda are moving near one another and in the same direction? Benvenuto (1380) glosses the tercet simply. In the old days some nymphs wanted to leave the shade for the sun, while others desired to leave the sun for the shade. Beginning with Tommaseo (1837), some commentators have suggested a relationship with Virgil's two bands of nymphs (*Georgics* IV.383), one hundred guarding the woods, another one hundred guarding the streams ("centum quae silvas, centum quae flumina servant"). Neither the gloss nor the citation, however, answers the question, above, that has bothered many commentators, none more than Porena (1946), who posits a lost classical source to explain our puzzlement but has not convinced others of this hypothesis. It would seem that Dante wishes to express only the thought that, just as in the distant (classical) past nymphs would move purposefully from one place to another in the forest, so did he and Matelda move from where they had been standing to go somewhere else. However, the brightness that they shall soon find would seem intrinsically to associate them with those nymphs who move from shade to sunshine.

7–12.   Since the stream normally flows east to west but now makes a 90-degree veer to the north, Matelda, followed by Dante, heads south for fifty paces until it makes a second 90-degree bend, and they are once again heading due east. Why the poet wanted to have this bend in the river, which accomplishes the removal of Dante and Matelda to a point some fifty feet south of where they had been and from which they resume movement in an easterly direction, has not been clear to the commentators.

15.   Matelda's addressing Dante as "frate" (brother) reminds him (and the reader) of his earlier misunderstanding of the nature of her affection for him (see *Purg.* XXVIII.43–45).

16–21.   The lustrous presence is so bright that the protagonist, forgetting his recent and abundant instruction by Matelda on the absence of "real" weather here (*Purg.* XXVIII.85–126), at first takes this shining for lightning, until its duration makes it clear that it is something altogether other. In this way the poet builds suspense for the pageant yet to come.

It is probably not without purpose that, near the beginning of each of these cantos (XXVIII and XXIX), in which his will is finally integral and good (see *Purg.* XXVII.140 and note to XXVII.139–141), Dante reveals that his problems now center in his weak understanding. Thus this second part of the poem anchors itself in the program of the correction of his intellect, which will last until *Paradiso* XXX. (See the note to *Purg.* XXVII.139–141.)

22–30.   The protagonist hears a melody (we will be allowed to know its lyric component at verse 51) so beautiful that righteous indignation causes him to condemn Eve for depriving him of immortal life in this beautiful garden.

The veil that she would not accept is variously glossed, from the first commentators onward, either as being negative (ignorance) or positive (obedience), and some (e.g., Grabher [1934]) have believed that it has both valences.

31–33.   The *primizie* (first fruits) are the first fruits of God's eternal love as these are found here in Eden, "this foretaste of eternal bliss," promising the joys of eternity.

36. This second reference to the growing intensity of this *son et lumière* again whets the reader's appetite to know what lies just ahead (see verse 21).

37–42. This is the fourth of the *Commedia*'s nine invocations (see the note to *Inf.* II.7–9).

Fallani (1965) rightly explains that "the marvelous vision is entirely contained in the poet's memory" and that Dante now requires aid only in finding the correct words to express it. (See the note to *Inferno* XXXII.10–12 in response to a similar second invocation in the first *cantica*.) In other words, he now requires aid from holy Muses to express in poetry the deeper truth of what he has seen in the pageant representing the Church Triumphant. For the increasing importance of the notion of a prior "conception" of God's truth to Dante's evolving self-presentation as poet, see the note to *Inferno* XXXII.1–9 and Hollander (Holl.2001.1), p. 59.

Two authors stand behind this passage, as has been variously understood in the commentary tradition. The first is St. Paul (II Corinthians 11:27): "in labor and hardships, in many a vigil, in hunger and thirst, in fastings often, in cold and nakedness." Paul tells us of his trials and tribulations that prepared him for his visionary rapture, when he was taken up into the third heaven (II Corinthians 12:2). The first commentator to make this connection, which now seems fairly obvious, was apparently Torraca (1905). The context fits: we are about to witness a Pauline vision (one which happens, however, to be more Johannine in nature, as we shall see). However, there is another source, a much less apparently appropriate one, given the religious context of the entire scene: Virgil's invocation in his seventh book (*Aeneid* VII.641): "now, goddesses, cast Helicon forth and move your song": "Helicon, celebrated range of mountains in Boeotia, sacred to Apollo and the Muses, in which rose the famous fountains of the Muses, Aganippe and Hippocrene. Dante (perhaps through a misunderstanding of *Aen.* VII.641; X.163) speaks of Helicon itself as a fountain" **(T)**. (He may, on the other hand, be indicating all the sources of poetic expression by their common site.) This invocation in Virgil's poem marks the transition to the "Iliadic" military second half of the epic. That might not seem particularly promising as a parallel here. On the other hand, just as Virgil, some 600 lines into the second half of his martial epic places another invocation, so does Dante, some 185 lines into the second half of his theological epic, insert one of his. For the first notice of the Virgilian reference see Tommaseo (1837). For the meaning of the word *mercé* (translated as "reward"), we follow the reasoning of Bosco/Reggio (1979), who argue that the more common understanding ("aid" or "help") is countered by the rhetoric of the tercet, in which Dante presents himself as having suffered for the Muses and as now claiming what is due him.

As for Urania, here the highest of the Muses and their leader (where Calliope, muse of epic, had held that role in *Purg.* I.9–12), as the muse of astronomy, of "high things," she is needed to give the poet fit words to convey the conceptual truth of the pageant to come. Dante has seen it, but now, coming to write of it, he requires an understanding of its theological meaning in order to give it proper expression.

42.   The thoughts behind the verses are "hard" because of their exalted and difficult subject—allegories of the Bible—according to De Fazio (DeFa.1993.1), p. 435.

43–45.   Like Matelda, who also seemed other than what she finally comes to mean to the protagonist, the seven candlesticks (verse 50) are perceived first and erroneously by him as seven trees. Carroll (1904) comments upon them as follows: "They represent the seven 'gifts of the Spirit,' as named in the Vulgate of Isaiah 11:2–3, namely, Wisdom, Intellect, Counsel, Fortitude, Knowledge, Piety, and Fear of the Lord." Dante discusses them in *Convivio* IV.xxi.11–12.

47–51.   The "common object" is a technical term derived from Scholastic discussions of sense perception. Strictly speaking, it refers to things that can be perceived simultaneously by more than one of the five senses (e.g., taste and touch and perhaps smell for something in one's mouth; or sight, smell, and hearing [an animal in a field]) and are thus more likely to be misperceived. For instance, one might have a pebble in one's mouth and smell a clove and think the pebble is a candy; or one might be looking at a horse in the distance in a cow pasture and smell manure, thus taking horse for cow. Dante discusses the term as the *sensibile comune* (that which is perceivable by several senses) in *Convivio* III.ix.6.

Dante here has two senses in play, sight and hearing. He was thus at first unable to make out what is being uttered (see verse 36) nor what is present at the uttering. By now he realizes that the "trees" are candlesticks and the song "Hosanna." Dante is, strictly speaking, "cheating," in that it is not the combination of confused senses that caused his problem, but merely distance, in each case.

The word *Osanna*, an untranslatable expression of joyous praise, is

Dante's most frequent Hebraism in the *Comedy* (see the note to *Purg.* XI.11). It derives from the salute to Jesus offered as he enters Jerusalem (Matthew 21:19 ["Hosanna in altissimis"]; Mark 11:10 ["Hosanna in excelsis"]).

52–54. The candlesticks, now seen as a single shape, are all flaming at their tips, brighter than the full moon at its apex in the sky on a clear night. This image, and many that are to follow, reflect passages in the Book of Revelation, here Apocalypse 4:5, the seven lamps burning before the great throne of Judgment, "which are the seven spirits of God," as was first noted by Pietro di Dante (1340).

55–57. For a useful discussion of the meaning of *stupore* (amazement) see De Fazio (DeFa.1993.1), pp. 436–45. She considers this passage alongside its precursor, with which it has evident similarities (*Purg.* XXVIII.139–148), in which Statius and Virgil smile at the revelation that this place, the earthly paradise, was what they understood as Parnassus. Now Dante seeks only to see the reaction of Virgil to the pageant of Revelation and finds that his guide is amazed as are those who cannot understand, for all their wonder and reverence, what they are gazing at. Thus, for her, Dante's *ammirazione* and Virgil's *stupore* have different valences. For this to be Virgil's final observed behavior in the poem shows Dante's desire to control his admiration for his *auctor*.

60. The reference to the modest gait of newly wedded brides as they leave the church to go to their husband's house introduces the theme of the wedding ceremony to the procession and to the poem, where it will reappear in a number of guises, including parody, throughout the rest of the scenes in the earthly paradise.

61–63. Matelda calls Dante's and our attention to what will be, at that moment, the theological high point in the poem, the pageant of the Church Triumphant. For useful studies of the entirety of the scene that follows, see Moore (Moor.1903.1), pp. 178–220, "The Apocalyptic Vision"; Cristaldi (Cris.1988.1); Pertile (Pert.1998.2), pp. 23–42 (for the particular relevance of the Song of Songs). For the artistic sources of this procession, particularly those found in mosaics in and near Ravenna, see Bosco/Reggio (1979). For the iconography and meaning of the symbolic elements in it, see Friedman (Frie.1987.1). And see Lansing (Lans. 1994.1) for the way in which Dante has designed the earthly paradise as an "eighth terrace."

64–66. Those dressed in the white of faith in Christ to come (we will soon find out that they represent the Hebrew Scriptures) are presented as followers of the seven Gifts of the Holy Spirit or of the seven spirits of God (Apocalypse 4:4), not as the leaders they surely were on their own terms.

67–69. Dante, facing east, has the stream to his left, as he has all along, and sees the pageant approach him on the far side of the narrow water.

That the poet emphasizes his left side so strongly may indicate his sense of his mortal unworthiness to look upon such wonders.

73–78. The candlestick-paintbrushes leave streaks above the entire procession, as the sun colors the rainbow and the moon (Delia, Diana, born on the island of Delos) its halo.

79–81. These banners form, as it were, a canopy over the entire procession. The ten paces that separate the two outer ones are sometimes allegorized by commentators. On the other hand, they may simply imply the triumphal perfection of the procession, since ten is known as the number of God's perfection (as is 100, 1,000, etc.), since $1 + 0 = 1$.

83–84. The twelve ranks, two abreast, dressed in white (see vv. 64–66) and crowned with white lilies, are the twenty-four books of the Old Testament. In the Book of Revelation (Apocalypse 4:4) there are twenty-four elders, clothed in white, seated around the throne of Judgment. They are sometimes interpreted as representing the twelve tribes of Israel and the twelve apostles. Here they clearly represent the books of the Old Testament according to St. Jerome's accountancy in his Prologue to his Latin translation of the Bible. (Pietro di Dante [1340] cites Jerome's discussion of the books of the Old Testament in his Prologue to the Book of Daniel.) It is clear also that Dante is in this part of the procession referring to books and not authors, for these would be fewer (e.g., Moses was "author" of five of them). He will change tactics when he comes to the New Testament. See vv. 133–144, below.

85–87. The faith in Christ to come of the Hebrew Scriptures is indicated by the elders' salute to Mary as mother of Christ. See Luke 1:28: "Blessèd are you among women." Mary does not appear in the procession.

92–93.   The four creatures clad in the green of hope are the representations of the four Gospels, Matthew, Mark, Luke, and John, traditionally portrayed, respectively, as angel (or man), lion, ox, and eagle. These identifications derive from Ezechiel 10:4–14 and Apocalypse 4:6–8.

94–96.   The six wings are found in the Apocalypse (4:8) but not in Ezechiel (1:6), where they are four (see verse 105). The reference is to the hundred eyes of Ovid's Argus (see *Metam.* I.568–723). Jove chose Io as a victim of his desire. When jealous Juno came near them, he changed Io into a heifer, but Juno remained suspicious and sent Argus, with his hundred eyes, to watch over Io. Jove dispatched Mercury to slay him, which he did after telling a long tale that closed his eyes in sleep. Juno put those hundred eyes into the feathers of the peacock.

   Dante's reference intrinsically distinguishes between the eyes of dead Argus and these living visionary eyes that have loftier purpose than guarding pretty heifers. For a study of the resonances of the Io narrative in the following cantos see Levenstein (Leve.1996.1).

97–99.   This is the fifth address to the reader in this *cantica*. For the poet's insistence on the constraints on his ability to expand his verse, see *Purgatorio* XXXIII.139–141 and note.

100–104.   Dante refers us to the lengthy passage in Ezechiel (see the note to vv. 94–96) for the details of the appearance of the four Gospel beasts.

   Lombardi (1791) is perhaps unique in his understanding of why Dante preferred John's six to Ezechiel's four. Bishop Primasius, he says, the student of St. Augustine, commenting on Revelation 4, said that the beasts have six wings because six is the number of the sixth and final age, after which we will come to the fullness of time *(plenitudo temporum)*. There is nothing like consensus on a solution for this problem, but Lombardi's thesis is, if nothing else, original.

105.   Dante's claim here mirrors the pretext of the entire poem; his experience of the otherworld is to be treated as actual and not as imagined. As a result, his authority as teller of the tale is absolute, and even biblical testimony is secondary to his own.

106–107.   The chariot, as will become evident, represents the Church, an opinion for which there is essential consensus. Its two wheels, however, are variously interpreted. Do they represent the two Testaments (but these are fully represented in the pageant, as Bosco/Reggio [1979] rightly object)? Wisdom and Love? The active and the contemplative life? We probably need to understand literally that Dante wanted his chariot to look something like, not a four-wheeled oxcart, but a two-wheeled Roman triumphal chariot. It may be better to leave allegory to one side. Scartazzini (1900) offers a scathing review of the attempts mentioned above and still others.

108.　　The griffin has only recently become a cause for controversy, even though for six hundred years it was assumed to signify Christ (e.g., Pietro di Dante [1340], to whom "Gryphon . . . figurat Christum" [the griffin figures Christ]). Beginning with Scartazzini (1900), commentators point to Isidore of Seville's description (*Etym.* XII.xxii.17) of the griffin as being half lion and half eagle, and then going on to say that Christ is like both lion and eagle. For a review of the question and close to definitive restatement of the traditional view (the griffin symbolizes Christ), see Cristaldi (Cris.1988.2), answering Armour's main objections to this understanding (e.g., Dante would not have used a hybrid creature to symbolize Christ) even before Armour (Armo.1989.1) made them. And now see Pertile (Pert.1998.2), pp. 143–62, whose arguments in favor of the griffin as symbolizing Christ seem difficult to counter.

109–111.　　The griffin's enormous wings go up, one on either side of the central pennon made by the fourth of the seven candlesticks' flaming paintbrush, so as not to disturb the canopy in any way.

113–114.　　His mixture of immortal gold in the part of him that was eagle and the more "human" red-and-white parts of the lion would surely seem further to identify him with Christ.

115–120.　　This chariot is not only more splendid than those awarded either to Scipio Africanus (185–129 B.C.), conqueror of Hannibal and destroyer of Carthage, or to the great Augustus himself (63 B.C.–A.D. 14), the emperor at the "fullness of time," when Christ was born in a world at peace under the rule of Augustus. Dante goes still further: this chariot makes the sun, become a chariot for Phaeton's wild misadventure (Ovid, *Metam.* II.47–324), seem a poor thing by comparison. It is striking that this third chariot involves a tragic event—Phaeton's death—while the first two are used to glorious purpose. We are reminded of God's mercy and of his justice.

That the most significant element in the procession is a triumphal chariot makes it difficult not to see that this pageant represents the Church Triumphant, i.e., the Church as it shall be in eternity. It is only in *Purgatorio* XXXII that we shall observe a representation of the Church Militant. There is a resemblance in this rhythm to that which we have experienced on all the seven terraces, namely *exempla* of the opposed virtue preceding those of the vice to be purged. Here the perfected Church precedes its temporally prior and persecuted self in all its tribulations. For this observation, see Lansing (Lans.1994.1), pp. 106–8.

121–129.   This part of the allegory escapes no one: the three ladies represent the three theological virtues, charity (red), hope (green), and faith (white). They stand at the right wheel of the cart, its better side. Faith, necessary to a proper form of love, first leads their dance; then it is the turn of Charity, necessary to a proper form of Hope.

130–132.   At the left wheel we find the four cardinal virtues, associated with Roman virtue by their purple robes: temperance, justice, fortitude, and prudence (represented by the three-eyed lady, since she is knowledgeable about past, present, and future).

133–141.   We now come to the second Christian section of the pageant, those who came after Christ. We recognize Luke as the doctor he was, author of the Acts of the Apostles; Paul as the sword-bearer (see Ephesians 6:17, where Paul speaks of the sword of the spirit, that is, the word of God). And, as Singleton points out (1973), the sword also represents Paul's martyrdom.

Here Dante uses the authors of New Testament texts to represent their works, and not vice versa, as he had done for the Old Testament. See the note to vv. 83–84.

142–144.   The writers of the lesser Epistles (James, Peter, John, and Jude) are followed by the Apocalypse, its author John depicted as sleeping the mystic sleep of vision.

145–150.   These seven authors or books all are typified not by the white of faith, as was the Old Testament, but by the red of love (for Christ come).

Pierotti (Pier.1981.1), p. 220, n. 12 has offered the following census of the pageant:

1)   24 books of the Old Testament
2)   4 Gospels: Matthew, Mark, Luke, John
3)   1 griffin
4)   3 theological virtues (love, hope, faith)
5)   4 cardinal virtues (prudence, fortitude, temperance, justice)
6)   2 "authors" of Book of Acts & major Epistles: Luke and Paul
7)   4 "authors" of lesser Epistles: Peter, James, John, Jude
8)   1 Apocalypse: John

Total: 43

Canto XXX will add 100 angels and Beatrice to bring the number to 144, the mystical number (144,000) of the Church Triumphant. See Apocalypse 7:4, 14:1, 14:3.

151–154.   The canto ends with the thunderclap, arresting all, from the front to the back of the procession, as they await an obviously momentous event.

PURGATORIO XXX

Quando il settentrïon del primo cielo,
che né occaso mai seppe né orto
3   né d'altra nebbia che di colpa velo,

e che faceva lì ciascuno accorto
di suo dover, come 'l più basso face
6   qual temon gira per venire a porto,

fermo s'affisse: la gente verace,
venuta prima tra 'l grifone ed esso,
9   al carro volse sé come a sua pace;

e un di loro, quasi da ciel messo,
"Veni, sponsa, de Libano" cantando
12   gridò tre volte, e tutti li altri appresso.

Quali i beati al novissimo bando
surgeran presti ognun di sua caverna,
15   la revestita voce alleluiando,

cotali in su la divina basterna
si levar cento, *ad vocem tanti senis*,
18   ministri e messagger di vita etterna.

Tutti dicean: *"Benedictus qui venis!"*
e fior gittando e di sopra e dintorno,
21   *"Manibus, oh, date lilïa plenis!"*

Io vidi già nel cominciar del giorno
la parte orïental tutta rosata,
24   e l'altro ciel di bel sereno addorno;

e la faccia del sol nascere ombrata,
sì che per temperanza di vapori
27   l'occhio la sostenea lunga fïata:

When the seven-starred Wain of highest heaven—
which never sets and never rises
and never wore a veil of fog except for sin

3

and which had made all of them mindful of their duty,
as lower down those seven stars direct
the helmsman making for his port—

6

came to a stop, the chosen people
that first appeared between it and the griffin
turned toward the chariot as to their peace.

9

One of them, who seemed dispatched from Heaven,
sang out aloud three times: 'Veni, sponsa,
de Libano,' and all the others echoed him.

12

As quickly as from their graves at the last trumpet
the blessèd shall arise, their voices
rejoined to flesh in joyous Hallelujahs,

15

there, on the sacred chariot, rose up
ad vocem tanti senis, one hundred
ministers and messengers of life eternal.

18

All were chanting: 'Benedictus qui venis' and,
tossing flowers up into the air and all around them,
'Manibus, oh, date lilia plenis!'

21

At break of day, I have seen the sky,
its eastern parts all rosy
and the rest serene and clear

24

even as the sun's face rose obscured
so that through tempering mist
the eye could bear it longer,

27

così dentro una nuvola di fiori
che da le mani angeliche saliva
30   e ricadeva in giù dentro e di fori,

sovra candido vel cinta d'uliva
donna m'apparve, sotto verde manto
33   vestita di color di fiamma viva.

E lo spirito mio, che già cotanto
tempo era stato ch'a la sua presenza
36   non era di stupor, tremando, affranto,

sanza de li occhi aver più conoscenza,
per occulta virtù che da lei mosse,
39   d'antico amor sentì la gran potenza.

Tosto che ne la vista mi percosse
l'alta virtù che già m'avea trafitto
42   prima ch'io fuor di püerizia fosse,

volsimi a la sinistra col respitto
col quale il fantolin corre a la mamma
45   quando ha paura o quando elli è afflitto,

per dicere a Virgilio: "Men che dramma
di sangue m'è rimaso che non tremi:
48   conosco i segni de l'antica fiamma."

Ma Virgilio n'avea lasciati scemi
di sé, Virgilio dolcissimo patre,
51   Virgilio a cui per mia salute die'mi;

né quantunque perdeo l'antica matre,
valse a le guance nette di rugiada
54   che, lagrimando, non tornasser atre.

"Dante, perché Virgilio se ne vada,
non pianger anco, non piangere ancora;
57   ché pianger ti conven per altra spada."

thus, within that cloud of blossoms
rising from angelic hands and fluttering
30   back down into the chariot and around it,

olive-crowned above a veil of white
appeared to me a lady, beneath a green mantle,
33   dressed in the color of living flame.

And in my spirit, which for so long a time
had not been overcome with awe
36   that used to make me tremble in her presence—

even though I could not see her with my eyes—
through the hidden force that came from her I felt
39   the overwhelming power of that ancient love.

As soon as that majestic force,
which had already pierced me once
42   before I had outgrown my childhood, struck my eyes,

I turned to my left with the confidence
a child has running to his *mamma*
45   when he is afraid or in distress

to say to Virgil: 'Not a single drop of blood
remains in me that does not tremble—
48   I know the signs of the ancient flame.'

But Virgil had departed, leaving us bereft:
Virgil, sweetest of fathers,
51   Virgil, to whom I gave myself for my salvation.

And not all our ancient mother lost
could save my cheeks, washed in the dew,
54   from being stained again with tears.

'Dante, because Virgil has departed,
do not weep, do not weep yet—
57   there is another sword to make you weep.'

Quasi ammiraglio che in poppa e in prora
viene a veder la gente che ministra
60 per li altri legni, e a ben far l'incora;

in su la sponda del carro sinistra,
quando mi volsi al suon del nome mio,
63 che di necessità qui si registra,

vidi la donna che pria m'appario
velata sotto l'angelica festa,
66 drizzar li occhi ver' me di qua dal rio.

Tutto che 'l vel che le scendea di testa,
cerchiato de le fronde di Minerva,
69 non la lasciasse parer manifesta,

regalmente ne l'atto ancor proterva
continüò come colui che dice
72 e 'l più caldo parlar dietro reserva:

"Guardaci ben! Ben son, ben son Beatrice.
Come degnasti d'accedere al monte?
75 non sapei tu che qui è l'uom felice?"

Li occhi mi cadder giù nel chiaro fonte;
ma veggendomi in esso, i trassi a l'erba,
78 tanta vergogna mi gravò la fronte.

Così la madre al figlio par superba,
com' ella parve a me; perché d'amaro
81 sente il sapor de la pietade acerba.

Ella si tacque; e li angeli cantaro
di sùbito *"In te, Domine, speravi"*;
84 ma oltre *"pedes meos"* non passaro.

Sì come neve tra le vive travi
per lo dosso d'Italia si congela,
87 soffiata e stretta da li venti schiavi,

Just like an admiral who moves from stern to prow
to see the men that serve the other ships
60 and urge them on to better work,

so on the left side of the chariot—
as I turned when I heard her call my name,
63 which of necessity is here recorded—

I saw the lady, who had just appeared
veiled beneath the angels' celebration,
66 fix her eyes on me from across the stream.

Although the veil, encircled with Minerva's leaves
and descending from her head,
69 did not allow me unrestricted sight,

regally, with scorn still in her bearing,
she continued like one who, even as he speaks,
72 holds back his hottest words:

'Look over here! I am, I truly am Beatrice.
How did you dare approach the mountain?
75 Do you not know that here man lives in joy?'

I lowered my eyes to the clear water.
But when I saw myself reflected, I drew them back
78 toward the grass, such shame weighed on my brow.

As a mother may seem overbearing to her child,
so she seemed to me, for the taste
81 of such stern pity is a bitter taste.

Then she fell silent and at once
the angels sang: *'In te, Domine, speravi,'*
84 but did not sing past *'pedes meos.'*

Even as the snow among those living beams
that grow along the spine of Italy is frozen
87 when blown and packed by the Slavonian winds

poi, liquefatta, in sé stessa trapela,
pur che la terra che perde ombra spiri,
90   sì che par foco fonder la candela;

così fui sanza lagrime e sospiri
anzi 'l cantar di quei che notan sempre
93   dietro a le note de li etterni giri;

ma poi che 'ntesi ne le dolci tempre
lor compartire a me, par che se detto
96   avesser: "Donna, perché sì lo stempre?"

lo gel che m'era intorno al cor ristretto,
spirito e acqua fessi, e con angoscia
99   de la bocca e de li occhi uscì del petto.

Ella, pur ferma in su la detta coscia
del carro stando, a le sustanze pie
102   volse le sue parole così poscia:

"Voi vigilate ne l'etterno die,
sì che notte né sonno a voi non fura
105   passo che faccia il secol per sue vie;

onde la mia risposta è con più cura
che m'intenda colui che di là piagne,
108   perché sia colpa e duol d'una misura.

Non pur per ovra de le rote magne,
che drizzan ciascun seme ad alcun fine
111   secondo che le stelle son compagne,

ma per larghezza di grazie divine,
che sì alti vapori hanno a lor piova,
114   che nostre viste là non van vicine,

questi fu tal ne la sua vita nova
virtüalmente, ch'ogne abito destro
117   fatto averebbe in lui mirabil prova.

but then, dissolving, melts into itself
if the land that casts no shadow merely breathes,
90   acting like a flame that makes a candle melt,

just so was I with neither tears nor sighs
before they sang who always are in tune
93   with notes set down in the eternal spheres,

but, when their lovely harmonies revealed
their sympathy for me, more than if they'd said:
96   'Lady, why do you torment him so?'

the ice that had confined my heart
was turned to breath and water and in anguish
99   flowed from my breast through eyes and mouth.

As yet she stood, motionless,
on the same side of the chariot,
102   then turned her words to the pitying angels:

'You keep your watch in the eternal day
so neither night nor sleep deprives you
105   of a single step that time takes in its course.

'Therefore my response is made with greater care
that he who is weeping over there should listen,
108   so that his sin and sorrow be of equal measure.

'Not only by the working of the wheels above
that urge each seed to a certain end
111   according to the stars that cluster with them,

'but by grace, abundant and divine,
which rains from clouds so high above
114   our sight cannot come near them,

'this man in his new life potentially was such
that each good disposition in him
117   would have come to marvelous conclusion,

Ma tanto più maligno e più silvestro
si fa 'l terren col mal seme e non cólto,
120   quant' elli ha più di buon vigor terrestro.

Alcun tempo il sostenni col mio volto:
mostrando li occhi giovanetti a lui,
123   meco il menava in dritta parte vòlto.

Sì tosto come in su la soglia fui
di mia seconda etade e mutai vita,
126   questi si tolse a me, e diessi altrui.

Quando di carne a spirto era salita,
e bellezza e virtù cresciuta m'era,
129   fu' io a lui men cara e men gradita;

e volse i passi suoi per via non vera,
imagini di ben seguendo false,
132   che nulla promession rendono intera.

Né l'impetrare ispirazion mi valse,
con le quali e in sogno e altrimenti
135   lo rivocai: sì poco a lui ne calse!

Tanto giù cadde, che tutti argomenti
a la salute sua eran già corti,
138   fuor che mostrarli le perdute genti.

Per questo visitai l'uscio d'i morti,
e a colui che l'ha qua sù condotto,
141   li preghi miei, piangendo, furon porti.

Alto fato di Dio sarebbe rotto,
se Letè si passasse e tal vivanda
fosse gustata sanza alcuno scotto
145   di pentimento che lagrime spanda."

with more blessing comes more respons- ibility

'but the richer and more vigorous the soil,
when planted ill and left to go to seed,
120   the wilder and more noxious it becomes.

'For a time I let my countenance sustain him.
Guiding him with my youthful eyes,
123   I drew him with me in the right direction.

'Once I had reached the threshold of my second age,
when I changed lives, he took himself from me
126   and gave himself to others.

'When I had risen to spirit from my flesh,
as beauty and virtue in me became more rich,
129   to him I was less dear and less than pleasing.

'He set his steps upon an untrue way,
pursuing those false images of good
132   that bring no promise to fulfillment—

'useless the inspiration I sought and won for him,
as both with dreams and other means
135   I called him back, so little did he heed them.

'He sank so low that every instrument
for his salvation now fell short—
138   except to make him see souls in perdition.

'And so I visited the threshold of the dead
and, weeping, offered up my prayers
141   to the one who has conducted him this far.

'Broken would be the high decree of God
should Lethe be crossed and its sustenance
be tasted without payment of some fee:
145   his penitence that shows itself in tears.'

1–7.   This first simile in a canto that is heavily similetic seems deliber-
ately difficult. Puzzled out, it compares the sevenfold spirit of the
Church Triumphant, toward which all in the procession now turn for
guidance as they do above in the Empyrean, to the Little Dipper, which
locates the North Star for earthly navigators. The sevenfold Spirit of God
[see the note to *Purg.* XXIX.64–66]) seems clearly to be identified with
the Holy Spirit, one aspect of the triune God in the Empyrean. Porena
(1946) points out that the stars of the constellation Ursa (whether Major
or Minor) were construed as seven plowing oxen, *septem triones*, as is
reflected in Dante's word "settentrïon" (which may reflect Virgil's
"septem . . . trioni" at *Georgics* III.381). This higher sevenfold spirit, un-
like Ursa Minor, never rises or sets but is constantly glowing with char-
ity; it is also never hidden by a clouded sky, even though it is not visible
to us because we exist in a "cloud" of our own sinfulness.

8–9.   The twenty-four elders, representing the Old Testament, turn
toward the chariot as to the awaited messiah who, in His first coming,
crowned their time of militance with peace and who now will come in
Judgment. See Ephesians 2:14, "Ipse enim est pax nostra" [For He is our
peace], a text cited by Singleton (1973). Since the procession in the gar-
den represents the Church Triumphant, the Mystical Body of Christ *after*
its progress through history, it seems advisable to realize that we deal
here with a scene that is meant to reflect the final advent of Christ for
the Day of Judgment. See Singleton (Sing.1958.1), pp. 72–85, citing St.
Bernard on the three advents of Christ (*Patrologia Latina* 183, col. 35ff.).
See also Thomas Merton (Mert.1953.1), Mark Musa (Musa.1974.1), and
the note to *Purgatorio* VIII.103–108.

10–12.   The elder who sings alone is clearly the Song of Songs, whether
the book itself or its "author," Solomon, his words repeating the phras-
ing "Veni . . . , veni . . . , veni" of the Canticle of Canticles 4:8 ("Come
from Lebanon, my bride, come from Lebanon, come"). We would be
forgiven if we believed we were about to witness a wedding ceremony
of some kind, featuring Beatrice in the role of bride. A strange "wed-
ding" it will turn out to be, characterized by tears more than by smiles.
In fact, no canto in the poem displays more words for weeping than this
one (*Inferno* XXXIII has exactly as many): *lagrime* (vv. 91, 145), *lagrimando*
(54), *piangere* (56, 57, 107, 141).

Chiarini (Chia.1967.2), p. 1112, points out that these verses consti-
tute the longest sentence (twelve lines) in the poem.

13–15.   The reference is to the trumpet blast that will summon the souls
of the dead to judgment (I Corinthians 15:52).

The word "hallelujah" seems so familiar that it may be surprising to
discover that it occurs (and occurs four times) only in a single biblical
text, the nineteenth chapter of John's Book of Revelation, where the
saints (Apocalypse 19:1, 19:3), the elders and the four Gospel beasts
(Apocalypse 19:4), and a great multitude (Apocalypse 19:6, reasonably
understood as the souls of the blessed, to whom, in fact, Dante refers
here) all cry out this word in welcome of the coming reign of the true
God and of his Judgment.

16–18.   As will arise all those who will be saved at the Last Judgment, a
hundred angels ("ministers and messengers of life eternal") rise up upon
the chariot itself to welcome Beatrice, who, in a moment, will come to
it. Where do these angels come from? We are not told whether they sud-
denly manifest themselves upon the chariot now just as Beatrice comes,
or descended from the Empyrean with her, or with the chariot when it
came to show itself to Dante in Eden. See the notes to *Purgatorio*
XXXI.77–78 and XXXII.89–90.

These Beatricean angels have a prehistory. In *Vita nuova* XXIII.7,
Dante imagines Beatrice's death and sees a band of angels who return
with her to heaven, mounting after a little white cloud, and singing
"Osanna in altissimis." Charles Singleton (Sing.1954.1), p. 57, was per-
haps the first to make the necessary connections between that scene and
this one. This procession began with voices singing "Hosanna" (*Purg.*
XXIX.51); Beatrice returns with her host of angels and again she is ob-
scured by a cloud.

These verses draw Dante's imagining of Beatrice's departure from
this life in *Vita nuova* into obvious relation to his presentation of her re-
turn to earth here in the garden of Eden. In both cases the word
"Hosanna" associates her with Christ's triumphal entry into Jerusalem:
in the *Vita nuova*, the New Jerusalem that is life eternal in the Empyrean;
here, a triumphant descent to earth modeled on Christ's return in judg-
ment.

16.   The rare word *basterna* has caused difficulty. Benvenuto (1380) says
that it is a vehicle made of soft skins, used to transport noblewomen; he
suggests that it fits the context here because it is drawn by two animals

(this chariot, he notes, is pulled by a two-natured beast) and because Beatrice is the most noble of women. According to Servius's gloss of *Aeneid* VIII.666 (cited first by Lombardi [1791] and then by Trucchi [1936]), the *basterna* was a cart, festooned with veils, found in Gaul, where it was used to transport chaste matrons to sacred festivals.

17.   The Latin phrase *ad vocem tanti senis* (at the words of so great an elder) is Dante's own, opening a series of three rhyming Latin endings of lines, the next two from Mark and Virgil respectively. The effect is to make three Latin "authors," Dante, Mark, and Virgil, each contribute part of a Latin verse for the advent of Beatrice.

19.   Beatrice's hundred angels cite the first of the two master texts for this poem found in this tercet, the Bible and the *Aeneid*. The clause "Blessèd are you who come" (with the adjective given a startling masculine ending, not the feminine that would seem a more fitting accompaniment to Beatrice) is derived from the account of Christ's entry into Jerusalem found in Mark 11:9–10: "And they that went before, and they that followed, cried, saying, 'Hosanna; Blessèd is he that comes *(Benedictus qui venit)* in the name of the Lord. Blessèd be the kingdom of our father David, that comes in the name of the Lord: Hosanna in the highest' *(Hosanna in excelsis)*." While Matthew (31:9) and John (12:13) also report the "Hosanna" and the blessedness of him who comes in fulfillment of the prophecy in Zechariah 9:9, only Mark has the words almost exactly as Dante has them in this passage and in *Vita nuova* XXIII.7 (see the note to vv. 16–18 and Hollander [Holl.1973.1], p. 146).

Dante could just as easily have said "benedicta" as "benedictus"; neither rhyme nor meter forced his hand. We must therefore understand that the scandalous regendering of Beatrice caused by the correct citation of Mark's Gospel is deliberate. It seems clear that the poet wants his reader to realize that her meaning, her eventual identity, is totally involved in Christ. And thus she comes as Christ, not as herself.

20.   The angelic strewing has reminded commentators, at least since the time of Daniello (1568), of the strewing of palm fronds in the path of Jesus on what became known as Palm Sunday.

21.   The Latin is Virgilian (*Aen.* VI.883): "Give lilies with full hands." This is the climax of Anchises' tearful and prophetic speech about the future of Rome and the dreadful loss of Marcellus, the adoptive son of

Augustus who was to rule Rome after the emperor's death, but who beat his "father" to the grave. In Virgil's text the lilies are flowers of mourning; in Dante's they seem rather to be associated with (according to Pietro di Dante [1340]) the Song of Songs (2:1), when the bride describes herself as the *lilium convallium*, "lily of the valley," a wildflower, not a cultivated plant. Dante will later associate lilies with the apostles (*Par.* XXIII.74). Traditionally, a flowering bough in the form of a lily was borne by the angel Gabriel in depictions of the Annunciation, denoting the chastity of Mary (see Fallani's comment [1965] to *Par.* 32.112]). It seems clear that here the lilies are relocated symbolically, losing their tragic tone for a "comic" and celebratory one; they have a positive and redemptive valence, not the funerary significance that they have in Virgil's line. At the same time, for those of us who are thinking of Virgil as well as of Beatrice, they do underline our (and soon Dante's) sadness at this "death" of Virgil in the poem. In that respect the verse functions in both a "Beatricean" and a "Virgilian" mode.

This is the closest Dante comes to giving a piece of Virgil's Latin text an uninterrupted verbatim presence in his poem. His Italian "oh," however, does interrupt the flow of the Virgilian line. It seems more than possible that the exclamation is spoken, since it is uttered by her angels, to mark the moment of Beatrice's appearance on the chariot.

31–33. Beatrice, described first by her apparel, is crowned with the olive branch, traditionally symbolic of peace but also associated with wisdom, since the olive was sacred to the goddess of wisdom, Minerva. The three colors that she wears associate her with faith (white), hope (green), and charity (red), the three theological virtues we have already seen in the procession (*Purg.* XXIX. 121–126).

34–36. Beatrice died in June 1290; it is now either the end of March or early April 1300 (see note to *Inf.* I.1) and thus about two months fewer than ten years since she died.

Virgil had been overcome by *stupore* (amazement) a short while ago (see note to *Purg.* XXIX.55–57); now it is Dante's turn. Not even the man who wrote of Beatrice can encompass the fact of her miraculous nature now that he finally experiences it directly and completely. It will take him another *cantica* adequately to understand what she means.

39. The line is clearly reminiscent (if the reminiscence was apparently only first noted by Torraca [1905]) of the opening of Dante's lyric (*Rime*

XCI), "Io sento sì d'Amor la gran possanza" (So much do I feel Love's mighty power). Just as was the case with Matelda (see the note to *Purg.* XXVIII.43–48), Dante's concupiscent memories and thoughts are at odds with the nature of Beatrice. Yes, she looks exactly like the woman with whom he fell in love in Florence; but now it is clear (as it should have been then) that she loves him only in Christ. This distinction will be insisted on at *Purgatorio* XXXII.7–9.

40–42.   For Dante's earlier references to his first being smitten by Beatrice while he was still in his childhood, in fact in his ninth year (i.e., while he was still eight), see *Vita nuova* II.2 (Andreoli [1856]); *Vita nuova* XII.7 (Poletto [1894]); and *Rime* CXI.1–2 (Singleton [1973]).

43–48.   Again Virgil is thought of as a *mamma*, that strikingly "vernacular" word we have heard applied to him before (in company with the same rhyme words) in the salutation addressed to him by Statius (see *Purg.* XXI.95–99 and the note to *Purg.* XXI.97–99). See also *Inferno* XXXII.9 and the note to XXXII.1–9.

Virgil, it may seem, is strangely feminized in Dante's gesture toward him. However, if we consider his nurturing role in the eyes of the protagonist, the term is less disturbing. And once we observe Dante's attempt to deal with Beatrice's asperity and her "masculine" demeanor, we can see that the dynamic of this scene is built upon the reversal of gender roles, Virgil now seeming gentle and mothering, while Beatrice, coming as Christ in judgment (see the note to vv. 16–18), like an admiral (see verse 58 and note), seems more like an unforgiving father.

48.   This verse is a translation of Dido's climactic utterance admitting that she has fallen in love with Aeneas, thus breaking her vows of chastity to her dead husband, Sichaeus (*Aen.* IV.23): "Agnosco veteris vestigia flammae" (I recognize the traces of the ancient flame).

49–51.   Near the conclusion of Virgil's tragic fourth *Georgic* (vv. 525–527), Orpheus's severed head cries out to his lost Eurydice. It is a moment that could define the tragic spirit, a decapitated voice giving vent to Orpheus's misery at the loss of his wife:

> . . . Eurydicen vox ipsa et frigida lingua,
> a miseram Eurydicen! anima fugiente vocabat,
> Eurydicen toto referebant flumine ripae.

> . . . "Eurydice" that very voice and frozen tongue,
> "Oh wretched Eurydice!" it called as the soul escaped,
> "Eurydice" the banks gave back along the stream.

It seems more than clear that Dante's three-verse farewell to Virgil is modeled on Orpheus's three-verse farewell to Eurydice. While surprisingly few twentieth-century commentators have heard that echo in these lines, even they seem unaware that it had been heard a few centuries earlier by Bernardino Daniello (1568), as was pointed out by Hollander (Holl.1983.1), pp. 132–34. Now that we have a published text of the commentary of Trifon Gabriele (1525), we can see that he was the first to notice this clear citation.

Freccero (Frec.1986.1), pp. 207–8, has noted a program of "effacement" in Dante's three citations of Virgil here. In verse 21 a Latin quotation; in verse 48 a literal Italian translation; in these lines, what he characterizes as "the merest allusion." This last may seem a bit too "effacing." See Hollander (Holl.1993.1), pp. 249, 317–18, who believes it is a full-fledged citation.

52. The sense of this verse is that all that Eve lost and Dante has now regained could not ease his pain at the loss of Virgil.

54. Dante's tears have reminded a number of readers, beginning with Tommaseo (1837), of the tears of Boethius that were wiped away by Lady Philosophy in the *Consolation of Philosophy* I.ii(pr).

55. This verse is perhaps the climax of the poem. Everything before it leads here. And once Dante is named, his new mission begins to take form, first as Beatrice has him cleanse himself of his past crimes and misdemeanors. (His "vacation" in the garden of Eden is over.) For the uniqueness of this self-nomination, see the note to v. 63, below.

It is in response to this verse that Dante's son Pietro offered his celebrated "etymology" of his father's Christian name (1340): ". . . nominatus erat auctor Dantes, ita dabat, sive dedit se ad diversa; scilicet primo ad theologiam, secundo ad poetica" (the author was named Dante, as in "he was giving" or "he gave" himself to diverse things, first of all to theology and then to poetry).

56–57. The thrice-repeated verb *piangere* (weep) offered by Beatrice in reproof to Dante echoes and rebukes the thrice-repeated plangent calling of Virgil's name by Dante in vv. 49–51.

58.   This striking and unsettling similetic presentation of Beatrice as admiral has drawn a mixed press. It is all very well to argue, as Hollander has done (Holl.1969.1), pp. 122–23, 159, 190, that Dante has prepared for this moment by staging a significant series of voyages within the poem in which he calls attention to a commanding officer standing on a poop deck. (The word *poppa* appears at some highly charged moments: *Inf.* XXVI.124, when Ulysses turns his poop deck away from the east, and XXVI.140, when the poop of his sinking vessel rises from the swallowing sea before its final plunge; *Purg.* II.43, the afterdeck upon which the "heavenly pilot" stands as the saved souls come to shore; and now, in its penultimate appearance in the poem, the place where Beatrice seems to stand as she joins the pageant. The word will appear only once more, at *Par.* XXVII.146, in the last world-prophecy in the poem, when an eventually benevolent storm at sea will set our erring "fleet" right, turning our poops to where our prows had been in our misdirected quests.) "Admiral Beatrice" seems, nonetheless, a bit overdone to most of Dante's readers, including Scott (Scot.1972.1), who, like Hollander, sees the necessary theological trappings of her role, but is not altogether happy with the resultant poetic image.

No other segment of the *Commedia* is as filled with similes as the first ninety-nine verses of this canto; there are seven in all. And they take up more than half of the text, fully fifty-five lines of it. This one (and we will not be confronted by another in this canto) is clearly meant to be read as climactic. If we are troubled by Dante's "Admiral Beatrice," we must also realize that the poet has chosen to disturb us in this way.

63.   Dante's insistence that he names himself only from necessity echoes a passage in *Convivio* (I.ii.12–14), in which Dante says that there are two reasons that excuse an author's speaking of himself: first, and as in the case of Boethius's *Consolatio*, in order to defend oneself from harm or against infamy; second, as in the case of Augustine's *Confessions*, in order to bring greatly useful instruction to others. Freccero (Frec.1986.1), in his article "Dante's Prologue Scene" (1966), deals with the Augustinian confessional mode as modeling and justifying Dante's own (pp. 1–3).

There was a tradition honored by many classical and medieval writers that one should only name oneself at the *incipit* and/or *explicit* of one's work (i.e., "Here begins [or concludes] the such-and-such of so-and-so"). Years ago the present writer (Holl.1983.1, p. 133, n. 24) thought that he had discovered a notable fact. It is widely appreciated that Dante only named himself once in the body of any of his extended works, here in verse 55. What had not been noted was that his self-nomination echoed the only self-nomination found in the extended works of Virgil, indeed in the very *Georgic* (IV.563, "Vergilium") that Dante had cited a few lines earlier (vv. 525–527 at *Purg.* XXX.49–51). With the publication of Trifon Gabriele's commentary (Gabr.1993.1), it became apparent that at least one earlier commentator had made the same discovery in his comment to this verse, where he says that, in naming himself, Dante wished to imitate Virgil's self-nomination ("volendo imitar Virgilio . . . *illo Vergilium me tempore*").

For the resonance here of an earlier claim, that his book is a true record of events, recording only what had actually occurred, see the note to *Inferno* XXIX.54–57.

65. The veil *(velo)* worn by Beatrice is insisted on fully three times (at vv. 31 and 67 as well), and the canto has also begun with this word (verse 3). (No other canto contains so many occurrences of the word.) The climax of this scene with Beatrice will occur when she, bridelike, unveils herself at the end of the next canto (*Purg.* XXXI.136–145).

68. The second (and now overt) reference to Minerva in association with Beatrice (see the note to vv. 31–33) probably, in conjunction with other references that are still more direct, associates her with Christ, or Sapience, the Word made flesh, the second person of the Trinity.

73–75. Verse 73 is problematic, as Singleton (1973) explains clearly: "*Guardaci*: Commentators differ in their interpretation of *ci* here. It could be the pronoun, in which case Beatrice, in her regal manner, would be using the plural of majesty, speaking as a monarch would, in the first person plural. This reading is often accompanied by "ben sem, ben sem" in the rest of the verse, continuing such a plural (*sem = siamo*). Or *ci* might be construed as the adverb *qui*, in which case the rest of the verse is usually given in the reading here adopted."

That Beatrice speaks the word *ben* (here meaning "really," but also carrying its root sense, "good" or "well") three times in order to echo the triple iteration of "Virgil" (vv. 49–51) and of "weep" (vv. 56–57) was first noted by Tommaseo (1837).

Beatrice's anger at wayward Dante, saved by mercies in Heaven that seem hardly to have been predictable, given his behavior, is not difficult to fathom. But he has survived. Now, face to face with the beatified woman who has interceded for him, he weeps for Virgil, compounding his failing past behavior by now missing his pagan guide instead of rejoicing in the presence of Beatrice.

76–78.   This fairly obvious reference to Ovid's Narcissus (*Metam.* III.339–510) was perhaps first discussed by Brownlee (Brow.1978.1). See the note to *Inferno* XXX.126–129 and that to vv. 85–99, below.

82–84.   For the commentators' failure to recognize the problematic nature of this tercet, see Hollander (Holl.1973.1), p. 149, n. 2. As for the pointed reference to *pedes meos* (my feet), among the few who have believed that there is a "solution" to Dante's riddle, there are two schools. What does it mean to say the angels "did not sing past '*pedes meos*' "? Freccero (Frec.1961.2) and Pézard (Peza.1965.1), p. 1335, both believe that the reference is limited to the end of the ninth verse ("You [God] have not given me over to my enemies, but have *set my feet in a spacious place*") of Psalm 30 (31:8), the words *pedes meos* understood as reflecting Dante's newly gained freedom of the will to move about the garden as he chooses. Mineo (Mine.1968.1) and Hollander, partly because Dante's very way of expressing himself asks us to (if someone tells us he has not gone farther than nine we realize he is telling us that he did not reach ten), argue for the relevance of the next verse in Psalm 30, which is a citation of the opening verse of Psalm 50, "Have mercy on me, O Lord," the *Miserere* of David's penitential song that serves as source for Dante's first spoken words in the *Commedia* (*Inf.* I.65). In this understanding, the angels, intervening on Dante's behalf with stern Beatrice, deliberately stop short of the *Miserere* out of sympathy for poor Dante, so heavily chastised by Beatrice. (See the note to vv. 103–108, below.)

85–99.   For a history of the exegesis examining Dante's tears, mainly given over to attack and counterattack over the issue of the contorted and artificial nature of the simile, see Mazzoni (Mazz.1988.1), pp. 180–89. Mazzoni goes on (pp. 189–90) to bring three sources to bear: first two similes in Ovid: the melting of Ovid's Narcissus in his self-love (*Metam.* III.486–490, a passage discussed in this context in the nineteenth century by Luigi Venturi and Cesari, according to Trucchi [1936]; and see Brownlee [Brow.1978.1] and Shoaf [Shoa.1989.1]) and the liquefaction of Biblis when her brother, Caunus, rejects her incestuous love (*Metam.* IX.659–665, also previously noted by Trucchi [1936]). Mazzoni's major interpretive novelty (pp. 207–12) lies in his seeing Dante's tears as reflecting the liquefaction in Psalm 147:16–18 as commented on by St.

Augustine (in *Ps. CLVIII Enarratio* [Patrologia Latina, XXXVIII, col. 1931]): "He gives snow like wool; he scatters the hoarfrost like ashes. / He casts forth his ice like morsels; who can stand before his cold? / He sends out his word, and melts *[liquefacit]* them; he causes his wind to blow, and the waters flow." Augustine's gloss has it that a sinner, "frozen" in his sinfulness, may yet "liquefy" and be saved.

85.   The phrase "living beams" is Dante's way of referring to trees as the eventual source of wooden beams that may be hewn from them.

103–108.   The point of Beatrice's gentle rebuke of the angels is that they, aware of Dante's past sins and of his eventual salvation, are now seeing him primarily as a saved soul rather than as a formerly sinful one, as Beatrice now (and vehemently) does. In her view, they are celebrating his salvation prematurely because they are seeing it *sub specie eternitatis,* beyond the time that still holds him bound.

103–105.   For the resonance of Ovid's tale of Argus (*Metam.* I.625–721), with his vision that seems limited, for all its seeing, when compared with the total sight of these angels, see Levenstein (Leve.1996.1), pp. 194–95.

109–114.   Pietrobono (1946) points out that in *Convivio* IV.xxi. 7–8, Dante had already revealed his theory of the relationship among the elements of the individual human soul: the fathering sower, the embryo, and the astral influences of the constellations of the zodiac that shape its human talents. In this passage we hear about God, who breathes in last the vital element, the intellectual, or rational, soul. The passage at *Purgatorio* XXV.68–75 explains that the generation of the rational soul is performed directly by God; here we learn that not even the saved in the Empyrean nor the angels can understand the love that moves God in the creation of that soul in each of his human creatures.

115–117.   It seems obvious to most readers today that the phrase *vita nova* refers, if in its Latin form, to Dante's first prosimetrum, the thirty-one poems collected with prose commentary known as *The New Life*. And it seemed so to at least one very early commentator, the Ottimo (1333). However, here is the commentary of Benvenuto da Imola to this passage (1380): "This man, i.e., Dante, was such in his new life, i.e., in his boyhood; others, however, refer to his treatise *De vita nova,* which he composed in his youth. But it is surely ridiculous to do so, seeing that the author was ashamed of it in his maturity." Benvenuto's enthusiastic pre-humanist reading of the *Comedy* will only accept an allegorical, theologized Beatrice who bears no resemblance to the mortal girl of the early work.

One finds, even among recent commentators, a certain desire to avoid committing oneself to what seems completely obvious: the phrase *vita nova* cannot help but call to mind, in this context, the work that records Beatrice's lasting impact on Dante, first in his "new life" (when they were both children, a time to which Dante refers in verse 42: "before I had outgrown my childhood") and then later on, as recorded in the book called "The New Life."

118–138. Moore's essay, "The Reproaches of Beatrice" (Moor.1903.1), pp. 221–52, remains one of the most valuable attempts to deal with this convoluted expression of the single most important explanation Dante offers with regard to what he now conceives to have been his chief errors before he wrote the *Commedia*.

118–123. Beatrice offers an epitome of the main narrative of the *Vita nuova*, according to which for some sixteen years (1274–1290) she attempted to lead Dante to God, despite his natural sinful disposition. Unfortunately, even while she lived, the "rich soil" of his soul grew weeds.

124–126. Upon Beatrice's death, and according to Dante's own report in the *Vita nuova* (chapters XXXV–XXXIX), he did indeed give himself to at least one other (*altrui* can be either singular or plural in Dante). His probably most egregious dalliance was with the *donna gentile* (noble lady) who sympathized with his distress.

The lady is later allegorized, in Dante's *Convivio*, as the Lady Philosophy. (For discussion, see the note to *Purg.* XXXIII.85–90.)

134. The sort of dream Beatrice prayed God to send Dante is probably well represented by the dream of the Siren in *Purgatorio* XIX. 7–32. That accounts for the first part of Beatrice's formulation, i.e., Dante was given negative dreams about his disastrous love for the wrong lady. What about the second? What God-sent "inspirations" was she granted in order to call him back to loving her even after her death? Scartazzini (1900) offers a simple and compelling hypothesis (apparently silently acceded to by any number of later commentators, who make the same point without even

a mention of his name). In *Vita nuova* XXXIX.1, Dante receives the image of the girlish Beatrice in his phantasy, the image-receiving part of his mind (one may compare the ecstatic visions vouchsafed him for the exemplary figures on the terrace of Wrath [and see the note to *Purg.* XV.85–114]). As he recounts (*VN* XXXIX.2–6), this vision of Beatrice had the necessary effect, and he resolved to love her yet again, turning away his affection from the *donna gentile*. And then, Scartazzini continues, he was allowed the final vision of Beatrice seated in the Empyrean (*VN* XLII.1). Thus, as seems clear, while Dante slept, God sent him dreams of what was unworthy in his love for the *donna gentile;* while he was awake, positive images of Beatrice. If this program is correctly perceived, it matches precisely the mode employed to teach penitents on the mountain, positive and negative examples teaching what to follow and what to flee. Unfortunately, even after such encouragement, Dante would fall again. See the note to *Purgatorio* XXXIII.85–90.

139–141.   Poor Virgil! He has done the Christians sixty-four cantos' worth of service, guiding their great poet to his redemption and vision, and now the very lady who sought his help does not even mention his name; he is but "colui" (the one who). Where is Virgil now? On his way back to Limbo, we must assume. And thus, we may also assume, to another sad welcome from his fellow poets once he is again (less than a week after he had already returned once [see note to *Inf.* IV.80–81]) among them in his *etterno essilio* (eternal exile—*Purg.* XXI.18). We shall only hear his name twice more (*Par.* XVII.19 and XXVI.118) and never again from Beatrice, who uses it only once, in her first words, coupling it with Dante's (verse 55), and then to shame Dante for his affection for Virgil when there are more important feelings he should feel.

142–145.   As Beatrice wept in Virgil's presence in hell for Dante's sake (verse 141), so now it is Dante's turn to weep for the sins that made her intervention necessary. The angels may want to celebrate the eventual triumph of this saved Christian; Beatrice is here to make sure that he observes the ritual of the completion of purgation correctly, even on this trial run.

PURGATORIO XXXI

OUTLINE

The Church Triumphant in the Garden: climax
I. Confession

II. Contrition

heavy, subject to other bowshots: the young bird
may stay still for two or three, but in the sight of
the adult bird arrows and nets are deployed in vain

III. Satisfaction

Postlude: the eyes and smile of Beatrice

"O tu che se' di là dal fiume sacro,"
volgendo suo parlare a me per punta,
3   che pur per taglio m'era paruto acro,

ricominciò, seguendo sanza cunta,
"dì, dì se questo è vero; a tanta accusa
6   tua confession conviene esser congiunta."

Era la mia virtù tanto confusa,
che la voce si mosse, e pria si spense
9   che da li organi suoi fosse dischiusa.

Poco sofferse; poi disse: "Che pense?
Rispondi a me; ché le memorie triste
12   in te non sono ancor da l'acqua offense."

Confusione e paura insieme miste
mi pinsero un tal "sì" fuor de la bocca,
15   al quale intender fuor mestier le viste.

Come balestro frange, quando scocca
da troppa tesa, la sua corda e l'arco,
18   e con men foga l'asta il segno tocca,

sì scoppia' io sottesso grave carco,
fuori sgorgando lagrime e sospiri,
21   e la voce allentò per lo suo varco.

Ond' ella a me: "Per entro i mie' disiri,
che ti menavano ad amar lo bene
24   di là dal qual non è a che s'aspiri,

quai fossi attraversati o quai catene
trovasti, per che del passare innanzi
27   dovessiti così spogliar la spene?

'O you on the far side of the sacred stream,'
turning the point of her words on me

3   that had seemed sharp enough when I felt their edge,

she then went on without a pause: 'Say it,
say if this is true. To such an accusation

6   your confession must be joined.'

My faculties were so confounded
that my voice struggled up but spent itself

9   before it made its way out of my mouth.

For a moment she held back, then asked:
'What are you thinking? Speak, for your memories

12   of sin have not been washed away by water yet.'

Confusion and fear, mixed together,
drove from my mouth a *yes*—

15   but one had need of eyes to hear it.

As a crossbow breaks with too much tension
from the pulling taut of cord and bow

18   so that the arrow strikes the target with less force,

thus I collapsed beneath that heavy load
and, with a flood of tears and sighs,

21   my voice came strangled from my throat.

At that she said to me: 'In your desire for me
that guided you to love that good

24   beyond which there is nothing left to long for,

'what ditches or what chains did you encounter
across your path to make you cast aside

27   all hope of going forward?

E quali agevolezze o quali avanzi
ne la fronte de li altri si mostraro,
30   per che dovessi lor passeggiare anzi?"

Dopo la tratta d'un sospiro amaro,
a pena ebbi la voce che rispuose,
33   e le labbra a fatica la formaro.

Piangendo dissi: "Le presenti cose
col falso lor piacer volser miei passi,
36   tosto che 'l vostro viso si nascose."

Ed ella: "Se tacessi o se negassi
ciò che confessi, non fora men nota
39   la colpa tua: da tal giudice sassi!

Ma quando scoppia de la propria gota
l'accusa del peccato, in nostra corte
42   rivolge sé contra 'l taglio la rota.

Tuttavia, perché mo vergogna porte
del tuo errore, e perché altra volta,
45   udendo le serene, sie più forte,

pon giù il seme del piangere e ascolta:
sì udirai come in contraria parte
48   mover dovieti mia carne sepolta.

Mai non t'appresentò natura o arte
piacer, quanto le belle membra in ch'io
51   rinchiusa fui, e che so' 'n terra sparte;

e se 'l sommo piacer sì ti fallio
per la mia morte, qual cosa mortale
54   dovea poi trarre te nel suo disio?

Ben ti dovevi, per lo primo strale
de le cose fallaci, levar suso
57   di retro a me che non era più tale.

'And what profit or advantage showed
in the face of other things so that you felt
30   you must parade yourself before them?'

After heaving a bitter sigh
I hardly had the voice to give the answer
33   my lips were laboring to shape.

In tears, I said: 'Things set in front of me,
with their false delights, turned back my steps
36   the moment that Your countenance was hidden.'

'Had you stayed silent or denied what you confess,'
she said, 'your fault would not be any less apparent
39   since it is known to such a Judge.

'But when a man's own blushing cheek reveals
the condemnation of his sin, in our high court
42   the grindstone dulls the sharp edge of the sword.

'Nonetheless, so that you now may bear
the shame of your shameful straying and next time,
45   when you hear the Sirens' call, be stronger,

'stop sowing tears and listen.
Then you shall hear just how my buried flesh
48   should have directed you to quite a different place.

'Never did art or nature set before you beauty
as great as in the lovely members that enclosed me,
51   now scattered and reduced to dust.

'And if the highest beauty failed you
in my death, what mortal thing
54   should then have drawn you to desire it?

'Indeed, at the very first arrow
of deceitful things, you should have risen up
57   and followed me who was no longer of them.

Non ti dovea gravar le penne in giuso,
ad aspettar più colpo, o pargoletta
60   o altra novità con sì breve uso.

Novo augelletto due o tre aspetta;
ma dinanzi da li occhi d'i pennuti
63   rete si spiega indarno o si saetta."

Quali fanciulli, vergognando, muti
con li occhi a terra stannosi, ascoltando
66   e sé riconoscendo e ripentuti,

tal mi stav' io; ed ella disse: "Quando
per udir se' dolente, alza la barba,
69   e prenderai più doglia riguardando."

Con men di resistenza si dibarba
robusto cerro, o vero al nostral vento
72   o vero a quel de la terra di Iarba,

ch'io non levai al suo comando il mento;
e quando per la barba il viso chiese,
75   ben conobbi il velen de l'argomento.

E come la mia faccia si distese,
posarsi quelle prime creature
78   da loro aspersïon l'occhio comprese;

e le mie luci, ancor poco sicure,
vider Beatrice volta in su la fiera
81   ch'è sola una persona in due nature.

Sotto 'l suo velo e oltre la rivera
vincer pariemi più sé stessa antica,
84   vincer che l'altre qui, quand' ella c'era.

Di penter sì mi punse ivi l'ortica,
che di tutte altre cose qual mi torse
87   più nel suo amor, più mi si fé nemica.

'You should not have allowed your wings to droop,
leaving you to other darts from some young girl
60   or other novelty of such brief use.

'The fledgling may allow even a third attempt,
but all in vain is the net flung or arrow shot
63   in sight of a full-fledged bird.'

As children in their shame stand mute, their eyes
upon the ground, listening,
66   acknowledging their fault, repentant,

just so I stood. And then she said: 'Now that
you are grieved by what you hear, lift up your beard
69   and you shall have more grief from what you see.'

With less resistance is the sturdy oak
torn from the earth, whether by our northern wind
72   or by the one that blows from Iarbas' lands,

than was my chin nudged up by her command.
When by my beard she sought my face
75   I recognized the venom in her words.

And when I had raised my head
my eyes saw that those first-created beings
78   had paused in scattering their flowers

and, my vision blurred and still uncertain,
saw Beatrice turning toward the beast
81   that is one person in two natures.

Even beneath her veil, even beyond the stream,
she seemed to surpass her former self in beauty
84   more than she had on earth surpassed all others.

The nettle of remorse so stung me then
that whatever else had lured me most to loving
87   had now become for me most hateful.

Tanta riconoscenza il cor mi morse,
ch'io caddi vinto; e quale allora femmi,
90   salsi colei che la cagion mi porse.

Poi, quando il cor virtù di fuor rendemmi,
la donna ch'io avea trovata sola
93   sopra me vidi, e dicea: "Tiemmi, tiemmi!"

Tratto m'avea nel fiume infin la gola,
e tirandosi me dietro sen giva
96   sovresso l'acqua lieve come scola.

Quando fui presso a la beata riva,
"*Asperges me*" sì dolcemente udissi,
99   che nol so rimembrar, non ch'io lo scriva.

La bella donna ne le braccia aprissi;
abbracciommi la testa e mi sommerse
102   ove convenne ch'io l'acqua inghiottissi.

Indi mi tolse, e bagnato m'offerse
dentro a la danza de le quattro belle;
105   e ciascuna del braccio mi coperse.

"Noi siam qui ninfe e nel ciel siamo stelle;
pria che Beatrice discendesse al mondo,
108   fummo ordinate a lei per sue ancelle.

Merrenti a li occhi suoi; ma nel giocondo
lume ch'è dentro aguzzeranno i tuoi
111   le tre di là, che miran più profondo."

Così cantando cominciaro; e poi
al petto del grifon seco menarmi,
114   ove Beatrice stava volta a noi.

Disser: "Fa che le viste non risparmi;
posto t'avem dinanzi a li smeraldi
117   ond' Amor già ti trasse le sue armi."

Such knowledge of my fault was gnawing at my heart
that I was overcome, and what I then became
90   she knows who was the reason for my state.

Then, when my heart restored my vital signs,
I saw the lady I first found alone above me,
93   saying: 'Hold on to me and hold me fast!'

She drew me into the river up to my throat
and, pulling me along behind her, moved
96   upon the water as lightly as a skiff.

When I had come close to the blessèd shore
I heard *'Asperges me'* so sweetly sung
99   that I cannot recall nor write it down.

The lovely lady spread her arms,
then clasped my head, and plunged me under,
102   where I was forced to swallow water.

Then she drew me out and led me, bathed,
into the dance of the four lovely ladies
105   as each one raised an arm above my head.

'Here we are nymphs and in heaven we are stars.
Before Beatrice descended to the world
108   we were ordained to serve her as her handmaids.

'We will bring you to her eyes. But to receive
the joyous light they hold, the other three,
111   who look much deeper into things, shall sharpen yours.'

Thus they began their song and then
they took me to the griffin's breast,
114   where Beatrice stood and faced us.

They said: 'Do not withhold your gaze.
We have placed you here before the emeralds
117   from which, some time ago, Love shot his darts.'

Mille disiri più che fiamma caldi
strinsermi li occhi a li occhi rilucenti,
120   che pur sopra 'l grifone stavan saldi.

Come in lo specchio il sol, non altrimenti
la doppia fiera dentro vi raggiava,
123   or con altri, or con altri reggimenti.

Pensa, lettor, s'io mi maravigliava,
quando vedea la cosa in sé star queta,
126   e ne l'idolo suo si trasmutava.

Mentre che piena di stupore e lieta
l'anima mia gustava di quel cibo
129   che, saziando di sé, di sé asseta,

sé dimostrando di più alto tribo
ne li atti, l'altre tre si fero avanti,
132   danzando al loro angelico caribo.

"Volgi, Beatrice, volgi li occhi santi,"
era la sua canzone, "al tuo fedele
135   che, per vederti, ha mossi passi tanti!

Per grazia fa noi grazia che disvele
a lui la bocca tua, sì che discerna
138   la seconda bellezza che tu cele."

O isplendor di viva luce etterna,
chi palido si fece sotto l'ombra
141   sì di Parnaso, o bevve in sua cisterna,

che non paresse aver la mente ingombra,
tentando a render te qual tu paresti
là dove armonizzando il ciel t'adombra,
145   quando ne l'aere aperto ti solvesti?

A thousand desires hotter than any flame
bound my eyes to those shining eyes,
120   which still stayed fixed upon the griffin.

Even as the sun in a mirror, not otherwise
the twofold beast shone forth in them,
123   now with the one, now with its other nature.

Consider, reader, whether I was struck by wonder
when I saw the thing itself remain as one
126   but in its image ever changing.

While my soul, filled with wonder and with joy,
tasted the food that, satisfying in itself,
129   yet for itself creates a greater craving,

the other three, who by their bearing
showed themselves of a higher order, moved forward,
132   dancing to their angelic roundelay.

'Turn, Beatrice, turn your holy eyes
upon your faithful one'—thus ran their song—
135   'who, to see you, now has come so far.

'Of your grace do us a grace: unveil
your mouth to him so that he may observe
138   the second beauty that you still conceal.'

O splendor of eternal living light—
even he who has grown pale in the shadow of Parnassus
141   or has drunk deeply from its well,

would not even he appear to have his mind confounded,
attempting to describe you as you looked,
Heaven with its harmonies reflected in you,
145   when in the wide air you unveiled yourself?

1.   Beatrice's words, perhaps reminiscent of Virgil's to the cowering, hiding Dante in *Inferno* XXI.88–90, call his (and our) attention to the fact that he has not yet crossed Lethe, i.e., he still has his sins in mind, as will be hammered home by vv. 11–12.

2–3.   The metaphor of Beatrice's speech as a "sword" picks up her earlier promise that Dante will weep for "another sword" beside that of Virgil's departure (*Purg.* XXX.57). The lengthy speech that she had directed to the angels (*Purg.* XXX.103–145) was in fact aimed squarely at him, using the angels as her apparent primary auditors in such a way as to publicize his sins and thus shame the protagonist. In this sense, then, the point of her "sword" had seemed aimed at them, while she was wounding Dante (if painfully enough, as we have seen) with only the edge of the blade. Now he finds her sword pointing straight at his heart.

5–6.   Beatrice calls for Dante's confession with specific reference to the list of charges against him that she had leveled in the last canto (*Purg.* XXX.124–132).

10–11.   *Che pense?* (What are you thinking?): Tommaseo was apparently the first to hear the resonance of Virgil's identical question to Francesca-dazzled Dante in *Inferno* V.111. Now see Pertile (Pert.1993.3), p. 389.
    It is perhaps not coincidental that Dante's first two guides, in scenes that are confessional in nature, both prod him to consider the conflicting natures of lust and charity with the same question.

16–21.   Dante's attempt to discharge the dart of his speech from the crossbow that collapses under the tension of his situation produces a more audible emission of tears and sighs than of true confessions, which he can barely whisper.

22–24.   Perhaps nowhere before or after does the poet make the nature of the love the protagonist should have had for Beatrice clearer than here. His desire for her should have led him to God.

25–30.   Beatrice, given Dante's muteness, rehashes the charges we had heard in the last canto (*Purg.* XXX.124–132), now substituting a fresh set of metaphors for those we found there (see the note to *Purg.*

XXX.118–138). There we heard that after Beatrice's death (1) he gave himself to another (or "to others"; the Italian *altrui* is ambiguous and may be singular or plural); (2) he chose a wrong path, "pursuing false images of good." Now he is presented first as warrior and then as lover. In the first tercet he is like a soldier (or an army) cut off from his pursuit of his goal by the defensive ditches or chains deployed by an enemy; in the second he is like a courting swain who parades before the house of the woman with whom he is infatuated. In the first case, once he loses his Beatrice he no longer advances toward God; in the second, he moves toward another and improper destination. He was turned by his love for the *donna gentile*, who, we may remember (*VN* XXXV.2), was seated at her window and looked pityingly at Dante, who then "parades" before her a pair of sonnets (*VN* XXXV.15–18; XXXVI.14–15). If, in the *Vita nuova*, he finally returns to his love for Beatrice and is rewarded with a vision of her in the Empyrean, in *Convivio* he is writing about the *donna gentile* again, now as having finally displaced Beatrice in his affections. He had looked for consolation from this lady, he says, but he had instead found gold (*Conv.* II.xii.5).

For this writer's view of this complex matter see Hollander (Holl.1969.1), pp. 159–69. And see, more recently, Picone (Pico.1992.1), pp. 205–12.

31–33.   Here begins Dante's confession. Mazzoni (Mazz.1965.2), p. 62, rightly observes (as, for instance, Singleton [1973] does not) that the confession will be followed by his contrition and then by his giving satisfaction. These three elements in the rite of confession, in that perhaps puzzling order, occupy the first 102 verses of this canto, with first confession and then contrition, occupying vv. 31–90 (for the traditional order, see the note to *Purg.* IX.94–102).

34–36.   Finally Dante confesses, summarizing his transgressions as delight in false things set before him after Beatrice was dead. Exactly what these pleasures were is a question that greatly exercises Dante scholars. It does seem clear that they are presented in so vague and encompassing a way as to allow two primary interpretations, that is, both carnal and intellectual divagations from the love he owed God, awakened in him by Beatrice.

36.   Dante's first words to Beatrice set a pattern that will not be broken until *Paradiso* XXXI.80: Dante addresses her with the honorific *voi*. See the note to *Purgatorio* XIX.131.

37–39.   Beatrice accepts his confession. That word has already been used at verse 6, underlining the precise nature of what is happening here (words for "confession" only occur three times in *Purgatorio*, where we might expect them to be more common, twice in this canto).

45.   The reference to the Sirens draws us back to *Purgatorio* XIX.19–33, the dream of the Siren and (as at least a few interpreters agree) Beatrice's intervention in Dante's dream to have Virgil show him the ugliness of the object of his infatuation. See the note to *Purgatorio* XIX.31–33.

The Ottimo (1333) is one of the very few commentators to think of Boethius's dismissal of the Sirens (who have so harmed him) in favor of the Muses of Lady Philosophy (*Cons.* I.i[pr]).

46.   Tommaseo (1837) was apparently the first to explain the strange phrase "to sow tears" by referring to the Bible, Psalm 125:5 (126:5), "those that sow in tears shall reap in joy." Even so, Dante has made the Psalmist more difficult than he had in fact been: "sowing tears" is not quite the same thing as "sowing in tears" (i.e., planting seed while weeping).

47–54.   Beatrice's phrasing offers a good example of the cause of the difficulty many have in interpreting her role in this poem. She tells Dante that her buried flesh should have led him elsewhere from where he elected to go (in this context, clearly to other women [*cosa mortale*, "mortal thing"]). This is not because she was more beautiful in her fleshly being than they, but because she offered him what they did and could not, "il sommo piacer" (the highest beauty). The verbal noun *piacer* is used only once in the first half of the poem (it describes Paolo's physical attractiveness at *Inf.* V.104). When it is found again (at *Purg.* XVIII.21), it then occurs thirty-four times in the second half, twenty-one of these in *Paradiso*. It is often used to denote the highest beauty of all, that of God. The word is used three times in this canto (vv. 35, 50, 52), its densest presence in the *Comedy*. The false beauty of Beatrice's rivals (verse 35) should have been countered by the highest beauty that he had found in her. The phrase "sommo piacer" was traditionally interpreted as referring to Beatrice as the most beautiful of all mortals. I.e., Dante's failure was in chasing after women who were not as beautiful as she was. This disastrous interpretation, undermined by the very antithesis present in Beatrice's formulations, *sommo piacer / cosa mortale*, which polarizes divine and human beauty, was intelligently dismissed in Mazzoni's gloss

(Mazz.1965.2), pp. 67–72. Mazzoni demonstrates that Dante is relying upon the Victorine tradition that discussed the beauty of God, even as it was manifest in individual human beings, the *summa pulchritudo* (highest beauty) in the phrase of Hugh of St. Victor (p. 68). (For a study of Dante's ideas about beauty see John Took [Took.1984.1].)

55–57.   Beatrice's next installment drives the point home, again separating the spiritual from the physical—if readers tend to fail to notice what she has done. The "deceitful" things of this world are distinguished from those of the next in that Beatrice tells Dante that, once she was no longer associated with this world, his affection should have followed her upward.

58–60.   We are given yet another (now the third) version of Dante's sins after Beatrice's death (see the note to vv. 25–30). Instead of flying up after dead Beatrice's spirit, the wings of his affection drooped down to earth in search of a *pargoletta* (young girl)—the sexual note is struck again—or "other novelty of such brief use," a phrasing that would again allow the understanding that Dante's divagation also involved some sort of intellectual experiment that now seems without eventual value.

62–63.   See Proverbs 1:17, "Frustra autem iacitur rete ante oculos pennatorum" (In vain is the net cast forth before the eyes of full-fledged birds). (The citation was first observed by Pietro Alighieri [1340].) Dante, as grown up "bird," should have been able to avoid capture by his huntress(es).

64–67.   Understandably, Dante is now compared, in simile, not to a mature man, who should have known better, but to a naughty boy.

68.   Continuing the motif introduced in the preceding simile, this verse has had the effect of convincing some readers that the usual portraits and busts of Dante are all incorrect in showing him as clean-shaven. However, all that is probably meant is that he was old enough to know better because he was old enough to shave. In the same vein, some have argued that Beatrice only indicates Dante's chin (*mento*, referred to in verse 73). Even so, his chin is "bearded" if he has to shave it. For a brief and cogent review of the argument, see Mazzoni (Mazz.1965.2), pp. 73–74. And for a hypothetical meditation on the iconographic valence of Dante's beardedness that essentially bypasses the issue that attracts most readers (and

which involves an astonishingly large bibliography)—whether Dante
meant us to understand that his face was bearded or not—see Shoaf
(Shoa.1986.1).

70–75. The formal "classical" simile is clear in its intent: Dante, for all
the reticence of his contrition, is finally won over. Its resonance, how-
ever, is subtle and not observed in the commentary tradition. Shoaf
(Shoa.1986.1), pp. 176–77, decodes the passage well. He points out that
Aeneid IV.196–278 presents Iarbas's appeal to Jupiter to intervene on his
behalf in his suit for widow Dido's hand, an appeal that results in
Mercury's coming to Aeneas to spur him to his Italian voyage. The sim-
ile that gives birth to this one is found, Shoaf continues, at *Aeneid*
IV.441–449, when Aeneas is compared to a deeply rooted oak tree buf-
feted by north winds when Dido makes her last-ditch appeal to him to
stay with her in Carthage. In the end, he remains strong enough in his
new resolve to deny her request and set sail. Here, the "new Aeneas,"
buffeted by the south wind, gives over his stubborn recalcitrance and ac-
cedes to the insistent demand of Beatrice, a new and better Dido, that he
express his contrition. Where it was good for Aeneas to resist the en-
treaties of his woman, it is also good for Dante to yield to Beatrice's.

77–78. Since Beatrice's hundred angels are not referred to directly
again, we can only conclude that, after this last act of theirs, they disap-
pear, either into thin air or else to fly back up to the Empyrean, along
with the rest of the Church Triumphant (see *Purg.* XXXII.89–90).
While the text guarantees no solution, the second hypothesis seems the
better one, if only because we have no reason to exempt them from the
general exodus that occurs at that point, even if their arrival is not clearly
accounted for (see the notes to *Purg.* XXX.16–18 and XXXII.89–90).

81. The phrasing "one person in two natures" makes it difficult to ac-
cept the arguments of those who believe the griffin is *not* a symbol of
Christ.

82. The word *velo* (veil) reminds us that the climactic moment of an
unveiling still lies before us. See the note to *Purgatorio* XXX.66.

85–90. The climax of Dante's contrition is performed as a fainting fit.
He is now ready to perform his act of satisfaction, forgetting all his diva-
gations, canceling them from his memory.

91–102. Dante's immersion in Lethe, supervised by Matelda, marks his final satisfaction of his confessor's demands on him. As we will see (*Purg.* XXXIII.91–99), his forgetting that he ever transgressed against Beatrice's instruction will be used by her as proof that he had indeed done so. Here we understand that his act of forgetting is an act of atonement, and is rewarded with absolution, indicated by the Latin song he hears as he completes his crossing of Lethe.

As for Dante's drinking of the waters, it has a Virgilian source, according to Pietro di Dante (1340) and, among the moderns, Mattalia (1960): in Lethe's waters the souls "longa oblivia potant" (drink in long forgetfulness [*Aen.* VI.715]). As we shall see at Eunoe (*Purg.* XXXIII.138), the ingestion of the waters of these two rivers is essential to the accomplishment of (here) leaving one's sins in oblivion and (there) securing in memory all the good things accomplished in one's mortal life.

Does Statius also drink of these waters? And does Matelda have oversight for his crossing of Lethe as well as Dante's? See the note to *Purg.* XXXIII.128–135.

The Ottimo (1333) identifies the phrase "Asperges me . . ." (Purge me [with hyssop, that I may be purified; wash me, and I shall be whiter than snow]) as deriving from "the penitential Psalm" (50:9 [51:7]) and goes on to report that the phrase is repeated in the rite of absolution when the priest blesses the confessed sinner with holy water. We have less certain information about who it is that sings the words. Among those commentators who venture an opinion, most assume it is the angels who sing, but it could be the (still unnamed) Matelda (as Porena [1946] admits, even though he prefers the angels). Since the angels have served as singers before (*Purg.* XXX.19, XXX.21, XXX.83–84), the most reasonable hypothesis seems to be that it is they who sing now, as well.

103–108. The four nymphs represent the four cardinal virtues (Justice, Prudence, Temperance, and Fortitude) in their primal form, i.e., as they were infused in Adam and Eve (and not acquired, as they have had to be ever after). God created the first humans, and no others, in this state. They are "nymphs" in that, like some classical nymphs, they inhabit a woodland landscape (Lombardi [1791]). The stars they are in heaven are probably (there is debate about this) identical with those we saw in *Purgatorio* I.23 (also referred to in I.37–39) and VIII.91, irradiating the face of Cato with their light. Dante thus seems to suggest that both Cato and Beatrice are of such special virtue that it seems that original sin did not affect them—a notion that could only be advanced in the sort of suggestive logic possible in poetry, for it is simply heretical. Dante never did say (or would have said) such a thing in prose.

The exact sense in which they served as the handmaids of Beatrice before she lived on earth is less easily determined. For two similar views of the problem see Singleton (Sing.1958.1), pp. 159–83, and Mazzoni (Mazz.1965.2), pp. 82–86. Both link the infused cardinal virtues to Beatrice's special role on earth, reflected in such passages as *Inferno* II.76–78, where she is addressed by Virgil as "donna di *virtù*" (lady of such virtue that by it alone / the human race surpasses all that lies / within the smallest compass of the heavens).

Botticelli-like (as in his *Primavera*, surely shaped by this scene), the four dancing maidens make a composite sign of the cross with their up-raised arms, which join over Dante's head. All redeemed sinners leave the garden of Eden on their way to glory in the moral condition that marked the creation of the first humans, before the Fall: primal innocence.

109–111.   The four cardinal virtues, representing the active life, insist that, while they are able to escort Dante to the eyes of Beatrice, their sister virtues, the theological three, at the right wheel of the chariot, are more appropriate presences to prepare Dante's vision for that moment.

112–114.   Beatrice has moved down from the chariot, from its left side, where she was looking at Dante across the stream (*Purg.* XXX.61 and 100), to, now that he has crossed it, a point in front of the chariot and of the griffin that draws it, so as to confront him.

115–117.   The four virtues prepare Dante to do something that will become, very quickly, the standard way of learning for the protagonist in this new Beatricean realm of the poem: gaze into her mirroring eyes.

123.   The word *reggimenti* (regiments, governments, regimes [in modern Italian]) would seem to give aid and comfort to those who have argued that this passage makes it difficult to argue for the traditional interpretation of the griffin as Christ. However, beginning with Venturi (1732), commentators have understood that here the word is synonymous with *atteggiamento* (in the sense of bearing, self-presentation). Daniello (1568 [118–123]) had previously understood the word as indicating that the griffin behaved "now as man, now as God."

124–126.   Dante's sixth address to his readers in *Purgatorio* asks that we share his wonder (see the note to *Inferno* VIII.94–96). The griffin himself is constant in his appearance, while his reflection in Beatrice's eyes, revealing his truer aspect, reflects, in turn, his divine and human natures.

127. *Stupore* (amazement, wonder) is again Dante's condition, now for the marvelous nature of his simultaneous perception of God's two natures. See the note to *Purgatorio* XXX.34–36.

128–129. Once again Scartazzini is the first commentator to find the likely citation behind Dante's words and to be followed, always without acknowledgment, by any number of twentieth-century discussants of the passage: Wisdom speaks in Ecclesiasticus 24:29: "He who eats of me will hunger again, who drinks of me will thirst again." That the speaker in this passage is Wisdom, the second person of the Trinity in Christian eyes, pleases Singleton (1973), who had argued earlier for the close relationship between Beatrice and Christ as Sapience (Sing.1958.1), pp. 122–34.

131. The "other three" are obviously the three theological virtues, Faith, Hope, and Charity, equally obviously of higher "rank" than the older classical cardinal virtues.

132. The word *caribo* has had extensive discussion among Dantists. Most currently agree that it indicates a particular dance, even if not an identifiable one. For extensive bibliography see Mazzoni (Mazz.1965.2), pp. 89–91.

133–138. The three theological virtues sing their appeal to Beatrice, requesting that she unveil her mouth. The moment recalls an experience recorded in *Convivio*. "Here it is necessary to know that the eyes of wisdom are her demonstrations, by which truth is seen with the greatest certainty, and her smiles are her persuasions, in which the inner light of wisdom [Sapienza] is revealed behind a kind of veil; and in each of them is felt the highest joy of blessedness, which is the greatest good of paradise. This joy cannot be found in anything here below except by looking into [her] eyes and upon her smile" (*Conv.* III.xv.2–3, trans. Lansing). It is important to know that these words are directed to *another* lady, also known as Wisdom, in the *Convivio*, namely the Lady Philosophy, the one who came as the replacement for the then supposedly less worthy Beatrice.

138. The *seconda bellezza* (second beauty) of Beatrice also may remind the reader of the "corollary" or extra gift that Matelda bestowed upon the three poets at the end of *Purgatorio* XXVIII (verse 136).

139–145.   The *luce etterna* (eternal living light) that is God has its *etterno piacer* (eternal beauty) reflected in Beatrice, her loveliness the mirror of the beauty of God.

This passage is reminiscent of that in *Purgatorio* XXVIII.139–148, the description of the smiles of recognition on the part of Virgil and of Statius when they discover that Eden represents the true Golden Age. No pagan poet, no matter how deeply inspired by drinking of the Castalian spring on Parnassus, could have written of the meaning of his vision of the Golden Age in a way that could come near to equaling what this Christian poet (by virtue of his faith, not of his talent), having now drunk of Lethe, can tell of God's love in making his first human creature innocent and allowing His creature a chance to regain that lost innocence, which is what Dante has been allowed to accomplish here, while still in the flesh, and what he will finally accomplish after his death.

143.   The pronoun *te* (the second person singular of "you") is jarring, in that we have already learned that Beatrice is to be addressed by Dante with the honorific *voi* (at verse 36). It takes us a moment to realize that it is not Beatrice whom he apostrophizes here, but her smile.

PURGATORIO XXXII

The pageant of the Church Militant

73–84   simile: Moses and Elijah disappeared from the view of Peter, John, and James after Christ was transfigured as Dante comes to himself and sees only Matelda

85–99   to Dante's query ("where is Beatrice?") Matelda replies that she is seated on the root of the tree

100–108 Beatrice's promise and command: here Dante will be a "forester" and then a citizen of the city of God; he must observe the chariot and record what he sees

109–160 the transformations of the Church in this world:

    109–117   1) eagle strikes the car [imperial persecutions]

    118–123   2) fox leaps into car [heresies]

    124–129   3) eagle feathers car [Donation of Constantine]

    130–135   4) dragon drives tail through car and makes off with some of its flooring [Mohammed]

    136–141   5) eagle feathers again [Charlemagne and Pepin]

    142–147   6) seven heads with ten horns [corrupt Church]

    148–160   7) harlot and giant; when she lusts after Dante, the giant drags her off, with the car [Avignon]

Tant' eran li occhi miei fissi e attenti
a disbramarsi la decenne sete,
3   che li altri sensi m'eran tutti spenti.

Ed essi quinci e quindi avien parete
di non caler—così lo santo riso
6   a sé traéli con l'antica rete!—;

quando per forza mi fu vòlto il viso
ver' la sinistra mia da quelle dee,
9   perch' io udi' da loro un "Troppo fiso!"

e la disposizion ch'a veder èe
ne li occhi pur testé dal sol percossi,
12   sanza la vista alquanto esser mi fée.

Ma poi ch'al poco il viso riformossi
(e dico "al poco" per rispetto al molto
15   sensibile onde a forza mi rimossi),

vidi 'n sul braccio destro esser rivolto
lo glorïoso essercito, e tornarsi
18   col sole e con le sette fiamme al volto.

Come sotto li scudi per salvarsi
volgesi schiera, e sé gira col segno,
21   prima che possa tutta in sé mutarsi;

quella milizia del celeste regno
che procedeva, tutta trapassonne
24   pria che piegasse il carro il primo legno.

Indi a le rote si tornar le donne,
e 'l grifon mosse il benedetto carco
27   sì, che però nulla penna crollonne.

My eyes were fixed and so intent
to satisfy ten years of thirst
3   that all my other senses were undone,

walled off from anything around them, enclosed
in their indifference, so did the holy smile
6   ensnare them in its old, familiar net,

when by the power of those goddesses
my gaze was forced to travel left
9   as they cried out: 'Too fixed!'

And then I shared the temporary blindness
of those whose eyes have just been smitten by the sun,
12   leaving me sightless for a time.

But after my eyes again became accustomed
to lesser sights—lesser, I mean, when compared
15   to the greater from which they'd been forced to turn—

I noted that the glorious army had wheeled around
on its right flank and now faced east,
18   with the seven candles and the sun before it.

As under cover of its shields a squadron
faces about to save itself, following the colors,
21   before the entire force can rearrange its ranks,

the soldiers of the heavenly kingdom
who were marching in the front passed by
24   before the chariot turned upon its yoke.

Then the ladies went back to their wheels
and the griffin moved its blessèd load,
27   but so that not a feather on it shook.

La bella donna che mi trasse al varco
e Stazio e io seguitavam la rota
30   che fé l'orbita sua con minore arco.

Sì passeggiando l'alta selva vòta,
colpa di quella ch'al serpente crese,
33   temprava i passi un'angelica nota.

Forse in tre voli tanto spazio prese
disfrenata saetta, quanto eramo
36   rimossi, quando Bëatrice scese.

Io senti' mormorare a tutti "Adamo";
poi cerchiaro una pianta dispogliata
39   di foglie e d'altra fronda in ciascun ramo.

La coma sua, che tanto si dilata
più quanto più è sù, fora da l'Indi
42   ne' boschi lor per altezza ammirata.

"Beato se', grifon, che non discindi
col becco d'esto legno dolce al gusto,
45   poscia che mal si torce il ventre quindi."

Così dintorno a l'albero robusto
gridaron li altri; e l'animal binato:
48   "Sì si conserva il seme d'ogne giusto."

E vòlto al temo ch'elli avea tirato,
trasselo al piè de la vedova frasca,
51   e quel di lei a lei lasciò legato.

Come le nostre piante, quando casca
giù la gran luce mischiata con quella
54   che raggia dietro a la celeste lasca,

turgide fansi, e poi si rinovella
di suo color ciascuna, pria che 'l sole
57   giunga li suoi corsier sotto altra stella;

The fair lady who had pulled me through the stream
and Statius and I were following the wheel
30   that in a smaller arc had made its turn.

Then, passing on beneath a vaulting forest,
emptied through fault of her who trusted in the snake,
33   we measured our steps to an angelic song.

We had proceeded perhaps as far as an arrow,
loosed three times from the string, would carry,
36   when Beatrice descended from the car.

I heard all of them murmuring 'Adam.'
Then they circled a tree stripped of its leaves
39   and any other flowering on its branches.

The higher its branches grew, the wider was their spread.
Its height would cause even the Indian,
42   in his towering forest, to gaze in wonder.

'Blessed are you, griffin, for not plundering
with your beak this tree's sweet-tasting fruit
45   that later wrenches bellies with its pain.'

Thus did those around the mighty tree cry out,
and the double-natured animal replied:
48   'This is how the seed of justice is preserved.'

Turning to the shaft that he had pulled,
he drew it to the foot of the widowed trunk
51   and left it bound to the tree from which it came.

As our plants, when the great light falls on them,
mingled with the light that shines
54   in the rays that follow the celestial carp,

begin to swell their buds and are renewed,
each in its proper color, before the sun
57   hitches his steeds to other stars,

men che di rose e più che di vïole
colore aprendo, s'innovò la pianta,
60   che prima avea le ramora sì sole.

Io non lo 'ntesi, né qui non si canta
l'inno che quella gente allor cantaro,
63   né la nota soffersi tutta quanta.

S'io potessi ritrar come assonnaro
li occhi spietati udendo di Siringa,
66   li occhi a cui pur vegghiar costò sì caro;

come pintor che con essempro pinga,
disegnerei com' io m'addormentai;
69   ma qual vuol sia che l'assonnar ben finga.

Però trascorro a quando mi svegliai,
e dico ch'un splendor mi squarciò 'l velo
72   del sonno, e un chiamar: "Surgi: che fai?"

Quali a veder de' fioretti del melo
che del suo pome li angeli fa ghiotti
75   e perpetüe nozze fa nel cielo,

Pietro e Giovanni e Iacopo condotti
e vinti, ritornaro a la parola
78   da la qual furon maggior sonni rotti,

e videro scemata loro scuola
così di Moïsè come d'Elia,
81   e al maestro suo cangiata stola;

tal torna' io, e vidi quella pia
sovra me starsi che conducitrice
84   fu de' miei passi lungo 'l fiume pria.

E tutto in dubbio dissi: "Ov' è Beatrice?"
Ond' ella: "Vedi lei sotto la fronda
87   nova sedere in su la sua radice.

so, taking on a hue less red than roses
yet deeper than violets, the tree renewed itself
60   where its branches just before had been so bare.

The hymn that company then chanted
is not sung on earth nor could I make it out,
63   nor bear to hear that music to its end.

Could I describe how those pitiless eyes,
hearing of Syrinx, were lulled to sleep,
66   the eyes whose lengthy vigil cost so dear,

I would fashion, as a painter does
when painting from a model, how I fell asleep.
69   But let him, who can do it, portray his nodding off.

I move along, therefore, to when I came awake
and say a brightness broke my veil of sleep,
72   as did the call: 'Arise, what are you doing?'

As, when brought to see the blossoms on the apple-tree
that makes the angels hungry for its fruit
75   and celebrates perpetual marriage-feasts in Heaven,

Peter and John and James were overcome,
called back into themselves at the word
78   by which still deeper sleep was broken,

and saw their company diminished
both by Moses and Elijah
81   and their teacher's raiment changed,

such did I become. I saw, standing above me,
the same compassionate lady
84   who had guided my steps along the river.

All in doubt I asked: 'Where is Beatrice?'
And she: 'Look there beneath the new-sprung blossoms
87   of the tree where she is seated on the root.

Vedi la compagnia che la circonda:
li altri dopo 'l grifon sen vanno suso
90   con più dolce canzone e più profonda."

E se più fu lo suo parlar diffuso,
non so, però che già ne li occhi m'era
93   quella ch'ad altro intender m'avea chiuso.

Sola sedeasi in su la terra vera,
come guardia lasciata lì del plaustro
96   che legar vidi a la biforme fera.

In cerchio le facevan di sé claustro
le sette ninfe, con quei lumi in mano
99   che son sicuri d'Aquilone e d'Austro.

"Qui sarai tu poco tempo silvano;
e sarai meco sanza fine cive
102   di quella Roma onde Cristo è romano.

Però, in pro del mondo che mal vive,
al carro tieni or li occhi, e quel che vedi,
105   ritornato di là, fa che tu scrive."

Così Beatrice; e io, che tutto ai piedi
d'i suoi comandamenti era divoto,
108   la mente e li occhi ov' ella volle diedi.

Non scese mai con sì veloce moto
foco di spessa nube, quando piove
111   da quel confine che più va remoto,

com' io vidi calar l'uccel di Giove
per l'alber giù, rompendo de la scorza,
114   non che d'i fiori e de le foglie nove;

e ferì 'l carro di tutta sua forza;
ond' el piegò come nave in fortuna,
117   vinta da l'onda, or da poggia, or da orza.

'See the company encircling her.
The others all ascend behind the griffin
90   with a song more sweet and more profound.'

I do not know if she had more to say,
for now, before my eyes, appeared the one
93   who had closed me off from any other thought.

On the bare ground she sat alone,
as if left behind to guard the chariot
96   I had seen the twofold beast make fast.

The seven nymphs encircled and enclosed her,
holding up lights that would not waver
99   should winds blow even from the north or south.

'Here for a time you shall be a woodsman
and then forever a citizen with me
102   of that Rome where Christ Himself is Roman.

'Therefore, to serve the world that lives so ill,
keep your eyes upon the chariot and write down
105   what now you see here once you have gone back.'

Thus Beatrice. And I, overwhelmed,
prostrate at the feet of her commands,
108   gave my mind and eyes to what she wished.

Never did fire descend with such swift motion
out of thickened banks of clouds,
111   plunging from the farthest zone of air,

as I saw the bird of Jove swoop down and plummet
through the tree, ripping the bark,
114   shredding flowers and fresh leaves.

It struck the chariot with its full force
so that it reeled like a ship tossed in a tempest,
117   now leeward, now windward, driven by the waves.

Poscia vidi avventarsi ne la cuna
del trïunfal veiculo una volpe
120   che d'ogne pasto buon parea digiuna;

ma, riprendendo lei di laide colpe,
la donna mia la volse in tanta futa
123   quanto sofferser l'ossa sanza polpe.

Poscia per indi ond' era pria venuta,
l'aguglia vidi scender giù ne l'arca
126   del carro e lasciar lei di sé pennuta;

e qual esce di cuor che si rammarca,
tal voce uscì del cielo e cotal disse:
129   "O navicella mia, com' mal se' carca!"

Poi parve a me che la terra s'aprisse
tr'ambo le ruote, e vidi uscirne un drago
132   che per lo carro sù la coda fisse;

e come vespa che ritragge l'ago,
a sé traendo la coda maligna,
135   trasse del fondo, e gissen vago vago.

Quel che rimase, come da gramigna
vivace terra, da la piuma, offerta
138   forse con intenzion sana e benigna,

si ricoperse, e funne ricoperta
e l'una e l'altra rota e 'l temo, in tanto
141   che più tiene un sospir la bocca aperta.

Trasformato così 'l dificio santo
mise fuor teste per le parti sue,
144   tre sovra 'l temo e una in ciascun canto.

Le prime eran cornute come bue,
ma le quattro un sol corno avean per fronte:
147   simile mostro visto ancor non fue.

Then I saw, flinging itself into the very cradle
of the triumphal car, a fox so wasted
120   it seemed deprived of any nourishment.

But my lady, railing at its foul offenses,
drove it back in such retreat
123   as its fleshless bones allowed.

Then, from where it had swept down before,
I saw the eagle plummet to the chariot's floor
126   and leave it feathered with its plumage.

Such a voice as issues from a grieving heart
I heard break forth from Heaven, saying:
129   'O my little bark, how badly are you laden!'

Then it seemed to me the earth was cleft
between the wheels, and I saw a dragon issue,
132   thrust its tail up through the car

and, as a wasp withdraws its sting, so it drew back
its venomed tail, ripping out part of the floor,
135   and then slithered off on its own errant way.

What was left was once more covered,
as is fertile soil with weeds, by plumage,
138   offered perhaps with kind and innocent intent,

and both the wheels and shaft
were completely covered over
141   in less time than a sigh may part the lips.

Thus transformed, the holy edifice
put forth heads on all its parts,
144   three on the shaft and one at every corner—

the first three bore horns like oxen, the others
had a single horn upon their foreheads—
147   such a monster as never seen before.

Sicura, quasi rocca in alto monte,
seder sovresso una puttana sciolta
150   m'apparve con le ciglia intorno pronte;

e come perché non li fosse tolta,
vidi di costa a lei dritto un gigante;
153   e basciavansi insieme alcuna volta.

Ma perché l'occhio cupido e vagante
a me rivolse, quel feroce drudo
156   la flagellò dal capo infin le piante;

poi, di sospetto pieno e d'ira crudo,
disciolse il mostro, e trassel per la selva,
tanto che sol di lei mi fece scudo
160   a la puttana e a la nova belva.

Secure, like a fortress on a towering mountain,
I saw a disheveled harlot sitting there,
150   casting provocative glances this way and that.

I saw a giant who stood beside her,
perhaps to prevent her being taken from him.
153   They were kissing each other again and again.

But because she turned on me
her lustful, roving eye, that savage lover
156   thrashed her body from head to foot.

Then, full of suspicion and cruel in his rage,
he unhitched the monster and dragged it through the wood
so far that the wood itself now screened
160   the harlot and the strange brute from my sight.

1–3.   Dante would seem to be looking back in time, seeing Beatrice now, in 1300, as she was in Florence in 1290 (the year in which she died). That his eyes are so "fixed" will be noted by the theological virtues at verse 9—and not with approval.

This is the longest canto in the *Comedy*. For consideration of the various lengths of Dante's cantos, see the note to *Inferno* VI.28–32.

4–6.   The love that Dante feels now for Beatrice is described in terms that indicate its "Carthaginian" dimension. The "antica rete" (old, familiar net) reminds us of the "antica fiamma" (ancient flame—*Purg.* XXX.48) that flared in Dido and then in Dante, Dido's words become his own. Dante's morals may have been cleansed on the mountain, and Lethe may have made him forget his now forgiven sins, but his intellect is surely not working at its highest level. Having seen Beatrice as God loves her, he still contrives to think she is that pretty girl from Florence. The poet records her "holy smile"; the protagonist remembers his earthly feelings.

The word *rete* (net) was used in the last canto (*Purg.* XXXI.63) to denote the instrument with which a hunter catches birds (as a girl [or girls] caught incautious Dante, according to Beatrice), and may also remind us of the net in which Vulcan caught his adulterous wife Venus *in flagrante delicto* with Mars, as Allen Tate (Tate.1961.1), p. 103, has suggested.

8.   Dante, facing Beatrice, the griffin, and the front of the chariot, turns to his left to pay attention to the three theological virtues, facing him as they stand at the chariot's right wheel (see *Purg.* XXIX.121).

9.   How can Dante love Beatrice too much? Only if he does not love her in God. And that, we should realize, is why he is rebuked here by the theological virtues (not the least of them being Charity), who understand that his gaze is fixed on the image of the young woman he loved and lost rather than on the saved soul who has made his journey possible. (See the note to *Purg.* XXX.58.) The problem is as old as Plato's *Phaedrus*. How do we love physical beauty in such ways as to see it as only the manifestation of a higher beauty (in Dante, of the *etterno piacer* [*Purg.* XXIX.32])? See Mazzeo's "Dante and the *Phaedrus* Tradition of Poetic Inspiration" (Mazz.1958.1, pp. 1–24). The virtues intercede be-

cause they sense that Dante is caught up in carnal appreciation of a spiritual entity.

13–15. The poet at first may seem to be making exactly the same sort of mistake the protagonist has just made, a second idolatrous praising of his lady who, he now seems to be saying, is of even greater worth than the entirety of the Church Triumphant (or so Singleton [1973] implies, referring to these "strong words, calling the whole procession 'poco' in comparison!").

The passage has caused difficulty over the years. The partial insights of several help us make sense of what Dante said. John of Serravalle (1416) points out that the word *sensibile* is a technical term, reflecting such discussions as those found in Aristotle (*De anima* II and *De senso et sensato*). The sensation encountered by any particular sense organ is what is meant, and the commentator's first example fits perfectly here. If one looks at the sun (a *sensibile*, an object of sense perception, in this case by the eyes), anything else will seem less bright by comparison (see the discussion of the *sensibile comune* [the objects of sensory perception] in the note to *Purg.* XXIX.47–51). Tozer (1901) reminds the reader of the similar passage at *Purgatorio* XV.15, in which Dante's sense of sight is overwhelmed. And Steiner (1921) distinguishes between the light of the sun and the blinding effulgence of God.

The context here is the "isplendor di viva luce etterna" (splendor of eternal living light), that is, the smile of Beatrice glowing with the direct light of God's rays. Her mouth is illumined by the "sun" that is God, while all else in the garden is lit by the light of the natural sun, and thus is less available to the sense of sight than Beatrice's smile, as vv. 10–12 make all but apparent: Dante has been blinded by the Light.

16–18. The Church, in metaphor a "glorious army," has reversed its course, is heading back toward the east, whence it came. In this poem, until we hear the penitents cry out in joy for the liberation of Statius's soul (*Purg.* XX.136), the words *gloria* and *glorioso* have referred to worldly fame. But here, as there, the word has the meaning it will have in *Paradiso*, referring to those who live in Glory, that is, in the shining effulgence of God. (The American nineteenth-century locution "going to glory" meant "headed for heaven.") This army is not famous for its worldly accomplishments; it dwells with God and does not care for the world's rewards. The word "glory" has 25 of its 39 occurrences in the poem in *Paradiso*; thus nearly two-thirds of them are found in one-third of the available poetic space.

19–24.   The elaborate military simile, in which the vanguard of the Church Triumphant had turned and was already moving eastward while the chariot was still facing west (an effect striven for and achieved by marching bands between the halves of American football games) may have an ulterior purpose. Dante has reversed temporal order to present first the Church in triumph as it will be after time, and only then the Church in its earthly travail (see the note to *Purg.* XXIX.115–120). As preparation for that change, from Church Triumphant to Church Militant, he may have chosen this introductory military simile, one in which the forces with which we identify are under attack and in strategic retreat.

27.   Benvenuto's gloss (1380) suggests that, while the mortal aspect of Christ may be mutable, His divine being (represented by his wings) is not.

28–30.   Matelda, Statius, and Dante are at the right wheel of the chariot, since that is the one that turns in the smaller arc, given the fact that the "army" has turned to its right in its retreat. Statius's presence has not been referred to since *Purgatorio* XXVIII.146 and his name has not been heard since *Purgatorio* XXVII.47. He is named a total of eight times between Cantos XXI and XXXIII of this *cantica*, this being the seventh; nonetheless, his presence almost always catches us by surprise.

31–37.   If paradise has been regained in this Eden, it is now time to consider how it was lost in the first place; the usual suspects are Eve and Adam (in that order, since she sinned first, but he still more disastrously). Eve is referred to periphrastically by the poet (verse 32), but it is Adam's name that is murmured by all the others present in the procession.

That the procession has paused, with Beatrice descending from the chariot, indicates that we have arrived at a "destination" of some importance.

38–42.   The tree, given the context, is, literally, the Tree of the Knowledge of Good and Evil. However, some of the first commentators (e.g., the Anonymus Lombardus [1322], Jacopo della Lana [1324]), disregarding that context, think its withered condition indicates the Tree of Life after the original sin, when humankind lost eternal life, a perfectly sensible (if almost certainly erroneous) conclusion. Benvenuto (1380), paying attention to what is said of the tree in the next canto (*Purg.*

XXXIII.61–63), only reasonably concludes that this tree, eaten of by Adam when he followed Eve in sin, must be the Tree of the Knowledge of Good and Evil. We probably should also assume that this tree, like those found on one of the terraces below (see *Purg.* XXII.131–135; XXIV.103–105), has its boughs pointed downward so as to prevent its being climbed.

43–48. This exchange between the members of the Church Triumphant and the griffin (his only spoken words in the poem) has puzzled the commentators, like so much else in this difficult canto. His faithful celebrate the griffin's un-Adamic restraint; not only will he not despoil the tree a second time, he will bring the dead tree back to life (vv. 58–60).

The griffin's words, as was first pointed out by Scartazzini (1900) and now by many another commentator, derive from Matthew 3:15. Christ insists on being baptized by John the Baptist: "For so it becomes us to fulfill all justice." That the griffin speaks a version of the very words of Christ is still further evidence that he is meant to be understood as representing Him here.

51. The griffin now binds the *temo* (shaft), by means of which he had been drawing the chariot, to the tree. Most discussants currently believe that this instrument represents Christ's cross. The first commentators argued that, since Adam's sin had been disobedience, this scene showed the obedience to which Christ enjoined his Church, a reasonable enough understanding. While embracing it, Benvenuto (1380) reports that some others believe that this ligature is symbolic of the Incarnation, while still others believe it is related to the cross. This last interpretation eventually became dominant, and remains so today.

It was only with Scartazzini (1900), however, that the most likely source for this tercet, the fourteenth chapter of the apocryphal Gospel of Nicodemus, which Scartazzini claims is also the source of the lengthy paraphrase found in the gloss to the passage by Francesco da Buti (1385), came to light. Any number of medieval legends were developed from this text (see Longfellow [1867]). In it, Adam's noncanonical son Seth visits the gates of the garden of Eden, now a wasteland, in search of some oil to ease Adam's aching head (Adam has been in Limbo for nearly five thousand years). Seth is not allowed to enter by the guardian angel, but does see a very tall tree, denuded of its leaves. The angel gives him a branch from the tree (it is the Tree of the Knowledge of Good and Evil) which he brings back to Adam, who has died before Seth returns to Limbo with the branch. Planted, it soon supplied the wood that would serve for the crucifixion of Jesus.

For a brief discussion of the "Legend of the Wood of the Cross" as being applicable to Dante's phrasing here see Moore (Moor.1903.1), pp. 219–20. For these legends see Mussafia (Muss.1869.1). It is remarkable that the Gospel of Nicodemus has not made its way into other commentaries to this tercet, since it has been a staple of commentators since Torraca (1905 [to *Inf.* IV.54]) as a probable source for Dante's sense of the harrowing of hell, witnessed by Virgil, as it is described in *Inferno* IV.52–63.

52–60.   The rays referred to are those of the sun when it moves from Pisces into Aries, i.e., at the first buds of springtime, and before the sun moves on and into Taurus. Our natural season of blossoming is compared, in this simile, to the miraculous and instantaneous flowering of the tree that had so long been dead, the color of its blossoms reminiscent of Christ's blood.

61–62.   Dante leaves us with another of his little mysteries. What was the "hymn" that he heard sung but could not understand, except to know that it is not sung on earth? Dante tells us as much and, as a result, the Ottimo (1333) reasons, we cannot identify it. However, is there a hymn, known to be sung in Heaven, that we on earth have never heard?

The word *inno* (hymn) occurs six times in the poem in five passages (*Inf.* VII.125; *Purg.* VIII.17; XXV.127 & 129; here; *Par.* XIV.123). In the occurrences previous to this one the word has been used once antiphrastically, to denigrate Plutus's unintelligible shout, and then, in its next two appearances, to refer to the hymns "Te lucis ante" and "Summae Deus clementiae," respectively. In other words, until now *inno* has either been used antiphrastically and thus in a general sense (i.e., "an utterance not like a hymn") or with exactitude to indicate a particular Christian hymn. (For the final appearance of *inno* see the note to *Par.* XIV.118–126.) Are we supposed to be able to identify this song? It would be unusual for Dante to have introduced a riddle without offering us the grounds for solving it. We are looking for a song with two characteristics: it must be unknown on earth and it almost certainly must be in celebration of Jesus' victory over death. Is there such a song? John of Serravalle (1416) thought so: the last book of the Bible speaks of a *canticum novum* (new song) that is sung before the throne of God

(Apocalypse 14:3), a citation found, surprisingly enough, only once again in the commentary tradition (Steiner [1921] and then possibly again, referred to glancingly but not definitively by Trucchi [1936]). Kaske (Kask.1974.1), pp. 206–7, however, while unaware that he had at least two precursors, also sees a reference here to the *canticum novum* of Revelation. Kaske cites Apocalypse 5:9, which is also apposite, if the similar passage at 14:3 has a certain priority, as we shall see. In Revelation 5, Christ comes as a slain lamb (Apocalypse 5:6) to judge humankind, at which the twenty-four elders and the four Gospel beasts lower themselves before the king (5:8) and sing a "new song" *(canticum novum):* "You are worthy to take the book, and to open the seals thereof; *for you were slain and have redeemed us to God. . . .*" (5:9, italics added). The related passage (Apocalypse 14:3) deepens the resonances with *Purgatorio XXXII:* "And they sang as it were a new song *[canticum novum]* before the throne, and before the four beasts and the elders; *and no man could learn that song* but the hundred and forty and four thousand, who were redeemed from earth" (italics added). It seems clear both what the song was and why it is not sung on earth. For the number of those in the procession as 144, the number of the 144,000 of the Church Triumphant, see the note to *Purg.* XXIX.145–150.

63. Dante's mystic sleep closes his experience of the Church Triumphant. Once he awakens, it will have returned to Heaven (vv. 89–90).

64–69. Dante is willing to live dangerously. What other medieval poet, in a serious moment of a serious poem, would turn to Ovid and to self-conscious literary humor in a moment like this? Dante has already (*Purg.* XXIX.94–96; and see the note to that tercet) referred to this Ovidian material (*Metam.* I.568–723) in these cantos dedicated to the recovery of Eden. He compares himself to Argus of the hundred eyes (Dante of the hundred cantos?), watching over Io at Juno's behest so that Jove cannot get at his bovine girlfriend, set to drowsiness and slumber (disastrously for him) by Mercury's tale of Syrinx and Pan. At what point does Argus fall asleep? Just when Mercury's tale reports on the musical sound that issues from the reeds that were Syrinx, who had escaped Pan's lustful pursuit and vanished. Music and a disappearance are features of Dante's scene, as well. The parallel scene is done with witty aplomb but is dealt with by the commentators only as serious business. It is funny, as is Dante's aside to us that, if he could portray the moment of falling asleep, he would do so.

70–71.   Dante's sleep and awakening in the garden is verbally reminiscent of Ugolino's description of his awakening from his dreadful dream (*Inf.* XXXIII.27), the phrase "squarciò il velame" (the veil was rent) remembered in "squarciò il velo" (broke my veil of sleep [these are the only two occurrences of that verb in the poem]). It also reminds us that each of the three previous days on the mountain have ended in sleep and dream. On this fourth day, which will conclude his experience of the earthly paradise at noon, instead he has this mystic sleep *after* he has had a final visionary experience of the griffin and his Church.

72.   Rather than a reference to the "Surgite, et nolite timere" of Matthew 17:7, frequently cited in the commentaries (first by Jacopo della Lana [1324]), Aversano (Aver.1988.1), p. 168, prefers to believe that Matelda refers to Paul's words (Ephesians 5:14), "Surge qui dormis" (Rise, you who are sleeping). And see his remarks on Paul's overall importance for Dante, pp. 185–88. Nonetheless, the passage in Matthew seems still closer to the context here, so much so that it is all but impossible not to see it as controlling this scene: "And Jesus came and touched them and said, 'Arise *[Surgite]* and be not afraid.' And when they had lifted up their eyes they saw no man, save Jesus only." See the next note.

73–84.   In the scene of the transfiguration of Jesus (Matthew 17:1–8) the three apostles Peter, James, and John ascend a mountain with Jesus, see him transformed in visage (it shines with light) and raiment (his clothes become white), then see him in the company of Moses and Elijah (who, representing the law and the prophets, respectively, both promised his advent), and then hear the voice of God from a cloud proclaim that Jesus is his Son, and finally find Moses and Elijah vanished. Just so, this simile insists, Dante thinks he finds himself (in the role of an apostle) in the company of Matelda alone.

78.   This verse also clearly refers to Christ's resurrections of Jairus's daughter and of Lazarus (Luke 8:54 and John 11:43).

85.   Dante's phrase, "Where is Beatrice?" will be remembered when she leaves him for the final time at *Paradiso* XXXI.64 and he asks St. Bernard, "Ov' è ella?" (Where is she?), as Poletto (1894) noted.

86–87.   Beatrice's pose is one of humility, seated on the ground on a root of the newly reflorescent tree. Thus she who, rather than Matelda, really corresponds to Christ in the biblical parallel is the one who is "transfigured," "changed in raiment," as we shall see in a moment.

88.   Those who remain behind in the garden with Beatrice are her "handmaids," the seven virtues, and Matelda. And of course there is the chariot. Dante and Statius are the spectators of the show that is to follow.

89–90.   We learn that the Church Triumphant has now returned to the Empyrean, just as it will do after it descends for Dante's sake a second time, in the sphere of the Fixed Stars (*Par.* XXIII.70–72). (For the logistics of the arrival and departure of the participants in this pageant, see the notes to *Purg.* XXX.16–18 and XXXI.77–78.)

94.   That Beatrice is described as seated "on the bare ground" associates her with humility in general and, perhaps more pointedly, with St. Francis, who raised humility to an art form. See the note to *Purgatorio* XI.135; and see the portrait of Francis in *Paradiso* XI.

95.   No longer the triumphant figure who came into the garden by descending to her chariot, Beatrice is now here to witness its devastation and, once, to protect that chariot; she is no longer in the role of conqueror.

98–99.   Since the nymphs are seven and since the "candles" leading the procession (last referred to at verse 18) are seven, and since Benvenuto (1380) lent the hypothesis his considerable authority, some commentators have believed that those candles are the lamps held by the seven virtues. Both because the seven candles seem a part of the procession of the Church Triumphant and because they are extremely large, this hypothesis has not convinced every reader. On the other hand, other suggestions are all minority opinions. Francesco da Buti (1385) believed they represent the seven gifts of the Holy Spirit, but many find his argument overly subtle and unsupported by the text. Torraca (1905) suggested the seven sacraments ordained by Christ. Bosco/Reggio (1979), uncomfortable with all earlier identifications, thought the reference was to the lamps of the wise virgins in the parable (Matthew 25:1–13) of the ten wise and foolish virgins; but the wise ones number only five. Pertile (1998.2), p. 198n., points (via Alain de Lille) to the "seven lamps of fire burning before the throne, which are the seven spirits of God" (Apocalypse 4:5), thus giving support to Francesco da Buti's view, which

does seem the most palatable. For the biblical and postbiblical under-
standing of the winds from north (Aquilo) and south (Auster) as being
the most destructive, see Pertile (Pert.1998.2), pp. 197–202.

100–102.   Beatrice's words are clear in their promise. (Those who be-
lieve that she is speaking not of Dante's next stay in the garden but of that
time left him on earth cannot rationalize the disjunction caused by the
fact that when Dante returns to earth he will be without Beatrice, who
speaks here only of being with him in Heaven.) Most commentators
now also agree that Beatrice is not alluding to the few minutes he will
now be with her in the garden, but to the short stay he will have in his
second visit to the earthly paradise, after his death and ascent. She then
looks past his first and upcoming visit to paradise in order to fasten his
attention on his final destination, when he, too, will be, with her, a cit-
izen of the City of God, the new Jerusalem in which Christ is "Roman."
The "city of man" that is our militancy on earth is to become the heav-
enly Rome presided over by Christ as emperor, at least it will be for all
those who will find themselves saved.

103–105.   Beatrice's charge to Dante is reminiscent of God's to John, au-
thor of the Revelation: "What you see, write in a book, and send it to
the seven churches. . . ." (Apocalypse 1:11).

109–160.   The second pageant in the garden of Eden is both dramatically
different from the first and exactly like it. In the first instance we were
given a description of the Church Triumphant (which exists as an ideal
out of time and can only be gathered once history is done) that comes
in a temporal form, moving from Genesis to the Apocalypse before
Dante's eyes. Now he sees real history, from just after the founding of the
Church until the present, unfolding as a series of events performed in a
sort of "dumbshow" in a single place. However, both pageants are pre-
sented as allegories, reflecting history, to be sure, but experienced as
though they were literally fictive (e.g., the books of the Bible, the grif-
fin, the depredations of the Church), requiring the kind of critical pro-
cedure that we expect for what Dante himself referred to (Convivio
II.i.4–5) as allegory as practiced by the poets.
      The rest of the canto will present the history of the Church and of the
empire as these two entities make their related voyages through history.

109–117.   The first tribulation of the new Church was to be persecuted
by the emperors of Rome, beginning with Nero (54–68) while Peter was

its first pope (and was crucified in the emperor's persecution of Christians ca. A.D. 68), and extending to the reign of Diocletian (284–305).

While the eagle of Jove may signify variously, there is no doubt that here and through the rest of the pageant of the persecution of the Church Militant it represents the empire.

116. The phrase *nave in fortuna* (ship tossed in a tempest) will find its way to the final world prophecy in the poem (*Par.* XXVII.145).

118–123. Beatrice, acting as the embodiment of the Church's spirit (the chariot representing its physical being, as it were), is able to defeat the forces of heresy, the traditional interpretation of the fox. Portirelli (1804) identified the fox with the "vulpes insidiosos" (insidious foxes) of the Song of Solomon (Canticle 2:15). His adjective, however, is not found in the biblical text, where the foxes are described only as "little," and the phrase in fact comes from St. Augustine, who identifies heresy and exactly such foxes in his *Enarrationes in Ps. LXXX*, as was noted by Tommaseo (1837). The temporal progression of these scenes would indicate that Dante is thinking of the early centuries of the Church's history, after the first persecutions and before the Donation of Constantine (see the next note).

124–129. All commentators agree that this invasion of the chariot by the eagle of empire represents the Donation of Constantine in the first third of the fourth century (see note to *Inf.* XIX.115–117). The Church was meant to operate independently of the empire (this is the essential theme of Dante's *Monarchia*). Here, by being given the "feathers" that belong to empire alone, it is adulterated from its pure form. In this formulation Dante reverses his usual view, which involves seeing the empire's rights and privileges as being curtailed by the Church. In a sense the point is even stronger expressed this way: the Church is harmed by exercising its authority in the civil realm.

Since the gloss of the Ottimo (1333), the voice from heaven is generally taken to be that of St. Peter. From the time of the earliest commentators, however, there was an understanding that Dante's voice from heaven was a sort of calque on the story that, on the day of the Donation, a voice from heaven was heard calling out: "Hodie diffusum est venenum in ecclesia Dei" (Today the church of God is suffused by poison).

130–135. While there is some debate about the nature of this particular calamity, most commentators believe it refers to the "schism" in the

Church brought about by Mohammed just after the middle years of the seventh century (see the note to *Inf.* XXVIII.22–31 for Dante's understanding of the relation of Islam to Christianity).

136–141.   In a sort of replay of the second calamity (the Donation of Constantine), the chariot is once again covered in imperial feathers. The standard interpretation of these verses is that they refer to the grants of lands to the Church by two French kings, Pepin and Charlemagne, in the second half of the eighth century.

The "plumage," which the poet suggests was "offered perhaps with kind and innocent intent," represents once again that which belonged to the empire by God's intent, and legally, in Dante's view, could not be surrendered to ecclesiastical authority, even though kings had chosen to do so. See *Paradiso* XX.55–57, where a similar expression is used to indicate that Constantine had sinned grievously, if without meaning to.

142–147.   The language and the imagery are clearly indebted to the Apocalypse (Apoc. 13:1) for the beast with seven heads and ten horns. Exactly what this symbolic transformation of the Church signifies is much discussed, with little resolution. In general, all can agree, we here see the corruption wrought by the clergy upon their own institution. In other words, in Dante's view, the Church had weathered all attacks upon it from within and without until the time of Charlemagne. In the next five centuries she would do such harm to herself as to make those earlier wounds mortal. This period is marked by corruption from the papacy down to the most modestly avaricious friar; Christianity has no enemies as implacable as its own ecclesiastical institutions or its own clergy.

148–160.   Strictly speaking, this seventh and final calamity is a vision, since the Church only moved to Avignon in 1309 after the election to the papacy of Clement V in 1305. We have now surveyed, in 52 verses, nearly thirteen centuries of the history of the Church.

The harlot and the giant, the whore of Babylon "with whom the kings of the earth have committed fornication" (Apocalypse 17:2) and Philip IV of France, bring the terrible history to its conclusion. The chariot no longer has to do with Beatrice, replaced by this wanton spirit that gives herself to all and any, and is now controlled by France. Dante's reaction to the "Avignonian captivity" is proof, if any is needed, that he is not the Protestant *avant la lettre* that some have tried to find in him.

Indeed, the last and only potentially (if fleeting) hopeful sign we find in the gradually darkening antitriumph of the Church Militant is that the whore gazes on Dante, thus gaining for herself a beating from her gigantic paramour. What does Dante represent now? Is he the embodiment of the truly faithful Christians who hope that their Church will be cleansed? of the Italian faithful left back on this side of the Alps? or is he Dante himself? This penultimate detail of a difficult and encompassing allegorical pageant has left many readers perplexed. Its final one is clear in its pessimism. The giant responds to his lover's wayward glance by releasing the chariot from its binding to the tree and dragging it deeper into the forest, which now looks less like Eden than it resembles France.

PURGATORIO XXXIII

had not become [the calcifying] water of Elsa about your mind, and your delight in these thoughts a Pyramus to the mulberry [covering their true color], by even such few circumstances [i.e., tree's height and inverted branches] you would even now recognize God's justice in his having forbidden you the tree; however, since I perceive that your intellect is indeed turned to stone and dyed another color so that my speech only dazzles you, I nonetheless desire that you carry the truth back within you (if not written, then at least in images) for the same reason that the pilgrim's staff is wreathed with the palm."

"Deus, venerunt gentes," alternando
or tre or quattro dolce salmodia,
3　　le donne incominciaro, e lagrimando;

e Bëatrice, sospirosa e pia,
quelle ascoltava sì fatta, che poco
6　　più a la croce si cambiò Maria.

Ma poi che l'altre vergini dier loco
a lei di dir, levata dritta in pè,
9　　rispuose, colorata come foco:

*"Modicum, et non videbitis me;
et iterum*, sorelle mie dilette,
12　　*modicum, et vos videbitis me."*

Poi le si mise innanzi tutte e sette,
e dopo sé, solo accennando, mosse
15　　me e la donna e 'l savio che ristette.

Così sen giva; e non credo che fosse
lo decimo suo passo in terra posto,
18　　quando con li occhi li occhi mi percosse;

e con tranquillo aspetto "Vien più tosto,"
mi disse, "tanto che, s'io parlo teco,
21　　ad ascoltarmi tu sie ben disposto."

Sì com' io fui, com' io dovëa, seco,
dissemi: "Frate, perché non t'attenti
24　　a domandarmi omai venendo meco?"

Come a color che troppo reverenti
dinanzi a suo maggior parlando sono,
27　　che non traggon la voce viva ai denti,

'*Deus, venerunt gentes,*' the ladies,
now three, now four, in alternation sang,
beginning their sweet psalmody in tears,

3

and Beatrice, sighing and compassionate,
was listening, her face so changed in its expression
that Mary's, at the cross, was hardly more transformed.

6

But when the other virgins stopped their song,
allowing her to speak, she answered, rising
to her feet and blazing like a fire:

9

'*Modicum, et non videbitis me; et iterum,*
my beloved sisters,
modicum, et vos videbitis me.'

12

Then she arranged the seven before her
and, with a gesture, signaled me, the lady,
and the sage who had remained, to follow.

15

Thus she moved forward. I do not believe
she had left her tenth step on the ground
when her piercing eyes met mine

18

and, with a calmer look, she said: 'Follow me
more closely, so that, if I should speak to you,
you will be able to hear me better.'

21

And as soon as I, obeying, drew up near her,
she asked: 'My brother, since we are together,
why do you not dare to ask me questions?'

24

As with those who are too shy
when speaking to their betters and thus fail
to bring their words distinctly to their lips,

27

avvenne a me, che sanza intero suono
incominciai: "Madonna, mia bisogna
30   voi conoscete, e ciò ch'ad essa è buono."

Ed ella a me: "Da tema e da vergogna
voglio che tu omai ti disviluppe,
33   sì che non parli più com' om che sogna.

Sappi che 'l vaso che 'l serpente ruppe,
fu e non è; ma chi n'ha colpa, creda
36   che vendetta di Dio non teme suppe.

Non sarà tutto tempo sanza reda
l'aguglia che lasciò le penne al carro,
39   per che divenne mostro e poscia preda;

ch'io veggio certamente, e però il narro,
a darne tempo già stelle propinque,
42   secure d'ogn' intoppo e d'ogne sbarro,

nel quale un cinquecento diece e cinque,
messo di Dio, anciderà la fuia
45   con quel gigante che con lei delinque.

E forse che la mia narrazion buia,
qual Temi e Sfinge, men ti persuade,
48   perch' a lor modo lo 'ntelletto attuia;

ma tosto fier li fatti le Naiade,
che solveranno questo enigma forte
51   sanza danno di pecore o di biade.

Tu nota; e sì come da me son porte,
così queste parole segna a' vivi
54   del viver ch'è un correre a la morte.

E aggi a mente, quando tu le scrivi,
di non celar qual hai vista la pianta
57   ch'è or due volte dirubata quivi.

so it was with me, and in a failing voice
I began: 'My lady, You know what I lack
30   and exactly how You may provide it.'

And she: 'Free yourself at once
from the snares of fear and shame,
33   no longer speaking as a man does from his dream.

'Know that the vessel which the serpent broke
was and is not. Let those who are to blame
36   take heed: God's vengeance fears no hindrance.

'The eagle that left its feathers on the car
so that it first was monster and then prey
39   shall not remain without an heir forever.

'For I see clearly and do thus declare:
stars already near at hand promise us a time
42   safe from all delay, from all impediment,

'when a Five Hundred Ten and Five,
sent by God, shall slay the thieving wench
45   and the giant sinning there beside her.

'Perhaps my words, obscure as those of Themis
or the Sphinx, persuade you less
48   because, like theirs, they cloud your mind.

'Events soon to occur shall be the Naiads
that solve this hard enigma
51   without the loss of flocks or ears of corn.

'Mark them, and, as they come from me,
set these words down for those
54   who live the life that is a race to death.

'And keep in mind, when you shall write them,
not to conceal the story of the tree
57   that now not once but twice has here been plundered.

Qualunque ruba quella o quella schianta,
con bestemmia di fatto offende a Dio,
60   che solo a l'uso suo la creò santa.

Per morder quella, in pena e in disio
cinquemilia anni e più l'anima prima
63   bramò colui che 'l morso in sé punio.

Dorme lo 'ngegno tuo, se non estima
per singular cagione essere eccelsa
66   lei tanto e sì travolta ne la cima.

E se stati non fossero acqua d'Elsa
li pensier vani intorno a la tua mente,
69   e 'l piacer loro un Piramo a la gelsa,

per tante circostanze solamente
la giustizia di Dio, ne l'interdetto,
72   conosceresti a l'arbor moralmente.

Ma perch' io veggio te ne lo 'ntelletto
fatto di pietra e, impetrato, tinto,
75   sì che t'abbaglia il lume del mio detto,

voglio anco, e se non scritto, almen dipinto,
che 'l te ne porti dentro a te per quello
78   che si reca il bordon di palma cinto."

E io: "Sì come cera da suggello,
che la figura impressa non trasmuta,
81   segnato è or da voi lo mio cervello.

Ma perché tanto sovra mia veduta
vostra parola disïata vola,
84   che più la perde quanto più s'aiuta?"

"Perché conoschi," disse, "quella scuola
c'hai seguitata, e veggi sua dottrina
87   come può seguitar la mia parola;

'Whoever robs that tree or does it harm
by blasphemous act gives great offense to God,
60   since He, with hidden purpose, made it sacred.

'By eating of that tree the first soul longed
in pain and in desire five thousand years and more
63   for Him who in Himself redeemed that bite.

'Your wits are sleeping if they do not grasp
that for a special reason it stands so tall
66   and is inverted, growing wider at its top.

'And if vain thoughts had not been water of the Elsa
to your mind, and your delight in them
69   a Pyramus to make the mulberry turn red,

'by such attributes alone you might have seen
the moral sense of the justice of God
72   in His interdiction of the tree.

'But since I see your mind has turned to stone
and, petrified, has gone so dark
75   that the light of what I say confounds you,

'I wish that, if not written, then sketched out,
you carry what I've said inside you, just as
78   a pilgrim brings his staff back wreathed with palm.'

And I: 'Even as wax maintains the seal
and does not alter the imprinted image,
81   my brain now bears Your stamp.

'But why is it that Your longed-for words
soar up so far beyond my sight
84   the more it strives the more it cannot reach them?'

'So that you may come to understand,' she said,
'the school that you have followed
87   and see if what it teaches follows well my words,

e veggi vostra via da la divina
distar cotanto, quanto si discorda
90   da terra il ciel che più alto festina."

Ond' io rispuosi lei: "Non mi ricorda
ch'i' stranïasse me già mai da voi,
93   né honne coscïenza che rimorda."

"E se tu ricordar non te ne puoi,"
sorridendo rispuose, "or ti rammenta
96   come bevesti di Letè ancoi;

e se dal fummo foco s'argomenta,
cotesta oblivïon chiaro conchiude
99   colpa ne la tua voglia altrove attenta.

Veramente oramai saranno nude
le mie parole, quanto converrassi
102   quelle scovrire a la tua vista rude."

E più corusco e con più lenti passi
teneva il sole il cerchio di merigge,
105   che qua e là, come li aspetti, fassi,

quando s'affisser, sì come s'affigge
chi va dinanzi a gente per iscorta
108   se trova novitate o sue vestigge,

le sette donne al fin d'un'ombra smorta,
qual sotto foglie verdi e rami nigri
111   sovra suoi freddi rivi l'alpe porta.

Dinanzi ad esse Ëufratès e Tigri
veder mi parve uscir d'una fontana,
114   e, quasi amici, dipartirsi pigri.

"O luce, o gloria de la gente umana,
che acqua è questa che qui si dispiega
117   da un principio e sé da sé lontana?"

'and see that your way is as far from God's
as that highest heaven, which spins the fastest,
90   is distant from the earth.'

To that I answered: 'As far as I remember
I have not ever estranged myself from You,
93   nor does my conscience prick me for it.'

'But if you cannot remember that,'
she answered, smiling, 'only recollect
96   how you have drunk today of Lethe,

'and if from seeing smoke we argue there is fire
then this forgetfulness would clearly prove
99   your faulty will had been directed elsewhere.

'But from now on my words shall be
as naked as is needed
102   to make them plain to your crude sight.'

Now more resplendent and with slower steps
the sun was keeping its meridian circle, which,
105   now here, now there, shifts with one's point of view,

when, just as a man escorting others
comes to a halt if he discovers
108   something unexpected—or some sign of it,

the seven ladies halted just beside dim shadows,
such as, beneath green leaves and darker boughs,
111   mountains cast above their icy streams.

In front of the ladies it seemed to me I saw
Tigris and Euphrates issue from a single source
114   and, like friends, slowly part from one another.

'O light, O glory of the human race,
what water pours here from a single source,
117   then separates, departing from itself?'

Per cotal priego detto mi fu: "Priega
Matelda che 'l ti dica." E qui rispuose,
come fa chi da colpa si dislega,

120

la bella donna: "Questo e altre cose
dette li son per me; e son sicura
che l'acqua di Letè non gliel nascose."

123

E Bëatrice: "Forse maggior cura,
che spesse volte la memoria priva,
fatt' ha la mente sua ne li occhi oscura.

126

Ma vedi Eünoè che là diriva:
menalo ad esso, e come tu se' usa,
la tramortita sua virtù ravviva."

129

Come anima gentil, che non fa scusa,
ma fa sua voglia de la voglia altrui
tosto che è per segno fuor dischiusa;

132

così, poi che da essa preso fui,
la bella donna mossesi, e a Stazio
donnescamente disse: "Vien con lui."

135

S'io avessi, lettor, più lungo spazio
da scrivere, i' pur cantere' in parte
lo dolce ber che mai non m'avria sazio;

138

ma perché piene son tutte le carte
ordite a questa cantica seconda,
non mi lascia più ir lo fren de l'arte.

141

Io ritornai da la santissima onda
rifatto sì come piante novelle
rinovellate di novella fronda,

145 puro e disposto a salire a le stelle.

To my question she replied: 'Ask your question
of Matelda.' And that fair lady answered,
120   as one who would be free from any blame:

'This and other things I have already told him.
And I am certain that Lethe's waters
123   did not conceal it from him.'

And Beatrice: 'Perhaps a greater care,
which often strips us of remembrance,
126   has veiled the eyes of his mind in darkness.

'But see Eunoe streaming forth there.
Bring him to it and, as you are accustomed,
129   revive the powers that are dead in him.'

As a gentle spirit that makes no excuses
but makes another's will its own
132   as soon as any signal makes that clear,

so, once she held me by the hand, the lady moved
and, as though she were mistress of that place,
135   said to Statius: 'Now come with him.'

If, reader, I had more ample space to write,
I should sing at least in part the sweetness
138   of the drink that never would have sated me,

but, since all the sheets
readied for this second canticle are full,
141   the curb of art lets me proceed no farther.

From those most holy waters
I came away remade, as are new plants
renewed with new-sprung leaves,
145   pure and prepared to rise up to the stars.

1–3.   The last canto of *Purgatorio* begins, like those of *Inferno* and *Paradiso*, with poetry (see *Inf.* XXXIV.1 and *Par.* XXXIII.1–39). In all three cases, the poem cited is in another voice than Dante's. In the first two cases this voice is Latin, first that of Venantius Fortunatus (his hymn of the cross), now that of David (his hymn for the desolation of Jerusalem, Psalm 78 [79], which begins, "O God, the heathen have come into your inheritance"). Thus do the seven virtues respond to the present culminating moment in the history of the Church Militant. As Benvenuto explains (1380), just as the various gentile nations had invaded and oppressed the Holy Land because of the sins of the Jews, so now has God again allowed foreigners, in this case the French, to take possession of Holy Church because of the sins of the latter-day "Romans."

7–12.   The words that Beatrice sings reflect closely Jesus' words to his disciples (John 16:16), "*A little while and you shall not see me; and again a little while and you shall see me,* because I go to the Father." Since the disciples are puzzled by these words, Jesus explains them: Now they may weep, but their sorrow will be turned to joy (John 16:20). The disciples are finally won over, finally believe that Jesus comes from God (John 16:30). Jesus ends his remarks by promising them peace after their tribulation and concludes, "I have overcome the world" (John 16:33). Thus do these twelve opening verses of the last canto of *Purgatorio* move from a tragic sense of loss to a celebratory and comic vision of the eventual triumph of Christ and his Church.

Beatrice's words also have a particular and local meaning for Dante, who wept at her death and thought he had lost her forever; she has come back into his life.

13–15.   This tercet reminds the reader exactly who is present in this scene (see the note to *Purg.* XXXII.88), Beatrice, her handmaids (the seven virtues), Dante, Matelda, and Statius. Not only is the Church Triumphant no longer in sight, the Church Militant has been dragged off to France.

The way in which Statius is referred to ("the sage who had remained") reminds the reader, yet again, of the absence of Virgil, denied this moment.

16–18.   Those that allegorize the nine steps taken by Beatrice argue that they represent the years between the accession of Pope Clement V in

1305, who agreed to King Philip's desire to move the papacy to France (which he did in 1309), and the deaths of Clement and Philip in 1314, thus possibly allowing the tenth step to point to the advent of the new leader in 1315. About such things there can be little or no certainty, but the hypothesis is attractive. Nonetheless, one should probably be aware that, except for a rather contorted effort by Francesco da Buti (1385), none of the early commentators, generally so fond of allegorizing, offers anything more than a literal reading of the detail. The allegorical reading of the ten steps as ten years is a nineteenth- and twentieth-century discovery, e.g., as it is found in Carroll (1904).

23.   This is the first time Beatrice addresses Dante as "brother." One senses, again, that her desire to rebuke Dante is (temporarily) suspended. But see vv. 85–90.

Beatrice for the first time, and in keeping with the spirit of her citation of John 16:16 in vv. 10–12, turns her attention to the future, and to Dante's future, now that the world's and his own sinful past have been dealt with.

25–28.   Benvenuto (1380) compares Dante to a student in the presence of his teacher, and indeed this is the opening moment in what might be called Dante's education in theology, which will last for another thirty cantos.

31–33.   Before she presents her prophecy, Beatrice charges Dante with the responsibility for reporting it precisely, not in the mode of a man who is talking in his sleep. Almost all the commentators take the passage literally and as applying in some general way. But Beatrice's words are very hard on poor Dante, since she makes it clear that, at least in her (infallible) opinion, his actual words, uttered at some previous time, have indeed been correctly characterized in this way. But when? Perhaps the later passage in this canto (vv. 85–90) that is devoted to his previous intellectual meanderings may shed some light on exactly what she means. For now the subject is left unexplored.

34–36.   The language, referring to the destruction of the Church as detailed in the preceding canto, is distinctly reflective of the Apocalypse (Apoc. 17:8, "The beast that you saw was, and is not").

The word *suppe* (here translated "hindrance" only to make sense in its context) has been variously understood. Many of the early commentators believed it referred to the cakes left on the tomb of a murderer's victim in a Greek custom reborn in Florence; if the murderer came to the tomb and ate of these cakes for nine consecutive days, he would then be safe from the offended family's vengeance (and for that reason the families of the slain person would keep watch over the tomb). See Portirelli (1804) for a restatement of this interpretation, which is at least as old as the commentary of Jacopo della Lana. Others think the reference is to the bread soaked in wine on which an oath is sworn between vassal and lord; still others of the offal which the *veltro* will despise (see *Inf.* I.103), and which is related to the "sop" to Cerberus of *Aeneid* VI.420. None of these "sops," however, would seem to offer a cause for fear, and are thus difficult to rationalize in this context.

37–42. The opening verses of Beatrice's extended prophecy seem clearly to indicate that the one who will come is related to the eagle of empire, i.e., that beneficent Roman empire that had begun so well under Augustus and then had become corrupt. It seems difficult to believe that this, as some maintain, is not an imperial prophecy.

43–45. This enigmatic passage has drawn an extraordinary amount of contradictory opinion. For a review of the entire question, see Pietro Mazzamuto, "Cinquecento diece e cinque," *ED* II (1970), pp. 10b–14b. It is also helpful to consult Charles Davis's similar review of the first and similar prophecy in the poem, the *veltro* (hound) of *Inferno* I.101 ("veltro," *ED* V [1976], pp. 908a–912b). Most now argue, whether or not they believe that the number, if expressed by the Roman numerals DXV, is an anagram of *DUX* (or "leader" [the Roman "V" and "U" being equivalent letters]), that the context of the passage makes it apparent that Beatrice is here indicating the advent of a temporal leader, one who will deal with the excesses of the king of France and the delinquent Church. Further, if the canto is taken as having been written before his death in August 1313, many believe that the prophecy points to Henry VII. Some also believe that if the first reference is to a political leader, it also points beyond him to the second coming of Christ, the final emperor. See Hollander (Holl.1969.1), pp. 184–90, and the note to *Inferno* I.100–105. A standard and useful treatment of the problem remains that of Moore (Moor.1903.1), pp. 253–83.

46–51. The general sense of this passage is clear: future events will make plain the terms of the cloudy prophecy, which is compared to those made by Themis (Ovid, *Metam.* I.375–394) and by the Sphinx. Both of these monstrous females later appear in the same passage in Ovid (*Metam.* VII.759–765), where their hatred of humans is, as here, described in terms of the loss of human and animal life in the countryside. The key lines in the modern text of Ovid run as follows: "Carmina Laïades non intellecta priorum / solverat ingeniis . . ." (The son of Laius [Oedipus] solved the riddles which had baffled the intellects of all before him). We are close to being absolutely sure, however, that the text as Dante knew it substituted "Naïades" for "Laïades" and showed a plural form of the verb (*solverant*). And so Dante believed that it was the Naiads, water nymphs, who had solved the riddle of the Sphinx. This was the cruel monster who cast herself down from her rock, whence she had been killing clueless Thebans, once Oedipus realized that the variously footed creature in her riddle was man (the story that we know from Sophocles' *Oedipus*, unknown, like nearly all of Greek letters, to Dante).

Dante does not "nod" often, but this is one of the most egregious errors in the *Comedy*, even if it has some reasonable excuse behind it. In fact, all of the early commentators accept Dante's reading, thus indicating that *their* texts also had "Naiads" where they should have had Laius's son. The better reading had to wait for Nikolaes Heinsius (1620–81), the Dutch Latin poet and scholar, one of the great Renaissance textual editors of the Latin classics. His edition (Florence, 1646) of the *Metamorphoses* restored the reading *Laïades*. It is thus only with the commentary of Venturi (1732) that the better reading is made known to the world of Dante's commentators, and even then some of them try to object to it, seeking a way to understand the Naiads as interpreters of prophetic utterance. Ghisalberti (Ghis.1932.1) offers a comprehensive discussion of the problem.

52. Beatrice's use of the verb *notare* here may remind us of its last use with this sense (setting something down as a text) in Dante's self-description as inspired poet, one who only records what he hears from the "dictator" (*Purg.* XXIV.53).

54. Dante's often admired phrase, describing life as a *"correre alla morte"* (race to death) reflects St. Augustine (*DcD* XIII.10): "Our time for this life is nothing other than a race to death *(cursus ad mortem)*," as was suggested by Mattalia (1960).

55–57. As her scribe, Dante is instructed by Beatrice not to conceal from his eventual readers the condition of the tree, now robbed of its possessions twice. Bosco/Reggio (1979) review the divided opinions of the early commentators, who variously believe that the reference is to Adam and the giant, to Adam and the eagle, or to the eagle and the giant. In their view, all three seem plausible glosses. However, it has seemed to others that, since, from Beatrice's words we gather that Dante has witnessed these two devastations (and not that of Adam, which is referred to in a following tercet [vv. 61–63]), it is the first and last attacks upon the tree that are referred to here: its defoliation by the eagle (the imperial persecutions of *Purg.* XXXII.112–114) and its having the chariot detached from it by the giant (the removal to Avignon, referred to in *Purg.* XXXII.158).

58–63.   Beatrice's accusation now widens, blaming Adam as the first despoiler of the tree and praising Christ for redeeming him. For the calculation of the length of Adam's life (930 years) and of his punishment in Limbo (4,302 years) see *Paradiso* XXVI.118–120 and the note to that passage. After 25 March the year 1300 is the 6,499th year since the creation of Adam.

66.   For the downward-pointing branches of the tree, set at an angle that makes climbing it difficult or impossible, see *Purgatorio* XXXII.40–42.

67–78.   For a paraphrase of this somewhat contorted utterance see the Outline of this canto.

67.   The river Elsa in Tuscany, because of its high concentration of minerals, was known for the crusting overlay it would leave on objects immersed in it.

69.   For Pyramus, Thisbe, and the mulberry tree, see the note to *Purgatorio* XXVII.37–42.

72.   'The word "moralmente" was understood, even in some of the earliest commentators (e.g., Jacopo della Lana [1324]), as having a technical meaning here, i.e., "con lo senso tropologico" (with the tropological [i.e., third] sense [of fourfold exegesis of the Bible]). See the section on allegory in the introduction to *Inferno*. Various later commentators are of the same opinion, e.g., Tommaseo (1837), Scartazzini (1900), Poletto (1894). What this signifies is that the meaning applies now to current his-

tory. God's original "interdiction," broken by Adam, whose sin was re-
deemed by the cross on which Christ sacrificed Himself, is now binding
on us, as well, even though we are at least potentially saved. Even now
we, new Adams, are not meant to eat of the Tree of the Knowledge of
Good and Evil.

77–78.   That is, Dante, bringing back this message, will seem like a pil-
grim returned from the Holy Land, his "staff" decorated with the sign
of the distant and holy place to which he has been.

79–84.   These lines offer a fairly rare instance of a speaker in the poem
expressing himself by use of a simile. Dante is saying that what Beatrice
tells him seems to be completely clear, but that he really cannot under-
stand what she means.

85–90.   Beatrice is charging Dante with having attempted to eat of the
Tree of the Knowledge of Good and Evil. As some commentators (e.g.,
the Ottimo [1333], Scartazzini [1900]) have understood, the point here
seems to be that Dante turned from theology to philosophy in his effort
to do that. The current majority view of the nature of Dante's aberra-
tion is well represented by Bosco/Reggio (1979): Dante had, in the
Convivio, set theology to one side in order to study philosophy, a deci-
sion he now deplores. For the notion that this fairly common view is in-
correct, see Scott (Scot.1991.1).

94–99.   Beatrice's response to Dante is worthy of the Inquisition. That
he can no longer remember his sins (because he has drunk from Lethe,
the river of oblivion) is proof that he had committed them.

97.   Dante's phrasing, "if from seeing smoke we argue there is fire,"
might remind a reader of St. Augustine's discussion of signs in *De doct-
rina christiana* (II.i.1): "A sign is a thing that causes us to think of some-
thing beyond the impression the thing itself makes on the senses. Thus,
if we see a track, we think of the animal that made the track; *if we see
smoke, we know that there is a fire* that causes it" (translation adapted from
that of D. W. Robertson, Jr., italics added).

100–102.   Not only does Beatrice speak more plainly for the rest of this
canto, but the poet does as well, allowing most of his verse to be more
immediately understandable than is his custom.

103–105.   The sun takes "slower steps" the higher it is above us, moving quickest at dawn and dusk, slowest as it approaches and departs from noon. While the absolute position of the sun is not in doubt, the earthly observer will have a sense of the location of the meridian circle containing it that varies according to that observer's position.

112.   Dante indicates to the reader that he knows very well that the rivers in the garden of Eden in fact (i.e., in Genesis 2:14) include Tigris and Euphrates (and not Lethe and Eunoe, which are here by his invention). See the note to *Purgatorio* XXVIII.127–131.

119.   While it is only now that we hear Matelda's name, we have observed her actions so long that we may feel that we understand her function. See the notes to *Purgatorio* XXVIII.1 and 40–42.

121–123.   Matelda did indeed tell Dante the name of this river (Eunoe) at *Purgatorio* XXVIII.131. As opposed to his forgetting his sins in Lethe he is now forgetting the promise of that good resolution of his plight, so deeply, we may well imagine, has he been stung by Beatrice's accusations.

128–135.   Only now, and in less than completely clear terms, do we learn about Matelda's function in the garden, which seems to be to serve as "baptizer" of the souls as they finish their purification, first in Lethe (as she draws Dante through that river at *Purg.* XXXI.91–102) and finally in Eunoe. There is a dispute as to whether or not Matelda's role in the garden is Dante-specific (which it has been, from all that we have seen, until now) or "universal" (see the note to *Purg.* XXVIII.40–42). Indeed, Contini has argued (Cont.1976.1), p. 174n., that the verb *usa* (as you are accustomed) in the present tense should be understood as a past definite (*già praticasti* [as once you used to]) and thus implies that Matelda had such a role in Dante's earlier life. This is a case of interpreting (or indeed revising) the text in order to create or preserve a desired interpretation. Contini's point would be worth considering except for a single, crucial, and indeed determinative final point, Matelda's last words in the poem, which are addressed to Statius (vv. 134–135): "Now come with him." Thus, and only at the very last moment, we learn that Matelda's function in the garden is not limited to ministrations on behalf of Dante alone (i.e., she deals either with all the saved souls who come through here or with some of them). (See Filippo Villani's similar view in Bellomo's edition of his commentary to *Inf.* I [Bell.1989.1], p. 92, n. 90.) To be sure,

Dante alone is mentioned as receiving her ministrations at the river Lethe (*Purg.* XXXI.91–105). From this later passage, however, we are probably forced to consent to the notion that she there presided over Statius's submersion as well as Dante's, a scene that, like much involving Statius's (and Virgil's) presence in the garden, is allowed to disappear from Dante's page. For this view see Singleton (Sing.1958.1), p. 181, n. 17.

136–141.   This seventh and last Purgatorial address to the reader opens a new subject that the poet will share with us, the formal requirements of his poem. If he had more space (another few lines? another canto?), he would tell us what Eunoe tasted like. The early commentators think that he means that he has run out of cantos (i.e., he cannot have a thirty-fourth as he did for *Inferno*). Tozer (1901) was perhaps the first to think that it was the number of verses in each *cantica* (4,720, 4,755, 4,758 respectively) that Dante refers to. That seems a possible, if dubious, hypothesis. We might also note that he had just completed the longest canto in the entire work in the preceding one (XXXII is 160 lines long), and ostensibly thus had available at least fifteen more lines. Thomas Hart (Hart.1995.1) reviews his copious work that would have us believe, among other things, that all the canto lengths of the poem were decided by Dante early on. (For a rejoinder see the note to *Inf.* VI.28–32.)

142–145.   The phrasing, with all its repeated "ri" sounds, reminiscent of the resurrective surge at the opening of the *cantica* (*Purg.* I.18), underlines the reconstituted innocence of this Adamic being. Scartazzini suggests that we should hear, in verse 144, a resonance of St. Paul (Ephesians 4:23), "And be renewed in the spirit of your mind."

That the three *cantiche* all end with the word *stelle* (stars) is no longer a surprise. It is important to attempt to imagine the effect of this repetition on a reader who does not know that it is coming, who is suddenly jarred into realizing the pattern, into realizing the shaping force of divine beauty on this poem.

Index of these items (in their English forms, where these exist) in the Italian text of *Purgatorio*. NB: (1) if a character or place is mentioned more than once in a canto, only the first reference is indicated; (2) no distinction has been made between direct and indirect references; i.e., one will find "Amata" instead of "Lavinia, mother of."

This index is meant to help the reader find subjects, treated in the notes, that may not be readily remembered as being related to a particular passage.

What follows is precisely that, not an inclusive bibliography of studies relevant to Dante or even to his *Purgatorio*, which alone would be voluminous. Abbreviated references in the texts of the notes are keyed to this alphabetical listing. For those interested in the general condition of Dantean bibliography, however, a few remarks may be helpful.

Since an extended bibliography for the study of Dante includes tens of thousands of items, those who deal with the subjects that branch out from the works of this writer are condemned to immoderate labor and a sense that they are always missing something important. While even half a century ago it was possible to develop, in a single treatment, a fairly thorough compendium of the most significant items (e.g., S. A. Chimenz, *Dante*, in *Letteratura italiana. I maggiori* [Milan: Marzorati, 1954], pp. 85–109), the situation today would require far more space. Fortunately, the extraordinary scholarly tool represented by the *Enciclopedia dantesca*, dir. U. Bosco, 6 vols. (Rome, Istituto della Enciclopedia Italiana, 1970–78—henceforth *ED*), has given Dante studies its single most important bibliographical resource, leaving only the last quarter century—which happens to be the most active period in the history of Dante studies—uncovered. However, for the years 1965–90, Enzo Esposito has edited a helpful guide, *Dalla bibliografia alla storiografia: la bibliografia dantesca nel mondo dal 1965–1990* (Ravenna: Longo, 1995). A closer analysis of a shorter period is available in "Bibliografia Dantesca 1972–1977," ed. Leonella Coglievina, *Studi Danteschi* 60 (1988): 35–314 (presenting 3121 items for this five-year period). The bibliography in *ED*, vol. 6, pp. 499–618 (a length that gives some sense of the amount of basic information available), contains ca. 5,000 items and is of considerable use, breaking its materials into convenient categories. (Its bibliography of bibliographies alone runs six double-column pages, pp. 542–47.)

The *ED* also, of course, contains important bibliographical indications in many of its entries. A major new English source for bibliographical information is *The Dante Encyclopedia*, ed. Richard Lansing (New York: Garland, 2000).

In the past dozen years, Dante studies, perhaps more than any other postclassical area of literature, has moved into "the computer age." There is a growing online bibliography available, developed from the bibliography of American Dante studies, overseen by Richard Lansing for the Dante Society of America, which includes an increasing number of Italian items (http://www.princeton.edu/~dante). Some seventy commentaries to the *Commedia* are now available through the Dartmouth Dante Project (opened 1988), still best reached via Telnet (telnet ddp.dartmouth.edu; at the prompt type "connect dante"), but soon to be available on the Web as well. There is also the Princeton Dante Project (http://www.princeton.edu/dante), a multimedia edition of the *Commedia* (open to public use since 1999) overseen by Robert Hollander, which also functions as an entry point to most of the many Dante sites on the Web, including Otfried Lieberknecht's site in Berlin, which is a source of an enormous amount of information about Dante in electronic form, and, since the autumn of 2000, the site being developed by the Società Dantesca Italiana (www.danteonline.it).

LIST OF WORKS CITED IN THE NOTES

Abra.1985.1
Abrams, Richard, "Illicit Pleasures: Dante among the Sensualists (*Purgatorio* XXVI)," *Modern Language Notes* 100 (1985): 1–41.

Alfi.1998.1
Alfie, Fabian, "For Want of a Nail: The Guerri-Lanza-Cursietti Argument Regarding the *Tenzone*," *Dante Studies* 116 (1998): 141–59.

Anto.2001.1
Antonelli, Roberto, "Cavalcanti e Dante: al di qua del Paradiso," in *Dante: da Firenze all'aldilà. Atti del terzo Seminario dantesco internazionale,* ed. Michelangelo Picone (Florence: Cesati, 2001), pp. 289–302.

Ardi.1990.1
Ardissino, Erminia, "I Canti liturgici nel *Purgatorio* dantesco," *Dante Studies* 108 (1990): 39–65.

Armo.1981.1
Armour, Peter, "The Theme of Exodus in the First Two Cantos of the *Purgatorio*," in *Dante Soundings*, ed. David Nolan (Dublin: Irish Academic Press, 1981), pp. 59–99.

Armo.1989.1
Armour, Peter, *Dante's Griffin and the History of the World: A Study of the Earthly Paradise ("Purgatorio" XXIX–XXXIII)* (Oxford: Clarendon, 1989).

Armo.1990.1
Armour, Peter, "Divining the Figures: Dante's Three Dreams in the *Purgatorio*," in *Melbourne Essays in Italian Language and Literature in Memory of Colin McCormick*, ed. Tom O'Neill (Dublin: Irish Academic Press, 1990), pp. 13–26.

Armo.1993.1
Armour, Peter, "Words and the Drama of Death in *Purgatorio* V," in *Word and Drama in Dante: Essays on the "Divina Commedia,"* ed. John C. Barnes and Jennifer Petrie (Dublin: Irish Academic Press, 1993), pp. 93–122.

Arti.1967.1
Artinian, Robert, "Dante's Parody of Boniface VIII," *Dante Studies* 85 (1967): 71–74.

Auri.1970.1
Aurigemma, Marcello, "Il Canto XII del *Purgatorio*," in *Nuove letture dantesche*, vol. IV (Florence: Le Monnier, 1970), pp. 105–27.

Aust.1932.2
Austin, H. D., "The Arrangement of Dante's Purgatorial Reliefs," *PMLA* 47 (1932): 1–9.

Aust.1933.1
Austin, H. D., "*Aurea Justitia*: A Note on *Purgatorio*, XXII, 40f," *Modern Language Notes* 48 (1933): 327–30.

Aver.1988.1
Aversano, Mario, "Il canto XXXII del *Purgatorio*," in *La quinta rota: Studi sulla "Commedia"* (Turin: Tirrenia, 1988), pp. 149–84.

Aver.2000.1
Aversano, Mario, "Sulla poetica dantesca nel canto XXIV del *Purgatorio*," *L'Alighieri* 16 (2000): 123–38.

Bald.1985.1
Baldelli, Ignazio, "Visione, immaginazione e fantasia nella *Vita nuova*," in *I sogni nel Medioevo*, ed. Tullio Gregory (Rome: Edizioni dell'Atene, 1985), pp. 1–10.

Bald.1999.3
Balducci, Marino A., "Il preludio purgatoriale e la fenomenologia del sinfonismo dantesco: percorso ermeneutico," *Publications of the Carla Rossi Academy Press (in Affiliation with the University of Connecticut [www.rossiacademy.uconn.edu])*, 1999.

Bara.1989.1
Barański, Zygmunt G., "Dante's Three Reflective Dreams," *Quaderni d'italianistica* 10 (1989): 213–36.

Bara.1993.1
Barański, Zygmunt G., "Dante e la tradizione comica latina," in *Dante e la "bella scola" della poesia: Autorità e sfida poetica*, ed. A. A. Iannucci (Ravenna: Longo, 1993), pp. 225–45.

Bara.1993.2
Barański, Zygmunt G., " 'Sordellus . . . qui . . . patrium vulgare deseruit': A Note on *De vulgari eloquentia*, I, 15, sections 2–6," in *The Cultural Heritage of the Italian Renaissance: Essays in Honour of T. G. Griffith*, ed. C. E. J. Griffiths and R. Hastings (Lewiston, N.Y.: Edwin Mellen Press, 1993), pp. 19–45.

Bara.2001.2
Barański, Zygmunt G., "Canto VIII," in *Lectura Dantis Turicensis: Purgatorio*, ed. Georges Güntert and Michelangelo Picone (Florence: Cesati, 2001), pp. 389–406.

Barb.1934.1
Barbi, Michele, *Problemi di critica dantesca* (Florence: Sansoni, 1934).

Barb.1984.1
Bàrberi Squarotti, Giorgio, "Ai piedi del monte: il prologo del *Purgatorio*," in *L'arte dell'interpretare: studi critici offerti a Giovanni Getto* (Turin: L'Arciere, 1984), pp. 19–44.

Barn.1993.1
Barnes, John C., "*Purgatorio XX*," in *Dante's "Divine Comedy," Introductory Readings II: "Purgatorio,"* ed. Tibor Wlassics (*Lectura Dantis [virginiana]*, 12, supplement, Charlottesville: University of Virginia, 1993), pp. 288–301.

Baro.1984.1
Barolini, Teodolinda, *Dante's Poets* (Princeton: Princeton University Press, 1984).

Baro.1992.1
Barolini, Teodolinda, *The Undivine "Comedy": Detheologizing Dante* (Princeton: Princeton University Press, 1992).

Baro.1997.1
Barolini, Teodolinda, "Guittone's *Ora parrà*, Dante's *Doglia mi reca*, and the *Commedia's* Anatomy of Desire," in *Seminario Dantesco Internazionale: Atti del primo convegno tenutosi al Chauncey Conference Center, Princeton, 21–23 ottobre 1994*, ed. Z. G. Barański (Florence: Le Lettere, 1997), pp. 3–23.

Basi.1990.1
Basile, Bruno, "Dante e l'idea di *peregrinatio*," in his *Il tempo e le forme: studi letterari da Dante a Gadda* (Modena: Mucchi, 1990 [1986]), pp. 9–36.

Batt.1961.1
Battaglia, Salvatore, and Giorgio Bárberi Squarotti, eds., *Il Grande Dizionario della lingua italiana* (Turin: UTET, 1961–96 [up to "Sik"]).

Bell.1989.1
Bellomo, Saverio, ed., Filippo Villani, *Expositio seu comentum super "Comedia" Dantis Allegherii* (Florence: Le Lettere, 1989).

Berg.1965.1
Bergin, Thomas G., "Dante's Provençal Gallery," *Speculum* 40 (1965): 15–30.

Berk.1979.1
Berk, Philip R., "Shadows on the Mount of Purgatory," *Dante Studies* 97 (1979): 47–63.

Bigi.1955.1
Bigi, Emilio, "Genesi di un concetto storiografico: 'dolce stil novo,' " *Giornale storico della letteratura italiana* 132 (1955): 333–71.

Bigo.1964.1
Bigongiari, Dino, *Essays on Dante and Medieval Culture*, ed. Henry Paolucci (New York: The Bagehot Council, 2000 [1964]).

Binn.1955.1
Binni, Walther, "Lettura del canto III del *Purgatorio*," in his *Ancora con Dante* (Ravenna: Longo, 1983 [1955]), pp. 9–27.

Biso.1971.1
Bisogni, Fabio, "Precisazioni sul Casella dantesco," *Quadrivium* 12 (1971 [1974]): 81–91.

Bloo.1952.1
Bloomfield, Morton W., *The Seven Deadly Sins* (East Lansing: Michigan State College Press, 1952).

Bocc.1974.1
Boccaccio, Giovanni, *Trattatello in laude di Dante*, ed. P. G. Ricci (Milan: Mondadori, 1974).

Bona.1902.1
Bonaventura, Arnaldo, *Il canto XV del "Purgatorio"* (["Lectura Dantis Orsanmichele"] Florence: Sansoni, 1902).

Bosc.1942.1
Bosco, Umberto, "Particolari danteschi," *Annali della Reale Scuola Normale di Pisa, Lettere, storia e filosofia* 11 (1942): 131–47.

Boyd.1981.1
Boyde, Patrick, *Dante Philomythes and Philosopher: Man in the Cosmos* (Cambridge: Cambridge University Press, 1981).

Brow.1978.1
Brownlee, Kevin, "Dante and Narcissus (*Purg*. XXX, 76–99)," *Dante Studies* 96 (1978): 201–6.

Brow.1984.1
Brownlee, Kevin, "Phaeton's Fall and Dante's Ascent," *Dante Studies* 102 (1984): 135–44.

Brug.1969.1
Brugnoli, Giorgio, "Stazio in Dante," *Cultura Neolatina* 29 (1969): 117–25.

Brug.1988.1
Brugnoli, Giorgio, "Statius Christianus," *Italianistica* 17 (1988): 9–15.

Brug.1993.2
Brugnolo, Furio, "Cino (e Onesto) dentro e fuori la *Commedia*," in *Omaggio a Gianfranco Folena*, ed. Pier Vincenzo Mengaldo (Padua: Editoriale Programma, 1993), pp. 369–86.

Bund.1927.1
Bundy, Murry Wright, *The Theory of Imagination in Classical and Medieval Thought* (Urbana: University of Illinois, 1927).

Cach.1993.1
Cachey, Theodore, "*Purgatorio* XV," in *Dante's "Divine Comedy," Introductory Readings II: "Purgatorio,"* ed. Tibor Wlassics (*Lectura Dantis [virginiana]*, 12, supplement, Charlottesville: University of Virginia, 1993), pp. 212–34.

Cart.1944.1
Carter, A. E., "An Unrecognized Virgilian Passage in Dante," *Italica* 21 (1944): 149–53.

Cass.1978.1
Cassell, Anthony K., " 'Mostrando con le poppe il petto' (*Purg.* XXIII, 102)," *Dante Studies* 96 (1978): 75–81.

Cass.1984.1
Cassell, Anthony K., *Dante's Fearful Art of Justice* (Toronto: University of Toronto Press, 1984).

Cass.1984.2
Cassell, Anthony K., "The Letter of Envy: *Purgatorio* XIII–XIV," *Stanford Italian Review* 4 (1984): 5–22.

Cecc.1990.2
Cecchetti, Giovanni, "The Statius Episode: Observations on Dante's Conception of Poetry," *Lectura Dantis [virginiana]*, 7 (1990): 96–114.

Ceri.2000.1
Ceri, Giovangualberto, "L'Astrologia in Dante e la datazione del 'viaggio' dantesco," *L'Alighieri* 15 (2000): 27–57.

Cerv.1986.1
Cervigni, Dino S., *Dante's Poetry of Dreams* (Florence: Olschki, 1986).

Cesa.1824.1
Cesari, Antonio, *Bellezze della "Divina Commedia"* (Verona: P. Libanti, 1824–26).

Cher.1989.1
Cherchi, Paolo, "Gervase of Tillbury and the Birth of Purgatory," *Medioevo romanzo* 14 (1989): 97–110.

Chia.1967.2
Chiarini, Eugenio, *"Purgatorio* Canto XXX," in *Lectura Dantis Scaligera* (Florence: Le Monnier, 1967), pp. 1103–38.

Chia.1984.2
Chiavacci Leonardi, Anna Maria, "Le beatitudini e la struttura poetica del *Purgatorio*," *Giornale storico della letteratura italiana* 161 (1984): 1–29.

Chia.1994.1
Chiavacci Leonardi, Anna Maria, *Purgatorio, con il commento di A. M. C. L.* (Milan: Mondadori, 1994).

Chia.1995.1
Chiamenti, Massimiliano, *Dante Alighieri traduttore* (Florence: Le Lettere, 1995).

Chia.1999.2
Chiamenti, Massimiliano, "Corollario oitanico al canto ventottesimo del *Purgatorio*," *Medioevo e rinascimento* 13 (1999): 207–20.

Ciof.1991.1
Cioffari, Vincenzo, "Dante's Use of Lapidaries: A Source Study," *Dante Studies* 109 (1991): 149–62.

Ciof.1985.1
Cioffi, Caron Ann, " 'Dolce color d'oriental zaffiro,' a Gloss on *Purgatorio* 1.13," *Modern Philology* 82 (1985): 355–64.

Ciof.1992.1
Cioffi, Caron Ann, "Fame, Prayer, and Politics: Virgil's Palinurus in *Purgatorio* V and VI," *Dante Studies* 110 (1992): 179–200.

Cont.1960.1
Contini, Gianfranco, ed., *Poeti del Duecento*, 2 vols. (Milan-Naples: Ricciardi, 1960).

Cont.1976.1
Contini, Gianfranco, *Un' idea di Dante* (Turin: Einaudi, 1976).

Cook.1999.1
Cook, Eleanor, "Scripture as Enigma: Biblical Allusion in Dante's Earthly Paradise," *Dante Studies* 117 (1999): 1–19.

Corn.2000.1
Cornish, Alison, "Angels," *The Dante Encyclopedia*, ed. Richard Lansing (New York: Garland, 2000), pp. 37–45.

Corn.2002.2
Cornish, Alison, *Reading Dante's Stars* (New Haven: Yale University Press, 2000).

Cors.1987.1
Corsi, Sergio, *Il "modus digressivus" nella "Divina Commedia"* (Potomac, Md.: Scripta humanistica, 1987).

Crac.1984.1
Cracco, Giorgio, "Tra Marco e Marco: un cronista veneziano dietro al canto XVI del *Purgatorio*?" in AA. VV., *Viridarium floridum: Studi di storia veneta offerti dagli allievi a Paolo Sambin*, a cura di M. C. Billanovich, G. Cracco, A. Rigon (Padua: Antenore, 1984), pp. 3–23.

Cris.1988.1
Cristaldi, Sergio, "Dalle beatitudini all'*Apocalisse*: Il Nuovo Testamento nella *Commedia*," *Letture classensi* 17 (1988): 23–67.

Cris.1988.2
Cristaldi, Sergio, " 'Per dissimilia.' Saggio sul grifone dantesco," *Atti e memorie dell'Arcadia* 9 (1988–89): 57–94.

Curs.1995.1
Cursietti, Mauro, *La falsa Tenzone di Dante con Forese Donati* (Anzio: De Rubeis, 1995).

Curs.1997.1
Cursietti, Mauro, "Nuovi contributi per l'apocrifia della cosiddeta 'Tenzone di Dante con Forese Donati': ovvero la 'Tenzone del Panìco,' " in *Bibliologia e critica dantesca: saggi dedicati a Enzo Esposito*, ed. V. De Gregorio, vol. II: *Saggi danteschi* (Ravenna: Longo, 1997), pp. 53–72.

Curs.2000.1
Cursietti, Mauro, "Dante e Forese alla taverna del Panìco: le prove documentarie della falsità della tenzone," *L'Alighieri* 16 (2000): 7–22.

Curt.1948.1
Curtius, Ernst Robert, *European Literature and the Latin Middle Ages*, trans. W. R. Trask (New York: Harper & Row, 1963 [1948]).

Cuzz.2002.1
Cuzzilla, Tony, "The Perception of Time in the *Commedia: Purg.*
IV.10–12," *Electronic Bulletin of the Dante Society of America* (May 2002).

Davi.1984.1
Davis, Charles T., *Dante's Italy and Other Essays* (Philadelphia: University
of Pennsylvania Press, 1984).

Debe.1906.1
Debenedetti, Santorre, "Documenti su Belacqua," *Bulletino della Società
Dantesca Italiana* 13 (1906): 222–33.

DeFa.1993.1
De Fazio, Marina, "*Purgatorio* XXIX," in *Dante's "Divine Comedy,"
Introductory Readings II: "Purgatorio,"* ed. Tibor Wlassics (*Lectura Dantis
[virginiana]*, 12, supplement, Charlottesville: University of Virginia,
1993), pp. 433–47.

Delc.1989.1
Delcorno, Carlo, *Exemplum e letteratura: Tra Medioevo e Rinascimento*
(Bologna: Il Mulino, 1989).

Dema.1987.1
Demaray, John G., *Dante and the Book of the Cosmos* (Philadelphia:
American Philosophical Society, 1987).

DeRo.1980.1
De Robertis, Domenico, ed., *Vita nuova* (Milan: Ricciardi, 1980).

DiBe.1985.1
Di Benedetto, Arnaldo, "Simboli e moralità nel II canto del *Purgatorio*,"
Giornale storico della letteratura italiana 162 (1985): 161–80.

Dovi.1906.1
D'Ovidio, Francesco, *Nuovi studii danteschi: Il "Purgatorio" e il suo preludio*
(Milan: Hoepli, 1906).

Dovi.1926.1
D'Ovidio, Francesco, "Esposizione del canto XX dell'*Inferno*," in his
Nuovo volume di studi danteschi (Caserta-Rome: A. P. E., 1926), pp.
313–55.

Durl.1996.1
Durling, Robert M., *The "Divine Comedy" of Dante Alighieri: Inferno*,
Notes by R. M. Durling and Ronald Martinez (New York and Oxford:
Oxford University Press, 1996).

Durl.2001.1
Durling, Robert, " 'Mio figlio ov'è?' (*Inferno* X, 60)," in *Dante: da
Firenze all'aldilà. Atti del terzo Seminario dantesco internazionale*, ed.
Michelangelo Picone (Florence: Cesati, 2001), pp. 303–29.

Elsh.1971.1
Elsheikh, Mahmoud Salem, "I musicisti di Dante (Casella, Lippo,
Schochetto) in Nicolò de' Rossi," *Studi Danteschi* 48 (1971): esp. 156–58.

Fasa.2001.1
Fasani, Remo, "Canto XXVII," in *Lectura Dantis Turicensis: Purgatorio*,
ed. Georges Güntert and Michelangelo Picone (Florence: Cesati, 2001),
pp. 423–33.

Fava.1975.1
Favati, Guido, *Inchiesta sul Dolce Stil Nuovo* (Florence: Le Monnier, 1975).

Ferg.1953.1
Fergusson, Francis, *Dante's Drama of the Mind* (Princeton: Princeton
University Press, 1953).

Ferr.1975.1
Ferrante, Joan M., *Woman as Image in Medieval Literature from the Twelfth
Century to Dante* (New York: Columbia University Press, 1975).

Fole.1977.1
Folena, Gianfranco, "Il canto di Guido Guinizzelli," *Giornale storico della
letteratura italiana* 154 (1977): 481–508.

Fosc.2002.1
Fosca, Nicola, *Commento alla "Commedia" di Dante*, unpublished, 2002.

Fosc.2002.2
Fosca, Nicola, "Beatitudini e processo di purgazione," *Electronic Bulletin
of the Dante Society of America* (February 2002).

Fran.1984.1
Frankel, Margherita, "Dante's Anti-Virgilian *villanello*," *Dante Studies* 102 (1984): 81–109.

Fran.1989.1
Frankel, Margherita, "La similitudine della zara (*Purg.* VI, 1–12) ed il rapporto fra Dante e Virgilio nell'Antepurgatorio," in *Studi Americani su Dante*, ed. G. C. Alessio and R. Hollander (Milan: F. Angeli, 1989), pp. 113–43.

Frec.1961.2
Freccero, John, "Adam's Stand," *Romance Notes* 2 (1961): 115–18.

Frec.1986.1
Freccero, John, *Dante: The Poetics of Conversion*, ed. Rachel Jacoff (Cambridge: Harvard University Press, 1986).

Frie.1987.1
Friedman, Joan Isobel, "La processione mistica di Dante: allegoria e iconografia nel canto XXIX del *Purgatorio*," in *Dante e le forme dell'allegoresi*, ed. M. Picone (Ravenna: Longo, 1987), pp. 125–48.

Gabr.1993.1
Gabriele, Trifon, *Annotationi nel Dante fatte con M. Trifon Gabriele in Bassano*, ed. Lino Pertile (Bologna: Commissione per i testi di lingua, 1993 [1525–27]).

Gall.1909.1
Galletti, Alfredo, *Il canto XXII del "Purgatorio"* (["Lectura Dantis Orsanmichele"] Florence: Sansoni, n.d. [read in 1909]).

Ghis.1932.1
Ghisalberti, Fausto, "L'enigma delle Naiadi," *Studi Danteschi* 16 (1932): 105–25.

Giam.1966.1
Giamatti, A. Bartlett, *The Earthly Paradise and the Renaissance Epic* (Princeton: Princeton University Press, 1966).

Gian.1989.1
Giannantonio, Pompeo, "Canto I," in *Lectura Dantis Neapolitana: "Purgatorio,"* ed. Pompeo Giannantonio (Naples: Loffredo, 1989), pp. 3–22.

Glen.1999.1
Glenn, Diana C., "Women in Limbo: Arbitrary Listings or Textual Referents? Mapping the Connections in *Inferno* IV and *Purgatorio* XXII," *Dante Studies* 117 (1999): 85–115.

Gmel.1955.1
Gmelin, Hermann, *Kommentar: der Läuterungsberg* (Stuttgart: Klett, 1955).

Gorn.1982.1
Gorni, Guglielmo, "Costanza della memoria e censura dell'umano nell'Antipurgatorio," *Studi Danteschi* 54 (1982): 53–70.

Grop.1962.1
Groppi, Felicina, *Dante traduttore*, 2nd ed. (Rome: Editrice "Orbis Catholicus" Herder, 1962).

Gunt.2001.1
Güntert, Georges, "Canto VIII," in *Lectura Dantis Turicensis: Purgatorio*, ed. Georges Güntert and Michelangelo Picone (Florence: Cesati, 2001), pp. 109–20.

Hart.1995.1
Hart, Thomas, " 'Per misurar lo cerchio' (*Par.* XXXIII.134) and Archimedes' *De mensura circuli*: Some Thoughts on Approximations to the Value of π," in *Dante e la scienza*, ed. P. Boyde and V. Russo (Ravenna: Longo, 1995), pp. 265–335.

Heff.1993.1
Heffernan, James A. W., *Museum of Words: The Poetics of Ekphrasis from Homer to Ashbery* (Chicago: University of Chicago Press, 1993), pp. 37–45.

Heil.1972.1
Heilbronn, Denise, "Dante's Valley of the Princes," *Dante Studies* 90 (1972): 43–58.

Heil.1977.1
Heilbronn, Denise, "The Prophetic Role of Statius in Dante's *Purgatory*," *Dante Studies* 95 (1977): 53–67.

Heil.1984.1
Heilbronn, Denise, "*Concentus musicus*: The Creaking Hinges of Dante's Gate of Purgatory," *Rivista di studi italiani* 2 (1984): 1–15.

Heil.2001.1
Heil, Andreas, *Alma Aeneis: Studien zur Vergil- und Statiusrezeption Dante Alighieris,* Inauguraldissertation zur Erlangung der Doktorwürde der Philosophischen Fakultät der Ruprecht-Karl-Universität Heidelberg, 2001.

Holl.1969.1
Hollander, Robert, *Allegory in Dante's "Commedia"* (Princeton: Princeton University Press, 1969).

Holl.1973.1
Hollander, Robert, "Dante's Use of the Fiftieth Psalm," *Dante Studies* 91 (1973): 145–50.

Holl.1974.1
Hollander, Robert, "*Vita Nuova*: Dante's Perceptions of Beatrice," *Dante Studies* 92 (1974): 1–18.

Holl.1975.1
Hollander, Robert, "*Purgatorio* II: Cato's Rebuke and Dante's *scoglio*," *Italica* 52 (1975): 348–63.

Holl.1976.2
Hollander, Robert, "The Invocations of the *Commedia*," *Yearbook of Italian Studies* 3 (1976): 235–40.

Holl.1980.1
Hollander, Robert, "The Tragedy of Divination in *Inferno* XX," in *Studies in Dante* (Ravenna: Longo, 1980), pp. 131–218.

Holl.1980.2
Hollander, Robert, "Babytalk in Dante's *Commedia*," in *Studies in Dante* (Ravenna: Longo, 1980), pp. 115–29.

Holl.1982.1
Hollander, Robert, "Dante's 'Book of the Dead': A Note on *Inferno*
XXIX, 57," *Studi Danteschi* 54 (1982): 31–51.

Holl.1983.1
Hollander, Robert, *Il Virgilio dantesco: tragedia nella "Commedia"*
(Florence: Olschki, 1983).

Holl.1983.3
Hollander, Robert, "*Purgatorio* XIX: Dante's Siren/Harpy," in *Dante,
Petrarch, Boccaccio: Studies in Honor of Charles S. Singleton*, ed. Aldo S.
Bernardo and Anthony L. Pellegrini (Binghamton, N.Y.: Medieval &
Renaissance Texts and Studies, 1983), pp. 77–88.

Holl.1984.4
Hollander, Robert, "Dante's 'Georgic' (*Inferno* XXIV, 1–18)," *Dante
Studies* 102 (1984): 111–21.

Holl.1986.1
Hollander, Robert, and Albert Rossi, "Dante's Republican Treasury,"
Dante Studies 104 (1986): 59–82.

Holl.1990.1
Hollander, Robert, "*Purgatorio* II: The New Song and the Old," *Lectura
Dantis [virginiana]* 6 (1990): 28–45.

Holl.1992.2
Hollander, Robert, "Dante and Cino da Pistoia," *Dante Studies* 110
(1992): 201–31.

Holl.1992.3
Holloway, Julia Bolton, *The Pilgrim and the Book* (New York: Peter Lang,
1992).

Holl.1993.1
Hollander, Robert, "Le opere di Virgilio nella *Commedia* di Dante," in
Dante e la "bella scola" della poesia: Autorità e sfida poetica, ed. A. A.
Iannucci (Ravenna: Longo, 1993), pp. 247–343.

Holl.1994.1
Hollander, Robert, "Dante's Self-Laureation (*Purgatorio* XI, 92),"
Rassegna europea di letteratura italiana 3 (1994): 35–48.

Holl.1996.1
Hollander, Robert, "Dante's Harmonious Homosexuals (*Inferno*
16.7–90)," *Electronic Bulletin of the Dante Society of America* (June 1996).

Holl.1999.1
Hollander, Robert, "Dante's 'dolce stil novo' and the *Comedy*," in *Dante:*
mito e poesia. Atti del secondo Seminario dantesco internazionale, ed. M.
Picone and T. Crivelli (Florence: Cesati, 1999), pp. 263–81.

Holl.1999.2
Hollander, Robert, "Dante as Uzzah? (*Purg.* X 57, and *Epistle* XI 9–12),"
in *Sotto il segno di Dante: Scritti in onore di Francesco Mazzoni,* ed. L.
Coglievina & D. De Robertis (Florence: Le Lettere, 1999), pp. 143–51.

Holl.2000.2
Hollander, Robert, "Dante's Antaeus (*Inferno* 31.97–132)," *Electronic*
Bulletin of the Dante Society of America (May 2000).

Holl.2001.1
Hollander, Robert, *Dante: A Life in Works* (New Haven: Yale University
Press, 2001).

Holl.2001.2
Hollander, Robert, " 'La concubina di Titone antico': *Purgatorio* IX.1,"
Electronic Bulletin of the Dante Society of America (July 2001).

Holl.2002.1
Hollander, Robert, "The Letters on Dante's Brow (*Purg.* 9.112 and
21.22–24)," *Electronic Bulletin of the Dante Society of America* (January
2002).

Ilie.1971.1
Iliescu, Nicolae, "Gli episodi degli abbracci nelle strutture del *Purgatorio*,"
Yearbook of Italian Studies 1 (1971): 53–63.

Ioli.1989.1
Ioli, Giovanna, *La Divina Commedia: Purgatorio*, ed. S. Jacomuzzi, A. Dughera, G. Ioli, V. Jacomuzzi (Turin: S.E.I., 1989).

Jaco.1988.1
Jacoff, Rachel, "Transgression and Transcendence: Figures of Female Desire in Dante's *Commedia*," *Romanic Review* 79 (1988): 129–42.

Jenn.1972.1
Jenni, Adolfo, "Il Canto XXIII del *Purgatorio*," in *Nuove letture dantesche*, vol. V (Florence: Le Monnier, 1972), pp. 1–31.

Kant.1957.1
Kantorowicz, Ernst, *The King's Two Bodies* (Princeton: Princeton University Press, 1957).

Kask.1971.1
Kaske, Carol V., "Mount Sinai and Dante's Mount Purgatory," *Dante Studies* 89 (1971): 1–18.

Kask.1974.1
Kaske, Robert E., "Dante's *Purgatorio* XXXII and XXXIII: A Survey of Christian History," *University of Toronto Quarterly* 43 (1974): 193–214.

Kirk.1989.1
Kirkham, Victoria, "Eleven Is for Evil: Measured Trespass in Dante's *Commedia*," *Allegorica* 10 (1989): 27–50.

Koni.2001.1
König, Bernhard, "Canto XXVIII," in *Lectura Dantis Turicensis: Purgatorio*, ed. Georges Güntert and Michelangelo Picone (Florence: Cesati, 2001), pp. 435–45.

Kuhn.1976.1
Kuhn, Reinhard, *The Demon of Noontide: Ennui in Western Literature* (Princeton: Princeton University Press, 1976).

LaFa.1973.1
La Favia, Louis M., "Per una reinterpretazione dell'episodio di Manfredi," *Dante Studies* 91 (1973): 81–100.

LaFa.1984.1
La Favia, Louis, " '. . . ché quivi per canti,' (*Purg.* XII, 113): Dante's Programmatic Use of Psalms and Hymns in the *Purgatory*," *Studies in Iconography* 9 (1984–86): 53–65.

Lans.1977.1
Lansing, Richard, *From Image to Idea: A Study of the Simile in Dante's "Commedia"* (Ravenna: Longo, 1977).

Lans.1994.1
Lansing, Richard, "Narrative Design in Dante's Earthly Paradise," *Dante Studies* 112 (1994): 101–13.

Lans.2000.1
Lansing, Richard, ed., *Dante Encyclopedia* (New York: Garland, 2000).

Lanz.1997.1
Lanza, Antonio, "A norma di filologia: ancora a proposito della cosiddetta 'Tenzone tra Dante e Forese,' " *L'Alighieri* 10 (1997): 43–54.

LeGo.1981.1
Le Goff, Jacques, *The Birth of Purgatory*, trans. A. Goldhammer (Chicago: University of Chicago Press, 1984 [1981]).

Leon.2001.1
Leonardi, Lino, "Cavalcanti, Dante e il nuovo stile," in *Dante: da Firenze all'aldilà. Atti del terzo Seminario dantesco internazionale*, ed. Michelangelo Picone (Florence: Cesati, 2001), pp. 331–54.

Leva.1957.1
Levavasseur, A., "Les pierres précieuses dans la *Divine Comédie*," *Revue des études italiennes* 4 (1957): 31–100.

Leve.1996.1
Levenstein, Jessica, "The Pilgrim, the Poet, and the Cowgirl: Dante's Alter-*Io* in *Purgatorio* XXX–XXXI," *Dante Studies* 114 (1996): 189–208.

LoCa.1967.1
Lo Cascio, Renzo, "La nozione di cortesia e di nobiltà dai siciliani a Dante," in *Atti del Convegno di studi su Dante e la Magna Curia* (Palermo: Luxograph, 1967), pp. 113–84.

Mall.1984.1
Mallin, Eric S., "The False Simile in Dante's *Commedia*," *Dante Studies* 102 (1984): 15–36.

Mani.2000.1
Manica, Raffaele, "Belacqua," in *Studi di letteratura, critica e linguistica offerti a Riccardo Scrivano* (Rome: Bulzoni, 2000), pp. 35–45.

Marc.2001.1
Marchesi, Simone, "La rilettura del *De Officiis* e i due tempi della composizione del *Convivio*," *Giornale storico della letteratura italiana* 178 (2001): 84–107.

Marc.2002.1
Marchesi, Simone, "Dante's 'active' hermeneutics in *Purgatorio* XXII: Virgil and Statius as readers of poetry," article awaiting publication.

Mari.1975.1
Mariotti, Scevola, "Il cristianesimo di Stazio in Dante secondo il Poliziano," in *Letteratura e critica: Studi in onore di Natalino Sapegno*, ed. Walther Binni et al., vol. II (Rome: Bulzoni, 1975), pp. 149–61.

Mark.1992.1
Marks, Herbert, "Hollowed Names: *Vox* and *Vanitas* in the *Purgatorio*," *Dante Studies* 110 (1992): 135–78.

Mart.1962.1
Marti, Mario, "Dolcezza di memorie ed assoluto etico nel canto di Casella (*Purg.* II)," in his *Studi su Dante* (Galatina: Congedo, 1984 [1962]), pp. 81–99.

Mart.1966.1
Marti, Mario, *Con Dante fra i poeti del suo tempo* (Lecce: Milella, 1966).

Mart.1989.2
Martinez, Ronald L., "La *sacra fame dell'oro* (*Purgatorio* 22, 41) tra Virgilio e Stazio: dal testo all'interpretazione," *Letture classensi* 18 (1989): 177–93.

Mast.1979.1
Mastrobuono, Antonio C., *Essays on Dante's Philosophy of History* (Florence: Olschki, 1979).

Mazz.1958.1
Mazzeo, Joseph A., *Structure and Thought in the "Paradiso"* (Ithaca: Cornell University Press, 1958).

Mazz.1965.2
Mazzoni, Francesco, "*Purgatorio* Canto XXXI," in *Lectura Dantis Scaligera* (Florence: Le Monnier, 1965).

Mazz.1977.2
Mazzoni, Francesco, ed., Dante Alighieri, *La Divina Commedia: Purgatorio. Con i commenti di T.Casini/S.A. Barbi & A. Momigliano* (Florence: Sansoni, 1977).

Mazz.1979.1
Mazzotta, Giuseppe, *Dante, Poet of the Desert* (Princeton: Princeton University Press, 1979).

Mazz.1988.1
Mazzoni, Francesco, "Un incontro di Dante con l'esegesi biblica (A proposito di *Purg.* XXX, 85–99)," in *Dante e la Bibbia*, ed. G. Barblan (Florence: Olschki, 1988), pp. 173–212.

Mert.1953.1
Merton, Thomas, "Le Sacrement de l'Avent dans la spiritualité de saint Bernard," *Dieu Vivant* 23 (1953): 23–43.

Mezz.1990.1
Mezzadroli, Giuseppina, "Dante, Boezio e le sirene," *Lingua e stile* 25 (1990): 25–56.

Mine.1968.1
Mineo, Nicolò, *Profetismo e Apocalittica in Dante* (Catania: Università di Catania, Facoltà di Lettere e Filosofia, 1968).

Mode.1995.1
Modesto, Diana, "Virgil, Man or shade: The 'Mancato abbraccio' of *Purgatorio* XXI, 132," *Spunti e ricerche* 11 (1995): 3–17.

Moev.2000.1
Moevs, Christian, "Pyramus at the Mulberry Tree: De-petrifying Dante's Tinted Mind," in *Imagining Heaven in the Middle Ages: A Book of Essays*, ed. Jan Swango Emerson and Hugh Feiss (New York: Garland, 2000), pp. 211–44.

Mole.1980.1
Moleta, Vincenzo, *Guinizzelli in Dante* (Rome: Edizioni di Storia e Letteratura, 1980).

Mont.1962.1
Montano, Rocco, *Storia della poesia di Dante*, vol. I (Naples: Quaderni di Delta, 1962).

Moor.1889.1
Moore, Edward, *Contributions to the Textual Criticism of the "Divina Commedia"* (Cambridge: Cambridge University Press, 1889).

Moor.1896.1
Moore, Edward, *Studies in Dante*, First Series: *Scripture and Classical Authors in Dante* (Oxford: Clarendon, 1969 [1896]).

Moor.1899.1
Moore, Edward, *Studies in Dante*, Second Series: *Miscellaneous Essays* (Oxford: Clarendon, 1968 [1899]).

Moor.1903.1
Moore, Edward, *Studies in Dante*, Third Series: *Miscellaneous Essays* (Oxford: Clarendon, 1968 [1903]).

Moor.1917.1
Moore, Edward, *Studies in Dante*, Fourth Series: *Textual Criticism of the "Convivio" and Miscellaneous Essays* (Oxford: Clarendon, 1968 [1917]).

Morg.1990.1
Morgan, Alison, *Dante and the Medieval Other World* (Cambridge: Cambridge University Press, 1990).

Musa.1974.1
Musa, Mark, *Advent at the Gates* (Bloomington: Indiana University Press, 1974).

Muss.1869.1
Mussafia, Adolfo, "Sulla legenda del legno della Croce," *Sitzungsberichte der philosophisch-historischen Classe der kaiserlichen Akademie der Wissenschaften* [Vienna] 63 (1869): 165–216.

Musu.1967.1
Musumarra, Carmelo, "*Purgatorio* Canto XIII," in *Lectura Dantis Scaligera* (Florence: Le Monnier, 1967), pp. 441–71.

Nard.1966.1
Nardi, Bruno, "Dante e il buon Barbarossa," *L'Alighieri* 7 (1966): 3–27.

Olso.1999.1
Olson, Glending, "*Inferno* XXVII and the Perversions of Pentecost," *Dante Studies* 117 (1999): 21–33.

Pacc.2001.1
Pacchioni, Paola, "Lia e Rachele, Matelda e Beatrice," *L'Alighieri* 18 (2001): 47–74.

Pado.1959.1
Padoan, Giorgio, "Il mito di Teseo e il cristianesimo di Stazio," *Lettere Italiane* 11 (1959): 432–57.

Pado.1967.1
Padoan, Giorgio, "*Purgatorio* Canto XVIII," in *Lectura Dantis Scaligera* (Florence: Le Monnier, 1967 [1964]), pp. 657–92.

Pado.1970.1
Padoan, Giorgio, "Il Canto XXI del *Purgatorio*," in *Nuove letture dantesche*, vol. IV (Florence: Le Monnier, 1970), pp. 327–54.

Para.1968.1
Paratore, Ettore, *Tradizione e struttura in Dante* (Florence: Sansoni, 1968).

Pare.1996.1
Parenti, Giovanni, "Ercole al bivio e il sogno della femmina balba," in *Operosa parva per Gianni Antonini*, ed. D. De Robertis & F. Gavazzeni (Verona: Valdonega, 1996), pp. 57–66.

Pasc.1902.1
Pascoli, Giovanni, *La mirabile visione* (Bologna: Zanichelli, 1923 [1902]).

Pasq.1965.1
Pasquazi, Silvio, "Catone," *Cultura e scuola* 13–14 (1965): 528–39.

Pasq.1970.1
Pasquazi, Silvio, "Il Canto XVII del *Purgatorio*," in *Nuove letture dantesche*, vol. IV (Florence: Le Monnier, 1970), pp. 221–50.

Pasq.1996.1
Pasquini, Emilio, "Il *Paradiso* e una nuova idea di figuralismo," *Intersezioni* 16 (1996): 417–27.

Pert.1993.1
Pertile, Lino, "Dante's *Comedy*: Beyond the *Stilnovo*," *Lectura Dantis [virginiana]* 13 (1993): 47–77.

Pert.1993.3
Pertile, Lino, "*Purgatorio* XXVI," in *Dante's "Divine Comedy," Introductory Readings II: "Purgatorio,"* ed. Tibor Wlassics (*Lectura Dantis [virginiana]*, 12, supplement, Charlottesville: University of Virginia, 1993), pp. 380–97.

Pert.1996.1
Pertile, Lino, "Bonconte e l'anafonesi (*Purg.*, V 109–18)," *Filologia e critica* 21 (1996): 118–26.

Pert.1997.1
Pertile, Lino, "Dante Looks Forward and Back: Political Allegory in the Epistles," *Dante Studies* 115 (1997): 1–17.

Pert.1998.2
Pertile, Lino, *La puttana e il gigante: Dal Cantico dei Cantici al Paradiso Terrestre di Dante* (Ravenna: Longo, 1998).

Pert.2001.1
Pertile, Lino, "Quale amore va in Paradiso?" in *"Le donne, i cavalieri, l'arme, gli amori": Poema e romanzo: la narrativa lunga in Italia*, ed. Francesco Bruni (Venice: Marsilio, 2001), pp. 59–70.

Peru.1978.1
Perugi, Maurizio, "Arnaut Daniel in Dante," *Studi Danteschi* 51 (1978): 59–152.

Peru.1983.1
Perugi, Maurizio, "Il Sordello di Dante e la tradizione mediolatina dell'invettiva," *Studi Danteschi* 55 (1983): 23–135.

Petr.1969.1
Petrocchi, Giorgio, *Itinerari danteschi*, Premessa a cura di C. Ossola (Milan: Franco Angeli, 1994² [Bari: Laterza, 1969]).

Peza.1950.1
Pézard, André, *Dante sous la pluie de feu* (Paris: Vrin, 1950).

Peza.1965.1
Pézard, André, ed., Dante Alighieri, *Oeuvres complètes* (Paris: Gallimard, 1965).

Pico.1987.2
Picone, Michelangelo, "*Purgatorio* XXVII: passaggio rituale e *translatio* poetica," *Medioevo romanzo* 12 (1987): 389–402.

Pico.1992.1
Picone, Michelangelo, " 'Auctoritas' classica e salvezza cristiana: una lettura tipologica di *Purgatorio* XXII," in *Studi in memoria di Giorgio Varanini. I: Dal Duecento al Quattrocento* (Pisa: Giardini [= *Italianistica* 21], 1992), pp. 379–95.

Pico.1993.1
Picone, Michelangelo, "L'Ovidio di Dante," in A. Iannucci, ed., *Dante e la "bella scola" della poesia* (Ravenna: Longo, 1993), pp. 107–44.

Pico.1993.2
Picone, Michelangleo, *"Purgatorio XXII,"* in *Dante's "Divine Comedy," Introductory Readings II: "Purgatorio,"* ed. Tibor Wlassics (*Lectura Dantis [virginiana],* 12, supplement, Charlottesville: University of Virginia, 1993), pp. 321–35.

Pico.1995.1
"Guittone e Dante" [three articles, by Guglielmo Gorni, Roberto Antonelli, and Francesco Mazzoni], in *Guittone d'Arezzo nel settimo centenario della morte: Atti del Convegno Internazionale di Arezzo (22–24 aprile 1994),* ed. M. Picone (Florence: Franco Cesati, 1995), pp. 307–83.

Pico.1997.1
Picone, Michelangelo, *"Inferno VIII: il viaggio contrastato,"* *L'Alighieri* 9 (1997): 35–50.

Pico.1998.1
Picone, Michelangelo, "All'ombra di Sordello: una lettura di *Purgatorio* VII," *Rassegna europea di letteratura italiana* 12 (1998): 61–77.

Pico.1999.2
Picone, Michelangelo, "Canto V," in *Lectura Dantis Turicensis: Purgatorio,* ed. Georges Güntert and Michelangelo Picone (Florence: Cesati, 2001 [1999]), pp. 71–83.

Pier.1981.1
Pierotti, Gian Luca, "La *filia solis* di Bonaventura e i cambiamenti di colore in *Par.* XXVII," *Lettere Italiane* 33 (1981): 216–21.

Piet.1984.1
Pietropaolo, Domenico, "The Figural Context of Buonconte's Salvation," *Dante Studies* 102 (1984): 123–34.

Prot.1912.1
Proto, Enrico, "Nuove ricerche sul Catone dantesco," *Giornale storico della letteratura italiana* 59 (1912): 193–248.

Raim.1962.1
Raimondi, Ezio, "Rito e storia nel I canto del *Purgatorio,*" in his *Metafora e storia* (Turin: Einaudi, 1970 [1962]), pp. 65–94.

Raim.1967.2
Raimondi, Ezio, "*Purgatorio* Canto I," in *Lectura Dantis Scaligera* (Florence: Le Monnier, 1967), pp. 3–42.

Raim.1968.1
Raimondi, Ezio, "Semantica del canto IX del *Purgatorio*," in his *Metafora e storia: Studi su Dante e Petrarca* (Turin: Einaudi, 1970 [1968]), pp. 95–122.

Rajn.1874.1
Rajna, Pio, *La materia e la forma della "Divina Commedia": I mondi oltraterreni nelle letterature classiche e nelle medievali*, ed. Claudia Di Fonzo (Florence: Le Lettere, 1998 [1874]).

Ricc.1970.1
Ricci, Pier Giorgio, "Il Canto XVIII del *Purgatorio*," in *Nuove letture dantesche*, vol. IV (Florence: Le Monnier, 1970), pp. 251–65.

Rigo.1994.1
Rigo, Paola, *Memoria classica e memoria biblica in Dante* (Florence: Olschki, 1994).

Roma.1902.1
Romani, Fedele, *Il canto XIX del "Purgatorio"* (["Lectura Dantis Orsanmichele"] Florence: Sansoni, 1902).

Ronc.1958.1
Ronconi, Alessandro, *Interpretazioni grammaticali* (Padua: Liviana, 1958).

Ronc.1965.1
Ronconi, Alessandro, "L'incontro di Stazio e Virgilio," *Cultura e scuola* 13–14 (1965): 566–71.

Ross.1993.1
Rossi, Luca Carlo, "Prospezioni filologiche per lo Stazio di Dante," in *Dante e la "bella scola" della poesia: Autorità e sfida poetica*, ed. A. A. Iannucci (Ravenna: Longo, 1993), pp. 205–24.

Russ.1969.1
Russo, Vittorio, "Il canto II del *Purgatorio*," *Nuove letture dantesche*, vol. III (Florence: Le Monnier, 1969), pp. 229–65.

Sals.1967.1
Salsano, Fernando, "*Purgatorio* Canto XV," in *Lectura Dantis Scaligera*
(Florence: Le Monnier, 1967), pp. 537–76.

Sant.2001.1
Santelli, Tullio, "Il canto XX del *Purgatorio*," *L'Alighieri* 17 (2001): 7–35.

Saro.1957.1
Sarolli, Gian Roberto, "Noterella biblica sui sette P.," *Studi Danteschi* 34
(1957): 217–22.

Scor.2000.1
Scorrano, Luigi, "Dall'abbandono alla bontà riconquistata (*Purgatorio*
III)," *L'Alighieri* 16 (2000): 53–71.

Scot.1972.1
Scott, John A., "Dante's Admiral," *Italian Studies* 27 (1972): 28–40.

Scot.1991.1
Scott, John A., "Beatrice's Reproaches in Eden: Which 'School' Had
Dante Followed?" *Dante Studies* 109 (1991): 1–23.

Scot.1996.1
Scott, John A., *Dante's Political Purgatory* (Philadelphia: University of
Pennsylvania Press, 1996).

Scot.2001.1
Scott, John A., "Canto XII," in *Lectura Dantis Turicensis: Purgatorio*, ed.
Georges Güntert and Michelangelo Picone (Florence: Cesati, 2001), pp.
173–97.

Scri.1992.1
Scrivano, Riccardo, "Stazio personaggio, poeta e cristiano," *Quaderni
d'italianistica* 13 (1992): 175–97.

Seem.1991.1
Seem, Lauren Scancarelli, "Dante's Drunkenness and Virgil's Rebuke
(*Purg.* 15.115–138)," *Quaderni d'italianistica* 12 (1991): 71–82.

Shoa.1975.1
Shoaf, R. A., "Dante's *colombi* and the Figuralism of Hope in the *Divine Comedy*," *Dante Studies* 93 (1975): 27–59.

Shoa.1978.1
Shoaf, R. A., " 'Auri sacra fames' and the Age of Gold (*Purg.* XXII, 40–41 and 148–150)," *Dante Studies* 96 (1978): 195–99.

Shoa.1986.1
Shoaf, R. A., "Dante's Beard: *Sic et non* (*Purgatorio* 31.68)," in *Magister Regis: Studies in Honor of Robert E. Kaske*, ed. Arthur Groos and others (New York: Fordham University Press, 1986), pp. 171–77.

Shoa.1989.1
Shoaf, R. A., " 'Lo gel che m'era intorno al cor' (*Purg.* 30.97) and 'Frigidus circum praecordia sanguis' (*Geo.* 2.484): Dante's Transcendence of Virgil," *Lectura Dantis [virginiana]* 5 (1989): 30–45.

Sing.1949.1
Singleton, Charles S., *An Essay on the "Vita Nuova"* (Baltimore: The Johns Hopkins University Press, 1977 [1949]).

Sing.1954.1
Singleton, Charles S., *Commedia, Elements of Structure* (Cambridge: Harvard University Press, 1965 [1954]).

Sing.1958.1
Singleton, Charles S., *Journey to Beatrice* (Cambridge: Harvard University Press, 1967 [1958]).

Sing.1960.1
Singleton, Charles S., " 'In exitu Israel de Aegypto,' " *Annual Report of the Dante Society* 78 (1960): 1–24.

Smit.1980.1
Smith, Nathaniel B., "Arnaut Daniel in the *Purgatorio*: Dante's Ambivalence toward Provençal," *Dante Studies* 98 (1980): 99–109.

Spit.1946.1
Spitzer, Leo, "A Note on the Poetic and the Empirical 'I' in Medieval Authors," *Traditio* 4 (1946): 414–22.

Stab.1983.1
Stabile, Giorgio, "Cosmologia e teologia nella *Commedia*: la caduta di Lucifero e il rovesciamento del mondo," *Letture classensi* 12 (1983): 139–73.

Stef.1985.1
Stefanini, Ruggero, "I tre sogni del *Purgatorio*: Struttura e allegoria," in *Studies in the Italian Renaissance: Essays in Memory of Arnolfo B. Ferruolo*, ed. G. P. Biasin, A. N. Mancini, and N. J. Perella (Naples: Società Editrice Napoletana, 1985), pp. 43–66.

Stef.1995.1
Stefanini, Ruggero, "Buonconte and Palinurus: Dante's Re-Working of a Classical Source," in *Dante: Summa Medievalis*, ed. C. Franco and L. Morgan (Stony Brook, N.Y.: Forum Italicum, 1995), pp. 100–11.

Stef.1996.1
Stefanini, Ruggero, " 'Tenzone' sì e 'tenzone' no," *Lectura Dantis [virginiana]*, 18–19 (1996): 111–24.

Step.1983.1
Stephany, William A., "Biblical Allusions to Conversion in *Purgatorio* XXI," *Stanford Italian Review* 3 (1983): 141–62.

Step.1991.1
Stephany, William A., "*Purgatorio* XIII," *Lectura Dantis [virginiana]* 9 (1991): 72–89.

Stie.2001.1
Stierle, Karlheinz, "Canto XI," in *Lectura Dantis Turicensis: Purgatorio*, ed. Georges Güntert and Michelangelo Picone (Florence: Cesati, 2001), pp. 157–72.

Stul.1991.1
Stull, William, and Robert Hollander, "The Lucanian Source of Dante's Ulysses," *Studi Danteschi* 63 (1991 [1997]): 1–52.

Tand.1969.1
Tandoi, Vincenzo, "Il ricordo di Stazio 'dolce poeta' nella *Sat.* VII di Giovenale," *Maia* 21 (1969): 103–22.

Taro.1901.1
Tarozzi, Giuseppe, *Il canto XVIII del "Purgatorio"* (["Lectura Dantis Orsanmichele"] Florence: Sansoni, 1901).

Tate.1961.1
Tate, Allen, "The Symbolic Imagination: A Meditation on Dante's Three Mirrors," in *Discussions of the "Divine Comedy,"* ed. Irma Brandeis (Boston: Heath, 1961), pp. 102–11.

Took.1984.1
Took, John, *"L'etterno piacer": Aesthetic Ideas in Dante* (Oxford: Clarendon, 1984).

Tosc.1989.1
Toscano, Tobia R., "Canto X," in *Lectura Dantis Neapolitana: "Purgatorio,"* ed. Pompeo Giannantonio (Naples: Loffredo, 1989), pp. 205–25.

Tron.1995.1
Trone, George Andrew, "The Cry of Dereliction in *Purgatorio* XXIII," *Dante Studies* 113 (1995), 111–29.

Tuck.1960.1
Tucker, Dunstan J., " 'In exitu Isräel de Aegypto': the *Divine Comedy* in the Light of the Easter Liturgy," *American Benedictine Review* 11 (1960): 43–61.

Vaso.1988.1
Vasoli, Cesare, and Domenico De Robertis, eds., *Il Convivio*, in Dante Alighieri, *Opere minori*, vol. I, part ii (Milan: Ricciardi, 1988).

Vazz.1970.1
Vazzana, Steno, "Il Canto X del *Purgatorio,"* in *Nuove letture dantesche*, vol. IV (Florence: Le Monnier, 1970), pp. 57–79.

Vazz.1981.1
Vazzana, Steno, "Il Canto IX del *Purgatorio*," in *Purgatorio: letture degli anni 1976–79*, ed. Silvio Zennaro, Casa di Dante in Roma (Roma: Bonacci, 1981), pp. 175–98.

Vesc.2002.1
Vescovini, Graziella Federici, "Dante e l'astronomia del suo tempo," *Letteratura italiana antica* 3 (2002): 291–309.

Vick.1983.1
Vickers, Nancy, "Seeing is Believing: Gregory, Trajan, and Dante's Art," *Dante Studies* 101 (1983): 67–85.

Vill.1987.1
Villa, Claudia, "In favore della Gran Contessa," *Quaderni del Dipartimento di lingue e letterature neolatine dell'Istituto universitario di Bergamo* 2 (1987): 67–76.

Wenz.1965.1
Wenzel, Siegfried, "Dante's Rationale for the Seven Deadly Sins (*Purgatorio* XVII)," *Modern Language Review* 60 (1965): 529–33.

Wenz.1967.1
Wenzel, Siegfried, *The Sin of Sloth: "Acedia" in Medieval Thought and Literature* (Chapel Hill: University of North Carolina Press, 1967).

Weth.1984.1
Wetherbee, Winthrop, "*Poeta che mi guidi*: Dante, Lucan, and Virgil," in *Canons*, ed. R. Von Hallberg (Chicago: University of Chicago Press, 1984), pp. 131–48.

Wilk.1927.1
Wilkins, Ernest Hatch, "Dante and the Mosaics of his *Bel San Giovanni*," *Speculum* 2 (1927): 1–10.

Wlas.1989.1
Wlassics, Tibor, "Il canto XV del *Purgatorio*," in *Filologia e critica dantesca: Studi offerti a Aldo Vallone* (Florence: Olschki, 1989), pp. 161–74.

Wolf.1935.1
Wolfson, Harry Austryn, "The Internal Sense in Latin, Arabic, and Hebrew Philosophic Texts," *Harvard Theological Review* 28 (1935): 69–133.

Wood.1977.1
Woody, Kennerly M., "Dante and the Doctrine of the Great Conjunctions," *Dante Studies* 95 (1977): 119–34.